Get the eBooks FREE!

(PDF, ePub, Kindle, and liveBook all included)

We believe that once you buy a book from us, you should be able to read it in any format we have available. To get electronic versions of this book at no additional cost to you, purchase and then register this book at the Manning website.

Go to https://www.manning.com/freebook and follow the instructions to complete your pBook registration.

That's it!
Thanks from Manning!

Praise for the First Edition

A thorough look at PowerShell from three of the best writers in the PowerShell community.
—Mike Shepard, Solutions Architect
Jack Henry & Associates

The most wonderful PowerShell administrative guide.
—Kais Ayari, PowerShell Expert, Microsoft

Another great PowerShell book for my desk!
—Thomas Lee, PowerShell Consultant, PS Partnership

Hicks, Jones, and Siddaway have come together to deliver the ultimate PowerShell resource.
—James Berkenbile, Principal Consultant
Berkenbile Consulting

I have many books on my shelves. This is one that will be on my desk!
—Trent Whiteley, Software Engineer, Fiserv

The authors know their audience and never lose sight of their readers. They use their knowledge and understanding in very clever ways to help readers understand even complex subjects.
—Rolf Åberg, Platform Architect Active Directory, SEB

An end-all, be-all resource in the working man's hands. I can finally give Google a rest.
—Eric Stoker, Network Administrator, Spokane Teacher's Credit Union

Hands-down the best PowerShell book to date. The authors are some of the most respected in the PowerShell community and this book illustrates why! These guys know this stuff inside and out.
—Adam Bell, Solution Architect, ZOE Systems Pty Ltd.

Priceless, practical guidance.
—Klaus Schulte, System administrator, www.kvwl.de

PowerShell in Depth
Second Edition

DON JONES
JEFFERY HICKS
RICHARD SIDDAWAY

MANNING
SHELTER ISLAND

For online information and ordering of this and other Manning books, please visit
www.manning.com. The publisher offers discounts on this book when ordered in quantity.
For more information, please contact

    Special Sales Department
    Manning Publications Co.
    20 Baldwin Road
    PO Box 261
    Shelter Island, NY 11964
    Email: orders@manning.com

Manning Publications Co.
20 Baldwin Road
PO Box 261
Shelter Island, NY 11964

Development editor: Karen Miller
Copyeditor: Liz Welch
Proofreaders: Toma Mulligan, Andy Carroll
Typesetter: Dennis Dalinnik
Cover designer: Marija Tudor

ISBN: 9781617292187
Printed in the United States of America

brief contents

contents

preface

Windows PowerShell is viewed by many IT professionals as a necessary evil, but we see it as a management marvel. The challenge from the beginning has been to wrap one's head around the PowerShell paradigm of an object-based shell. Some people view PowerShell as just another scripting language like VBScript, but the truth is that Power-Shell is an automation and management engine. You can run this engine in a traditional console application, which is how most IT pros are first exposed to it. You can also run it in a graphical environment like the PowerShell Integrated Scripting Environment (ISE), or through a third-party tool like PowerGUI or PowerShell Plus.

As you might imagine, the fourth version of a product offers substantially more features and benefits than the first, and PowerShell 4.0 fits this model. This version of PowerShell naturally builds on what came before, but it takes off from there. If you think of Windows 8.1 and Windows Server 2012 R2 as operating systems for the cloud, then PowerShell 4.0 is the automation and management engine for the cloud, although PowerShell "scales down" to help you better manage any size environment.

Collectively, we have close to 70 years of IT experience. We have worked with PowerShell from its days as a beta product and have written on the topic for nearly as long. Our goal is to bring this knowledge and experience into a single reference book. Notice the key word, "reference." This is not a how-to or teach yourself PowerShell book, although you can learn much from reading it cover to cover. Rather, this book is intended as the reference guide you keep at your desk or on your mobile device so that when you need to better understand a topic, like PowerShell remoting, you have a place to which you can turn.

We have tried to keep our examples practical and targeted towards IT professionals responsible for Windows system administration. It is our hope that this will be the book you go to for answers.

acknowledgments

As you can imagine, a book of this scope and magnitude is not an easy undertaking, even with three coauthors. There are many, many people who had a hand in making this possible. First, we'd like to thank the entire PowerShell product team at Microsoft. Many of them took time from their busy schedules to answer our questions and offer guidance on a number of new features, even while they were still being developed!

The authors would also like to thank the fine folks at Manning Publications: Cynthia Kane, Karen Miller, Maureen Spencer, Liz Welch, Linda Recktenwald, Andy Carroll, Janet Vail, and Mary Piergies. They have taken what can be a grueling process and turned it into something pleasant yet productive in helping us bring this book to publication. That is not easy.

We also thank the cadre of what we think of as "real-world" reviewers who offered their opinions on how we could make this a book that they, and you, would want on your bookshelf. They include Arthur Zubarev, Braj Panda, David Moravec, Jan Vinterberg, Jim Gray, Lincoln Bovee, Michel Clomp, Nick Selpa, Stuart Caborn, and Wayne Boaz.

We would especially like to thank Aleksandar Nikolić for his time and dedication in reviewing the technical content of our book. Aleksandar shares our desire to produce the best possible PowerShell reference and we truly appreciate his efforts.

DON would like to thank everyone at Manning for their support of, and commitment to, this project. He'd also like to thank his coauthors for their hard work, and his family for being so giving of their time.

JEFF would like to thank the members of the PowerShell community who make a book like this possible. He would also like to thank his coauthors for making this one of the best authoring experiences possible.

RICHARD would like to thank everyone who has taken the time to comment on the book and the PowerShell community for their willingness to share. He would like to thank Don and Jeff for making this a very enjoyable experience—working across eight time zones makes for some interesting conversations.

about this book

This book was written as a reference for system administrators. You can read the book cover to cover, and we've tried to arrange the chapters in a logical progression, but in the end it works best as a reference, where you can explore a topic more deeply in the chapter that is devoted to a particular subject. Chapter 1 will tell you more about what you will learn in the book, and what you need to know before you start.

The 41 chapters in the book are arranged into four parts, as follows:

- Part 1, "PowerShell Fundamentals," includes chapters 1 through 9, which cover the basics associated with using PowerShell. Although we didn't write this book as a tutorial, there are a few basics you'll need to explore before you can use PowerShell effectively: the pipeline, the concept of PowerShell hosts, the shell's help system, and so forth. We'll dive deeper into some of these topics than a tutorial normally would, so even if you're already familiar with these foundational concepts, it's worth a quick read-through of these chapters.

- Part 2, "PowerShell management," covers topics such as remote control, background jobs, regular expressions, and HTML and XML. These are just a few of the core technologies accessible within PowerShell that make server and client management easier, more scalable, and more effective. Chapters 10 through 18 tackle these technologies individually, and we dive as deeply as we can into them, so that you can master their intricacies and subtleties.

- Part 3, "PowerShell scripting and automation," includes chapters 19 through 33, which have a single goal: repeatability. Using PowerShell's scripting language, along with associated technologies like workflow, you can begin to create reusable tools that automate key tasks and processes in your environment.

- Part 4, "Advanced PowerShell," consists of chapters 34 through 41. One of PowerShell's greatest strengths is its ability to connect to other technologies, such as WMI, CIM, COM, .NET, and a host of other acronyms. The chapters in part 4 look at each of these and demonstrate how PowerShell can utilize them. We give you a starting place for doing this, and then we provide you with some direction for further independent exploration.

Code conventions and downloads

All source code in listings or in text is in a `fixed-width font like this` to separate it from ordinary text. Code annotations accompany many of the listings, highlighting important concepts. In some cases, numbered bullets link to explanations that follow the listing.

The code samples are based on PowerShell 4.0. We intended the samples to be instructive, but we did not design them for production use. They may not always be the "best" PowerShell—our code examples were designed to reinforce concepts and make points.

We have tried to fit code samples into the confines of a printed page, which means that sometimes we have had to bend some rules. You are welcome to try the code snippets on your computer, but remember that the book is not intended as a tutorial. Longer code samples are displayed as code listings; we don't expect you to type these. If you want to try them, the files can be downloaded from the book's page on the publisher's website at www.manning.com/PowerShellinDepthSecondEdition.

We, along with our technical reviewer, strove to test and retest everything, but sometimes errors will still sneak through. We encourage you to use the Author Online forum for this book at www.manning.com/PowerShellinDepthSecondEdition to post any corrections, as well as your comments or questions on the book's content.

Author Online

Purchase of *PowerShell in Depth, Second Edition* includes free access to a private web forum run by Manning Publications, where you can make comments about the book, ask technical questions, and receive help from the authors and from other users. To access the forum and subscribe to it, point your web browser to www.manning.com/PowerShellinDepthSecondEdition. This page provides information on how to get on the forum once you are registered, what kind of help is available, and the rules of conduct on the forum.

Manning's commitment to our readers is to provide a venue where a meaningful dialogue between individual readers and between readers and the authors can take place. It is not a commitment to any specific amount of participation on the part of the authors, whose contribution to the book's forum remains voluntary (and unpaid). We suggest you try asking the authors some challenging questions, lest their interest stray!

The Author Online forum and the archives of previous discussions will be accessible from the publisher's website as long as the book is in print.

About the authors

DON JONES has more than 20 years of experience in the IT industry and is a recognized expert in Microsoft's server platform. He's a multiple-year recipient of Microsoft's prestigious Most Valuable Professional (MVP) award and writes the "Windows PowerShell" column for Microsoft TechNet Magazine. Don has authored more than 50 books on information technology topics, including three books in the popular *Learn PowerShell in a Month of Lunches* series from Manning. He is a regular and top-rated speaker at numerous technology conferences and symposia worldwide, and a founding director of PowerShell.org, a community-owned and community-operated resource for PowerShell users.

JEFFERY HICKS is an IT veteran with over 25 years of experience, much of it spent as an IT infrastructure consultant specializing in Microsoft server technologies with an emphasis in automation and efficiency. He is a multi-year recipient of the Microsoft MVP Award in Windows PowerShell. He works today as an independent author, trainer, and consultant. Jeff has authored or co-authored numerous books written for a variety of online sites and print publications, is a contributing editor at Petri.com, and is a frequent speaker at technology conferences and user groups. You can keep up with Jeff at his blog (http://jdhitsolutions.com/blog) or on Twitter (@jeffhicks).

RICHARD SIDDAWAY has been working with Microsoft technologies for over 25 years, having spent time in most IT roles. He has always been interested in automation techniques (including automating job creation and submission on mainframes many years ago). PowerShell caught his interest, and Richard has been using it since the early beta versions. He regularly blogs about PowerShell, and using PowerShell, at http://blogs.msmvps.com/richardsiddaway/. Richard founded the UK PowerShell User Group and has been a PowerShell MVP for the last seven years. He's a regular speaker and writer on PowerShell topics, and his previous Manning books include *PowerShell in Practice* and *PowerShell and WMI*.

THE AUTHORS would love to hear from you and are eager to help spread the good news about PowerShell. We hope you'll come up to us at conferences like TechEd and let us know how much (hopefully) you enjoyed the book. If you have any other PowerShell questions, we encourage you to use the forums at PowerShell.org, where we all are active participants, or Manning's Author Online forum at www.manning.com/PowerShellinDepthSecondEdition.

About the cover illustration

The figure on the cover of *PowerShell in Depth, Second Edition* is captioned a "Man from Split, Dalmatia." The illustration is taken from the reproduction published in 2006 of a nineteenth-century collection of costumes and ethnographic descriptions entitled *Dalmatia* by Professor Frane Carrara (1812–1854), an archaeologist and historian and the first director of the Museum of Antiquity in Split, Croatia. The illustrations were obtained from a helpful librarian at the Ethnographic Museum (formerly the Museum of Antiquity), itself situated in the Roman core of the medieval center of Split: the ruins of Emperor Diocletian's retirement palace from around AD 304. The book includes finely colored illustrations of figures from different regions of Croatia, accompanied by descriptions of the costumes and of everyday life.

The man on the cover is wearing dark blue woolen trousers and a black vest over a white linen shirt. Over his shoulder is a brown jacket, and a red belt and a red cap complete the outfit; in his hand he holds a long pipe. The elaborate and colorful embroidery on his costume is typical for this region of Croatia.

Dress codes have changed since the nineteenth century and the diversity by region, so rich at the time, has faded away. It is now hard to tell apart the inhabitants of different continents, let alone different towns or regions. Perhaps we have traded cultural diversity for a more varied personal life—certainly for a more varied and fast-paced technological life.

We at Manning celebrate the inventiveness, the initiative, and, yes, the fun of the computer business with book covers based on the rich diversity of regional life of two centuries ago, brought back to life by the pictures from this collection.

Part 1

PowerShell fundamentals

In part 1, we'll cover some of the basics associated with using PowerShell. Although we didn't write this book as a tutorial, there are nonetheless a few basics you'll need to explore before you can use PowerShell effectively: the pipeline, the concept of PowerShell hosts, the shell's help system, and so forth. We'll dive a bit deeper into some of these topics than a tutorial normally might do, so even if you're already familiar with these foundational concepts, it's worth a quick read-through of these chapters.

Introduction

This chapter covers

- What the book will and won't teach
- The boundaries of this book
- Going beyond PowerShell

As of this writing, Windows PowerShell is on to its seventh year of existence and in its fourth major release, with a fifth version in preview. In that time, it's changed the way people look at administering many Microsoft, and even some non-Microsoft, products. Although the graphical user interface (GUI) will always be an important part of administration in many ways, PowerShell has given administrators options: Use an easy, intuitive GUI; manage from a rich, interactive command-line console; or fully automate with a simple scripting language. We're delighted that so many administrators have started using PowerShell, and we're honored that you've chosen this book to further your own PowerShell education.

1.1   Who this book is for

We wrote this book for system administrators, not developers. In the Microsoft world, administrators go by the catchall title "IT professional" or "IT pro" and that's who we had in mind. As such, we assume you're not a full-time programmer, although if you have some programming or scripting experience it'll make certain parts of Power-Shell easier to learn.

We assume you're primarily interested in automating various administrative tasks and processes, or at least being more efficient, but we don't make any assumptions about the products with which you work. You may be an Exchange Server administrator, or maybe SharePoint or SQL Server is your thing. Perhaps you manage Active Directory, or you're in charge of file servers. You may even manage a Citrix or VMware environment (yes, they can be managed by PowerShell). It doesn't matter, because what we'll focus on in this book is the core technologies of PowerShell itself: the techniques and features you'll need to use no matter what products you're administering. We do use Active Directory in a few examples, but every technique, pattern, practice, and trick we show you will apply equally well, no matter where you've chosen to use PowerShell.

1.2   *What this book will teach you*

You can certainly read this book cover to cover, and we've tried to arrange the chapters in a logical progression. But in the end, we intend for this book to be a reference. Need to figure out PowerShell Remoting? Skip to that chapter. Confused about how commands pipe data from one to another? We've written a chapter for that. Need to access a database from within a PowerShell script? There's a chapter for that.

We've no intention of making you a programmer—we don't claim to be programmers—we all have backgrounds as IT pros. Yes, PowerShell can support some robust scripts, but you can also accomplish a lot by running commands. If you have programming experience, it'll serve you well, and you may be tempted to approach PowerShell more as a scripting language, which is fine. If you've never scripted or programmed a single line of code, you'll probably see PowerShell as a pure command-line interface, where you run commands to make stuff happen, and that's fine, too. Either way you win because you get to automate your tedious, repetitive work. The other winning feature is that what you learn by using PowerShell at the command line is directly usable when you start writing scripts—there's no wasted learning with PowerShell.

1.3   *What this book won't teach you*

We assume you're already an experienced administrator and that you're familiar with the inner workings of whatever technology you manage. We aren't going to teach you what an Active Directory user account is, or what an Exchange mailbox does, or how to create a SharePoint site. PowerShell is a tool that lets you accomplish administrative tasks, but like any tool it assumes you know what you're doing.

To use a noncomputer analogy, PowerShell is a hammer, and this book will teach you how to swing that hammer and not smash your thumb. We won't teach you about building houses, though—we assume you already know how to do that and that you're looking for a more efficient way to do it than pounding nails with a rock.

1.4 *Where we drew the line*

It's safe to say that PowerShell can't do everything for you. You'll find some things with which it's completely incapable of helping, as with any technology. But you'll also find tasks for which PowerShell works well. And you'll encounter that weird middle ground where you *could* do something in PowerShell, but to do it you'd have to go beyond the strict boundaries of what PowerShell is. For example, PowerShell doesn't natively contain a way to map a network printer.

> **NOTE** There is a PrintManagement module containing an Add-Printer cmd-let, but it's part of Windows (specifically Windows 8/2012 and later) rather than PowerShell.

You could instantiate a Component Object Model (COM) object to accomplish the task from *within* PowerShell, but it has nothing to do with PowerShell. Instead, it's the shell giving you a way to access completely external technologies. In these cases (which are becoming increasingly rare in the latest version of Windows), we'll only say, "You can't do that in PowerShell yet." We know our statement isn't 100% true, but we want to keep this book focused on what PowerShell is and what it does natively. If we turn this book into "everything you can do with PowerShell natively, plus all the external stuff like .NET and COM and so on that you can get to from PowerShell," it'd grow to 7,000 pages in length and we'd never finish.

That said, we're including material in the book on using some of these external technologies, along with some guidance on where you can find resources to educate yourself on them more completely if you've a mind to do so.

1.5 *Beyond PowerShell*

PowerShell is a lot like the Microsoft Management Console (MMC), with which you're probably familiar. On its own, it's useless. Both the MMC and PowerShell only become useful when you add extensions, which in the MMC would be "snap-ins," and in Power-Shell would be either a "snap-in" or a "module." Those extensions give you access to Exchange, Active Directory, SharePoint, SQL Server, and so on. The later versions of Windows (Windows 8 and later) ship with over 50 additional modules, not counting the Remote Server Administration Tools (RSAT) modules. This additional functionality is blurring the boundaries of PowerShell. The thing to remember is that in this book we're concentrating on the core of PowerShell so that you understand how it works. Using the other modules will become obvious once you understand PowerShell itself.

Understand that the folks at Microsoft who write PowerShell *don't* write the extensions. They provide some tools and rules for the developers who do create extensions, but their job is to create the core PowerShell stuff. Extensions are made by other product teams: The Exchange team makes the Exchange PowerShell extension, the Active Directory team makes its extension, and so on. If you're looking at a particular extension and don't like what you see, blame the product team that produced it, not PowerShell. If you'd like to administer something—maybe Windows Internet Name

Service (WINS) Server, for example—and PowerShell has no way to administer it, it's not the PowerShell team's fault. Blame the owners of the technology you're trying to work with, and encourage them to get on board and produce a PowerShell extension for their product.

This division of labor is one reason why we're keeping this book focused on the core of PowerShell. That core is what you'll use no matter what extensions you end up deploying to achieve your administrative goals.

1.6   *Ready?*

Okay, that's enough of an introduction. If you want to follow along, make sure you have PowerShell v4 installed on a Windows 7 or later client. You'll also find it useful to have a test server running PowerShell v4, ideally on Windows Server 2012 R2.

> **NOTE**   The examples and code in this book will work with PowerShell v5 if you have that installed. The major new feature in PowerShell v5 is software management through the OneGet module.

Now, pick a chapter and jump in.

PowerShell hosts

This chapter covers

- The purpose of PowerShell hosts
- The PowerShell console and ISE hosts
- The differences between 64-bit and 32-bit hosts
- PowerShell transcripts

PowerShell can be confusing to use because it behaves differently in different situations. Here's an example from PowerShell v2: When you run the `Read-Host` command in the PowerShell.exe console, it behaves differently than if you run that same command in the PowerShell Integrated Scripting Editor (ISE). The reason you encounter these differences has to do with the fact that you don't interact directly with PowerShell. Instead, you give commands to the PowerShell engine by means of a *host*. It's up to the host to determine how to interact with the PowerShell engine.

> **NOTE** The difference in the response of `Read-Host` between the console and the ISE has been eliminated in PowerShell v3 and later.

The PowerShell engine is a set of .NET Framework classes stored in a DLL file. You can't interact with it directly. Instead, the application you interact with loads the engine. For example, if you've ever used the Exchange Server 2007 (or later) graphical management console (called the Exchange Management Console, or EMC), then you've used a PowerShell host. The EMC lets you interact by clicking icons, filling in dialog boxes, and so forth, but it's PowerShell that performs the actions it takes. You never "see" the shell, but it's hiding under the GUI. That's why it can show you the PowerShell commands for the actions it has performed. Exchange also provides a console-based shell that exposes the underlying PowerShell engine together with the Exchange cmdlets.

When we talk about "using PowerShell," we're most often talking about using it through a host that looks more like a command-line shell. Microsoft provides two different hosts for that purpose: the *console* and the *ISE*. Third-party vendors can also produce host applications, and many popular PowerShell editors—PrimalScript, Power-GUI, PowerShell Plus, PowerSE, and so forth—all host the PowerShell engine. You can write your own .NET programs to run PowerShell scripts or even call the underlying classes directly. How you interact with the shell and what your results look like will depend on the host you're using. Results might look and work one way in the Microsoft-supplied console, but they might look and work differently in a third-party application—or in some cases may not work at all. Conversely, some things that have worked in a third-party host don't work in the Microsoft hosts.

> **TIP** Remember that if things work in one host but not in another, it's mostly likely due to the differences in the hosts rather than it being a PowerShell error. If you have an error in a third-party host that you can't resolve, make sure you test it in the Microsoft PowerShell console as a lowest common denominator.

For this book, we'll assume you're using one of the two Microsoft-supplied hosts, which we'll describe in this chapter.

2.1 *32-bit vs. 64-bit, and administrator vs. not*

The way you access the shortcuts for Microsoft's PowerShell host applications depends on the version of the operating system and the install options you've chosen. The first thing you need to be aware of is that PowerShell v4 isn't available on all versions of Windows. It's installed as part of the base build on

- Windows 8.1 x86 and x64
- Windows Server 2012 R2 x64

The Windows Management Framework (WMF) download (PowerShell v4, WinRM v3 [the version of WinRM hasn't changed between PowerShell v3 and v4], and the new WMI API) is available for

- Windows 7 SP1 (or above) x86 and x64
- Windows Embedded Standard 7
- Windows Server 2008 R2 SP1 (or above) x64
- Windows Server 2012

The WMF download is available from www.microsoft.com/en-us/download/details .aspx?id=40855. Check the version you need for your system in the download instructions. You'll notice that PowerShell v4 isn't available for Windows 8. This is deliberate because it's included in the free Windows 8.1 upgrade.

> **NOTE** If you're using Windows XP, Windows Vista, Windows Server 2008, or any flavor of Windows Server 2003, you can't install PowerShell v4. Check appendix C for further information on the differences between the Power-Shell versions.

Application incompatibilities

Don't install WMF 4.0 on a system running any of the following:

- System Center 2012 Configuration Manager (but you can install SP1 to remove the incompatibility)
- Microsoft Exchange Server 2013
- Microsoft Exchange Server 2010
- Microsoft Exchange Server 2007
- Microsoft SharePoint Server 2013
- Microsoft SharePoint Server 2010
- Windows Small Business Server 2011 Standard

These restrictions also apply to WMF 3.0 (PowerShell 3.0), but they may be changed with the issue of Service Packs for these applications. Please check the application documentation to see if there are any changes.

You'll need to install Microsoft .NET Framework 4.5 (use the full offline installer from http://msdn.microsoft.com/en-us/library/5a4x27ek(v=vs.110).aspx) before installing WMF 4.0. The 4.5 version of the framework is preinstalled on Windows 8.1 and Windows Server 2012 R2.

Microsoft, and other vendors, have produced tablet devices with Windows RT installed. These devices, such as the Microsoft Surface, do have PowerShell installed, but the instance of PowerShell is constrained in that you can't access some features. Which features are unavailable depends on whether the device is running Windows 8 or Windows 8.1 RT, but here are some examples:

- You can't remote into the device.
- You can't run workflows.
- You can't use Desired State Configuration.

In addition, the ISE isn't available on Surface devices.

> **NOTE** The Microsoft Surface Pro devices run a full version of PowerShell, including the ISE.

In the Windows 8/2012 family of products, the way you access applications has changed. You use the Start screen instead of the Start menu. If you're on the Windows

Desktop, press the Win button to access the Start screen or click the Start button in Windows 8.1/2012 R2. Scroll to the right to find the PowerShell icon. Alternatively, press Win-Q to access the application search menu.

On earlier versions of Windows you'll find shortcuts to Microsoft's host applications on your computer's Start menu. If you're on a Server Core (Windows Server 2008 R2 or later) system that doesn't have a Start menu, run `powershell` to start the console host. You'll need to install PowerShell because it isn't part of the default Windows Server 2008 R2 server core install. The shortcuts can usually be found under Accessories > Windows PowerShell.

> **NOTE** PowerShell and the old command prompt use the same underlying console technology, which means you can type `Powershell` in a command prompt or `cmd` in a PowerShell console and "switch" to the other shell. Typing `exit` will revert back to the starting shell.

On a 32-bit system (on any Windows version), you'll find shortcuts for PowerShell—what we refer to as "the console"—and for the PowerShell ISE. Obviously, these shortcuts both point to 32-bit versions of PowerShell. But on a 64-bit system you'll find four shortcuts:

- Windows PowerShell—the 64-bit console
- Windows PowerShell ISE—also 64-bit
- Windows PowerShell (x86)—the 32-bit console
- Windows PowerShell ISE (x86)—also 32-bit

It's important to run the proper version, either 32-bit or 64-bit. PowerShell itself behaves the same either way, but when you're ready to load extensions you can only load ones built on the same architecture. The 64-bit shell can only load 64-bit extensions. If you have a 32-bit extension, you'll have to load it from the 32-bit shell. Once you launch, the window title bar will also display "(*x86*)" for the 32-bit versions, which means you can always see which one you're using.

> **TIP** We recommend that you pin PowerShell to your taskbar. Doing so makes access much quicker. Right-clicking the icon on the taskbar provides access to the PowerShell console and the ISE in addition to providing links to run as Administrator for both hosts.

On computers that have User Account Control (UAC) enabled, you'll need to be a bit careful. If your PowerShell window title bar doesn't say "Administrator," you're not running PowerShell with Administrator authority.

> **WARNING** Watch the top-left corner of the host as it starts. It will say "Administrator: Windows PowerShell" or "Administrator: Windows PowerShell ISE" during at least some of the startup period. Some of us, like Richard, modify the title bar to display the path to the current working directory so the title bar won't show "Administrator" once the profile has finished executing.

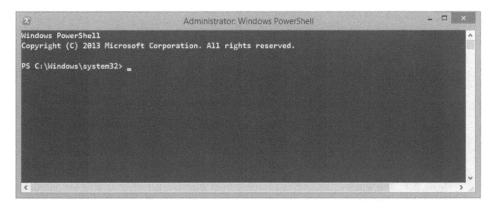

Figure 2.1 An elevated PowerShell session from Windows 8.1. Notice the Administrator label in the caption.

If you're not running as an Administrator, some tasks may fail with an "Access Denied" error. For example, you can only access some WMI classes when you're using PowerShell with the elevated privileges supplied by running as Administrator. If your title bar doesn't say "Administrator" and you need to be an Administrator to do what you're doing, close the shell. Reopen it by right-clicking one of the Start menu shortcuts and selecting Run as Administrator from the context menu. That'll get you a window title bar like the one shown in figure 2.1, which is what you want. In Windows 8, either right-click the taskbar shortcut or right-click the title on the Start screen to access the Run as Administrator option.

It's always worth taking a moment to verify whether your session is elevated before continuing with your work. One way you can do this is to modify your profile so that the console top border indicates whether PowerShell is elevated (in addition to specifying whether it's x86 or x64 and the current folder). You can then set a smaller prompt so that you have more of the console to type in. By default the current path is shown at the prompt, as you can see in figure 2.1. The function you need to add to your profile appears in listing 2.1.

Listing 2.1 Prompt function for PowerShell profile

```
function prompt {
if ([System.IntPtr]::Size -eq 8) {$size = '64 bit'}      ① Determine 64-
else {$size = '32 bit'}                                     or 32-bit

$currentUser = [Security.Principal.WindowsIdentity]::GetCurrent()    ② Get Windows-
$secprin = New-Object Security.Principal.WindowsPrincipal $currentUser   Principal
                                                                         object

if ($secprin.IsInRole([Security.Principal.WindowsBuiltinRole]::Administrator))
{$admin = 'Administrator'}                          ③ Determine if
else {$admin = 'non-Administrator'}                    elevated

$host.ui.RawUI.WindowTitle = "$admin $size $(get-location)"    ④ Set window
"£> "                                                            title
}                                        ⑤ Set prompt
```

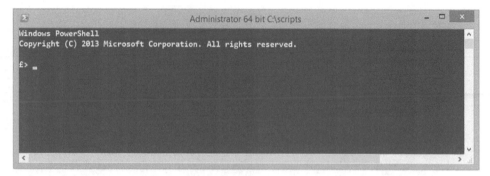

Figure 2.2   The Windows PowerShell console from Windows 8.1 after running the function in listing 2.1 in your profile.

The function in listing 2.1 specifies whether you're running the 32- or 64-bit version of PowerShell ❶. The current user is retrieved and used to create a `Security.Principal` `.WindowsPrincipal` object ❷. That object is then used to determine whether the user is running PowerShell as Administrator—that is, with elevated privileges ❸. The window title is set using the information gathered earlier ❹, and then the prompt is set ❺. Any string you want can be used as the prompt. The results of including listing 2.1 in your profile are shown in figure 2.2. The ISE will also run this function at startup.

  The PowerShell console is the simpler of the two available hosts, which is why we'll consider it before ISE.

2.2   *The console*

Most people's first impression of PowerShell is the Microsoft-supplied console, shown in figure 2.2 in the previous section. This console is built around an older piece of console software that's built into Windows—the same one used for the old Cmd.exe shell. Although PowerShell's programmers tweaked the console's initial appearance— it has a blue background rather than black, for example—it's still the same piece of software that's been more or less unchanged since the early 1990s. As a result, it has a few limitations. For example, it can't properly display double-byte character set (DBCS) languages, making it difficult to use with Asian languages that require a larger character set. The console also has primitive copy-and-paste functionality, along with fairly simplistic editing capabilities.

  You may wonder then, why use the console? If you've ever used a command-line shell before, even one in a Unix or Linux environment, the console looks and feels familiar. That's the main reason. If you're using Server Core, then the console is your only choice, because the ISE won't run on Server Core.

> **NOTE**   "Server Core" is a term that originated in Windows Server 2008. In Windows Server 2012 and later, Server Core is the default server installation that doesn't have the Server Graphical Shell feature installed. PowerShell wasn't available on the Windows Server 2008 version of Server Core, but it's available in Windows Server 2008 R2 and later.

Within the console, you can use a few tricks to make it a bit easier to work with:

- Pressing the up and down arrows on your keyboard will cycle through the command history buffer, enabling you to recall previous commands, edit them, and run them again.
- Pressing F7 will display the command history buffer in a pop-up window. Use the up and down arrow keys to select a previous command, and then either press Enter to rerun the command or press the right arrow key to display the command for editing.
- Use your mouse to highlight blocks of text by left-clicking and dragging. Then, press Enter to copy that block of text to the Windows clipboard. Quick Edit Mode must be enabled in the console's properties for this to work.
- Right-click to paste the Windows clipboard contents into the console.
- Use the Tab key to complete the PowerShell cmdlet, function, and parameter names. In PowerShell v4, variable names and .NET classes can also be completed in this way.

You can also do a few things to make the console more comfortable for yourself. Click the control box, which is at the top-left corner of the console window, and select Properties. You'll want to make a few adjustments in this dialog box:

- On the Options tab, you can increase the command history buffer. A bigger buffer takes more memory but preserves more of the commands you've run, allowing you to recall them and run them again more easily.
- On the Colors tab, choose text and background colors you're comfortable reading.
- On the Font tab, select a font face and size you like. This is important: You want to be sure you can easily distinguish between the single quote and backtick characters, between parentheses and curly brackets, and between single and double quotes. Distinguishing these characters isn't always easy to do using the default font. The backtick and single quote confusion is particularly annoying. The Consolas font is a good choice. Consider changing the text color to pure white (RGB 255:255:255) for better readability.

NOTE On a U.S. or U.K. keyboard, the backtick character is located on the upper-left key, under the Esc key. It shares space with the tilde (~) character. It's also referred to as a "grave accent mark." On other keyboards, you may find it in a different location.

- On the Layout tab, make sure both Width settings are the same. The bottom one controls the physical window size, whereas the top one controls the logical width of the window. When they're both the same, you won't have a horizontal scrollbar. If the upper "screen buffer" width is larger than the "window size," you'll have a horizontal scrollbar. That means viewing much of PowerShell's output will require horizontal scrolling, which can become cumbersome and annoying to work with.

As you're customizing your console window, take a moment to make sure it can display all the characters from the character set with which you work. If any characters aren't displaying properly, you may want to switch to the PowerShell ISE instead. Its ability to use TrueType fonts and to display DBCS languages makes it a real advantage.

2.3 *The PowerShell ISE*

The PowerShell Integrated Scripting Environment, or ISE (usually pronounced "aye ess eee," not "ice"), was created to offer a better script-editing experience than Windows Notepad, as well as provide a console experience that supports the use of DBCS languages and TrueType fonts. In general, the ISE works similarly to the console host, with a few exceptions:

- The ISE can maintain several PowerShell *runspaces* in a single window by placing each onto a separate tab. Each runspace is an instance of PowerShell, much like opening multiple console windows.
- The ISE can have multiple PowerShell scripts open simultaneously. Each is available through a separate tab.
- The ISE displays graphical dialog boxes for many prompts and messages, rather than displaying them on a command line as text.
- The ISE doesn't support transcripts, which we'll describe later in this chapter (this changes in PowerShell v5).
- You can change the font, starting size, and color schemes by selecting Tools from the menu and then selecting the appropriate options. To adjust the text display size, use the slider at the bottom right of the ISE window.

NOTE Some server operating systems don't have the ISE installed by default. If you need it, and it isn't present, you can install it using Server Manager like any other Windows feature. You can also use PowerShell to install ISE on servers. The command syntax is `Add-WindowsFeature -Name PowerShell-ISE`. The ISE may be installed but not exposed through the Start screen, in which case you need to pin it to the Start screen and/or taskbar.

The ISE supports two basic layouts, which are controlled by the three buttons on its toolbar. The default layout, shown in figure 2.3, uses two vertically stacked panes.

The top pane is the script editor, and the bottom pane is where you can interactively type commands and receive output. In PowerShell v3, the interactive and output panes were combined to effectively duplicate the PowerShell console. This configuration is maintained in PowerShell v4.

Clicking the second layout button in the toolbar gives you the layout shown in figure 2.4, where the script editor takes up one side and the console takes up the other.

Finally, the last button switches to a full-screen editor, which is useful if you're working on a long script. In some views, you'll notice that the script pane has a little blue arrow in the top-right corner. This can be used to hide or expose the script pane.

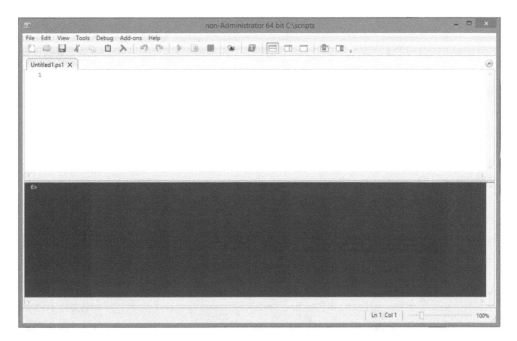

Figure 2.3   The default ISE layout uses two vertically stacked panes together with the Command Add-on pane (which we've removed here). The title shows that ISE is being run in a nonelevated manner—using the function in listing 2.1 as part of our profile.

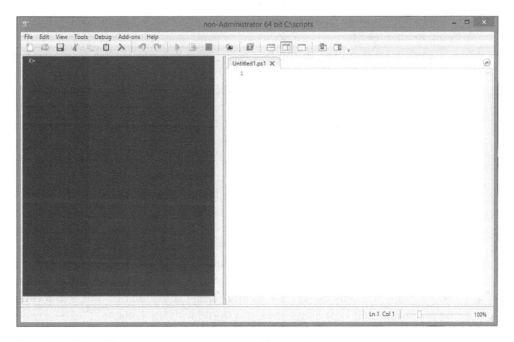

Figure 2.4   The split view gives you more room to edit a script.

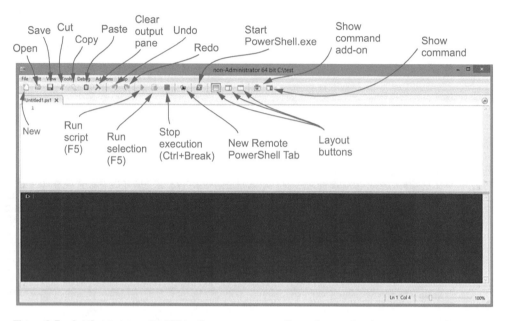

Figure 2.5   Getting to know the ISE toolbar can save you time when performing common tasks.

The other toolbar buttons, labeled in figure 2.5, provide access to the majority of the ISE's functions (the button layout is identical in PowerShell v3 and v4). You'll also find additional options on the menu. The File, Edit, and View menus are self-explanatory, and we'll discuss the Debug menu when we come to the topic of debugging in chapter 31.

Let's try something: In the ISE, select New PowerShell Tab from the File menu. (You'll also see a New Remote PowerShell Tab option. We'll discuss that in chapter 10 on Remoting.) What pops up is a whole new instance of PowerShell, called a runspace, which we mentioned earlier. Each tab has its own set of script file tabs, with each file tab representing a single script file. Each PowerShell tab also has its own output area and command-line pane. Each PowerShell tab is truly separate: If you load an extension into one, for example, it's only available in that one. To load an extension into every open PowerShell tab, you have to manually load it into each one, one at a time. Figure 2.6 shows what the ISE looks like with two PowerShell tabs open and with several script files opened within one PowerShell tab.

A lot of folks tend to think of the ISE as "just a script editor," but it's designed to be a complete, usable replacement for the PowerShell console host. The ISE offers better copy-and-paste capabilities (using the standard Ctrl-C, Ctrl-X, and Ctrl-V shortcut keys), better color-coding for PowerShell syntax, and more. Even if you hide the script editor pane and only use the ISE as an interactive command line, you'll often have a better PowerShell experience than you would with the console. The ISE even supports the up/down arrow keys for recalling previous commands and lets you edit those commands by putting your cursor anywhere on the line and typing away.

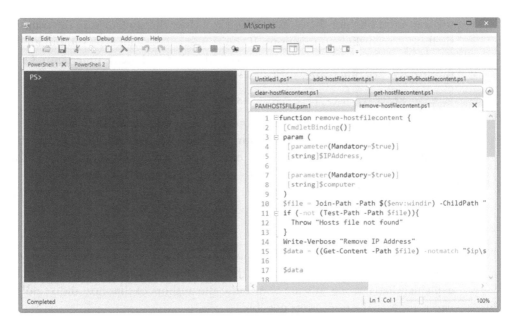

Figure 2.6   The ISE supports multiple PowerShell tabs, as well as multiple script files within each tab.

The ISE is also extensible. Information on some of the available extensions, sample code, and guidance on writing your own extensions to the ISE can be found at http:// social.technet.microsoft.com/wiki/contents/articles/2969.windows-powershell-ise-add-on-tools.aspx.

2.4   *Command history buffer vs. PowerShell's history*

The console application maintains its own command history buffer, which contains a list of the commands you've run. It holds the 50 most recent commands by default, and we explained earlier how you can adjust that number. When you're using the up and down arrow keys, or pressing F7 in the console, you're accessing this buffer.

PowerShell maintains its own independent list of the commands you've run, and you can view that list by running the `Get-History` command. By default this buffer maintains the last 4,096 commands. We're not going to dive into a lot of detail on PowerShell's history at this point, although we'll work it into the discussion in upcoming chapters as needed. For now, you should be aware of the two different histories, being maintained in two different ways. Also be aware that a number of cmdlets are available for viewing and working with the PowerShell history (`Get-Help *history`).

2.5   *Transcripts*

The PowerShell console—but not the ISE currently—supports the `Start-Transcript` and `Stop-Transcript` commands. When you start a transcript, every PowerShell command you run, along with its output and errors, will be saved to a text file. Legacy commands such as `ping` and `ipconfig` will have the command recorded only in the transcript file, not the output. When you close the shell or stop the transcript, the shell stops recording your actions. If you run `Start-Transcript` without any parameters, it creates a file in your Documents folder that includes a timestamp. Or you can specify your own filename:

```
PS C:\> Start-Transcript c:\work\Monday.txt
```

You'll find transcripts useful when you're experimenting with the shell, because they enable you to keep a log of everything you've tried. You can then review the file in Notepad or another text editor, copy out the parts you want, and save them for future use. If necessary, you can append to an existing transcript file. This can be handy when you're working with PowerShell features that can exist between PowerShell sessions, such as workflows. Use the –append parameter:

```
PS C:\> Start-Transcript c:\work\mytranscript.txt -append
```

Non-Microsoft hosts often don't support transcripts. If you try to start a transcript in a host that doesn't support it (such as the ISE), you'll get an error message that clearly explains what's wrong. It's not your fault; the authors of that host didn't do the work necessary to make transcripts possible.

2.6   *Summary*

You can use Windows PowerShell within a variety of host applications, and the ones you'll probably use most commonly are the Microsoft-supplied console and ISE hosts. The ISE offers a richer experience, but it lacks support for a small number of features such as transcripts. On 64-bit systems, Microsoft supplies 32-bit and 64-bit versions of both hosts, although on server operating systems you may have to take extra steps to install them. You should spend a little time familiarizing yourself with these hosts' user interfaces, as well as some time customizing them to suit your needs.

Using the PowerShell
help system

3

This chapter covers

- Defining PowerShell help commands
- Updating help
- Saving help
- Using help
- Working with common parameters

One of the difficulties associated with command-line interfaces is their inherent lack of discoverability. You won't find any tooltips, toolbars, context menus, or menus—none of the elements that a graphical user interface (GUI) offers to help you figure out what you can do and how to do it. PowerShell attempts to make up for this shortcoming with an effective and comprehensive help system. We firmly believe that becoming proficient at using the help system is a critical factor in anyone's ability to succeed at PowerShell. "Be prepared to read the help," Don says, "or you'll fail at PowerShell."

3.1 The help commands

PowerShell's official command for searching and retrieving help is Get-Help. But you'll often see people using help or man instead. These aren't technically nicknames (or aliases, which we cover in the next chapter), but rather they're a function (`help`) and an alias to that function (`man`). Both `help` and `man` run `Get-Help` under the hood, but they pipe its output to `more` (much like running `Get-Help Get-Service|more`), resulting in a page-at-a-time display (that you can advance one line at a time by pressing Enter) or a screenful at a time (by pressing the spacebar). For this chapter, we'll mostly show our examples using `help`. Note that the page display doesn't work in the PowerShell ISE, because it doesn't directly support the use of `more`. The help in the PowerShell v2 ISE is provided as a compiled help file. Creating a shortcut on your desktop to that file gives an alternative method of accessing help information. In PowerShell v3 and later, the updatable help functionality takes over and there isn't a compiled help file available for the PowerShell cmdlets.

> **NOTE**   Technically, `help` is a function and `man` is an alias to `help`. They both accomplish the same thing.

`Get-Help` produces output, like all other cmdlets, as objects; we'll get to those in chapter 7, which focuses on working with objects. Piping those to `more`, as happens with `help` and `man`, results in output that's pure text. For the most part, the conversion to pure text won't have any impact on you accessing help information whatsoever, which means you can feel free to use any of the commands with which you feel more comfortable.

3.2   *Where's the help?*

PowerShell v3 introduced a new feature called *updatable help*. This is a great feature that has, unfortunately, led to a lot of confusion and gnashing of teeth. For a number of reasons, both technical and nontechnical, Microsoft doesn't include any of Power-Shell's help files with PowerShell itself. Instead, you must download and install those help files on any computer where you'll want to read them. To do so, run `Update-Help`. The command can even download updated help for non-Microsoft shell extensions that have been designed to take advantage of this feature. You should also set yourself a reminder to run it every month or so in order to have the most recent help files on your system, possibly as a scheduled job using another feature introduced in PowerShell v3 (see chapter 11). You can also subscribe to an RSS feed at http://sxp.microsoft.com/feeds/msdntn/PowerShellHelpVersions that will provide information when new versions of the help files are made available. If you don't download help, you'll be prompted to do so the first time you use the `Get-Help` cmdlet.

> **WARNING**   If you don't download the help files (which are XML files), Power-Shell will automatically generate a fairly stripped-down help display when you ask for help. Needless to say, we strongly recommend taking the 30 seconds you'll need to download the help before you start using the shell.

The `Update-Help` command has a few parameters that let you customize its behavior. Some of these are designed to accommodate specific operational restrictions that some organizations deal with, so we'll cover those:

- The `-Module` parameter accepts one or more module names (in a comma-separated list) and attempts to update help for only those modules. This can be quicker than forcing the shell to check for updated help for every installed module, if you know that only one or two have been updated.
- The `-SourcePath` parameter provides a comma-separated list of local file paths (UNCs, or Universal Naming Conventions, are valid) where you can find help files. Use this to pull updated help that you've downloaded to a file server, for example, rather than attempting to download help directly from the internet.

You don't need to restart the shell once you've downloaded and updated help; it'll start using the new help immediately. But we have a great big caveat to alert you to about updating the help: Because the Microsoft-provided PowerShell extensions live in the Windows System32 folder, their help files also must live there. Because System32 is protected, you *must* be running the shell under elevated credentials in order for `Update-Help` to have permission to write to the necessary folders. You'll want to make sure the shell's window title bar says "Administrator" before running `Update-Help`. You can run `Update-Help` as often as you like, but it won't do anything after the first attempt of the day unless you use the `-Force` parameter.

Help has three cmdlets associated with it:

- `Get-Help`—Displays help information
- `Save-Help`—Downloads help files for later use via `Update-Help`
- `Update-Help`—Downloads and immediately updates help files (as discussed earlier)

You can use `Save-Help` in situations where you want to download help files to a network location that all machines can access, and update their help files from this one location:

```
Save-Help -DestinationPath c:\source\powershellhelp -UICulture en-US -Force
  -Verbose
```

You'll see a progress bar and messages for each help file that's downloaded, like the following:

```
VERBOSE: Resolving URI: "http://go.microsoft.com/fwlink/?linkid=285756"
VERBOSE: Your connection has been redirected to the following URI:
"http://download.microsoft.com/download/F/1/8/F184E1E5-22B3-4899-9C45-
    5C0E757A7E9A/"
VERBOSE: Microsoft.PowerShell.Management: Saved
C:\Source\PowerShellhelp\Microsoft.PowerShell.Management_eefcb906-b326-4e99-
    9f54-8b4bb6ef3c6d_en-US_HelpContent.cab.
Culture en-US Version 4.0.3.0
```

By design Microsoft limits you to one update per day, although you can use the `-Force` parameter to override that behavior, which allows you to run a `Save-Help` or `Update-Help` command for the same module more than once each day. We've found it's sometimes necessary to run `Save-Help` or `Update-Help` a couple of times to get all the files downloaded. Notice the use of the –UICulture parameter. The help files come as a pair, for example:

```
Microsoft.PowerShell.Management_eefcb906-b326-4e99-9f54-8b4bb6ef3c6d_en-
    US_HelpContent.cab
Microsoft.PowerShell.Management_eefcb906-b326-4e99-9f54-
    8b4bb6ef3c6d_HelpInfo.xml
```

The correct culture has to be downloaded to match your system. You can test the UI culture:

```
PS C:\> Get-UICulture | select -ExpandProperty Name
en-US
```

You can also test the culture of your system:

```
PS C:\> Get-Culture | select -ExpandProperty Name
en-GB
```

> **PowerShell culture**
>
> The use of Get-Culture and Get-UICulture may seem confusing, but there's a difference.
>
> The Get-Culture cmdlet gets information about the current culture settings. This includes information about the current language settings on the system, such as the keyboard layout, and the display format of such items as numbers, currency, and dates.
>
> The Get-UIculture cmdlet gets information on the user interface (UI) culture. The UI culture determines which text strings are used for UI elements, such as menus and messages.

The help files can then be updated like the following:

```
Update-Help -Source c:\source\powershellhelp -UICultureen-US -Force -Verbose
```

You'll get messages like the following:

```
VERBOSE: Microsoft.PowerShell.Management: Updated
C:\Windows\System32\WindowsPowerShell\v1.0\en-
    US\Microsoft.PowerShell.Commands.Management.dll-help.xml. Culture en-US
Version 4.0.3.0
VERBOSE: Microsoft.PowerShell.Management: Updated
C:\Windows\SysWOW64\WindowsPowerShell\v1.0\en-
    US\Microsoft.PowerShell.Commands.Management.dll-help.xml. Culture en-US
Version 4.0.3.0
```

> **TIP** Use Group Policy to set the Source value. Under the Computer Configuration, go to Policies > Administrative Templates > Windows Components > Windows PowerShell and configure the setting "Set the default source path for Update-Help."

If you're running a 64-bit OS, the previous example shows that the help for 64-bit and 32-bit versions of PowerShell is updated simultaneously. Updatable help is a great feature that'll ensure your help information is kept up to date. We strongly recommend that you update your help on a regular basis because Microsoft fixes documentation issues in the help files as they're reported.

3.3 *Saving help*

As we mentioned earlier, you can save help to a local share and direct your clients to it. In PowerShell v3 you could download help only for modules installed on your computer. We generally recommended running `Save-Help` from a Windows 8 desktop that had Remote Server Administration Tools (RSAT) installed (this machine had to be using the en-US culture for RSAT to be installable). With this approach you were likely to include help for most server-based modules. But this approach was not 100% effective because some modules are only installed on servers, which meant you had to download or save help on those computers.

In PowerShell v4, you can download help content for modules that *aren't* located on your computer. All you need to do is get the module from the remote computer, which will include the `HelpInfoUri`, and pass that information to `Save-Help`. Here's an example:

```
PS C:\> Get-Module -Name Hyper-V -CimSession chi-hvr2
➥ -ListAvailable | Save-Help -DestinationPath
➥ \\chi-fp02\PSHelp -Force
```

We ran this command on a Windows 8.1 desktop (CHI-FP02). The computer CHI-HVR2 is running Hyper-V on Windows Server 2012 R2. We retrieved the module and passed it to `Save-Help`, saving the help content locally.

Even though your Windows 8.1 desktop has RSAT installed, there are still some gaps. But using PowerShell you can identify the modules that don't exist locally and save help. First, you need to create a variable with the names of all the locally installed modules:

```
PS C:\> $local = (Get-Module -ListAvailable).name
```

Then you can get all the modules on a remote server that aren't on your local machine:

```
PS C:\> Get-Module -CimSession chi-hvr2.globomantics.local -ListAvailable |
➥    where {$local -notcontains $_.name}
```

ModuleType	Version	Name	ExportedCommands
Manifest	1.1	Hyper-V	
Manifest	1.0.0.0	NetWNV	{Get-NetVirtualiza...
Manifest	1.0.0.0	ServerCore	{Get-DisplayResolu...
Manifest	1.0.0.0	SoftwareInventoryLogging	{Get-SilComputer, ...
Manifest	1.0.0.0	UserAccessLogging	{Enable-Ual, Disab...
Manifest	1.0.0.0	WindowsServerBackup	

Once you've confirmed this works as expected, you can pipe this to `Save-Help`:

```
PS C:\> Get-Module -CimSession chi-hvr2.globomantics.local -ListAvailable |
    where {$local -notcontains $_.name} |
    Save-Help -DestinationPath \\chi-fp02\PSHelp -Force
```

The benefit is that you can set up a scheduled PowerShell job on a single computer running PowerShell v4 and have it save help for all of the servers in your enterprise. Each server can then have a separate job to periodically download help from the local source, assuming you need updated help on the server.

> **NOTE**   If you'll be in a mixed PowerShell environment—that is, running PowerShell v3 and v4—and plan on saving help, you'll have to take some extra steps. Help files for the different versions are generally not interchangeable. You wouldn't want to download v4 help files for a PowerShell v3 system. If you plan on saving help, you'll need to have separate processes and paths for each version.

3.4   *Using the help*

The help system in PowerShell v3 is smart. For example, it supports the use of wildcards (the * character), enabling you to search for help topics when you don't know the name of the specific command you need. When executing a search, it searches not only the shell extensions loaded into memory at the time but also any other installed extensions that are located in the defined module path. That way, you're searching across not only what's in memory but also what's available on the entire computer. If your search term isn't found in the name of a command or a help file, the help system will proceed to perform a full-text search across the help files' synopses and descriptions. That can be a bit more time-consuming, but it can help uncover obscure help topics for you.

For example, if you want to find a command for working with services, you might do the following:

```
PS C:\> help *service*
Name                   Category Module                           Synopsis
----                   -------- ------                           --------
Get-Service            Cmdlet   Microsoft.PowerShell.Management   Gets ...
New-Service            Cmdlet   Microsoft.PowerShell.Management   Creat...
New-WebServiceProxy    Cmdlet   Microsoft.PowerShell.Management   Creat...
Restart-Service        Cmdlet   Microsoft.PowerShell.Management   Stops...
Resume-Service         Cmdlet   Microsoft.PowerShell.Management   Resum...
Set-Service            Cmdlet   Microsoft.PowerShell.Management   Start...
Start-Service          Cmdlet   Microsoft.PowerShell.Management   Start...
Stop-Service           Cmdlet   Microsoft.PowerShell.Management   Stops...
Suspend-Service        Cmdlet   Microsoft.PowerShell.Management   Suspe...
Stop-DnsService        Cmdlet   DnsShell                          Stop-...
Start-DnsService       Cmdlet   DnsShell                          Start...
Get-NetFirewallServiceFilter Function NetSecurity ...
Set-NetFirewallServiceFilter Function NetSecurity ...
```

Notice that the last four results are from modules you haven't loaded into memory yet. PowerShell v3 and v4, by default, automatically load all modules on your module path for you. The shell will search as broadly as possible for you.

This isn't Bing or Google; the help system is only capable of doing basic pattern matches, not a contextual search. When choosing your search "keyword," follow these tips:

- Choose a single word or partial word, not multiple words and not phrases.
- Put wildcards (*) on either side of your word. The help system will sometimes do this implicitly. For example, run `help iscsi` and, because "iscsi" doesn't match the name of a command or help file, the shell will implicitly run `help *iscsi*` for you.
- Stick with singular words rather than plurals: "Service" rather than "Services," for example.
- Go with partial words: "*serv*" will generate more hits than "*service*" will.

WARNING The help system isn't searching for available commands; it's searching for available help files. Because Microsoft ships help files for all of its commands, it amounts to much the same thing. But it's possible for a command to exist without a corresponding help file, in which case the help system won't find it. A separate command, `Get-Command`, also accepts wildcards and searches across available commands, so it's a good companion to the help system.

Once you've located the command you want, ask for the help on that specific command in order to learn how to use it:

```
PS C:\> help Invoke-Command
NAME
    Invoke-Command
SYNOPSIS
    Runs commands on local and remote computers.
SYNTAX
    Invoke-Command [-ScriptBlock] <ScriptBlock> [-ArgumentList<Object[]>]
 [-InputObject<PSObject>] [-NoNewScope [<SwitchParameter>]]
[<CommonParameters>]
    Invoke-Command [[-ConnectionUri] <Uri[]>] [-ScriptBlock] <ScriptBlock>
 [-AllowRedirection [<SwitchParameter>]]
[-ArgumentList<Object[]>] [-AsJob [<SwitchParameter>]]
[-Authentication <AuthenticationMechanism>]
[-CertificateThumbprint<String>] [-ConfigurationName<String>]
[-Credential <PSCredential>] [-Disconnected[<SwitchParameter>]]
[-HideComputerName [<SwitchParameter>]]
[-InputObject<PSObject>] [-JobName<String>]
[-SessionOption<PSSessionOption>] [-ThrottleLimit<Int32>]
 [<CommonParameters>]
    Invoke-Command [[-ConnectionUri] <Uri[]>] [-FilePath] <String>
[-AllowRedirection [<SwitchParameter>]]
[-ArgumentList<Object[]>] [-AsJob [<SwitchParameter>]]
[-Authentication <AuthenticationMechanism>]
[-ConfigurationName<String>] [-Credential <PSCredential>]
```

```
[-Disconnected [<SwitchParameter>]] [-HideComputerName
[<SwitchParameter>]] [-InputObject<PSObject>] [-JobName<String>]
[-SessionOption<PSSessionOption>]
[-ThrottleLimit<Int32>] [<CommonParameters>]
...
```

You can include a few options when you're getting help for a command, and these are specified with the following parameters:

- -Full—Displays the full help, including details for each command parameter and usually including usage examples. We suggest you get into the habit of always viewing the full help, because it reveals a lot more detail about the command and its various use cases.

- -Examples—Displays usage examples only. That's useful for learning how to use the cmdlet.

- -Detailed—Displays details on each command parameter but doesn't display usage examples.

- -Online—Opens the help in the system's default web browser, loading from Microsoft's website. This is a great way to check for the most up-to-date help, and it displays the help in a separate window so that you can look at it as you're typing a command.

- -ShowWindow—Opens full help in a pop-up window. This makes it much easier to browse through help without giving up your PowerShell prompt. You can also search the help content in this window. See figure 3.1; the display was produced

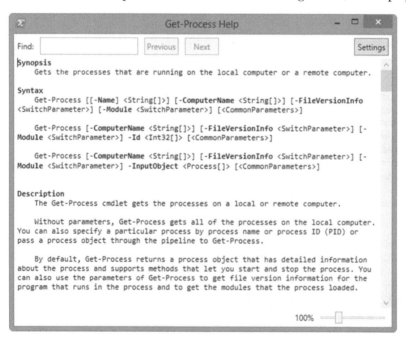

Figure 3.1   Results of using the –ShowWindow parameter with Get-Help

with the command Get-Help Get-Process -ShowWindow. Using -ShowWindow doesn't lock your PowerShell prompt; the help display is separate. You can have multiple help files open simultaneously by using -ShowWindow and still have a working PowerShell prompt.

Sometimes you may want the detail on a specific parameter. You don't have to wade through pages of full help; instead, use the Get-Help cmdlet. You may want to run help on Get-Help. If you do, you'll see that you can run commands like the following:

```
PS C:\> Get-Help Get-service -Parameter name
-Name <String[]>
    Specifies the service names of services to be retrieved. Wildcards are
permitted. By default, Get-Service gets all of the services on the
computer.
    Required?                  false
    Position?                  1
    Default value              All services
    Accept pipeline input?     true (ByPropertyName, ByValue)
    Accept wildcard characters? true
```

3.5   *"About" help files*

In addition to providing help on commands, PowerShell includes help for general concepts, troubleshooting, and so forth. Usually referred to as "about" files because their filenames start with the word "about," these files act as PowerShell's formal documentation. To see a complete list you can run the command yourself, but we'll truncate it as follows:

```
PS C:\> help about*
Name                              Category  Module
----                              --------  ------
about_AliasesHelpFile
about_Arithmetic_OperatorsHelpFile
about_ArraysHelpFile
about_Assignment_OperatorsHelpFile
about_Automatic_VariablesHelpFile
about_BreakHelpFile
about_Command_PrecedenceHelpFile
about_Command_SyntaxHelpFile
about_Comment_Based_HelpHelpFile
about_CommonParametersHelpFile
about_Comparison_OperatorsHelpFile
about_ContinueHelpFile
about_Core_CommandsHelpFile
about_Data_SectionsHelpFile
about_DebuggersHelpFile
about_DoHelpFile
about_Environment_VariablesHelpFile
about_Escape_CharactersHelpFile
about_EventlogsHelpFile
about_Execution_PoliciesHelpFile
```

To view any of these files, you can ask for help on the complete help filename:

```
PS C:\> help about_debuggers
TOPIC
about_Debuggers
SHORT DESCRIPTION
    Describes the Windows PowerShell debugger.
LONG DESCRIPTION
    Debugging is the process of examining a script while it is running in
    order to identify and correct errors in the script instructions. The
    Windows PowerShell debugger is designed to help you examine and
Identify
```

These files are also part of the updatable help system. We strongly recommend using the -ShowWindow parameter with about files because it makes them much easier to read.

3.6   *Provider help*

As you'll learn in upcoming chapters, PowerShell relies heavily on providers (technically, PSProviders) to connect PowerShell to various external data stores and systems such as Active Directory or the Registry. Both of these elements can provide help. For example, here's how to get help on the FileSystem provider:

```
PS C:\> help filesystem
PROVIDER NAME
FileSystem
DRIVES
    C, D
SYNOPSIS
    Provides access to files and directories.
DESCRIPTION
    The Windows PowerShell FileSystem provider lets you get, add, change,
    clear, and delete files and directories in Windows PowerShell.
    The FileSystem provider exposes Windows PowerShell drives that
    correspond to the logical drives on your computer, including drives
    that are mapped to network shares. This lets you reference these
    drives from within Windows PowerShell.
```

The help for providers can be quite extensive, and it often includes valuable details on how to use the provider for various management tasks, including usage examples. These files also document the dynamic changes that providers make to cmdlets. You can find the providers installed on your system by using Get-PSProvider.

3.7   *Interpreting command help*

Despite the usefulness of provider help and the about help files, you'll find yourself working primarily with help for individual commands. Learning to interpret the help displays is an incredibly important skill—perhaps one of the *most* important skills in PowerShell. Let's look at a quick overview (listing 3.1).

Listing 3.1   Sample help

```
NAME
    Get-Service
SYNOPSIS
    Gets the services on a local or remote computer.
SYNTAX
SYNTAX
    Get-Service [[-Name] <String[]>] [-ComputerName<String[]>]      Parameter
    [-DependentServices] [-Exclude <String[]>]                      set 1
    [-Include <String[]>] [-RequiredServices] [<CommonParameters>]

    Get-Service [-ComputerName<String[]>] [-DependentServices]      Parameter
    [-Exclude <String[]>] [-Include <String[]>]                     set 2
    [-RequiredServices] -DisplayName<String[]> [<CommonParameters>]

    Get-Service [-ComputerName<String[]>] [-DependentServices]
    [-Exclude <String[]>] [-Include <String[]>]                     Parameter
    [-InputObject<ServiceController[]>] [-RequiredServices]         set 3
    [<CommonParameters>]
```

What you're looking at are three different *parameter sets*, each of which represents a slightly different way to use this cmdlet. These parameter sets can be a big source of confusion, so we'll provide a simple rule to remember: When you're running the command, you can only choose parameters from a single parameter set to use together. In this case, that means you couldn't use both –Name and –InputObject at the same time, because they appear in different parameter sets. You can mix and match parameters from one set, but you can't mix and match parameters from multiple sets.

Now let's focus on the syntax display by looking at help for Get-WmiObject:

```
SYNTAX
    Get-WmiObject [-Class] <String> [[-Property] <String[]>] [-Amended]
    [-AsJob] [-Authentication {Default | None | Connect | Call | Packet |
     PacketIntegrity | PacketPrivacy | Unchanged}] [-Authority <String>]
    [-ComputerName <String[]>] [-Credential <PSCredential>]
    [-DirectRead] [-EnableAllPrivileges] [-Filter <String>]
    [-Impersonation {Default | Anonymous | Identify | Impersonate |
    Delegate}]  [-Locale <String>] [-Namespace <String>]
    [-ThrottleLimit <Int32>]   [<CommonParameters>]
```

If you know the meaning of all the punctuation, you can extract quite a bit of information from this concise display. Note that the meaning of the punctuation within the help file isn't the same as when these same symbols are used elsewhere in the shell. Here's what we know:

- We know that the –Class parameter is positional, because the parameter name (but not its data type <String>) is contained in square brackets. Positional means that you don't have to type –Class, provided you put the String value in the first position, because –Class is listed first in this help file. In other words you can type Get-WmiObject Win32_ComputerSystem instead of Get-WmiObject -Class Win32_ComputerSystem. Positional parameters are fine to use at the command line, but we recommend you don't use them in your scripts.

- We know that the -Class parameter is mandatory, because its name and data type aren't both contained in square brackets.

- We know that the -Property parameter is entirely optional for this command. That's because the entire parameter, both its name and data type, is contained in square brackets: [[-Property]<String[]>].

- We know that the -Amended parameter doesn't accept a value—it's a *switch*. This means you either provide the parameter or not, but if you do, it doesn't need a value.

- We know that the -Class parameter accepts a String value, meaning a string of characters. If the string contains a space, tab, or other whitespace, it must be enclosed within single or double quotes.

- We know that the -Property parameter accepts one or more strings, because its value is shown with two square brackets jammed together: <String[]>. That's a PowerShell indication for an array. You could provide those multiple values as a comma-separated list.

- We know that the -Authentication and -Impersonation parameters are limited to a discrete set of values because those values are supplied in curly braces {}.

TIP   Try to avoid using parameters positionally if you're getting started with PowerShell. Positional parameters make it harder to interpret commands, and you're taking on the responsibility of getting everything lined up in perfect order. By typing the parameter names, you're removing the worry of getting everything in the right order. The order doesn't matter if you type the parameter names. You're also making the command line easier to read. Positional parameters should be avoided in scripts or functions. Typing the parameter name now makes reading and maintenance in the future a whole lot easier.

Yes, that's a lot of information. You can find most of that in a more detailed fashion when you're viewing the detailed or full help. For example, what follows is the section specifically for the -Class parameter:

```
-Class <String>
    Specifies the name of a WMI class. When this parameter is used,
    the cmdlet retrieves instances of the WMI class.
    Required?                    true
    Position?                    1
    Default value
    Accept pipeline input?       false
    Accept wildcard characters?  False
```

In this example, you can see that the parameter is mandatory (required), that its value can be passed in position 1, and that it accepts data of the String type. There's also a bit more detail about what the parameter does—some parameters' detailed help even includes brief examples. The list of acceptable values is also often provided in the case of parameters only taking values from a restricted group, as follows:

```
PS C:\> Get-Help Get-EventLog -Parameter EntryType
-EntryType<string[]>
    Gets only events with the specified entry type. Valid values are Error,
    Information, FailureAudit, SuccessAudit, and Warning. The default is all
    events.
    Required?                      false
    Position?                      named
    Default value                  All events
    Accept pipeline input?         false
    Accept wildcard characters?    false
```

3.8   *Common parameters*

You'll notice that every command's help file references <CommonParameters> at the end of each parameter set. These are a set of parameters that are automatically added by PowerShell to every command. You can read about them in an about file:

```
PS C:\> help about_common*
TOPIC
about_CommonParameters
SHORT DESCRIPTION
    Describes the parameters that can be used with any cmdlet.
LONG DESCRIPTION
    The common parameters are a set of cmdlet parameters that you can
    use with any cmdlet. They are implemented by Windows PowerShell, not
    by the cmdlet developer, and they are automatically available to any
    cmdlet.
    You can use the common parameters with any cmdlet, but they might
    not have an effect on all cmdlets. For example, if a cmdlet does not
    generate any verbose output, using the Verbose common parameter
    has no effect.
```

The common parameters are:

- Debug
- ErrorAction
- ErrorVariable
- OutVariable
- OutBuffer
- PipelineVariable
- Verbose
- WarningAction
- WarningVariable

We'll address each of the common parameters throughout this book, in the chapters that deal with each one's specific function, so we won't cover them any further here.

Most commands that modify the system in some way support two other "semi-common" parameters:

- -Confirm—Asks you to confirm each operation before performing it.
- -WhatIf—Doesn't perform the operation, but instead indicates what would've been done. This is kind of a "test run" and generally must only be used with the

last command on the command line, because it prevents the command from doing anything. This parameter is usually available only on cmdlets that can perform modifications to your system.

These parameters (referred to in the help file as risk mitigation parameters) must be defined by the cmdlet and supported by the provider. For example, Stop-Service has a -WhatIf parameter that you can see when you're looking at help:

```
PS C:\> Stop-Service wuauserv -WhatIf
What if: Performing operation "Stop-Service" on Target "Windows Update
 (wuauserv)".
```

-WhatIf is an example of a great sanity check to make sure your command will execute what you intend. You may also have to check the PSProvider to see if it supports ShouldProcess:

```
PS C:\> Get-PSProvider | where {$_.Capabilities -match "ShouldProcess"} |
     Select name
     Name
     ----
     Alias
     Environment
     FileSystem
     Function
     Registry
     Variable
```

For example, New-Item supports -WhatIf and it works fine in the filesystem. But you may have a snap-in or a module that adds a new provider that might not support it. If in doubt, check the provider.

3.9   *Summary*

PowerShell's help system is a powerful tool—and because it's fundamental to using the shell, we included this chapter in the beginning of the book in hopes you'd find it right away. PowerShell v3 introduced a couple of caveats, such as the need to download the help to your computer before the help system becomes fully functional, but we hope that'll be a minor hurdle for most administrators. The ability to download help based on the modules installed on a remote machine is an additional feature introduced with PowerShell v4.

The basics of PowerShell syntax

Any time you're learning to use a new tool, particularly one that involves typed commands, the syntax can be the biggest "gotcha." We won't pretend that every single bit of PowerShell's syntax is easy to remember, makes perfect sense, and is totally consistent. In the end, the syntax is what it is—we (and you) have to learn it and deal with it.

If you've used PowerShell a bit already, and if you've picked up some of its syntax from reading other people's blogs and articles on the internet, you may have an inaccurate view of the syntax. You also need to remember that best practice has evolved over the eight-plus years we've had between the original release of Power-Shell and the latest version. This chapter will help set you straight.

4.1   Commands

PowerShell has four features that we think of as *commands*:

- Internal cmdlets, which only run inside PowerShell and are written in a .NET Framework language such as Visual Basic or C#
- Functions, which are written in PowerShell's scripting language
- PowerShell v3 and v4 cmdlets, which are produced from WMI (Windows Management Instrumentation) classes using the "cmdlets over objects" capabilities
- External commands, such as ping.exe, which could also be run from the old cmd.exe shell

In this chapter, we'll focus only on the first two command types.

> **NOTE**   What's in a name? Sometimes, a lot of cleverness. Microsoft chose the name "cmdlet" for PowerShell's internal commands, because that word hadn't been used for anything else, ever. If you hop on your favorite search engine and include "cmdlet" in your search query, the results you get will be almost 100% PowerShell-related, because the word "cmdlet" isn't used in any other context.

PowerShell cmdlets have a specific naming convention. Functions *should* follow this same convention, but PowerShell doesn't require them to do so. That convention is called *verb-noun*. A cmdlet name starts with a verb, which is followed by a dash, which is followed by a singular noun. PowerShell isn't case sensitive, so capitalization of commands is a matter of personal preference and convention. Tab completion will capitalize for you according to convention. Consider some of these cmdlet names:

- `Get-Service`
- `New-ADUser`
- `Set-Service`
- `Write-EventLog`
- `Enter-PSSession`

Microsoft strictly controls the verbs that everyone can use for a cmdlet name. Although it's possible for someone to create a cmdlet—or a function—that uses non-standard verbs, PowerShell will display a warning when loading those into memory. You can find the official list of approved verbs at http://msdn.microsoft.com/en-us/library/windows/desktop/ms714428(v=vs.85).aspx, which is part of the PowerShell Software Development Kit (SDK) documentation. You can also see the list by running the `Get-Verb` cmdlet (`Get-Verb` is actually a function but it's treated as a cmdlet).

> **NOTE**   The approved verbs list hasn't changed between PowerShell v3 and PowerShell v4.

Nouns aren't controlled, but they should always be singular ("Service" versus "Services"), and they should clearly describe whatever it is they're examining or manipulating. For example, we recommend using "Mailbox," which is clearer than something like "mbx."

Why are these rules in place? They're for your benefit. If you'd never worked with System Center Virtual Machine Manager, you could guess that the cmdlet used to retrieve a list of virtual machines would be named something like "Get-VirtualMachine." You could then use PowerShell's help functionality to look for help on that cmdlet name, which would validate your guess.

> **TIP** Wildcard searching is often the best way to start. `Get-Command *net*` will give a significant number of responses but will enable you to quickly discover the networking cmdlets.

But with the exception of Microsoft Exchange Server, you'll find that most products that offer PowerShell-based tools have cmdlet nouns that include a short prefix. It's not "Get-User," but rather "Get-**AD**User." The idea behind the prefixes is to tie a cmdlet to a specific technology or vendor. For example, Quest (now a part of Dell) has a set of cmdlets for managing Active Directory. Their user cmdlet is called "Get-QADUser." By using a prefix, the cmdlet name is clear about what kind of user it's working with or at least what product. It's not a SQL Server user, it's not a local user, it's an **AD**User or a **QAD**User. This is important because the Microsoft and Quest cmdlets produce different object types, which would confuse PowerShell's formatting engine, along with everyone else. Exchange Server is an exception: It uses "Get-Mailbox" rather than "Get-ExMailbox." If they had it to do over, we're sure Microsoft would've chosen the latter, but Exchange Server shipped before anyone thought of using the noun prefixes.

> **WARNING** When people speak aloud about cmdlets, they tend to be a bit lazy. They'll say, "Get Service," which might lead you to believe that you could type "Get Service" and have it work. Nope. Never forget that there's always a dash between the verb and noun. Even though people might not say "Get dash Service," you'd type `Get-Service`.

You might feel that cmdlet names are long and hard to type. They certainly can be—`Reset-ADAccountPassword` is a mouthful whether you're saying it or typing it. PowerShell offers two features to help make typing easier.

4.1.1 *Aliases: nicknames for commands*

An alias is a nickname for a command name. Aliases can point to cmdlets or to functions, and they provide a short way to type the command's name. Typing `dir` is a lot easier than typing `Get-ChildItem`, for example.

An alias is *only* a shortcut for a command's *name.* As you'll learn in a moment, commands can be accompanied by parameters, which specify and modify a command's behavior. An alias never includes any parameters. You can't create an alias to run `dir $env:temp -File -Recurse`, although you could create a simple function and define an alias for the function.

We strongly recommend using aliases only when you're interactively typing commands into the PowerShell console. If you decide to create a script, or even if you copy and paste a command into a script, use full command names (some commercial editors can expand aliases into their full command names for you).

> **WARNING** Never use your own created aliases in scripts that you're distributing to others. They may not have those aliases or, even worse, they may have defined those aliases to something else. Never assume the presence or meaning of an alias.

Although the aliases are easy to type, they're more difficult to read, particularly for someone with less PowerShell experience. Using full command names helps make it clearer what a script is doing, making the script easier to maintain.

4.1.2 Command name tab completion

Most PowerShell hosts—including the console and ISE provided by Microsoft—provide a feature called *tab completion*. It's a way of letting the shell type for you. For example, open a PowerShell console window and type Get-P. Then, press the Tab key on your keyboard. Keep pressing Tab, and you'll see PowerShell cycle through all of the available commands that match what you'd already typed. Press Shift+Tab to cycle backward.

We think this is a great way to use full command names without having to type so much.

4.2 Parameters

Even if you've never used PowerShell before, we can guarantee you've used parameters. Take a look at figure 4.1, a dialog box you've probably seen before. It shows the User Properties dialog box from Active Directory Users and Computers.

The labels in the dialog box in figure 4.1—"First name," "Last name," "Description," and so forth—are parameters. What you type into the text boxes are parameter values. PowerShell uses a more text-friendly way of representing parameters and values. Take a look at figure 4.2 and you'll see what we mean.

In figure 4.2, we're running a command called New-ADUser that's part of Microsoft Active Directory module. It has several parameters, which all start with a hyphen or a dash, followed by the parameter name. Because parameter names can't contain spaces, the parameter names sometimes look a little strange, like -GivenName. After the parameter name you have a space and then the parameter value. You always have to enclose string values in quotation marks (either single or double, it doesn't matter) when the string contains a space. None of our values included spaces, so we didn't have to use the quotes, but it doesn't hurt to do so anyway.

> **TIP** PowerShell's cmdlet and parameter names aren't case sensitive. If you use tab completion, you'll get capitalization, but if you type the names, any old case will do. We regularly work interactively in lowercase. We will say that capitalization of cmdlet and parameter names makes your scripts easier to read.

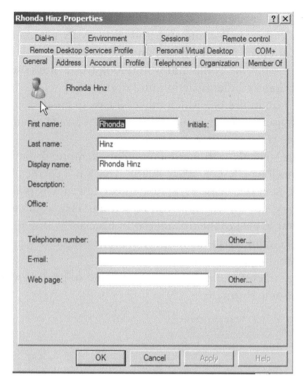

Figure 4.1 **Even dialog boxes have parameters.**

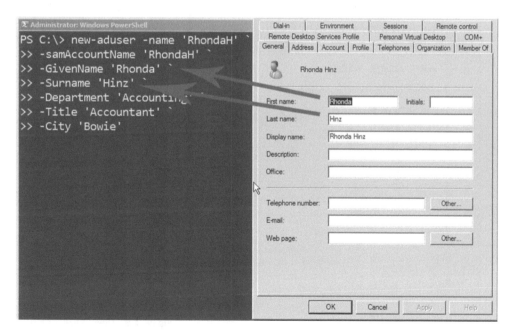

Figure 4.2 **Graphical parameters map to the text-based parameters used by PowerShell.**

PowerShell v3 introduced a new cmdlet called Show-Command (also present in v4 and later), which takes another PowerShell command and displays its parameters in a graphical dialog box. You can fill in the dialog box and either run the command or click a different button to see what the command would look like written out in text. Figure 4.3 shows the Show-Command cmdlet in action on Windows 8.

This cmdlet is also turned on in the ISE, which makes it easy to create a command by checking parameters and inserting it into your script. Show-Command is available as a docked window in the ISE; see chapter 2 to learn more.

We sometimes see people struggle with parameters. For example, if they want to get a service named BITS, they'll type "Get-Service –BITS." That's not correct. The correct command would be Get-Service -Name BITS. Remember, after the hyphen comes the parameter name—the piece of information you're setting. That's followed by a space, then the value you want to give to the parameter. In his classes, Don makes students chant "dash name space value, dash name space value, dash name space value" for several minutes, to be sure the pattern sinks in.

Like command names, parameter names can get a bit tedious to type. As with commands, PowerShell provides some shortcuts.

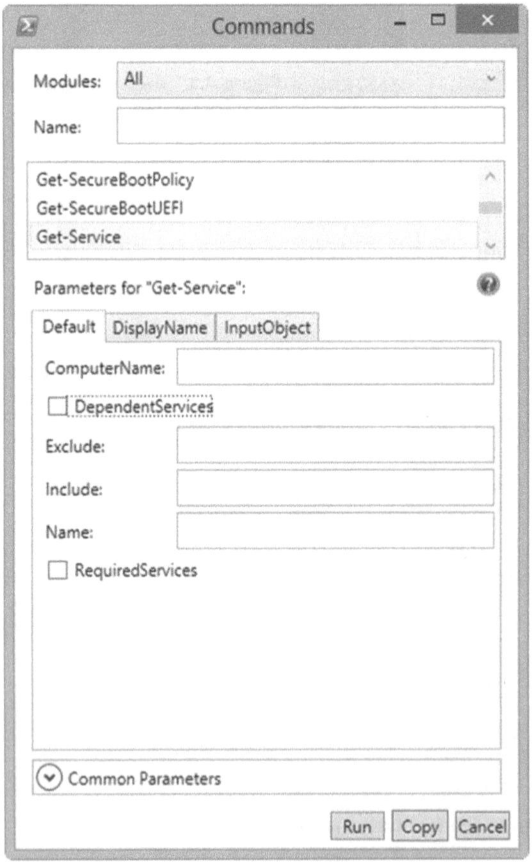

Figure 4.3   PowerShell's Show-Command **cmdlet graphically prompts you to fill in a command's parameters.**

4.2.1 *Truncating parameter names*

PowerShell requires that you type only enough of the parameter name to differentiate it from the other parameters available to the command. For example, consider the Get-Service cmdlet, which has the following syntax:

```
Get-Service [[-Name] <string[]>] [-ComputerName <string[]>]
[-DependentServices] [-RequiredServices]
[-Include <string[]>] [-Exclude <string[]>]
[<CommonParameters>]

Get-Service -DisplayName <string[]> [-ComputerName <string[]>]
[-DependentServices] [-RequiredServices]
[-Include <string[]>] [-Exclude <string[]>]
[<CommonParameters>]

Get-Service [-InputObject <ServiceController[]>]
[-ComputerName <string[]>]
[-DependentServices] [-RequiredServices]
[-Include <string[]>] [-Exclude <string[]>]
[<CommonParameters>]
```

Only one parameter starts with the letter "C," and that's -ComputerName. Therefore, instead of typing Get-Service -ComputerName SRV23 you could type Get-Service -c SRV23. Two parameters start with the letter "D," though: -DependentServices and -DisplayName. You couldn't shorten those to only one letter; you'd need to type -de or -di at a minimum.

As with command aliases, shortened parameter names are easy to type but hard to read. When someone else comes along and reads a script with lines like the following:

```
gsv -di BITS -c SERVER2 -de
```

they're likely to be a little confused, don't you think? Coming back to that code six months after writing it, you may be confused as well. That's why we suggest including full, complete parameter names when you're putting commands into a script. With tab completion available it's just as easy to use the full name and saves having to remember all of the aliases.

4.2.2 *Parameter name tab completion*

The good news is that tab completion works for parameter names, too. Type Get-S, press Tab multiple times to complete the command name to Get-Service, and then type -c and press Tab. PowerShell will fill in -ComputerName for you. You can still truncate your parameter names when you're typing, or one or two extra keystrokes on the Tab key will get you the fully spelled-out name that's easier to read. Not sure about any of the parameters? After entering a cmdlet name, if you type a dash and then press Tab you can cycle through all the parameters.

While we're talking about parameter completion, later versions of PowerShell can also guess what value you want. Try this: At a PowerShell prompt type Get-Service -n and press Tab. That should complete -Name. Then press the spacebar and hit the Tab key again. PowerShell should display the first service. You can keep pressing Tab to find the service you want. Use Shift-Tab to go backwards. This even works for positional parameters. At a new prompt type `Get-Service` followed by a space. Then start pressing the Tab key. How cool is that!

> **TIP** This tab completion trick works with other things in PowerShell like WMI classes. Start typing a command like `Get-WmiObject win32_` then wait a few seconds and start pressing Tab. You should be able to cycle through the class names. The names should be cached so that the next time you use `Get-WmiObject` or `Get-CimInstance` you can start tabbing immediately.

4.3   *Typing trick: line continuation*

Sometimes, typing in PowerShell can be frustrating. For example, you might find yourself looking at a strange prompt, like the following:

```
PS C:\> Get-Process -Name "svchost
>>
```

What the heck?

That ">>" prompt is PowerShell's way of telling you, "I know you're not finished typing, so keep going!" If you look carefully, you'll notice that we forgot to include the closing quotation mark after "svchost." PowerShell knows that quotes always come in pairs, so it's waiting for us to finish typing the last quote. In this case, we goofed, so we press Ctrl-C to break out of that "continuation prompt" and try our command again.

Sometimes, this can be a useful trick. PowerShell will let you "continue" like this whenever you have an unclosed structure: Quotation marks, square brackets, curly brackets, and parentheses all enclose a structure. PowerShell will also let you "continue" when a line ends in a comma, pipe character, or semicolon, because those all tell it that there's "more to come." Finally, if a line ends in a backtick (`) and a carriage return, that also tells the shell to let you continue typing. Using these tricks, you can break a long, complex command onto several lines, as follows:

```
PS C:\> Get-Service -Name B*,
>> A*,
>> C* |
>> where {
>>        $_.Status -eq 'Running'
>> } |
>> sort Status
>>

Status    Name            DisplayName
------    ----            -----------
Running   COMSysApp       COM+ System Application
Running   CryptSvc        Cryptographic Services
Running   BFE             Base Filtering Engine
Running   ADWS            Active Directory Web Services
Running   AppHostSvc      Application Host Helper Service
```

We ran the following command in the example:

```
Get-Service –Name B*,A*,C* | where { $_.Status -eq 'Running' } | sort Status
```

But we used PowerShell's little "continuation" tricks to break it onto several lines. Notice that we had to press Enter on the final, blank line, to tell the shell that we were finally finished typing and that it should execute the command.

These same "continuation rules" apply when you're in a script, too, and folks will use these rules to help format a script's commands so that they're more readable. In our case, we use them to help keep each line of the script short enough to fit in this book. In scripts we recommend the pipe character, braces, and commas. The backtick is usually not needed unless you have a very long line of code.

4.4　*Parenthetical commands and expressions*

Do you remember algebra? Whether you loved it or hated it, we hope you remember one thing: parentheses. In algebra, parentheses mean "do this first." Take a mathematical expression like this one:

```
(5 + 5) * 10
```

The answer is 100, because you first add the 5 and 5, getting 10, and then multiply that by 10. When you were first learning algebra, you probably wrote out each step:

```
(5 + 5) * 10
   10    * 10
          100
```

PowerShell works the same way, both with mathematical expressions and with more complex commands.

For example, use Notepad to create a simple text file that includes one computer name per line. Figure 4.4 shows the text file.

Next, return to PowerShell and display the contents of the file. You do this by running the `Get-Content` cmdlet, although you may be more familiar with the `type` or `cat` alias:

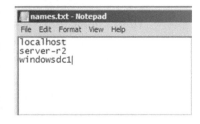

Figure 4.4　Creating a list of computer names in Notepad

```
PS C:\> Get-Content names.txt
localhost
server-r2
windowsdc1
```

Suppose you want to retrieve a list of running processes from each of those computers. One way to do so involves typing their names:

```
Get-Process –ComputerName localhost,server-r2,windowsdc1
```

That's going to become tedious if you have to keep doing it over and over. Because you've got the names in a text file, why not let PowerShell type the names for you?

```
Get-Process –ComputerName (Get-Content names.txt)
```

Think about algebra when you read this: PowerShell executes whatever's inside the parentheses first. The parentheses will, in effect, be replaced by whatever is produced. So if you were going to write this out, step by step, as you would in algebra, it might look like the following:

```
Get-Process -ComputerName (Get-Content names.txt)
Get-Process -ComputerName localhost,server-r2,windowsdc1
```

That second version is exactly what you could've typed manually—but you let Power-Shell arrive at that on its own. This demonstrates that a parenthetical expression, or parenthetical command, can stand in for any manually typed data. You only need to make sure that the command is producing the exact type of data that you'd have provided manually.

You'll see a lot more examples of parenthetical commands as we progress through this book. It's an important technique in PowerShell and one that we'll reinforce as we go.

4.5 Script blocks

PowerShell supports a special kind of structure called a *script block*. A script block can contain any set of PowerShell commands, and it can contain as many of them as you need. In the same way that strings are enclosed in quotation marks, a script block is enclosed in curly brackets, or braces:

```
$sb={ Get-CimInstance -ClassName Win32_OperatingSystem ; Get-CimInstance
➥ -ClassName Win32_ComputerSystem }
```

This example uses a semicolon to separate two commands, which allows them to each execute sequentially and independently. The script block has been saved to a variable, $sb. You could also have written the script block as follows:

```
$sb={
 Get-CimInstance -ClassName Win32_OperatingSystem
 Get-CimInstance -ClassName Win32_ComputerSystem
}
```

Separate code lines like the second example are generally easier to read if you have a complicated block of code. In any event, both commands are contained within that same script block. This can be passed as a single unit to anything capable of accepting a script block such as Invoke-Command. Script blocks can also be invoked using the call operator (&). We're a bit early in the book to provide a real-world example of using script blocks, but we want to bring them to your attention. We'll remind you of them when we're ready to put them to use.

4.6 Summary

We've looked at some of the basics of PowerShell's syntax. We have more to cover, but most of what's ahead will build on these basics. Yes, PowerShell uses a lot of punctuation in its syntax: You've seen dashes, curly brackets, parentheses, semicolons, quotation marks, and a bit more in this chapter. Keeping track of all of them is the price of admission for using PowerShell. The shell can do a lot for you, but only after you learn to speak its language, so that you can tell it what you need. You're on the right track, and this chapter covered some of the most important bits that you'll need.

PowerShell is an extensible environment. We've mentioned the Active Directory and Exchange cmdlets in this chapter, both of which are delivered as extensions to the PowerShell base. In chapter 5 you'll learn how to work with the PowerShell snap-ins and modules used to provide these extensions.

Working with PSSnapins and modules

PowerShell's real value lies not in the hundreds of built-in commands that it ships with but in its ability to have more commands added. PowerShell extensions—our collective term for the PSSnapins and modules that can be loaded—permit Power-Shell to manage anything: IIS, Exchange, SQL Server, VMware, Citrix, NetApp, SharePoint, Cisco, you name it. Being able to efficiently work with these extensions is probably one of the most important things you'll do in the shell.

5.1 There's only one shell

Before we jump into working with these extensions, let's get something straight: There's no such thing as a product-specific version of PowerShell. It's easy to get the impression that such a thing exists, because Microsoft tends to create Start menu shortcuts with names like "Exchange Management Shell," "SharePoint Man-agement Shell," and so forth.

NOTE The PowerShell functionality in SQL Server 2008 and 2008 R2 is the only exception to this rule of which we know. It had its own version of Power-Shell—sqlps.exe—that was a recompiled version of PowerShell with the SQL Server functionality added and the snap-in functionality removed. SQL Server 2012 delivers its PowerShell functionality as a module (confusingly called sqlps) so we'll forget (and possibly even forgive) the oddity that was sqlps.exe.

The fact is that these Start menu shortcuts are running plain ol' powershell.exe and passing a command-line argument that has the shell do one of four things:

- Autoload a PowerShell console (.psc) file, which specifies one or more PSSnap-ins to load into memory at startup
- Autorun a PowerShell script (.ps1) file, which can define commands, load extensions, show a "tip of the day," and whatever else the authors desire
- Autoload a module
- Autoload a PSSnapin

You can look at the properties of these Start menu shortcuts to see which of these four tricks they're using to provide the illusion of a product-specific shell—and you can manually perform the same task in a "plain" PowerShell console to replicate the results. There's nothing stopping you from loading the Exchange stuff into the same shell where you've already loaded the SharePoint stuff, creating a "custom" shell in much the same way that you could always create a custom graphical Microsoft Management Console (MMC) environment. In fact, it's less confusing if you do this because you don't have to worry about which "shell" supplies which functionality.

5.2 *PSSnapins vs. modules*

PowerShell has two types of extensions: PSSnapins and modules. Both are capable of adding cmdlets and PSProviders to the shell (we'll get into PSProviders in chapter 15); modules are also capable of adding functions to the shell (we refer to functions and cmdlets as "commands" because they do the same thing in the same way).

PSSnapins are the "v1 way" of extending the shell, although they're still supported in v2, v3, and v4. Microsoft's advice is for folks to not make PSSnapins anymore, but it isn't preventing anyone from doing so. PSSnapins are written in a .NET language like C# or Visual Basic, and they're packaged as DLL files. They have to be installed and registered with the system before PowerShell can see them and load them into memory.

Modules, introduced in v2, are the preferred way of extending the shell. Sometimes they have to be installed, but most of the time they can be copied from system to system—it depends a bit on the underlying dependencies the module may have on other components or code. Modules can benefit from autoloading, too, which we'll discuss next.

5.3   *Loading, autoloading, and profiles*

Prior to PowerShell v3, you had to figure out what extensions were on your system and manually load them into memory. Doing so could be tricky, and you had to load them each time you started a new shell session.

As a workaround, you could also create a PowerShell *profile*. A profile is a PowerShell script file stored in a specific folder and with a specific filename. If the file exists when PowerShell starts, it runs it. The script could therefore be programmed to load whatever extensions you want, every time the shell started, eliminating some manual effort on your part. You can read more about profiles by running `help about_profiles` in the shell.

In PowerShell v3 and later, much of that is unnecessary for many extensions, thanks to a feature called *module autoloading*. This feature makes modules look "available" even when they're not loaded, and it implicitly loads them into memory when you try to run one of their commands. Let's look at some specific rules about which extensions can take advantage of this feature:

- Only modules, not PSSnapins, support autoloading.
- Only modules stored in specific locations are eligible. These locations are defined in the `PSModulePath` environment variable, which you can modify to include additional locations (such as a shared location on a file server).
- Autoloading behavior can be changed, which we'll discuss later in this chapter.

5.4   *Using extensions*

Using extensions involves three steps: discovering what you've installed, loading them, and discovering what they've added to the shell.

5.4.1   *Discovering extensions*

To see the PSSnapins that are installed on your system, use the following command:

```
PS C:\> Get-PSSnapin -Registered
```

This command displays the registered snap-ins, excluding the core PowerShell snap-ins in PowerShell v2, regardless of whether they're loaded. If you want to see only the loaded snap-ins, use `Get-PSSnapin`, which shows the core PowerShell snap-ins.

> **NOTE**   In PowerShell v3 and v4 the core PowerShell functionality is delivered as modules. In PowerShell v3 they're also listed as `PSSnapins` by `Get-PSSnapin` but PowerShell v4 only lists the `Microsoft.PowerShell.Core` snap-in.

You can do the same trick for modules, using a different command:

```
PS C:\> Get-Module -ListAvailable
    Directory: C:\Windows\system32\WindowsPowerShell\v1.0\Modules
ModuleType Name                            ExportedCommands
---------- ----                            ----------------
Manifest   ADDeploymentWF                  Invoke-ADCommand
Manifest   AppLocker                       {Get-AppLockerFileInform...
```

```
Manifest    Appx                            {Add-AppxPackage, Get-Ap...
Manifest    BestPractices                   {Get-BpaModel, Get-BpaRe...
Manifest    BitsTransfer                    {Add-BitsFile, Complete-...
Manifest    BranchCache                     {Add-BCDataCacheExtensio...
Manifest    CimCmdlets                      {Get-CimAssociatedInstan...
Manifest    DirectAccessClientComponents    {Disable-DAManualEntryPo...
```

We want to point out a few more caveats about this command. Because there's no central registration of modules, as there is for PSSnapins, the command can only include those modules that are installed to specific locations. Those locations are defined in a systemwide environment variable, `PSModulePath`:

```
PS C:\> $env:psmodulepath
C:\Users\Administrator\Documents\WindowsPowerShell\Modules;C:\Program
Files\WindowsPowerShell\Modules;C:\windows\system32\WindowsPowerShell\v1.0\
Modules\
```

> **NOTE** In PowerShell v4, C:\Program Files\WindowsPowerShell\Modules has been added to the module path (for Desired State Configuration primarily). You won't see that in earlier versions.

As with any Windows environment variable, you can change this variable to include alternate or additional locations that should be autosearched for modules. In fact, some third-party PowerShell solutions might update this variable.

> **NOTE** You'll still need to use the –ListAvailable parameter of Get-Module, because even though PowerShell v4 "sees" all modules automatically, thanks to its autoloading feature Get-Module sees only modules that are fully loaded—either by using Import-Module or by using a command in a module that triggers a full load in the background.

In chapter 10, we'll discuss PowerShell Remoting, which is the shell's ability to maintain a connection with remote computers. The Get-Module cmdlet has a special feature that uses Remoting to list the modules available on a remote machine. For example, create a Remoting session to another computer, and then see what modules it contains:

```
PS C:\> $session = New-PSSession -ComputerName Win8
PS C:\> Get-Module -PSSession $session -ListAvailable
ModuleType Name                            ExportedCommands
---------- ----                            ----------------
Manifest   ActiveDirectory                 {Set-ADAccountPassword, ...
Manifest   ADDeploymentWF                  Invoke-ADCommand
Manifest   ADDSDeployment                  {Install-ADDSForest, Add...
Manifest   AppLocker                       {Set-AppLockerPolicy, Ne...
Manifest   Appx                            {Remove-AppxPackage, Get...
Manifest   BestPractices                   {Get-BpaResult, Set-BpaR...
Manifest   BitsTransfer                    {Complete-BitsTransfer, ...
Manifest   BranchCache                     {Get-BCNetworkConfigurat...
Manifest   CimCmdlets                      {Get-CimSession, New-Cim...
Manifest   DirectAccessClientComponents    {New-DAEntryPointTableIt...
Script     Dism                            {Use-WindowsUnattend, Ad...
```

```
Manifest    DnsClient                        {Resolve-DnsName, Remove...
Manifest    International                     {Set-Culture, Get-WinHom...
Manifest    iSCSI                            {Disconnect-iSCSITarget,...
Manifest    IscsiTarget                      {Convert-IscsiVirtualDis...
Manifest    Kds                              {Get-KdsConfiguration, G...
```

This example reveals a great trick for discovering the modules that exist on a remote machine. In chapter 10, we'll also explore a technique called *implicit remoting*, which lets you load those remotely stored modules into your own, local PowerShell session—which means once you've discovered modules, it's easy to start using them.

5.4.2 *Loading extensions*

To load a PSSnapin, you *add* it to your session:

```
PS C:\> Add-PSSnapin microsoft.sqlserver.cmdletsnapin.100
```

Specify the PSSnapin name as revealed by Get-PSSnapin –Registered. Modules are loaded similarly, although in this case you *import* them:

```
PS C:\> Import-Module storage
```

Note that some modules are script modules, meaning they can load only if you've enabled execution of scripts. If you try to load one on a default PowerShell configuration where scripting isn't enabled, you'll get an error message. You'll need to enable script execution, which we cover in chapter 17, or you can read the help for the Set-ExecutionPolicy command to learn how to load such a module.

> **NOTE** For modules stored in one of the PSModulePath locations, you won't need to import the module explicitly. PowerShell will import the module automatically through its autoloading feature the first time you try to run one of the commands in the module.

If modules aren't stored in one of the PSModulePath locations, you can import them by providing the full path to the module's folder, rather than providing only the module's name. For example, a module stored in C:\MyModules\Fred would be loaded by running Import-Module C:\MyModules\Fred. Because that module doesn't live in one of the autosearched locations, it wouldn't be autoloaded, nor would it be revealed by running Get-Module –ListAvailable.

5.4.3 *Discovering extensions' additions*

Once an extension is loaded, you can see what commands it contains:

```
PS C:\> Get-Command -Module storage
CommandType     Name                               ModuleName
-----------     ----                               ----------
Alias           Initialize-Volume                  storage
Function        Add-InitiatorIdToMaskingSet        storage
Function        Add-PartitionAccessPath            storage
Function        Add-PhysicalDisk                   storage
```

```
Function          Add-TargetPortToMaskingSet                              storage
Function          Add-VirtualDiskToMaskingSet                             storage
Function          Clear-Disk                                              storage
Function          Connect-VirtualDisk                                     storage
```

This technique works with both modules and PSSnapins. From here, you can ask for help on a specific command to learn how to use it.

> **NOTE** The –Module parameter has an alias, -PSSnapin, which makes it also legal to run Get-Command –PSSnapin My.Snapin.Name. It's the same effect.

Keep in mind that extensions can add more than commands; they can also add providers. To see what providers are available on your machine, run the following:

```
PS C:\> Get-PSProvider
Name              Capabilities                Drives
----              ------------                ------
Alias             ShouldProcess               {Alias}
Environment       ShouldProcess               {Env}
FileSystem        Filter, ShouldProcess, ...  {C, A, D}
Function          ShouldProcess               {Function}
Registry          ShouldProcess, Transact...  {HKLM, HKCU}
Variable          ShouldProcess               {Variable}
WSMan             Credentials                 {WSMan}
Certificate       ShouldProcess               {Cert}
```

This is the list from a standard Windows 8.1 machine. You may see more providers if you have other modules loaded such as those for Active Directory or SQL Server. In a newly opened PowerShell console, you may not see the WSMan or Certificate provider in the list until you have accessed them because they aren't part of the core PowerShell load.

We didn't filter for a specific module or PSSnapin, so you'll see all available providers. Remember that you can ask for help on a provider (help alias, for example) once it's loaded.

5.4.4 Managing extensions

You can use the following commands to manage extensions:

- Remove-Module unloads a module.
- Get-Module displays a list of all loaded modules in the current PowerShell session.
- Remove-PSSnapin removes a PSSnapin.
- Get-PSSnapin displays a list of all loaded PSSnapins in the current PowerShell session.

Generally, when you remove a module or a snap-in all of its commands are removed from your PowerShell session. But be aware that some items, such as custom type or format extensions, might persist. This may not be a big deal, but you may get an exception if you reimport or readd the module or PSSnapin in the same session. If so, you can ignore the error message. Using a new PowerShell console is one way to avoid these messages.

5.5   *Command name conflicts*

When you start loading up a bunch of modules or PSSnapins, it's obviously possible for two of them to contain commands having the same name. So what happens?

By default, when you run a command, PowerShell runs the last version of that command that was loaded into memory—that is, whichever one was loaded most recently. That command has the effect of "hiding" commands having the same name that were loaded earlier. There's a specific purpose for that behavior: It enables something called *proxy functions*, which we'll discuss in chapter 37.

But you can access any specific command you want to by providing a fully qualified name. That name combines the name of the PSSnapin or module that contains the command you want, a backslash, and then the command name. `ActiveDirectory\Get-ADUser`, for example, will run the `Get-ADUser` command contained in the Active-Directory module or PSSnapin, even if some other extension has more recently loaded a different "Get-ADUser" command.

An alternative is to use the `-Prefix` parameter of `Import-Module`, which enables you to add a prefix to the noun for each of the cmdlets (or functions) in your module. Assume you had a module called `MyModule` that contains

```
Get-MyNoun
Set-MyNoun
```

If you import it as `Import-Module MyModule -Prefix DJR`, the functions would have a prefix applied and would become

```
Get-DJRMyNoun
Set-DJRMyNoun
```

Now you can run these commands without worrying about naming collisions.

In PowerShell v4, you can also get modules by a fully qualified name. If for some reason you have two modules with the same name but they're different versions (don't ask us why you would), you can specify the module you want. `FullyQualifiedname` is a special hash table of the format `@{ModuleName="MyModule";ModuleVersion="1.0"}`. Both `Get-Module` and `Get-Module -ListAvailable` provide the version number and name as part of the default display:

```
PS C:\> Get-Module -FullyQualifiedName @{ModuleName="Applocker";
➥ ModuleVersion="2.0"} -ListAvailable

    Directory: C:\WINDOWS\system32\WindowsPowerShell\v1.0\Modules

ModuleType Version    Name                    ExportedCommands
---------- -------    ----                    ----------------
Manifest   2.0.0.0    AppLocker               {Get-AppLockerFile...
```

You'll want to include `-ListAvailable`. If this is the module you wanted to import, the best thing is to pipe it to `Import-Module`:

```
PS C:\> Get-Module -FullyQualifiedName @{ModuleName="Applocker";
➥ ModuleVersion="2.0"} -ListAvailable | Import-Module
```

Now, there's an odd quirk here, or perhaps a bug. If you specify a version but the only version you have is *newer*, you'll get the newer version. We assume the reasoning is that the newer version is backwards compatible. But if you ask for a version that's newer than the one that's installed, you'll get nothing. In our example, the AppLocker module is at version 2.0. If we ask for version 1.0, we'll get this version. But if we ask for version 3.0, we'll get nothing.

5.6 *Managing module autoloading*

PowerShell has a built-in variable, `$PSModuleAutoLoadingPreference`, that controls autoloading behavior. You probably won't see this variable if you run `Get-Variable`. PowerShell's default behavior is to autoload all modules. But you can explicitly create the variable and assign it one of the following values:

- `All`—Automatically imports a module on first use of any command contained in the module.
- `ModuleQualified`—Modules are loaded automatically only if you use a qualified command name, such as `MyModule\Do-Something`. Running only `Do-Something` wouldn't load the module containing that command.
- `None`—Modules aren't loaded automatically.

This variable doesn't prevent you from explicitly loading a module using `Import-Module`. But autoloading makes it easier because all you have to do is run the command and let PowerShell handle any necessary module imports. Be aware that this applies only to modules; you still need to manually add a PSSnapin before you can use any of its commands.

5.7 *Summary*

Managing PowerShell extensions is one key to being successful with the shell. Much of the functionality you'll rely on to accomplish administrative tasks comes from extensions rather than from the shell's core functionality. Being able to find, load, and inventory extensions is the primary way you can get needed functionality to the shell and have it available for your use.

Operators 6

This chapter covers

- Logical and comparison operators
- Bitwise operators
- Arithmetic operators
- Type operators
- Other special operators

In any computer language, *operators* provide a means of comparing and manipulating pieces of data. PowerShell's no exception, offering a wide variety of operators for different tasks.

Powershell supplies a number of help files on the various operators. We recommend that you read them in conjunction with this chapter. The help files contain numerous examples that will aid your understanding. The following help files are available:

- about_Operators
- about_Arithmetic_Operators
- about_Assignment_Operators
- about_Comparison_Operators

- about_Logical_Operators
- about_Operator_Precedence
- about_Type_Operators

All of these operators have a common syntactical form. Practically all PowerShell operators start with a dash or a hyphen, followed by the operator name. You'll see plenty of examples of this in the following sections and throughout the rest of the book. If you have prior experience with other scripting or programming languages, PowerShell's operators can seem confusing or odd at first, but you'll get used to them as you work with them.

6.1 Logical and comparison operators

Comparison operators are designed to take two pieces of data and compare them. They always return either True or False, known as Boolean values, based on whether or not the comparison was true.

> **NOTE** PowerShell has built-in variables ($True and $False) that represent the Boolean values True and False. Variables are covered in detail in chapter 16.

There are some cases where you may get an answer that isn't a Boolean value:

```
PS C:\> $a = 1,2,3
PS C:\> $a -eq 1
1
```

In reality, you're performing a comparison that doesn't make sense in that you're trying to compare an array of values to a single value. The correct comparison would be:

```
PS C:\> $a -contains 1
True
```

Or possibly:

```
PS C:\> $a[0] -eq 1
True
```

Table 6.1 shows the primary comparison operators in PowerShell. In the middle column, we've included the more common equivalent from other languages to allow you to match up operators with whatever prior experience you may have.

Table 6.1　PowerShell's comparison operators

Operator	Other languages	Purpose
-eq	= or ==	Equal to
-ne	<> or !=	Not equal to
-gt	>	Greater than

Table 6.1   PowerShell's comparison operators *(continued)*

Operator	Other languages	Purpose
-lt	<	Less than
-le	<=	Less than or equal to
-ge	>=	Greater than or equal to
-like, -notlike	n/a	Wildcard string comparison

> **NOTE**   Another comparison operator set, -match, -cmatch, -notmatch, and -cnotmatch, is used with regular expressions. Because it's a big topic, we're devoting an entire chapter to it (chapter 13). The PowerShell help file called about_comparison_operators also discusses -contains, -notcontains, and -replace. These, together with the bitwise operators, are the subject of later sections in this chapter.

All string comparisons are case *insensitive* by default. The following example would return True (try running it in the shell to prove it):

```
"HELLO" -eq "hello"
```

There may be times when you explicitly need to perform a case-sensitive string comparison, and PowerShell offers a set of alternate, case-sensitive operators for those times. Add a "c" after the dash in the operator: -ceq, -cne, and so forth. For example

```
PS C:\> "Hello" -ceq "hello"
False
```

> **NOTE**   It's also possible to use an "i" to force a case-insensitive comparison, for example, —ieq, -ine, and so on. It may seem odd to have these available when PowerShell is case-insensitive by default, but consider the situation where you have multiple comparisons to perform and some have to be case-sensitive and some case-insensitive. It'd be useful to be able to easily differentiate the type of comparison.

Be careful with the way you build your comparison. These all return the same result:

```
"Hello" -eq "hello"
"Hello" -ieq "hello"
"Hello" -cne "hello"
```

We recommend that you always use the simplest possible operator to aid debugging and working with the code in the future.

The size operators, -gt, -ge, -lt, and -le, are self-explanatory when used with numerical data:

```
PS C:\> 10 -gt 9
True
```

They really come into their own when you're using branching constructs, as explained in chapter 19. You may come across this apparent oddity:

```
PS C:\> 9 -gt "10"
False
PS C:\> 9 -lt "10"
True
```

PowerShell is converting the string to an integer so that it can perform the comparison. Any conversion activity involves the value on the right-hand side; that value is converted to the same type as the value on the left-hand side.

The -like operator, along with the case-sensitive -clike operator (case-insensitive versions exist as well), permits you to use ? and * as wildcards. For example, the following would return True:

```
"PowerShell" -like "*sh*"
```

You'll also find the -notlike and -cnotlike operators, which reverse the normal logic. This would return False:

```
"PowerShell" -notlike "*sh*"
```

You can type any of these examples directly into the PowerShell console, press Enter, and see the result. It offers an easy way to test different comparisons before using them in a longer command or script.

6.1.1   *The –contains operator*

We want to call special attention to this operator because it's often confused for -like. For example, you'll see folks try the following example, which won't work:

```
"PowerShell" -contains "*sh*"
```

The previous comparison will work fine if you use the -like operator, because its job is to compare strings using a wildcard comparison. But -contains is different. It's designed to look inside a collection of objects and see if that collection contains another object. For example, you could create a collection containing three strings and then test to see if the collection contains a fourth string:

```
$collection = "one","two","three"
$collection -contains "one"
```

That comparison would return True. The -contains operator is easy to understand with simple objects like strings or numbers. But with more complicated objects it becomes less straightforward. For example, consider the following:

```
PS C:\> $collection = Get-Process
PS C:\> $process = Get-Process | select -first 1
PS C:\> $collection -contains $process
False
```

Wait, False? What's going on?

You started by getting all processes on the system and placing them into the $collection variable. Next, you retrieved the first running process and put it into the variable, $process. Surely $collection contains $process, right?

> **NOTE** If you're curious about variables, we devoted an entire chapter to them (chapter 16). For now, think of them as storage boxes that contain things—in this case, processes.

Well, sort of. On our system, the first running process was Conhost, and $collection definitely contains Conhost. The problem is in the way -contains works. When it looks for a match, it tries to match every single property of the object. In addition to looking at the name Conhost, it'll look at the other 65 properties of a process object. Some of those properties—such as memory and CPU consumption—are constantly changing. In the short span of time between filling $collection and then filling $process, some properties of that Conhost process changed. That means the snapshot of Conhost in $collection is slightly different from the snapshot in $process; therefore, the -contains operator doesn't believe they're the same, and it returns False.

You can show that -contains does work by trying the following:

```
PS C:\> $collection = Get-Process
PS C:\> $process = $collection | select -First 1
PS C:\> $collection -contains $process
True
```

In the previous example, the $process variable is populated by selecting the first member of the collection. The collection has to contain the first member to return a result of True. As long as you understand that -contains compares every property when dealing with objects, you're fine.

> **NOTE** You'll also find -notcontains, which is the logical opposite of -contains.

6.1.2 *The -in and -notin operators*

Related to -contains is an operator introduced in PowerShell v3 called -in, which also has an inverse, -notin. You can use this operator to test whether a value is part of a collection of values. This operator always returns a Boolean value:

```
PS C:\>  "Bruce" -notin "Don","Jeff","Richard"
True
PS C:\>  "Bruce" -in "Don","Jeff","Richard"
False
```

The only difference between the previous and the -contains lies in the order. With -contains you're testing if an array contains something:

```
PS C:\> "Don","Jeff","Richard" -contains "don"
True
```

With -in you're testing whether a value is in an array. This is a subtle distinction. In practical terms no real differences exist between the two operators. The choice of which to use may come down to how you like to read code. For example, consider the following:

```
$names = Get-Process | select -ExpandProperty Name
If ($names -contains "calc"){
 Stop-Process -Name "calc" -WhatIf
}
if ("notepad" -in $names) {
 Stop-Process -Name "notepad" -WhatIf
}
```

As you can see, you get a list of process names and then test whether a particular process name is in the list. Using -in reads a little more simply, but both if statements do the same job. If you're using the simplified syntax for Where-Object (see chapter 7) you need to use -in rather than -contains; that's why it was invented.

6.1.3 *Boolean, or logical, operators*

The comparison operators we've discussed accept only two values. They compare them and return either True or False. But what if you need to compare more than one thing? That's where Boolean, or logical, operators come into play.

   Generally speaking, these operators are designed to take two subcomparisons, or subexpressions, which each produce a True or a False. The Boolean operators then take both True/False results and compare them, returning a True or a False for the entire expression. Typically, you limit the number of subexpressions to two, but you can have as many as you want, each separated by an operator.

> **NOTE** On a practical basis, the more logical operators and subexpressions you put into the comparison, the more difficult it becomes to understand and debug. Think carefully about what you're doing if you find yourself building huge comparison strings. Usually, you can find a better way to accomplish the same thing.

Table 6.2 lists these Boolean operators.

Table 6.2 PowerShell's Boolean operators

Operator	Purpose
-and	Return True if all subexpressions are True.
-or	Return True if any subexpression is True.
-not or !	Return the opposite: True becomes False, and False becomes True.
-xor	Return True if one subexpression is True, but not if both are True.

Let's look at some examples. Note that we've used parentheses to group the subexpressions. You don't necessarily need to do that in comparisons that are this simple, but we think it makes them easier to read (and debug):

```
PS C:\> (5 -gt 100) -and (5 -eq 5)
False
PS C:\> (5 -gt 100) -or (5 -eq 5)
True
PS C:\> (500 -gt 100) -and (5 -eq 5)
True
PS C:\> (500 -gt 100) -or (5 -eq 5)
True
PS C:\> (500 -gt 100) -xor (5 -eq 5)
False
```

You can make these comparisons as complex as you wish. Again, we find that using parentheses to contain each subexpression makes complex, multipart comparisons easier for your brain to digest and to edit when you revisit the code six months later. Keep in mind that PowerShell, like algebra, processes from the innermost parenthetical expression and works outward. The following is an example of a complex expression:

```
PS C:\> (((500 -gt 100) -or (1 -eq 2) -and 5 -eq 5) -and (10 -eq 10))
True
```

Did you get all that? It's easier, sometimes, to break it down as PowerShell would. Start with the innermost parentheses and evaluate their expressions, and then work your way outward:

- `(((500 -gt 100) -or (1 -eq 2) -and 5 -eq 5) -and (10 -eq 10))`
- `((True -or False -and 5 -eq 5) -and True)`
- `((True -or False -and True) -and True)`
- `((True -and True) -and True)`
- `(True -and True)`
- `True`

But letting PowerShell do the work is a lot faster.

6.1.4   *Bitwise operators*

Technically, these operators are comparison operators, but the way in which they perform their comparison requires a little explanation.

First, keep in mind that you can render any integer number in binary. For example, 18 in binary is 00010010. A bitwise operator takes two binary numbers and compares each digit, or *bit*, one at a time. The result is the total number of bits that passed the comparison. Table 6.3 shows the operators.

Table 6.3   PowerShell's bitwise operators

Operator	Purpose
-band	Return 1 if both compared bits are 1
-bor	Return 1 if either compared bit is 1
-bxor	Return 1 if one compared bit is 1, but not if both are 1

Keep in mind that this comparison is executed on each bit, one at a time. Table 6.4 shows an example comparison.

NOTE   When dealing with a binary, the least significant (first) bit is on the right-hand side.

Table 6.4   Example bitwise comparison using `-band`

Number	Binary							
129	1	0	0	0	0	0	0	1
19	0	0	0	1	0	0	1	1
`-band (1)`	0	0	0	0	0	0	0	1

In table 6.4, you ran `129 -band 19`. PowerShell converted both 129 and 19 to binary, and those bits are shown in the table. The first bit, with a value of 1, was present in both 129 and 19. No other bits were present in both, so the final result is the first bit turned on, with a value of 1. Now look at table 6.5, which shows the same two numbers being compared with `-bxor`: `129 -bxor 19`.

Table 6.5   Example bitwise comparison using `-bxor`

Number	Binary							
129	1	0	0	0	0	0	0	1
19	0	0	0	1	0	0	1	1
`-bxor (146)`	1	0	0	1	0	0	1	0

In table 6.5, the second, fifth, and eighth bits return 1, because those bits were set to 1 in one, but not both, of the two numbers being compared. The individual values of those bits are 2, 16, and 128, respectively. The result is $128 + 16 + 2 = 146$.

Table 6.6 presents the use of `-bor` for completeness. In this case the resultant bit is a 1 if either of the numbers being operated on contains a 1 at that location. The result is $128 + 16 + 2 + 1 = 147$.

Table 6.6   Example bitwise comparison using `-bor`

Number	Binary							
129	1	0	0	0	0	0	0	1
19	0	0	0	1	0	0	1	1
`-bor (147)`	1	0	0	1	0	0	1	1

In practice, bitwise operators are generally used to test whether a certain bit is set or to set a specific bit. For example, some directory services store certain attributes as *bitmasks*, where each bit has a specific meaning. The first bit, for example, might indicate whether an account is locked out, and the second bit would indicate if a password is due to be changed. If you loaded that entire bit mask attribute into a variable named $flag, you'd test to see if the account was locked out by running $flag -band 1. If you got 1 as your result, then you'd know bit 1 is set in $flag. Similarly, to set bit 1 you'd run $flag -bor 1. The result would include bit 1 being set, with the other 7 bits in $flag left as they were. The following listing offers a slightly more practical example.

Listing 6.1 Comparing bitwise values

```
Param ([string]$ComputerName=$env:COMPUTERNAME)
New-Variable -Name ADS_UF_DONT_EXPIRE_PASSWD -Value 0x10000 -Option
➥ Constant
[ADSI]$server="WinNT://$computername"
$users=$server.children | where {$_.schemaclassname -eq "user"}
foreach ($user in $users) {
  if ($user.userflags.value -band $ADS_UF_DONT_EXPIRE_PASSWD) {     ◁── Perform
      $pwdNeverExpires=$True                                           bitwise
  }                                                                    comparison
  else {
      $pwdNeverExpires=$False
  }
  New-Object -TypeName PSObject -Property @{
   Computername=$server.name.value
   Username=$User.name.value
   PasswordNeverExpires=$pwdNeverExpires
  }
}
```

Listing 6.1 connects to a remote machine and gets all of the local user accounts. The userflags property is a bitmask value.

> **NOTE** In listing 6.1 the value 0x10000 given for the variable is expressed in hexadecimal (base 16). Its decimal value is 65536.

If you perform a binary and a (-band), you can determine whether an account has been set with a nonexpiring password:

```
Username                           PasswordNeverExpires Computername
--------                           -------------------- ------------
Administrator                                      True QUARK
Guest                                              True QUARK
Jeff                                               True QUARK
Lucky                                             False QUARK
```

Okay, we'll admit that the previous example is esoteric stuff. But it's handy in the right situation.

6.2　*Arithmetic operators*

PowerShell supports the standard arithmetic operators, shown in table 6.7.

Table 6.7　PowerShell's arithmetic operators

Operator	Purpose
+	Addition or string concatenation
-	Subtraction
/	Division
*	Multiplication (numeric or string)
%	Modulo (remainder)
++	Unary addition (increment)
--	Unary subtraction (decrement)
+=, -+, /=, *=	Shortcuts

The unary operators come from classic C syntax: $var++ means "add 1 to whatever is in $var, and put the result in $var." The shortcut operators have a similar origin. For example, $var += 7 means "add 7 to whatever is in $var, and put the result in $var." The equivalent—and also legal in PowerShell—syntax would be $var = $var + 7.

The + operator does double duty for both the concatenation of strings and the addition of numbers. Generally, PowerShell will look at the type of the first operand to decide what to do:

```
PS C:\> $string = "5"
PS C:\> $number = 5
PS C:\> $string + $number
55
PS C:\> $number + $string
10
```

When it's able to convert (or coerce) one type into another to make the operation make sense, it'll do so. In our first example, the number was treated as a string. In the second example, the string—because it was the second operand that time—was coerced into an integer.

The multiplication operator works exactly as you'd expect with numeric data:

```
PS C:\> 17*3
51
```

What you might not expect is the ability to multiply strings:

```
PS C:\> "PowerShell rocks  " * 3
PowerShell rocks  PowerShell rocks  PowerShell rocks
```

When you multiply a string you get a new string with the original data repeated, no matter how many times you specified it—up to the memory constraints in your system!

The modulo operator performs division but only returns the remainder:

```
PS C:\> 5 % 3
2
```

6.3   *Other operators*

PowerShell includes a number of other operators you'll find useful from time to time. These aren't operators you'll use constantly, but they'll come in handy for special situations.

6.3.1   *String and array manipulation operators*

Three operators are designed to facilitate string manipulation: -replace, -split, and -join.

The -replace operator searches for a substring within a string and replaces that substring with another, for example:

```
PS C:\> "SERVER-DC2" -replace "DC","FILE"
SERVER-FILE2
PS C:\> "SERVER-DC2","SERVER-DC7" -replace "DC","FILE"
SERVER-FILE2
SERVER-FILE7
```

As you can see, the input string can be a single string or an array of strings. In the latter case, each string in the array will be searched and replaced.

The -split and -join operators are designed to transform between single strings and arrays. The -split operator takes a single string, along with a delimiter, and returns an array, for example:

```
PS C:\> "one,two,three,four,five" -split ","
one
two
three
four
five
```

The default delimiter is a space, which means even though the example might look odd, it works:

```
PS C:\> -split "one two three four five"
one
two
three
four
five
```

It's also possible to control the number of elements returned by defining a maximum number of substrings:

```
PS C:\> "one,two,three,four,five" -split ",", 3
one
two
three,four,five
```

You've told PowerShell to return three substrings, so it performs the split to give the first two, as previously shown, and then puts what's left into the final element.

You also have the option of case sensitive or case insensitive splits (using -csplit and -isplit, respectively). These operators follow the same case rules as the logical and comparison operators discussed earlier:

```
PS C:\> "one,Two,three,four,five" -split "two"
one,
,three,four,five
PS C:\> "one,Two,three,four,five" -csplit "two"
one,Two,three,four,five
PS C:\> "one,Two,three,four,five" -isplit "two"
one,
,three,four,five
```

It's also possible to use regular expressions to determine how a string is split. This is well covered in the about_Split help file.

The -join operator does the opposite, taking the elements of an array and creating a single string, with the array elements separated by a delimiter:

```
PS C:\> $names = Get-Service | select -expand name
PS C:\> $names -join ','
ADWS,AeLookupSvc,ALG,AppHostSvc,AppIDSvc,Appinfo,AppMgmt,aspnet_state,Audi
oEndpointBuilder,AudioSrv,BFE,BITS,Browser,c2wts,CertPropSvc,clr_optimizat
ion_v2.0.50727_32,clr_optimization_v2.0.50727_64,COMSysApp,CryptSvc,CscSer
vice,DcomLaunch,defragsvc,Dfs,DFSR,Dhcp,DNS,Dnscache,dot3svc,DPS,EapHost,E
FS,eventlog,EventSystem,FCRegSvc,fdPHost,FDResPub,FontCache,FontCache3.0.0
.0,gpsvc,hidserv,hkmsvc,idsvc,IISADMIN,IKEEXT,IPBusEnum,iphlpsvc,IsmServ,k
dc,KeyIso,KtmRm,LanmanServer,LanmanWorkstation,lltdsvc,lmhosts,MMCSS,MpsSv
c,MSDTC,MSiSCSI,msiserver,MSMQ,MSSQL$SQLEXPRESS,MSSQLServerADHelper100,nap
agent,Netlogon,Netman,NetMsmqActivator,NetPipeActivator,netprofm,NetTcpAct
ivator,NetTcpPortSharing,NlaSvc,nsi,NTDS,NtFrs,PerfHost,pla,PlugPlay,Polic
yAgent,Power,ProfSvc,ProtectedStorage,RasAuto,RasMan,RemoteAccess,RemoteRe
gistry,RpcEptMapper,RpcLocator,RpcSs,RSoPProv,sacsvr,SamSs,SCardSvr,Schedu
le,SCPolicySvc,seclogon,SENS,SessionEnv,SharedAccess,ShellHWDetection,SNMP
```

Optionally, the -join operator can combine the array elements without a delimiter:

```
PS C:\> -join $names
ADWSAeLookupSvcALGAppHostSvcAppIDSvcAppinfoAppMgmtaspnet_stateAudioEndpoin
tBuilderAudioSrvBFEBITSBrowserc2wtsCertPropSvcclr_optimization_v2.0.50727_
32clr_optimization_v2.0.50727_64COMSysAppCryptSvcCscServiceDcomLaunchdefra
gsvcDfsDFSRDhcpDNSDnscachedot3svcDPSEapHostEFSeventlogEventSystemFCRegSvcf
dPHostFDResPubFontCacheFontCache3.0.0.0gpsvchidservhkmsvcidsvcIISADMINIKEE
XTIPBusEnumiphlpsvcIsmServkdcKeyIsoKtmRmLanmanServerLanmanWorkstationlltds
```

6.3.2 *Object type operators*

PowerShell provides three operators that identify and manipulate object types. First, the -is operator is used to test the type of an object:

```
PS C:\> "world" -is [string]
True
```

The second operator, -isnot, performs the converse action—it tests if an object is *not* of a specific type. We tend to avoid using this operator because it frequently puts us into double negative territory. Third, the -as operator attempts to convert an object of one type into another type. If it's unsuccessful in doing so, it'll usually produce no output, rather than an error:

```
PS C:\> "55.2" -as [int]
55
PS C:\> "string" -as [int]
PS C:\>
```

These conversions can be quite handy. For example, when converting a floating-point number to an integer, PowerShell follows standard rounding rules:

```
PS C:\> (185739 / 1KB) -as [int]
181
```

This also illustrates the use of the KB (kilobyte) shortcut; PowerShell also recognizes KB, MB, GB, TB, and PB for kilobytes, megabytes, gigabytes, terabytes, and petabytes, respectively. When you use any of these shortcuts, the returned values will be in bytes, unless you further manipulate them:

```
PS C:\> 1mb
1048576
PS C:\> 10mb
10485760
PS C:\> 250MB+1GB
1335885824
PS C:\> 4590932427/1gb
4.27563900779933
PS C:\> 4590932427/1gb -as [int]
4
```

6.3.3   *Format operator*

You can use the -f format operator to create formatted strings. On the left side of the operator, provide a string that includes one or more placeholders. On the right side of the operator, provide a comma-separated list of values to be placed into those placeholders:

```
PS C:\> "Today is {0} and your name is {1}" -f (Get-Date),($Env:USERNAME)
Today is 12/8/2013 3:13:29 PM and your name is Administrator
```

In this example, the right-side list includes two parenthetical expressions, each of which ran a command. The results of those commands are then placed into the numbered placeholders.

The placeholders can also contain instructions for formatting the right-side values. These work primarily for numbers, dates, and simple strings:

```
PS C:\> "Today is {0:d} and Pi is {1:N}" -f (Get-Date),[math]::pi
Today is 12/8/2013 and Pi is 3.14
```

The d specifies a short date format, whereas the N specifies a standard decimal display for numbers. A list of standard formatting codes for dates can be found at http://msdn.microsoft.com/en-us/library/az4se3k1.aspx, and a list of numbers is available at http://msdn.microsoft.com/en-us/library/dwhawy9k.aspx. These standard codes typically provide an entire predefined format; you'll also find custom codes:

```
PS C:\> "Today is {0:ddd d MMMM yyyy}" -f (Get-Date)
Today is Sat 8 December 2013
```

The previous example made use of the custom date codes documented at http://msdn.microsoft.com/en-us/library/8kb3ddd4.aspx; custom numeric codes are at http://msdn.microsoft.com/en-us/library/0c899ak8.aspx. You can also reference http://msdn.microsoft.com/en-us/library/txafckwd.aspx, which discusses the entire underlying .NET Framework formatting system and which provides additional links to formatting codes for time spans.

Note that the right-side values are expected to be simple values, including numbers, dates, and strings. If you provide an entire object on the right side, PowerShell will attempt to make a string representation of it. This approach may provide unexpected and less-than-useful results:

```
PS C:\> "Services running include {0}" -f (Get-Service)
Services running include ADWS
```

In the example, PowerShell retrieved all of the services but couldn't put them all into the single placeholder. Therefore, it selected only the first service and displayed its name. PowerShell tends to prefer a "Name" property if one exists, because "Name" properties typically include human-readable, useful text identifiers.

6.3.4 *Miscellaneous operators*

Finally, PowerShell has several other operators that perform a variety of tasks. We'll cover these in this chapter for completeness, but you'll see more detailed information on them throughout the rest of this book as you encounter situations where these operators can be used effectively.

First is the call operator, which is the & sign (ampersand). Sometimes this is referred to as an invoke operator. You can use this to execute strings or script blocks, assuming they contain executable commands:

```
PS C:\> $cmd = "dir"
PS C:\> & $cmd

    Directory: C:\

Mode                LastWriteTime     Length Name
----                -------------     ------ ----
d----        10/21/2013   9:44 AM            a00974d2e4c90e7814
d----        11/27/2011  11:00 AM            files
d----        10/21/2011   9:50 AM            inetpub
d----         7/13/2009   8:20 PM            PerfLogs
d-r--         11/1/2011   8:38 AM            Program Files
d-r--         11/1/2011   8:07 AM            Program Files (x86)
d----        11/27/2012  11:05 AM            Test
```

```
d-r--        10/21/2011   9:51 AM        Users
d----        11/1/2011    8:38 AM        Windows
```

Next is the subexpression operator, $(). Inside the parentheses, you can place expressions and PowerShell will execute them. This operator is primarily used within double quotation marks. Normally, PowerShell looks for escape characters and variables inside double quotes. Escape characters are executed, and variables are replaced with their contents. A subexpression enables you to have something more complicated than a single variable. For example, suppose $service contains a single Windows service, and you want to include its name. One way would be to first pull that name into a variable:

```
PS C:\> $service = Get-Service | select -first 1
PS C:\> $name = $service.name
PS C:\> "Service name is $name"
Service name is ADWS
```

Using a subexpression can result in more compact syntax, although many people find the $(syntax) difficult to read. The subexpression also avoids the creation of a variable, which saves a bit of memory:

```
PS C:\> $service = Get-Service | select -first 1
PS C:\> "Service name is $($service.name)"
Service name is ADWS
```

You may often want to work with a range of values, for example, the numbers 1 to 10. PowerShell has a range operator (designated by two dots, ..) that can be used for this task. A simple example will illustrate its use:

```
1..10 | foreach {Write-Host $_}
```

The numbers 1 to 10 will be written to your screen. You can also reverse the range so that the numbers decrement:

```
10..1 | foreach {Write-Host $_}
```

We've mentioned arrays a number of times, and though the full discussion of these objects is postponed until chapter 16, you need to know that the range operator can be used with arrays:

```
PS C:\> $procs = Get-Process
PS C:\> $procs[2..5]
```

Handles	NPM(K)	PM(K)	WS(K)	VM(M)	CPU(s)	Id	ProcessName
77	8	1952	6444	54	1.48	3152	conhost
403	11	1968	4052	44	1.20	516	csrss
351	39	2548	106424	169	16.69	580	csrss
351	18	4336	12560	73	0.09	1544	dasHost

There is one more type of operator you need to be aware of: The math operators are strictly .NET rather than PowerShell, but they're the way you have to access math functionality in PowerShell.

6.4 *Math operators*

The .NET System namespace contains a class called Math (see http://msdn.microsoft
.com/en-us/library/System.Math(v=vs.110).aspx). Chapter 7 explains classes, objects,
methods, and other terminology you'll need to know, but for now we'll just show you
how to use the math functionality.

The Math class has a number of methods (and a few fields) that supply the math
functionality you'll need in PowerShell. For example, if you need the value of pi,
use this:

```
[math]::pi
[System.Math]::pi
```

This code is telling PowerShell to use the Math class by putting the name of the class in
square brackets. The double colon (::) tells PowerShell to use a static field (or
method), and pi determines the field or method to be accessed.

> **NOTE** A static method is one in which you don't have to create an object
> from the class. You can use it directly.

Either example will give you the results you need. Case is optional, and the use of the
namespace (System) is also optional.

A few examples will illustrate the versatility of this class:

- [math]::Sqrt(16)—Calculates the square root of a number. The result is 4.
- [math]::Sin([math]::pi/2)—Calculates the sin of an angle of pi/2 radians
  (90 degrees). The result is 1.

Other standard trigonometry functions such as cos and tan are also available.

Many calculations produce results with a large number of decimal places. For example, the free disk space on the machine used to produce this chapter is 190400217088
bytes. You, like us, would probably prefer to see that value in GB:

```
PS C:\> 190400217088 / 1GB
177.324020385742
```

That level of precision is unnecessary; you only need two or three places after the decimal point. The Math class supplies a Round() method that performs a mathematical
rounding for you:

```
PS C:\> [math]::Round( (190400217088 / 1GB), 3)
177.324
```

The calculation is placed in parentheses to ensure it's performed first. The Round()
method takes two parameters: the value to be rounded and an integer that determines
the number of decimal places to which rounding will occur. If you read the Math class
documentation, you'll discover that other rounding options exist.

The Math class provides the mathematical functionality that extends PowerShell
without overwhelming you with an extra set of keywords to learn.

6.5   *Summary*

PowerShell's operators are the basis for its logic-making capabilities, and you'll use them extensively with scripting constructs such as If, Switch, and For. Obviously, the arithmetic operators have their uses, and the many miscellaneous operators come in handy as well.

Working with objects 7

This chapter covers

- Using objects in PowerShell
- Understanding object properties, methods, and events
- Working with objects in the pipeline

When you work with Windows PowerShell for, say, 10 minutes or so, you start to suspect that it isn't quite the standard command-line interface it appears to be. Many administrators, relying on previous experience with shells like Cmd.exe or Bash, struggle to use PowerShell efficiently and effectively. The reason for this is that—despite PowerShell doing its best to disguise this fact—it's an object-oriented shell, which is a significant difference from the text-based shells of yesterday. Wrapping your head around this paradigm shift, you can see that PowerShell's object-oriented nature is crucial to using the shell effectively.

> **NOTE** PowerShell is object oriented *but* that doesn't mean you have to become a programmer to use it. You need to learn enough about objects to get the most of the shell—enough to use the tool effectively.

Although Don's proverb "PowerShell *hates* text" isn't exactly true, it does give you an idea how important it is to embrace object-based operations over text-based operations. This is directly analogous to using SQL for set-based operations on a database as opposed to using a sequential programming technique. You use the tool in the best way by using it correctly.

7.1   *Introduction to objects*

If you have some experience with object-oriented programming, skip down to section 7.2. If you have no idea what "object oriented" means, or if you're starting to get concerned that this is a programming book (believe us, it's not), then definitely read this section before proceeding.

People make a big deal of objects when it comes to programming, although there's no reason to. You've probably used a spreadsheet before—probably Microsoft Excel. If you have, then you're completely prepared to deal with objects.

Open an Excel spreadsheet and type some column names into the first row. Perhaps you could use new user information, with columns named UserName, First-Name, LastName, Department, City, and Title. That's the example we'll go with, and you can see our spreadsheet in figure 7.1. We've also added some data rows underneath the first, and you should go ahead and do that, too.

If you thought of this spreadsheet as a database, you wouldn't be far off. It isn't a complicated database, but it certainly stores data in a columnar format, which is how most databases are presented—the innards of the database require another book. It'd

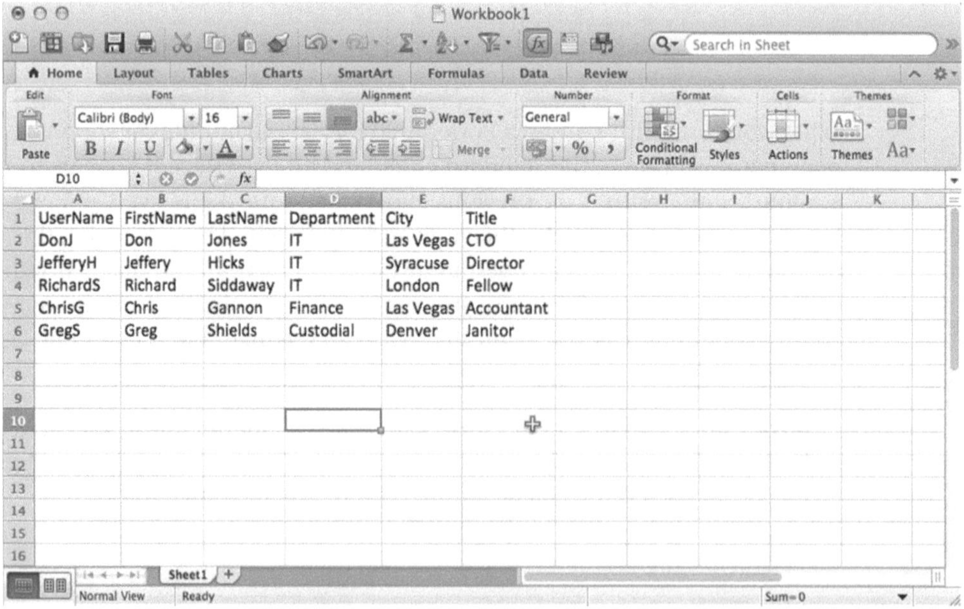

Figure 7.1 Creating a simple database as an Excel spreadsheet

be better if you thought of this as a *data structure*, which is a more generic term than *database*. This data structure has some visible features associated with it. There are six columns, for example, and five rows (the first row, which contains column names, doesn't count). Each row contains data for each of the six columns.

We could've put this information into lots of other data structures. For example, we could've put it into a SQL Server database, which would look visually similar, although it'd be physically quite different if you looked at how the data was saved to disk. The point is that they're both data structures. It's true that they use different names. For example, what Excel calls a column could be called either a *column* or a *domain* in SQL Server; what Excel refers to as a row would be called a *row,* a *tuple,* or an *entity* in SQL Server. Excel has a *sheet*, whereas SQL Server would have a *table*. The names are only names, and they don't affect what's being stored in those structures.

Objects, it turns out, are another kind of data structure. As with Excel or SQL Server, you don't ever get to see how objects physically store their data, nor do you need to. You only need to know that objects are a way of storing data, usually in memory, so that you can work with the data. Objects use a slightly different terminology than Excel or SQL Server:

- Excel stores a bunch of things on sheets, and SQL Server stores them in tables. In object lingo, a bunch of things is called a *collection.*
- Excel uses a row to represent a single thing, such as a user in our example. In object-speak, a row is an *object.*
- In Excel and SQL Server, you have columns to store the individual bits of data about a thing. In the world of objects, they're called *properties.*

Try to mentally visualize objects as looking like an Excel spreadsheet, with some minor changes in terminology. Instead of a *sheet* containing *rows* and *columns*, you have a *collection* consisting of *objects*, which have *properties*.

At this point, most object tutorials will indulge in a noncomputer, real-world analogy, and we're obligated by tradition to do the same. Let's say you wander onto a used car lot—you're standing in the middle of a *collection* of car *objects*. It's worth nothing that objects come in many different *types*. For example, a *car* object would look entirely different from a *television* object. All of those car objects have various *properties*, which describe the objects: color, number of doors, type of engine, and so forth. Some of these properties you can change, such as the color, and some you can't, such as the manufacturer. Thus some properties you can read and write and some are read-only. All this will become more relevant when you start working with PowerShell objects. But for now you can imagine making a spreadsheet, with columns for the color, doors, and so on, and with each row representing a single car on the lot.

7.2 Members: properties, methods, and events

It's obvious that objects have a lot of things associated with them, and this is where the spreadsheet analogy will start to break down, so we'll stick with cars. And maybe televisions, because who doesn't like a nice TV show now and again?

Consider some of the things you might use to describe a television or a car; these are the properties of the objects. Obviously, each different *type* of object will have a different set of properties, so one of the things you'll always want to keep in mind is the *type name* of the object you're working with. Table 7.1 provides some examples.

Table 7.1   Example properties for a car type and for a television type

TypeName: Car	TypeName: Television
Manufacturer	Manufacturer
Model	Model
Color	Size
EngineType	Resolution
Length	CurrentChannel

Both of these types of objects can perform various actions, which in the world of objects are called *methods*. Specifically, a method is something that you can tell an object to do or have done to it. Thinking in terms of cars and televisions, look at table 7.2 for some examples.

Table 7.2   Example methods for a car type and for a television type

TypeName: Car	TypeName: Television
Turn	ChangeChannel
Accelerate	PowerOn
Brake	PowerOff
DeployAirbags	RaiseVolume
Sell	LowerVolume

In the world of Windows, consider a service. What kinds of actions can a service take? You can stop them, start them, pause them (sometimes), resume them (from pause), and so on. Therefore, if you were looking at an object of the type Service, you might expect to find methods named Start, Stop, Pause, Resume, and so on.

Collectively, the properties and methods of an object are referred to as its *members*, as if the object type is some kind of exclusive country club and the properties and methods belong to it.

There's one other type of member, called *events*. You don't work with events in PowerShell a whole lot, but you'll see them, so we want you to know what they're for.

NOTE Their lack of use isn't a PowerShell deficiency, because you'll find many good cmdlets for working with WMI-, .NET-, and PowerShell-related events. We'll cover these more in later chapters. Based on our experiences, most administrators haven't explored working with events, which is somewhat complicated and often drifts into the world of .NET or systems programming. The adoption of PowerShell is a bit like the exploration of an unknown area. The pioneers push into unknown territory, such as events, whereas the bulk of the population slowly follows the trails they've created. Events are on the fringes of explored territory for most IT pros.

Basically, an event is a notification from the object to you that something has happened. A car object might have a "Crashed" event, letting you know that something bad happened. A service object might have a "FinishedStarting" event, letting you know that it was done starting. When you use events, you're simply writing commands that you want to run in response to the event—that is, when the car crashes, run the command to call for emergency services. Or sometimes you just want to see the notification.

　　PowerShell has a convenient way of showing you the members of an object: the `Get-Member` cmdlet. You should be using this cmdlet so much that you get tired of typing `Get-Member` and want to use the shorter alias, `gm`, instead. Go right ahead—this is going to be an important part of your life with PowerShell, so you should become familiar with it right away. To use `Get-Member`, run any command that creates output. That output goes into PowerShell's pipeline, and that output is always in the form of objects. You can pipe those objects to `gm` to see what members the objects have. Here's an example:

```
PS C:\> Get-Service | Get-Member
   TypeName: System.ServiceProcess.ServiceController

Name                        MemberType     Definition
----                        ----------     ----------
Name                        AliasProperty  Name = ServiceName
RequiredServices            AliasProperty  RequiredServices = ServicesDepen...
Disposed                    Event          System.EventHandler Disposed(Sys...
Close                       Method         void Close()
Continue                    Method         void Continue()
CreateObjRef                Method         System.Runtime.Remoting.ObjRef C...
Dispose                     Method         void Dispose(), void IDisposable...
Equals                      Method         bool Equals(System.Object obj)
ExecuteCommand              Method         void ExecuteCommand(int command)
GetHashCode                 Method         int GetHashCode()
GetLifetimeService          Method         System.Object GetLifetimeService()
GetType                     Method         type GetType()
InitializeLifetimeService   Method         System.Object InitializeLifetime...
Pause                       Method         void Pause()
Refresh                     Method         void Refresh()
Start                       Method         void Start(), void Start(string[...
Stop                        Method         void Stop()
WaitForStatus               Method         void WaitForStatus(System.Servic...
CanPauseAndContinue         Property       bool CanPauseAndContinue {get;}
CanShutdown                 Property       bool CanShutdown {get;}
CanStop                     Property       bool CanStop {get;}
Container                   Property       System.ComponentModel.IContainer...
DependentServices           Property       System.ServiceProcess.ServiceCo...
DisplayName                 Property       string DisplayName {get;set;}
```

```
MachineName             Property      string MachineName {get;set;}
ServiceHandle           Property      System.Runtime.InteropServices.S...
ServiceName             Property      string ServiceName {get;set;}
ServicesDependedOn      Property      System.ServiceProcess.ServiceCon...
ServiceType             Property      System.ServiceProcess.ServiceTyp...
Site                    Property      System.ComponentModel.ISite Site...
Status                  Property      System.ServiceProcess.ServiceCon...
ToString                ScriptMethod  System.Object ToString();
```

You can see all of the members in this output:

- Properties, which come in several variations, like `AliasProperty` and plain-old `Property` properties. Functionally, there's no difference in how you use any of them, so we'll generically refer to them as *properties*.
- Methods, like `Start`, `Stop`, `Pause`, and so on. Don't worry about trying to run these methods now. When the time comes, hopefully there will be cmdlets such as `Stop-Service` you can run that will wrap up the method.
- Events—well, one event—like `Disposed`. We have no idea what this does. Okay, we do but for our purposes you can ignore it. A lot of this information comes from the .NET Framework so more is exposed than most IT pros care to see.

The important, and easy-to-overlook, information is the `TypeName`, which in this case is `System.ServiceProcess.ServiceController`. You can punch that entire `TypeName` into an internet search engine to find Microsoft's detailed documentation on this kind of object, which is where you'd go if you wanted to figure out what `Disposed` is for.

Property types

As you explore different objects with `Get-Member`, you're likely to come across a number of property types. These will be listed under `MemberType`. Items that are `Property` should be what you find when reading the MSDN documentation for that object type. Some of these property names aren't necessarily intuitive for an IT pro, so PowerShell or the cmdlet developer often adds an `AliasProperty`. This is an alternative for the "official" property name. For example, the members of `Get-Service` show an `AliasProperty` of `Name`. When you use that property name, PowerShell will "redirect" to the original property name of `ServiceName`. Most Windows admins would think of the `Name` of a service and not a `ServiceName`.

You may also come across `ScriptProperty`. This is another PowerShell-added property that uses a PowerShell command to calculate a property value. A `NoteProperty` is a static property name, often added by `Select-Object` or `Add-Member`. Finally, you might also see `PropertySet`. Think of this as a prepackaged bundle of properties. These are defined by PowerShell or cmdlet developers—for example, a process object as a `PSResources` property set. So instead of typing

```
Get-Process | Select Name,ID,HandleCount,WorkingSet,PagedMemorySize,
PrivateMemorySize,VirtualMemorySize,TotalProcessorTime
```

you can simply type

```
Get-Process | select PSResources
```

NOTE Microsoft updates its documentation as new versions of .NET are released, but be careful to match the documentation version to the version of .NET you're using. How do you know that? Type $psversiontable at a PowerShell prompt and use the first two numbers given in the CLRVersion property. On a system using PowerShell v2, expect something like 2.0. For PowerShell v3 or v4 you should see a version starting with 4.0.

Get-Member is even smart enough to deal with multiple types of objects at once. For example, when you run Dir, you're potentially producing both Directory and File objects. They're similar but not exactly the same. A Directory, for example, won't have some of the data that a File would have, such as a length (size in bytes).

```
PS C:\windows> dir | get-member


    TypeName: System.IO.DirectoryInfo

Name                MemberType     Definition
----                ----------     ----------
Mode                CodeProperty   System.String Mode{get=Mode;}
Create              Method         System.Void Create(System.Secur...
CreateObjRef        Method         System.Runtime.Remoting.ObjRef ...
CreateSubdirectory  Method         System.IO.DirectoryInfo CreateS...
Delete              Method         System.Void Delete(), System.Vo...
...
PSChildName         NoteProperty   System.String PSChildName=ADWS
PSDrive             NoteProperty   System.Management.Automation.PS...
PSIsContainer       NoteProperty   System.Boolean PSIsContainer=True
PSParentPath        NoteProperty   System.String PSParentPath=Micr...
PSPath              NoteProperty   System.String PSPath=Microsoft....
PSProvider          NoteProperty   System.Management.Automation.Pr...
Attributes          Property       System.IO.FileAttributes Attrib...
CreationTime        Property       System.DateTime CreationTime {g...
CreationTimeUtc     Property       System.DateTime CreationTimeUtc...
Exists              Property       System.Boolean Exists {get;}
Extension           Property       System.String Extension {get;}
FullName            Property       System.String FullName {get;}
LastAccessTime      Property       System.DateTime LastAccessTime ...
LastAccessTimeUtc   Property       System.DateTime LastAccessTimeU...
LastWriteTime       Property       System.DateTime LastWriteTime {...
LastWriteTimeUtc    Property       System.DateTime LastWriteTimeUt...
Name                Property       System.String Name {get;}
Parent              Property       System.IO.DirectoryInfo Parent ...
Root                Property       System.IO.DirectoryInfo Root {g...
BaseName            ScriptProperty System.Object BaseName {get=$th...


    TypeName: System.IO.FileInfo

Name                MemberType     Definition
----                ----------     ----------
Mode                CodeProperty   System.String Mode{get=Mode;}
AppendText          Method         System.IO.StreamWriter AppendTe...
CopyTo              Method         System.IO.FileInfo CopyTo(strin...
Create              Method         System.IO.FileStream Create()
CreateObjRef        Method         System.Runtime.Remoting.ObjRef ...
...
```

```
PSChildName              NotePiroperty  System.String PSChildName=bfsvc...
PSDrive                  NoteProperty   System.Management.Automation.PS...
PSIsContainer            NoteProperty   System.Boolean PSIsContainer=False
PSParentPath             NoteProperty   System.String PSParentPath=Micr...
PSPath                   NoteProperty   System.String PSPath=Microsoft....
PSProvider               NoteProperty   System.Management.Automation.Pr...
Attributes               Property       System.IO.FileAttributes Attrib...
CreationTime             Property       System.DateTime CreationTime {g...
CreationTimeUtc          Property       System.DateTime CreationTimeUtc...
Directory                Property       System.IO.DirectoryInfo Directo...
DirectoryName            Property       System.String DirectoryName {get;}
Exists                   Property       System.Boolean Exists {get;}
Extension                Property       System.String Extension {get;}
FullName                 Property       System.String FullName {get;}
IsReadOnly               Property       System.Boolean IsReadOnly {get;...
LastAccessTime           Property       System.DateTime LastAccessTime ...
LastAccessTimeUtc        Property       System.DateTime LastAccessTimeU...
LastWriteTime            Property       System.DateTime LastWriteTime {...
LastWriteTimeUtc         Property       System.DateTime LastWriteTimeUt...
Length                   Property       System.Int64 Length {get;}
Name                     Property       System.String Name {get;}
BaseName                 ScriptProperty System.Object BaseName {get=if ...
VersionInfo              ScriptProperty System.Object VersionInfo {get=...
```

NOTE We removed some of the command's output to save space. We may do that from time to time when the output isn't germane to the discussion, but we'll stick in an ellipsis (...) so that you'll know we left some stuff out.

Keep this trick in mind: Any command that produces output can be piped to Get-Member to see what members that output had. But once you've done this, your output is removed and replaced with Get-Member's own output. In other words, Get-Member usually needs to be the last thing on the command line, because piping its output to something else doesn't usually make sense or do anything useful (Select-Object is sometimes useful if you need the member names, for instance).

Sometimes, PowerShell lies, but only for good. For example, take a look at the first few lines of output created by Get-Process:

```
PS C:\> get-process

Handles  NPM(K)    PM(K)     WS(K) VM(M)   CPU(s)     Id ProcessName
-------  ------    -----     ----- -----   ------     -- -----------
     87       8     2208      7780    79     1.06   1100 conhost
     33       5      980      3068    46     0.02   1820 conhost
     30       4      828      2544    41     0.00   2532 conhost
```

Guess what? There's no property named "NPM(K)." Of those eight columns, only Handles, Id, and ProcessName have the correct column headers. The rest of them were created by PowerShell for display purposes, but they're not the real property names. So, if you wanted to work with the information in those columns, you'd need to find the property names. Remember that you can use any property name you see from Get-Member in cmdlets like Where-Object and Select-Object. Don't assume a command's default output is all there is to the object or that those are the actual property names.

NOTE Go ahead and open PowerShell and run `Get-Process | Get-Member`. See if you can identify the properties that were used to create those other five columns.

7.3 Sorting objects

Once you know the properties that an object contains, you can start to have fun with those objects. For example, by default `Get-Process` produces a list that's sorted by process name. What if you wanted to sort the list by Virtual Memory size instead?

This is where PowerShell's object orientation proves to be vastly superior to older text-based shells. In a Unix operating system, for example, you'd have to do some fancy text manipulation. You'd need to know that the Virtual Memory column started at character 27 and went on for five character columns. If the output of the command ever changed, you'd be out of luck and would have to rewrite all your commands that depended on Virtual Memory being in characters 27 through 31. In PowerShell, you don't need to worry about it. Because the data isn't text until the command has finished running, you can take advantage of the flexibility of the object data structure and run something like the following:

```
PS C:\> Get-Process | Sort-Object -Property vm

Handles  NPM(K)    PM(K)      WS(K) VM(M)   CPU(s)     Id ProcessName
-------  ------    -----      ----- -----   ------     -- -----------
      0       0        0         24     0                0 Idle
    486       0      108        304     3                4 System
     29       2      348       1020     5     0.05      228 smss
     48       4      824       2688    14     0.02     1408 svchost
    144       8     2284       4068    18     0.02      484 lsm
     68       6     1356       4244    29     0.05     2828 svchost
    261      18     3180       7424    31     0.16      712 svchost
    233      13     3848       7720    34     1.15      468 services
     96      13     2888       4868    34     0.00     1352 ismserv
    125      13     2324       5712    35     0.05     1468 dfssvc
```

We hope you used `Get-Member` to discover that the "VM(M)" column is being produced from the `VM` property (if you didn't, here's a hint: look at the members with a member type of `AliasProperty`). We took the output of `Get-Process` and passed the information to `Sort-Object`. The `Sort-Object` cmdlet has a parameter, `-Property`, that lets you specify one or more properties—that is, columns—on which to sort. As you can see from the first few lines of output, it's now sorting on the `VM` property. Note that sorting is in ascending order by default; if you want descending order, there's another parameter for that:

```
PS C:\> Get-Process | Sort-Object -Property vm –Descending

Handles  NPM(K)    PM(K)      WS(K) VM(M)   CPU(s)     Id ProcessName
-------  ------    -----      ----- -----   ------     -- -----------
    256      38    88116      74268   692     1.89     2188 powershell_ise
    403      21    56032      54320   566     2.31     2656 powershell
    248      39    38920      35684   545     0.84     1248 Microsoft.Acti...
    146      24    29336      21924   511     0.37      164 PresentationFo...
```

```
 985      43    19344     35604   387    8.52    848 svchost
1118     103    21460     27752   358    2.87    476 lsass
```

Now, we have to be honest and tell you that you won't see most people run the command that way. They'll usually use aliases instead of the full cmdlet names. They'll often know that the -Property parameter is positional, meaning you don't have to type the parameter name as long as your list of sort properties appears immediately after the cmdlet name or alias. When you type less, you can specify the descending option, because it's the only parameter that starts with the letters "desc." In other words, the following is more common:

```
PS C:\> Get-Process | sort vm -desc

Handles  NPM(K)    PM(K)      WS(K) VM(M)    CPU(s)     Id ProcessName
-------  ------    -----      ----- -----    ------     -- -----------
    256      38    88116      74268   692      1.89   2188 powershell_ise
    400      21    86920      87024   567      3.32   2656 powershell
    248      39    38920      35684   545      0.84   1248 Microsoft.Acti...
    146      24    29336      21924   511      0.37    164 PresentationFo...
    998      44    19536      35712   389      8.52    848 svchost
```

Keep in mind that the property name—vm, in this case—can't be shortened in any way. The shortening bit only applies to parameter names, not their values. Although you didn't type the parameter name (it's -Property), vm is still being passed to that parameter as a value. You can tell because it's vm and not –vm.

7.4   Selecting objects

The next cmdlet we'll discuss is Select-Object. This cmdlet can do several distinct things, and it can do some of them at the same time. Because we find that newcomers to PowerShell get *very* confused about this command's functionality, we recommend you pay close attention to what we're describing.

7.4.1   Use 1: choosing properties

Select-Object includes a -Property parameter, which accepts a comma-separated list of properties that you want to display. You use this to override the default display for that object type. PowerShell will still control how this information is formatted (we'll show you how to control formatting in chapter 9).

> **TIP** Remember, if you're curious about what properties are available to be selected, pipe the object to Get-Member. Don't assume that the formatted column headers you may have seen are the property names.

```
PS C:\> Get-Process | Select-Object -Property Name,ID,VM,PM

Name                             Id               VM                PM
----                             --               --                --
conhost                        1100         82726912           2166784
conhost                        1820         48480256           1003520
conhost                        2532         42979328            847872
csrss                           324         45211648           2027520
```

```
csrss                       372          74035200           31252480
dfsrs                      1288         363728896           14540800
dfssvc                     1468          36069376            2326528
```

As you can see from those first few lines of output, you got exactly the "columns" (remember our spreadsheet example?) you asked for. Also note that PowerShell isn't terribly sensitive about case—it displayed "Id" even though you typed it as "ID".

Here's something interesting about Select-Object:

```
PS C:\> Get-Process | Select Name,ID,VM,PM | Get-Member

   TypeName: Selected.System.Diagnostics.Process

Name        MemberType   Definition
----        ----------   ----------
Equals      Method       bool Equals(System.Object obj)
GetHashCode Method       int GetHashCode()
GetType     Method       type GetType()
ToString    Method       string ToString()
Id          NoteProperty System.Int32 Id=1100
Name        NoteProperty System.String Name=conhost
PM          NoteProperty System.Int32 PM=2162688
VM          NoteProperty System.Int32 VM=82726912
```

> **TIP** Select-Object can be shortened to its alias, Select. Its -Property parameter is positional (like it was for Sort), so in that last example you provided the list of properties in the correct position.

After Select-Object runs, the objects it sends to the pipeline have only the properties you specified. Everything else is gone. You can see that the objects' type names have changed too, indicating that they've been "Selected." That's a cue to you that this isn't a complete process object; it's a subset of information that would normally be available. This behavior creates some interesting problems for newbies. Can you tell the difference between these two commands?

1 Get-Process | Select Name,Id,PM,NPM | Sort VM -Descending
2 Get-Process | Sort VM -Descending | Select Name,Id,PM,NPM

Here's the difference:

1 The process objects are generated first. Then, you're selecting a subset of their columns (that is, properties), including only Name, ID, PM, and NPM. Only those four properties will exist in the output. Yet the final command is trying to sort on the VM property, which wasn't one of the ones you picked. This command will run without error, but you won't get the results you were expecting.

2 The process objects are generated first, and then you sort them on the VM property. This will work, because at this stage the objects still have a VM property. Then you choose the properties you want to see.

These two examples illustrate how important it is to think about what each command is doing, about what each command is outputting, and about what the next command is going to do with that output—think in pipelines, not commands. This is another situation where Get-Member is invaluable. If you run a command and don't get the result you expect, break your command into small commands and pipe each part to Get-Member so you can verify exactly what type of object PowerShell is writing to the pipeline.

7.4.2   Use 2: choosing a subset of objects

The other, and almost completely unrelated, thing that Select-Object can do is select a subset of "rows" or objects. It can select a chunk of objects either from the beginning of the set, or from the end, or even from the middle. But that's it.

> **NOTE**   This is a big "gotcha" for newcomers. Select-Object doesn't apply any intelligence when it's grabbing a chunk of rows. It's either "the first 10," or "the last 5," or something like that. *It doesn't care about the data*—it's merely counting off a specified number of rows. That's it.

In this example, you grab the five processes that are using the most virtual memory:

```
PS C:\> Get-Process | sort VM -Descending | select -first 5

Handles  NPM(K)    PM(K)     WS(K) VM(M)   CPU(s)      Id ProcessName
-------  ------    -----     ----- -----   ------      -- -----------
    256      38    88116     74268   692     1.89    2188 powershell_ise
    483      21    69624     70160   567     3.87    2656 powershell
    248      38    38880     35648   543     0.84    1248 Microsoft.Acti...
    146      24    29336     21924   511     0.37     164 PresentationFo...
    993      43    19352     35620   387     8.52     848 svchost
```

Or maybe you'd like to see the five using the least amount of paged memory:

```
PS C:\> Get-Process | sort PM -Descending | select -last 5

Handles  NPM(K)    PM(K)     WS(K) VM(M)   CPU(s)      Id ProcessName
-------  ------    -----     ----- -----   ------      -- -----------
     30       4      828      2544    41     0.00    2532 conhost
     48       4      824      2688    14     0.02    1408 svchost
     29       2      348      1020     5     0.05     228 smss
    485       0      108       304     3                4 System
      0       0        0        24     0                0 Idle
```

Or perhaps—and this gets tricky—you want to see the five biggest consumers of paged memory, skipping the top three:

```
PS C:\> Get-Process | sort PM -Descending | select -skip 3 -first 5

Handles  NPM(K)    PM(K)     WS(K) VM(M)   CPU(s)      Id ProcessName
-------  ------    -----     ----- -----   ------      -- -----------
    525      21    69980     70776   567     4.10    2656 powershell
    248      39    38928     35684   545     0.84    1248 Microsoft.Acti...
    606      42    32704     39540   192     1.98    1788 explorer
    206      14    30520     19504    71     1.40     372 csrss
    146      24    29336     21924   511     0.37     164 PresentationFo...
```

Keep in mind that it doesn't matter in which order you specify the parameters to Select-Object; it will always execute -Skip first and then grab whatever -First or -Last you specify.

When used in this context, `Select-Object` writes the original object to the pipeline. So in this example if you piped the command to `Get-Member` you'd see PowerShell is writing `System.Diagnostics.Process` to the pipeline.

> **NOTE** We want to remind you again that –First and –Last don't care about the data in your objects. They're only grabbing the "top five consumers of memory" because you'd first sorted them on that data. After sorting you need to blindly grab the first five or last five or whatever—the first or last "n" that are presented to `Select-Object` by the pipeline. That's the extent of `Select-Object`'s ability to filter out some of the objects you've produced.

An important change was made to `Select-Object` starting in PowerShell v3. In PowerShell v2, when you selected, say, the first 5 objects, PowerShell continued to get all the remaining objects. For small data sets this was no big deal. But if your command was returning 5,000 objects and you just wanted the first 5, you had to wait until all 5,000 were processed—hardly performance friendly. Starting in v3, once PowerShell gets the first or last X number of objects, it stops processing, which means a much faster performing expression. If for some reason you'd like to revert to the v2 approach, use the –Wait parameter. If you don't believe us, you can test this for yourself with `Measure-Command`.

```
PS C:\> measure-command {1..5000 | select -first 5 -wait}

Days               : 0
Hours              : 0
Minutes            : 0
Seconds            : 0
Milliseconds       : 98
Ticks              : 983903
TotalDays          : 1.13877662037037E-06
TotalHours         : 2.73306388888889E-05
TotalMinutes       : 0.00163983833333333
TotalSeconds       : 0.0983903
TotalMilliseconds  : 98.3903

PS C:\> measure-command {1..5000 | select -first 5}

Days               : 0
Hours              : 0
Minutes            : 0
Seconds            : 0
Milliseconds       : 0
Ticks              : 6005
TotalDays          : 6.95023148148148E-09
TotalHours         : 1.66805555555556E-07
TotalMinutes       : 1.00083333333333E-05
TotalSeconds       : 0.0006005
TotalMilliseconds  : 0.6005
```

In the first command, which simulates the v2 approach, it took 98 milliseconds. But the optimized approach introduced in v3 only took *.6 milliseconds*. That's a performance gain we can all get behind.

7.4.3 *Use 3: making custom properties*

This is a super-cool feature: `Select-Object`'s `-Property` parameter accepts a combination of property names, which you've seen us do, and custom properties, which are properties you define on the fly using a special syntax. We'll admit up front that the syntax is kind of ugly and involves a lot of punctuation, but it's worth learning. Let's start with a one-line example:

```
PS C:\> Get-Process | Select -Property
    Name,ID,@{name="TotalMemory";expression={$_.PM + $_.VM}}

Name                                    Id          TotalMemory
----                                    --          -----------
conhost                                 1100           84889600
conhost                                 1820           49483776
conhost                                 2532           43827200
csrss                                    324           47239168
```

Here you're creating a new property called `TotalMemory`. The value for this property comes from adding the `PM` and `VM` properties of each object in the collection.

Hmm, looking at this it turns out the `VM` and `PM` properties are in bytes. You're used to seeing them in kilobytes and megabytes, because PowerShell's default output obviously tweaks them. Because you're working with the raw values, you'll have to do some math. The following is a one-line command that wraps on the printed page:

```
PS C:\> Get-Process | Select -Property
    Name,ID,@{Name="TotalMemory(M)";Expression={($_.PM + $_.VM) /
    1MB -as [int]}}

Name                                    Id       TotalMemory(M)
----                                    --       --------------
conhost                                 1100                 81
conhost                                 1820                 47
conhost                                 2532                 42
csrss                                    324                 45
csrss                                    372                100
dfsrs                                   1288                361
```

NOTE Keep your math skills in mind. You needed to enclose the addition operation in parentheses to force it to occur first. Otherwise, math rules dictate that PowerShell run `$_.VM / 1MB` first and then add `$_.PM`, which would still be in bytes. Also, remember that converting the value to an integer causes it to be rounded to the nearest integer.

Okay, so what the heck is all that?

- The structure starting with an `@` sign is called a *hash table* (also referred to as dictionaries or associative arrays). Hash tables consist of one or more key-value pairs. In this case, we've used two pairs. Each pair is separated by a semicolon. See the About_Hash_Tables help topic and chapter 16.
- The first key is `Name`, and it's a key that `Select-Object` has been designed to look for. We didn't make this up—it's listed in the examples in the help file for

`Select-Object`. The value that goes along with this key is what you want to appear in the column header for your new custom property.

- The second key is `Expression`, and we didn't make that up, either. Again, it's a special key that the command is hardcoded to look for. Its value goes in curly brackets, and everything inside the curly brackets is run by PowerShell to create the value for this column for each row. You can have as much PowerShell code as you need between the curly braces.

- The `$_` is a placeholder that PowerShell looks for in special situations. This is one of those situations. PowerShell will replace `$_` with whatever object is in the row that's currently being produced. So, `$_` will represent one process object at a time. Because this placeholder trips up many people, in PowerShell v3 and later you can also use `$psitem` in its place and achieve the same result.

- You don't want to work with the entire process object—it has more than 65 properties! You only want to work with one of those properties at a time. In other words, you want to work with a piece, or a fraction, of the object. In math, what character indicates a fraction? A decimal point! So you follow `$_` with a period, or decimal point, to indicate that you're going to specify the portion of the object you want. In the first case, it's the `PM` property, and in the second it's the `VM` property.

- Each `@` structure represents a single property in your output. You can specify as many of those structures as you want, as part of the comma-separated property list, to create additional columns.

One use for this trick is to come up with new column names that you like better than the originals:

```
PS C:\> Get-Process | Select -Property Name,ID,
    @{Name="VirtMem";Expression={$psitem.vm}},
    @{Name="PhysMem";Expression={$psitem.pm}}

Name                            Id        VirtMem          PhysMem
----                            --        -------          -------
conhost                       1100       82726912         2166784
conhost                       1820       48480256         1003520
conhost                       2532       42979328          847872
csrss                          324       45211648         2027520
```

In this example we opted for the newer `$psitem` instead of `$_` to indicate the current object in the pipeline. As with all other cases where you use `Select-Object` and its `-Property` parameter, the output objects contain only the properties you specified:

```
PS C:\> Get-Process | Select -Property Name,ID,
    @{Name="VirtMem";Expression={$psitem.vm}},
    @{Name="PhysMem";Expression={$psitem.pm}} | get-member

   TypeName: Selected.System.Diagnostics.Process

Name       MemberType   Definition
----       ----------   ----------
Equals     Method       bool Equals(System.Object obj)
```

```
GetHashCode Method       int GetHashCode()
GetType     Method       type GetType()
ToString    Method       string ToString()
Id          NoteProperty System.Int32 Id=1100
Name        NoteProperty System.String Name=conhost
PhysMem     NoteProperty System.Int32 PhysMem=2166784
VirtMem     NoteProperty System.Int32 VirtMem=82726912
```

You need to remember the following about these custom properties:

- The key `Name` can be replaced with `n` or `N` as a shortcut. You could also use `Label`, `L` or `l` (the letter L). We don't like using a lowercase L all by itself, because it's easily mistaken for the number 1. If you do abbreviate use `L`.
- The key `expression` can be replaced with `e` or `E` as a shortcut.
- Use `$_` or `$psitem` to reference the current object in the pipeline.

NOTE Why does PowerShell let you use `name`, `n`, `label`, or `l`? In v1 of Power-Shell, some cmdlets accepted custom properties and required `Name`. Other cmdlets that did the same thing used `Label` instead. It made no sense, so beginning with v2 Microsoft let all of those cmdlets use any of those keys.

7.4.4 *Use 4: extracting and expanding properties*

Okay, this will get a bit cerebral, but bear with us while we walk you through some examples. We're going to focus on exclusively using the `-ExpandProperty` parameter of `Select-Object` for all of these.

EXTRACTING PROPERTY VALUES

First, let's suppose you have a bunch of computers in Active Directory. Hopefully that isn't too hard to imagine. Now, let's say you want to get a list of running processes from every computer in the WebFarm organizational unit (OU) of the company.pri domain.

NOTE In these examples we're assuming you're using the Microsoft AD cmdlets, which aren't part of PowerShell out of the box but must be added separately, usually by installing Remote Server Administration Tools (RSAT). If that's not the case, you'll need to modify them to fit with your toolset.

You run the following to get the computers themselves:

```
Get-ADComputer -Filter * -SearchBase "ou=WebFarm,dc=company,dc=pri"
```

This command produces a bunch of computer objects, each of which will have a `Name` property containing the computer's name. The `Get-Process` cmdlet accepts multiple computer names on its `-ComputerName` parameter, so in theory it might seem like you could do this:

```
Get-Process -computerName (
  Get-ADComputer -Filter * -SearchBase "ou=WebFarm,dc=company,dc=pri"
)
```

The problem is, `Get-ADComputer` produces objects of the type Computer, whereas the `-ComputerName` parameter wants input of the type String (it says so in the command's help file). So that won't work. Instead, you need to extract only the contents of the Name property from those computers, and that's where the `-ExpandProperty` parameter comes in:

```
Get-Process -computerName (
  Get-ADComputer -Filter * -SearchBase "ou=WebFarm,dc=company,dc=pri" |
  Select-Object -ExpandProperty Name
)
```

> **NOTE** We're writing these commands in a more formatted style to make them more readable in the book. You can type them exactly as they're written (press Enter on a blank line when you're finished to run them), or type them all into a single line. It's your choice.

When PowerShell executes this expression, the command within the parentheses is evaluated first. This expression is getting all computer objects from the WebFarm organizational unit and expanding the Name property. This has the effect of writing a collection of strings, such as the computer name, to the pipeline, instead of a bunch of computer objects. Using `-ExpandProperty` is also a handy technique when you want to save a property value to a variable.

For example, let's say you have some code to use the `DisplayName` property from a service object. This works, but it's a little complicated:

```
PS C:\> $svc = Get-Service spooler | select displayname
PS C:\> Write-Host "Checking $($svc.Displayname)"
Checking Print Spooler
```

The `Get-Service` cmdlet wrote a service object to `$svc` so you need to use a subexpression to access the `DisplayName` property. Or you can expand the property:

```
PS C:\> $svc = Get-Service spooler | Select -ExpandProperty Displayname
PS C:\> Write-Host "Checking $svc"
Checking Print Spooler
```

Depending on your situation this might be easier to understand. You can expand only a single property, but you can do it for a bunch of objects. This is a great way of creating an array of simple values.

```
PS C:\> $sources = Get-Eventlog system -Newest 1000 |
    select -Unique -ExpandProperty Source
PS C:\> $sources | sort | select -first 10
BTHUSB
DCOM
disk
EventLog
HTTP
Microsoft-Windows-Dhcp-Client
Microsoft-Windows-DHCPv6-Client
Microsoft-Windows-DNS-Client
Microsoft-Windows-DriverFrameworks-UserMode
Microsoft-Windows-FilterManager
```

With this technique, $sources is a collection of strings and not eventlog objects.

Starting in PowerShell v3, you can also take a shortcut and have PowerShell implicitly expand a property:

```
PS C:\> (Get-Service m*).Displayname
Multimedia Class Scheduler
Windows Firewall
Distributed Transaction Coordinator
Microsoft iSCSI Initiator Service
Windows Installer
Microsoft Keyboard Filter
```

This is much easier to type than:

```
PS C:\> Get-Service m* | select -ExpandProperty Displayname
Multimedia Class Scheduler
Windows Firewall
Distributed Transaction Coordinator
Microsoft iSCSI Initiator Service
Windows Installer
Microsoft Keyboard Filter
```

> **Service names**
>
> Services have a Name property and a DisplayName property. The two are usually different. Consider this example:
>
> ```
> (Get-Service m*).Displayname
> ```
>
> You're filtering on Name but listing DisplayName. The differences between Name and DisplayName are easily shown:
>
> ```
> PS C:\> Get-Service m* | Format-Table Name, DisplayName -AutoSize
>
> Name            DisplayName
> ----            -----------
> MMCSS           Multimedia Class Scheduler
> MpsSvc          Windows Firewall
> MSDTC           Distributed Transaction Coordinator
> MSiSCSI         Microsoft iSCSI Initiator Service
> msiserver       Windows Installer
> MsKeyboardFilter Microsoft Keyboard Filter
> ```
>
> When working with Services, just be careful which type of name you're specifying.

although it's perhaps not necessarily easier to understand, especially if you're new to PowerShell. But when used interactively in the console, you can get the same results with a single command that previously took several steps:

```
PS C:\> (Get-Eventlog system -Newest 1000).Source | sort | Get-Unique |
➥ select -first 10
BTHUSB
DCOM
disk
```

```
EventLog
HTTP
Microsoft-Windows-Dhcp-Client
Microsoft-Windows-DHCPv6-Client
Microsoft-Windows-DNS-Client
Microsoft-Windows-DriverFrameworks-UserMode
Microsoft-Windows-FilterManager
```

If you use syntax like this in a PowerShell script, be sure to clearly document the expression.

EXPANDING COLLECTIONS

Sometimes, you'll find that a property is a collection of other objects. For example, the DependentServices property of a service object is a collection of other services:

```
PS C:\> Get-Service | Select-Object -Property Name,DependentServices

Name                          DependentServices
----                          -----------------
ADWS                          {}
AeLookupSvc                   {}
ALG                           {}
AppIDSvc                      {}
Appinfo                       {}
AppMgmt                       {}
AudioEndpointBuilder          {AudioSrv}
AudioSrv                      {}
BFE                           {SharedAccess, RemoteAccess, Polic...
```

These collections get printed in curly brackets as you see here, but you can use -ExpandProperty to "expand" them into their full, stand-alone objects. This is often useful when you're getting a single top-level object, such as getting the BFE service (which appears to have several dependent services):

```
PS C:\> Get-Service -Name BFE | Select -Expand DependentServices

Status   Name          DisplayName
------   ----          -----------
Running  WdNisSvc      Windows Defender Network Inspection...
Running  WdNisDrv      Windows Defender Network Inspection...
Stopped  SharedAccess  Internet Connection Sharing (ICS)
Stopped  RemoteAccess  Routing and Remote Access
Running  PolicyAgent   IPsec Policy Agent
Stopped  NcaSvc        Network Connectivity Assistant
Running  MpsSvc        Windows Firewall
Stopped  IKEEXT        IKE and AuthIP IPsec Keying Modules
```

Now you can see the *contents* of the DependentServices property. Those contents are themselves services, so they have the same familiar-looking output.

You can also use the enumeration trick we showed earlier:

```
PS C:\> (Get-Service BFE).DependentServices

Status   Name          DisplayName
------   ----          -----------
Running  WdNisSvc      Windows Defender Network Inspection...
```

```
Running   WdNisDrv          Windows Defender Network Inspection...
Stopped   SharedAccess      Internet Connection Sharing (ICS)
Stopped   RemoteAccess      Routing and Remote Access
Running   PolicyAgent       IPsec Policy Agent
Stopped   NcaSvc            Network Connectivity Assistant
Running   MpsSvc            Windows Firewall
Stopped   IKEEXT            IKE and AuthIP IPsec Keying Modules
```

You can even continue the enumeration to the next level:

```
PS C:\> (Get-Service BFE).DependentServices.Displayname
Windows Defender Network Inspection Service
Windows Defender Network Inspection System Driver
Internet Connection Sharing (ICS)
Routing and Remote Access
IPsec Policy Agent
Network Connectivity Assistant
Windows Firewall
IKE and AuthIP IPsec Keying Modules
```

7.4.5 *Use 5: choosing properties and a subset of objects*

You can also combine the "first or last" functionality with the ability to pick the columns (properties) that you want:

```
PS C:\> Get-Process | sort PM -Descending |
➥ select -Skip 3 -First 5 -Property name,id,pm,vm
```

Name	Id	PM	VM
----	--	--	--
powershell	2656	72245248	594939904
Microsoft.Activ...	1248	39858176	571244544
explorer	1788	33488896	200929280
csrss	372	31252480	74035200
PresentationFon...	164	30040064	536096768

> **NOTE** Normally, you'll see people specify the properties they want without using the –Property parameter name: Select-Object Name,ID,PM,VM. We didn't do that, because we didn't specify the list of properties in the first position. When you use parameter names, as you did in this example, you can put the parameters in any order you want. We're big fans of using parameter names, specifically because you don't have to remember any special order. If you omit the parameter names and only provide values, then it's on you to make sure you get the order right, and it's easy to get that wrong.

7.5 *Filtering objects*

We howed you how Select-Object can grab a subset of objects, but we took pains to point out that it's non-intelligent, grabbing hunks of objects from the beginning or end of the set. The Where-Object cmdlet, on the other hand, has much more powerful capabilities for truly filtering out objects you don't want.

7.5.1   *Simplified syntax*

PowerShell v3 introduced a new, simplified syntax for `Where-Object`, so we'll cover that first. PowerShell v3 and later still support the full syntax, which is all that'll work in older versions of PowerShell, and we'll cover that last.

To use this syntax, you'll need to know two things:

- The name of the property that contains the data you want to filter on
- The property values that you want to keep (everything else will be discarded)

Here's an example:

```
PS C:\> Get-Service | Where Status -ne Running

Status   Name              DisplayName
------   ----              -----------
Stopped  AeLookupSvc       Application Experience
Stopped  ALG               Application Layer Gateway Service
Stopped  AppIDSvc          Application Identity
Stopped  Appinfo           Application Information
Stopped  AppMgmt           Application Management
Stopped  AudioEndpointBu... Windows Audio Endpoint Builder
```

We included the first few lines of output. As you can see, we used the `Where` alias instead of the `Where-Object` cmdlet name; you'll also see people use the alias ? (this is harder for newcomers to understand so we don't recommend it), as in this example:

```
PS C:\> Get-Service | ? Status -ne Running

Status   Name              DisplayName
------   ----              -----------
Stopped  AeLookupSvc       Application Experience
Stopped  ALG               Application Layer Gateway Service
Stopped  AppIDSvc          Application Identity
Stopped  Appinfo           Application Information
Stopped  AppMgmt           Application Management
Stopped  AudioEndpointBu... Windows Audio Endpoint Builder
```

After the command (or alias), you type the name of the property you want the command to look at. In this case, we chose the `Status` property. Then, you specify one of PowerShell's comparison operators, which we covered in the previous chapter. Finally, you specify the value that identifies objects you want to keep—we wanted to keep all services that didn't have a status of "Running."

To use this simplified syntax, you need to know a few rules:

- You can only perform a single comparison. In other words, you can't look for services that have a service type of "Win32OwnProcess" and a status of "stopped" —you can only do one of those things. You *could* use two consecutive `Where-Object` commands to achieve that goal, though: `get-service | where status -eq stopped | where servicetype -eq Win32OwnProcess`.
- You can only use the core comparison operators specifically supported by the command—read its help for a full list.

If you need to do anything more complicated, you'll have to switch to the full syntax for the command.

> **NOTE** Keep in mind that the simplified syntax was new for PowerShell v3. You're likely to run across lots of examples that seem like they could use the simplified syntax but instead use the full syntax. It's likely those examples were written for older versions of PowerShell, or that the examples' authors are used to the full syntax. It's okay, because that full syntax still works fine in v3 and later.

7.5.2 *Full syntax*

The full syntax for `Where-Object` involves a script block, which is basically a comparison contained within curly brackets. This syntax uses the same `$_` or `$psitem` that you could've used in `Select-Object`. Remember, PowerShell looks for `$_` (or `$psitem`) in special instances, and the script block of `Where-Object` is one of those. If you don't need to work with the entire piped-in object (and you rarely will), use a period to specify a single property. For example, here are three versions of the exact same command. We'll start with the fullest possible syntax and work down to the briefest using aliases and positional parameters:

- `Get-Process | Where-Object -FilterScript {$_.workingset -gt 1mb -AND $_.company -notmatch "Microsoft"}`
- `Get-Process | Where {$_.workingset -gt 1mb -AND $_.company -notmatch "Microsoft"}`
- `ps | ? {$_.ws -gt 1mb -AND $_.company -notmatch "Microsoft"}`

These all do exactly the same thing, and you're welcome to run them in PowerShell to see what you get. You'll notice that, with this full syntax, you're able to specify multipart comparisons using some of the Boolean operators that we introduced in chapter 6.

If you're writing a script that might be executed on a system running PowerShell v2, you'll need to stick with `$_`. Otherwise you can use `$psitem`, but the only thing you gain is potential clarity.

7.5.3 *The Where method*

PowerShell v4 introduced another way to filter a collection of objects. This method isn't well documented, nor is it easily discoverable, yet it's relatively easy to use and performs well. Basically, you can use `Where` as a method:

```
PS C:\> (Get-Service m*).Where{$_.status -eq "stopped"}

Status    Name               DisplayName
------    ----               -----------
Stopped   MozillaMaintenance Mozilla Maintenance Service
Stopped   MSDTC              Distributed Transaction Coordinator
Stopped   MSiSCSI            Microsoft iSCSI Initiator Service
Stopped   msiserver          Windows Installer
```

When you use Where in this way, you must include $psitem or $_ to indicate a pipe-lined object. You aren't required to use parentheses, but we think you should get in the habit anyway. This command will give you the same results:

```
(Get-Service m*).Where({$psitem.status -eq "stopped"})
```

The reason is that there's a second parameter to the Where method. You can specify any one of the following: First, Last, SkipUntil, Until, or Split.

```
PS C:\> $p = (Get-Process).Where({$_.ws -gt 100mb},"split")
```

We retrieved all processes and split them into two parts based on the filter. The first element of the array will contain those processes where the WorkingSet (the property is abbreviated to ws by Get-Process) is greater than 100 MB:

```
PS C:\> $p[0].count
13
PS C:\> $p[0][0]

Handles  NPM(K)    PM(K)      WS(K) VM(M)   CPU(s)     Id ProcessName
-------  ------    -----      ----- -----   ------     -- -----------
    201      67    86224     102668   261   197.91   1240 chrome
```

The second element of the array ($p) will contain everything else:

```
PS C:\> $p[1].count
75
```

Here are a few other ways to use this cool trick:

```
PS C:\> (Get-Process).Where({$_.ws -gt 100mb},"First",3)

Handles  NPM(K)    PM(K)      WS(K) VM(M)    CPU(s)     Id ProcessName
-------  ------    -----      ----- -----    ------     -- -----------
    414      39   126472     141540   476 1,279.25   2196 chrome
   1764     102   164760     216800   480 3,609.66   3856 chrome
    814      54    99444     107804   504   383.08   7260 chrome
PS C:\> (Get-Process).Where({$_.ws -gt 100mb},"Last",2)

Handles  NPM(K)    PM(K)      WS(K) VM(M)    CPU(s)     Id ProcessName
-------  ------    -----      ----- -----    ------     -- -----------
    778      39    85344     103384   160 2,350.08   1308 svchost
    680      96   142976     176404   409    31.45   3252 thunderbird
```

The number is the number of objects to return. Yes, you could get the same results with more traditional expressions like this:

```
PS C:\> Get-Process | Where {$_.ws -gt 100mb} | Select -First 3
```

For a small data set like this, you may not notice much of a performance difference. But in a large set you will:

```
PS C:\> measure-command {(1..1000).where({$psitem%2})}

Days            : 0
Hours           : 0
Minutes         : 0
Seconds         : 0
```

```
Milliseconds      : 41
Ticks             : 413475
TotalDays         : 4.78559027777778E-07
TotalHours        : 1.14854166666667E-05
TotalMinutes      : 0.000689125
TotalSeconds      : 0.0413475
TotalMilliseconds : 41.3475

PS C:\> measure-command {(1..1000) | where {$psitem%2}}

Days              : 0
Hours             : 0
Minutes           : 0
Seconds           : 0
Milliseconds      : 118
Ticks             : 1185579
TotalDays         : 1.37219791666667E-06
TotalHours        : 3.293275E-05
TotalMinutes      : 0.001975965
TotalSeconds      : 0.1185579
TotalMilliseconds : 118.5579
```

Here we filtered to get the odd numbers between 1 and 1000. Using the traditional syntax took 118 ms whereas the newer v4 syntax took only 41 ms.

We haven't covered the Skip and SkipUntil options yet. The best way to think of them is that they provide an additional filter that supplies the data that matches the condition or the data that doesn't match. Let's start by looking at the complete set of processes:

```
PS C:\> Get-Process | sort Handles

Handles  NPM(K)    PM(K)     WS(K) VM(M)   CPU(s)      Id ProcessName
-------  ------    -----     ----- -----   ------      -- -----------
      0       0        0        24     0                0 Idle
     43       6      664      2988    40     0.00     2932 TabTip32
     44       2      280       620     4     2.55      364 smss
     72       8      992      4600    70     0.03     3148 jusched
     75       8     1916      6544    57     1.16     7088 conhost
     81       7      968      1308    44     0.00     1488 armsvc
    ...
    810      44    38500     83228   492     4.59     6060 EXCEL
    838      50    97772    183120   627    17.27      412 WINWORD
    843      45    13884     19960   105    12.09      380 svchost
    872      32    21636     24776   132    13.31      932 svchost
    971      46    27568     33388   137    97.02      980 svchost
   1010     156   155984    206096   549    26.56     6668 WWAHost
   1073      39    34984     50056   878    22.28     4292 livecomm
   1095       0      128      9196    13 4,138.06        4 System
   1164      27     8692     25700   288     0.56     2120 UcMapi
   1324      20     8400     13340    54    38.69      652 lsass
   1327      50    67388     95364   537    20.25     5680 ONENOTE
   1983      61    44424     45640   449    59.27     1008 svchost
   2015      89    53904    113196   570    81.89     3140 explorer
   2244      64    72928    117012   664     7.25     2820 lync
```

If you want to see only the data where the `Handles` property is greater than 1000, use the following:

```
PS C:\> Get-Process | sort Handles | Where Handles -gt 1000

Handles  NPM(K)    PM(K)      WS(K) VM(M)    CPU(s)      Id ProcessName
-------  ------    -----      ----- -----    ------      -- -----------
   1010     156   155984     206096   549     26.56    6668 WWAHost
   1078      39    34996      50788   878     22.48    4292 livecomm
   1094       0      128       9196    13  4,140.78       4 System
   1170      28     8720      25720   289      0.56    2120 UcMapi
   1314      48    67304      95364   535     20.27    5680 ONENOTE
   1322      20     8316      13296    53     38.72     652 lsass
   1980      61    44372      45608   449     59.27    1008 svchost
   2015      88    53904     113208   570     82.88    3140 explorer
   2236      64    72884     116980   663      7.36    2820 lync
```

You could modify this as follows:

```
PS C:\> (Get-Process | sort Handles).Where({$_.Handles -gt 1000})

Handles  NPM(K)    PM(K)      WS(K) VM(M)    CPU(s)      Id ProcessName
-------  ------    -----      ----- -----    ------      -- -----------
   1010     156   155984     206096   549     26.56    6668 WWAHost
   1116       0      128       9196    13  4,141.44       4 System
   1126      42    36836      53436   889     23.36    4292 livecomm
   1174      28     8728      25728   289      0.56    2120 UcMapi
   1332      50    67536      95420   537     20.34    5680 ONENOTE
   1337      20     8396      13332    54     38.89     652 lsass
   1984      61    44372      45608   449     59.27    1008 svchost
   2106      93    54676     113484   576     83.33    3140 explorer
   2236      64    72912     116996   664      7.38    2820 lync
```

To see the data that doesn't match, you have to modify the filter or use the `Until` parameter:

```
PS C:\> (Get-Process | sort Handles).Where({$_.Handles -gt 1000}, "Until")

Handles  NPM(K)    PM(K)      WS(K) VM(M)    CPU(s)      Id ProcessName
-------  ------    -----      ----- -----    ------      -- -----------
      0       0        0         24     0                  0 Idle
     43       6      664       2988    40      0.00    2932 TabTip32
     44       2      280        620     4      2.55     364 smss
     72       8      992       4600    70      0.03    3148 jusched
     75       8     1932       6568    57      1.55    7088 conhost
     81       7      968       1308    44      0.00    1488 armsvc
    ...
    812      44    38500      83260   492      4.64    6060 EXCEL
    841      50    62776     145108   586     87.06     412 WINWORD
    842      45    13884      19964   105     12.09     380 svchost
    871      32    21112      24180   132     13.38     932 svchost
    971      46    27568      33388   137     97.33     980 svchost
```

If you don't sort the processes, data will be displayed until the first process is met that has a `Handles` property with a value greater than 1000.

If you add an integer as a third property:

```
(Get-Process | sort Handles).Where({$_.Handles -gt 1000}, "Until", 3)
```

you'll see the first three processes that don't have a `Handles` property greater than 1000. Unfortunately there isn't a way to get the last N processes that don't match the criterion.

The `SkipUntil` parameter is the opposite of `Until`. It skips all processes that don't match the filter. These options yield the same result:

```
(Get-Process | sort Handles).Where({$_.Handles -gt 1000}, "First")
(Get-Process | sort Handles).Where({$_.Handles -gt 1000}, "First", 1)
(Get-Process | sort Handles).Where({$_.Handles -gt 1000}, "SkipUntil", 1)
```

So why would you use `SkipUntil`? The best reason is that it's a bit faster than the alternatives, so you get your data sooner.

> **TIP** Because this syntax can be so efficient, it's great for interactive sessions. Normally, we hesitate to use such a shortcut in a script, but because of the performance gains it's hard to argue against it. So if you include syntax like this in a PowerShell script, we encourage you to document and clearly explain it, especially if the script will be used by other people.

This syntax can be confusing, so we recommend that you practice with it by building on the examples we've provided.

7.6 *Grouping objects*

Most of the time, the PowerShell pipeline handles groups of objects fine. But sometimes you want to take matters into your own hands. The `Group-Object` cmdlet takes a bunch of objects and puts them into buckets, or groups, based on a key property:

```
PS C:\> Get-Service | Group-Object -property Status

Count Name                    Group
----- ----                    -----
   95 Running                 {System.ServiceProcess.ServiceController, Sy...
   99 Stopped                 {System.ServiceProcess.ServiceController, Sy...
```

Here you're taking all the service objects and piping them to `Group-Object`, organizing them into groups based on the `Status` property. What you get back is a different object. Even though you started with service objects, `Group-Object` writes a different type of object to the pipeline. You can verify this by piping your command to `Get-Member`:

```
PS C:\> Get-Service | group status | Get-Member

   TypeName: Microsoft.PowerShell.Commands.GroupInfo
Name        MemberType Definition
----        ---------- ----------
Equals      Method     bool Equals(System.Object obj)
GetHashCode Method     int GetHashCode()
GetType     Method     type GetType()
ToString    Method     string ToString()
Count       Property   System.Int32 Count {get;}
Group       Property   System.Collections.ObjectModel.Collection`1[[Syst...
Name        Property   System.String Name {get;}
Values      Property   System.Collections.ArrayList Values {get;}
```

You can simplify your typing by taking advantage of aliases and positional parameters. As you can see, you have something called a `Microsoft.PowerShell.Commands.Group-Info` object, which has properties of `Group`, `Name`, and `Values`. The `Group` property is the collection of objects. In this example, that will be service objects.

Let's run that command again:

```
PS C:\> $services = Get-Service | group status
PS C:\> $services
Count Name            Group
----- ----            -----
  100 Stopped         {System.ServiceProcess.ServiceController, Sy...
   94 Running         {System.ServiceProcess.ServiceController, Sy...
```

The variable `$services` contains the `GroupInfo` objects. Let's look at the `Group` property of the first element of `$services` and display the first few items:

```
PS C:\> $services[0].group[0..5]

Status   Name            DisplayName
------   ----            -----------
Stopped  AeLookupSvc     Application Experience
Stopped  ALG             Application Layer Gateway Service
Stopped  AppIDSvc        Application Identity
Stopped  Appinfo         Application Information
Stopped  AppMgmt         Application Management
Stopped  aspnet_state    ASP.NET State Service
```

Grouping objects can come in handy when you're more interested in the collective results. For example, suppose you want to find out what types of files are in a given folder. We'll look at a local folder, but this would easily translate to a shared folder on one of your file servers:

```
PS C:\> $files = dir c:\work -recurse -file | Group Extension
PS C:\> $files | sort Count -descending | select -first 5 Count,Name
                          Count Name
                          ----- ----
                            215 .txt
                             90 .ps1
                             42 .csv
                             40 .xml
                             15 .abc
```

We'll deal with formatting later, but at a glance you can see which file types are most in use. If you were curious about the files themselves, you could get them in the `Group` property.

Depending on what you need to do with the grouped objects, you might find it easier to work with a hash table. `Group-Object` can help you with the `–AsHashTable` parameter:

```
PS C:\> $services = Get-WmiObject -Class Win32_Service |
     group StartMode -AsHashTable

PS C:\> $services
Name                    Value
----                    -----
Manual                  {\\SERENITY\root\cimv2:Win32_Service.Name...
```

```
Unknown                             {\\SERENITY\root\cimv2:Win32_Service.Name...
Auto                                {\\SERENITY\root\cimv2:Win32_Service.Name...
Disabled                            {\\SERENITY\root\cimv2:Win32_Service.Nam....

PS C:\> $services.Disabled.count
11
PS C:\> $services.Disabled.displayname
Bluetooth Support Service
HomeGroup Listener
HomeGroup Provider
Net.Tcp Port Sharing Service
Routing and Remote Access
Remote Registry
Smart Card
Internet Connection Sharing (ICS)
Windows Biometric Service
Windows Media Player Network Sharing Service
Family Safety
```

Finally, sometimes you don't care about the grouped items themselves, only the results of the grouping. In those situations you can use the -NoElement parameter, which omits the Group property:

```
PS C:\> dir c:\scripts -file | group extension -NoElement |
➥   sort count -desc | select -first 5

Count Name
----- ----
 1170 .ps1
  313 .txt
   57 .zip
   26 .xml
   25 .csv
```

Here we got all files from the Scripts folder, grouped by extension but omitting the files themselves.

7.7   *Measuring objects*

Sometimes, you need to know how many objects you have, and PowerShell is happy to help. Allow us to introduce the Measure-Object cmdlet and its alias, Measure:

```
PS C:\> Get-Command -Verb Get | Measure-Object

Count    : 508
Average  :
Sum      :
Maximum  :
Minimum  :
Property :
```

You can also get count information with Group-Object as we showed previously. But as the previous output implies, Measure-Object can do more than count, if you give it a single property that you know contains numeric data:

```
PS C:\> Get-Process | Measure-Object -Property PM -Average -Sum -Min -Max

Count    : 45
Average  : 14478631.8222222
Sum      : 651538432
Maximum  : 90230784
Minimum  : 0
Property : PM
```

Like `Group-Object`, this cmdlet writes a new object to the pipeline with properties like `Sum` and `Average`. But as you can imagine, this is certainly a useful tool. Let's continue with our group of file extensions and find out how much space they're using:

```
PS C:\> $files | sort count -descending |
    select -first 5 Count,Name,@{Name="Size";Expression={
    ($_.Group | Measure-Object Length -sum).sum}}

          Count Name                                            Size
          ----- ----                                            ----
            215 .txt                                        22386907
             90 .ps1                                          663866
             42 .csv                                         7928346
             40 .xml                                        26003578
             15 .abc                                         4564272
```

Here you created a custom property called `Size` that took the `Group` property from each `GroupInfo` object and piped it to `Measure-Object` to get the sum of the `length` property. This is a nice example of the PowerShell's flexibility and capability. You started out by running a simple `DIR` command and ended up with completely different but extremely valuable output.

7.8   Enumerating objects

Enumerating basically means "going through a whole bunch of things, one at a time." In other words, imagine that you have a big stack of comic books and need to pick out all the ones that Neil Gaiman worked on. You're going to go through that stack, one at a time, open each one up, and look to see if Neil's mentioned in the credits. It's going to be time-consuming, and you're going to wish you could get your little brother to do it, but it's what you have to do.

PowerShell does this with the `ForEach-Object` cmdlet. As with `Where-Object`, PowerShell v3 introduced a simplified syntax—but this time, we'll start with the full syntax.

7.8.1   Full syntax

You'll usually pass a script block to its `-Process` parameter, and in that script block you'll have access to good-old `$_`, which will represent a single piped-in object, or use the newer `$psitem`. For example, let's say that you were fed up with work and needed to shut down every computer in the domain. We're not saying you should do that, but if you needed to, this would accomplish it:

```
Get-ADComputer -filter * | ForEach-Object -Process {
  Stop-Computer -computerName $_.Name
}
```

In real life, if someone were crazy enough to do this, you'd probably see it written with an alias as well as abbreviated and positional parameters:

```
Get-ADComputer -filter * | ForEach {
  Stop-Computer -comp $_.Name
}
```

You might even see a shorter alias used. This isn't one we care for, because it gets hard to read scripts that have a lot of these, but people use it a lot:

```
Get-ADComputer -filter * | % {
  Stop-Computer -comp $_.Name
}
```

You could type any of those all on one line, but you could also type them exactly as we did in the example. Press Enter on a blank line when you're finished, and PowerShell will start shutting everything down.

Before you do that (and possibly tank your career), we want to revisit this concept of enumerating. We're not going to pretend you'll never need to use this cmdlet, because you will. We're not even going to tell you that using it should be a rare occurrence, because it might not be. But any time you do use ForEach-Object, sit down and ask yourself if you really have to. For example, we notice that the Stop-Computer cmdlet has a –ComputerName parameter, which accepts data of the type string[], which means it can accept more than one computer name at a time. Thus, the following would work:

```
Stop-Computer -computername (
  Get-ADComputer -Filter * | Select -Expand Name)
```

See? No need to use the confusing old ForEach-Object at all, with its curly brackets and $_ and whatnot. In many cases, a properly used cmdlet can work against several things at once, without you needing to go through them one at a time. It's as if you had a magic scanner into which you could pour your comic collection and have it spit out the ones you want without you having to manually look at each one.

7.8.2   *Simplified syntax*

The simplified syntax for ForEach-Object is a bit restrictive in what it lets you do, but it does away with the ugly $_ or $psitem placeholder. The simplified syntax of Foreach-Object has similar restrictions to Where-Object in that you can only use a single simple command. As an example, you can use calc.exe:

```
PS> Start-Process calc
PS> Get-Process calc
Handles   NPM(K)    PM(K)      WS(K) VM(M)   CPU(s)     Id ProcessName
-------   ------    -----      ----- -----   ------     -- -----------
     72       18     6152      11060    85     0.11   2320 calc
```

A new calculator process is started. Richard used to use Notepad for this sort of example until a reviewer complained because the code shut down Notepad and destroyed his notes. We trust you aren't. In the full syntax, you'd use

```
Get-Process calc | foreach {$_.Kill()}
```

In the real world you'd use `Get-Process calc | Stop-Process`, but the explanation wouldn't work as well.

With the simplified syntax, you'd use

```
Get-Process calc | foreach Kill
```

But something like this won't work:

```
Get-Process | foreach if (Id -eq 2120){Kill}
```

You need to use the full syntax:

```
Get-Process | foreach {if ($_.Id -eq 2120){$_.Kill()}}
```

The simplified syntax is probably of more use with `Where-Object`, but having options is always good, and you should take the opportunity to type less code to achieve the desired result where applicable.

7.8.3   The ForEach method

In PowerShell v4 you also get a `ForEach` method, which like the `Where` method we discussed earlier, isn't easy to discover. But the syntax is essentially the same:

```
PS C:\> ("don","jeff","richard").foreach({$_.toupper()})
DON
JEFF
RICHARD
```

As with `Where`, you can use `$_` or `$psitem`. The method offers performance gains. Here's the traditional way to use it:

```
PS C:\> measure-command {(1..1000) | foreach {$_ *3}}
```

```
Days              : 0
Hours             : 0
Minutes           : 0
Seconds           : 0
Milliseconds      : 92
Ticks             : 929776
TotalDays         : 1.07612962962963E-06
TotalHours        : 2.58271111111111E-05
TotalMinutes      : 0.00154962666666667
TotalSeconds      : 0.0929776
TotalMilliseconds : 92.9776
```

And here's the new syntax:

```
PS C:\> measure-command {(1..1000).foreach({$_ *3})}
```

```
Days              : 0
Hours             : 0
Minutes           : 0
Seconds           : 0
Milliseconds      : 40
Ticks             : 400475
TotalDays         : 4.63512731481481E-07
TotalHours        : 1.11243055555556E-05
```

```
TotalMinutes      : 0.000667458333333333
TotalSeconds      : 0.0400475
TotalMilliseconds : 40.0475
```

The larger the data set, the greater the gain:

```
PS C:\> (measure-command {(1..100000) | foreach {$_ *3}}).TotalMilliseconds
2854.1627
PS C:\> (measure-command {(1..100000).foreach({$_ *3})}).TotalMilliseconds
801.3789
```

As before, if you use this syntax in a script be sure to clearly document it.

7.9   *Importing, exporting, and converting objects*

Now we're going to cover PowerShell's core, built-in commands for getting data in and out of the shell and various other formats. First, let's define the four verbs you'll be working with:

- *Import* refers to the process of reading data from some external format, usually a file, and bringing that data into the shell in the form of objects. So this is a two-step process: *read* the data, and then *convert* the data into objects.
- *Export* refers to the process of taking objects in the shell, converting them to some other data structure, and then writing that data out to an external form—usually a file. As with import, this is a two-step process: *convert* the data, and then *write* it out.
- *ConvertTo* refers to the process of taking objects in the shell, changing them into some other data structure, and then leaving that converted data in the shell so that other commands can work with it.
- *ConvertFrom* refers to the process of taking some data structure and converting it into the object data structure that the shell uses. The objects remain in the shell for other commands to work with.

WARNING   We see folks get confused about these four verbs all the time. Remember, Import and Export deal with external files; ConvertTo and ConvertFrom deal entirely with data that's contained within PowerShell.

Here's a quick rundown of *some* of the cmdlets you'll find yourself using. This isn't an exhaustive list, but it's a good one to start with:

- ConvertTo-HTML
- ConvertTo-CSV
- Export-CSV
- Import-CSV
- Export-CliXML
- Import-CliXML

Let's work with the CSV cmdlets first. Technically, they only create comma-separated value (CSV) data structures by default; using their -Delimiter parameter, you can also have them create files that use delimiters other than a comma. We've seen people create tab-delimited format (TDF) files using these cmdlets, for example.

Here's the first example:

```
PS C:\> Get-Process | select name,id,vm,pm | ConvertTo-Csv

#TYPE Selected.System.Diagnostics.Process
"Name","Id","VM","PM"
"conhost","1100","82726912","2883584"
"conhost","1820","48480256","1003520"
"conhost","2532","42979328","847872"
"csrss","324","45211648","2027520"
"csrss","372","74035200","31252480"
"dfsrs","1288","364253184","14684160"
"dfssvc","1468","36069376","2326528"
"dllhost","1016","58023936","4202496"
"dns","1324","122880000","86794240"
"dwm","1964","55918592","1712128"
"explorer","1788","200929280","33488896"
```

As you can see, this obviously took the objects we had and made them into a CSV representation—*not* a CSV file, mind you, because there's no file involved. The data was converted from objects (one kind of data structure) to CSV (another kind of data structure), but the data stayed in the shell, which is what the ConvertTo verb means.

> **NOTE** The first line in the CSV is a comment, indicating what type of data was converted. You can eliminate this, if necessary, by using a parameter of the ConvertTo-CSV cmdlet. We'll let you read the help file for the cmdlet to find that parameter. It's for your own good.

So what if you need that in a file? Simple: redirect the output using the legacy console redirection characters.

```
PS C:\> Get-Process | select name,id,vm,pm | ConvertTo-Csv > procs.csv
```

That's an alternative to the Out-File cmdlet, so you could use that instead:

```
PS C:\> Get-Process | select name,id,vm,pm | ConvertTo-Csv |
    Out-File procs.csv
```

If you're a fan of shortcuts, then you're going to love Export-CSV. As implied by the Export verb, it basically combines ConvertTo-CSV and Out-File into a single, handy utility:

```
PS C:\> Get-Process | select name,id,vm,pm | Export-Csv procs.csv
```

But be careful. Run the following command in PowerShell:

```
PS C:\> Get-Process | Export-Csv myprocs.csv
```

Then open the CSV file in Notepad or view it in PowerShell:

```
PS C:\> Get-Content .\myprocs.csv | select -first 2
#TYPE System.Diagnostics.Process
"__NounName","Name","Handles","VM","WS","PM","NPM","Path","Company","CPU","
FileVersion","ProductVersion","Description","Product","BasePriority","ExitC
```

```
ode","HasExited","ExitTime","Handle","HandleCount","Id","MachineName","Main
WindowHandle","MainWindowTitle","MainModule","MaxWorkingSet","MinWorkingSet
","Modules","NonpagedSystemMemorySize","NonpagedSystemMemorySize64","PagedM
emorySize","PagedMemorySize64","PagedSystemMemorySize","PagedSystemMemorySi
ze64","PeakPagedMemorySize","PeakPagedMemorySize64","PeakWorkingSet","PeakW
orkingSet64","PeakVirtualMemorySize","PeakVirtualMemorySize64","PriorityBoo
stEnabled","PriorityClass","PrivateMemorySize","PrivateMemorySize64","Privi
legedProcessorTime","ProcessName","ProcessorAffinity","Responding","Session
Id","StartInfo","StartTime","SynchronizingObject","Threads","TotalProcessor
Time","UserProcessorTime","VirtualMemorySize","VirtualMemorySize64","Enable
RaisingEvents","StandardInput","StandardOutput","StandardError","WorkingSet
","WorkingSet64","Site","Container"
```

What happened? Exactly what you told PowerShell to do: get all processes on the local computer and export them to a CSV file. Don't assume that exporting, or converting for that matter, works on the cmdlet's default output. The export or convert cmdlet processes *all* objects *and all* their properties. If that isn't what you want, you'll need to select the properties you're interested in:

```
PS C:\> Get-Process | Select Name,ID,WS,VM,PM,Path | Export-Csv myprocs.csv
PS C:\> Get-Content .\myprocs.csv | select -first 3

#TYPE Selected.System.Diagnostics.Process
"Name","Id","WS","VM","PM","Path"
"cmd","2036","208896","79732736","5902336","C:\Windows\system32\cmd.exe"
```

That's more like it. The other fact to keep in mind when exporting or converting to the CSV format is that properties that are nested objects don't translate well:

```
PS C:\> Get-Service | Select Name,Displayname,DependentServices,status |
➥  Convertto-CSV | Select -first 4

#TYPE Selected.System.ServiceProcess.ServiceController"Name","DisplayName",
 "DependentServices","Status"
"AeLookupSvc","Application
Experience","System.ServiceProcess.ServiceController[]","Stopped"
"ALG","Application Layer Gateway
Service","System.ServiceProcess.ServiceController[]","Stopped"
```

The DependentServices property is a collection of nested service objects. When you attempt to turn this into a CSV-formatted item, you end up with System.Service-Process.ServiceController[], which is hardly meaningful. The bottom line is that when using the CSV format, stick with properties that have simple values. We'll show you how to handle these nested objects in a bit.

Hopefully that illustrates the main difference between converting and exporting:

- *Convert* = Changes the data structure
- *Out* = Put into external storage
- *Export* = Convert + Out

That leaves us with Import-CSV. Let's say you start with the following CSV file and data:

```
Name,Department,City
Don,IT,Las Vegas
```

```
Jeffery,IT,Syracuse
Richard,IT,London
Greg,Custodial,Denver
```

You can now run the following command to bring that data into the shell as objects:

```
PS C:\> Import-Csv .\data.csv
Name                    Department              City
----                    ----------              ----
Don                     IT                      Las Vegas
Jeffery                 IT                      Syracuse
Richard                 IT                      London
Greg                    Custodial               Denver
```

As you can see, PowerShell does the work of interpreting the CSV file. At the start of this chapter, we explained that "rows" and "columns" in a spreadsheet become "objects" and "properties" when they're made into objects, and that's exactly what `Import-CSV` has done. You can then manipulate those objects as you've manipulated others:

```
PS C:\> Import-Csv .\data.csv | where { $psitem.Department -eq "IT" } |
       Sort Name

Name                    Department              City
----                    ----------              ----
Don                     IT                      Las Vegas
Jeffery                 IT                      Syracuse
Richard                 IT                      London
```

How cool is that? Everything in PowerShell is geared to make working with objects easy. By getting the shell to convert other data structures into objects, you get to work with that stuff more easily.

Now for a quick look at HTML. The only cmdlet here is `ConvertTo-HTML`; for some reason, there's no `Export-HTML`, so you'll generally have to redirect the output to a file on your own. There's also no `Import` or `ConvertFrom` option here; it's a one-way trip to HTML. As with the CSV format, make sure you're only converting simple property values. No nested objects. Here's the example, and figure 7.2 shows the results.

```
PS C:\> Get-Service | Where { $_.Status -eq "Stopped" } |
       ConvertTo-HTML -Property Name,Status,DisplayName |
       Out-File Stopped.html
```

> **NOTE** The `ConvertTo-HTML` cmdlet has many more uses for its many different parameters. We'll make heavy use of them toward the end of the book, in chapter 33 on creating reports.

Finally, a quick word on the CliXML format: It's XML. It's a simple XML that Power-Shell understands natively. It's a great way to persist objects over time, such as creating a snapshot of some objects for later examination. We're going to use it in the next section for that purpose.

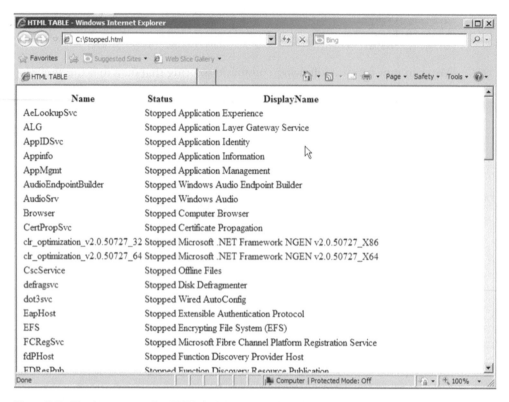

Figure 7.2   Viewing converted-to-HTML data in Internet Explorer

7.10   *Comparing objects*

The last cmdlet you'll learn in this chapter is Compare-Object, which has an alias named Diff. You're going to use it in conjunction with Export-CliXML and Import-CliXML to perform a cool, and incredibly useful, trick.

Do you do configuration change reporting in your environment? Many organizations do, and PowerShell can make it easy. You start by creating a baseline, or reference file, that represents the way you want things to be configured. For example:

```
PS C:\> Get-Process | Export-CliXML proc-baseline.xml
```

That takes a snapshot of the currently running processes and puts it into PowerShell's XML format, in an external file. CliXML is better than CSV for this task, because XML can represent deeply nested data, whereas CSV can only represent a single, flat level of data. Let's say you do this on a server, where the processes that are running should be pretty fixed. If new processes crop up over time, you'll definitely want to know about it. So, you'll come along in a month or so and see what's new. The following is a one-line PowerShell command:

```
PS C:\> Compare-Object -ReferenceObject (Import-CliXML .\proc-baseline.xml)
     -DifferenceObject (Get-Process) -Property Name
```

```
Name                                   SideIndicator
----                                   -------------
calc                                   =>
mspaint                                =>
notepad                                =>
svchost                                =>
```

A blank result set would have been good news—what the heck is going on here? MSPaint running on a server? You clearly need to have a group meeting about proper uses for servers.

Here's what you need to do:

- Run `Compare-Object`.
- The first parameter is `-ReferenceObject`, which is your baseline. To provide the baseline data, use a parenthetical command that imports your baseline data from the XML file. The entire contents of that XML file are converted into objects, and those become the values for the parameter.
- The second parameter is `-DifferenceObject`, which is what you want to compare the reference to. You have the current process objects as the values for the parameter, again by using a parenthetical command.
- The properties of a process are always changing: Memory, processor, and so forth are always different. So you don't want to compare those values, which `Compare-Object` would normally do. Instead, use the `-Property` parameter to tell it to only look at one property. That property is `Name`, which won't ever change during a process's lifetime.
- The results include a "side indicator." It's a little arrow, and if it points right, it means the difference set has something (in this case, the current processes) that doesn't exist in the reference set. A left-pointing arrow means the opposite—a process existed in the baseline but doesn't currently exist.

We've seen companies build scripts that are little more than dozens, or even hundreds, of those `Compare-Object` commands, each one comparing a different baseline to some portion of the existing configuration. They'll even pipe the output to an HTML file, and then email the file (as an attachment, using `Send-MailMessage`) to someone.

7.11 *Summary*

Well, we covered a lot. The goal of this chapter was to introduce you to the idea of objects and to show you some of the core PowerShell cmdlets that manipulate objects. We dare say that you'll use these commands all the time, whether you're working with Windows, Active Directory, Exchange Server, SQL Server, SharePoint Server, VMware, Citrix, or anything else that's manageable with PowerShell. The skills you learned in this chapter, and the ones you'll learn in the next couple of chapters, are as fundamental to PowerShell as the mouse is to Windows itself. We covered a lot of ground, so be prepared to come back to this chapter to refresh your memory any time you need to and be sure to read any help topics we eferenced.

The PowerShell pipeline

8

This chapter covers

- Using PowerShell's pipeline mechanism
- Working with parameter binding
- Troubleshooting the pipeline

Okay, we'll admit it: We're big PowerShell fans. You probably could have guessed that, but you might not know exactly why. It's the pipeline. Although not everyone realizes it, PowerShell is incredibly different from other command-line shells in any other operating system, or even in older versions of Windows, and that difference is due primarily to the pipeline. It's easy to use PowerShell without knowing much about the pipeline, but mastering PowerShell requires you to master the pipeline. That's what this chapter will help you do.

8.1 How the pipeline works

We started using the pipeline almost from the very start of this book, and the previous chapter made heavy use of it. Heck, you've used it yourself if you've ever run a command like `Dir | More`, or `Get-Service | Out-File`, or `Get-Process | Sort | Select`, or any other combination of commands. That vertical bar, |, is the *pipe character*, and it indicates that you're using PowerShell's pipeline.

8.1.1   *The old way of piping*

In pretty much every other operating system shell we're aware of, including Windows' old Cmd.exe shell, you can pipe stuff from command to command. It's worth understanding how older shells do it so that you can better appreciate what PowerShell's up to.

In those older shells, utilities—such as `Ping`, `Ipconfig`, `Tracert`, `NSlookup`, and so forth—are generally written to a specific set of rules, which require them to implement three interfaces:

- `StdIn`
- `StdOut`
- `StdErr`

When you run a command, it outputs *text* to `StdOut`. If you just run a single command, the shell captures whatever comes out of `StdOut` and displays it on the screen. Thus, when you run `Ipconfig`, you see output on the screen. Input is given to the command via `StdIn`. So, when you run an interactive utility like `NSlookup`, the shell takes whatever you type and jams it into the utility's `StdIn` so that you can interact with the utility. `StdErr` is where errors are written.

Run a command like `Dir | More` in an older shell and you're basically telling the shell to "connect the `StdOut` of the first command to `StdIn` of the second command." Figure 8.1 shows how this arrangement works.

The output sent from command to command is *always* text. That's why Unix and Linux administrators tend to have strong string-manipulation skills and really strong regular expression skills—because they're working with text in their shell, they need those skills to get by.

8.1.2   *The PowerShell way of piping*

PowerShell works completely differently. For one, its cmdlets don't implement `StdOut`, `StdIn`, or `StdErr` the way old-school commands do (although PowerShell knows how to interact with those standard interfaces, because it has to do so in order to run older commands like `Ping` and `Ipconfig`; we'll cover those at the end of this chapter).

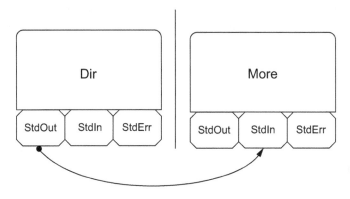

Figure 8.1 Piping in old shells just connects `StdOut` to `StdIn`.

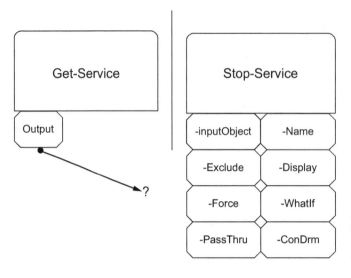

Figure 8.2   PowerShell has to decide which parameter of the second command will receive the output from the first command.

Instead, when two PowerShell commands are connected to each other, the first command places its output, in the form of objects, into the pipeline. The pipeline is something that the shell itself maintains as a way of getting objects from one command to another. In a way, the pipeline is a bit like StdOut; it's the one place that all PowerShell commands must send their output.

> **NOTE** Technically, PowerShell has several pipelines: one for output (which is like StdOut), one for errors (similar to StdErr), one for warnings, one for verbose command messages, and one for debugging information. Right now, we're just concerned with the output pipeline.

The real PowerShell difference happens with the next command in the pipeline: There's no StdIn for the shell to use. There's no single way for whatever's in the pipeline to be handed off to the next command. Instead, PowerShell has to attach the objects in the pipeline to one of the next command's parameters. For example, let's say you were to run Get-Service | Stop-Service (*don't* actually do so—it'll crash your machine). As shown in figure 8.2, PowerShell has to decide which parameter of Stop-Service will receive the objects that Get-Service put into the pipeline.

This decision-making process is called *pipeline parameter binding*, and PowerShell has two techniques it can use: ByValue and ByPropertyName. Both of these techniques rely on the programmer who created the cmdlet having hooked it up to participate in this process.

8.2   *Parameter binding ByValue*

With this technique, PowerShell figures out which parameters of the cmdlet are capable of accepting pipeline input via the ByValue technique. This capability, as we mentioned, is built into the cmdlet when it's created by a programmer. The programmer decides which parameters will support ByValue, and that information is documented in the cmdlet's help file. For example, if you run Help Stop-Service -Full, you can scroll down to the help for each individual parameter. Here's what two of them look like:

```
-Include <string[]>
    Stops only the specified services. The value of this parameter
    qualifies the Name parameter. Enter a name element or pattern,
    such as "s*". Wildcards are permitted.
    Required?                    false
    Position?                    named
    Default value
    Accept pipeline input?       false
    Accept wildcard characters?  false
-InputObject <ServiceController[]>
    Specifies ServiceController objects representing the services to be
     stopped. Enter a variable that contains the objects, or type a
     command or expression that gets the objects.
    Required?                    true
    Position?                    1
    Default value
    Accept pipeline input?       true (ByValue)
    Accept wildcard characters?  False
```

The -Include parameter doesn't support pipeline input at all—it says so right in the help. The -InputObject parameter does accept pipeline input, and it does so using the ByValue technique, which is what PowerShell is attempting. PowerShell reads through all of the available parameters and figures out which ones support ByValue. The result is shown in figure 8.3.

Each parameter can accept only a certain kind of input, which is also documented in the help. The -Name parameter accepts objects of the type String, whereas the -InputObject parameter accepts objects of the type ServiceController. PowerShell looks at the objects in the pipeline to see what type they are. You can do the same thing by using the Get-Member cmdlet:

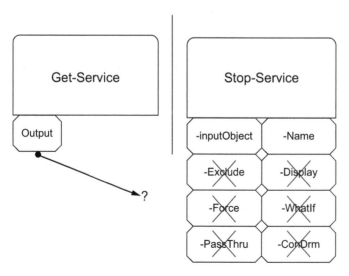

Figure 8.3 PowerShell eliminates parameters that don't support ByValue pipeline input.

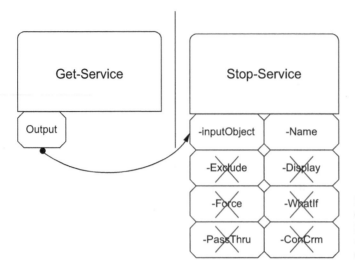

Figure 8.4   The output of Get-Service will be attached to the -InputObject parameter of Stop-Service.

```
PS C:\> Get-Service | Get-Member

    TypeName: System.ServiceProcess.ServiceController

Name                    MemberType      Definition
----                    ----------      ----------
Name                    AliasProperty   Name = ServiceName
RequiredServices        AliasProperty   RequiredServices = ServicesDepen...
Disposed                Event           System.EventHandler Disposed(Sys...
```

The first line of output says it all: Get-Service produces objects of the type System .ServiceProcess.ServiceController. As a shortcut, you usually just look at the last part of the name, which is ServiceController. That's the exact type of object that -InputObject will accept ByValue, and so, as shown in figure 8.4, PowerShell sends the objects in the pipeline to the -InputObject parameter. The help file for Stop-Service says that the -InputObject parameter

```
Specifies ServiceController objects representing the services to be Stopped
```

So whatever service objects are in the pipeline—which is all of them—will be stopped.

PowerShell always does ByValue parameter binding first; it will only go on to the next technique, ByPropertyName, if there was no parameter capable of accepting the type of object that's in the pipeline by using the ByValue technique. You'll also see that only one parameter per cmdlet can use ByValue. If the cmdlet had two parameters that supported ByValue, PowerShell would have no way of knowing what input gets hooked into each parameter.

> **NOTE**   PowerShell recognizes the object type "Object" as a generic type. If you look at the help for cmdlets such as Sort-Object and Select-Object, you'll see that they too have an -InputObject parameter, which accepts pipeline input ByValue and which accepts the generic type "Object." In other words, any kind of object can be given to -InputObject, and that's why all of the

examples in the previous chapter worked. Parameters that accept the type "Object" are kind of "universal recipients," capable of accepting anything that comes along the pipeline.

8.3 *Pipeline binding ByPropertyName*

If PowerShell can't make ByValue binding work, it'll shift to Plan B, which is ByProp-erty-Name. Let's change our example just a bit. Take a look at figure 8.5 to see what you'll try next (again, don't actually run this command just yet because it might crash your machine).

You might not think it makes any sense to run Get-Service | Stop-Process, but PowerShell is going to give it a try anyway. First, the shell will look to see which parameters accept pipeline input ByValue, and figure 8.6 shows what it comes up with.

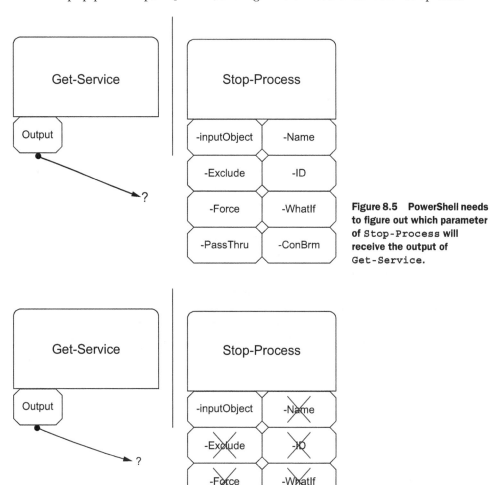

Figure 8.5   PowerShell needs to figure out which parameter of Stop-Process will receive the output of Get-Service.

Figure 8.6   Finding the parameters that accept pipeline input ByValue

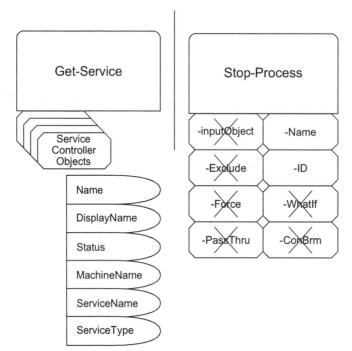

Figure 8.7 PowerShell starts trying `ByPropertyName` binding by listing the properties of the objects in the pipeline.

That's right, `Stop-Process` has only one parameter that accepts pipeline input `ByValue`, and it's `-InputObject`. Unfortunately, the help file says that this parameter accepts objects of the type Process. That isn't what you have in the pipeline, and you can't turn a `ServiceController` into a `Process` so `ByValue` will fail. On to Plan B!

Now the shell looks to see which parameters accept pipeline input `ByProperty-Name`. It also does the internal equivalent of running `Get-Member` again, to see what properties the objects in the pipeline have. Figure 8.7 shows this step.

`PropertyName` is simple: The values from every property of every object in the pipeline will be sent to any parameters that have the same name. In this case, only two `Stop-Process` parameters work with `ByPropertyName`: `-Name` and `-ID`. The objects in the pipeline don't have an `ID` property, so the `-ID` parameter gets nothing. The objects in the pipeline have a `Name` property, so that property's values get attached to the `-Name` parameter, simply because the property name matched the parameter name!

Figure 8.8 shows how PowerShell connects the two commands, and you can run this with the `-WhatIf` switch to see what would've happened.

```
PS C:\> Get-Service | Stop-Process –whatif
Stop-Process : Cannot find a process with the name "Dhcp". Verify the
process name and call the cmdlet again.
At line:1 char:27
+ Get-Service | Stop-Process <<<<  -whatif
    + CategoryInfo          : ObjectNotFound: (Dhcp:String) [Stop-Process]
    , ProcessCommandException
```

```
     + FullyQualifiedErrorId : NoProcessFoundForGivenName,Microsoft.PowerSh
  ell.Commands.StopProcessCommand
What if: Performing operation "Stop-Process" on Target "dns (1324)".
Stop-Process : Cannot find a process with the name "Dnscache". Verify the
process name and call the cmdlet again.
At line:1 char:27
+ Get-Service | Stop-Process <<<<  -whatif
    + CategoryInfo          : ObjectNotFound: (Dnscache:String) [Stop-Proc
  ess], ProcessCommandException
    + FullyQualifiedErrorId : NoProcessFoundForGivenName,Microsoft.PowerSh
  ell.Commands.StopProcessCommand
```

We've truncated most of the output to save space, but you can see what's happening: Service names rarely match their executable names. For example, the DHCP service doesn't run as Dhcp.exe; it runs in Svchost.exe (service host). So Stop-Process fails to stop that one. But the DNS service does run as Dns.exe, meaning its service name and process name match, so Stop-Process would've tried to stop it. We boldfaced that in the output, so you can see it more easily.

The point of this example was to illustrate how ByPropertyName works, but you probably want to see an example of it working *properly*, right? No problem. Start by creating a CSV file named Users.csv. You can do this in Notepad, and you'll put this into the file:

```
samAccountName,Name,Department,City,Title
DonJ,DonJ,IT,Las Vegas,CTO
JefferyH,JefferyH,IT,Syracuse,Director
RichardS,RichardS,IT,London,Writer
GregS,GregS,Custodial,Denver,Janitor
```

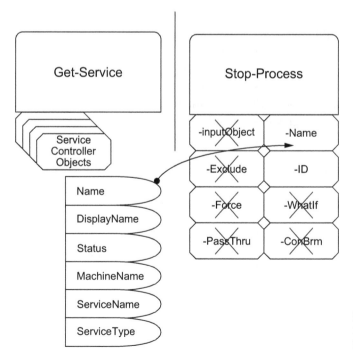

Figure 8.8 `ByProperty-Name` **binding matches property names to parameter names.**

Now, you'll use `Import-CSV` to have the shell read this file. Specifically, you're going to pipe it to `Get-Member` to see what type of objects the `Import-CSV` command produces:

```
PS C:\> import-csv .\users.csv | Get-Member

   TypeName: System.Management.Automation.PSCustomObject

Name           MemberType   Definition
----           ----------   ----------
Equals         Method       bool Equals(System.Object obj)
GetHashCode    Method       int GetHashCode()
GetType        Method       type GetType()
ToString       Method       string ToString()
City           NoteProperty System.String City=Las Vegas
Department     NoteProperty System.String Department=IT
Name           NoteProperty System.String Name=DonJ
samAccountName NoteProperty System.String samAccountName=DonJ
Title          NoteProperty System.String Title=CTO
```

Okay, we know some interesting facts that we'll refer back to in a moment. The command produces objects of the type `PSCustomObject`, and the objects have properties that correspond to your CSV file columns: `City`, `Department`, `Name`, `samAccountName`, and `Title`.

Take a look at the help for the `New-ADUser` cmdlet (if you don't have this installed on your computer, you can read the help online at http://technet.microsoft.com/en-us/library/ee617253.aspx). You'll notice that none of its parameters support pipeline binding `ByValue` (if you're viewing the help online, just use your browser's Find function to search for "ByValue" on the page). That means PowerShell's Plan A, `ByValue` binding, fails. `New-ADUser` simply doesn't support it.

On to Plan B! You'll notice that lots of the command's parameters support pipeline input `ByPropertyName`, including the `-City`, `-Department`, `-Name`, `-samAccount-Name`, and `-Title` parameters. Goodness, those names sound familiar...because they're the exact names that you used as column headers in your CSV file! That means you could create four new users (that's how many objects your CSV file produces) simply by running this (although you shouldn't run it just yet):

```
PS C:\> Import-CSV users.csv | New-ADUser
```

Think about that for a long moment. What a powerful technique! Because the first command produced objects whose properties correspond to parameters of the second cmdlet, you can accomplish a time-consuming task with just a couple of commands in a single pipeline. Wow! Problem is, this isn't a realistic example. That CSV file, in a real organization, will probably originate with Personnel or Human Resources—and they're never going to get the format right. They'll see "samAccountName" and think, "There's nobody named 'Sam' here, so that can't be right." More likely, you'll get something like this from them:

```
UserName,Department,City,Title
DonJ,IT,Las Vegas,CTO
JefferyH,IT,Syracuse,Director
```

```
RichardS, IT, London, Writer
GregS, Custodial, Denver, Janitor
```

That won't work. For one, it lacks the `Name` column, which is a mandatory parameter of `New-ADUser`. It also lacks the `samAccountName` column, and user objects need to have that property. You could just edit the CSV file every time you got one—but that sounds like a lot of work. Why not have PowerShell do it? In the previous chapter, we showed you a custom property-creation trick with `Select-Object`, and that trick will serve you well right now:

```
PS C:\> import-csv .\users.csv | select-object *,
>> @{name="samAccountName";expression={$_.UserName}},
>> @{name="name";expression={$_.UserName}}
>>

UserName        : DonJ
Department      : IT
City            : Las Vegas
Title           : CTO
samAccountName  : DonJ
name            : DonJ

UserName        : JefferyH
Department      : IT
City            : Syracuse
Title           : Director
samAccountName  : JefferyH
name            : JefferyH

UserName        : RichardS
Department      : IT
City            : London
Title           : Writer
samAccountName  : RichardS
name            : RichardS

UserName        : GregS
Department      : Custodial
City            : Denver
Title           : Janitor
samAccountName  : GregS
name            : GregS
```

Cool! You told `Select-Object` to grab all of the properties from the input objects (that's what `*` does in the property list), and then you also created two brand-new properties named `samAccountName` and `Name`. Those were populated with the contents of the old `UserName` property. We left `UserName` in the output to demonstrate a point: Because that property doesn't map to any parameters of `New-ADUser`, it'll just get ignored. Now you can create those users! You'll add the `-passThru` switch so that the resulting user objects are displayed as output:

```
PS C:\> import-csv .\users.csv | select-object *,
>> @{name='samAccountName';expression={$_.UserName}},
>> @{name='name';expression={$_.UserName}} |
```

```
>> New-ADUser -passThru
>>

DistinguishedName : CN=DonJ,CN=Users,DC=company,DC=pri
Enabled           : False
GivenName         :
Name              : DonJ
ObjectClass       : user
ObjectGUID        : 1c6d89b1-a70b-471e-8a11-797b4569f7a1
SamAccountName    : DonJ
SID               : S-1-5-21-29812541-3325070801-1520984716-1104
Surname           :
UserPrincipalName :

DistinguishedName : CN=JefferyH,CN=Users,DC=company,DC=pri
Enabled           : False
GivenName         :
Name              : JefferyH
ObjectClass       : user
ObjectGUID        : 577569a3-4e2b-4145-944f-868a591be6fc
SamAccountName    : JefferyH
SID               : S-1-5-21-29812541-3325070801-1520984716-1105
Surname           :
UserPrincipalName :

DistinguishedName : CN=RichardS,CN=Users,DC=company,DC=pri
Enabled           : False
GivenName         :
Name              : RichardS
ObjectClass       : user
ObjectGUID        : 2863a36b-6ee2-4ea8-8058-64e8f536f863
SamAccountName    : RichardS
SID               : S-1-5-21-29812541-3325070801-1520984716-1106
Surname           :
UserPrincipalName :

DistinguishedName : CN=GregS,CN=Users,DC=company,DC=pri
Enabled           : False
GivenName         :
Name              : GregS
ObjectClass       : user
ObjectGUID        : 18e2ad39-a4bf-4ccb-bfaa-b35ddd15121a
SamAccountName    : GregS
SID               : S-1-5-21-29812541-3325070801-1520984716-1107
Surname           :
UserPrincipalName :
```

Awesome! Of course, you could add more columns to the CSV file to fill in more attributes, and we expect you'd do that in a real organization. And there's no reason you can't use other parameters with New-ADUser. For example, you might want to specify the parent container for all of the new accounts:

```
PS C:\> import-csv .\users.csv | select-object *,
>> @{name='samAccountName';expression={$_.UserName}},
>> @{name='name';expression={$_.UserName}} |
>> New-ADUser -path "ou=employees,dc=company,dc=pri" -passThru
```

The –passThru switch

Most of the time in PowerShell, cmdlets that do something—those with verbs like New, Stop, Set, and so forth—don't produce any output. They'll display errors if something goes wrong, but generally speaking it's the Get cmdlets that produce output.

Many so-called action cmdlets have a –passThru switch. This tells the cmdlet, "When you get done doing whatever it is you do, place the objects you acted on into the pipeline." This can enable some pretty powerful one-liner commands: Imagine piping the output of New-ADUser (which is one or more new user objects) to another cmdlet that sets their password...and another cmdlet that enables their account...and another cmdlet that adds them to a group...and so on, and so on, and so on. It becomes even more powerful if you have the Exchange tools installed on your workstation because you can continue the pipeline into Enable-Mailbox and create their mailbox as well!

You won't find this switch on every cmdlet, but it's worth looking at cmdlets' help files to see if it exists (you can also type Get-Command -ParameterName Passthru to get a list of cmdlets supporting the –Passthru parameter) and to think about how you might use it. Remember, if nothing is written to the pipeline, you can't pipe into the next command in your expression. This ability to pipe objects between cmdlets is a compelling feature of Windows PowerShell.

8.4 Troubleshooting parameter binding

It's extremely common to try to connect commands together and to become disappointed when they don't connect in quite the way you'd hoped. There are two steps to troubleshooting those problems: carefully considering the process itself, which we've described in this chapter, and getting PowerShell to tell you what it's doing.

As a quick reference, figure 8.9 is a flowchart of the entire process, including both ByValue and ByPropertyName phases.

PowerShell's Trace-Command cmdlet can help you see what PowerShell's doing with parameter binding.

> **CAUTION** When you trace a command, the command you specify actually executes. Be careful not to trace any command that you don't want to run! You can use the –whatIf switch (if supported) on the final command of your command line to prevent it from doing anything.

The output of Trace-Command can be complicated, so we'll help you break it down by walking through it one chunk at a time. First, run the command. You're going to trace the command that you ran earlier to create the new users in Active Directory:

```
PS C:\> trace-command -pshost -name parameterbinding -Expression {
>> import-csv .\users.csv | select-object *,
>> @{name="samAccountName";expression={$_.UserName}},
>> @{name="name";expression={$_.UserName}} |
>> New-ADUser -whatif
>> }
>>
```

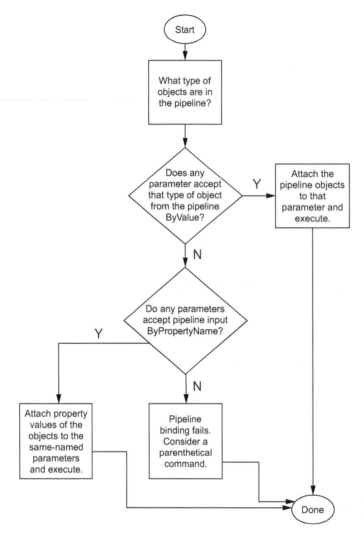

Figure 8.9 The complete parameter binding process

The first chunk of output is for your Import-CSV command. Here you'll see it bind the argument .\users.csv to the -Path parameter. It did so positionally because you didn't actually type the -Path parameter name. The -Path parameter accepts an array of strings, but you provided only one, so PowerShell internally creates an array and adds your one item to it. You can also see PowerShell checking to make sure all mandatory parameters were provided (they were). Each of these steps is outlined in the trace:

```
DEBUG: ParameterBinding Information: 0 : BIND NAMED cmd line args
[Import-Csv]
DEBUG: ParameterBinding Information: 0 : BIND POSITIONAL cmd line args
[Import-Csv]
DEBUG: ParameterBinding Information: 0 :    BIND arg [.\users.csv] to
parameter [Path]
```

```
DEBUG: ParameterBinding Information: 0 :        Binding collection
parameter Path: argument type [String], parameter type [System.String[]],
collection type Array, element type [System.String], no coerceElementType
DEBUG: ParameterBinding Information: 0 :        Creating array with
element type [System.String] and 1 elements
DEBUG: ParameterBinding Information: 0 :        Argument type String is
not IList, treating this as scalar
DEBUG: ParameterBinding Information: 0 :        Adding scalar element of
type String to array position 0
DEBUG: ParameterBinding Information: 0 :        BIND arg [System.String[]]
 to param [Path] SUCCESSFUL
DEBUG: ParameterBinding Information: 0 : MANDATORY PARAMETER CHECK on
cmdlet [Import-Csv]
```

Next up is your `Select-Object` command. There were no named parameters on this one, but there was a positional parameter where you specified your property list. Again, a check for mandatory parameters (there aren't any) is run:

```
DEBUG: ParameterBinding Information: 0 : BIND NAMED cmd line args
[Select-Object]
DEBUG: ParameterBinding Information: 0 : BIND POSITIONAL cmd line args
[Select-Object]
DEBUG: ParameterBinding Information: 0 :        BIND arg [System.Object[]] to
parameter [Property]
DEBUG: ParameterBinding Information: 0 :        BIND arg [System.Object[]]
 to param [Property] SUCCESSFUL
DEBUG: ParameterBinding Information: 0 : MANDATORY PARAMETER CHECK on
cmdlet [Select-Object]
```

In the next chunk, you can see PowerShell working with the `New-ADUser` parameters. Now, keep in mind that at this point the shell is just worrying about the obvious parameters—the ones you specified by typing parameter names or values. It hasn't gotten to pipeline input yet, because it hasn't run any of these commands. You're still in a sort of "pre-flight" mode. You can see the `-WhatIf` parameter being bound, along with the standard mandatory parameter check:

```
DEBUG: ParameterBinding Information: 0 : BIND NAMED cmd line args
[New-ADUser]
DEBUG: ParameterBinding Information: 0 :        BIND arg [True] to parameter
[WhatIf]
DEBUG: ParameterBinding Information: 0 :        COERCE arg to
[System.Management.Automation.SwitchParameter]
DEBUG: ParameterBinding Information: 0 :            Parameter and arg
types the same, no coercion is needed.
DEBUG: ParameterBinding Information: 0 :        BIND arg [True] to param
[WhatIf] SUCCESSFUL
DEBUG: ParameterBinding Information: 0 : BIND POSITIONAL cmd line args
[New-ADUser]
DEBUG: ParameterBinding Information: 0 : BIND cmd line args to DYNAMIC
parameters.
DEBUG: ParameterBinding Information: 0 :        DYNAMIC parameter object:
[Microsoft.ActiveDirectory.Management.Commands.NewADUserParameterSet]
DEBUG: ParameterBinding Information: 0 : MANDATORY PARAMETER CHECK on
cmdlet [New-ADUser]
```

Now the fun begins. PowerShell begins executing your commands. There are three of them total, so you'll see three statements in the output:

```
DEBUG: ParameterBinding Information: 0 : CALLING BeginProcessing
DEBUG: ParameterBinding Information: 0 : CALLING BeginProcessing
DEBUG: ParameterBinding Information: 0 : CALLING BeginProcessing
```

At this point, Import-CSV starts to run and produces its first object. That object goes into the pipeline. If you remember what you put into that CSV file, this should be the user information for DonJ. In the trace, you can see PowerShell attempting to bind this object to the Select-Object cmdlet. It sees that the object is of the type PSCustom-Object, and it successfully binds the object to the -InputObject parameter. You can see a breakdown of the object's contents, including the UserName, Department, City, and Title properties. PowerShell also does another check to make sure all mandatory parameters have been specified:

```
DEBUG: ParameterBinding Information: 0 : BIND PIPELINE object to
parameters: [Select-Object]
DEBUG: ParameterBinding Information: 0 :     PIPELINE object TYPE =
[System.Management.Automation.PSCustomObject]
DEBUG: ParameterBinding Information: 0 :     RESTORING pipeline parameter's
 original values
DEBUG: ParameterBinding Information: 0 :     Parameter [InputObject]
PIPELINE INPUT ValueFromPipeline NO COERCION
DEBUG: ParameterBinding Information: 0 :     BIND arg [@{UserName=DonJ;
Department=IT; City=Las Vegas; Title=CTO}] to parameter [InputObject]
DEBUG: ParameterBinding Information: 0 :         BIND arg [@{UserName=DonJ;
 Department=IT; City=Las Vegas; Title=CTO}] to param [InputObject]
SUCCESSFUL
DEBUG: ParameterBinding Information: 0 : MANDATORY PARAMETER CHECK on
cmdlet [Select-Object]
```

Now Select-Object does its magic and produces its output—just one object, because you're doing this one object at a time. PowerShell now needs to bind that to New-ADUser:

```
DEBUG: ParameterBinding Information: 0 : BIND PIPELINE object to
parameters: [New-ADUser]
DEBUG: ParameterBinding Information: 0 :     PIPELINE object TYPE =
[Selected.System.Management.Automation.PSCustomObject]
DEBUG: ParameterBinding Information: 0 :     RESTORING pipeline parameter's
 original values
```

Now you're going to see PowerShell start binding ByPropertyName. It does this for every single parameter of New-ADUser, so there's quite a bit of output in this part of the trace. For this example, you're just going to include the first handful of properties. Notice the two we've highlighted in bold? That's your Name property being bound to -Name and your City property being bound to -City. The -Name parameter has an internal validation programmed into it, which ensures that the parameter doesn't receive a null or empty value. Because you've provided the value DonJ, the validation passes and PowerShell continues:

```
DEBUG: ParameterBinding Information: 0 :     Parameter [Name] PIPELINE
INPUT ValueFromPipelineByPropertyName NO COERCION
DEBUG: ParameterBinding Information: 0 :     BIND arg [DonJ] to parameter
[Name]
DEBUG: ParameterBinding Information: 0 :     Executing VALIDATION
metadata: [System.Management.Automation.ValidateNotNullOrEmptyAttribute]
DEBUG: ParameterBinding Information: 0 :     BIND arg [DonJ] to param
[Name] SUCCESSFUL
DEBUG: ParameterBinding Information: 0 :     Parameter [DisplayName]
PIPELINE INPUT ValueFromPipelineByPropertyName NO COERCION
DEBUG: ParameterBinding Information: 0 :     Parameter [Description]
PIPELINE INPUT ValueFromPipelineByPropertyName NO COERCION
DEBUG: ParameterBinding Information: 0 :     Parameter
[AccountExpirationDate] PIPELINE INPUT ValueFromPipelineByPropertyName NO
COERCION
DEBUG: ParameterBinding Information: 0 :     Parameter
[AccountNotDelegated] PIPELINE INPUT ValueFromPipelineByPropertyName NO
COERCION
DEBUG: ParameterBinding Information: 0 :     Parameter [AccountPassword]
PIPELINE INPUT ValueFromPipelineByPropertyName NO COERCION
DEBUG: ParameterBinding Information: 0 :     Parameter
[AllowReversiblePasswordEncryption] PIPELINE INPUT
ValueFromPipelineByPropertyName NO COERCION
DEBUG: ParameterBinding Information: 0 :     Parameter
[CannotChangePassword] PIPELINE INPUT ValueFromPipelineByPropertyName NO
COERCION
DEBUG: ParameterBinding Information: 0 :     Parameter [Certificates]
PIPELINE INPUT ValueFromPipelineByPropertyName NO COERCION
DEBUG: ParameterBinding Information: 0 :     Parameter
[ChangePasswordAtLogon] PIPELINE INPUT ValueFromPipelineByPropertyName NO
COERCION
DEBUG: ParameterBinding Information: 0 :     Parameter [City] PIPELINE
INPUT ValueFromPipelineByPropertyName NO COERCION
DEBUG: ParameterBinding Information: 0 :     BIND arg [Las Vegas] to
parameter [City]
DEBUG: ParameterBinding Information: 0 :     BIND arg [Las Vegas] to
param [City] SUCCESSFUL
DEBUG: ParameterBinding Information: 0 :     Parameter [Company] PIPELINE
INPUT ValueFromPipelineByPropertyName NO COERCION
DEBUG: ParameterBinding Information: 0 :     Parameter [Country] PIPELINE
INPUT ValueFromPipelineByPropertyName NO COERCION
```

This goes on for quite a while because there are so many parameters. Eventually, PowerShell runs a final check to make sure all mandatory parameters have been given a value, and it executes the command. You can see the "what if" output indicating what New-ADUser would've done:

```
DEBUG: ParameterBinding Information: 0 : MANDATORY PARAMETER CHECK on
cmdlet [New-ADUser]
What if: Performing operation "New" on Target "CN=DonJ,CN=Users,DC=company,D
C=pri".
```

It's important to understand that PowerShell executes all the cmdlets in the pipeline more or less simultaneously. In other words, there are objects streaming through the pipeline one at a time, in parallel. You've just seen the first object, the DonJ user, travel through the pipeline. This entire process repeats for the other three objects created by `Import-CSV`.

The point of this exercise is to see what PowerShell is actually doing. If you're having difficulty getting a particular command line to work, this is a useful technique to see if PowerShell is doing what you thought it would do.

8.5 *When parameter binding lets you down*

Sometimes, cmdlets just aren't rigged up the way you want them to be. Consider this example:

```
Get-ADComputer -filter * |
Select-Object @{name='computername';expression={$_.Name}} |
Get-WmiObject -class Win32_OperatingSystem
```

Here's what we think this is going to do:

1 The first command will produce a bunch of Active Directory computer objects, which we know have a `Name` property.

2 The second command will produce a `PSCustomObject` that has a `ComputerName` property. This property will contain the contents of the computer object's original `Name` property.

3 The third command has a `-computerName` parameter. We're expecting those `PSCustomObject` objects to bind `ByPropertyName`, thus specifying the computer names we want to query information from.

A wonderful plan. Sadly, the `-ComputerName` parameter of `Get-WmiObject` doesn't accept pipeline input. It just never got rigged up for that functionality. (We're basing this example on v3 of PowerShell; it might work in a later version if Microsoft recodes the parameter to accept pipeline input, but it's unlikely given that Microsoft's development effort is concentrated on the CIM cmdlets rather than the older WMI cmdlets. The differences between the two sets of cmdlets are explained in chapter 39.) If we'd looked at help for this parameter, we'd have seen that it doesn't take pipeline input:

```
PS C:\> Get-Help Get-WmiObject -Parameter computername | select pipelineInput
pipelineInput
-------------
false
```

In these situations, a parenthetical command can usually take the place of pipelining objects:

```
Get-WmiObject -class Win32_OperatingSystem -computerName (
  Get-ADComputer -filter * | Select-Object -expand Name
)
```

This revised command is simply expanding the computers' `Name` property into plain strings, which is what the parameter expects. Parenthetical commands are powerful this way, because they don't rely on parameters being designed to accept pipeline input.

When pipeline input won't do what you need, a parenthetical command often will. Alternatively, fall back on using `Foreach-Object` to work with one or more commands, or even a complete pipeline of commands, for each object passing along the pipeline.

8.6   *Nested pipelines*

The pipeline is viewed as a sequential process: A | B | C | D. Sometimes you may need to reuse the values from B in later parts of the pipeline. This can be difficult to achieve and usually involves nested pipelines and using variables to store data.

Imagine you need to print out the multiplication tables for the values 1 to 10. You could do something like this:

```
1..10 |
Foreach-Object -Process {
 $value = $psitem
 1..10 | ForEach-Object -Process { "$value * $($_) = " + ($value * $_)}
}
```

Put the values 1 through 10 onto the pipeline. In the `Process` block of `ForEach-Object`, the current pipeline object (`$psitem` - introduced in PowerShell v3 as an alternative to using `$_`) is put into the variable `$value`. A second pipeline has the values 1 to 10 placed in it and each is multiplied by `$value` with the results written to screen. The output would look like this:

```
1 * 1 = 1
1 * 2 = 2
1 * 3 = 3
...
10 * 9 = 90
10 * 10 = 100
```

PowerShell v4 introduced a new common parameter, `PipelineVariable`, that's designed for these cases. The parameter has an alias of `PV`. You can discover this example in the help file `about_CommonParameters`:

```
1..10 |
Foreach-Object -PipelineVariable Left -Process { $_ } |
Foreach-Object -PV Right -Process { 1..10 } |
Foreach-Object -Process { "$Left * $Right = " + ($Left * $Right) }
```

Using the range operator, integers 1 through 10 are placed on the pipeline. In the first `Foreach-Object` call, the values are put into the `$Left` variable. The pipeline progresses to the second `Foreach-Object`, where for each object on the pipeline the values 1 through 10 are added to the `$Right` variable.

In the third `Foreach-Object`, the value of `$Left` is multiplied by the corresponding value of `$Right` to produce output similar to the previous version of the code.

NOTE   Each value of `$Left` is multiplied by every value in `$Right`.

As a more practical example, consider the need to create a folder hierarchy. You need 10 folders called Server*N*, where *N* is a value 1 through 10. Each of those folders will have 10 subfolders, called Log1 to Log10. You can generate the folder structure like this:

```
$folders = 1..10 |
ForEach-Object -PipelineVariable TLfolder -Process {"Server$_"} |
ForEach-Object -PipelineVariable ChildFolder -Process {1..10 | foreach
    {"Log$_"}} |
ForEach-Object -Process {"$TLfolder\$childFolder"}

New-Item -Path C:\ -Name "Logs" -ItemType  Directory
foreach ($folder in $folders){
 New-Item -Path C:\Logs -ItemType Directory -Name $folder
}
```

The folder names are generated by putting the values 1 to 10 onto the pipeline. The value is appended to "Server" and saved in the TLfolder variable. The pipeline progresses, and in the second Foreach-Object, the values 1 to 10 are appended to "Logs" and saved to the PipelineVariable ChildFolder. The final Foreach-Object combines the contents of the two pipeline variables to produce the full folder name. New-Item is used to create a folder in the root of C:, and then foreach is used to iterate over the folder names to create the folder.

8.7   *The pipeline with external commands*

So if this pipeline binding stuff all relies on objects, what happens if you try to use external command-line utilities in PowerShell?

Simple: When a command-line utility, such as Ipconfig, is run in PowerShell, PowerShell captures its StdOut, which will contain text. Each line of text is brought into PowerShell as a String object. This usually works well, as long as you know what to expect. You'll often pipe those String objects to a command like Select-String, which lets you search the strings for specific patterns.

Similarly, if you try to pipe objects to an external command-line utility, PowerShell will convert those objects to text (much as it does when creating an onscreen display for you to look at) and send that text to the external command's StdIn. This rarely works well, except in cases where the external command doesn't care about what the strings actually say. The More command—famous from the Dir | More example—is a command that works well with this technique. It doesn't care what the strings say—it just displays them one page at a time and pauses until you press Enter to continue.

8.8   *Summary*

In this chapter, we've revealed one of the most important inner workings in PowerShell. If your head is still spinning a bit, don't worry—it's taken us years to grasp and use the pipeline effectively. It's something you should practice, and if you get stuck ask someone for help. Online forums like PowerShell.org, PowerShell.com, Scripting-Answers.com, and so on are all good places to ask questions, especially for tricky pipeline-binding problems.

Formatting

PowerShell, as you've learned in the preceding chapters, works primarily with objects. Objects are just an in-memory data structure. But the time comes when PowerShell needs to share information from those objects with us humans. Power-Shell has to take those in-memory data structures and convert them into something a person can view. PowerShell's formatting system is designed to accomplish that task.

9.1 The time to format

Whenever you construct a command line, those commands all run in a pipeline. What you don't see is an invisible cmdlet hanging out at the end of every pipeline: `Out-Default`. It's hardcoded into the shell, and you can't get rid of it. You also never have to explicitly call it. Its sole purpose is to kick off the formatting process, using whatever objects happen to be in the pipeline at that point.

That's an important concept, so let's linger on it for a second. Consider this command line:

```
Get-Service | Export-CSV -Path services.csv
```

What output does that command create? You might be tempted to say "a file on disk," but that's completely external to PowerShell. Maybe a better question is "What objects does that command leave in the pipeline?" Try running the command, right now, and see what appears on the screen. The answer: nothing. Nothing appears on the screen, because no objects were produced by the command. Get-Service certainly produced objects and put them in the pipeline, but Export-CSV consumed those objects and didn't put any of its own into the pipeline. So, no objects in the pipeline means Out-Default has nothing to work with, and so that's what you see on the screen: nothing.

But let's say you run a command that does leave objects in the pipeline. Those go to Out-Default, which simply passes them on to another cmdlet, Out-Host, that's invoked by default. You don't have to do anything. Out-Host can't make heads or tails of those objects, though, because it only understands a special kind of object we call formatting directives (that isn't their official name, but it's one we use a lot because we don't know if they even have an official name). So when Out-Host gets anything that isn't formatting directives, it calls on the shell's formatting system. That system kicks in, extracts data from the objects, and uses the data to create formatting directives.

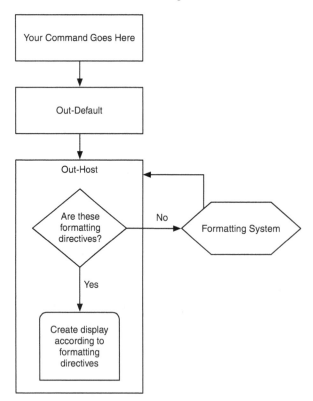

Figure 9.1 How PowerShell turns objects into text

Those are passed back to `Out-Host`, and output appears on your screen. Figure 9.1 shows all of this in action.

Most of the time you blindly accept the formatting directives. But by understanding the mystery behind them, you can control them.

9.2 *The formatting system*

Microsoft has provided the formatting system with a few rules, and a lot of configuration defaults, that let it produce decent-looking output without any work on your part. The process involves a few steps, which we'll cover here.

9.2.1 *Is there a predefined view?*

Microsoft ships PowerShell with a whole mess of *predefined views*. You can also create your own views and load them into memory for PowerShell to use; we've devoted chapter 26 to showing you how. Look in PowerShell's installation folder and you'll see Microsoft's predefined views:

```
PS C:\> dir $pshome -filter *.format.ps1xml


    Directory: C:\Windows\System32\WindowsPowerShell\v1.0

Mode                LastWriteTime     Length Name
----                -------------     ------ ----
-a---        18/06/2013     15:50      27338 Certificate.format.ps1xml
-a---        18/06/2013     15:50      27106 Diagnostics.Format.ps1xml
-a---        18/06/2013     15:50     147702 DotNetTypes.format.ps1xml
-a---        18/06/2013     15:50      14502 Event.Format.ps1xml
-a---        18/06/2013     15:50      21293 FileSystem.format.ps1xml
-a---        18/06/2013     15:50     287938 Help.format.ps1xml
-a---        18/06/2013     15:50      97880 HelpV3.format.ps1xml
-a---        18/06/2013     19:30     105230 PowerShellCore.format.ps1xml
-a---        18/06/2013     15:50      18612 PowerShellTrace.format.ps1xml
-a---        18/06/2013     15:50      13659 Registry.format.ps1xml
-a---        18/06/2013     15:50      17731 WSMan.Format.ps1xml
```

These are some of the ones that we found on our Windows 8.1 computers. They're XML files, and they contain formatting instructions for a wide variety of types of objects. So when PowerShell needs to display a process object, or a service object, or whatever, it looks through these files (which it's programmed to automatically load each time it starts) to see if that object type is covered by a view. If the object being displayed is covered by a view within one of these files, then that view is used. That's why running `Get-Process`, `Get-Service`, and most other commands produces the output they do: because Microsoft took the time to create that nice-looking display as a predefined view—in other words, a default format.

Predefined views tell PowerShell what kind of layout—such as a table or a list—to use. They tell the shell what properties to display, how wide columns should be, whether data should be left- or right-aligned, and so on.

9.2.2   *What properties should be displayed?*

If there's no predefined view, PowerShell looks to see if the object in the pipeline has a DefaultDisplayPropertySet. That's a special property set, defined as a type extension (we have a chapter on those later in the book, too, chapter 27) in another XML file. As you might expect, Microsoft defines this property set for a lot of object types. Try running this:

```
Get-WmiObject -Class Win32_OperatingSystem
```

You'll see a DefaultDisplayPropertySet at work.

If a DefaultDisplayPropertySet exists, PowerShell will display only those properties. If one doesn't exist, it'll display every property that the object has.

9.2.3   *List or table?*

Based on the number of properties it's been asked to display, PowerShell chooses between a table layout or a list layout. Tables are used only when there are four or fewer properties, on the theory that the screen should have enough room to display them all. Five or more properties automatically trigger a list layout—although you can override this behavior by explicitly calling the Format cmdlet of your choice.

Keep in mind that this happens only if a predefined view wasn't found. Process objects, for example, display in an eight-column table because there's a predefined view that tells the shell to do it that way.

9.3   *The Format cmdlets*

If you want to display something other than the defaults, you have to do it yourself, by piping your command output to one of PowerShell's Format cmdlets:

- Format-Wide
- Format-Table
- Format-List
- Format-Custom

Let's look at these in a bit more detail.

9.3.1   *Formatting wide lists*

The Format-Wide cmdlet generates a multicolumn list that focuses on a single piece of information. If you don't tell it differently, it looks for the Name property of the objects it's displaying, because most objects have a Name property.

```
PS C:\> Get-Process | Format-Wide

calc                          conhost
conhost                       conhost
csrss                         csrss
dfsrs                         dfssvc
dllhost                       dns
dwm                           explorer
Idle                          iexplore
```

iexplore	ismserv
lsass	lsm
Microsoft.ActiveDirectory.WebServices	msdtc
mspaint	notepad
notepad	powershell
powershell_ise	PresentationFontCache
services	smss
spoolsv	svchost
svchost	svchost
svchost	svchost
svchost	svchost
svchost	svchost
svchost	svchost
svchost	System
taskhost	TPAutoConnect
TPAutoConnSvc	vds
vmtoolsd	vmtoolsd
VMwareTray	wininit
Winlogon	

Peruse the help for this cmdlet (whose alias is fw, by the way) and you'll see that it lets you specify the number of columns to display and lets you pick an alternate property. You can also ask it to autosize the display, which tells it to create as many columns as it can while accommodating the data that needs to be displayed. The two parameters –Autosize and –Column are mutually exclusive. Here are some examples:

```
PS C:\> Get-Process | Format-Wide -Property ID -Column 4
```

1892	1100	1820	2532
324	372	1288	1468
1016	1324	1964	1788
0	1728	3036	1352
476	484	1248	668
2988	1476	2880	2656
2188	164	468	228
1216	540	640	712
808	848	896	940
980	1408	1792	2388
2828	4	2564	804
1940	1880	1536	2908
2996	364	408	

```
PS C:\> Get-Process | Format-Wide -Property ID –Autosize
```

```
1892  1100 1820 2532 324   372  1288 1468 1016 1324 1964 1788 0    1728 3036
1352  476  484  1248 668   2988 1476 2880 2656 2188 164  468  228  1216 540
640   712  808  848  896   940  980  1408 1792 2388 2828 4    2564 804  1940
1880  1536 2908 2996 364   408
```

Not much to it. We'll agree that these aren't the most compelling real-world examples, but they help illustrate the cmdlet. Format-Wide is most useful when you have data to scan through that's easier to view in a smaller number of rows. The output from Get-Verb (viewing the standard PowerShell verbs) is a good example. The default display is two columns. Using Format-Wide produces a display that's easier to work with. Try it and see.

9.3.2 *Formatting tables*

The `Format-Table` cmdlet (alias `ft`) is one of the most flexible of the bunch. By default, it formats things in a columnar table display. Note that this has no special effect if it's displaying a type of object that uses a table by default—you'll just get the same old thing. But using the `-Property` parameter, you can choose the properties you want to display. Like `Format-Wide`, an `-AutoSize` parameter tries to fit each column to its largest piece of data. Without that, the table will attempt to fill the screen, which can result in an empty-looking display, for example:

```
PS C:\> Get-Service | Format-Table -Property Name,Status

Name                                                            Status
----                                                            ------
ADWS                                                            Running
AeLookupSvc                                                     Stopped
ALG                                                             Stopped
AppIDSvc                                                        Stopped
Appinfo                                                         Stopped
AppMgmt                                                         Stopped
AudioEndpointBuilder                                            Stopped
AudioSrv                                                        Stopped
BFE                                                             Running
...
PS C:\> Get-Service | Format-Table -Property Name,Status -AutoSize

Name                          Status
----                          ------
ADWS                          Running
AeLookupSvc                   Stopped
ALG                           Stopped
AppIDSvc                      Stopped
Appinfo                       Stopped
AppMgmt                       Stopped
AudioEndpointBuilder          Stopped
AudioSrv                      Stopped
BFE                           Running
BITS                          Running
Browser                       Stopped
CertPropSvc                   Stopped
clr_optimization_v2.0.50727_32 Stopped
...
```

Quite a difference. Sometimes, it's possible to include so many columns that some data gets truncated with an ellipsis (...); in those cases, adding the `-Wrap` parameter will allow data to wrap across multiple rows without being truncated.

Notice that the `-Property` parameter is positional, so you'll usually see the command written like this:

```
PS C:\> Get-Process | ft Name,ID -auto

Name                           Id
----                           --
calc                         1892
```

```
conhost                          1100
conhost                          1820
conhost                          2532
csrss                             324
csrss                             372
dfsrs                            1288
dfssvc                           1468
dllhost                          1016
dns                              1324
dwm                              1964
explorer                         1788
Idle                                0
iexplore                         1728
iexplore                         3036
...
```

We also used the cmdlet's alias, `ft`, and truncated `-AutoSize` to just `-auto` or even `-a`. You'll see other common shortcuts in the wild.

> **NOTE** In PowerShell v2, if you used `-AutoSize` and PowerShell couldn't display all the properties because of display width, you'd get a warning that some columns wouldn't fit and were removed. In PowerShell v3 and later, columns that don't fit will still be removed, but you won't get the warning.

There's also a `-GroupBy` parameter, which tells the cmdlet to watch a particular property's values. Every time the value changes, the cmdlet generates a new table header. This can initially seem kind of annoying, as shown by this output excerpt:

```
PS C:\> Get-Service | Format-Table -GroupBy Status

   Status: Running

Status    Name            DisplayName
------    ----            -----------
Running   ADWS            Active Directory Web Services

   Status: Stopped

Status    Name            DisplayName
------    ----            -----------
Stopped   AeLookupSvc     Application Experience
Stopped   ALG             Application Layer Gateway Service
Stopped   AppIDSvc        Application Identity
Stopped   Appinfo         Application Information
Stopped   AppMgmt         Application Management
Stopped   AudioEndpointBu... Windows Audio Endpoint Builder
Stopped   AudioSrv        Windows Audio

   Status: Running

Status    Name            DisplayName
------    ----            -----------
Running   BFE             Base Filtering Engine
Running   BITS            Background Intelligent Transfer Ser...
...
```

The trick is to first sort the data on that same property so that the property isn't flipping back and forth between the same value:

```
PS C:\> Get-Service | Sort Status | Format-Table -GroupBy Status

   Status: Stopped

Status    Name                DisplayName
------    ----                -----------
Stopped   TPVCGateway         TP VC Gateway Service
Stopped   NtFrs               File Replication
Stopped   TrkWks              Distributed Link Tracking Client
Stopped   TrustedInstaller    Windows Modules Installer
Stopped   NetTcpPortSharing   Net.Tcp Port Sharing Service
Stopped   PolicyAgent         IPsec Policy Agent
Stopped   Themes              Themes
Stopped   THREADORDER         Thread Ordering Server
Stopped   PerfHost            Performance Counter DLL Host
...
   Status: Running

Status    Name                DisplayName
------    ----                -----------
Running   ADWS                Active Directory Web Services
Running   BFE                 Base Filtering Engine
Running   BITS                Background Intelligent Transfer Ser...
...
```

There's also a -HideTableHeaders parameter, which preserves the normal table layout but eliminates the two header lines.

Format-Table wildcard limitation in early PowerShell versions

One thing that may come as a surprise in PowerShell v3 and earlier is that Format-Table has a limitation on the number of properties it can display when using the wildcard for property names. As an experiment, try this code:

```
Get-Service spooler | Format-Table *
```

You'll get no more than 10 properties. Yet if you do this

```
Get-Service spooler | select *
```

you can count and see there are more than 10 properties (15 properties exist to be precise). You never get more than 10 properties displayed when using the wildcard with the -Property parameter. As far as we're aware, this isn't documented anywhere, but Format-Table appears to be limited to displaying 10 columns.

That said, try this:

```
Get-Service spooler | Format-Table
    Name,Req*,Can*,Dis*,Dep*,Mach*,Ser*,St*,Si*,Co*
```

Now you'll get all properties to the limits of your display. You can display more than 10 properties but you have to ask for them.

(continued)

The wildcard limitation in PowerShell versions v3 and lower probably won't affect your day-to-day work, but you need to be aware of it when using the wildcard and how to overcome it.

In PowerShell v4 this behavior has changed. `Format-Table *` will attempt to display all of the properties of the object. To see the effect of this, try:

```
Get-Process | Format-Table *
```

Bottom line? You still need to think about what you want to display.

If some of your column properties truncate, you can tell `Format-Table` to wrap the lines with, what else, `-Wrap`. Use this with `-AutoSize` to maximize the amount of formatted data:

```
PS C:\> Get-Eventlog system -Newest 5 | ft Source,Message -Wrap -auto

Source                          Message
------                          -------
Service Control Manager         The start type of the Background
                                Intelligent Transfer Service service was
                                changed from auto start to demand start.
Service Control Manager         The start type of the Background
                                Intelligent Transfer Service service was
                                changed from demand start to auto start.
Microsoft-Windows-Kernel-General The description for Event ID '16' in
                                Source 'Microsoft-Windows-Kernel-General'
                                cannot be found.  The local computer may
                                not have the necessary registry
                                information or message DLL files to
                                display the message, or you may not have
                                permission to access them.  The following
                                information is part of the event:'72', '\?
                                ?\GLOBALROOT\Device\HarddiskVolumeShadowCo
                                py4\Users\default\ntuser.dat', '496', '27'
Microsoft-Windows-Kernel-General The description for Event ID '15' in
                                Source 'Microsoft-Windows-Kernel-General'
                                cannot be found.  The local computer may
                                not have the necessary registry
                                information or message DLL files to
                                display the message, or you may not have
                                permission to access them.  The following
                                information is part of the event:'171', '\
                                ??\Volume{d32e13b1-e760-11e1-be66-806e6f6e
                                6963}\System Volume Information\SPP\SppCbs
                                HiveStore\{cd42efe1-f6f1-427c-b004-033192c
                                625a4}{12AC1A68-9D32-4816-A377-DD750018528
                                C}', '57552896', '57614336'
Microsoft-Windows-Kernel-General The description for Event ID '16' in
                                Source 'Microsoft-Windows-Kernel-General'
                                cannot be found.  The local computer may
                                not have the necessary registry
```

```
information or message DLL files to
display the message, or you may not have
permission to access them.  The following
information is part of the event:'171', '\
??\Volume{d32e13b1-e760-11e1-be66-806e6f6e
6963}\System Volume Information\SPP\SppCbs
HiveStore\{cd42efe1-f6f1-427c-b004-033192c
625a4}{A5499462-B89D-4433-9EF2-FC721EF1102
2}', '198', '24'
```

Finally, like `Select-Object`, `Format-Table` supports custom properties (we also refer to them as calculated fields) in its property list. The cool thing is that, unlike `Select-Object`, `Format-Table` is explicitly dealing with formatting, so it picks up a few extra keys:

- `N` or `Name` and `L` or `Label` specify the column header, just as in `Select-Object` they specify the custom property name. In PowerShell v1 only `Label` could be used in `Format-Table`. In PowerShell v2 and later, this changed so `Name` or `Label` could be used.

- `E` or `Expression` specifies the contents of the column, the same as in `Select-Object`.

- `FormatString`, unavailable in `Select-Object`, applies formatting. For example, `N2` is a number with two decimal places. This is .NET string formatting. A good starting reference for the formatting you can use is available at http://msdn .microsoft.com/en-us/library/26etazsy(v=vs.110).aspx.

- `Alignment` or `Align`, also unavailable in `Select-Object`, will accept `'Left'`, `'Center'`, or `'Right'`.

- `Width`, also unavailable in `Select-Object`, lets you specify a column width as a number of characters.

Here's a one-line example:

```
PS C:\> get-process | ft Name,ID,@{name='VM';expression={$_.VM /
⇒ 1MB};formatstring='N2';align='right';width=8}

Name                                                           Id      VM
----                                                           --      --
conhost                                                      1100   78.89
conhost                                                      1820   46.23
conhost                                                      2532   40.99
csrss                                                         324   43.12
csrss                                                         372   72.04
dfsrs                                                        1288  347.19
dfssvc                                                       1468   34.40
```

This is an awesome trick. But be sure to read section 9.4 so that you can avoid mistakes folks commonly make when employing this and other formatting tricks.

9.3.3 *Formatting lists*

After the joy of `Format-Table`, `Format-List` (alias `fl`) may seem a bit mundane. Really, it works a lot like `Format-Table`. You can specify properties, including custom ones. You can specify * to list all properties, which is a useful trick, especially when you want to quickly bypass the default formatting. It even supports -GroupBy. But there's no autosizing, and if you construct a custom property you don't get to specify width or alignment, although FormatString is still legal.

The business of being able to specify and see (technically Format-Table accepts * as a property also, but it's rarely practical) all properties is a great debugging tool. Although Get-Member will show you all of the properties an object has, Format-List -Property * (or just fl *, which is what folks commonly type) lets you see all of the properties *and* all of their values. Wondering what the DriveType property is for? Pipe the object to fl * and see what the property *contains*:

```
PS C:\> Get-WmiObject win32_logicaldisk -Filter "Deviceid='c:'" | fl *
PSComputerName                 : QUARK
Status                         :
Availability                   :
DeviceID                       : C:
StatusInfo                     :
__GENUS                        : 2
__CLASS                        : Win32_LogicalDisk
__SUPERCLASS                   : CIM_LogicalDisk
__DYNASTY                      : CIM_ManagedSystemElement
__RELPATH                      : Win32_LogicalDisk.DeviceID="C:"
__PROPERTY_COUNT               : 40
__DERIVATION                   : {CIM_LogicalDisk, CIM_StorageExtent, CIM...}
__SERVER                       : QUARK
__NAMESPACE                    : root\cimv2
__PATH                         : \\QUARK\root\cimv2:Win32_LogicalDisk.Devi...
Access                         : 0
BlockSize                      :
Caption                        : C:
Compressed                     : False
ConfigManagerErrorCode         :
ConfigManagerUserConfig        :
CreationClassName              : Win32_LogicalDisk
Description                    : Local Fixed Disk
DriveType                      : 3
ErrorCleared                   :
ErrorDescription               :
ErrorMethodology               :
FileSystem                     : NTFS
FreeSpace                      : 127647277056
InstallDate                    :
LastErrorCode                  :
MaximumComponentLength         : 255
MediaType                      : 12
Name                           : C:
NumberOfBlocks                 :
PNPDeviceID                    :
PowerManagementCapabilities    :
PowerManagementSupported       :
ProviderName                   :
Purpose                        :
```

```
QuotasDisabled                  :
QuotasIncomplete                :
QuotasRebuilding                :
Size                            : 201504845824
SupportsDiskQuotas              : False
SupportsFileBasedCompression    : True
SystemCreationClassName         : Win32_ComputerSystem
SystemName                      : QUARK
VolumeDirty                     :
VolumeName                      :
VolumeSerialNumber              : B0CEF5BA
Scope                           : System.Management.ManagementScope
Path                            : \\QUARK\root\cimv2:Win32_LogicalDisk.Devi...
Options                         : System.Management.ObjectGetOptions
ClassPath                       : \\QUARK\root\cimv2:Win32_LogicalDisk
Properties                      : {Access, Availability, BlockSize, Captio...}
SystemProperties                : {__GENUS, __CLASS, __SUPERCLASS, __DYNAS...}
Qualifiers                      : {dynamic, Locale, provider, UUID}
Site                            :
Container                       :
```

Sometimes it's just easier to read a list than a table. But there's another hidden gem with `Format-List` as well as `Format-Table`.

9.3.4   *Same objects, different formats*

Sometimes PowerShell has a few surprises. Here's one:

```
PS C:\> Get-Process -id $pid | Format-Table

Handles  NPM(K)    PM(K)     WS(K) VM(M)  CPU(s)     Id ProcessName
-------  ------    -----     ----- -----  ------     -- -----------
    562      15    82660     78432   232   22.39   1516 powershell
```

That looks pretty normal. The default format output for a process object is a table, so explicitly piping to `Format-Table` gives the same expected result. Now watch what happens when you pipe the same command to `Format-List`:

```
PS C:\> Get-Process -id $pid | Format-List

Id      : 1516
Handles : 589
CPU     : 22.464144
Name    : powershell
```

The same object but different properties are presented, depending on the format. This happens because, in PowerShell's format type extension files for the `Process` object, there are different default property sets, depending on whether you use a list or a table. You might be surprised at what information is readily available. The only way to know for sure is to pipe a command to a Format cmdlet that isn't what you normally see.

At some stage you may need more control over the format of output data. You can create your own custom formats.

9.3.5 Custom formatting

For all intents and purposes, you won't use Format-Custom much, if at all. Sure, you can pipe things to it, but by default all it does is show you a complete breakdown of each object's properties, enumerating through collections and so forth. The cmdlet is primarily designed to work along with predefined custom views, like the one Power-Shell uses to construct directory listings or its own help displays. That said, you can create your own custom configuration file and then use it with Format-Custom. We cover formatting extensions in chapter 26 but in the meantime listing 9.1 shows a sample file.

Listing 9.1 Demo-CustomFormat.ps1xml

```xml
<?xml version="1.0" encoding="utf-8" ?>
<Configuration>
    <ViewDefinitions>
        <View>
            <Name>System.IO.FileInfo</Name>
            <ViewSelectedBy>
                <TypeName>System.IO.FileInfo</TypeName>
            </ViewSelectedBy>
            <CustomControl>
            <!-- ############### CUSTOM DEFINITIONS ############### -->
             <CustomEntries>
                <CustomEntry>
                    <CustomItem>
                        <ExpressionBinding>
                            <ScriptBlock>
                             $_.VersionInfo.Filename
                            </ScriptBlock>
                        </ExpressionBinding>
                        <Text> (</Text>
                                <ExpressionBinding>
                                  <PropertyName>Attributes</PropertyName>
                                </ExpressionBinding>
                                <Text>)</Text>
                        <NewLine/>
                        <Frame>
                            <LeftIndent>4</LeftIndent>
                            <CustomItem>
                                <Text>FileVersion: </Text>
                                <ExpressionBinding>
                                    <ScriptBlock>
                                     $_.VersionInfo.Fileversion
                                    </ScriptBlock>
                                </ExpressionBinding>
                                <NewLine/>
                                <Text>Modified Age: </Text>
                                <ExpressionBinding>
                                    <ScriptBlock>
                                     ((Get-Date) -
➡  $_.LastWriteTime).toString()
                                    </ScriptBlock>
```

```
                                    </ExpressionBinding>
                                    <NewLine/>
                                    <Text>Created: </Text>
                                    <ExpressionBinding>
                                        <PropertyName>
                                         CreationTime
                                    </PropertyName>
                                    </ExpressionBinding>
                                    <Text>   Modified: </Text>
                                    <ExpressionBinding>
                                        <PropertyName>
                                          LastWriteTime
                                        </PropertyName>
                                    </ExpressionBinding>
                                    <NewLine/>
                                    <Text>SizeBytes: </Text>
                                    <ExpressionBinding>
                                        <PropertyName>Length</PropertyName>
                                    </ExpressionBinding>
                                    <NewLine/>
                                     <Text>Owner: </Text>
                                    <ExpressionBinding>
                                        <ScriptBlock>
                                           ($_ | Get-ACL).Owner
                                        </ScriptBlock>
                                    </ExpressionBinding>
                                    <NewLine/>
                                </CustomItem>
                            </Frame>
                        </CustomItem>
                    </CustomEntry>
                </CustomEntries>
            </CustomControl>
        </View>
    </ViewDefinitions>
</Configuration>
```

You'll need to jump to chapter 26 if you want to understand how it's constructed. This file defines a custom view, System.Io.FileInfo, for file objects. Once you have this file, you need to import it into your PowerShell session:

```
PS C:\> Update-FormatData -AppendPath C:\scripts\Demo-FormatCustom.ps1xml
```

Once it's loaded, you can format the display of any file object by piping it to Format-Custom:

```
PS C:\> dir c:\work -file | Format-Custom

C:\work\a.ps1 (Archive)
    FileVersion:
    Modified Age: 18.00:30:41.0124823
    Created: 12/6/2013 1:33:17 PM   Modified: 12/6/2013 1:37:16 PM
    SizeBytes: 349
    Owner: BUILTIN\Administrators
```

```
C:\work\ComputerData.xml (Archive)
   FileVersion:
   Modified Age: 18.21:48:15.1495274
   Created: 12/5/2013 2:12:22 PM   Modified: 12/5/2013 4:19:42 PM
   SizeBytes: 228
   Owner: BUILTIN\Administrators

C:\work\Install.txt (Archive)
   FileVersion:
   Modified Age: 1323.12:28:53.2247604
   Created: 5/11/2010 1:39:04 AM   Modified: 5/11/2010 1:39:04 AM
   SizeBytes: 1639
   Owner: JH-WIN81-ENT\Jeff

C:\work\mydata.xml (Archive)
   FileVersion:
   Modified Age: 18.04:35:36.7160348
   Created: 12/6/2013 8:45:48 AM   Modified: 12/6/2013 9:32:20 AM
   SizeBytes: 1352
   Owner: BUILTIN\Administrators

C:\work\Server1.mof (Archive)
   FileVersion:
   Modified Age: 18.00:18:51.0901805
   Created: 12/6/2013 1:49:06 PM   Modified: 12/6/2013 1:49:06 PM
   SizeBytes: 1670
   Owner: BUILTIN\Administrators

C:\work\WMIExplorer.exe (Archive)
   FileVersion: 1.1.3910.1261
   Modified Age: 582.00:35:42.2588165
   Created: 12/24/2013 1:45:01 PM   Modified: 5/21/2012 1:32:15 PM
   SizeBytes: 462848
   Owner: BUILTIN\Administrators
```

Because the custom format works with file objects only, our expression only gets file objects. Piping it to `Format-Custom` gives you a custom view of the file object with the information you need for reporting purposes. You can also create named views to provide custom formatting; you'll learn about that in chapter 26.

9.4   *Eliminating confusion and "gotchas"*

Finally, we're getting far enough along that we need to try to stop you from making some of the same confusing mistakes that we've seen our students sometimes make. There are three of them we want to cover.

9.4.1   *Formatting is the end of the line*

In this section, we aim to make sure you don't get caught by what's probably one of PowerShell's biggest traps. When you see a cmdlet named `Format-Table`, you probably assume that it formats things into a table form, right? And if your goal is to have, say, an HTML table, then you should be able to do this:

```
PS C:\> Get-Service | Format-Table -Property Name,Status |
➥ ConvertTo-HTML | Out-File services.html
```

Go ahead and try that. Don't worry, you won't break anything, but the final HTML won't be very attractive. Why not? Remember that PowerShell's formatting system—including the Format cmdlets—produce *formatting directives*, not normal objects. Those formatting directives are intended to be used to construct an onscreen display, or a plain-text file, or a piece of paper. The directives can *only* be used for those purposes, and no other cmdlet can make any sense of them.

So, to stay out of trouble, just remember two simple rules (well, one rule and one exception):

- If you use a Format cmdlet, it needs to be the last command on your command line.
- The only exceptions are the `Out-File`, `Out-Printer`, and `Out-Host` cmdlets. Because `Out-Host` is the default, you'll probably never type it, leaving you with just `Out-File` and `Out-Printer`. Those are the only commands that can come after a Format cmdlet.

Follow those rules, and you'll be fine. Don calls this the "Format Right" rule, meaning you want to move your formatting as far to the right—toward the end—of the command line as possible.

9.4.2 *Select or format?*

You've probably noticed that both `Select-Object` and the Format cmdlets let you specify the properties you want to see (just one for `Format-Wide`, but multiple properties are accepted by the other two). You'll also notice that `Select-Object`, `Format-List`, and `Format-Table` all support the same custom property syntax.

So which one do you use? It depends on what you want to do:

- If you've finished manipulating your objects and you're ready to display them, it's probably easier to select properties, and make custom properties, using `Format-Table` or `Format-List`. Keep in mind, though, that the output from that point has to go to the screen, to a plain-text file, or to a printer.
- If you haven't finished manipulating your objects, then use `Select-Object`. Keep in mind that it isn't dealing with formatting, so it doesn't have the ability to set column widths, alignment, or formatting strings. But the output can be sent on to other cmdlets.

Sometimes you'll end up using both, or you'll end up needing to be very clever. For example, suppose you want to query a computer and get information about its local disk drives. You want to display each drive's drive letter, total size in gigabytes, and free space in gigabytes. You want both of those values to carry two decimal places. You want to display only drives whose free space is less than 20 percent of the total space.

This is like one of those logic puzzles, where you're told that Jill lives in a red house, Joe lives next door to Jill, and Kim lives in a small house, and then you have to figure out who lives where. Here are the facts:

- You can use WMI to query the drive information. WMI is covered in chapter 39, so we won't focus on it now. It works a lot like the other Get cmdlets you've seen.

- You need to filter out the drives that you don't want displayed. This is best done as early as possible in the command line.

- You have some formatting requirements (two decimal places) that Format-Table can accommodate, but you need to decide if that'll be the last thing you want to do with the objects.

Here's one example of how you could construct the command:

```
Get-WmiObject -Class Win32_LogicalDisk -Filter "Drivetype=3" |
Select-Object @{name='DriveLetter';expression={$_.DeviceID}},
        @{name='Size';expression={$_.Size / 1GB}},
        @{name='FreeSpace';expression={$_.FreeSpace / 1GB}},
        @{name='PercentFree';expression={$_.FreeSpace / $_.Size * 100}} |
Where-Object { $_.PercentFree -lt 20 } |
Format-Table DriveLetter,
    @{name='Size';FormatString='N2';expression={$_.Size}},
    @{name='FreeSpace';FormatString='N2';expression={$_.FreeSpace}} -auto
```

Let's walk through this. You start by getting your WMI objects. Easy enough. Then, you use Select-Object to do the math needed to generate values in gigabytes, rather than the default bytes provided by WMI. Then, you filter out the drives you don't want by using Where-Object. Finally, you need to use Format-Table, because it's the only thing that can do the formatting necessary to get just two decimal places.

Was this the easiest way? Probably not. Here's a better approach:

```
Get-WmiObject -Class Win32_LogicalDisk -Filter "Drivetype=3" |
Where-Object { ($_.FreeSpace / $_.Size) -lt .2 } |
Format-Table @{name='DriveLetter';expression={$_.DeviceID}},
@{name='Size';expression={$_.Size / 1GB};FormatString='N2'},
@{name='FreeSpace';expression={$_.FreeSpace / 1GB};FormatString='N2'} -auto
```

This example shortens the command line to just three commands. You're filtering much earlier in the process, which is always good and means this expression runs a bit faster than the first example. Next, there's no reason to convert the values to gigabytes before doing that filtering, because you can do the division operation with bytes just as easily. You don't need to make a "PercentFree" column at all, because you don't want that in your output. You only have to go through the ugly custom-property–making syntax once, at the very end, where it can also handle your formatting instructions. Remember, though, that all this will do is send pretty output to the screen or a text file, assuming you piped to Out-File. You can't do anything else with it.

So it's largely a matter of being careful and clever and spending some time thinking about what's happening and what you want to achieve.

9.4.3 *Format, out, export—which?*

By this point in this book, we've thrown at you a lot of different ways to get information in and out of the shell:

- Import-CSV and Export-CSV
- Get-Content
- Out-File
- Format-Table

If you're following along, you're probably starting to wonder what the difference is. We certainly see classroom students trying to run stuff like this:

```
Get-Content data.csv | Where { $_.Column1 -eq 'value' } |
Select Column1,Column2,Column3
```

And that just won't work. Here's the deal:

- Get-Content and Out-File both work with plain, unstructured text. If you use Get-Content to read in a CSV file, it doesn't attempt to interpret the file or break apart its contents. It just spews the text onto the screen, including the column headers. You can't treat that as data objects. Out-File doesn't do any conversion of the data; what appears in the file is exactly what would've otherwise appeared on the screen.
- Import-CSV and Export-CSV deal with structured data. Export-CSV takes objects, which is one kind of data structure, and transforms them into CSV, which is another kind of data structure. Import-CSV does the opposite. If you want to be able to work with columns as properties, you use these.
- Format cmdlets discard your data structure and instead create a visual display that's only meaningful to humans. There's no practical way to bring that information back into the shell in any usable form.

We know, it's a lot to keep track of, but that's the price of being a PowerShell guru!

9.5   *Summary*

Formatting is one of the great powers of PowerShell. With a bit of planning and cleverness, you can produce incredible-looking reports, send them out to files or to a printer, or just look at them onscreen—all without much effort. There are some caveats and gotchas involved, and we've tried to cover those thoroughly for you here. Practice is the best thing for formatting, so jump in and start seeing what you can do.

Part 2

PowerShell management

Remote control. Background jobs. Regular expressions. HTML and XML. These are just a few of the core technologies accessible within PowerShell that you'll use to make server and client management easier, more scalable, and more effective than ever before. The chapters in part 2 tackle these technologies individually, diving as deeply as we can, so that you can master their intricacies and subtleties.

PowerShell Remoting

10

This chapter covers

- Outlining Remoting technologies and protocols
- Configuring and securing Remoting endpoints
- Exploring Remoting scenarios
- Using implicit Remoting

Remoting was one of the major new technologies introduced in PowerShell v2 and in the broader Windows Management Framework v2 (WMF v2), of which Power-Shell is a part. With v4, Microsoft has continued to invest in this important foundational technology. Most Windows machines, client or server, can be used as the local or remote machine—that is, you can create remote connections *to* them and you can create remote connections *from* them. The one exception is Windows RT—you can only remote from machines running that version.

> **NOTE** There's very little difference between Remoting in PowerShell v3 and v4. Unless we state otherwise, everything in this chapter applies equally to PowerShell v3 and v4.

Remoting is a complex technology, and we'll do our best to explore it as thoroughly as possible. But some uses for Remoting are outside the purview of an administrator: Programming custom-constrained runspaces, for example, requires software development skills that are outside the scope of this book.

> **NOTE**   Everything in this chapter focuses on PowerShell v4 and v3, but the majority of the material also applies to v2. The three versions of the shell can talk to each other via Remoting—that is, a v2 shell can connect to a v3 or v4 shell, and vice versa. PowerShell Remoting between v3 and v4 works seamlessly.

10.1   *The many forms of remote control*

The first thing we need to clear up is the confusion over the word *remote*. PowerShell v2 offers two means for connecting to remote computers:

- Cmdlets, which have their own -ComputerName parameter. They use their own proprietary communications protocols, most often DCOM or RPC, and are generally limited to a single task. They don't use PowerShell Remoting (with a couple of exceptions that we'll cover later in this chapter).
- Cmdlets that specifically use the Remoting technology: Invoke-Command, anything with the -PSSession noun, and a few others that we'll cover in this chapter.

In this chapter, we're focusing exclusively on the second group. The nice thing about it is that any cmdlet—whether it has a -ComputerName parameter or not—can be used through Remoting.

> **NOTE**   PowerShell v3 introduced another type of Remoting: CimSessions. These are analogous to PowerShell Remoting sessions and also work over WSMAN by default. They are covered in detail in chapter 39.

What exactly is Remoting? It's the ability to send one or more commands over the network to one or more remote computers. The remote computers execute the commands using their own local processing resources (meaning the command must exist and be loaded on the remote computers). The results of the commands—like all PowerShell commands—are objects, and PowerShell *serializes* them into XML. The XML is transmitted across the network to the originating computer, which *deserializes* them back into objects and puts them into the pipeline. The serialize/deserialize part of the process is crucial, because it offers a way to get complex data structures into a text form that's easily transmitted over a network. Don't overthink the serializing thing, though: It's not much more complicated than piping the results of a command to Export-CliXML and then using Import-CliXML to load the results back into the pipeline as objects. It's almost exactly like that, in fact, with the additional benefit of having Remoting taking care of getting the data across the network.

PowerShell Web Access (PWA—Microsoft uses PSWA but the PowerShell community prefers PWA as an acronym) was introduced in Windows Server 2012 and enhanced in Windows Server 2012 R2. PWA is covered in appendix B. PWA uses PowerShell Remoting "under the hood." It's best to consider PWA as a presentation layer superimposed on PowerShell Remoting, which is why we don't cover it here.

10.2 Remoting overview

Terminology gets a lot of people messed up when it comes to Remoting, so let's get that out of the way.

- *WSMAN* is the network protocol used by PowerShell Remoting. It stands for Web Services for Management, and it's more or less an industry-standard protocol. You can find implementations on platforms other than Windows, although they're not yet widespread. WSMAN is a flavor of good-old HTTP, the same protocol your web browser uses to fetch web pages from a web server.
- *Windows Remote Management*, or *WinRM*, is a Microsoft service that implements the WSMAN protocol and that handles communications and authentication for connections. WinRM is designed to provide communications services for any number of applications; it isn't exclusive to PowerShell. When WinRM receives traffic, that traffic is tagged for a specific application—such as PowerShell—and WinRM takes care of getting the traffic to that application as well as accepting any replies or results that the application wants to send back.
- *Remoting* is a term applied to PowerShell's use of WinRM. Therefore, you can't do "Remoting" with anything other than PowerShell—although other applications could certainly have their own specific uses for WinRM.

One of the features introduced in PowerShell v3 was a set of Common Information Model (CIM) cmdlets. Over time, they'll replace the legacy Windows Management Instrumentation (WMI) cmdlets that have been in PowerShell since v1, although for now the WMI and CIM cmdlets live side by side and have a lot of overlapping functionality. Both sets of cmdlets use the same underlying WMI data repository; one of the primary differences between the two sets is in how they communicate over the network. The WMI cmdlets use remote procedure calls (RPCs), whereas the CIM cmdlets use WinRM. The CIM cmdlets *aren't using Remoting*—they provide their own utilization of WinRM (more details in chapter 39). We point this out only as an example of how confusing the terminology can be. In the end, you don't have to worry about it all the time, but when it comes to troubleshooting you'll definitely need to understand which parts are using what.

Now for a bit more terminology, this time diving into some of the specific implementation details:

- An *endpoint* is a particular configuration item in WinRM. An endpoint represents a specific application for which WinRM can receive traffic, along with a group of settings that determine how the endpoint behaves. It's entirely possible for a single application, like PowerShell, to have multiple endpoints set up. Each endpoint might be for a different purpose and might have different security, network settings, and so forth associated with it.
- A *listener* is another configuration item in WinRM, and it represents the service's ability to accept incoming network traffic. A listener is configured to have a TCP port number, is configured to accept traffic on one or more IP addresses, and so

forth. A listener also is set up to use either HTTP or HTTPS; if you want to be able to use both protocols, then you must have two listeners set up.

10.2.1   *Authentication*

WinRM has two levels of authentication: machine-level and user-level. User-level authentication involves the delegation of your logon credentials to the remote machine that you've connected to. The remote machine can undertake any tasks you've specified using your identity, meaning you'll be able to do whatever you have permission to do and no more. By default, the remote machine can't delegate your credentials to any other machines—which can lead to a problem called "the second hop" where you attempt, and usually fail, to perform an action on a third machine from within your remote session. We'll deal with that later in the chapter.

Remoting also supports machine-level authentication. In other words, when you connect to a remote machine, your computer must trust that machine. Trust normally comes through mutual membership in an Active Directory domain, although it can also be manually configured in a number of ways. The practical upshot is that your computer will refuse to connect to any remote machine that it doesn't know and trust. That can create complications for some environments where the machines aren't all in the same domain, requiring additional configuration to get Remoting to work.

10.2.2   *Firewalls and security*

One of the joys of Remoting is that it operates over a single port: 5985 for HTTP and 5986 for HTTPS, by default, although you can reconfigure them if you like. It's therefore easy to set up firewall exceptions that permit Remoting traffic.

Some organizations, mainly those with very tight network security, may have some trepidation about enabling Remoting and its firewall exceptions. Our only advice is to "get over it." Remoting is now a foundational, mandatory technology in Windows. Not allowing it would be like not allowing Ethernet. Without Remoting, you'll find that many of Windows' administrative tools and features simply don't work, especially in Windows Server 2012 and later.

Remoting is more secure than what we've used in the past for these tasks. It authenticates, by default, using the Kerberos protocol, which never transmits passwords on the network (encrypted or otherwise). Remoting uses a single, customizable port, rather than the thousands required by older protocols like RPCs. WinRM and Remoting have a huge variety of configuration settings that let you control who can use it, how much they can use it, and soon.

10.3   *Using Remoting*

In the next few sections, we're going to walk you through the complete process of setting up and using Remoting. This will specifically cover the "easy scenario," meaning that both your computer and the remote computer are in the same Active Directory domain. After we go over these basics, we'll dive into all of the other scenarios that you might have to configure.

10.3.1 Enabling Remoting

Remoting needs to be enabled on any machine that will receive connections, which can include computers running either the server or a client version of the Windows operating system. Windows Server 2012, and later versions of the server OS, has Remoting enabled by default though client version of Windows don't. The easy way to set up Remoting is to run `Enable-PSRemoting` (you need to be running PowerShell with elevated privileges). You could perform all of the steps manually but we don't recommend it.

> **NOTE** You have to set up PowerShell Remoting on the machine itself. You can't do it remotely. Having it enabled by default is a good step forward—one less configuration step on new machines.

The `Enable-PSRemoting` command performs several tasks:

- Starts (or restarts, if it's already started) the WinRM service.
- Sets the WinRM service to start automatically from now on.
- Creates a WinRM listener for HTTP traffic on port 5985 for all local IP addresses.
- Creates a Windows Firewall exception for the WinRM listener. Note that this will fail on client versions of Windows if any network cards are configured to have a type of "Public," because the firewall will refuse to create new exceptions on those cards. If this happens, change the network card's type to something else (like "Work" or "Private," as appropriate—Windows 8/2012 provides the `Set-NetConnectionProfile` cmdlet for this task) and run `Enable-PSRemoting` again. Alternately, if you know you have some Public network cards, add the `-SkipNetworkProfileCheck` parameter to `Enable-PSRemoting`. Doing so will successfully create a Firewall exception that allows incoming Remoting traffic only from the computer's local subnet.

The command will also set up one or more of these endpoints:

- Microsoft.PowerShell
- Microsoft.PowerShell32
- Microsoft.ServerManager (for Server Manager)
- Microsoft.Windows.ServerManagerWorkflows (for Server Manager workflows)
- Microsoft.PowerShell.Workflow (for PowerShell workflow)

You'll be prompted several times as the command runs; be sure to reply "Y" for "Yes" so that each step can complete properly. You can avoid the prompts by using the `-Force` parameter.

Discovering WSMAN endpoints

You can find the endpoints that exist on your system through the WSMAN provider. The configuration information is exposed through a PowerShell drive—WSMAN:

```
PS C:\> dir WSMan:\localhost\Plugin

   WSManConfig: Microsoft.WSMan.Management\WSMan::localhost\Plugin

Type        Keys                           Name
----        ----                           ----
Container   {Name=Event Forwarding Plugin} Event Forwarding Plugin
Container   {Name=microsoft.powershell}    microsoft.powershell
Container   {Name=microsoft.powershell...  microsoft.powershell.workflow
Container   {Name=microsoft.powershell32}  microsoft.powershell32
Container   {Name=WMI Provider}            WMI Provider
```

This example is taken from a Windows 8.1 64-bit machine. You'll notice what appears to be two endpoints that we haven't mentioned:

- Event Forwarding Plugin
- WMI Provider

Windows servers have another apparent endpoint that we haven't mentioned: SEL Plugin.

The simple reason we haven't mentioned them is that they aren't Remoting endpoints as such. Their purpose is to provide WSMAN connectivity for other activities. Event forwarding and WMI are self-explanatory whereas SEL is for hardware management.

The WSMAN configurations that are purely for Remoting can be discovered by using `Get-PSSessionConfiguration`:

```
PS C:\> Get-PSSessionConfiguration | format-table Name, PSVersion -auto

Name                          PSVersion
----                          ---------
microsoft.powershell          4.0
microsoft.powershell.workflow 4.0
microsoft.powershell32        4.0
```

Table 10.1 illustrates some example endpoint configurations. On a 32-bit machine, the endpoint is referred to as PowerShell rather than PowerShell32.

Table 10.1 Example endpoint configurations. The table reports the "out-of-the-box" configuration. Any machine originally running PowerShell v3 that has been upgraded to PowerShell v4 will show the PowerShell version as 4.

	PowerShell version	PowerShell 32-bit	PowerShell 64-bit	Server Manager	Server Manager workflow	PowerShell workflow
Windows Server 2008 R2	2	Y	Y	Y		
Windows 7 64-bit	2	Y	Y			Y

Table 10.1 Example endpoint configurations. The table reports the "out-of-the-box" configuration. Any machine originally running PowerShell v3 that has been upgraded to PowerShell v4 will show the PowerShell version as 4. *(continued)*

	PowerShell version	PowerShell 32-bit	PowerShell 64-bit	Server Manager	Server Manager workflow	PowerShell workflow
Windows 8 32-bit client	3	Y				Y
Windows 8.1 64-bit client	4	Y	Y			Y
Windows Server 2012	3	Y	Y		Y	Y
Windows Server 2012 R2	4	Y	Y		Y	Y
Windows 7 client 32-bit stand-alone	2	Y				

In an enterprise you'll probably use Group Policy to configure Remoting. That approach has slightly a different outcome compared to using `Enable-PSRemoting`, as shown in table 10.2.

Table 10.2 The outcome when enabling Remoting through different mechanisms

	`Enable-PSRemoting`	Group Policy	Manually step-by-step
Set WinRM to auto-start and start the service	Yes	Yes	Yes; use `Set-Service` and `Start-Service`.
Configure HTTP listener	Yes	You can configure autoregistration of listeners, but you can't create custom listeners.	Yes; use the Winrm command-line utility and WSMan: drive in PowerShell
Configure HTTPS listener	No	No	Yes; use the winrm command-line utility and WSMan: drive in PowerShell
Configure endpoints/ session configurations	Yes	No	Yes; use `PSSession-Configuration` cmdlets
Configure Windows Firewall exception	Yes, but not on a Public network	Yes, but not on a Public network	Yes, but not on a Public network

10.3.2 *1-to-1 Remoting*

The most straightforward way to use Remoting is called *1-to-1 Remoting*, in which you essentially bring up an interactive PowerShell prompt on a remote computer. It's pretty simple, once Remoting is enabled on the remote machine:

```
PS C:\> Enter-PSsession -ComputerName Win8
[Win8]: PS C:\Users\Administrator\Documents>
```

> **NOTE** If you want to experiment with this, just use localhost as the computer name, once you've enabled Remoting on your computer. You'll be "remotely controlling" your local machine, but you'll get the full Remoting experience.

Notice how the PowerShell prompt changes to include the name of the computer you're now connected to. From here, it's almost exactly as if you were physically standing in front of that computer, and you can run any command that the remote machine contains. Keep these important caveats in mind:

- By default, when the PowerShell prompt contains any computer name (even localhost), you can't execute any other commands that initiate a Remoting connection. Doing so would create a "second hop," which won't work by default.
- You can't run any commands that start a graphical application. If you do so, the shell may appear to freeze; press Ctrl-C to end the process and regain control.
- You can't run any command program that has its own "shell" like nslookup or netsh—though you can run them as commands rather than interactively.
- You can only run scripts on the remote machine if its execution policy permits you to do so (we discuss that in chapter 17).
- You aren't connected to an interactive desktop session; your connection will be audited as a "network logon," much as if you were connecting to a file share on the remote machine. As a result of the connection type, Windows won't execute profile scripts, although you'll be connected to your profile home folder on the remote machine.
- Nothing you do will be visible by any other user who's connected to the same machine, even if they're interactively logged onto its desktop console. You can't run some application and have it "pop up" in front of the logged-on user.
- You must specify the computer's name as it appears in Active Directory or in your local Trusted Hosts list; you can't use IP addresses or DNS CNAME aliases unless they've been added to your Trusted Hosts list.

When you've finished with the remote machine, run `Exit-PSSession`. This will return you to your local prompt, close the connection to the remote machine, and free up resources on the remote machine. This will also happen automatically if you just close the PowerShell window.

```
[Win8]: PS C:\Users\Administrator\Documents> Exit-PSSession
PS C:\>
```

The way we've used `Enter-PSSession` will always connect to the remote machine's default PowerShell endpoint. On a 64-bit operating system, that'll be the 64-bit version of PowerShell. Later, we'll show you how to connect to other endpoints (remembering that `Enable-PSRemoting` will create multiple endpoints).

10.3.3 *1-to-many Remoting*

One-to-many Remoting, also known as fan-out Remoting, is a powerful technique that highlights the value of Remoting. You transmit a command (or a series of commands) to multiple remote computers. They each execute the command, serialize the results into XML, and send the results back to you. Your copy of PowerShell deserializes the XML into objects and puts them in the pipeline. For example, suppose you want to get a list of all processes whose names start with the letter "s," from two different computers:

```
PS C:\> Invoke-Command -ScriptBlock { Get-Process -name s* } -ComputerName
    localhost,win8
```

Handles	NPM(K)	PM(K)	WS(K)	VM(M)	CPU(s)	Id	ProcessN ame	PSCompu terName
217	11	3200	7080	33	1.23	496	services	win8
50	3	304	980	5	0.13	248	smss	win8
315	16	2880	8372	46	0.03	12	spoolsv	win8
472	36	8908	11540	60	0.31	348	svchost	win8
306	12	2088	7428	36	0.19	600	svchost	win8
295	15	2372	5384	29	0.61	636	svchost	win8
380	15	17368	19428	55	0.56	728	svchost	win8
1080	41	12740	25456	120	2.19	764	svchost	win8
347	19	3892	8812	93	0.03	788	svchost	win8
614	52	13820	18220	1129	2.28	924	svchost	win8
45	4	508	2320	13	0.02	1248	svchost	win8
211	18	9228	8408	1118	0.05	1296	svchost	win8
71	6	804	3540	28	0.00	1728	svchost	win8
2090	0	120	292	3	10.59	4	System	win8
217	11	3200	7080	33	1.23	496	services	loca...
50	3	304	980	5	0.13	248	smss	loca...
315	16	2880	8372	46	0.03	12	spoolsv	loca...
469	36	8856	11524	59	0.31	348	svchost	loca...
306	12	2088	7428	36	0.19	600	svchost	loca...
295	15	2372	5384	29	0.61	636	svchost	loca...
380	15	17368	19428	55	0.56	728	svchost	loca...
1080	41	12740	25456	120	2.19	764	svchost	loca...
347	19	3892	8812	93	0.03	788	svchost	loca...
607	49	13756	18132	1129	2.28	924	svchost	loca...
45	4	508	2320	13	0.02	1248	svchost	loca...
211	18	9228	8408	1118	0.05	1296	svchost	loca...
71	6	804	3540	28	0.00	1728	svchost	loca...
2089	0	120	292	3	10.59	4	System	loca...

The command is `Invoke-Command`. Its –`ScriptBlock` parameter accepts the commands (use semicolons to separate multiple commands) you want transmitted to the remote machines; the -ComputerName parameter specifies the machine names. Alternatively, for longer commands a script block object could be created:

```
$sb = {Get-Process -Name s*}
Invoke-Command -ComputerName localhost,win8 -ScriptBlock $sb
```

As with Enter-PSSession, you must specify the computer's name as it appears in Active Directory or in your local Trusted Hosts list; you can't use IP addresses or DNS CNAME aliases unless they've been added to your Trusted Hosts list.

Notice anything interesting about the output? It contains an extra column named PSComputerName, which contains the name of the computer each result row came from. This is a handy way to separate, sort, group, and otherwise organize your results. This property is always added to the incoming results by PowerShell; if you'd rather not see the property in the output, add the -HideComputerName parameter to Invoke-Command. The property will still exist (and can be used for sorting and so forth), but it won't be displayed in the output by default.

As with Enter-PSSession, Invoke-Command will use the default PowerShell endpoint on the remote machine—which in the case of a 64-bit OS will be the 64-bit shell. We'll cover how to connect to a different endpoint later in this chapter.

By default, Invoke-Command will talk to only 32 computers at once. Doing so requires it to maintain a PowerShell instance in memory for each remote machine it's talking to; 32 is a number Microsoft came up with that seems to work well in a variety of situations. If you specify more than 32 computers, the extra ones will just queue up, and Invoke-Command will start working with them as the first 32 begin to complete. You can change the level of parallelism by using the command's -ThrottleLimit parameter, keeping in mind that higher numbers place a greater load on your computer but no extra load on the remote machines.

10.3.4 Remoting caveats

The data sent from a remote machine to your computer has to be packaged in a way that makes it easy to transmit over the network. Serialization and deserialization, which we've already mentioned, make it possible—but with some loss of functionality. For example, consider the type of object produced by Get-Service:

```
PS C:\> Get-Service | Get-Member

   TypeName: System.ServiceProcess.ServiceController

Name                    MemberType     Definition
----                    ----------     ----------
Name                    AliasProperty  Name = ServiceName
RequiredServices        AliasProperty  RequiredServices = ServicesDepe...
Disposed                Event          System.EventHandler Disposed(Sy...
Close                   Method         System.Void Close(
Continue                Method         System.Void Continue()
CreateObjRef            Method         System.Runtime.Remoting.ObjRef ...
Dispose                 Method         System.Void Dispose()
Equals                  Method         bool Equals(System.Object obj)
```

```
ExecuteCommand              Method        System.Void ExecuteCommand(int ...
GetHashCode                 Method        int GetHashCode()
GetLifetimeService          Method        System.Object GetLifetimeService()
GetType                     Method        type GetType()
InitializeLifetimeService   Method        System.Object InitializeLifetim...
Pause                       Method        System.Void Pause()
Refresh                     Method        System.Void Refresh()
Start                       Method        System.Void Start(), System.Voi...
Stop                        Method        System.Void Stop()
WaitForStatus               Method        System.Void WaitForStatus(Syste...
CanPauseAndContinue         Property      bool CanPauseAndContinue {get;}
CanShutdown                 Property      bool CanShutdown {get;}
CanStop                     Property      bool CanStop {get;}
Container                   Property      System.ComponentModel.IContaine...
DependentServices           Property      System.ServiceProcess.ServiceCo...
DisplayName                 Property      string DisplayName {get;set;}
MachineName                 Property      string MachineName {get;set;}
ServiceHandle               Property      System.Runtime.InteropServices....
ServiceName                 Property      string ServiceName {get;set;}
ServicesDependedOn          Property      System.ServiceProcess.ServiceCo...
ServiceType                 Property      System.ServiceProcess.ServiceTy...
Site                        Property      System.ComponentModel.ISite Sit...
Status                      Property      System.ServiceProcess.ServiceCo...
ToString                    ScriptMethod  System.Object ToString();
```

As you can see, these objects' members include several methods, which let you stop the service, pause it, and so on. Now consider that exact same kind of object retrieved, via Remoting, from a remote machine:

```
PS C:\> Invoke-Command -ComputerName win8 -ScriptBlock { Get-Service } |
➡  Get-Member


    TypeName: Deserialized.System.ServiceProcess.ServiceController

Name                    MemberType   Definition
----                    ----------   ----------
ToString                Method       string ToString(), string ToString(str...
Name                    NoteProperty System.String Name=AeLookupSvc
PSComputerName          NoteProperty System.String PSComputerName=win8
PSShowComputerName      NoteProperty System.Boolean PSShowComputerName=True
RequiredServices        NoteProperty Deserialized.System.ServiceProcess.Ser...
RunspaceId              NoteProperty System.Guid RunspaceId=00e784f7-6c27-4...
CanPauseAndContinue     Property     System.Boolean {get;set;}
CanShutdown             Property     System.Boolean {get;set;}
CanStop                 Property     System.Boolean {get;set;}
Container               Property     {get;set;}
DependentServices       Property     Deserialized.System.ServiceProcess.Ser...
DisplayName             Property     System.String {get;set;}
MachineName             Property     System.String {get;set;}
ServiceHandle           Property     System.String {get;set;}
ServiceName             Property     System.String {get;set;}
ServicesDependedOn      Property     Deserialized.System.ServiceProcess.Ser...
ServiceType             Property     System.String {get;set;}
Site                    Property     {get;set;}
Status                  Property     System.String {get;set;}
```

The methods (except for the universal ToString() method) are gone. That's because you're looking at a deserialized version of the object (it says so right in the TypeName at the top of the output), and the methods are stripped off. Essentially, you're getting a read-only, static version of the object.

This isn't necessarily a downside; serialization and the removal of methods doesn't occur until the remote commands finish executing and their output is being packaged for transmission. The objects are still "live" objects when they're on the remote computer, so you have to start them, stop them, pause them, or whatever on the remote machine. In other words, any "actions" you want to take must be part of the command you send to the remote machine for execution.

10.3.5 *Remoting options*

Both Invoke-Command and Enter-PSSession offer a few basic options for customizing their behavior.

ALTERNATE CREDENTIALS

By default, PowerShell delegates whatever credential you used to open the shell on your computer. That may not always be what you want, so you can specify an alternate username by using the -Credential parameter. You'll be prompted for the account's password, and that account will be used to connect to the remote machine (or machines) and run whatever commands you supply.

> **NOTE** In chapter 17, on PowerShell security, we discuss the -Credential parameter in more detail and offer other ways in which it can be used.

ALTERNATE PORT NUMBER

PowerShell defaults to using port 5985 for Remoting; you can change that when you set up WinRM listeners. You can also change your computer to use a different port when it initiates connections, which makes sense if you've changed the port your servers are listening to.

You'll find the port being listened to (the port on which traffic will be accepted) by examining your WSMan drive in PowerShell. Here's an example. (Note that your computer's listener ID will be different than the Listener_1084132640 shown here, but you can find your ID by getting a directory listing of WSMan:\localhost\Listener.)

```
PS WSMan:\localhost\Listener\Listener_1084132640> ls

   WSManConfig:
Microsoft.WSMan.Management\WSMan::localhost\Listener\Listener_1084132640
```

Type	Name	SourceOfValue	Value
System.String	Address		*
System.String	Transport		HTTP
System.String	Port		5985
System.String	Hostname		
System.String	Enabled		true
System.String	URLPrefix		wsman

```
System.String    CertificateThumbprint
System.String    ListeningOn_1638538265                         10.211.55.6
System.String    ListeningOn_1770022257                         127.0.0.1
System.String    ListeningOn_1414502903                         ::1
System.String    ListeningOn_766473143                          2001:0:4...
System.String    ListeningOn_86955851                           fdb2:2c2...
System.String    ListeningOn_1728280878                         fe80::5e...
System.String    ListeningOn_96092800                           fe80::98...
System.String    ListeningOn_2037253461                         fe80::c7...
```

Keep in mind that to work with the WSMAN PSDrive, you must be in an elevated PowerShell session. To change the port (using port 1000 as an example), type this:

```
PS C:\> Set-Item WSMan:\localhost\listener\*\port 1000
```

Now let's look at the client-side configuration, which tells your computer which port the server will be listening to:

```
PS WSMan:\localhost\Client\DefaultPorts> dir

   WSManConfig:
Microsoft.WSMan.Management\WSMan::localhost\Client\DefaultPorts
```

Type	Name	SourceOfValue	Value
System.String	HTTP		5985
System.String	HTTPS		5986

If you've set all of your servers to port 1000 (for example), then it makes sense to also reconfigure your clients so that they use that port by default:

```
PS C:\> Set-Item WSMan:\localhost\client\DefaultPorts\HTTP 1000
```

Alternately, both `Invoke-Command` and `Enter-PSSession` have a `-Port` parameter, which can be used to specify a port other than the one listed in the `DefaultPorts` configuration. That's useful if you have to use an alternate port for just one or two servers in your environment and don't want to change the client's defaults.

> **TIP** If you want to change default ports for your enterprise, we suggest you use Group Policy to push out these settings.

The default ports should only be changed if you have a good reason. If you do change the ports, make sure that your change is documented and applied across your enterprise (including firewalls) to avoid unnecessary troubleshooting efforts if Remoting connections fail.

USING SSL

If a server is configured with an HTTPS endpoint (which isn't the case after running `Enable-PSRemoting`; you have to set that up manually, which we'll get to later), then specify the `-UseSSL` parameter of `Invoke-Command` or `Enter-PSSession` to use the HTTPS port. That's port 5986 by default.

SENDING A SCRIPT INSTEAD OF A COMMAND

Our example of Invoke-Command showed how to send just one command, or even a few commands separated by semicolons. For example, to run a command that's located in a module, you first need to load the module:

```
PS C:\> Invoke-Command –ScriptBlock { Import-Module ActiveDirectory;
➥ Get-ADUser –filter * } –ComputerName WINDC1
```

PowerShell v3 and v4 autoloads modules by default, though you won't see them using Get-Module -ListAvailable until you've used them. Forcing the module to load is required for PowerShell v2 and does no harm in v3 or later. In a mixed environment, it's essential. The module has to be available on the remote machine. Invoke-Command can also send an entire script file, if you prefer. The file path and name are provided to the –FilePath parameter, which you'd use in place of –ScriptBlock. PowerShell will read the contents of the file from the local machine and transmit them over the network—the remote machines don't need direct access to the file itself.

10.4   PSSessions

So far, your use of Remoting has been ad hoc. You've allowed PowerShell to create the connection, it's run your commands, and then it closes the connection. Without realizing it, you've been creating a temporary *PowerShell session*, or *PSSession*. A PSSession represents the connection between your computer and a remote one. Some overhead is involved in setting up a connection and then closing it down, and if you plan to connect to the same computer several times within a period of time, you may want to create a persistent connection to avoid that overhead.

Persistent connections have another advantage: They represent a running copy of PowerShell on a remote machine. Using the ad hoc Remoting that we've shown you so far, every single command you send runs in a new, fresh copy of the shell. With a persistent connection, you could continue to send commands to the same copy of PowerShell, and the results of those commands—such as importing modules—would remain in effect until you closed the connection.

10.4.1   Creating a persistent session

The New-PSSession command sets up one or more new sessions. You might want to assign these session objects to a variable so that you can easily refer to them in the future:

```
PS C:\> $win8 = New-PSsession –ComputerName win8
PS C:\> $domaincontrollers = New-PSsession –ComputerName win8,windc1
```

Here, you've created a variable, $win8, that contains a single session object, and a variable, $domaincontrollers, that contains two session objects.

> **NOTE**   New-PSSession offers the same options for using alternate credentials, using SSL, and using port numbers as Enter-PSSession and Invoke-Command.

10.4.2 Using a session

Both `Invoke-Command` and `Enter-PSSession` can use an already-open session object. Provide the object (or objects) to the commands' `-Session` parameter, instead of using the `-ComputerName` parameter. For example, to initiate a 1-to-1 connection to a computer, use this:

```
PS C:\> Enter-PSSession -Session $win8
[win8]: PS C:\Users\Administrator\Documents>
```

Be careful to pass only a single session to `Enter-PSSession`; if you give it multiple objects, the command can't function properly. `Invoke-Command`, though, can accept multiple sessions:

```
PS C:\> Invoke-Command -Session $domaincontrollers -ScriptBlock {
➥ get-eventlog -LogName security -Newest 50 }
```

As we mentioned, it's a lot easier to work with sessions if you keep them in a variable. That isn't mandatory, though, because you can use `Get-PSSession` to retrieve sessions. For example, if you have an open session to a computer named `WINDC1`, you can retrieve the session and connect to it like this:

```
PS C:\> Enter-PSSession -Session (Get-PSSession -computername WINDC1)
```

The parenthetical `Get-PSSession` runs first, returning its session object to the `-Session` parameter of `Enter-PSSession`. If you have multiple sessions open to the same computer, the command will fail.

10.4.3 Managing sessions

Session objects will remain open and available for quite some time by default; you can configure a shorter idle timeout if you want. You can display a list of all sessions, and their status, by running `Get-PSSession` with no parameters:

```
PS C:\> Get-PSSession
```

Id	Name	ComputerName	State	ConfigurationName	Ava ila bil ity
6	Session6	win8	Opened	Microsoft.PowerShell	ble
7	Session7	win8	Opened	Microsoft.PowerShell	ble

Note that the output includes both the state (Opened, in this case) and availability (Available, although our output here is a bit truncated). You can also see the name of the endpoint that the session is connected to—Microsoft.PowerShell in both instances in this example. One reason you might maintain multiple connections to a single remote machine is to connect to different endpoints—perhaps, for example, you might want a connection to both a 64-bit and a 32-bit PowerShell session.

When you've finished with a session, you can close it to free up resources. For example, to close all open sessions, use this:

```
PS C:\> Get-PSSession | Remove-PSSession
```

Get-PSSession is quite flexible. It provides parameters that let you retrieve just a subset of available sessions without having to get them all and then filter them through Where-Object:

- -ComputerName retrieves all sessions for the specified computer name.
- -ApplicationName retrieves all sessions for the specified application.
- -ConfigurationName retrieves all sessions connected to the specified endpoint, such as Microsoft.PowerShell.

10.4.4 Disconnecting and reconnecting sessions

PowerShell v3 introduced the ability to disconnect a session and then later reconnect it. A disconnected session is still running on the remote machine, meaning you can potentially start a long-running process, disconnect, and then reconnect later to check your results. You can even receive the results from a disconnected session without having to explicitly reconnect.

Note that the disconnection isn't necessarily automatic. If you just close your shell window, or if your computer crashes, PowerShell won't automatically put the remote session into a disconnected state. Instead, it'll shut the session down. Disconnecting is something you have to explicitly do, although PowerShell *can* automatically put a session into a disconnected state after a long timeout period or a network outage. The neat thing is that you can start a session from one computer, disconnect it, and then reconnect to that session from another computer. For example, to start a session and then disconnect it, use this:

```
PS C:\> New-PSSession -ComputerName win8

Id Name           ComputerName   State     ConfigurationName    Ava
                                                                ila
                                                                bil
                                                                ity
-- ----           ------------   -----     -----------------    ---
16 Session16       win8           Opened    Microsoft.PowerShell ble
```

Availability value when the session is open is -Available

```
PS C:\> Get-PSSession -ComputerName win8 | Disconnect-PSSession

Id Name           ComputerName   State        ConfigurationName    Ava
                                                                   ila
                                                                   bil
                                                                   ity
-- ----           ------------   -----        -----------------    ---
16 Session16       win8           Disconnected Microsoft.PowerShell one
```

Availability value when the session is disconnected is – None.

Now you can shut down your shell window, move to an entirely different computer, and reconnect the session from there. To do so, run Connect-PSSession and specify the computer name on which the session is running (you can also specify an application name and configuration name using the appropriate parameters):

```
PS C:\> Connect-PSSession -ComputerName win8
```

Id	Name	ComputerName	State	ConfigurationName	Ava ila bil ity
--	----	------------	-----	-----------------	---
16	Session16	win8	Opened	Microsoft.PowerShell	ble

Here's an important thing to note: You can reconnect to someone else's session. For example, it's possible for Bob to "grab" a session that was originally opened by, and disconnected by, Jane. You need to be an administrator to seize someone else's session as long as you have the credentials.

Invoke-Command can be used in its ad hoc mode—when you specify a computer name rather than a session—and told to create a disconnected session. The command will start up a session, send the command you specify, and then leave the session disconnected and still running that command. You can reconnect later or receive the results from the session. Here's an example:

```
PS C:\> Invoke-Command -ComputerName win8 -ScriptBlock { get-eventlog
➥   -LogName security -Newest 1000 } –Disconnected
```

Id	Name	ComputerName	State	ConfigurationName	Ava ila bil ity
--	----	------------	-----	-----------------	---
13	Session12	win8	Disconnected	http://schemas.mi...	one

```
PS C:\> Receive-PSSession -Session (Get-PSSession -ComputerName win8)
```

Index	Time	EntryType	Source	InstanceID	Me ss ag e	PS Co mp ut er Na me
-----	----	---------	------	----------	--	--
299	Mar 14 16:24	SuccessA...	Microsoft-Windows...	4616	Th	wi
298	Mar 14 15:23	SuccessA...	Microsoft-Windows...	4616	Th	wi
297	Mar 14 14:22	SuccessA...	Microsoft-Windows...	4616	Th	wi
296	Mar 14 13:21	SuccessA...	Microsoft-Windows...	4616	Th	wi

Here, you can see that we invoked the command and asked it to create a disconnected session. The -Disconnected parameter we used is an alias for -InDisconnectedSession. Normally, when you specify a computer name the session will start, run the command, and then send you the results and close. In this case, you anticipate the command taking a few moments to complete, so you leave the session running and disconnected. Receive-PSSession is used to retrieve the results. The session is still running and disconnected, but if you want to run further commands in it, you can easily reconnect it to do so:

```
PS C:\> Get-PSSession -ComputerName win8 | Connect-PSSession
```

Id	Name	ComputerName	State	ConfigurationName	Availability
--	----	-----------	-----	-----------------	---
13	Session12	win8	Opened	http://schemas.mi...	ble

```
PS C:\> invoke-command -ScriptBlock { get-service } -Session (Get-PSSession
➡  -ComputerName win8)
```

Status	Name	DisplayName	PSComputerName
------	----	-----------	-------
Stopped	AeLookupSvc	Application Experience	win8
Stopped	ALG	Application Layer Gateway Service	win8
Stopped	AllUserInstallA...	Windows All-User Install Agent	win8
Stopped	AppIDSvc	Application Identity	win8
Stopped	Appinfo	Application Information	win8
Stopped	AppMgmt	Application Management	win8

10.5 *Advanced session techniques*

There's a lot more you can do with sessions. Keep in mind that Remoting always involves a session—even if it's one that's created, used, and closed automatically. Therefore, most of the options we'll discuss in the next two sections apply both to the -PSSession cmdlets as well as Invoke-Command, because all of them involve the use of Remoting sessions.

10.5.1 *Session parameters*

Several common parameters are used by the Remoting cmdlets:

- -Authentication specifies an authentication mechanism. Kerberos is the default; you can also specify Basic, CredSSP, Digest, Negotiate, and Negotiate-WithImplicitCredential. CredSSP is a common alternative that offers a solution to the "second hop" problem, which we'll discuss later. Note that the protocol you specify must be enabled in WinRM before it can be used, and only Kerberos is enabled by default. You can see the authentication protocols configured on the client by using this:

    ```
    dir wsman:\localhost\client\auth
    ```

    The remote authentication configuration can be viewed like this:

    ```
    Connect-WSMan -ComputerName server02
    dir wsman:server02\service\auth
    ```

    -SessionOption specifies a Session Options object, which wraps up a number of advanced configuration settings. We'll discuss those next.

- -AllowRedirection allows your Remoting session to be redirected from the computer you originally specified and handled by another remote machine instead. It's unusual to use this on an internal network, but it's common when you're connecting to a cloud infrastructure. Microsoft Office 365 is an excellent example: You'll often connect PowerShell to a generic computer name and then be redirected to the specific server that handles your organization's data.

- `-ApplicationName` connects a session to the specified application name, such as http://localhost:5985/WSMAN. The application name is always a URI starting with http:// or https://.

- `-ConfigurationName` connects a session to the specified configuration or endpoint. This can either be a name, like Microsoft.PowerShell, or a full URI, such as http://schemas.microsoft.com/powershell.

- `-ConnectionURI` specifies the connection endpoint—this is more or less an alternate way of specifying a computer name, port number, and application name in one easy step. These look something like http://SERVER2:5985/PowerShell, including the transport (http or https), the computer name, the port, and the application name.

When creating a new session with either `Invoke-Command` or `New-PSSession`, you can specify a friendly name for the session. Just use `-SessionName` with `Invoke-Command`, or use `-Name` with `New-PSSession`. Once you've done so, it's a bit easier to retrieve the session again: Just use `Get-PSSession` and the `-Name` parameter to specify the friendly name of the desired session.

10.5.2 Session options

On most of the Remoting-related commands you'll notice a `-SessionOption` parameter, which accepts a Session Options object. This object consolidates a number of advanced parameters that can be used to set up a new session. Typically, you'll create the options object using `New-PSSessionOption`, export the session to an XML file (or store it in a variable), and then reimport it (or specify the variable) to utilize the options. `New-PSSessionOption` supports a number of parameters, and you can read all about them in its help file.

For example, suppose you occasionally want to open a new session with no compression or encryption. Here's how you could create a reusable options object and then use it to open a new session:

```
PS C:\> New-PSSessionOption -NoCompression
➥   -NoEncryption | Export-Clixml NoCompNoEncOption.xml
PS C:\> New-PSSession -ComputerName win8
➥   -SessionOption (Import-Clixml .\NoCompNoEncOption.xml)
```

NOTE This particular set of session options won't work by default, because the default client profile doesn't permit unencrypted traffic. We modified our test computer to permit unencrypted traffic to help ease troubleshooting and experimentation in our lab.

`New-PSSessionOption` has a whole slew of parameters; none of them are mandatory. Specify the ones you want, and omit the ones you don't care about, when creating a new session options object.

10.6   *Creating a custom endpoint*

The New-PSSessionConfigurationFile cmdlet makes it easy to set up new endpoints. You're not technically creating anything related to a PSSession, despite what the cmdlet name implies; you're creating a new Remoting configuration, also known as an *endpoint*, that will run Windows PowerShell. The command uses a number of parameters, most of which are optional. We'll let you read the command's help for full details and stick with the most important parameters. The first, -Path, is mandatory and specifies the path and filename of the session configuration file that you want to create. You must give the file the ".pssc" filename extension.

Everything else is optional. Some of the parameters, such as –AliasDefinitions, accept a hash table (we cover those in chapter 16). This parameter, for example, defines a set of aliases that'll be available to anyone who connects to this new endpoint. You'd specify something like –AliasDefinitions @{Name='hlp';definition='Get-Help'; options='ReadOnly'} to define an alias named hlp that runs the Get-Help cmdlet and that isn't modifiable by anyone using the endpoint (ReadOnly).

Here's an example:

```
PS C:\> New-PSSessionConfigurationFile -Path Restricted.pssc
➡   -LanguageMode Restricted -VisibleProviders FileSystem
➡   -ExecutionPolicy Restricted -PowerShellVersion 3.0
```

This code creates a new configuration file that specifies:

- The endpoint will be in Restricted Language mode. Users will be able to run cmdlets and functions, but they may not create script blocks or variables and may not use other scripting language features. Only basic comparison operators will be available (all of this is documented in the command's help for the -LanguageMode parameter).
- The endpoint will be PowerShell 3.0. If you omit this parameter the newest available version of Windows PowerShell is used. Valid values are 2.0 and 3.0 even in PowerShell v4 and later. We recommend using the newest available version.
- Only the FileSystem PSProvider will be available; other forms of storage won't be connected as drives.
- Script execution won't be permitted, meaning that only cmdlets will be available to run.

Next, you ask the shell to use that configuration file to create the new endpoint, registering it with WinRM:

```
PS C:\> Register-PSSessionConfiguration -Path .\Restricted.pssc -Force
➡   -Name MyEndpoint

    WSManConfig: Microsoft.WSMan.Management\WSMan::localhost\Plugin

Type            Keys                          Name
----            ----                          ----
Container       {Name=MyEndpoint}             MyEndpoint
```

You define the name MyEndpoint for this new endpoint, so to create a session that connects to it, you go to another computer and use `New-PSSession`:

```
PS C:\> $sess = New-PSSession -ComputerName win8
➡    -ConfigurationName MyEndpoInt
```

Now you can use that session object with `Enter-PSSession` or `Invoke-Command`, as you learned earlier in this chapter.

There are other commands used for unregistering a configuration, disabling and enabling them (while leaving them registered), and so forth:

```
PS C:\> Get-Command -Noun pssessionconfiguration*

Capability      Name
----------      ----
Cmdlet          Disable-PSSessionConfiguration
Cmdlet          Enable-PSSessionConfiguration
Cmdlet          Get-PSSessionConfiguration
Cmdlet          New-PSSessionConfigurationFile
Cmdlet          Register-PSSessionConfiguration
Cmdlet          Set-PSSessionConfiguration
Cmdlet          Test-PSSessionConfigurationFile
Cmdlet          Unregister-PSSessionConfiguration
```

When you create a custom session configuration file, as you've seen, you can set its language mode. The language mode determines what elements of the PowerShell scripting language are available in the endpoint, and the language mode can be a bit of a loophole. With the `Full` language mode, you get the entire scripting language, including *script blocks.* A script block is any executable hunk of PowerShell code contained within curly brackets {}. They're the loophole. Any time you allow the use of script blocks, they can run any legal command, even if your endpoint used `-VisibleCmdlets` or `-VisibleFunctions` or another parameter to limit the commands in the endpoint.

In other words, if you register an endpoint that uses `-VisibleCmdlets` to expose `Get-ChildItem` but you create the endpoint's session configuration file to have the full language mode, *then any script blocks inside the endpoint can use any command.* Someone could run:

```
PS C:\> & { Import-Module ActiveDirectory; Get-ADUser -filter * |
➡  Remove-ADObject }
```

Eek! This can be especially dangerous if you configured the endpoint to use a RunAs credential to run commands under elevated privileges. It's also somewhat easy to let this happen by mistake, because you set the language mode when you create the new session configuration file (`New-PSSessionConfigurationFile`), not when you *register* the session (`Register-PSSessionConfiguration`). So if you're using a session configuration file created by someone else, pop it open and confirm its language mode before you use it!

You can avoid this problem by setting the language mode to `NoLanguage`, which shuts off script blocks and the rest of the scripting language. Or, go for `RestrictedLanguage`, which blocks script blocks while still allowing some basic operators if you want users of the endpoint to be able to do basic filtering and comparisons.

Understand that this isn't a bug—the behavior we're describing here is by design. But it can be a problem if you don't know about it and understand what it's doing.

> **NOTE**   Much thanks to fellow MVP Aleksandar Nikolic for helping us understand the logic of this loophole!

10.6.1 *Custom endpoints for delegated administration*

One of the coolest things you can do with a custom endpoint is called *delegated administration.* You set up the endpoint so that it runs all commands under a predefined user account's authority, rather than using the permissions of the user who connected to the endpoint. This is especially useful for PowerShell Web Access.

To start, you create a custom endpoint, just as we showed you earlier. When creating the new session configuration file, you restrict the endpoint. So, when you're running `New-PSSessionConfigurationFile`, you'll generally do something like this:

- Use `-ExecutionPolicy` to define a `Restricted` execution policy if you don't want people running scripts in the endpoint.
- Use `-ModulesToImport` to specify one or more modules to load into the session.
- Use `-FunctionDefinitions` to define custom functions that will appear within the session.
- Potentially use `-LanguageMode` to turn off PowerShell's scripting language; this is useful if you want people to run only a limited set of commands.
- Use `-SessionType` to set the session type to `RestrictedRemoteServer`. This turns off most of the core PowerShell commands, including the ability to import any modules or extensions that aren't part of the session configuration file.
- Use `-VisibleCmdlets` to specify which commands you want visible within the session. You have to make sure their module is imported, but this lets you expose less than 100 percent of the commands in a module. Use `-VisibleFunctions` to do the same thing for imported functions, and use `-VisibleProviders` to make specific PSProviders available.

Register the new session configuration using `Register-PSSessionConfiguration`. When you do so, use the `-RunAsCredential` parameter to specify the username that all commands within the session will run as. You'll be prompted for the password. You might also want to consider these parameters:

- `-AccessMode` lets you specify that the endpoint can only be used by local users ("Local") or by local and remote ("Remote").
- `-SecurityDescriptorSddl` lets you specify, in the Security Descriptor Definition Language (SDDL), who can use the endpoint. Users must have, at a minimum, "Execute(Invoke)" in order to be able to use the session. We find SDDL to be complex, so you could specify the `-ShowSecurityDescriptorUI` parameter,

which lets you set the endpoint permissions in a GUI dialog box. See, GUIs are still useful for some things!

In the end, you've created an endpoint that (a) only certain people can connect to, and that (b) will run commands under an entirely different set of credentials. Delegated administration! The people using the endpoint don't need permission to run the commands you've allowed within it!

10.7 Connecting to non-default endpoints

To connect to an endpoint other than the default PowerShell endpoint, you need to know the endpoint name, also called its configuration name. You can run Get-PSSessionConfiguration to see all of the endpoints configured on the local machine:

```
PS C:\> Get-PSSessionConfiguration

Name          : microsoft.powershell
PSVersion     : 4.0
StartupScript :
RunAsUser     :
Permission    : BUILTIN\Administrators AccessAllowed,
                BUILTIN\Remote Management Users AccessAllowed

Name          : microsoft.powershell.workflow
PSVersion     : 4.0
StartupScript :
RunAsUser     :
Permission    : BUILTIN\Administrators AccessAllowed,
                BUILTIN\Remote Management Users AccessAllowed

Name          : microsoft.powershell32
PSVersion     : 4.0
StartupScript :
RunAsUser     :
Permission    : BUILTIN\Administrators AccessAllowed,
                BUILTIN\Remote Management Users AccessAllowed
```

This output shows you the configuration name, which you provide to the New-PSSession -ConfigurationName parameter when creating a new session:

```
PS C:\> New-PSSession -ComputerName win8
➥  -ConfigurationName 'microsoft.powershell32'
 Id Name            ComputerName     State       ConfigurationName     Ava
                                                                       ila
                                                                       bil
                                                                       ity
 -- ----            ------------     -----       -----------------     ---
 19 Session19       win8             Opened      microsoft.powersh... ble
```

You'll also find a -ConfigurationName parameter on Invoke-Command and Enter-PSSession, which enables those cmdlets to connect to an alternate endpoint without creating a persistent session object first.

`Get-PSSessionConfiguration` only works on the local machine. If you need to discover the endpoints on a remote machine, you can do one of two things. Your first option is to create a session to the remote machine and use `Get-PSSessionConfiguration`:

```
PS C:\> Enter-PSSession -ComputerName dc02
[dc02]: PS C:\Users\Richard\Documents> Get-PSSessionConfiguration
```

Alternatively, you could use `Connect-WSMan` like this:

```
PS C:\> Connect-WSMan -ComputerName w12standard
PS C:\> dir wsman:\w12standard\plugin
```

Both methods work and give the required results as long as Remoting is enabled on the remote system.

10.8   *Enabling the "second hop"*

We've mentioned this "second hop" thing a number of times. It's essentially a built-in, default limitation on how far your credentials can be delegated. Here's the scenario:

- You're using a computer named CLIENT. You open PowerShell, making sure that the shell is run as Administrator. You can run whatever commands you like.
- You use `Enter-PSSession` to remote to a machine named SERVER1. Your credentials are delegated via Kerberos, and you can run whatever commands you like.
- While still remoted into SERVER1, you use `Invoke-Command` to send a command, via Remoting, to SERVER2. Your credentials can't delegate across this "second hop," and so the command fails.

There are two workarounds to solve this problem. The first is easy: Specify a `-Credential` parameter any time you're launching a new Remoting connection across the second and subsequent hops. In our example scenario, while running `Invoke-Command` on SERVER1 to connect to SERVER2, provide an explicit credential. That way, your credential doesn't need to be delegated, and you avoid the problem.

> **NOTE** If you're a domain administrator and the local machine (CLIENT in this example) is a domain controller, some elements of the delegation to enable "second hop" processing are available by default. We don't recommend using domain controllers as administration workstations!

The second technique requires that you enable, and then use, the CredSSP authentication protocol on all machines involved in the chain of Remoting, starting with your computer (CLIENT in our example scenario) and including every machine that you'll remote to. Enabling CredSSP is most easily done through Group Policy, where you can configure it for entire groups of computers at once. You can, though, enable it on a per-machine basis using the WSMan: drive in PowerShell:

```
PS WSMan:\localhost\Service\Auth> dir

   WSManConfig: Microsoft.WSMan.Management\WSMan::localhost\Service\Auth

Type            Name                        SourceOfValue    Value
----            ----                        -------------    -----
```

```
System.String    Basic                                          false
System.String    Kerberos                                       true
System.String    Negotiate                                      true
System.String    Certificate                                    false
System.String    CredSSP                                        false
System.String    CbtHardeningLevel                              Relaxed

PS WSMan:\localhost\Service\Auth> set-item ./credssp $true
PS WSMan:\localhost\Service\Auth> dir

    WSManConfig: Microsoft.WSMan.Management\WSMan::localhost\Service\Auth

Type             Name                          SourceOfValue    Value
----             ----                          ------------     -----
System.String    Basic                                          false
System.String    Kerberos                                       true
System.String    Negotiate                                      true
System.String    Certificate                                    false
System.String    CredSSP                                        true
System.String    CbtHardeningLevel                              Relaxed
```

Here, we've shown the protocol before and after enabling it in WSMan:\localhost\
Service\Auth. Once it's enabled, specify –Authentication CredSSP when using Invoke-
Command, Enter-PSSession, or New-PSSession to use the protocol. An alternative,
and possibly simpler, technique is to use the Enable-WSManCredSSP cmdlet on the relevant machines.

On the client machine, run:

```
Enable-WSManCredSSP -Role Client -DelegateComputer SERVER1
```

We recommend that you only enable CredSSP when required rather than as a permanent configuration.

On the remote machine, run:

```
Enable-WSManCredSSP -Role Server
```

10.9 *Setting up WinRM listeners*

Enable-PSRemoting creates a single WinRM listener that listens on all enabled IP
addresses on the system. You can discover the existing listeners by using this:

```
PS C:\> Get-WSManInstance winrm/config/Listener -Enumerate

cfg                   : http://schemas.microsoft.com/wbem/wsman/1/config/
                        listener
xsi                   : http://www.w3.org/2001/XMLSchema-instance
lang                  : en-US
Address               : *
Transport             : HTTP
Port                  : 5985
Hostname              :
Enabled               : true
URLPrefix             : wsman
CertificateThumbprint :
ListeningOn           : {10.10.54.165, 127.0.0.1, 192.168.2.165, ::1...}
```

And the IP addresses that are being listened on are discovered like this:

```
Get-WSManInstance winrm/config/Listener -Enumerate |
select -ExpandProperty ListeningOn
```

Alternatively, you can use the WSMAN provider:

```
PS C:\> dir wsman:\localhost\listener

   WSManConfig: Microsoft.WSMan.Management\WSMan::localhost\Listener

Type            Keys                             Name
----            ----                             ----
Container       {Address=*, Transport=HTTP}      Listener_809701527
```

Keep in mind that a single WinRM listener can service any number of endpoints and applications, as shown in figure 10.1; you only need to set up a new listener if the default one (which uses HTTP on port 5985) isn't what you want to use. It's easier to change the default listener to use different settings if you don't want to use its default settings at all. But if you want both that listener and an alternate one, then you need to create that alternate one.

Why might you want to create a new listener? The most probable answers are that you want to restrict the IP addresses, or ports, that are used for listening or you want to create a listener for secured traffic using HTTPS rather than HTTP. A combination of these conditions would allow only connections over HTTPS to a specific IP address and port. That approach is useful in an environment requiring secure transport and access—for example, to a server in the DMZ where you need to be able to connect over the management network but not from the internet-facing address.

10.9.1 *Creating an HTTP listener*

You can create a new listener by using the New-WSManInstance cmdlet:

```
PS C:\> New-WSManInstance winrm/config/Listener
    -SelectorSet @{Transport='HTTP'; Address="IP:10.10.54.165"}
    -ValueSet @{Port=8888}
```

The address, port, and transport protocol are specified, but notice that they're in two separate groups. That's because New-WSManInstance uses –SelectorSet to identify

Requests   Listener   Endpoints

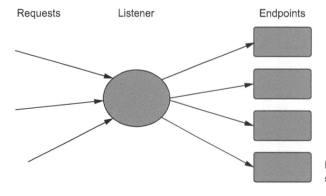

Figure 10.1 A single listener servicing multiple endpoints

the individual instance (see the Keys column in the following code) and -ValueSet to define property values. You can see the new listener like this:

```
PS C:\> dir wsman:\localhost\listener | Format-Table -AutoSize

    WSManConfig: Microsoft.WSMan.Management\WSMan::localhost\Listener

Type       Keys                                       Name
----       ----                                       ----
Container  {Address=*, Transport=HTTP}                Listener_809701527
Container  {Address=IP:10.10.54.165, Transport=HTTP}  Listener_886604375
```

10.9.2 *Adding an HTTPS listener*

Adding a listener for HTTPS is similar, but you need to go through a few steps first:

1 Create a certificate request. You can't do that in PowerShell and need to either ask your Certificate Services administrators for help or use the tools provided by your certificate provider.
2 Request the certificate using the request you've just created.
3 Download the certificate.
4 Install the certificate into the computer certificate store.
5 Find the new certificate in the PowerShell cert: drive and get its thumbprint.

You can now create the listener:

```
New-WSManInstance winrm/config/Listener
➥    -SelectorSet @{Transport='HTTPS'; Address="IP:10.10.54.165"}
➥    -ValueSet @{Hostname="<servername>";CertificateThumbprint="XXXXXXXX"}
```

where Hostname matches the server name in your SSL certificate.

You can remove a listener using Remove-WSManInstance:

```
PS C:\> Get-WSManInstance winrm/config/Listener
➥    -SelectorSet @{Transport='HTTP'; Address="IP:10.10.54.165"} |
Remove-WSManInstance
```

Or use

```
Remove-WSManInstance winrm/config/Listener
➥    -SelectorSet @{Transport='HTTP'; Address="IP:10.10.54.165"}
```

You remove the default listener like this:

```
Remove-WSManInstance winrm/config/Listener
➥    -SelectorSet @{Transport="HTTP"; Address="*"}
```

We recommend restarting the WinRM service after you modify the listeners.

There are two modifications you can make to a connection, whether using Invoke-Command, Enter-PSSession, or some other Remoting command that relates to HTTPS listeners. These are created as part of a session option object.

- -SkipCACheck causes WinRM to not worry about whether or not the SSL certificate was issued by a trusted CA. But untrusted CAs may in fact be untrustworthy! A poor CA might issue a certificate to a bogus computer, leading you to believe you're connecting to the right machine when in fact you're connecting to an imposter. Using this parameter is risky, so do so with caution.

- -SkipCNCheck causes WinRM to not worry about whether or not the SSL certificate on the remote machine was actually issued for that machine. Again, this is a great way to find yourself connected to an imposter. Half the point of SSL is mutual authentication, and this parameter disables that half.

10.10 Other configuration scenarios

So far in this chapter, we've tried to focus on the easy and common Remoting configuration scenarios, but we know there are other scenarios you'll have to confront. In the next few sections, we'll cover some of these "outside the lines" cases. There are certainly others, and you'll find most of those documented in PowerShell's about_remote_troubleshooting help file, which we heartily recommend that you become familiar with. That file also explains how to configure many of the Remoting configuration settings, set up firewall exceptions, and perform other tasks via Group Policy—which is a lot easier than configuring individual machines one at a time.

10.10.1 Cross-domain Remoting

Remoting doesn't work across Active Directory domains by default. If your computer is in DOMAINA, and you need to remote into a machine that belongs to DOMAINB, you'll have to do a bit of work first. You'll still need to ensure that your user account has permissions to do whatever it is you're attempting in DOMAINB—the configuration setting we're showing you only enables the Remoting connectivity. This is a Registry setting, so be careful when making this change:

```
PS C:\> New-ItemProperty -Name LocalAccountTokenFilterPolicy -Path
➥   HKLM:\SOFTWARE\Microsoft\Windows\CurrentVersion\Policies\System
➥   -PropertyType DWord -Value 1
```

This code will enable all members of a machine's Administrators group, regardless of the domain they're in, to use Remoting on the machine. So, in our example, you'd make this change on the machine in DOMAINB—the destination machine of the Remoting connection.

10.10.2 Quotas

The great thing about Remoting is that it exists and solves a number of administration problems. The bad thing (and there's always one of those) is that too much Remoting can damage your system health. Imagine the scenario where you've implemented a server to support a new business-critical application. The application is being rolled out across the enterprise and the number of users is growing rapidly. At a certain loading you realize that the application is breaking down and consuming more resources than it should. You need to restrict the amount of resources devoted to PowerShell Remoting. How? You set quotas.

If you look in the WSMAN provider, you'll see a number of possible quota sessions:

```
PS C:\> dir wsman:\localhost | select Name, Value
```

```
Name                                            Value
----                                            -----
MaxEnvelopeSizekb                               500
MaxTimeoutms                                    60000
MaxBatchItems                                   32000
MaxProviderRequests                             4294967295

PS C:\> dir wsman:\localhost\service | select Name, value

Name                                            Value
----                                            -----
MaxConcurrentOperations                         4294967295
MaxConcurrentOperationsPerUser                  1500
EnumerationTimeoutms                            240000
MaxConnections                                  300
MaxPacketRetrievalTimeSeconds                   120
```

We haven't come across a situation where the defaults needed to be changed, but just in case you should ever need to make a change, this is how you do it:

```
Set-Item wsman:\localhost\MaxEnvelopeSizeKB -value 200
```

This code sets a global value for the size of the envelope (message) to 200 KB. Quotas can be set on individual session configurations:

```
Set-PSSessionConfiguration -name microsoft.powershell
     -MaximumReceivedObjectSizeMB 11 -Force
```

This increases the maximum object size for the microsoft.powershell endpoint. Other quota values can be found in a number of areas of the listener and endpoint configurations:

```
dir wsman:\localhost\plugin\microsoft.powershell\quotas
dir wsman:\localhost\plugin\microsoft.powershell\InitializationParameters
```

10.10.3 Configuring on a remote machine

You may run into instances where you need to modify the WinRM configuration on a remote computer. WinRM needs to be up and running on that system, and you can use the Connect-WSMan cmdlet to create the connection:

```
PS WSMan:\> Connect-WSMan -ComputerName win8
PS WSMan:\> dir

   WSManConfig:

ComputerName                                    Type
------------                                    ----
localhost                                       Container
win8                                            Container
```

As you can see here, the new computer shows up alongside localhost in your WSMan: drive, enabling you to access the machine's WinRM configuration. You might also want to use the `Test-WSMan` cmdlet to verify everything:

```
PS C:\> Test-WSMan -comp quark -Authentication default

wsmid            : http://schemas.dmtf.org/wbem/wsman/identity/1/
                   wsmanidentity.xsd
ProtocolVersion : http://schemas.dmtf.org/wbem/wsman/1/wsman.xsd
ProductVendor   : Microsoft Corporation
ProductVersion  : OS: 6.2.8250 SP: 0.0 Stack: 3.0
```

In addition to validating that Remoting is working, you can see the WinRM stack version (the `OS` and `SP` values will only be visible if the `-Authentication default` parameter is used). In this example, Quark is running PowerShell 3.0 and therefore WSMAN 3.0 is shown in the `Stack` property.

> **NOTE**   WSMAN version 3.0 is used in PowerShell v3 and v4.

For the most part you shouldn't run into any issues Remoting from a PowerShell 4.0, or 3.0, machine to one running PowerShell 2.0, but this is a handy tool for double-checking version information. You'll need this when we discuss CIM sessions in chapter 39.

10.10.4 Key WinRM configuration settings

All of these settings are located in your WSMan: drive; we'll cover the ones of most common interest but you can explore the drive to discover others. Many of these can also be configured via Group Policy—look for the "Windows Remote Management" section of the Group Policy object, under the Computer Configuration container.

- \Shell\IdleTimeout—The number of milliseconds a Remoting session can sit idle before being disconnected
- \Shell\MaxConcurrentUsers—The maximum number of Remoting sessions any number of users can have to a machine
- \Shell\MaxShellRunTime—The maximum time any Remoting session can be open, in milliseconds
- \Shell\MaxProcessesPerShell—The maximum number of processes any Remoting session can run
- \Shell\MaxMemoryPerShellMB—The maximum amount of memory any Remoting session can utilize
- \Shell\MaxShellsPerUser—The maximum number of Remoting sessions any one user can open to the machine

To change one of these settings manually, use the `Set-Item` cmdlet:

```
PS C:\> Set-Item WSMAN:\Localhost\Shell\IdleTimeout -Value 3600000
```

> **WARNING**   The updated configuration might affect the operation of the plug-ins having a per-plug-in quota value greater than 3600000. Verify the configuration of all the registered plug-ins and change the per-plug-in quota values for the affected plug-ins.

Some WSMAN settings can be configured at a global and individual plug-in level (a plug-in is another way of looking at a session configuration). This is especially true when the plug-in needs to use the capability of the shell. If you run this code

```
Get-Item -Path wsman:\localhost\shell\IdleTimeout
Get-ChildItem wsman:\localhost\plugin |
foreach {
 Get-Item "wsman:\localhost\plugin\$($_.Name)\quotas\IdleTimeoutms"
}
```

you'll get back something like this:

```
    WSManConfig: Microsoft.WSMan.Management\WSMan::localhost\Shell

Type              Name                              SourceOfValue   Value
----              ----                              -------------   -----
System.String     IdleTimeout                                       7200000

    WSManConfig:
Microsoft.WSMan.Management\WSMan::localhost\Plugin\microsoft.powershell
\Quotas

Type              Name                              SourceOfValue   Value
----              ----                              -------------   -----
System.String     IdleTimeoutms                                     7200000

    WSManConfig: Microsoft.WSMan.Management\WSMan::localhost\Plugin\microsoft
      .powershell.
workflow\Quotas

Type              Name                              SourceOfValue   Value

----              ----                              -------------   -----
System.String     IdleTimeoutms                                     7200000
```

As the error message on the `Set-Item` call explains, if you change the timeout setting at the shell level it will conflict with the setting at the plug-in level. The plug-in needs to be modified to match the shell. As with quotas, the default settings work very well and we don't know any reason for changing them in normal operating conditions.

10.10.5 Adding a machine to your Trusted Hosts list

Remoting doesn't like to connect to machines that it doesn't trust. You might think you're connecting to a remote machine named SERVER1, but if an attacker could somehow spoof DNS or perform some other trickery, they could hijack your session and have you connect to the attacker's machine instead. They could then capture all manner of useful information from you. Remoting's concept of trust prevents that from happening. By default, Remoting trusts only machines that are in the same Active Directory domain as your computer, enabling it to use Kerberos authentication to confirm the identity of the remote machine. That's why, by default, you can't remote to a machine using an IP address or hostname alias: Remoting can't use those to look up the machine's identity in Active Directory.

You can modify this behavior by manually adding machine names, IP addresses, and other identifiers to a persistent, static Trusted Hosts list that's maintained by WinRM. WinRM—and thus Remoting—will always trust machines on that list, although it doesn't actually authenticate them. You're opening yourself up to potential hijacking attempts—although it's rare for those to occur on an internal network.

You modify the list by using the WSMan: drive, as shown here:

```
PS WSMan:\localhost\Client> dir

    WSManConfig: Microsoft.WSMan.Management\WSMan::localhost\Client

Type              Name                         SourceOfValue     Value
----              ----                         -------------     -----
System.String     NetworkDelayms                                 5000
System.String     URLPrefix                                      wsman
System.String     AllowUnencrypted                               false
Container         Auth
Container         DefaultPorts
System.String     TrustedHosts

PS WSMan:\localhost\Client> Set-Item .\TrustedHosts *

WinRM Security Configuration.
This command modifies the TrustedHosts list for the WinRM client. The
computers in the TrustedHosts list might not be authenticated. The client
might send credential information to these computers. Are you sure that
you want to modify this list?
[Y] Yes  [N] No  [S] Suspend  [?] Help (default is "Y"): y
PS WSMan:\localhost\Client>
```

We've added * to TrustedHosts, essentially meaning we'll be able to use Remoting with any computer. We don't necessarily recommend that as a best practice, but it's useful in a lab environment where you just want stuff to work. In a production environment, we generally prefer to see a managed list of trusted hosts rather than the * wildcard. For example, *.company.pri would trust all hosts in the company.pri domain. Read the about_remote_troubleshooting PowerShell help file for a lot more detail and examples.

10.10.6 Using Group Policy to configure Remoting

This is a reminder that in a production environment the best way to configure Remoting is to use Group Policy. Full details on configuring Remoting via Group Policy can be found in the help file about_remote_troubleshooting.

We strongly recommend that you fully understand the settings by configuring manually in a lab before applying a Group Policy to your enterprise.

10.11 *Implicit Remoting*

Implicit Remoting is an incredibly cool trick and one that you'll get more and more use out of in the future. The basic idea is this: Rather than installing every possible PowerShell module on your computer, you leave the modules installed out on servers. You can then "import" the modules into your current PowerShell session, making it look like the commands in the modules all live locally. In reality, your computer will contain "shortcuts" to the commands, and the commands will execute out on the servers you got them from. The results—and even the commands' help—will be brought to your computer via Remoting.

Here's an example where you'll import the ServerManager module from a remote server:

```
PS C:\> $sess = New-PSSession -ComputerName win8
PS C:\> Invoke-Command -Session $sess -ScriptBlock { Import-Module
➥  servermanager }
PS C:\> Import-PSSession -Session $sess -Module ServerManager -Prefix RemSess

ModuleType Name                             ExportedCommands
---------- ----                             ----------------
Script     tmp_1hn0kr5w.keb                 {Get-WindowsFeature, Ins...
```

Here's what you did:

1. You opened a session to the remote machine, saving the session object in a variable for easy use later.
2. You invoked a command against that session, asking it to load the desired module into memory.
3. You imported that session, grabbing only the commands in the ServerManager module. To make these commands easy to distinguish, you added the prefix "RemSess" to the noun of all imported commands. The prefix is optional but is recommended especially if you're importing to a Windows 8, Windows Server 2012, or later system with the greatly increased number of cmdlets.

You can quickly check to see which commands you brought over:

```
PS> Get-Command -Noun RemSess*

CommandType Name
----------- ----
Alias       Add-RemSessWindowsFeature
Alias       Remove-RemSessWindowsFeature
Function    Disable-RemSessServerManagerStandardUserRemoting
Function    Enable-RemSessServerManagerStandardUserRemoting
Function    Get-RemSessWindowsFeature
Function    Install-RemSessWindowsFeature
Function    Uninstall-RemSessWindowsFeature
```

NOTE The module name column has been removed to enable the display to fit the page width.

You can now run these commands, just as if they were locally installed, and can even access their help (provided the server has had `Update-Help` run so that it has a copy of the help locally). The only caveat is the one that applies to all results in Remoting: The results of your commands won't have any methods attached to them, because the results will have been through the serialization/deserialization process.

These "imported" commands will exist as long as your session to the remote machine is open and available. Once it's closed, the commands will vanish. If you want to make these commands always available to you, save the remote session information to a module using the `Export-PSSession` cmdlet.

There are a few ways you might want to use this. First, take your current session and export everything to a module:

```
PS C:\> Export-PSSession -Session $q -OutputModule QuarkAll
```

The session $q is to the computer named Quark. This command will create a module called QuarkAll under $home\Documents\WindowsPowerShell\Modules:

```
PS C:\> Get-Module -ListAvailable QuarkAll

ModuleType Name                          ExportedCommands
---------- ----                          ----------------
Manifest   QuarkAll                      {}
```

Later, you can import this module as you would with implicit Remoting. Because the imported cmdlet names may conflict, add a prefix:

```
PS C:\> Import-Module QuarkAll -Prefix Q
```

The first time you try to run one of the commands, PowerShell dynamically creates the necessary session and establishes a remote connection:

```
PS C:\> Get-Qsmbshare
Creating a new session for implicit Remoting of "Get-SmbShare" command...
```

If you check sessions, you should see a new one created for this module:

```
PS C:\> Get-PSSession | select *
State                 : Opened
ComputerName          : quark
ConfigurationName     : Microsoft.PowerShell
InstanceId            : 662484ed-d350-4b76-a146-865a8d43f603
Id                    : 2
Name                  : Session for implicit Remoting module at
                        C:\Users\Jeff\Documents\WindowsPowerShell\Modules\
                        QuarkAll\QuarkAll.psm1
Availability          : Available
ApplicationPrivateData : {PSVersionTable}
Runspace              : System.Management.Automation.RemoteRunspace
```

If you remove the module, the session is also automatically removed.

You can also create a limited module by only exporting the commands you want. First, create a session:

```
PS C:\> $q=New-PSSession Quark
```

Then, create a new module exporting only the Get cmdlets:

```
PS C:\> Export-PSSession -Session $q -OutputModule QuarkGet -CommandName
➥ Get* [CA] -CommandType cmdlet
```

When you import the module, the only commands you can run remotely on Quark are the Get cmdlets:

```
PS C:\> Import-Module QuarkGet -Prefix Q
PS C:\> Get-Command -module QuarkGet

CommandType      Name                         Definition
-----------      ----                         ----------
Function         Get-QAppLockerFileInformation  ...
Function         Get-QAppLockerPolicy           ...
Function         Get-QAppxProvisionedPackage    ...
Function         Get-QAutoEnrollmentPolicy      ...
Function         Get-QBitsTransfer              ...
...
```

One thing we should point out is that when you export a session, any commands with names that might conflict on your local computer are skipped unless you use the -AllowClobber parameter. In the examples with Quark, you're connecting from a computer running PowerShell 2.0 to one running PowerShell 4.0, or 3.0, and thus are able to use the cmdlets of the later versions of PowerShell just as if they were installed locally:

```
PS C:\> get-qciminstance win32_operatingsystem | Select
➥ CSName,BuildNumber,Version
Creating a new session for implicit Remoting of "Get-CimInstance" command...

CSName                BuildNumber              Version
------                -----------              -------
QUARK                 8250                     6.2.8250
```

Implicit Remoting is an incredibly powerful technique—and a necessity for working with remote Exchange servers—that lets you take advantage of modules, snap-ins, and tools that you may not have installed locally. If you find yourself needing these tools often, take the time to export a session to a module; then you'll be ready for anything.

10.12 Standard troubleshooting methodology

Troubleshooting can be difficult, especially with Remoting because there are so many layers in which something can go wrong. We strongly recommend that you read, learn, and inwardly digest the help file about_Remote_Troubleshooting. It contains a lot of useful information that will improve your knowledge of Remoting and enable you to troubleshoot problems. When you have to diagnose problems with Remoting, we recommend that you follow these four steps:

1. Test Remoting with its default configuration. If you've tinkered with it, undo your changes and start from scratch.
2. Start by attempting to connect from the initiating machine to the target machine by using something other than Remoting but that's still security-sensitive. For

example, use Windows Explorer to open the remote machine's C$ shared folder. If that doesn't work, you have broader security issues. Make a note of whether you need to provide alternate credentials—if you do, Remoting will need them as well.

3 Install a Telnet client on the initiating machine (a simple command-line client, like the Windows native one, will do). Attempt to connect to the HTTP WinRM listener by running `telnet machine_name:5985`. You should get a blank screen, and Ctrl-C will end the session. If this doesn't work, there's a basic connectivity problem (such as a blocked port) you need to resolve.

4 Use `Test-WSMan`, using an alternate credential if necessary. Make sure that you're using the machine's real name as it appears in Active Directory or that you've taken one of the other approaches (TrustedHosts plus a credential, or SSL plus a credential). If that doesn't work, you have a problem in the WSMAN configuration.

Walking through these four steps, in this order, can help you pinpoint at least the general cause of most problems.

10.13 *Summary*

Remoting was the most eagerly awaited feature in PowerShell v2. It moved Power-Shell's capabilities up by several levels. You can gain remote access to systems through a number of cmdlets that have a `-ComputerName` parameter or through the WSMAN-based Remoting technology.

Once you've mastered the material in this chapter, you'll be able to administer all the machines in your environment from the comfort of your own workstation.

Background jobs and scheduling

This chapter covers

- Creating jobs
- Retrieving job results
- Managing the job queue
- Using scheduled jobs

In PowerShell, jobs are one of the many extension points provided to the shell for you to build on. Jobs allow you to run tasks asynchronously—you get the prompt back to continue working while PowerShell runs the job in the background. Power-Shell v4 (beginning in v3) defines four broad but distinct types of jobs: those based on the Remoting architecture covered in the previous chapter (also known as background jobs)—though they don't use PowerShell Remoting directly—those based on WMI and CIM, and those based on a new "scheduled job" architecture.

NOTE The CIM cmdlets themselves don't have an -AsJob parameter you have to use Start-Job or Invoke-Command to wrap the command as a job. If you create a CDXML module using the cmdlet-over-objects technology (see chapter 39) you'll automatically get an -AsJob parameter added to your cmdlets.

PowerShell workflows can also be run as jobs, as you'll learn in chapter 23. Each of these jobs works slightly differently, but all of them represent the same essential thing: a unit of work that's run in the background.

11.1 Remoting-based jobs

You have two ways to start jobs that use the Remoting architecture: `Start-Job` and `Invoke-Command`. `Start-Job` is designed to start a job that runs entirely on your local computer and technically doesn't use the Remoting subsystem to function because it doesn't use remote machines. `Invoke-Command` starts a job that's tracked on your local machine but that sends commands to remote computers for execution there. `Invoke-Command` is a great way to coordinate running a command on a bunch of remote computers.

> **NOTE** If you use `Invoke-Command` locally and use the `-Computername` or `-AsJob` parameter, PowerShell will use Remoting to the local computer, so it must be enabled.

11.1.1 Starting jobs

To start a local job use the `Start-Job` cmdlet and specify a script block:

```
PS C:\> Start-Job -ScriptBlock { Get-Eventlog -LogName security }

Id Name PSJobTypeName State    HasMoreData Location  Command
-- ---- ------------- -----    ----------- --------  -------
6  Job6 BackgroundJob Running  True        localhost get-eventlog -LogNa...
```

> **NOTE** Depending on the width of your PowerShell console, when you use the job cmdlets you might get a truncated view and some columns might not appear at all. We've tried to accommodate all columns in the confines of the printed page so you can get an idea of what to expect and look for.

The command's immediate result is a job object. Job IDs are numbered sequentially, starting with 1 for the first job you run when opening a new shell instance, although it's possible depending on your configuration that job numbers might start at 2 or higher. PowerShell v2 tended to start the job IDs at 1 whereas PowerShell v3 and later start at 2. Job names are also created sequentially based on the parent job name (which we'll explain in minute), such as Job1, although you can specify a custom name when starting a new job by using the `-Name` parameter of `Start-Job`.

> **TIP** Use the `-Name` parameter if you're working with a lot of jobs simultaneously—it makes keeping track of them easier.

Here are a few other parameters you should keep in mind:

- Use `-FilePath` instead of `-ScriptBlock` to specify the name of a script to run—the script is on the *local* machine. You can add `-ArgumentList` to specify a list of parameter values to be fed to that script.

- -Credential and -Authentication can be used to specify alternative credentials or an authentication mechanism for the job to run under.
- -InitializationScript is a script block that runs before the job starts. You might use this, for example, to first import a required module.
- -PSVersion can be either 2.0 or 3.0—the default is 3.0 even in later versions of PowerShell—and it specifies the version of PowerShell you want the job run under. It's mainly useful on machines that have PowerShell v2 and v3/v4 installed side by side.
- -RunAs32 runs the script in the 32-bit version of PowerShell. You'll need this if you're using a snap-in or module that only exists in a 32-bit flavor and you're on a 64-bit machine.
- -DefinitionName starts the job using a predefined job definition, which enables you to start custom job types. You can also use -DefinitionPath to start the job at the specified path. We'll use these in a bit for scheduled jobs.

Jobs run in a background PowerShell process, so the more jobs you have running at once, the more copies of PowerShell you'll have running at once in memory.

You can also start jobs using Invoke-Command. Run Invoke-Command as usual, adding the -AsJob parameter (and use the -JobName parameter if you want to give the job a nicer name than PowerShell will make up by default). Because Invoke-Command is specifically designed to send commands to remote computers, it's a good way to have all of that running in the background, for example:

```
PS C:\> Invoke-Command -ScriptBlock { Get-Service } -ComputerName win8,
➥ localhost -AsJob -JobName ServiceCheck

Id Name           PSJobTypeName State   HasMoreData Location      Command
-- ----           ------------- -----   ----------- --------      -------
12 ServiceCheck   RemoteJob     Running True        win8,local... get-se...
```

11.1.2 Checking job status

Run Get-Job to display a list of running jobs and to check their status, for example:

```
PS C:\> Get-Job

Id Name           PSJobTypeName State     HasMoreData Location    Command
-- ----           ------------- -----     ----------- --------    -------
6  Job6           BackgroundJob Completed True        localhost   get-event...
12 ServiceCheck   RemoteJob     Completed True        win8,l...   get-servi...
```

When a job is targeting multiple computers, the status shown here will be the worst-case scenario from all computers involved. In other words, if one computer failed, you'll see "Failed" as the status, even if every other computer succeeded. To drill down for more detail, you'll need to work with those child jobs directly.

11.1.3 *Working with child jobs*

Every job consists of a top-level parent job and at least one child job. Jobs that target multiple computers will have one child job per targeted computer. To examine the child jobs, you'll need the ID or name of the top-level job. For example:

```
PS C:\> Get-Job

Id Name          PSJobTypeName State     HasMoreData Location  Command
-- ----          ------------- -----     ----------- --------  -------
6  Job6          BackgroundJob Completed True        localhost get-event...
12 ServiceCheck  RemoteJob     Completed True        win8,1... get-servi...
```

PowerShell v3 added parameters to make it easier to work with child jobs. It's easy to see all the jobs at once by using -IncludeChildJob:

```
PS C:\> Get-Job -Name ServiceCheck -IncludeChildJob

Id Name          PSJobTypeName State     HasMoreData Location  Command
-- ----          ------------- -----     ----------- --------  -------
12 ServiceCheck  RemoteJob     Completed True        win8,1... get-servi...
13 Job13         RemoteJob     Completed True        win8      get-servi...
14 Job14         RemoteJob     Completed True        localhost get-servi...
```

This code demonstrates how you'd find the name of a job and its children. This also works with the job ID.

> **NOTE** Depending on your PowerShell installation, when you look at help for Get-Job you might not see the -IncludeChildJob parameter but rather -ShowChildJob. This appears to be a documentation bug. The correct parameter is -IncludeChildJob. PowerShell v4 documentation has the correct parameter name.

These job objects have more information than can be contained in a table; to see everything, use this:

```
PS C:\> Get-Job -id 13 | select *

State          : Completed
StatusMessage  :
HasMoreData    : True
Location       : serenity
Runspace       : System.Management.Automation.RemoteRunspace
Command        :  get-service
JobStateInfo   : Completed
Finished       : System.Threading.ManualResetEvent
InstanceId     : e6761f14-4ea4-488f-84e6-0e08f396b969
Id             : 13
Name           : Job13
ChildJobs      : {}
PSBeginTime    : 9/26/2012 12:58:06 PM
PSEndTime      : 9/26/2012 12:58:06 PM
PSJobTypeName  :
Output         : {AeLookupSvc, ALG, AllUserInstallAgent, AppIDSvc...}
Error          : {}
Progress       : {}
```

```
Verbose       : {}
Debug         : {}
Warning       : {}
```

Notice that the job object provides access to the Error, Progress, Verbose, Debug, and Warning streams (or pipelines) from the copy of PowerShell that ran the job. There's also data that indicates when the job started and when it ended if you need to track how long these things take to complete. Here's a handy one-liner you can use:

```
Get-Job -State Completed |
select Name, Location, *time, @{Name="RunTime";
Expression={$_.PSEndTime - $_.PSBeginTime}}
```

11.1.4 *Waiting for a job*

If you launch a job from within a script, you may want to have your script pause, or wait, until the job completes:

```
PS C:\> Wait-Job -id 13
```

Using other parameters of `Wait-Job`, you can also wait until all active jobs reach a given state. Finally, you can also specify a timeout, which will end the waiting period once the time has expired regardless of the job status. Nothing will happen to the jobs but you'll get your prompt back.

11.1.5 *Stopping jobs*

It's not impossible for a job to hang or otherwise fail. When that happens, you can stop it immediately. Any results that the job has already produced will be retained:

```
PS C:\> Stop-Job -Name ServiceCheck
```

It's also possible to stop all jobs that are in a particular status, such as stopping all running jobs:

```
PS C:\> Stop-Job -state 'Running'
```

Review the help for `Stop-Job` for more details.

11.1.6 *Getting job results*

PowerShell temporarily caches the results of jobs, enabling you to retrieve them whenever you're ready. There's a trick: By default, whatever results you receive are removed from the cache when they're given to you. You can, for example, retrieve the results of a job that's still running. You'll get whatever results are currently available, and new ones will continue to pile up.

To get the results of a job, specify it by name, ID, or other identifier. If you get the results from a parent job, you'll automatically get all of its child job results:

```
PS C:\> Receive-Job -Name ServiceCheck

Status    Name              DisplayName                    PSCompu
                                                           terName

------    ----              -----------                    -------
```

```
Stopped   AeLookupSvc       Application Experience              win8
Stopped   ALG               Application Layer Gateway Service   win8
Stopped   AllUserInstallA...Windows All-User Install Agent      win8
Stopped   AppIDSvc          Application Identity                win8
Stopped   Appinfo           Application Information             win8
Stopped   AppMgmt           Application Management              win8
Stopped   AudioEndpointBu...Windows Audio Endpoint Builder      win8
Stopped   Audiosrv          Windows Audio                       win8
Running   BFE               Base Filtering Engine               win8
Running   BITS              Background Intelligent Transfer Ser...win8
Running   BrokerInfrastru...Broker Infrastructure               win8
```

Jobs started with `Invoke-Command` will contain the `PSComputerName` property by default, showing you which result came from which computer. WMI job result objects also have a `PSComputerName` property that fills a similar purpose (you can use the WMI system property `__SERVER` if you prefer).

You can also direct PowerShell to deliver a *copy* of the results, keeping the original results in memory so that you can retrieve them again:

```
PS C:\> Receive-Job -id 13 -Keep

    Index Time          EntryType    Source              InstanceID Messa
                                                                     ge

    ----- ----          ---------    ------              ---------- -----
     2494 Jun 10 10:11  SuccessA...  Microsoft-Windows...     4616  Th...
     2493 Jun 10 09:10  SuccessA...  Microsoft-Windows...     4616  Th...
     2492 Jun 10 08:09  SuccessA...  Microsoft-Windows...     4616  Th...
     2491 Jun 10 07:08  SuccessA...  Microsoft-Windows...     4616  Th...
```

You can retrieve results from the job queue as often as you want as long as you use `-Keep`. The first time you don't, though, the results will be flushed from the queue.

The `Receive-Job` command has some interesting parameters:

- `-ComputerName` gets the results from all jobs run against the specified computers. Use this instead of `-ID` or `-Name`.
- `-Session` gets the results from all jobs run through a specified Remoting session. You specify the full session object as the value for this parameter.
- `-AutoRemoveJob` deletes the job object after getting the results from it.
- `-Wait` tells the shell to start receiving job results but to not display the command prompt again until all results have been received. In conjunction with this, you can specify `-WriteEvents` to display notices about changes in the job status while you're waiting for the results to finish. You can't use this with `-Keep` and you must use `-Wait`.
- `-WriteJobInResults` precedes the job results output with a copy of the job object itself. You can't use this with `-Keep` and you must use `-Wait`.

11.1.7 *Removing jobs*

Unless you have `Receive-Job` autoremove them, job objects linger until you close the shell or manually remove them:

```
PS C:\> Get-Job -id 13 | Remove-Job
```

Or you can just remove everything that's completed:

```
PS C:\> Remove-Job -State Completed
```

Other parameters of `Remove-Job` let you specify the jobs to remove in other ways, including by name, a hash table filter, the command that was run, and so forth.

11.1.8 Investigating failed jobs

Job objects have a `Reason` property that'll indicate why a job failed. For example, let's start a job that'll fail and see what happens:

```
PS C:\> Get-Job
PS C:\> Start-Job -ScriptBlock { Get-Eventlog -LogName Nothing }
```

Id	Name	PSJobTypeName	State	HasMoreData	Locat ion
--	----	-------------	-----	-----------	-----
17	Job17	BackgroundJob	Running	True	lo...

Eventually, we check the job and its children and see that it failed:

```
PS C:\> Get-Job -IncludeChildJob
```

Id	Name	PSJobTypeName	State	HasMoreData	Locat ion
--	----	-------------	-----	-----------	-----
17	Job17	BackgroundJob	Failed	False	lo...
18	Job18		Failed	False	lo...

You could also filter and get only failed child jobs like this:

```
PS C:\> Get-Job -ChildJobState Failed
```

The value for `-ChildJobState` is any job state such as running, stopped, or completed. The job object has a `JobStateInfo` property, which is an object. Let's look at the failed child job:

```
PS C:\> Get-Job 18 | select -ExpandProperty JobStateInfo
              State Reason
              ----- ------
             Failed System.Management.Automation.Remo...
```

Because this is also an object, you need to expand this as well to get to the root of the problem:

```
PS C:\> Get-Job 18 | select -ExpandProperty JobStateInfo |
➡ select -ExpandProperty Reason
The event log 'Nothing' on computer '.' does not exist.
```

That's pretty much what we expected.

You can read more about jobs, and job troubleshooting, in the about_jobs and about_Job_Details help files.

> **TIP** Even if you see that a job has failed, you might still want to try to receive results. It's possible your job may have partially completed before failing, and depending on your situation, some results may be better than nothing.

11.2   *WMI jobs*

WMI jobs work pretty much like the Remoting-based jobs we've discussed. You start them using `Get-WmiObject`, adding its –AsJob parameter. `Invoke-WmiMethod`, `Remove-WmiObject`, and `Set-WmiInstance` also have an –AsJob parameter. Apart from adding the –AsJob parameter, you use these cmdlets the same as you would otherwise.

> **NOTE**   `Test-Connection`, `Stop-Computer`, and `Restart-Computer` all have an –AsJob parameter. They should be considered part of this group because they use WMI "under the hood" to perform their functions.

There's one difference in these commands' normal operation: When run as a background job, computers are contacted in parallel rather than sequentially as is normally the case. The cmdlets support a –ThrottleLimit parameter to increase or decrease the parallelism from its default of 32 concurrent connections. WMI jobs continue to communicate over remote procedure calls (RPCs) and don't use or require PowerShell Remoting. For example:

```
PS C:\> Get-WmiObject -Class Win32_Service -ComputerName win8 -AsJob

Id     Name          PSJobTypeName    State        HasMoreData     Locat
                                                                   ion
--     ----          -------------    -----        -----------     -----
25     Job25         WmiJob           Running      True            win8
```

> **NOTE**   The CIM cmdlets, such as `Get-CimInstance`, don't support an -AsJob parameter. Because these cmdlets rely on WinRM by default (the same technology as PowerShell Remoting), you send the CIM command to the remote computers via `Invoke-Command`.

The job object is created locally with a child job for each remote computer. WMI jobs use the same cmdlets to retrieve job status, get job results, and so forth—everything from the first portion of this chapter applies.

11.3   *Scheduled jobs*

PowerShell v3 introduced a new job definition for scheduled jobs. Unlike the jobs discussed previously in this chapter, these scheduled jobs do have a lifespan outside the PowerShell console window. Once scheduled, they continue to exist and operate even if you close the shell. Several commands deal specifically with these jobs:

```
PS C:\> Get-Command -Noun ScheduledJob*

CommandType     Name                       ModuleName
-----------     ----                       ----------
Cmdlet          Disable-ScheduledJob       PSScheduledJob
Cmdlet          Enable-ScheduledJob        PSScheduledJob
Cmdlet          Get-ScheduledJob           PSScheduledJob
Cmdlet          Get-ScheduledJobOption     PSScheduledJob
Cmdlet          New-ScheduledJobOption     PSScheduledJob
Cmdlet          Register-ScheduledJob      PSScheduledJob
Cmdlet          Set-ScheduledJob           PSScheduledJob
```

```
Cmdlet          Set-ScheduledJobOption              PSScheduledJob
Cmdlet          Unregister-ScheduledJob             PSScheduledJob
```

These cmdlet names reveal three kinds of objects you'll work with: scheduled jobs themselves (which you can enable, disable, get, register, modify, and unregister), scheduled job triggers (which determine when a job runs), and scheduled job options (which you can get, create, and change).

11.3.1 Scheduled jobs overview

Scheduled jobs are a kind of hybrid entity introduced with PowerShell v3.

> **NOTE** The terminology between scheduled jobs and scheduled tasks can be very confusing—we recommend you spend a few moments working out the differences. A scheduled task runs a command (or script) on a trigger activated by the Windows Task Scheduler. A scheduled job runs a PowerShell job on a trigger activated by the Windows Task Scheduler. As an additional source of confusion, the module for scheduled jobs (PSScheduledJob) is available in PowerShell v3 and v4 when installed on older versions of Windows but the module for scheduled tasks (ScheduledTasks) isn't available on those legacy systems.

There's the scheduled job itself, which is registered with Windows Task Scheduler and can be managed from Task Scheduler. That scheduled job may have one or more options associated with it, and it'll have triggers that determine when the scheduled job runs. When a scheduled job does run, a normal PowerShell job object is created to contain the results. So, if a scheduled job runs 10 times, you'll have 10 job objects to play with. Those "result" job objects work identically to the ones we've already covered in this chapter; you can use `Receive-Job` to extract their results, `Remove-Job` to delete them, and so on.

> **NOTE** You'll find quite a bit of in-shell documentation on scheduled jobs. Run `Help about_scheduled*` for a list of topics.

11.3.2 Creating a scheduled job

To create a scheduled job, start by—at a minimum—creating a trigger. This is what tells the job when to run. That might be something simple, like "every day at 3 a.m.," or something more complex; review the help for `New-JobTrigger` to see your options. For example:

```
$trigger = New-JobTrigger -Daily -At '3 am'
```

Here, you're saving the trigger into a variable, `$trigger`, to make it easy to refer to later. You may also want to create a job options object. Doing so isn't mandatory, but reading the help for `New-ScheduledJobOption` lets you see what your options are. Here's a quick example:

```
$options = New-ScheduledJobOption -HideInTaskScheduler -RequireNetwork
```

This option, which you've also saved into a variable, will make the job invisible in Task Scheduler and will make the job fail if the network isn't available at the time the job runs. With the options and trigger created, you can register a new scheduled job. Note the verb on this one is Register, because it's creating something external to PowerShell:

```
Register-ScheduledJob -Name DailyRestart -ScriptBlock { Get-Process ;
Restart-Computer -force } -Trigger $trigger -ScheduledJobOption $options
```

You've created a new scheduled job that will get a list of running processes and then restart the local computer, each day at 3 a.m., provided the network is available at the time. Note that you didn't need to export the process list to anything—it'll be stored for you. For longer sets of commands, put them into a script file and use the -FilePath parameter to point to the script (on the local machine), rather than trying to jam everything into the script block.

When you create a scheduled job, PowerShell creates a folder for it on the disk of the computer where the job exists. This folder goes in your user profile directory by default, in \AppData\Local\Microsoft\Windows\PowerShell\ScheduledJobs, with a subfolder for each job name. For the earlier example, that would be \DailyRestart. This folder contains the scheduled job's XML definition file and an \Output folder. The \Output folder is further broken down with a subfolder for each time the job has executed—folder names are a timestamp. Within those timestamp folders you'll find the job's output in an XML file, along with the job's status. You have little need to work with any of these folders or files directly, because the job management commands handle them for you.

Like many PowerShell commands, Register-ScheduledJob (and Set-ScheduledJob) has a -Credential parameter, which specifies an alternate username for the job to run as.

A new feature introduced in v4 is the option to run the job immediately upon creating it. In v3 if you wanted to create a scheduled job and run it you had to jump through some hoops. Now you can simply use the -RunNow parameter.

In this example, we've created a scheduled job to run once a month on Sunday:

```
$trigger = New-JobTrigger -At 12:00 -WeeksInterval 4 -DaysOfWeek Sunday
➡ -Weekly
$action = { Get-Process | Export-Clixml -Path c:\work\WeeklyProcs.xml }
Register-ScheduledJob -Name "Weekly Process Snapshot" -ScriptBlock
➡ $action -Trigger $trigger -RunNow
```

But we also wanted it to run right immediately. Mission accomplished.

You can view the properties of a scheduled job:

```
PS C:\> Get-Scheduledjob "Weekly Process Snapshot"

Id     Name            JobTriggers      Command          Enabled
--     ----            -----------      -------          -------
1      Weekly Proce... 1                get-process | ... True
```

If you don't give a job name, you'll see all of the existing jobs.

11.3.3 *Managing scheduled jobs*

A number of cmdlets are available for managing scheduled jobs. Note that these apply only to the scheduled entity; they don't work with the results of jobs that have already run. First up are commands that deal with triggers:

- `Add-JobTrigger`—Adds a new trigger to an existing scheduled job
- `Disable-JobTrigger`—Turns off a scheduled job's triggers but doesn't delete them
- `Enable-JobTrigger`—Enables a previously disabled scheduled job trigger
- `Get-JobTrigger`—Gets the triggers of scheduled jobs
- `New-JobTrigger`—Creates a new job trigger
- `Remove-JobTrigger`—Removes a job trigger from the scheduled job
- `Set-JobTrigger`—Reconfigures a trigger on a scheduled job

Next are commands that deal with scheduled job options:

- `Get-ScheduledJobOption`—Gets the options for a scheduled job
- `New-ScheduledJobOption`—Creates a new option set
- `Set-ScheduledJobOption`—Reconfigures a scheduled job's options

Finally, these commands work with scheduled job entries:

- `Disable-ScheduledJob`—Disables, but doesn't delete, a scheduled job
- `Enable-ScheduledJob`—Reenables a previously disabled scheduled job
- `Get-ScheduledJob`—Gets the scheduled jobs on a computer
- `Register-ScheduledJob`—Creates and registers a new scheduled job
- `Set-ScheduledJob`—Reconfigures an existing scheduled job
- `Unregister-ScheduledJob`—Removes a scheduled job entry

It's possible to run a scheduled job on demand:

```
PS C:\> Start-Job -DefinitionName DailyRestart
```

Just give the scheduled job's name (which is its definition name), and the job will begin immediately. Even though you can see the scheduled job in the Task Scheduler, we recommend using PowerShell to manually run it.

11.3.4 *Working with scheduled job results*

Once a scheduled job has run, you can run `Get-Job` to see a list of available jobs. Each result job will have the same name as the scheduled job that ran it; in many cases, you'll need to use ID numbers to retrieve the specific results. For example, after setting up your job and letting it run for a few days, you have this:

```
PS C:\> Get-Job -Name DailyRestart

Id     Name          State       HasMoreData   Location
--     ----          -----       -----------   --------
45     DailyRestart  Completed   True          localhost
```

```
46      DailyRestart    Completed       True            localhost
47      DailyRestart    Completed       True            localhost
48      DailyRestart    Completed       True            localhost
49      DailyRestart    Completed       True            localhost
50      DailyRestart    Completed       True            localhost
51      DailyRestart    Completed       True            localhost
```

If you don't see anything, don't forget to import the PSScheduledJob module first. You can now use `Receive-Job -id 45` to get the first set of results, and so forth. All of the rules we covered earlier in this chapter for working with jobs still apply, and you'll need to take care to remove the jobs you're finished with, to free up memory and disk space.

> **NOTE** In the case of jobs created by a scheduled job, the results will remain on disk after being received, even if you don't specify the `-Keep` parameter of `Receive-Job`. Be sure to use `Remove-Job` to delete job results you're finished with so that you can free up disk space. You can also run something like `Remove-Job -Name DailyRestart` to remove all results associated with a given job name.

Worried about job results taking up too much space? You can control how many results are kept. A scheduled job has an `ExecutionHistoryLength` property, which determines how many saved results are retained on disk. As new results are created, older ones are deleted to make room. The default value is 32; use the `-MaxResultCount` parameter of `Set-ScheduledJob` or `Register-ScheduledJob` to modify this value for an existing or a newly scheduled job, respectively.

> **TIP** Use the `-ClearExecutionHistory` parameter of `Set-ScheduledJob` to completely delete a scheduled job's existing execution history and results.

11.3.5 Removing scheduled jobs

Because PowerShell scheduled jobs are stored in the Task Scheduler, you might be tempted to simply delete the job there. Don't. When you want to remove a scheduled job, first make sure you've saved any results. Then use the `Unregister-ScheduledJob` cmdlet:

```
PS C:\> Unregister-ScheduledJob -Name "Weekly Process Snapshot"
```

You can also pipe `Get-ScheduledJob` to `Unregister-ScheduledJob` to remove multiple jobs at once. When you use this approach, PowerShell will clean up job results and files written to disk. If you use the Task Scheduler, you'll be left with orphan files and `Get-ScheduledJob` will give you bad results.

> **NOTE** If you look at help for `Unregister-ScheduledJob`, you'll see a `WhatIf` parameter. In PowerShell v3 if you use it, you'll think the cmdlet behaved as you'd expect when using `-Whatif`, but it doesn't. The job will be removed, so be careful. This has been corrected in PowerShell v4.

11.4 Job processes

The preceding sections have described the three different types of jobs available within PowerShell:

- Remoting-based jobs
- WMI-based jobs
- Scheduled jobs

We provided a few hints as to where these jobs actually run. It's now time for us to summarize how and where jobs run because it's different for each of the job types. This will give you an indication of what's happening on your system when you run PowerShell jobs.

11.4.1 Jobs created with Start-Job

These jobs run as child processes of your interactive PowerShell process. Each background job creates a new instance of powershell.exe as a child to your interactive session.

> **NOTE** That's why you lose all of the running jobs when you close your session—because the child processes are automatically closed when you close the interactive parent session.

The child instances of powershell.exe are hidden, though they can be viewed by using a process monitoring tool. They're temporary sessions that are closed when the job is finished. Figure 11.1 illustrates this point. Open a PowerShell session and run Get-Process filtering on processes whose names begin with the letter "p." Figure 11.1 shows a single PowerShell instance with an ID of 1436.

A job is then started that'll continue running until it's forcibly stopped. This is achieved by a script block with an infinite loop:

```
do {sleep 1} while ($true)
```

PowerShell won't exit the loop because the condition is always true! Running Get-Process again shows that two PowerShell sessions now exist. The following WMI call shows that the new process (ID 3024) is a child of process 1436, your original PowerShell session:

```
PS> Get-WmiObject -Class Win32_Process -Filter "ProcessId = 3024" |
    Format-table ProcessName, Processid, ParentProcessId -auto

ProcessName     Processid ParentProcessId
-----------     --------- ---------------
powershell.exe       3024            1436
```

11.4.2 Jobs created with Invoke-Command

When a job is started using the –AsJob parameter of Invoke-Command, it runs under WSMAN in a wsmprovhost.exe process, as illustrated in figure 11.2.

No processes called wsmprovhost are running prior to the starting of the job. Once the job starts, you can see that a wsmprovhost.exe process exists. Running jobs in this manner may result in a performance boost.

```
Administrator: Windows PowerShell                                          _  □  x

PS C:\> get-process p*

Handles  NPM(K)    PM(K)      WS(K) VM(M)    CPU(s)      Id ProcessName
-------  ------    -----      ----- -----    ------      -- -----------
    697      52   181944      70300   789     12.97    1436 powershell

PS C:\> start-job -name test1 -ScriptBlock { do {sleep 1} while ($true)}

Id      Name            PSJobTypeName    State      HasMoreData    Location
--      ----            -------------    -----      -----------    --------
5       test1           BackgroundJob    Running    True           localhost

PS C:\> get-job

Id      Name            PSJobTypeName    State      HasMoreData    Location
--      ----            -------------    -----      -----------    --------
5       test1           BackgroundJob    Running    True           localhost

PS C:\> get-process p*

Handles  NPM(K)    PM(K)      WS(K) VM(M)    CPU(s)      Id ProcessName
-------  ------    -----      ----- -----    ------      -- -----------
    775      54   182188      86280   791     13.20    1436 powershell
    374      28    48524      59228   609      0.34    3024 powershell

PS C:\> _
```

Figure 11.1   Illustrating the creation of a child PowerShell session when a job is run

When the -AsJob parameter is used to start jobs on remote machines, one child job is
created per remote system. If you use Start-Job inside an Invoke-Command, one job
object (parent and child jobs) is created per remote system.

```
Administrator: Windows PowerShell                                          _  □  x

PS C:\> get-process ws*
PS C:\> invoke-command -ComputerName $env:COMPUTERNAME -scriptblock { do {sleep
1} while ($true)} -AsJob

Id      Name            PSJobTypeName    State      HasMoreData    Location
--      ----            -------------    -----      -----------    --------
7       Job7            RemoteJob        Running    True           CHI-WIN81

PS C:\> get-job

Id      Name            PSJobTypeName    State      HasMoreData    Location
--      ----            -------------    -----      -----------    --------
5       test1           BackgroundJob    Running    True           localhost
7       Job7            RemoteJob        Running    True           CHI-WIN81

PS C:\> get-process ws*

Handles  NPM(K)    PM(K)      WS(K) VM(M)    CPU(s)      Id ProcessName
-------  ------    -----      ----- -----    ------      -- -----------
    376      26    49244      59040   583      0.41    2648 wsmprovhost

PS C:\> _
```

Figure 11.2   Illustrating the processes involved when running a job through Invoke-Command

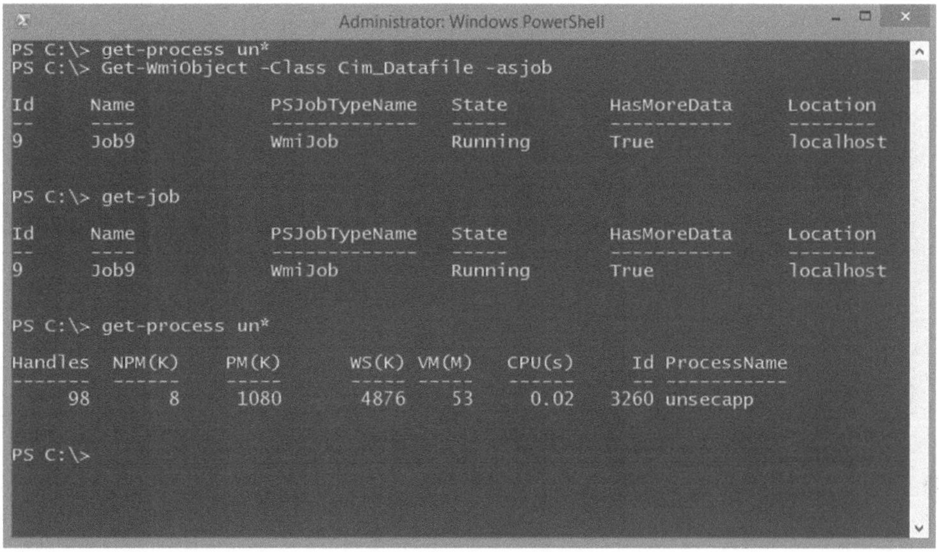

```
Administrator: Windows PowerShell                    _ □ x
PS C:\> get-process un*
PS C:\> Get-WmiObject -Class Cim_Datafile -asjob

Id      Name              PSJobTypeName    State      HasMoreData   Location
--      ----              -------------    -----      -----------   --------
9       Job9              WmiJob           Running    True          localhost

PS C:\> get-job

Id      Name              PSJobTypeName    State      HasMoreData   Location
--      ----              -------------    -----      -----------   --------
9       Job9              WmiJob           Running    True          localhost

PS C:\> get-process un*

Handles  NPM(K)    PM(K)      WS(K)  VM(M)   CPU(s)     Id ProcessName
-------  ------    -----      -----  -----   ------     -- -----------
     98       8     1080       4876     53     0.02   3260 unsecapp

PS C:\>
```

Figure 11.3 Illustrating the process used to run a WMI-based job

11.4.3 *Jobs created through the WMI cmdlets*

WMI-based jobs run in a completely different process. Figure 11.3 shows this in the unsecapp.exe process.

The unsecapp.exe application is part of the WMI installation and can be found in the C:\Windows\System32\wbem folder.

11.4.4 *Jobs created through the scheduler*

PowerShell jobs that are created as a scheduled task run in their own instance of PowerShell when the job is started. This runspace is automatically closed when the job completes.

11.5 *Summary*

Jobs are a good way to move long-running processes to the background to allow you to continue using the shell for other tasks. Remember, you may encounter many different kinds of jobs. Microsoft or even third parties may introduce job types that we haven't discussed in this chapter, and they may work entirely differently from the ones we've shown you.

Working with credentials

## 12

This chapter covers

- Creating a credential object
- Using credentials
- Supporting alternative credentials in your scripts

A great many PowerShell commands have a -Credential parameter. You can view the list by typing

```
Get-Help * -Parameter Credential
```

When you use this parameter, it generally allows the command to operate with the username and password you provide rather than the one you used to log on to the shell. It's a great way to enable the *principle of least privilege*. Do as much work as you can with unprivileged credentials, but when more privilege is required, specify alternative credentials for that purpose. You'll need to run PowerShell with elevated privileges ("Run as Administrator") to complete some actions regardless of the credentials you use.

12.1 *About credentials*

Most of the time, you'll find that a -Credential parameter will accept one of two objects: a string object or a credential object. The string object is easy: Provide a username, which can be a plain username, a DOMAIN\User-style username, or in User Principal Name (UPN) format, username@*domainname,* where *domainname* is fully qualified—that is, *domainname.com,* not just *domainname.* If you don't specify a domain component, the credential will be assumed to be an account on the local machine.

> **WARNING** Some cmdlets—such as Get-WmiObject—don't accept credentials when working against the local machine.

If you have a credential you want to use for a local account on a remote machine, use the format COMPUTERNAME\user. In any event, when you specify a string, you'll be graphically prompted for the password, as shown in figure 12.1, which depicts the ISE. You'll see a similar graphical prompt if Get-Credential is called from the PowerShell console.

> **NOTE** The password will be masked as you enter it, to keep it secure.

And before you ask, no, you can't also specify the password on the command line. Doing so would mean including a clear-text password, most likely for an administrator

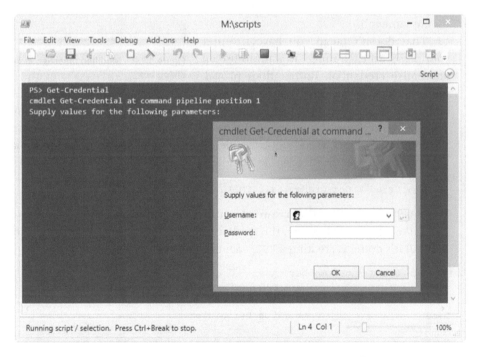

Figure 12.1 Using Get-Credential to get a username and password. The -username parameter can be used to partially complete the credential.

account, right on the command line or in a script. Because that'd be a horrible idea, Microsoft went to some lengths to make it impossible.

PowerShell v3 introduced an extra option to using `Get-Credential`. In PowerShell v2 you could use it with or without supplying a username like this:

```
Get-Credential
Get-Credential -Credential richard
Get-Credential -Credential mymachine\richard
Get-Credential -Credential mydomain\richard
```

That still applies in v3 and v4, but two parameters, –UserName and –Message, are now available that work like this:

```
Get-Credential -Message "Credentials needed for"
```

The message in the dialog box is replaced with the text you supply. Adding the username populates the dialog box, as shown in figure 12.2. This option remains in Power-Shell v4.

Figure 12.2 was generated by using `Get-Credential` from the console. Subtle differences exist between it and figure 12.1, which was generated in the ISE. Both dialog boxes do the same job.

That doesn't mean you have to enter your password each time you want to use an alternative credential. Rather than providing a username, you can create a complete

Figure 12.2 Modified message in credential dialog box

credential object ahead of time, often storing it in a variable. You'll be prompted for your password only once, and then the password will be stored as a secure string inside the credential object. Here's an example of creating, examining, and using a credential object with the `Get-Credential` cmdlet:

```
PS C:\> $cred = Get-Credential COMPANY\DJones
```

You'll be prompted for the password in the same graphical dialog box. Although this looks like a logon dialog box, the cmdlet isn't authenticating or verifying the credentials. All it's doing is creating a `PSCredential` object.

```
PS C:\> $cred | get-member

    TypeName: System.Management.Automation.PSCredential

Name                  MemberType Definition
----                  ---------- ----------
Equals                Method     bool Equals(System.Object obj)
GetHashCode           Method     int GetHashCode()
GetNetworkCredential  Method     System.Net.NetworkCredential GetNetworkC...
GetObjectData         Method     System.Void GetObjectData(System.Runtim...
```

```
GetType                 Method         type GetType()
ToString                Method         string ToString()
Password                Property       System.Security.SecureString Password {g...
UserName                Property       string UserName {get;}
```

When you use the credential, PowerShell will hand it off to Windows and carry out normal security and authentication protocols. As you can see by piping to Get-Member, this is a simple object:

```
PS C:\> $cred
UserName                                            Password
--------                                            --------
COMPANY\DJones                          System.Security.SecureString
```

Notice that the password isn't accessible in clear text, so it's somewhat safer in the credential object. The password can only be decrypted using the private key, which exists only on the computer where the credential was created. Even if you use the ConvertFrom-SecureString cmdlet, you don't get the plain-text password.

```
PS C:\> convertfrom-securestring $cred.password
01000000d08c9ddf0115d1118c7a00c04fc297eb01000000897b1b8a84101a498e418f03a19
495f000000000002000000000003660000c0000000100000004070c5b1564d0b5e59e355a4c8
a79fcf0000000004800000a000000010000000f77c0a3324fb6a51c52065d7ef21d6cf18000
000163f5bf2d8c230fab1053846c98cfa957e9f87f92aec22b214000000caad18fd9f97a94e
3ffa0c36a9cb3312fae1662b
PS C:\>
```

The only way to return the plain-text password is to invoke the GetNetwork-Credential() method:

```
PS C:\> $cred.GetNetworkCredential() | Select username, password
UserName                         Password
--------                         --------
DJones                           P@ssw0rd
```

Now before you start having a panic attack, understand that this command only works in the current session that created the $cred variable. As soon as you close the session, the variable is destroyed. All of this is in memory. If you have PowerShell sessions open and logged on with administrator credentials or saved credential objects, be sure to lock your desktop should you walk away. That should be Common Sense Security 101.

The benefit of all of this fuss with Get-Credential is that by specifying the entire credential object from a command, you won't be prompted for the password again. To use this credential object, provide the variable as the value for any cmdlet that has the –Credential parameter:

```
PS C:\> Get-WmiObject -Class Win32_BIOS -Computer SERVER1 -Credential $cred
```

When the Get-WmiObject cmdlet runs, it'll use the username and password in the $cred variable, not the credentials of the current user. Note that WMI only permits the use of alternative credentials for remote computers. You'll get an error if you try to specify and use a credential against the local machine.

Because security should be a big deal to you and credentials in PowerShell have a few quirks, let's spend a few minutes looking at how to use them.

12.2 *Using credentials*

Here are some tricks and caveats for using credentials:

- When a command targets multiple computers, such as when you specify multiple names to a -ComputerName parameter, whatever credential you provide to the -Credential parameter will be used for every one of the computers. There's no way to specify a different credential for each computer. If you have to do that, run the command one time for each credential you need to provide.

- You can run Get-Credential in your PowerShell profile (the script that runs when PowerShell starts) to have PowerShell create a credential object for you each time the shell starts. Assuming you have the profile store that credential in a variable, it'll be ready to use for as long as you keep that shell session open. This is a useful trick if there's a credential you commonly use. You can create as many credential objects as you need but remember that you'll be prompted for all of those passwords! You'll create a new set of credentials for each session because you can't use them across PowerShell sessions.

- Some commands default to a credential other than the one you opened the shell with. For example, the Active Directory module (included in Windows Server 2008 R2 and later) lets you map PSDrives to Active Directory domains, and you can specify a credential when doing so. When you change to an Active Directory "drive," any Active Directory commands will inherit the credential used to map the drive. This only works for accessing the drive, not if you use the cmdlets against a remote domain. This is meant to be a convenient way of having multiple authenticated connections opened at the same time, without the need to manage credential objects or constantly retype passwords.

- When creating Active Directory accounts, remember the following when adding a password to the account:
  - The Microsoft cmdlets and Active Directory provider can work directly with a secure string.
  - The Quest cmdlets and Active Directory Services Interfaces (ADSI)-based scripts expect a plain string, so it has to be passed as $cred.GetNetwork-Credential().Password.

- It's usually better to create a credential object and use that rather than attempt to create the credential in the call to the cmdlet. So use

```
$cred = Get-Credential
Get-WmiObject -Class Win32_OperatingSystem `
-ComputerName Myserver -Credential $cred
```

instead of

```
Get-WmiObject -Class Win32_OperatingSystem `
-ComputerName Myserver -Credential (Get-Credential)
```

This is because WMI may create the connection with your current credentials before generating the credential and it won't swap to using the new credential. As a result your connection will fail.

- The WMI cmdlets have an -Authentication parameter. This has nothing to do with credentials; it sets the level of Distributed Component Object Model (DCOM) authentication and encryption of DCOM connections.

For the majority of your work in PowerShell, this information should suffice. But sometimes you need to get a little crazy.

12.3 Crazy credentials ideas

We're *constantly* asked if there's any way to save the password so that a script can run some command and pass an alternative credential without anyone needing to type the password again. The general idea is that people want to write some script or tool and then give that to people who don't have permission to do whatever task the script performs. By "encoding" the password inside the script, they feel, they can have the command run without needing to give people the underlying permissions.

Generally speaking, this is a Bad Idea Of Epic Proportions. If you want someone to be able to do something, give them permission to do it. But we know how the real world works, and so we'll entertain this crazy notion and explore how you might do it—but we'll call out the associated risks, too, so that you're making a smart decision.

12.3.1 Packaging your script

First, we suggest using a commercial tool that can package (not compile, although some will use that term) your script into an executable and that enables you to specify alternative credentials. The tool generally encrypts the credentials, and it takes care of running the script under those credentials. This approach has several upsides:

- The password isn't in clear text, although it's encrypted with a static shared secret, which means it's hardly unbreakable. But it should be sufficient to deter most ordinary users.
- Your script can contain any commands, not just ones that offer a -Credential parameter.
- Users running the script won't even necessarily know it's a PowerShell script. Done properly, it'll look like a stand-alone Windows executable.

You'll have to have PowerShell installed on any machine where the packaged script runs, but that's become less of a burden now that PowerShell is a default part of the Windows operating system. Tools that can package scripts in this fashion include PrimalScript and PowerShellStudio (formerly known as PrimalForms) from SAPIEN Technologies (www.sapien.com/software) and PowerGUI (www.powergui.org); there may even be others by the time you read this.

12.3.2 *Saving a credential object*

What if you don't want to use a packager? Well, about the only other option is to save a credential object to disk and then have a script read it back in. This approach does limit you to commands that offer a –Credential parameter, which is far from every command on the planet.

> **TIP** The Start-Process and Invoke-Command cmdlets offer a -Credential parameter; you can use them to run about any other command or script, meaning you could potentially write a "bootstrap" script that launched a second one under alternative credentials.

We've emphasized what a bad idea this is, right? Okay, then here's how you'd do it. Start by creating the password as a secure string and saving it to disk:

```
Read-Host –Prompt "Password" –AsSecureString |
ConvertFrom-SecureString |
Out-File C:\Password.txt
```

The password.txt file (or whatever you name it) will look something like this:

```
PS C:\> get-content .\password.txt
01000000d08c9ddf0115d1118c7a00c04fc297eb010000007471fb40e68f7e488e168bee016
034c8000000000200000000000003660000c0000000100000000348a2572718ecdd58149fbd7fa
887d930000000004800000a00000001000000023ee801dc09d5a2ef1138d153f9a6d6b18000
000b0c6389e4e1919f844b4a3b435be2e9087e2e813ccb2921c14000000d9e7273e09fa337d
6b19d679bad775935705bdc3
```

Safe enough for ordinary users, perhaps. To read that back in and turn it into a credential object, use this:

```
PS C:\> $cred = New-Object -Type System.Management.Automation.PSCredential
⇒    -ArgumentList "username",(Get-Content C:\Password.txt | ConvertTo-
⇒    SecureString)
PS C:\> $cred
UserName                                        Password
--------                                        --------
username                                        System.Security.SecureString
```

That gives you a credential object in $cred, which you can then pass to whatever -Credential parameter you like. The downside? As written, this will all work only on a single computer. When PowerShell performs that encryption, it does so using a locally stored encryption key. Move the script and password file to another machine and it won't work, because the local encryption key will be different.

You can extend this technique by adding the –Key parameter to ConvertFrom-SecureString and ConvertTo-SecureString, supplying your own encryption/decryption key for each. Unfortunately, that puts your encryption key *in clear text for anyone to read,* making it trivial for even an unsophisticated user to decrypt the password. We told you this was a Bad Idea Of Epic Proportions. There isn't any way around it, unless you create some hidden place for encryption keys to live and hope that your users (or an attacker) won't think to look there.

> **NOTE** There's also a free utility called PShellExec that you can look into. It's intended to encode/encrypt a script's contents for more secure execution. Again, it isn't a perfect security mechanism, but you can decide if it's sufficient for your needs.

12.3.3 *Creating a credential without the GUI*

A variation on this theme is to create a credential object without resorting to `Get-Credential`. As easy as it is to use, it does require a graphical component that you may want to skip. Perhaps you want a console-only approach. First, prompt for the username:

```
PS C:\> $username=Read-Host "Enter a username"
Enter a username: mycompany\bill
```

Next, you need a password:

```
PS C:\> $password=Read-Host "Enter the password" -AsSecureString
Enter the password: ***********
```

Finally, create a new `PSCredential` object as you did earlier with the `New-Object` cmdlet:

```
PS C:\> $cred=New-Object System.Management.Automation.PSCredential
$username,$password
PS C:\> $cred
UserName                                              Password
--------                                              --------
Mycompany\bill                            System.Security.SecureString
```

You don't have to specify the username. Perhaps you have a script where you want to use the Domain Administrator account. You might include code like this:

```
$admin="$env:userdomain\Administrator"
$password=Read-Host "Enter the password for $admin" -AsSecureString
$adminCredential=New-Object System.Management.Automation.PSCredential
$admin,$password
```

The `$admin` variable will be the Administrator account from the current user's domain. By using the `%USERDOMAIN%` environment variable, you avoid hardcoding any domain names, which makes this code much easier to reuse.

Or if you want something handy that you can use as a one-liner, ideally something you'll use interactively and not in a script, you can do this:

```
PS C:\> $cred = new-object PSCredential "mydomain\admin",
➥ (convertto-securestring "P@ssw0rd" -AsPlainText -Force)
```

This will create a `PSCredential` object for MyDomain\Admin using the password. Anyone looking over your shoulder would see the password. It'd also be recorded if you're using a transcript. A compromise might be this variation of a previous command:

```
PS C:\> $cred = new-object PSCredential "mydomain\admin",
➥ ( (Read-Host "Enter Password" -AsSecureString)
Enter Password: ********
PS C:\>
```

There's not much benefit to a one-liner other than you might feel pretty cool.

12.3.4 Supporting credentials in your script

One last idea, and perhaps not that crazy at all, is to provide support for alternative credentials in your own scripts. This approach is useful if your script is running cmdlets that support alternative credentials. The following listing shows one way you might tackle this.

Listing 12.1 Supporting alternative credentials in a script

```
#requires -version 3.0                              ⟵   Set PowerShell
[cmdletbinding()]                                    ❶  minimum version
Param (
[Parameter(Position=0,HelpMessage="Enter a computername")]
[string]$computername=$env:COMPUTERNAME,             ❷  Get
[Parameter(Position=1)]                                  parameters
[object]$Credential
)                                                   ⟵
if ($credential -AND ($computername -eq $env:Computername)) {    ❸  Test
  Write-Warning "You can't use credentials for the local computer" ⟵   for local
  Break                                                              machine
}
$command="Get-WmiObject -Class Win32_OperatingSystem `   ❹  Create
-ComputerName $Computername"                         ⟵       command
if ($credential -is [System.Management.Automation.PSCredential]) { ⟵
  Write-Verbose "Using a passed PSCredential object"        ❺  Test is
  $Cred=$credential                                            credential
}
elseif ($credential -is [string]) {
    Write-Verbose "Getting credentials for $credential"   ❻  Get
    $Cred=Get-Credential -Credential $credential      ⟵      credential
}
if ($cred) {
    Write-Verbose "Appending credential to command"   ⟵   Execute
    $command+=" -Credential `$cred"                    ❼  command
}
else {
    Write-Verbose "Executing without credentials"
}
#invoke the command expression
Write-Verbose "Running the WMI command"
Invoke-Expression $command
```

The PowerShell version number ❶ sets the minimum version of PowerShell that can run this script. In this case it can run under version 3.0 or 4.0. The script has a -Credential parameter as well as a -ComputerName parameter ❷.

The script tests whether you're running on the local machine ❸ and reminds you that you can't use alternative credentials on the local machine before stopping. If it's not the local machine, a command is created ❹ that'll be executed using the alternative credentials.

If the value is already a PSCredential object, the script will use it ❺:

```
if ($credential -is [System.Management.Automation.PSCredential]) {
  Write-Verbose "Using a passed PSCredential object"
  $Cred=$credential
}
```

All you're doing is defining a new variable. Otherwise, any value will be treated as a string ❻, which is in turn passed to `Get-Credential`:

```
elseif ($credential -is [string]) {
    Write-Verbose "Getting credentials for $credential"
    $Cred=Get-Credential -credential $credential
}
```

If `$Cred` is defined, then the script runs a WMI command that uses it ❼. Otherwise, it runs without credentials:

```
if ($cred) {
    Write-Verbose "Appending credential to command"
    $command+=" -Credential `$cred"
}
else {
    Write-Verbose "Executing without credentials"
}
#invoke the command expression
Write-Verbose "Running the WMI command"
Invoke-Expression $command
```

12.4 *Summary*

This chapter has covered the basics of credentials in PowerShell, including how to make reusable credential objects and even, if you're bound and determined, how to persist a credential object or password on disk for later reuse. We beg you to be careful with credentials, and if you end up doing something silly and someone discovers your Domain Admin password as a result, well, we warned you.

Regular expressions

13

This chapter covers

- Regular expression syntax
- The `-match` operator
- Regular expressions in `Select-String`
- Regular expressions in the `switch` statement
- The REGEX object

Regular expressions are a powerful and complex language you can use to describe data patterns. Most pattern-based data, including email addresses, phone numbers, IP addresses, and more, can be represented as a "regex," as they're also known.

We need to set some limits for this chapter, because regular expressions are complex enough to deserve their own book. PowerShell uses industry-standard regex syntax and supports the full .NET regular expression library, but we'll only be covering the basics. Most of our focus will be on how PowerShell uses a regex once you've written one. If you'd like to explore regular expressions further, write more complex expressions, or look for a regex that meets a particular need, we recommend one of these two books as a starting place: *Mastering Regular Expressions* by Jeffrey E.F. Friedl (a favorite), and *Regular Expression Pocket Reference* by Tony Stubblebine, both from O'Reilly. You can also visit http://RegExLib.com, a free community repository of regular expressions for specific tasks.

13.1 *Basic regular expression syntax*

A simple regular expression is a literal string. For example, the regular expression "Don" will match any instance of "Don," although in PowerShell such matching is case insensitive by default. Where regular expressions show their power is when you start using wildcards, character classes, and placeholders instead of literal strings. Table 13.1 shows some of the basic syntax, which is also covered in PowerShell's about_regular_expressions help file. We've included some additional comments and clarified a few points.

Table 13.1   Basic regular expression syntax

Regex symbol	Purpose	Example
.	Any single character.	"d.n" would match both "don" and "dan" but not "dean."
[abc]	Matches at least one of the characters in the set enclosed by the square brackets. The comparison is *not* case sensitive.	"d[oae]n" would match "don" and "dan" but wouldn't match "dean," because the string contains an extra letter. It also wouldn't match "din" because "i" isn't in the set.
[a-z]	A shorter way of specifying an entire range of characters or numbers. The comparison is *not* case sensitive.	"d[a-e]n" would match "dan" and "den" but not "don."
[^o]	Matches any character except those in brackets; you can also precede a range with ^ to match any character except one in that range. The comparison is *not* case sensitive.	"d[^e]n" would match both "don" and "dan" but not "den."
^	Indicates that the pattern must start at the beginning of the string.	"^op" would match "operate," because the pattern—"op"—occurs at the start of the string. "Loop" wouldn't be a match, because "op" doesn't happen at the start of the string.
$	Indicates the end of the string in the pattern.	"op$" would match "hop," because "op" occurs at the end of the string. "Hope" wouldn't be a match, because "op" is followed by "e" rather than the end of the string.
*	Matches zero or more instances of the preceding character or character sets.	"g*" would match "bag" and "baggy," because both contain zero or more "g" characters. Be careful here because "baddy" will also be true, because there are zero instances of the character g. Perhaps a better example is matching 2.19 and .76 to "\d*\.\d*," which will match on any number with a decimal point, regardless of whether the decimal point contains a number to its left.

Table 13.1   Basic regular expression syntax *(continued)*

Regex symbol	Purpose	Example
+	Matches one or more repeating instances of the character or character set.	"abc+" would match on all instances of "abc" in a string like "abcDabcEabcF". Often this will give you the same result as using *.
?	Matches exactly zero or one instance of the preceding character or character set.	"g?" would match "bag" and "baggy," because both contain one "g." The fact that "baggy" contains an extra "g" doesn't stop the match. Be careful with this one as well because even if you have zero matches you'll still get a match. Your best approach may be to incorporate a quantifier, which we'll cover later in this chapter.
\	Escapes a character that normally is a regex symbol, treating it as a literal value.	"192\.168" would match "192.168" because the "\." matches a literal period. Conversely, "192.168" would match both "192.168" and "192x168," because the period is matching any single character.

Regular expressions work around the concept of matching: Either the pattern described by the regex matches a given string or it doesn't. If PowerShell has a match, it'll give you $True. We typically use regex matches in IF statements and Where-Object script blocks. You've already seen matching in a simplistic form when you used wildcards. In the filesystem, for example, the wildcard pattern "*.tmp" would match all files ending in ".tmp," including "this.tmp" and "that.tmp." Those filesystem wildcards are, in essence, a super-simplified kind of regex.

Typing out all the characters you might want in a match can be tedious, even when using ranges. For that reason, regex syntax includes character classes, several of which are shown in table 13.2. (Although the table isn't a comprehensive list, they're the ones you're most likely to use in PowerShell.) These classes stand in for any character contained within that class.

Table 13.2   Regular expression classes

Regex symbol	Purpose	Example
\w	Any word character, including any letter, number, or underscore, but not most punctuation and no whitespace.	"\w*" would match "Hello." It would also match "Hello There," because it would match the "Hello" portion before stopping at the space between the two words.
\s	Any whitespace, including tabs, carriage returns, and spaces.	"\s" would match the space between the two words in "Hello There." Reducing the comparison to "Hello" wouldn't match because there isn't any whitespace, even though "Hello " does match.
\d	Any digit—that is, numbers 0 through 9.	"\d" would match "10." It would also match the digits in "12 Monkeys" but wouldn't match "Zebras" at all.

Table 13.2   Regular expression classes *(continued)*

Regex symbol	Purpose	Example
\W	Match anything except a word character.	It would match on the spaces in " jeff" but not on "jeff."
\S	Match anything except a space character. This includes tabs.	Note that `"Hello " -match "\S"` `"Hello " -match "\S"` `"` `tHello" -match "\S"` all return TRUE because a nonspace character could be found. The matching character will be the H. We'll explain the `-match` operator in a moment.
\D	Match anything except a digit character.	The string "P0w3rShell" will match on everything except the 0 and 3.

The three examples for the \S regex symbol are where PowerShell is case sensitive, without being explicitly told to behave that way. The uppercase versions of those classes represent the "opposite," that is, anything that isn't contained in the class.

You can see from these class examples that it's not always sufficient to know that *some portion of a string has matched* your regex; you may also need to know that no portion of the string failed to match, or you may need to know which part of the string matched your expression. Those are somewhat trickier tasks, and we'll analyze them in some of the examples later in this chapter.

One way to be more precise with your expressions is to use quantifiers. The major ones are listed in table 13.3.

Table 13.3   Basic regular expression quantifiers

Regex symbol	Purpose	Example
*	Match zero or more instances.	"\w*" matches "hello."
+	Match repeating patterns of the preceding characters.	"xy\d+" would match "xy7xy6."
?	Match zero or one of the preceding characters.	"\w?" would match the "x" in "7x24."
{n}	Match exactly that many times.	"a{2}" would match "aa" but not "a."
{n,}	Match at least that many times, but also match more.	"a{2,} would match "aa" and "aaa" but not "a."
{n,m}	Match at least that many times (n) and no more than this many times (m).	"a{2,3}" would match "aa" and "aaa" but not "a." But it will also match "aaaa," because the match contains at least two characters but not more than three. The match will be on the first three characters. This is where anchors come in handy, for example, "^a{2,3}$."

Parentheses can also be used to group subexpressions. For example, "(\d{1,3}\.){3}" would match "192.168.12." because the group contains one to three digits followed by a period repeated three times. There'd be no match on "192.168." But be careful because "192.168.12.1.1" will also match unless you use an anchor like "^(\d{1,3}\.){3}$." where you force the match to occur at the beginning of the string.

13.2   *The –match operator*

PowerShell's -match operator, its case-sensitive -cmatch version, and the logical opposites -notmatch and -cnotmatch (case-insensitive versions -imatch and –inotmatch also exist but aren't used much because PowerShell is case insensitive by default) all use regular expressions. The left side of the operator is a string to test, whereas the right side is the regex to test against. If you match a single string, the result is $True if there's a match and $False if there's no match. In addition, PowerShell autopopulates a collection called $matches with the matches it's detected. Using that collection, you can see exactly what PowerShell matched against, for example:

```
PS C:\> 'don' -match '\w'
True
PS C:\> $matches
Name                           Value
----                           -----
d
```

In the previous example, you can see that "don" does match the regex "\w" and, more specifically, that it was the first letter, "d," that made the match.

You can also match multiple strings, in which case the result of the operator is a collection of the strings that matched:

```
PS C:\> 'one','two','three' -match '\w{3}'
one
two
three
```

When used in this fashion, $matches isn't populated. Looking at that example carefully, you might be surprised to see "three" in the output. There's the tricky bit of a regex. It was the "thr" that matched the regex, which in turn caused the entire string to output. If you want to have three characters and then the end of the string, use the $ anchor:

```
PS C:\> 'one','two','three' -match '\w{3}$'
one
two
three
```

Whoops—that time it matched the "ree" in "three." Let's also add the ^ anchor:

```
PS C:\> 'one','two','three' -match '^\w{3}$'
one
two
```

There you go. This illustrates the difficulty of working with regular expressions—you have to be careful to make sure they're rejecting the right data, as well as matching the right data. For example, see if you think this is a legitimate regex for a Universal Naming Convention (UNC) path such as \\Server\Share\Folder\File.txt:

```
PS C:\> '\\server\share\folder\file.txt' -match '\\\\\w+([\w\.]\\+)'
True
```

Seems fine, but let's try a deliberately malformed UNC:

```
PS C:\> 'x\\server\share\folder\file.txt' -match '\\\\\w+([\w\.]\\+)'
True
```

That shouldn't have matched, so you clearly need to tweak it:

```
PS C:\> 'x\\server\share\folder\file.txt' -match '^\\\\\w+([\w\.]\\+)'
False
```

And now you can make sure the original, valid UNC still works:

```
PS C:\> '\\server\share\folder\file.txt' -match '^\\\\\w+([\w\.]\\+)'
True
```

Again, these can be tricky. Can you think of any other ways to fool this regex or to improve it? Let's break down what it's doing in table 13.4.

Table 13.4 Deconstructing a regex

Regex pattern	Purpose
^	Anchors the start of the pattern to the start of a string, ensuring no characters can come before the leading \\.
\\\\	Matches the leading \\ in the UNC. Keep in mind that \ is a special character in regex syntax, so you have to double them up to "escape" them.
\w+	Matches one or more word characters—this is what picks up the server name in the UNC.
(	Starts a repeating pattern.
[\w\.]	Accepts a word character or a period.
\\	Followed by a backslash.
+	One or more times.
)	Ending the repetition.

Breaking it down like that, we suspect other problems may exist with it. You won't always end a UNC in a backslash, for example. Maybe the following would be better?

```
PS C:\> '\\server\share\folder\file.txt' -match '^\\\\\w+([\w\.\\]+)+'
True
```

We'll leave it to you to decipher and decide if you can improve on it. For what it's worth, the online regex library we use documents at least five regular expressions designed to detect various kinds of file paths, including UNCs: http://regexlib.com/ Search.aspx?k=unc&c=2&m=-1&ps=20. That reinforces how tricky a regex can be to write.

> **TIP** Even if you decide to write your own regex, it's always worth checking regexlib.com to determine if there's a more efficient way.

13.3 *The Select-String cmdlet*

The Select-String cmdlet is designed to look through a bunch of data, finding data that matches a pattern you provide. You can pipe in strings or, better yet, point the command to a directory full of files. Here's one example, which searches for all files containing the word "shell":

```
PS C:\Windows\System32\WindowsPowerShell\v1.0\en-US> Select-String -Pattern
    "shell" -SimpleMatch -Path *.txt -List
about_Aliases.help.txt:6:      PowerShell.
about_Arithmetic_Operators.help.txt:5:      Describes the operators that
perform arithmetic in Windows PowerShell.
about_Arrays.help.txt:9:     of the same type. Windows PowerShell supports
data elements, such as
about_Assignment_Operators.help.txt:13:     Windows PowerShell supports
the following assignment operators.

<display truncated for brevity>
```

This example used the command's –SimpleMatch parameter, which tells it to treat the pattern not like a regex but like a text string. As you can see, it lists all files with a match, the matching line number, and the matching line itself. Now try this with a regex:

```
PS C:\Windows\System32\WindowsPowerShell\v1.0\en-US> Select-String -Pattern
    "\sGet-\w{4,8}\s" -Path *.txt -List
about_Aliases.help.txt:89:          get-help about_profile
about_Arithmetic_Operators.help.txt:397:C:\PS> get-date + $day
about_Arrays.help.txt:50:    Microsoft .NET Framework. For example, the
    objects that Get-Process
about_Assignment_Operators.help.txt:113:          $a = get-service | sort
    name

<display truncated for brevity>
```

You asked for matches on a pattern that specified a space, "Get-," and four to eight characters followed by another space. These are only partial results; run the command on your own—in the same directory used here—to see the full list.

A variety of other parameters are available on the command to customize its behavior further, and it's a great way to (for example) scan through text log files looking for a particular pattern of characters.

13.4 *The Switch statement*

You can also use regular expressions in the `Switch` statement. You'll use the `-regex` parameter to indicate this. Consider the example in the following listing.

```
'abcd', 'Abcd', 'abc1', '123a', '!>@#' |
foreach {
 switch -regex -case ($_){
  "[a-z]{4}" {"[a-z]{4} matched $_"}
  "\d"    {"\d matched $_"}
  "\d{3}" {"\d{3} matched $_"}
  "\W"    {"\W matched $_"}
  default {"Didn't match $_"}
 }
}
```

Which of the input strings didn't match?

The tests can be decoded as follows:

- "[a-z]{4}" means match four characters, each of which is a letter in the range a to z.
- "\d" means match a digit.
- "\d{3}" means match three digits.
- "\W" means match a non-word character.

When we tested this code we received the following output:

```
[a-z]{4} matched abcd
Didn't match Abcd
\d matched abc1
\d matched 123a
\d{3} matched 123a
\W matched !>@#
```

Why didn't "Abcd" match? At a PowerShell prompt it works:

```
PS C:\> "Abcd" -match "[a-z]{4}"
True
```

So why did it not match in our code snippet? The catch is that we also used the `-case` parameter in the `Switch` statement. It makes the matches case sensitive, which is the equivalent of doing the following:

```
PS C:\> "Abcd" -cmatch "[a-z]{4}"
False
```

The next listing shows one more example that might be a bit more practical.

```
$Computername="LON-DC01"
Switch -regex ($Computername) {
```

```
"^SYR"  {
    #run Syracuse location code
    }
"^LAS"  {
    #run Las Vegas location code
    }
"^LON"  {
    #run London location code
    }
"DC"  {
    #run Domain controller specific code
    }
"FP"  {
    #run file/print specific code
    }
"WEB"  {
    #run IIS specific code
    }
Default {Write-Warning "No code found $computername"}
}
```

Listing 13.2 contains a code excerpt from something you might want to do. The Switch statement will evaluate the $computername variable using a series of regular expression patterns. Wherever there's a match, the corresponding script block will execute. In the example, this would mean PowerShell would run any code specific to the London location and the domain controller role, assuming our servers follow a standard naming convention.

13.5   *The REGEX object*

Most of the time simple matching or not matching is sufficient. But regular expressions have some special capabilities such as finding all the matches in a string or replacing matched text. To accomplish these tasks you need to create a REGEX object. The easiest approach is to use the [regex] type accelerator with a regular expression pattern. Start with something simple:

```
PS C:\> [regex]$rx="Don"
```

Piping the object to Get-Member reveals some interesting possibilities:

```
PS C:\> $rx | get-member

    TypeName: System.Text.RegularExpressions.Regex

Name                   MemberType Definition
----                   ---------- ----------
Equals                 Method     bool Equals(System.Object obj)
GetGroupNames          Method     string[] GetGroupNames()
GetGroupNumbers        Method     int[] GetGroupNumbers()
GetHashCode            Method     int GetHashCode()
GetType                Method     type GetType()
GroupNameFromNumber    Method     string GroupNameFromNumber(int i)
GroupNumberFromName    Method     int GroupNumberFromName(string name)
IsMatch                Method     bool IsMatch(string input), bool IsMatch(...
```

```
Match              Method      System.Text.RegularExpressions.Match Matc...
Matches            Method      System.Text.RegularExpressions.MatchColle...
Replace            Method      string Replace(string input, string repla...
Split              Method      string[] Split(string input), string[] Sp...
ToString           Method      string ToString()
Options            Property    System.Text.RegularExpressions.RegexOptio...
RightToLeft        Property    System.Boolean RightToLeft {get;}
```

Don't use the REGEX object with -Match. Instead, invoke the Match() method. With this object, case matters:

```
PS C:\> $rx.Match("don")

Groups    : {}
Success   : False
Captures  : {}
Index     : 0
Length    : 0
Value     :

PS C:\> $rx.Match("Don")
Groups    : {Don}
Success   : True
Captures  : {Don}
Index     : 0
Length    : 3
Value     : Don

PS C:\> $rx.Match("Richard")
Groups    : {}
Success   : False
Captures  : {}
Index     : 0
Length    : 0
Value     :
```

The object writes a new object to the pipeline. The Match() method returns an object only on the first match. Look at the following:

```
PS C:\> $rx.Match("Let me introduce Don Jones. Don is a PowerShell MVP")
Groups    : {Don}
Success   : True
Captures  : {Don}
Index     : 17
Length    : 3
Value     : Don
```

If you want to identify all of the matches of "Don," use the Matches() method:

```
PS C:\> $rx.Matches("Let me introduce Don Jones. Don is a PowerShell MVP")
Groups    : {Don}
Success   : True
Captures  : {Don}
Index     : 17
Length    : 3
Value     : Don
```

```
Groups    : {Don}
Success   : True
Captures  : {Don}
Index     : 28
Length    : 3
Value     : Don
```

This code will write a `Match` object for each match.

13.5.1 *Replacing with REGEX*

Where this gets even more interesting is when it comes time to replace matched text:

```
PS C:\> $rx.Replace("Let me introduce Don Jones. Don is a PowerShell
➥ MVP","Donald")
Let me introduce Donald Jones. Donald is a PowerShell MVP
```

The REGEX object replaces all the matching instances of the pattern "Don" in the string with "Donald."

The `Replace()` method from the String object as well as the `–Replace` operator are using regular expressions under the hood. You can use regular expression patterns:

```
PS C:\> "172.16.10.12" -replace "\d{3}","XXX"
XXX.16.10.12
```

13.5.2 *Splitting with REGEX*

Another technique we want to show with the REGEX object is splitting data on the regular expression match. Let's say you want to parse the contents of the Windows Update log. The log contains lines like the following:

```
$s="2012-03-14 18:57:35:321 1196 13f8 PT  Server URL =
➥ http://172.16.10.1/SimpleAuthWebService/SimpleAuth.asmx"
```

Suppose you want to split this line on the time stamp value (18:57:35:321) so you construct a REGEX object:

```
[regex]$r="\d{2}:\d{2}:\d{2}:\d{3}"
```

In order to split, it has to match, so you'll test:

```
PS C:\> $r.match($s)
Groups    : {18:57:35:321}
Success   : True
Captures  : {18:57:35:321}
Index     : 11
Length    : 12
Value     : 18:57:35:321
```

Excellent. Now you can split the string on the pattern match:

```
PS C:\> $r.split($s)
2012-03-14
 1196 13f8 PT  Server URL =
➥  http://172.16.10.1/SimpleAuthWebService/SimpleAuth.Asmx
```

The second line in the previous example is wrapping, but it worked. Notice that the matching data is gone. That happens because you used that as the split "character" so all you're left with is everything before it, the date, and everything after it. Depending on your pattern, you may have extra spaces to take care of, but that's simple to fix:

```
PS C:\> $a=$r.split($s) | foreach {$_.trim()}
PS C:\> $a[1]
1196 13f8 PT  Server URL =
➥ http://172.16.10.1/SimpleAuthWebService/SimpleAuth.aSmx
```

The `Trim()` method deletes any leading or trailing spaces from the string. Extending this to the entire file, you can split each line and save the second part to a variable:

```
PS C:\> $data=get-content C:\windows\WindowsUpdate.log |
➥   foreach {$r.split($_)[1].Trim()}
```

You can then do whatever you want with `$data`. We'll come back to the Windows Update log in a moment.

13.6 *Subexpressions and named captures*

The last item we want to demonstrate with regular expressions and PowerShell is the ability to use subexpressions and named captures. Consider this simple example:

```
PS C:\> "aaa 123 bbb 456" -match "\d{3}"
True
PS C:\> $matches

Name                      Value
----                      -----
0                         123
```

The `-Match` operator found the first three-digit match. A subexpression, at its simplest, is the pattern wrapped in parentheses:

```
PS C:\> "aaa 123 bbb 456" -match "(\d{3})"
True
PS C:\> $matches

Name                      Value
----                      -----
1                         123
0                         123
```

One subtle but important change is that the `Match` object has two values now. One of them is for the subexpression:

```
PS C:\> "aaa 123 bbb 456" -match "(\d{3}) (\w{3})"
True
PS C:\> $matches

Name                      Value
----                      -----
2                         bbb
1                         123
0                         123 bbb
```

Now we have subexpression matches for numbers and text. Let's take the next step and use a REGEX object so we can capture everything:

```
PS C:\> [regex]$rx = "(\d{3}) (\w{3})"
PS C:\> $m =$rx.Matches("aaa 123 bbb 456")
PS C:\> $m

Groups    : {123 bbb, 123, bbb}
Success   : True
Captures  : {123 bbb}
Index     : 4
Length    : 7
Value     : 123 bbb
PS C:\> $m.groups

Groups    : {123 bbb, 123, bbb}
Success   : True
Captures  : {123 bbb}
Index     : 4
Length    : 7
Value     : 123 bbb

Success   : True
Captures  : {123}
Index     : 4
Length    : 3
Value     : 123

Success   : True
Captures  : {bbb}
Index     : 8
Length    : 3
Value     : bbb
```

If we wanted to get the match of just the letters or numbers, that gets a little tricky. Fortunately, the solution is to use a named capture. All you need to do is to define a name for your capture like this:

```
PS C:\>  "aaa 123 bbb 456" -match "(?<word>\w{3}) (?<num>\d{3})"
True
```

Now for the cool part. The Match object now shows these names:

```
PS C:\> $matches

Name                           Value
----                           -----
word                           aaa
num                            123
0                              aaa 123
```

We can get the name we want like this:

```
PS C:\> $matches.num
123
PS C:\> $matches.word
aaa
```

When a REGEX object is used, you have to access the matches using the defined names:

```
PS C:\> [regex]$rx="(?<word>\w{3}) (?<num>\d{3})"
PS C:\> $m = $rx.Matches("aaa 123 bbb 456")
```

The tricky part is that $m contains several types of objects:

```
PS C:\> $m | foreach {$_.groups["num"].value}
123
456
PS C:\> $m | foreach {$_.groups["word"].value}
aaa
bbb
```

Here's a more practical example. Suppose you get a string that looks like a UNC and you want to get the server and share name:

```
PS C:\> $p = "\\server01\data"
```

You could split the string on the last \ into an array and know that the server name would be element 0 and the share name element 1. Or you could use a named capture:

```
PS C:\> $p -match "^\\\\(?<server>\w+)\\(?<share>\w+$)"
True
PS C:\> $matches.server
server01
PS C:\> $matches.share
Data
```

Let's end this section by returning to the Windows Update log. Earlier we showed you how to split each line. Because the log file has a known and consistent layout, you can use a regular expression named capture and "objectify" the log file.

> **NOTE** We realize there are other ways to import the log into PowerShell, but this is a log everyone has and serves as a good learning tool.

We'll walk through the process using a sample line from the log:

```
$t = "2014-01-07   10:23:48:211   880   a9c   IdleTmr   Incremented PDC
➥ RefCount for Network to 2"
```

The layout uses the format DATE TIME PID TID COMPONENT TEXT, so you need to define a set of regular expression patterns to capture the various elements:

```
$t -match "(?<Date>\d{4}-\d{2}-\d{2})\s+(?<Time>(\d{2}:)+\d{3})\s+
➥ (?<PID>\d+)\s+(?<TID>\w+)\s+(?<Component>\w+)\s+(?<Message>[.*)"
```

The match result shows success:

```
PS C:\> $matches

Name                      Value
----                      -----
Message                   Incremented PDC RefCount for Network to 2
Time                      10:23:48:211
Date                      2014-01-07
Component                 IdleTmr
```

```
PID                     880
TID                     a9c
1                       48:
0                       2014-01-07    10:23:48:211    880    a9c...
```

Now let's use the REGEX object:

```
[regex]$rx = "(?<Date>\d{4}-\d{2}-\d{2})\s+(?<Time>(\d{2}:)+\d{3})\s+
➥ (?<PID>\d+)\s+(?<TID>\w+)\s+(?<Component>\w+)\s+(?<Message>.*)"
```

An advantage with this approach is that you can identify the names:

```
PS C:\> $rx.GetGroupNames()
0
1
Date
Time
PID
TID
Component
Message
```

The first two aren't our names, so they can be filtered out:

```
$names = $rx.GetGroupNames() | where {$_ -match "\w{2}"}
```

For our proof of concept, we'll get the first five lines of the log file:

```
$t = get-content C:\windows\WindowsUpdate.log | select -first 5
```

The variable $t is a collection of five lines that need to be "decoded" individually:

```
$data = $t | foreach {
    $rx.Matches($_) | foreach {
      $match = $_
      $names | foreach -begin {$hash=[ordered]@{}} -process {
       $hash.Add($_,$match.groups["$_"].value)
      } -end { [pscustomobject]$hash}
      }
}
```

In the code we get all the matches using the REGEX object. Each match is then processed using a nested ForEach-Object loop to get the corresponding named match. Each match is added to an ordered hash table that's using the Name as the key and Match as the value. After processing all names, PowerShell writes a custom object to the pipeline using the hash table. Everything is saved to $data.

```
PS C:\> $data

Date      : 2014-01-20
Time      : 00:45:08:210
PID       : 1112
TID       : 24b4
Component : Report
Message   : WARNING: CSerializationHelper:: InitSerialize failed :
            0x80070002
```

```
Date      : 2014-01-20
Time      : 00:45:08:211
PID       : 1112
TID       : 24b4
Component : Report
Message   : CWERReporter::Init succeeded
Date      : 2014-01-20
Time      : 00:45:08:211
PID       : 1112
TID       : 24b4
Component : Agent
Message   : ********** Agent: Initializing Windows Update Agent
            **********
Date      : 2014-01-20
Time      : 00:45:08:211
PID       : 1112
TID       : 24b4
Component : Agent
Message   : * Found 2 persisted download calls to restore
Date      : 2014-01-20
Time      : 00:45:08:212
PID       : 1112
TID       : 24b4
Component : DnldMgr
Message   : Download manager restoring 1 downloads
```

Because everything is now an object, the log file can be viewed any way you want:

```
PS C:\> $data | where component -eq 'agent' |
    select Date,Time,Message | format-table –AutoSize -Wrap

Date       Time         Message
----       ----         -------
2014-01-20 00:45:08:211 ********** Agent: Initializing Windows
                        Update Agent **********
2014-01-20 00:45:08:211 * Found 2 persisted download calls to restore
```

You could use these techniques for just about any log file.

13.7 Summary

Remember, the REGEX object is based on a regular expression pattern that can be as complicated as necessary. Be careful to watch how matches are made and be sure to test for failures as well when developing a regular expression.

> **TIP** Don't try to reinvent the wheel. Visit sites like Regexlib.com to look for a pattern that someone has already developed. In most cases you can use the pattern as is in your PowerShell scripting.

Regular expressions are, no question, a complex language all their own. We've briefly touched on the main ways in which PowerShell uses them, as well as on the basics of regex syntax, including the REGEX object. We know there's more to regex than we could cover in this chapter, and if you'd like to explore them further, please check out the resources we mentioned in the beginning of the chapter.

Working with HTML and XML data

14

This chapter covers

- Working with HTML
- Creating HTML output
- Persisting data with XML
- Working with XML files

PowerShell includes some great capabilities for working with two common forms of structured data: HTML and XML. Why is this important? Because HTML is a great way to produce professional-looking reports and you can use XML in so many places within your environment. If you use PowerShell, the help, format, and type files are XML. The "cmdlet over objects" functionality introduced in PowerShell v3 is based on XML. The HTML- and XML-related functionality hasn't had any major changes in PowerShell v4. We'll cover the various capabilities and provide some concise examples of how you might want to use them.

14.1 Working with HTML

HTML—the Hypertext Markup Language—is a similar-to-XML language used to construct the content for web pages. Like XML, HTML documents consist of sets of nested tags, which form a document hierarchy:

```
<Body>
  <H1>This is a heading</H1>
  <p>This is some text</p>
</Body>
```

A full discussion of HTML and all its many features is beyond the scope of this book, but you can find some excellent tutorials at www.w3schools.com/html/ if you want to learn more. PowerShell v3 introduced unique new ways to work with HTML, which we'll cover in this chapter.

14.1.1 *Retrieving an HTML page*

Your first step will be to get some HTML into the shell. To do that, you'll ask Power-Shell to retrieve a page from a web server, in much the same way that a web browser would do the same task. PowerShell won't draw, or *render,* the page, but it'll let you work with the raw HTML.

> **NOTE** In this chapter we're concerned with the HTML only. In chapter 40 you'll learn more about using `Invoke-WebRequest` and other web-based cmd-lets for interacting with websites and web services.

PowerShell v3 introduced this cmdlet, which you can use with the following command:

```
PS C:\> $html = Invoke-WebRequest -uri http://bing.com
```

Nice and simple. The `Invoke-WebRequest` command has a lot of additional parameters that you can use, many of which require a bit of understanding into how HTTP requests are formed and sent to a web server. Let's review a few of the major ones:

- `-Credential` lets you attach a credential to the request, which is useful when you're accessing a server that requires authentication.
- `-Headers` is a dictionary (or hash table) of request headers that need to be sent. This can include any valid HTTP headers—a full list of which is outside the scope of this book, but http://en.wikipedia.org/wiki/List_of_HTTP_headers contains a list of valid options.
- `-MaximumRedirection` lets you specify the maximum number of times your request can be redirected from one server to another before the request fails.
- `-Method` specifies the type of request you're sending, and you'll usually specify either GET or POST. GET is the default and lets you use URLs that have embedded parameters, such as the following:

  http://www.bing.com/search?q=cmdlet&go=&qs=n&form=QBLH&pq=cmdlet& sc=8-6&sp=-1&sk=
- `-OutFile` accepts a file path and name and saves the resulting HTML to that file. This creates a static, local copy of the web page you requested. In our example, we captured the HTML to a variable instead.
- `-Proxy` accepts the URI for an HTTP proxy server, which will proxy the request for you. Depending on your network, you may need to also use `-ProxyCredential` or `-ProxyUseDefaultCredentials` to specify credentials for the proxy server.

- -UseBasicParsing is necessary when you're running the command on a computer that doesn't have Internet Explorer (IE) installed, such as on Server Core computers. This causes the command to skip the HTML Document Object Model (DOM) parsing, because IE is needed to perform that step.

- -UserAgent lets you specify a custom user agent string for the request. Web servers use this to identify the type of web browser you're using, and they may change their content based on this value. For example, mobile browsers might get different content than a desktop browser. The user agent string for IE11 on Windows 8.1 is "R" "Mozilla/5.0 (Windows NT 6.3; Trident/7.0; rv:11.0) like Gecko".

Those parameters will get you through basic requests to most websites. Things get tricky when you need to automate several back-and-forth requests with a web server; we'll cover this in detail in chapter 40. Typically, web servers send your browser a small piece of data called a *cookie*, which is used to identify your particular browser to the server.

NOTE   Cookie use in Europe is diminishing as a result of recent legislation.

That way, the server can, for example, maintain the state of things like a shopping cart. PowerShell isn't a web browser, though, and doesn't automatically handle cookies like a web browser would. So each request the shell sends is a fresh new relationship with the server, and that might not work for some scenarios.

Invoke-WebRequest does have the ability to maintain state information—you have to help it to do so. Two parameters, -SessionVariable and -WebSession, support this capability. You'll use one or the other but never both.

You'll generally use -SessionVariable when you're sending an initial, or first, request to the server. For example, if you're retrieving a server's login page, use this:

```
PS C:\> $r = Invoke-WebRequest http://www.facebook.com/login.php
➥ -SessionVariable fb
```

This code will result in the creation of a variable $fb as the session variable. PowerShell will populate $fb with a WebRequestSession object, and you'll use that for subsequent requests sent to that server. To do this, you'd pass the entire variable to the -WebSession parameter:

```
PS C:\> $r = Invoke-WebRequest http://whatever.com -WebSession $fb
```

NOTE   You'll find a complete walkthrough on how to log into Facebook from PowerShell in the help file for Invoke-WebRequest. It includes examples of how to construct the form contents to submit. We also suggest reading it, because it's a good example of how to maintain a multirequest, back-and-forth conversation with a web server.

14.1.2   Working with the HTML results

On a machine with IE installed, the result of your web request is a parsed HTML document. For example, our request for the home page of Bing.com resulted in the following being stored in our $html variable:

```
PS C:\> $html
StatusCode        : 200
StatusDescription : OK
Content           : <!DOCTYPE html PUBLIC "-//W3C//DTD XHTML 1.0
                    Transitional//EN" "http://www.w3.org/TR/xhtml1/DTD/xht
                    ml1-transitional.dtd"><html lang="en" xml:lang="en"
                    xmlns="http://www.w3.org/1999/xhtml"><head><meta ...
RawContent        : HTTP/1.1 200 OK
                    Connection: keep-alive
                    Content-Length: 32595
                    Cache-Control: private, max-age=0
                    Content-Type: text/html; charset=utf-8
                    Date: Tue, 13 Mar 2013 17:55:21 GMT
                    P3P: CP="NON UNI COM NAV...
Forms             : {sb_form}
Headers           : {[Connection, keep-alive], [Content-Length, 32595],
                    [Cache-Control, private, max-age=0], [Content-Type,
                    text/html; charset=utf-8]...}
Images            : {}
InputFields       : {@{innerHTML=; innerText=; outerHTML=<INPUT
                    id=sb_form_q title="Enter your search term"
                    class=sw_qbox name=q autocomplete="off">; outerText=;
                    tagName=INPUT; id=sb_form_q; title=Enter your search
                    term; class=sw_qbox; name=q; autocomplete=off},
                    @{innerHTML=; innerText=; outerHTML=<INPUT tabIndex=0
                    id=sb_form_go title=Search class="sw_qbtn sw_sb"
                    type=submit name=go>; outerText=; tagName=INPUT;
                    tabIndex=0; id=sb_form_go; title=Search;
                    class=sw_qbtn sw_sb; type=submit; name=go},
                    @{innerHTML=; innerText=; outerHTML=<INPUT id=sa_qs
                    type=hidden value=bs name=qs>; outerText=;
                    tagName=INPUT; id=sa_qs; type=hidden; value=bs;
                    name=qs}, @{innerHTML=; innerText=; outerHTML=<INPUT
                    type=hidden value=QBLH name=form>; outerText=;
                    tagName=INPUT; type=hidden; value=QBLH; name=form}}
Links             : {@{innerHTML=Explore ; innerText=Explore ;
                    outerHTML=<A onmousedown="return
                    si_T('&amp;ID=SERP,5002.1')"
                    href="/explore?FORM=BXLH">Explore </A>;
                    outerText=Explore ; tagName=A; onmousedown=return
                    si_T('&amp;ID=SERP,5002.1');
                    href=/explore?FORM=BXLH}, @{innerHTML=Images;
                    innerText=Images; outerHTML=<A
                    onclick="selectScope(this, 'images');"
                    onmousedown="return si_T('&amp;ID=SERP,5013.1')"
                    href="/images?FORM=Z9LH">Images</A>;
                    outerText=Images; tagName=A;
                    onclick=selectScope(this, 'images');;
                    onmousedown=return si_T('&amp;ID=SERP,5013.1');
                    href=/images?FORM=Z9LH}, @{innerHTML=Videos;
                    innerText=Videos; outerHTML=<A
                    onclick="selectScope(this, 'video');"
                    onmousedown="return si_T('&amp;ID=SERP,5014.1')"
                    href="/videos?FORM=Z9LH1">Videos</A>;
                    outerText=Videos; tagName=A;
```

```
                           onclick=selectScope(this, 'video');;
                           onmousedown=return si_T('&amp;ID=SERP,5014.1');
                           href=/videos?FORM=Z9LH1}, @{innerHTML=Shopping;
                           innerText=Shopping; outerHTML=<A
                           onclick="selectScope(this, 'commerce');"
                           onmousedown="return si_T('&amp;ID=SERP,5015.1')"
                           href="/shopping?FORM=Z9LH2">Shopping</A>;
                           outerText=Shopping; tagName=A;
                           onclick=selectScope(this, 'commerce');;
                           onmousedown=return si_T('&amp;ID=SERP,5015.1');
                           href=/shopping?FORM=Z9LH2}...}
ParsedHtml          : System.__ComObject
RawContentLength    : 32595
```

You can see that the resulting object contains the following properties:

- StatusCode—The HTTP status code for our request. A "200" is good news, indicating a successful request.
- StatusDescription—A textual version of the status code.
- Content—The raw, unparsed HTML content.
- RawContent—The entire response, including various headers.
- Forms—A collection of HTML forms on the page (which will be empty if there are no forms).
- Headers—A collection of HTML headers sent with the response.
- Images—A collection of the <IMG> tags from the page.
- InputFields—A collection of the <INPUT> tags from the page.
- Links—A collection of the <A> tags from the page.
- ParsedHTML—A DOM object with the page's tag hierarchy. We're not going to dive into this in detail because it's "developer-y," but if you'd like to explore further, you'll find a decent tutorial at www.javascriptkit.com/javatutors/dom.shtml.
- RawContentLength—The number of bytes in the response.

Of this set, the StatusCode, Forms, Headers, Images, InputFields, and Links properties are probably the easiest to use. StatusCode states the obvious; the others are all collections of tags. Each tag is presented as an object. For example, this is a link:

```
PS C:\> $html.links[0]
innerHTML    : Explore
innerText    : Explore
outerHTML    : <A onmousedown="return si_T('&amp;ID=SERP,5002.1')"
               href="/explore?FORM=BXLH">Explore </A>
outerText    : Explore
tagName      : A
onmousedown  : return si_T('&amp;ID=SERP,5002.1')
href         : /explore?FORM=BXLH
```

As you can see, there are subproperties for the link's HTML, text, destination URL, and so forth. This means you could create a list of all destination URLs on this page, as follows:

```
PS C:\> $links = $html.links | select -expand href
PS C:\> $links
/explore?FORM=BXLH
/images?FORM=Z9LH
/videos?FORM=Z9LH1
/shopping?FORM=Z9LH2
/news?FORM=Z9LH3
/maps/?FORM=Z9LH4
/travel/?cid=homenav&amp;FORM=Z9LH5
/entertainment?FORM=Z9LH6
/profile/history?FORM=Z9LH7
```

This technique created a collection of simple String objects, making it easy to enumerate through those, if you wanted to do so for some reason. Similarly, let's look at the one and only form on the page:

```
PS C:\> $html.forms[0] | format-list *

Id     : sb_form
Method : get
Action : /search
Fields : {[sb_form_q, ], [sb_form_go, ], [sa_qs, bs], [form, QBLH]}
```

This tells us there's a form named sb_form, which uses the GET request method, submits to a page called /search, and contains four form fields.

Obviously, one of the big tricks in working with HTML is to understand HTML itself, which isn't something we're going to teach you in this book. PowerShell only provides a means of getting to the HTML data, once you know what it is you're working with.

14.1.3 Practical example

As a simple yet practical example, you'll write a command that searches Bing.com for the term "cmdlet" and returns the URLs for the top 10 results:

```
PS C:\> Invoke-WebRequest -uri 'http://www.bing.com/search?q=cmdlet&
➥ form=APMCS1' | select -expand links | select -expand href -first 10
/?scope=web&amp;FORM=Z9FD
/images/search?q=cmdlet&amp;FORM=BIFD
/videos/search?q=cmdlet&amp;FORM=BVFD
/shopping/search?q=cmdlet&amp;mkt=en-US&amp;FORM=BPFD
/news/search?q=cmdlet&amp;FORM=BNFD
/maps/default.aspx?q=cmdlet&amp;mkt=en-US&amp;FORM=BYFD
/explore?q=cmdlet&amp;FORM=BXFD
http://www.msn.com/
http://mail.live.com/
```

Being able to easily send web requests and deal with the results opens up a wide range of possibilities in PowerShell. This capability was available in earlier versions of the shell but required you to use low-level .NET Framework classes that are now nicely wrapped up into a single handy cmdlet.

14.1.4 *Creating HTML output*

PowerShell can also create HTML output from almost any command (except commands that produce no output, or the `Format-` commands, which produce a specialized form of output). Here's a simple example:

```
PS C:\> Get-Service | where Status -eq 'Running' | ConvertTo-HTML |
    Out-File RunningServices.html
```

This code produces the HTML shown in figure 14.1. You can open the HTML file by passing its path to `Invoke-Item`:

```
PS C:\> Invoke-Item -Path ./RunningServices.html
```

> **TIP** Any file that's linked to an application through a file association can be opened using `Invoke-Item`. This includes Word documents, Excel spreadsheets, TXT files (Notepad), or CSV files (Excel).

Figure 14.1 shows a simple HTML table, but you can tweak it quite a bit. Notice that we explicitly needed to pipe the HTML content to `Out-File` in order to get it into a file;

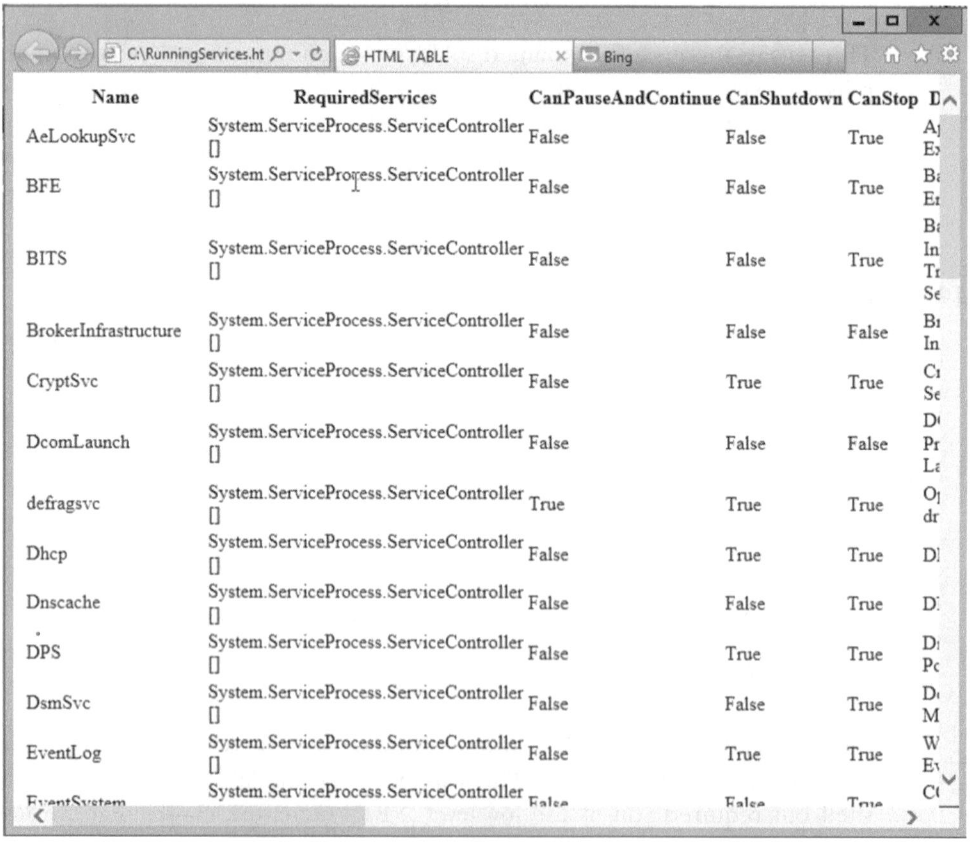

Figure 14.1 `ConvertTo-HTML` **creates simple HTML tables from the command output.**

the `ConvertTo` verb changes the format of something (to HTML in this case), but it leaves the converted data in the shell's pipeline.

The `ConvertTo-HTML` command has a number of useful parameters:

- `-Property` lets you specify the properties you want displayed. You could also do this by piping the output to `Select-Object` first. If you're bringing data across the network from a remote machine, then filter it when you retrieve the data.

- `-Head` lets you specify HTML-formatted text to be included in the `<HEAD>` section of the final HTML.

- `-Title` lets you specify a title for the page, which will appear in the browser's window title bar. Don't use this and `-Head` at the same time, because they modify the same section of the HTML page and `-Title` will be ignored.

- `-CssUri` lets you specify the URL of a Cascading Style Sheet (CSS) file, which can specify better-looking formatting directives for the page. A browser combines the CSS and HTML to render the final output. Figure 14.2 shows our example HTML page with CSS applied.

- You can use `-PostContent` and `–PreContent` to add textual content after or before the main HTML table constructed by the cmdlet. You can use them to briefly explain what's being shown or add other information to the page.

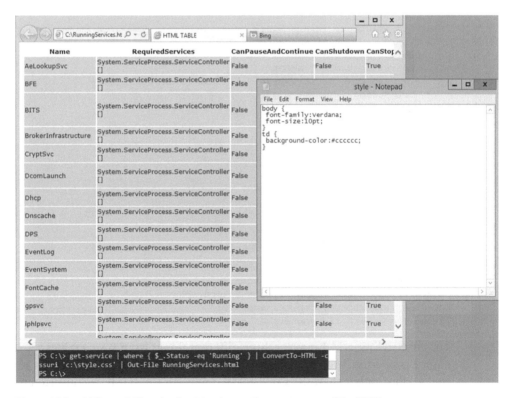

Figure 14.2   Adding a CSS style sheet to change the appearance of the HTML page

ConvertTo-HTML normally produces an entire HTML web page, including the outer <HTML> tags, the initial <HEAD> section, and so forth. But you can also use it to produce only an HTML fragment. Such fragments aren't intended for stand-alone use but can be used to construct a multisection HTML page. Combining it with the –As parameter, which lets you change the output from the default table form into a list, you can create some impressive-looking reports in HTML. The following listing shows an example.

Listing 14.1 Creating an HTML report

```
$computername = 'WIN8'
$b = Get-WmiObject -class Win32_ComputerSystem -Computer $computername |
  Select-Object -Property Manufacturer,Model,
  @{name='Memory(GB)';expression={$_.TotalPhysicalMemory / 1GB -as [int]}},
  @{name='Architecture';expression={$_.SystemType}},
  @{name='Processors';expression={$_.NumberOfProcessors}} |
  ConvertTo-HTML -Fragment -As LIST
  ➥   -PreContent "<h2>Computer Hardware:</h2>" |
  Out-String
$b += Get-WmiObject -class Win32_LogicalDisk -Computer $computername |
    Select-Object -Property @{n='DriveLetter';e={$_.DeviceID}},
    @{name='Size(GB)';expression={$_.Size / 1GB -as [int]}},
    @{name='FreeSpace(GB)';expression={$_.FreeSpace / 1GB -as [int]}} |
    ConvertTo-Html -Fragment -PreContent "<h2>Disks:</h2>" |
    Out-String
$b += Get-WmiObject -class Win32_NetworkAdapter -Computer $computername |
    Where { $_.PhysicalAdapter } |
    Select-Object -Property MACAddress,AdapterType,DeviceID,Name |
    ConvertTo-Html -Fragment
    ➥   -PreContent "<h2>Physical Network Adapters:</h2>" |
    Out-String
$head = @'
<style>
body { background-color:#dddddd;
      font-family:Tahoma;
      font-size:12pt; }
td, th { border:1px solid black;
        border-collapse:collapse; }
th { color:white;
    background-color:black; }
table, tr, td, th { padding: 2px; margin: 0px }
table { margin-left:50px; }
</style>
'@
ConvertTo-HTML -head $head -PostContent $b `
-Body "<h1>Hardware Inventory for $ComputerName</h1>" |
Out-File -FilePath "$computername.html"
Invoke-Item -Path "$computername.html"
```

The code in listing 14.1 queries three different things from WMI, creates some custom output properties, and converts the results to HTML fragments. The first one is created as a list rather than the usual HTML table. All the HTML is converted to a string (Out-String) and appended to a variable, $b.

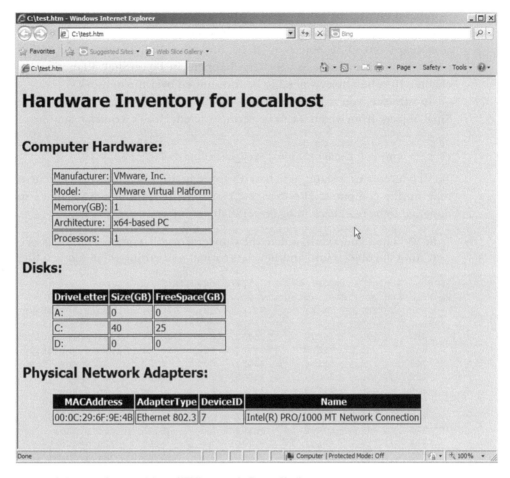

Figure 14.3 Creating a multipart HTML report in PowerShell

The $head variable is created to contain an embedded HTML style sheet, eliminating the need to put the CSS into a separate file. Everything is then fed to ConvertTo-HTML one last time to combine it all into a completed HTML page, which is shown in figure 14.3.

This is a powerful technique and one you can easily expand to include additional sections of information.

14.2 Using XML to persist data

Before we jump into using XML, let's explore a feature of PowerShell that's been available since PowerShell v1—persisting PowerShell data as XML. One common use of XML is to preserve complex, hierarchical data in a simple, text-based format that's easily transmitted across networks, copied as files, and so forth. XML's other advantage is that it can be read by humans if required. Objects, PowerShell's main form of command output, are one common kind of complex, hierarchical data, and a pair of PowerShell cmdlets can help convert objects to and from XML. This process is called *serializing* (converting objects to XML) and *deserializing* (converting XML back into objects), and it's almost exactly what happens in PowerShell Remoting (covered in chapter 10) when objects need to be transmitted over the network.

In this case, you're using XML as a format in which to save the data in the Power-Shell objects, from which it can be reconstructed. Here's a quick example:

```
PS C:\> $proc = Get-Process
PS C:\> $proc | Export-Clixml proc_baseline.xml
```

This code creates a static, text-based representation of the processes currently running on the computer. The Export-Clixml cmdlet produces XML that's specifically designed to be read back in by PowerShell:

> **NOTE**   The Export verb, unlike the ConvertTo verb, combines the acts of converting the objects into another data format *and* writing them out to a file.

```
PS C:\> $rproc = Import-Clixml .\proc_baseline.xml
PS C:\> $rproc | sort -property pm -Descending | select -First 10
```

Handles	NPM(K)	PM(K)	WS(K)	VM(M)	CPU(s)	Id	ProcessName
783	77	336420	285772	819	43.69	2204	powershell
544	41	196500	166980	652	13.41	2660	powershell
348	24	91156	39032	600	1.28	92	wsmprovhost
186	18	52024	35472	170	5.56	716	dwm
329	28	24628	24844	213	0.30	2316	iexplore
311	26	24276	22308	213	0.30	108	iexplore
210	14	20628	26228	69	5.95	1828	WmiPrvSE
1327	41	19608	33164	126	49.45	764	svchost
398	15	19164	21120	56	3.95	728	svchost
722	47	17992	23080	1394	13.45	924	svchost

The previous example demonstrates that the objects are imported from XML and placed, as objects, into the pipeline, where they can again be sorted, selected, filtered, and so forth.

If you now run:

```
PS C:\> $proc | sort -property pm -Descending | select -First 10
```

the data will appear the same whether you use $proc or $rproc. But there are differences. Try:

```
$proc | Get-Member
$rproc | Get-Member
```

Comparing the results shows that $rproc is a Deserialized.System.Diagnostics.Process object and $proc is a System.Diagnostics.Process object, as you'd expect from Get-Process. Deserialized objects are static, and their methods have been removed because they're no longer "live" objects against which actions can be taken. You can see this by comparing the outputs of Get-Member produced earlier. But because XML captures a hierarchy of object data, it's an excellent tool for capturing complex objects.

If you open proc_baseline.xml with Notepad or an XML editor, you'll see that it's incredibly verbose. We don't recommend that you use CliXml for anything but persisting PowerShell objects. If you want to work directly with XML, you need to use the techniques in the following sections.

JSON

PowerShell v3 introduced another potential intermediary form: JavaScript Object Notation (JSON). Two cmdlets are provided:

```
ConvertTo-Json
ConvertFrom-Json
```

When converting a PowerShell object to JSON, properties are converted to field names, the field values are converted to property values, and the methods are removed. This last point is important because it means you end up with an inert object when you convert back. In the CliXML example, you'd get a `Deserialized .System.Diagnostics.Process` object returned—that is, a Process object with the methods removed.

Try performing the same actions with JSON:

```
Get-Process | ConvertTo-Json | ConvertFrom-Json |
sort -property pm -Descending | select -first 10
```

This won't give the same results as the type returned by `ConvertFrom-Json`, which is a `System.Management.Automation.PSCustomObject`, and as such the default formatting for the Process object won't apply.

We recommend using the CliXML format as an intermediary rather than JSON. JSON as an output from web services is covered in chapter 40.

14.3 *XML basics*

PowerShell's XML abilities are no less amazing than its HTML abilities. XML (Extensible Markup Language) is perhaps one of the most useful text-based formats for storing a static copy of data. PowerShell provides rich functionality for working with XML data. Unlike comma-separated values (CSV) files, which can store only "flat" data, XML can store rich, hierarchical representations of data, yet it's still easy to import into the shell, modify, save, attach to emails, and so forth.

It's a little easy to overthink XML, when in fact XML has only a couple of rules. XML isn't technically a language—it's a *grammar*. It's a set of rules—only a couple of rules, really—for creating your own language. In other words, *you* get to make up most of the rules, which makes XML easy to work with. Take a look at this short example of an XML document:

```
<servers>
  <server name="SERVER2">
    <OSVersion>2012R2</OSVersion>
    <BIOS Version="1.2.662" Maker="Dell" />
  </server>
  <server name="SERVER1" />
</servers>
```

Let's walk through some of the important parts, most of which correspond to the official XML rules, and some of which are options that you get to decide on:

- The document starts with a single, top-level, *root element*. In this case, it's the <servers> element. We chose that—there's no rule that made us pick it, and no rule that forced us to make it plural. We could've called it <fred> and the document would still work the same way. But by choosing <servers> we make the document a bit more human-readable. It contains information on servers, and so it makes sense to have the root element indicate that.

- The XML elements, called *tags*, are case sensitive. The tag <Server> isn't the same as <server>.

- All elements have both an opening tag and a closing tag, such as <server> </server>. But it's common to use a *self-closing tag* when the element doesn't contain any information. That's what we chose to do with SERVER1's tag. We could also have written that as <server name="SERVER1"></server> and it'd have been just as valid.

- All elements must be completely nested within their parent. Because <servers> is our root element, everything appears between that opening tag and its closing counterpart. We indented each element a bit so that it was visually clearer to us how the nesting worked, but that indentation is purely for human convenience.

- There are two ways to attach data to an element, and we've used both. In the <OSVersion> element, "2012R2" is the *value of the element*. That's useful when you have only one piece of data that goes with the element. However, for <BIOS>, we included two *attributes,* Version and Maker, and attached values to those. Both approaches are equally valid. In fact, we could've broken the <BIOS> element out as follows:

```
<BIOS>
  <Version>1.2.662</Version>
  <Maker>Dell</Maker>
</BIOS>
```

The only reason we didn't do so is because, from a programming perspective, it's a little easier to use our first approach. We only have to get that <BIOS> element, which is a single operation, and then we get access to its attributes. Using the more expanded approach, we'd have to retrieve each element to access the values. But it's not *that* much extra work—how you decide to go about it is up to you.

TIP The PowerShell ISE "understands" XML. If you create a new document in it, and then save that document with an .xml or .ps1xml filename extension, the ISE will properly color-code the XML. It's a lot easier to work in than, say, Notepad.

For the running example in this chapter, we're going to use the XML in listing 14.2 as a starting point. If you want to follow along, know that we're running our code against two computers: one named MEMBER, and then the local computer, LOCALHOST. If you want to follow along with the chapter, replace LOCALHOST with your local computer name and MEMBER with the name of another computer.

Listing 14.2   ComputerData.xml

```
<computers>
    <computer name='localhost'>
        <biosserial />
        <osversion />
    </computer>
    <computer name='member'>
        <biosserial />
        <osversion />
    </computer>
</computers>
```

14.4 *Reading XML files*

PowerShell makes it easy to import an XML file. Now, we're not talking about the `Import-CliXML` cmdlet here. That cmdlet is designed to read a specific kind of XML—the kind produced by `Export-CliXML`. With that particular XML language, PowerShell makes the rules, and the result isn't meant to be especially human-readable. No, we're talking about importing any ol' XML you want, such as the snippet we offered earlier. Just do this:

```
[xml]$xml = Get-Content C:\ComputerData.xml
```

The `[xml]` part tells PowerShell to parse the text file as an XML document, so if your document isn't properly formed XML, you'll get an error. The resulting XML document is then stored in the `$xml` variable. We could've called that variable anything, but `$xml` seemed reasonable.

  Once you've got the XML document in a variable—and mind you, this is an *XML document* now, not just a big chunk of text—you can start manipulating it. For example, let's say we didn't know in advance how many `<computer>` elements the document contained and we wanted to enumerate them. We could do this in a script:

```
foreach ($computer in $xml.computers.computer) {
  Write-Output " Computer $($computer.name)"
}
```

Here, we've accessed the XML document in `$xml`, asked for the `<computers>` node, and then asked for the collection of `<computer>` nodes. We can access the attributes of a <computer> node by simply referring to it, as we've done with the name attribute. Because we're getting only a single attribute, we could also do something like this:

```
PS C:\> $xml.computers.computer.name
localhost
member
```

What are we enumerating?

Enumerating XML documents can seem a bit confusing. In our sample XML document, the <computers> node contains one or more <computer> child nodes, right? So why didn't we run `foreach ($computer in $xml.computers)`?

The answer requires that you realize XML doesn't restrict child nodes to being of a single type. That is, we could've created a <computers> root node (which we did), and underneath that could have put <client>, <server>, <phone>, and many other types of nodes. So in order to enumerate something—at least, the way PowerShell does it—you specify the kind of node you're enumerating:

```
foreach ($thing in $xml.computers.computer)
```

Or, if you prefer a more abstract example:

```
foreach ($item in $xml.root_node.child_node_type)
```

PowerShell treats the XML document like an object, with each node or tag as a nested object property.

You can also use an *XPath query* to access individual nodes. A full discussion is beyond the scope of this book (although you can find numerous XPath tutorials online, starting at www.w3schools.com), but here's a quick example:

```
$node = $xml.SelectSingleNode("//computer[@name='localhost']")
```

The $node variable will now contain the <computer> node whose name attribute is localhost:

```
PS C:\> $node

name                          biosserial                    osversion
----                          ----------                    ---------
localhost
```

We can also access properties with the new object:

```
PS C:\> $node.name
localhost

PS C:\> $node.osversion
PS C:\>
```

Obviously we're missing some data, so let's correct that.

14.5 *Modifying XML*

Once you have a node, you can modify it easily. Starting with our original example, let's try to populate the BIOS serial numbers, as shown in listing 14.3.

Listing 14.3   Modifying XML data

```
foreach ($computer in $xml.computers.computer) {
    $bios = Get-WmiObject -Class Win32_BIOS -ComputerName ($computer.name)
    $computer.biosserial = $bios.SerialNumber
}
```

Using the code in listing 14.3, we've enumerated the computers, queried each one by using WMI, and inserted the queried BIOS serial number into each computer's <biosserial> node. The resulting XML might look like this:

```
<computers>
  <computer name="localhost">
    <biosserial>VMware-56 4d bb 4e e8 ec 08 e</biosserial>
    <osversion />
  </computer>
  <computer name="member">
    <biosserial>VMware-56 4b d8 09 35 c4 f8 02 21</biosserial>
    <osversion />
  </computer>
</computers>
```

After modifying the XML, we used `$xml.InnerXML` to display the modified XML document, although it won't be as nicely formatted as we show here. Note that this doesn't save the XML back to disk. We've only modified the XML data currently in memory. To update the file, we can run this command, assuming the XML file is in the current directory:

```
$xml.Save(".\ComputerData.xml")
```

So it's easy to modify the existing elements, populating them with data as you see fit. What about adding new ones? Let's create a new element for each computer that shows the computer's manufacturer (listing 14.4).

Listing 14.4   Adding the manufacturer

```
foreach ($computer in $xml.computers.computer) {
    $bios = Get-WmiObject -Class Win32_BIOS -ComputerName ($computer.name)
    $sys = Get-WmiObject -Class Win32_ComputerSystem
➥    -ComputerName ($computer.name)

    $computer.biosserial = $bios.SerialNumber

    $new_node = $xml.CreateNode('element','manufacturer','')
    $new_node.InnerText = $sys.Manufacturer
    $computer.AppendChild($new_node) | Out-Null
}
```

Here's what the resulting XML might look like:

```
<computers>
  <computer name="localhost">
    <biosserial>VMware-56 4d bb 4e e8 ec 08 e</biosserial>
    <osversion />
    <manufacturer>VMware</manufacturer>
  </computer>
  <computer name="member">
    <biosserial>VMware-56 4b d8 09 35 c4 f8 02 21</biosserial>
    <osversion />
    <manufacturer>VMware</manufacturer>
  </computer>
</computers>
```

As you can see, an all-new node has been created for each computer, and we've populated its inner text with the manufacturer value that we queried through the WMI `Win32_ComputerSystem` class.

What about adding a new attribute to an existing element? For example, suppose we wanted to add the operating system build number as an attribute of the `<computer>` element (listing 14.5)?

Listing 14.5   Adding a new element

```
foreach ($computer in $xml.computers.computer) {
    $bios = Get-WmiObject -Class Win32_BIOS -ComputerName ($computer.name)
    $sys = Get-WmiObject -Class Win32_ComputerSystem
    -ComputerName ($computer.name)
    $os = Get-WmiObject -Class Win32_OperatingSystem
    -ComputerName ($computer.name)

    $computer.biosserial = $bios.SerialNumber

    $new_node = $xml.CreateNode('element','manufacturer','')
    $new_node.InnerText = $sys.Manufacturer
    $computer.AppendChild($new_node) | Out-Null

    $attr = $xml.CreateAttribute('build')
    $attr.Value = $os.BuildNumber
    $computer.SetAttributeNode($attr) | Out-Null
}
```

The resulting XML might look like this:

```
<computers>
  <computer build="3900" name="localhost">
    <biosserial>VMware-56 4d bb 4e e8 ec 08 e</biosserial>
    <osversion />
    <manufacturer>VMware</manufacturer>
  </computer>
  <computer build="3900" name="member">
    <biosserial>VMware-56 4b d8 09 35 c4 f8 02 21</biosserial>
    <osversion />
    <manufacturer>VMware</manufacturer>
  </computer>
</computers>
```

Notice that we used Out-Null in two places. That's because the methods SetAttribute-Node() and AppendChild() both produce an output object, and we didn't want to see it. Sending it to null effectively suppresses it. This is a useful technique that you can apply in any place where you want your script to run silently.

14.6 Creating XML

Now all of that's fine if you're starting with an existing XML document. But what about taking data from PowerShell and turning it into XML? Yes, there is Export-CliXML, which is great for storing data you intend to reuse in PowerShell. But the XML from that cmdlet can't be used outside of PowerShell. What you can use instead is ConvertTo-XML.

Like ConvertTo-CSV, ConvertTo-XML takes objects and serializes them:

```
PS C:\> Get-Service | ConvertTo-Xml

xml                                             Objects
---                                             -------
version="1.0"                                   Objects
```

The cmdlet writes an XML document to the pipeline, so you'll need to save it to a variable:

```
PS C:\> $svc = Get-Service | ConvertTo-Xml
PS C:\> $svc.GetType().name
XmlDocument
```

Because the XML is in memory, you can use the techniques we demonstrated earlier in the chapter, including saving the results to a file:

```
PS C:\> $svc.Save("c:\work\services.xml")
```

ConvertTo-Xml will save all data, but usually you only need a subset. In listing 14.6 we're gathering some WMI information from a few computers.

Listing 14.6 Creating an XML document

```
$computers = 'chi-dc01','chi-fp02','chi-dc04'
$data = Get-CimInstance -ClassName Win32_ComputerSystem -ComputerName
    $computers |
Select Name,TotalPhysicalMemory,NumberofProcessors,
NumberofLogicalProcessors,Manufacturer,Model,SystemType |
ConvertTo-Xml -NoTypeInformation
```

You'll notice we used the –NoTypeInformation parameter because we intend to use the resulting XML in something other than PowerShell. Here's what the XML looks like:

```
<?xml version="1.0"?>
<Objects>
  <Object>
    <Property Name="Name">CHI-DC01</Property>
    <Property Name="TotalPhysicalMemory">1073274880</Property>
    <Property Name="NumberofProcessors">1</Property>
    <Property Name="NumberofLogicalProcessors">1</Property>
    <Property Name="Manufacturer">Microsoft Corporation</Property>
```

```
      <Property Name="Model">Virtual Machine</Property>
      <Property Name="SystemType">x64-based PC</Property>
    </Object>
    <Object>
      <Property Name="Name">CHI-FP02</Property>
      <Property Name="TotalPhysicalMemory">750309376</Property>
      <Property Name="NumberofProcessors">1</Property>
      <Property Name="NumberofLogicalProcessors">2</Property>
      <Property Name="Manufacturer">Microsoft Corporation</Property>
      <Property Name="Model">Virtual Machine</Property>
      <Property Name="SystemType">x64-based PC</Property>
    </Object>
    <Object>
      <Property Name="Name">CHI-DC04</Property>
      <Property Name="TotalPhysicalMemory">1073270784</Property>
      <Property Name="NumberofProcessors">1</Property>
      <Property Name="NumberofLogicalProcessors">1</Property>
      <Property Name="Manufacturer">Microsoft Corporation</Property>
      <Property Name="Model">Virtual Machine</Property>
      <Property Name="SystemType">x64-based PC</Property>
    </Object>
</Objects>
```

Technically there's nothing wrong with this. But it might be nicer to revise so that we can see a collection of computer nodes. To accomplish that we need to rename nodes so that <Objects> becomes <Computers> and <Object> becomes <Computer>. We created a simple PowerShell function to get this done (listing 14.7).

Listing 14.7 Rename-XMLNode

```
Function Rename-XMLNode {
 [cmdletbinding()]
Param(
[Parameter(Position=0,Mandatory,HelpMessage="Specify an XML node")]
[System.Xml.XmlElement]$Node,
[Parameter(Position=1,Mandatory,
HelpMessage="Enter the new name of the node")]
[string]$NewName

)
$document = $Node.OwnerDocument                                    ⟵─  Get the XML document
$newNode = $Document.CreateNode('element',$NewName,$null)          ⟵─┐ Create a node with
                                                                     │ the new name
while ($Node.HasChildNodes) {
  $newNode.AppendChild($Node.FirstChild) | Out-Null                ⟵─┐
}                                                                    │ Copy child nodes
                                                                     │ to the new node
$Attributes = $node.Attributes

while ($attributes.count -gt 0) {                                      │ Copy attributes
                                                                     │ to the new node
  $newNode.attributes.append($attributes[0]) | Out-Null            ⟵─┘
}

$Node.ParentNode.ReplaceChild($newNode,$node) | Out-Null           ⟵─┐ Replace the old node
                                                                     │ with the new node
} #end function
```

The `Rename-XMLNode` function creates a new node, with the new name, copies data from the specified node, and replaces it. It won't write anything to the pipeline, but it'll update the XML document in memory:

```
PS C:\> Rename-XMLNode -Node $data.objects -NewName Computers
PS C:\> $data

xml                                              Computers
---                                              ---------
version="1.0"                                    Computers
```

We renamed the outer <Objects> node to <Computers>. Next we need to do the same for each of the child <Object> nodes with code like this:

```
foreach ($node in $data.computers.object) {
 rename-xmlnode -node $node -NewName Computer
}
```

Finally, we can save the modified XML document:

```
PS C:\> $data.Save("c:\work\mydata.xml")
```

Here's the new XML:

```
<?xml version="1.0"?>
<Computers>
  <Computer>
    <Property Name="Name">CHI-DC01</Property>
    <Property Name="TotalPhysicalMemory">1073274880</Property>
    <Property Name="NumberofProcessors">1</Property>
    <Property Name="NumberofLogicalProcessors">1</Property>
    <Property Name="Manufacturer">Microsoft Corporation</Property>
    <Property Name="Model">Virtual Machine</Property>
    <Property Name="SystemType">x64-based PC</Property>
  </Computer>
  <Computer>
    <Property Name="Name">CHI-FP02</Property>
    <Property Name="TotalPhysicalMemory">750309376</Property>
    <Property Name="NumberofProcessors">1</Property>
    <Property Name="NumberofLogicalProcessors">2</Property>
    <Property Name="Manufacturer">Microsoft Corporation</Property>
    <Property Name="Model">Virtual Machine</Property>
    <Property Name="SystemType">x64-based PC</Property>
  </Computer>
  <Computer>
    <Property Name="Name">CHI-DC04</Property>
    <Property Name="TotalPhysicalMemory">1073270784</Property>
    <Property Name="NumberofProcessors">1</Property>
    <Property Name="NumberofLogicalProcessors">1</Property>
    <Property Name="Manufacturer">Microsoft Corporation</Property>
    <Property Name="Model">Virtual Machine</Property>
    <Property Name="SystemType">x64-based PC</Property>
  </Computer>
</Computers>
```

To us, this is clearer and now ready to use outside of PowerShell.

14.7   *Select-XML*

PowerShell v3 and later also include a Select-Xml cmdlet. This cmdlet is designed to find text within an XML string or within an XML document. Specifically, it's designed to execute XPath queries (the same ones we mentioned earlier).

Let's start with a simple XML document:

```
<top>
  <mid attrib="1">Value 1</mid>
  <mid attrib="2">Value B</mid>
</top>
```

We'll save that in test.xml to make it easy to use. We might then run:

```
[xml]$xml = Get-Content test.xml
Select-XML -Xml $xml -Xpath "//mid[@attrib='1']"
```

Doing so would return the first <mid> node from the document, because it has an attribute equal to "1." Again, you have to know XPath for this to work. If you're still looking for a starting point on XPath, you'll find a good one at www.w3schools.com/xpath/xpath_syntax.asp.

The cmdlet can accept XML in one of several ways:

- Use the –Xml parameter to pass an XML node or document.
- Use the –Content parameter to pass a string that contains XML.
- Use the –Path or –LiteralPath parameter to specify file paths.

The result of the cmdlet is a result object, and it will have a Node property that provides access to the desired chunk of XML. For example:

```
PS C:\> [xml]$xml = Get-Content test.xml
PS C:\> $result = Select-Xml -Xml $xml -Xpath "//mid[@attrib='1']"
PS C:\> $result.node.InnerXML
Value 1
PS C:\> $result.node.attrib
1
```

In that example, we used the Node property to access the XML node that was found by the cmdlet, and then accessed its value via the InnerXML property and the value of its attrib attribute. Select-Xml isn't all that different from the SelectSingleNode() method that we showed you earlier; it's just done with a cmdlet, instead of accessing a method of the XML document itself.

14.8   *Summary*

With so much of the world's data in XML and/or HTML, being able to work in those formats can be handy. PowerShell provides a variety of capabilities that should be able to address most common situations; obviously, the more knowledge you have of those formats and how they're used, the more effective you'll be with PowerShell's ability to handle them.

HTML is the data format of the web and being able to work directly with the format opens up a number of possibilities. More importantly, from your viewpoint, being able to easily create reports in HTML gives you the opportunity to produce impressive-looking output with minimal effort on your part.

XML is easy to work with. You've seen how to manually set up a starting document, load it into the shell, and enumerate its elements. We've shown you how to add nodes and attributes, and how to write the final thing back to disk. It isn't a lot of work, and XML makes a wonderful, simple, text-based data file that's a lot more flexible than CSV. It's also a lot easier than working with something like an Excel spreadsheet.

PSDrives and PSProviders

This chapter covers

- Understanding PSProviders
- Working with PSDrives
- Using transactional processing

When you add a module or a PSSnapin to PowerShell, you usually take this step because of the commands contained within those extensions. But extensions can also add something called a *PSProvider* to the shell, and those providers can be useful in ways many administrators haven't realized are possible.

15.1 Why use PSProviders?

PSProviders, or *providers* for short, don't immediately seem like a good idea for administration, but they are. To better understand what providers are, and what advantages they offer, you have to understand the other way of managing things in PowerShell: using commands.

Think about what developers at Microsoft have to do when they're designing a set of commands. Take Active Directory as an example: First, they have to think of the nouns they'll create. In other words, what kinds of things exist in Active Directory? These can include users, computers, contacts, printers, organizational units, and so forth. Once they have a list of the available nouns, they think of what they can do with those things, and that's their list of verbs: create new ones, delete them, modify them, move them, and so on. Combine the two lists and you have the list of commands that you'll need to create: `New-ADUser`, `Set-ADUser`, `Remove-ADUser`, and on and on.

That technique works fine when the list of things—that is, the nouns—can all be known in advance. Technically, in Active Directory you can't ever know all the nouns in advance, because Active Directory can have its schema extended. You might, for example, add a class that represents a door, so that Active Directory can contain security information about your office building. There's no way Microsoft could know about that in advance, and so you wouldn't have commands for it, meaning you couldn't manage it directly. It may be possible to manage through a generic command (`*-ADObject`). In reality, companies don't like to extend their Active Directory schema that much, so the nouns Microsoft knows about—users, computers, and so forth—are likely the only ones you'll ever have.

But take another example, like Internet Information Services (IIS). IIS isn't only designed to be extensible; it almost insists on it! Some IIS machines have ASP.NET, whereas others have PHP. Some might have the URL Rewrite feature installed, whereas others might have that along with some advanced caching module. You never know in advance what might be installed.

That's where a provider comes in handy. For anything that can be represented as a hierarchy, a provider can dynamically discover what's available and give you a way of discovering it and manipulating it. A provider doesn't need to know in advance what the nouns and verbs are. Unfortunately, that makes providers a bit trickier to use. Without knowing in advance what the nouns and verbs are, you're stuck with a fairly generic set of commands that can manipulate almost anything a provider might see. Those commands have help files, of course, but the help is also generic, so it's difficult to find practical examples that apply to a specific technology. The same sets of commands are used to manage IIS, SQL Server, WSMAN, and many other technologies.

That difficulty is one reason the IIS team didn't commit 100% to a provider. They do know certain nouns in advance, because IIS will always contain things like websites, application pools, and so forth. Those are the things you're most likely going to manipulate in PowerShell, so the IIS team created regular commands for them. The provider for IIS exists to handle everything else.

15.2 What are PSProviders?

A PSProvider is essentially an adapter that connects PowerShell to some external technology and that represents that external technology as a hierarchical data store. It makes external systems look like disk drives.

You can see a list of all currently loaded providers by running `Get-PSProvider`. Keep in mind that when you load a module or snap-in, it can also load additional providers, so it's a good idea to periodically run `Get-PSProvider` and see what's available to you.

NOTE The `Certificate` and `WSMan` providers may not show when you use `Get-PSProvider`.

A good provider developer will always provide a help file for the provider, which is the one place they can offer nongeneric examples of how to use the provider. Most people don't even realize that provider help exists, but if you run `Help FileSystem`, you'll see an example of what provider help looks like. You use the normal `Help` command, along with the name of a provider (`FileSystem`, `Registry`, `WSman`, and so on) to learn how to use a provider.

In and of themselves, providers aren't useful, because you can't use them directly. Instead, they're used to create *PSDrives*.

NOTE Be aware that providers are designed for PowerShell. How they interact with the rest of the operating system varies. For example, changes you make using the `Registry` provider will be reflected in the operating system. But changes you make using the Environment provider affect only your current PowerShell session. If you change the value of an environment variable using the provider, it has no effect outside of PowerShell.

15.3   *What are PSDrives?*

A PSDrive is a provider in action. Keep in mind that a provider is an adapter that connects PowerShell to some external system; a PSDrive is an adapter being used to connect to a specific system.

PSDrives don't have drive letters; instead, they have drive *names*. That's because 26 letters wouldn't be enough to handle all the drives PowerShell might have connected at any one time, and because names are a bit easier to remember than single letters.

By default, PowerShell maps a number of PSDrives, using some of its built-in adapters, every time it starts. When a module or snap-in includes a provider, it'll usually map a PSDrive or two when the module or snap-in loads. To see a list of all currently available PSDrives, run `Get-PSDrive`:

```
PS C:\> Get-PSDrive

Name      Used (GB) Free (GB) Provider    Root
----      --------- --------- --------    ----
Alias                         Alias
C             64.47    167.39 FileSystem  C:\
Cert                          Certificate \
Env                           Environment
Function                      Function
HKCU                          Registry    HKEY_CURRENT_USER
HKLM                          Registry    HKEY_LOCAL_MACHINE
Variable                      Variable
WSMan                         WSMan
```

The command will show you the drives, where they're mapped to, which provider is handling the connection, and other information applicable to the individual drive. Your current location within the set of drives will also be shown.

NOTE Your currently attached disk drives will still retain their letters and be visible as PowerShell PSDrives.

To create a new PSDrive, you run the `New-PSDrive` command. What you'll normally want to do is change to an already-connected PSDrive that uses the same provider and then run the command. That's because each provider can provide its own specific version of `New-PSDrive`. For example, the `ActiveDirectory` module included with Windows Server 2008 R2 and later provides a special version of `New-PSDrive`. If you need to connect a PSDrive to an Active Directory domain, you must do so while in the default AD: drive that's created when you load the `ActiveDirectory` module. Not all providers include a special version of `New-PSDrive`, but by changing to an existing drive that uses the provider, you'll be assured of using any special version that might be in there. That specialized version, if one exists, will also include help that's specific for how it works, so you'll want to view the help from within an existing drive as well, for example:

```
PS C:\> Import-Module ActiveDirectory
PS C:\> Set-Location AD:
PS C:\> Help New-PSDrive
```

NOTE You'll usually see folks use the `cd` alias of `Set-Location` rather than using the full cmdlet name. You should also check the `Push-Location` and `Pop-Location` cmdlets if you aren't familiar with their actions. These cmdlets have aliases of `pushd` and `popd`, respectively, and come in handy when you're navigating around the shell, especially when changing between PSDrives from different providers.

15.4 Working with PSDrives

PowerShell includes about a dozen generic commands that are designed to work with the contents of a PSDrive. Many of these have aliases that correspond to old-school DOS or Cmd.exe commands, because the filesystem drives are some of the most commonly used PSDrives. The commands, and their most common aliases, are as follows:

- `Clear-Item (cli)`
- `Copy-Item (copy, cpi, or cp)`
- `Get-ChildItem (dir, ls, or gci)`
- `Get-Item (gi)`
- `Invoke-Item (ii)`
- `Move-Item (move, mv, or mi)`
- `New-Item (ni)`
- `Remove-Item (erase, del, rd, ri, or rm)`
- `Rename-Item (rni or ren)`
- `Set-Item (si)`
- `Clear-ItemProperty (clp)`
- `Copy-ItemProperty (cpp)`
- `Get-ItemProperty (gp)`

- Move-ItemProperty (mp)
- New-ItemProperty
- Rename-ItemProperty (rnp)
- Set-ItemProperty (sp)

As you can see from the command names, a PSDrive can contain two different generic kinds of object: an item and an item property. There are also the Set-Location command, which changes your location to a different PSDrive or within a PSDrive, and the Get-Location command, which displays the current location. Read Get-Help about_Core_commands and Get-Help about_providers for further information.

> **NOTE** The FileSystem provider is the one you tend to work with the most, and it's also the one around which the provider and PSDrive terminology are based. We'll focus on the filesystem for our main examples but also include examples using other providers so that you can see how the terminology and techniques carry over.

15.4.1 Filter, Include, and Exclude

One point that causes a lot of confusion is the use of the -Filter, -Include, and -Exclude parameters of the *Item cmdlets. Table 15.1 defines the parameters for Get-ChildItem.

Table 15.1 Definitions of the Exclude, Filter, and Include parameters

Parameter	Definition
-Exclude	Omits the specified items. The value of this parameter qualifies the Path parameter. Enter a path element or pattern, such as *.txt. Wildcards are permitted.
-Filter	Specifies a filter in the provider's format or language. The value of this parameter qualifies the Path parameter. The syntax of the filter, including the use of wildcards, depends on the provider. Filters are more efficient than other parameters, because the provider applies them when retrieving the objects, rather than having Windows PowerShell filter the objects after they're retrieved.
-Include	Gets only the specified items. The value of this parameter qualifies the Path parameter. Enter a path element or pattern, such as *.txt. Wildcards are permitted.

So, what does this mean in practice and how should you use these parameters? The first clue is in the definition of -Filter. Filters are the most efficient way to restrict the data because they're applied as data is retrieved rather than PowerShell filtering the result set. As Don always says, "Filter early." The -Filter parameter works like this:

```
PS C:\> Get-ChildItem -Path 'C:\MyData\PSHinDepth2E' -Filter *.txt

    Directory: C:\MyData\PSHinDepth2E

Mode                LastWriteTime     Length Name
----                -------------     ------ ----
-a---          16/12/2013     18:22     5371 pswa - Copy.ps1.txt
```

The filter modifies the `-Path` parameter. In effect it becomes:

```
Get-ChildItem -Path 'C:\MyData\PSHinDepth2E\*.txt'
```

Unfortunately, you can supply only a single filter. You can't do this, for instance:

```
Get-ChildItem -Path 'C:\MyData\PSHinDepth2E' -Filter *.txt, *.docx
```

If you only want to work with a subset of the items, then `-Filter` is the recommended way because of its efficiency. At times you may need to use the `-Include` and `-Exclude` parameters.

The `-Exclude` parameter is the simplest in concept. It excludes any item that matches the value of the parameter. In the following example you get everything but files that have a .txt extension.

```
Get-ChildItem -Path 'C:\MyData\PSHinDepth2E' -Exclude *.txt
```

Following that example, you may think to do this:

```
Get-ChildItem -Path 'C:\MyData\PSHinDepth2E' -Include *.txt
```

But you won't get anything returned. This is a point about which we see many questions in the forums. If you want to use `-Include`, you need to do it like this:

```
Get-ChildItem -Path 'C:\MyData\PSHinDepth2E\*' -Include *.txt
```

The value supplied to `-Path` has to end in a wildcard so that everything in the folder is returned. PowerShell then filters the data using the value given in the `-Include` parameter. Not only is this more complicated to remember, it's also slower, which is why we recommend using `-Filter`.

You can combine the parameters so these options will work:

```
Get-ChildItem -Path 'C:\MyData\PSHinDepth2E\*' -Include *.doc  -Exclude A*
Get-ChildItem -Path 'C:\MyData\PSHinDepth2E\*' -Filter *.doc -Exclude A*
Get-ChildItem -Path 'C:\MyData\PSHinDepth2E\*' -Filter *.doc -Include X*
```

But don't try:

```
Get-ChildItem -Path 'C:\MyData\PSHinDepth2E\*' -Filter *.doc -Include *.txt
```

15.4.2 *Working with PSDrive items*

In the filesystem, an "item" is either a folder or a file, because those are the only two things the filesystem can contain. When you're using other providers, objects are presented as a hierarchy of files and folders, as if they were also a filesystem. But under the hood, that isn't always the case.

Here's a simple sequence of commands that creates a text file, renames it, creates a folder, and moves the file to that folder:

```
PS C:\> dir > directory.txt
PS C:\> ren directory.txt dir.txt
PS C:\> md files

    Directory: C:\
```

```
Mode                LastWriteTime    Length Name
----                -------------    ------ ----
d----         11/27/2013  11:00 AM          files
PS C:\> move dir.txt files
```

If you're paying close attention, you'll see the use of md, which wasn't included on the list of aliases we provided earlier. That's because it isn't an alias to a command—it's an alias to a built-in function named Mkdir:

```
PS C:\> get-alias md

CommandType    Name                                  ModuleName
-----------    ----                                  ----------
Alias          md -> mkdir

PS C:\> get-content function:\mkdir
```

> **TIP** Try running Get-Content function:\mkdir. The output is long, but you'll see that it's a function that runs New-Item under the hood.

You don't have to use Md or Mkdir to create new folders. Instead, you could run the New-Item command, which is what Mkdir is running under the hood:

```
PS C:\> New-Item -Type Directory -Name Test
    Directory: C:\
Mode                LastWriteTime    Length Name
----                -------------    ------ ----
d----         11/27/2013  11:05 AM          Test
```

The Mkdir function takes care of adding the -Type Directory parameter so that you don't have to type it.

If you have experience using older command-line shells, whether from MS-DOS or a Unix or Linux system, then working with items will be familiar to you. It's true that the parameters of commands like Get-ChildItem (which you probably know as dir or ls) differ from the older commands that you've used in the past, but PowerShell's help system can show you the new syntax any time you need a reminder.

Two things that can trip you up about the item-related commands are the -Path and -LiteralPath parameters that they all support. The -Path parameter is what's used by default when you don't specify a parameter name:

```
PS C:\> dir windows
```

That command is using the -Path parameter. That parameter accepts wildcards, meaning the ? character stands in for any single character, and the * character stands in for any one or more characters:

```
PS C:\> dir win*
```

That's all well and good, and it's what you'd normally expect to happen in the filesystem. In the Windows filesystem, neither ? nor * is legal in a file or folder name. They're reserved, by the filesystem, as wildcard characters. You'd never have a file named D?n, but specifying that with one of the item commands would match Dan, Don, Dun, and so forth.

A problem arises when you remember that there are providers other than the
`FileSystem` one, and in other data stores both ? and * are legal characters. For example, it's completely legal to have a Registry key named "Modified?" or "Ex*tra." But if
you tried to use the normal `-Path` parameter with those, you'd get "Modified?" along
with "ModifiedA" and "ModifiedB," because the `-Path` parameter always treats ? and *
as wildcards. Therefore, you should use the `-LiteralPath` parameter, which treats ?
and * as literal characters rather than as wildcards. You'll need to use the `-Literal-Path` parameter any time a path contains ? or *, which might be the case in some of
the nonfilesystem providers.

If you have access to a Windows Server 2008 R2 or later computer, and if it has IIS
installed, try this:

```
PS C:\> import-module web*
PS C:\> cd iis:
PS IIS:\> dir
Name
----
AppPools
Sites
SslBindings
```

Here you load the `WebAdministration` module, which adds an IIS PSProvider and
automatically uses that provider to map an IIS: PSDrive. You then change to that drive
and list its top-level contents. As you can see, the IIS server has three top-level items:
AppPools, Sites, and SslBindings.

A word about PSDrive names

This can be a bit tricky, so we want to call your attention to it. As we've mentioned,
all PSDrives have a name, which is what you use to refer to them. Your computer
probably has a C: drive, an HKCU drive, an HKLM drive, and so forth. *The drive names
do not include a colon at the end.*

When you work with these drives, you'll often see a colon after the name. For example, running `cd hkcu` doesn't work, because PowerShell tries to treat the `hkcu` as the
name of an item. Putting a colon after a drive name is a cue to the shell that this is
a drive name. Running `cd hkcu:` will change you to the HKCU drive.

Normally, you'll only use the colon when you're including the drive name as part of a
path, such as when you're specifying a `-Path` or `-LiteralPath` parameter. If a command needs only the name of a drive—such as when you're using `New-PSDrive` to
connect a new drive—then you don't use the colon.

From here, you can use `cd` to move around the drive and use `dir` to see its contents:

```
PS IIS:\> cd .\AppPools
PS IIS:\AppPools> dir
Name                      State      Applications
----                      -----      ------------
1af7c46fb0ee418db1735836  Started    /Topology…
```

```
832e13c26dbd40e4a4a420a1  Started     /b7a2fc705e6945ef90251b9dc2e59b0d…
Classic .NET AppPool      Started
DefaultAppPool            Started     Default Web Site
SecurityTokenServiceAppl  Started     /SecurityTokenServiceApplicationPool…
SharePoint - 80           Started     SharePoint - 80
SharePoint Central Admin  Started     SharePoint Central Administration v4…
SharePoint Web Services   Stopped     SharePoint Web Services Root
```

You'll notice that the "directory listings" for different drives all look a bit different, depending on the provider in use. A directory listing for the C: drive, for example, won't include "State" and "Applications" columns, because those make no sense in the filesystem. In the IIS provider, those columns do make sense. This is the most confusing part about working with providers and PSDrives. You have to remember that every data store you connect to works a bit differently. Although PowerShell does its best to make them all look like files and folders, under the hood they aren't, and some differences are inevitable.

How useful are the providers in the real world?

One common question revolves around the usefulness of providers compared to using cmdlets. In certain cases, such as the Registry or certificate store, specific cmdlets aren't available, so you have to use the provider or a scripting technique.

Richard decided to experiment with the AD provider to determine just how many common administrative tasks could be performed using the provider. The experiments grew into a comparison of scripting techniques, the Microsoft cmdlets, the Quest cmdlets, and the AD provider. Surprisingly, it was possible to perform practically all common AD administrative tasks through the provider (though some involved jumping through a few hoops).

The interested reader is directed to the Active Directory posts on Richard's blog at http://blogs.msmvps.com/richardsiddaway/.

15.4.3   *Working with item properties*

In the filesystem, "items" are files and folders. These items all have properties, such as a file's "Read Only" attribute. The item property commands, such as Get-ItemProperty and Set-ItemProperty, enable you to work with those properties:

```
PS C:\> Get-ItemProperty test.ps1 | Format-List *
PSPath          : Microsoft.PowerShell.Core\FileSystem::C:\test.ps1
PSParentPath    : Microsoft.PowerShell.Core\FileSystem::C:\
PSChildName     : test.ps1
PSDrive         : C
PSProvider      : Microsoft.PowerShell.Core\FileSystem
VersionInfo     : File:            C:\test.ps1
                  InternalName:
                  OriginalFilename:
                  FileVersion:
                  FileDescription:
                  Product:
                  ProductVersion:
                  Debug:           False
```

```
                        Patched:          False
                        PreRelease:       False
                        PrivateBuild:     False
                        SpecialBuild:     False
                        Language:
BaseName            : test
Mode                : -a---
Name                : test.ps1
Length              : 2518
DirectoryName       : C:\
Directory           : C:\
IsReadOnly          : False
Exists              : True
FullName            : C:\test.ps1
Extension           : .ps1
CreationTime        : 11/1/2013 7:57:42 AM
CreationTimeUtc     : 11/1/2013 2:57:42 PM
LastAccessTime      : 11/1/2013 7:57:42 AM
LastAccessTimeUtc   : 11/1/2013 2:57:42 PM
LastWriteTime       : 11/26/2013 8:04:47 PM
LastWriteTimeUtc    : 11/27/2013 4:04:47 AM
Attributes          : Archive, NotContentIndexed
```

Obviously, the properties displayed will be different across different providers: Items in the Registry, for example, will have different properties than items in the filesystem.

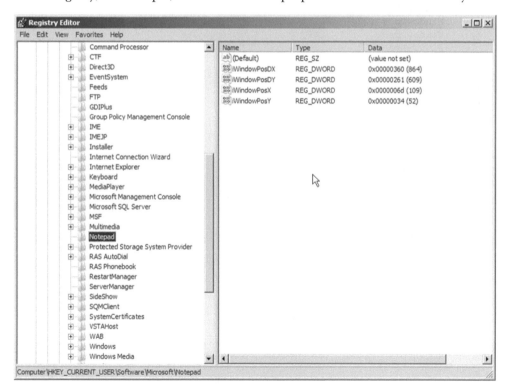

Figure 15.1 Examining a Registry key using the graphical Registry Editor

In fact, the Registry is a good example of where item properties get interesting. Take a look at figure 15.1, which shows Windows' graphical Registry Editor. We've opened it to HKEY_CURRENT_USER\Software\Microsoft\Notepad.

Now let's change to that same location using PowerShell:

```
PS C:\> cd hkcu:\software\microsoft\notepad
PS HKCU:\software\microsoft\notepad> dir
```

Wait, what? The directory listing is empty? Why wouldn't the directory listing include those four Registry values—iWindowPosDX, iWindowPosDY, and so forth?

In PowerShell's Registry provider, registry hives such as HKEY_LOCAL_MACHINE and HKEY_CURRENT_USER are connected as PSDrives. Registry keys, such as Software, Microsoft, and Notepad, are presented as items. If you run Dir HKCU:\Software, you'll get a listing of Registry keys under the Software key, because the dir alias points to Get-ChildItem, and because Registry keys are *items*.

But Registry *values* are presented as item properties, so they don't show up when you run Dir. Instead, you have to switch to using the item property commands, such as Get-ItemProperty, or its alias, gp. Here's what you need to do:

```
PS HKCU:\software\microsoft\notepad> cd ..
PS HKCU:\software\microsoft> gp notepad
iWindowPosX       : 246
iWindowPosY       : 64
iWindowPosDX      : 1199
iWindowPosDY      : 630
fWrap             : 0
StatusBar         : 0
lfEscapement      : 0
lfOrientation     : 0
lfWeight          : 400
lfItalic          : 0
lfUnderline       : 0
lfStrikeOut       : 0
lfCharSet         : 0
lfOutPrecision    : 3
lfClipPrecision   : 2
lfQuality         : 1
lfPitchAndFamily  : 49
lfFaceName        : Consolas
iPointSize        : 160
szHeader          :
szTrailer         :
iMarginTop        : 1000
iMarginBottom     : 1000
iMarginLeft       : 750
iMarginRight      : 750
PSPath            : Microsoft.PowerShell.Core\Registry::HKEY_CURRENT_USER
                    \Software\Microsoft\notepad
PSParentPath      : Microsoft.PowerShell.Core\Registry::HKEY_CURRENT_USER
                    \Software\Microsoft
PSChildName       : notepad
```

```
PSDrive        : HKCU
PSProvider     : Microsoft.PowerShell.Core\Registry
```

First, you change up a level in the hierarchy so that the shell is focused on HKCU:
\Software\Microsoft. Then, you ask the shell to display the item properties of the Notepad key. Essentially, the Notepad key looks like a file, and the settings (or values) underneath it look like properties of the file.

From this same point, you can start to make changes:

```
PS HKCU:\software\microsoft> Set-ItemProperty -Path Notepad -Name iWindowPosX
➥  -Value 120
PS HKCU:\software\microsoft> gp notepad -name iWindow*

iWindowPosX  : 120
iWindowPosY  : 64
iWindowPosDX : 1199
iWindowPosDY : 630
PSPath       : Microsoft.PowerShell.Core\Registry::HKEY_CURRENT_USER\Sof...
PSParentPath : Microsoft.PowerShell.Core\Registry::HKEY_CURRENT_USER\Sof...
PSChildName  : notepad
PSDrive      : HKCU
PSProvider   : Microsoft.PowerShell.Core\Registry
```

You change the iWindowPosX Registry setting to 120 and then redisplay the settings under Notepad to confirm your change. Presumably, the next time you open Notepad, its window will be in a slightly different position because of this change.

When you consider this technique for modifying the Registry, commands like New-ItemProperty should start making sense to you. It doesn't make sense to add new properties to an actual file on the filesystem; the filesystem recognizes only the properties that it was designed to work with. In the Registry, though, item properties are the way Registry values are presented, and it absolutely makes sense that you're able to create new ones, as well as delete old ones, copy them, and so on.

15.5 *Transactional operations*

One cool feature of some, but not all, providers is support for transactional operations. Running Get-PSProvider will reveal the providers that support this feature:

```
PS C:\> Get-PSProvider
Name            Capabilities                          Drives
----            ------------                          ------
Alias           ShouldProcess                         {Alias}
Environment     ShouldProcess                         {Env}
FileSystem      Filter, ShouldProcess, Credentials    {C, D, E, G...}
Function        ShouldProcess                         {Function}
Registry        ShouldProcess, Transactions           {HKLM, HKCU}
Variable        ShouldProcess                         {Variable}
Certificate     ShouldProcess                         {Cert}
WSMan           Credentials                           {WSMan}
```

You can see "Transactions" hiding at the end of the Registry provider's Capabilities column. A *transaction* consists of a set of operations that you've queued up but that haven't yet been implemented. As you add operations to the queue, PowerShell keeps track of them for you. When you've finished, you can either commit the entire batch or cancel the entire batch. The idea is to let you perform an entire set of tasks and ensure that either none of them completes or that all of them complete successfully. If an error crops up halfway through, you can cancel everything and start over.

Almost all of the item and item property commands include a –UseTransaction switch, which tells them to add something to the queue of an active transaction. To do that, you first have to start a transaction. Let's walk through an example. We'll start by evaluating the item properties of the HKCU:\Software\Microsoft\Notepad Registry key:

```
PS HKCU:\software\microsoft> get-itemproperty notepad

iWindowPosX      : 120
iWindowPosY      : 64
iWindowPosDX     : 1199
iWindowPosDY     : 630
fWrap            : 0
...
```

Next, start a transaction, and then make two changes to the Registry. Notice that each change is using the –UseTransaction parameter:

```
PS HKCU:\software\microsoft> Start-Transaction
Suggestion [1,Transactions]: Once a transaction is started, only commands t
hat get called with the -UseTransaction flag become part of that transactio
n.
PS HKCU:\software\microsoft> Set-ItemProperty -Path Notepad
➥ -Name iWindowPosX -Value 500 -UseTransaction
PS HKCU:\software\microsoft> Set-ItemProperty -Path Notepad
➥ -Name iWindowPosY -Value 50 -UseTransaction
```

Now, take a look at the Registry values again to see if your changes took effect:

```
PS HKCU:\software\microsoft> get-itemproperty Notepad -Name iWindowPos*
iWindowPosX  : 120
iWindowPosY  : 64
iWindowPosDX : 1199
iWindowPosDY : 630
PSPath       : Microsoft.PowerShell.Core\Registry::HKEY_CURRENT_USER\Sof...
PSParentPath : Microsoft.PowerShell.Core\Registry::HKEY_CURRENT_USER\Sof...
PSChildName  : notepad
PSDrive      : HKCU
PSProvider   : Microsoft.PowerShell.Core\Registry
```

The two changes seem to have been ignored. That's because they haven't happened, yet—they're queued up in the transaction. If you want to see what the Registry would look like after the transaction, you have to tell Get-ItemProperty to take the transaction's queue into account:

```
PS HKCU:\software\microsoft> get-itemproperty Notepad -Name iWindowPos*
➥   -useTransaction
iWindowPosDX : 1199
iWindowPosDY : 630
```

```
iWindowPosX  : 500
iWindowPosY  : 50
PSPath         : Microsoft.PowerShell.Core\Registry::HKEY_CURRENT_USER\Sof...
PSParentPath : Microsoft.PowerShell.Core\Registry::HKEY_CURRENT_USER\Sof...
PSChildName  : notepad
PSDrive        : HKCU
PSProvider     : Microsoft.PowerShell.Core\Registry
```

Ah, now you can see your changes. But they're still not real: The transaction is pending. You can run `Cancel-Transaction` to abandon your changes and shut down the transaction or run `Complete-Transaction` to go ahead and apply the pending changes:

```
PS HKCU:\software\microsoft> Complete-Transaction
PS HKCU:\software\microsoft> get-itemproperty Notepad -Name iWindowPos*
iWindowPosX  : 500
iWindowPosY  : 50
iWindowPosDX : 1199
iWindowPosDY : 630
PSPath         : Microsoft.PowerShell.Core\Registry::HKEY_CURRENT_USER\Sof...
PSParentPath : Microsoft.PowerShell.Core\Registry::HKEY_CURRENT_USER\Sof...
PSChildName  : notepad
PSDrive        : HKCU
PSProvider     : Microsoft.PowerShell.Core\Registry
```

With the transaction committed, `Get-ItemProperty` is able to show the finalized changes.

> **NOTE** Not every provider supports the use of transactions. Be sure to check a provider's capabilities before you assume that it'll support transactions. In PowerShell v3 and v4, of the base providers only the Registry provider supports transactions.

15.6 *Every drive is different*

Keep in mind that every drive in PowerShell can behave a bit differently, because every provider—and every underlying technology—works a bit differently. The basic commands that you'll use for manipulating items and item properties can even change slightly—each provider is capable of providing its own specialized versions of these commands. A bit of experimentation—and the fact that each PSProvider should offer its own help file—can usually get you on the right path.

The provider in SQL Server 2008 (and R2) is a little unusual. PowerShell support in these versions of SQL Server is provided by a closed-shell version of PowerShell (SQLPS.exe) that includes the SQL Server provider and cmdlets but has some aspects of PowerShell removed. This means that you can't add any other PowerShell functionality into it. But you can add the SQL Server components into a normal PowerShell session, which provides access to the full range of functionality. You can access SQLPS.exe by right-clicking an object such as a database in SQL Server Management Studio or by starting the executable (which isn't on the Start menu by default).

Assuming you've started a PowerShell session with the SQL Server components loaded, you can use `Get-PSDrive` to discover that the SQL Server provider installs a SQLSERVER: drive, which you can access as any other drive:

```
PS C:\> cd sqlserver:
PS C:\> dir
```

Name	Root	Description
SQL	SQLSERVER:\SQL	SQL Server Database Engine
SQLPolicy	SQLSERVER:\SQLPolicy	SQL Server Policy Management
SQLRegistration	SQLSERVER:\SQLRegistration	SQL Server Registrations
DataCollection	SQLSERVER:\DataCollection	SQL Server Data Collection

PowerShell and SQL Server deserve a book in their own right, so for now you'll get a quick look at using the provider concentrating on the database engine. One important point is that the functionality to create databases or associated objects wasn't implemented. You need to use PowerShell and Server Management Objects (SMO) to accomplish those tasks. You need to traverse a number of levels to get to the interesting bits:

```
cd sql\W08R2SQL08\default
```

The location you're changing to breaks down as SQL (for the database engine as shown earlier) followed by the server name followed by the instance name. If you think this may allow you to access the provider on remote machines, you're correct.

Within the instance are the objects you'd expect such as databases, logins, endpoints, and so forth. If you look at the databases

```
PS C:\> cd databases
PS C:\> Get-ChildItem | Get-Member
```

you'll see that you're dealing with an SMO object:

```
TypeName: Microsoft.SqlServer.Management.Smo.Database
```

The methods and properties of the objects can be accessed as with any other provider. One of the properties of a database is that it can be set to AutoClose—that is, it shuts down when the last user logs off. This setting is often used by inexperienced DBAs. It may sound like a good idea, but it means that your database won't be available for the overnight backup! The setting can be easily tested (assuming you're still in the databases container—if not, give the full path):

```
dir | select Name, AutoClose
```

Any databases that are incorrectly set can be quickly corrected. You might think to use this:

```
Set-ItemProperty -Path Test1 -Name Autoclose -Value $true
```

But unfortunately that functionality wasn't enabled in this provider and you'll get an error message. You can work in the provider—you need a little more effort:

```
Get-ChildItem |
where {$_.AutoClose} |
foreach {
 $_.AutoClose = $false
 $_.Alter()
}
```

This code sets the property to the desired value and then calls the `Alter()` method to save the change.

The SQL Server provider isn't straightforward, but its ability to combine Power-Shell and SMO in simple commands makes it hugely powerful. The ability to work through the provider with remote systems gives a large boost to productivity.

15.7 *Summary*

At first glance, providers can seem like an awkward, complicated way to perform management tasks. Because you're using a generic set of cmdlets to manipulate items and item properties, and because items and item properties refer to different things in different providers, it can be difficult to get help and examples specific to the task you're trying to accomplish. Sometimes, you might wish that there were commands for everything, instead of these crazy providers.

But providers offer what's probably the best solution to a difficult problem: dynamic systems. Without knowing in advance what a system will look like, Microsoft and other developers can't provide a concrete set of commands. A provider's ability to adapt to dynamic situations, along with the provider's model of using generic commands, is the most flexible way to address the situation. With a bit of practice, you'll find that working with providers becomes as straightforward as working with regular commands.

Variables, arrays, hash tables, and script blocks

16

Variables are a big part of any programming language or operating system shell, and PowerShell is no exception. In this chapter, we'll explain what they are and how to use them, and we'll cover some advanced variable-like data structures such as arrays, hash tables, and script blocks.

16.1 Variables

Variables are quite simply a temporary storage area for data. If you have some piece of data you plan to use over and over again, it makes sense to store it in a variable rather than having to retrieve it from where it's stored each time you need it. Or if you have a command that takes a long time to run and you want to try different things with the results, save the results to a variable so you don't have to keep executing the same long-running expression.

You can think of variables as a kind of box. The box has its own attributes, such as its size, but what you're generally interested in is what's *inside* the box. Boxes can contain anything: letters, numbers, processes, services, user accounts, you name it. It doesn't have to be a single value like "Richard." It could be a collection of job or process objects. But whatever's in a box remains static: It continues to look the same as it looked when you put it in there. Things in the box don't update themselves automatically, so it's possible for their information to be out of date, which isn't always a bad thing but something to keep in mind.

> **NOTE** You'll see in chapter 39 that the information in a variable created using the CIM cmdlets can be refreshed. The important point to remember is that the original variable isn't changed but is used to speed up the production of new data.

Think of a variable as holding a point-in-time snapshot.

16.1.1 *Variable names*

Remember the last time you moved? When you started packing, you were good about writing names on boxes: "Living room," "Kitchen," "Kids' room," and so on. Later on as you neared the finish you just started throwing random stuff in boxes and skipping the names, didn't you? But PowerShell *always* gives variables a name. In fact, variable names are one of the subtle little details that trip people up all the time. In PowerShell, a variable name generally contains a mixture of letters, numbers, and the underscore character. You typically see variable names preceded by a dollar sign:

```
$var = "Howdy"
```

But it's important to remember that *the dollar sign isn't part of the variable name*. The dollar sign is a sort of cue to PowerShell, telling it, "I don't want to work with the *box* named `var`, I want to work with the *contents* of that box." There are times when PowerShell will need to know the name of a variable so that it knows what box you want to use, and in those cases you *must not* include the dollar sign! To give you an example, consider the `-ErrorVariable` common parameter. Supported by all PowerShell cmdlets, this parameter lets you specify the name of a variable that you want any errors to be put into. That way, if an error occurs, you can easily see what it was just by looking in that variable. We constantly see people attempt to use it like this:

```
Get-Service -ErrorVariable $var
```

Given the previous example, which set `$var` = `"Howdy"`, this new example would put the error in a variable named `Howdy`, because the dollar signed accessed the contents of `$var`, which were "Howdy." Instead, the proper syntax is

```
Get-Service -ErrorVariable var
```

This little trip-up catches a lot of people, which is one reason we want to point it out nice and early.

> **NOTE** The *-Variable cmdlets are another source of confusion when working with variables. Their -Name parameter expects the name of the variable without the $ sign.

There's another little thing about variable names you should know: They can contain a lot more than letters, numbers, and underscores, provided you wrap the variable's name in curly brackets. This looks totally weird:

```
${this is a valid variable name} = 12345
```

Weird, but it works. We don't recommend using that technique, because it makes your scripts a lot harder to read and modify. We're definitely in favor of meaningful variable names, like $computerName instead of $c, especially in a script. When using PowerShell interactively, the emphasis is on command-line efficiency, so using a variable like $c makes sense because you know what it means. But in a script at line 267 if you see $c, it might not be so clear, especially if it's someone else's script. In any event we think the curly brackets let you go a bit too far.

16.1.2 *Variable types*

PowerShell keeps track of the type of object, or objects, contained within a variable. Whenever possible, PowerShell will elect to treat a type of data as a different type if doing so will make a particular operation make more sense. In programming, this is called *coercing* the variable, and it can lead to some odd results, such as

```
PS C:\> $a = 5
PS C:\> $b = "5"
PS C:\> $a + $b
10
PS C:\> $b + $a
55
```

That can freak you out the first time you see it or at least leave you scratching your head. Basically, PowerShell looks at the first operand's data type and then looks at the operator. Because + can mean addition or string concatenation, PowerShell makes a choice based on what came first: Give it an integer in $a first, and + means addition. So it coerces $b to be an integer (otherwise it'd be treated like a string because it's enclosed in quotes) and does the math. Give it a string in $b first, and + means concatenation, and so it treats $a like a string character and attaches it to $b.

This same behavior can create difficulties for you if you're not careful. For example, let's say you have a script, which contains a variable. You fully expect that variable to contain a number—perhaps the number of times a particular task should be performed. Somehow, a string—like a computer name—ends up in that variable instead. Boom, your script breaks. One way to help alleviate that error is to explicitly declare a type for your variable:

```
[int]$iterations = 5
```

When you do this, PowerShell will no longer put anything into that variable that isn't an integer or that PowerShell can't make into an integer, for example:

```
PS C:\> [int]$iterations = 5
PS C:\> $iterations+1
6
PS C:\> $iterations = 10
PS C:\> $iterations+1
11
PS C:\> $iterations = "20"
PS C:\> $iterations+1
21
PS C:\> $iterations = "Richard"
Cannot convert value "Richard" to type "System.Int32". Error: "Input
string was not in a correct format."
At line:1 char:12
+ $iterations <<<<  = "Richard"
+ CategoryInfo          : MetadataError: (:) [], ArgumentTransfo
rmationMetadataException
+ FullyQualifiedErrorId : RuntimeException
```

Here, everything worked fine even when you tried to put a string into the variable—provided that string consisted of nothing but digits. You always end up with a number. But when you tried to store something that couldn't be coerced to a number, you got an error. The error is descriptive, and if it occurred in a script it'd tell you the exact line number where things went wrong, making the problem easier to troubleshoot.

You can always re-declare the variable to put a different data type into it. Power-Shell won't do so on its own. Here's an example:

```
PS C:\> [string]$iterations = "Richard"
```

That works fine, because you explicitly changed the type of data that the variable was allowed to contain. Of course, this would be a silly variable name for a value of "Richard", so we hope that this points out the importance of proper variable naming.

Hungarian notation

In the days of VBScript, scripters often defined their variables using a technique known as *Hungarian notation*. This involved prepending a short prefix to indicate what type of data was stored in the variable. You'd see variables like strComputer and iCount. Sadly, you still see this in PowerShell with variables like $strComputer. Technically this is a legal name, but it screams that you haven't grasped PowerShell fundamentals yet. Make your variable names meaningful and the type will follow. If you see a script with a variable $Computername, you're going to assume it's a string. A variable of $Count will most likely be an integer. But you'd have no idea what $C might be without some sort of context.

A common use of Hungarian notation is to show that the variable contains an object–$objSomething. All variables in PowerShell are objects, so pointing this out in the variable name is a redundant action that just adds complications and extra typing.

(continued)

The only valid reason we can see for using Hungarian notation, or any variants, would be if you were performing a series of data type conversions. Putting the type into the name may make it easier to keep track of where you are in the process. In general, though, drop the Hungarian notation and use common sense.

16.1.3 Being strict with variables

PowerShell has another behavior that can make for difficult troubleshooting. For this example, you're going to create a very small script and name it test.ps1. The following listing shows the script.

Listing 16.1   Initial script—no testing on type

```
$test = Read-Host "Enter a number"
Write-Host $tset
```

That typo in the second line is deliberate. This is the exact kind of typo you could easily make in your own scripts. Let's see what PowerShell does with this by default:

```
PS C:\> ./test
Enter a number: 5
PS C:\>
```

Unexpected output and no error. That's because, by default, PowerShell assumes variables to have a default value of 0, or an empty string, or some other similar value associated with the data type assigned to the variable. If you don't assign a data type, the variable will contain $null.

```
PS C:\> [string]$t -eq ""
True
PS C:\> [int]$t -eq 0
True
PS C:\> $t -eq $null
True
```

This kind of behavior, which doesn't create an error when you try to access an uninitialized variable, can take hours to debug. The solution is to set a strict mode, which you can do generally in the shell or at the top of each script using the Set-StrictMode cmdlet. The effect of this cmdlet is similar to using Option Explicit in VBScript.

To use the cmdlet, you need to specify a PowerShell version value. The version will dictate how PowerShell handles uninitialized variables and a few other syntax elements that could cause problems. If you use a –version value of 1, PowerShell will complain when you reference an uninitialized variable. An exception is made for uninitialized variables in strings, which could still be difficult to troubleshoot. Let's add a bit more to our test script, which you should save as test2.ps1.

Listing 16.2   Using strict mode

```
$test = Read-Host "Enter a number"
Write-host $tset
$a=[system.math]::PI*($tset*$test)
Write-Host "The area is $tset"
```

Here's what happens with strict mode off. Go ahead and explicitly set it in the shell before running the script:

```
PS C:\> Set-StrictMode -off
PS C:\>.\test2.ps1
Enter a number: 5
The area is
PS C:\>
```

Now set the version value to 1:

```
PS C:\> Set-StrictMode -Version 1
PS C:\> .\test2.ps1
Enter a number: 5
The variable '$tset' cannot be retrieved because it has not been set.
At c:\test2.ps1:2 char:12
+ Write-Host $tset
+            ~~~~~
    + CategoryInfo          : InvalidOperation: (:) [], RuntimeException
    + FullyQualifiedErrorId : VariableIsUndefined
The variable '$tset' cannot be retrieved because it has not been set.
At c:\test2.ps1:3 char:23
+ $a=[system.math]::PI*($tset*$test)
+                       ~~~~~
    + CategoryInfo          : InvalidOperation: (:) [], RuntimeException
    + FullyQualifiedErrorId : VariableIsUndefined
The area is
PS C:\>
```

PowerShell complains that $tset hasn't been set on lines 2 and 3. The script fails but now you know what to fix. Notice PowerShell didn't complain about the last line that also had a variable typo because it's part of a string. Let's fix all typos but the last one and run it again (save the script as test3.ps1).

Listing 16.3   Removing most typos

```
$test = Read-Host "Enter a number"
Write-host $test
$a=[system.math]::PI*($test*$test)
Write-Host "The area is $tset"
```

This version (test3.ps1) behaves better:

```
PS C:\> Set-StrictMode -Version 1
PS C:\> .\test.ps1
Enter a number: 5
5
The area is
PS C:\>
```

Even though you didn't get an error, at least you recognize that there's a problem with the last line.

Using a -version value of 2 will do everything in version 1 as well as prohibit references to nonexistent properties of an object, prohibit function calls that use the syntax for calling methods, and not allow you to use a variable without a name, such as ${}.

```
PS C:\> Set-StrictMode -Version 2
PS C:\> .\test3.ps1
Enter a number: 5
5
The variable '$tset' cannot be retrieved because it has not been set.
At C:\test\test3.ps1:4 char:25
+ Write-Host "The area is $tset"
+                         ~~~~~
    + CategoryInfo          : InvalidOperation: (tset:String) [],
      RuntimeException
    + FullyQualifiedErrorId : VariableIsUndefined
```

Using:

```
Set-StrictMode –Version 3
```

or

```
Set-StrictMode –Version 4
```

will give the same results. Alternatively, you can use a -Version value of Latest. PowerShell will use the strictest version available—this is our recommended practice.

> **TIP** When a new version of PowerShell becomes available, we recommend that you read the release notes to determine if there are any changes to strict mode.

This is a great way to make your script future proof. When you use strict mode, set it at the beginning of your script to make it obvious it's on, as shown in the next listing.

Listing 16.4 Removing all typos

```
Set-Strictmode –Version Latest
$test = Read-Host "Enter a number"
Write-host $test
$a=[system.math]::PI*($test*$test)
Write-Host "The area is $test"
```

Be aware that if you have multiple errors like these, PowerShell will only throw an exception at the first one. If you have other errors, you won't see them until you rerun the script. We suggest that if you discover a variable typo, use your script editor's find-and-replace feature to look for other instances.

One thing missing in PowerShell, even version 4, is the ability to determine the current StrictMode setting. It's possible using a number of .NET programming techniques, but that's not something we want to get into. We recommend that you be aware of StrictMode and be explicit in your code as to when you use it.

> **TIP** Many scripts you obtain from the internet will fail if you turn StrictMode on. If you use it, be prepared to spend time rewriting the script.

The whole strict mode thing plays into something called *scope* in PowerShell, which we're not quite ready to talk about yet. We'll revisit strict mode in chapter 22.

16.2 Built-in variables and the Variable: drive

PowerShell starts up with a number of variables already created and ready to go. Most of these variables control various aspects of PowerShell's behavior, and you can change them in order to modify its behavior. Any changes you make will be lost when you exit the shell, and they won't be reflected in any other shell instances you may have open unless you put the changes in your profile. These variables load up with the same values in each new shell session, and they're specific to each session rather than being global for the entire PowerShell engine. You can get a look at these by getting a directory listing for the Variable: drive, which is where PowerShell stores all variables:

```
PS C:\> dir variable:
Name                          Value
----                          -----
$
?                             True
^
args                          {}
ConfirmPreference             High
ConsoleFileName
currentUser                   System.Security.Principal.WindowsIdentity
DebugPreference               SilentlyContinue
Error                         {}
ErrorActionPreference         Continue
ErrorView                     NormalView
ExecutionContext              System.Management.Automation.EngineIntrin...
false                         False
FormatEnumerationLimit        4
HOME                          C:\Users\Richard
Host                          System.Management.Automation.Internal.Hos...
input                         System.Collections.ArrayList+ArrayListEnu...
MaximumAliasCount             4096
MaximumDriveCount             4096
MaximumErrorCount             256
MaximumFunctionCount          4096
MaximumHistoryCount           4096
MaximumVariableCount          4096
MyInvocation                  System.Management.Automation.InvocationInfo
NestedPromptLevel             0
null
OutputEncoding                System.Text.ASCIIEncoding
PID                           2516
```

```
principal                        System.Security.Principal.WindowsPrincipal
PROFILE                          C:\Users\Richard\Documents\WindowsPowerSh...
ProgressPreference               Continue
PSBoundParameters                {}
PSCommandPath                    C:\Users\Richard\Documents\WindowsPowerSh...
PSCulture                        en-GB
PSDefaultParameterValues         {}
PSEmailServer
PSHOME                           C:\Windows\System32\WindowsPowerShell\v1.0
PSScriptRoot                     C:\Users\Richard\Documents\WindowsPowerShell
PSSessionApplicationName         wsman
PSSessionConfigurationName       http://schemas.microsoft.com/powershell/...
PSSessionOption                  System.Management.Automation.Remoting.PSS...
PSUICulture                      en-GB
PSVersionTable                   {PSVersion, WSManStackVersion,
                                 SerializationVersion, CLRVersion...}
PWD                              C:\MyData\SkyDrive\Data\scripts
role                             Administrator
ShellId                          Microsoft.PowerShell
StackTrace
true                             True
VerbosePreference                SilentlyContinue
WarningPreference                Continue
WhatIfPreference                 False
```

The list shows the state of the variables in a console session that has just been opened.
You can even find a variable that controls the maximum number of variables Power-
Shell can keep track of! Any variables that you create are also stored in this drive—so
can you think of how you might completely delete a variable? The same way you'd
delete a file: the `Del` (or `Remove-Item`) command! And yes, you can absolutely delete
the built-in variables, but they'll come right back when you open a new shell instance.
As a practical rule, though, be careful about deleting automatic variables because
many PowerShell commands rely on them. A number of help files are available that
deal with variables (get-help about*variable*).

16.3   *Variable commands*

PowerShell includes a dedicated set of commands for variable management:

```
PS C:\> Get-Command -noun Variable

CommandType     Name                    ModuleName
-----------     ----                    ----------
Cmdlet          Clear-Variable          Microsoft.PowerShell.Utility
Cmdlet          Get-Variable            Microsoft.PowerShell.Utility
Cmdlet          New-Variable            Microsoft.PowerShell.Utility
Cmdlet          Remove-Variable         Microsoft.PowerShell.Utility
Cmdlet          Set-Variable            Microsoft.PowerShell.Utility
```

For the most part, you never need to use these. For example, to create a new variable
you just use it for the first time and assign a value to it:

```
$x = 5
```

To assign a new value to it, you don't need to use Set-Variable; you can just do this:

```
$x = 10
```

The variable cmdlets are there if you decide to use them. One advantage to using them is that they let you modify variables in scopes other than your own. Again, scope is something we're going to come to later, so you may see these cmdlets in use then. Remember that when working with variables using the variable cmdlets the name of the variable is used without the $ prefix, so:

```
PS C:\> New-Variable -Name newvar -Value 10
```

not:

```
PS C:\> New-Variable -Name $newvar -Value 10
New-Variable : Cannot bind argument to parameter 'Name' because it is null.
At line:1 char:20
+ New-Variable -Name $newvar -Value 10
+                    ~~~~~~~
    + CategoryInfo          : InvalidData: (:) [New-Variable],
    ⇒ ParameterBindingValidationException
    + FullyQualifiedErrorId : ParameterArgumentValidationErrorNullNotAllowed,
    ⇒ Microsoft.PowerShell.Commands.NewVariable Command
```

> **NOTE** Folks with a programming background will ask if there's a way to make PowerShell require variable declaration, rather than letting you make up new variables on the fly. They'll often look at strict mode, and the New-Variable cmdlet, to see if they can create some kind of "declaration required" setting. They can't. PowerShell doesn't require you to announce your intention to use a variable, and there's no way to make it a requirement.

The other possibility for using New-Variable to create your variables is to make the variables read-only (which can be changed using –Force or deleted) or a constant (which can't be deleted or changed). You'd use New-Variable if you wanted to ensure that particular variables couldn't be modified once created.

16.4 *Arrays*

In many programming languages, there's a definite difference between an array of values and a collection of objects. In PowerShell, not so much. There's technically a kind of difference, but PowerShell does a lot of voodoo that makes the differences hard to see. So we'll tend to use the terms *array* and *collection* interchangeably. If you have a software development background, that might bug you. Sorry. It's just how Power-Shell is.

Simply put, an array is a variable that contains more than one value. In PowerShell, all values—like integers or strings—are technically objects. So it's more precise to say that an array can contain multiple objects. One way to get multiple objects into a variable is to run a command that returns more than one object:

```
$services = Get-Service
```

In PowerShell, the equals sign is the *assignment* operator. Whatever's on the right side of the operator gets put into whatever's on the left side. In this case, the right side contains a pipeline command—albeit a short pipeline, with only one command. Power-Shell runs the pipeline, and the result goes into $services. You can have more complex pipelines, too:

```
$services = Get-Service | Where Status -eq 'Running'
```

You can access individual elements in an array by using a special notation:

```
PS C:\> $services = Get-Service
PS C:\> $services[0]
Status    Name                DisplayName
------    ----                -----------
Running   ADWS                Active Directory Web Services
PS C:\> $services[1]
Status    Name                DisplayName
------    ----                -----------
Stopped   AeLookupSvc         Application Experience

PS C:\> $services[-1]

Status    Name                DisplayName
------    ----                -----------
Stopped   wudfsvc             Windows Driver Foundation - User-mo...
PS C:\> $services[-2]

Status    Name                DisplayName
------    ----                -----------
Running   wuauserv            Windows Update
```

The first *index* in an array is 0 (zero), which points to the first item in the array. Index 1 is the second item, and so on. Negative numbers start at the end of the array, so -1 is the last item, -2 the second-to-last, and so on.

> **NOTE** Be careful of the array indices if you're used to starting at 1. Power-Shell is .NET based and follows the .NET convention that the first element in an array is index 0. This is sometimes awkward but it's something we're stuck with.

Arrays can be created from simple values by using the array operator (the @ symbol) and a comma-separated list:

```
PS C:\> $names = @('one','two','three')
PS C:\> $names[1]
two
```

PowerShell will tend to treat any comma-separated list as an array, so you can generally skip the array operator and the parentheses:

```
PS C:\> $names = 'one','two','three'
PS C:\> $names[2]
three
```

This is exactly why some cmdlet parameters can accept multiple values in a comma-separated list. For example, look at the help for `Get-Service` and you'll see the following:

```
Get-Service [[-Name] <string[]>] [-ComputerName <string[]>]
[-DependentServices] [-Exclude <string[]>] [-Include <string[]>]
[-RequiredServices] [<CommonParameters>]
```

Back in chapter 3, on interpreting the help files, we pointed out that the `<string[]>` notation's double square brackets indicated that it could accept multiple values; technically, it's an array. Because PowerShell interprets comma-separated lists as arrays, this is legal:

```
PS C:\> get-service -name a*,b*
Status     Name              DisplayName
------     ----              -----------
Running    ADWS              Active Directory Web Services
Stopped    AeLookupSvc       Application Experience
Stopped    ALG               Application Layer Gateway Service
Stopped    AppIDSvc          Application Identity
Stopped    Appinfo           Application Information
Stopped    AppMgmt           Application Management
Stopped    AudioEndpointBu... Windows Audio Endpoint Builder
Stopped    AudioSrv          Windows Audio
Running    BFE               Base Filtering Engine
Running    BITS              Background Intelligent Transfer Ser...
Stopped    Browser           Computer Browser
```

> **NOTE** PowerShell is picky about parameter input. In this case, the `-Name` parameter not only can accept an array, it must accept only an array. If you provide only a single value, PowerShell converts that to an array of one object behind the scenes.

Arrays can hold different types of objects as well:

```
PS C:\> $a=42,"Jeff",(Get-Date).Month,(get-process -id $pid)
PS C:\> $a
42
Jeff
1

Handles  NPM(K)    PM(K)      WS(K) VM(M)   CPU(s)     Id ProcessName
-------  ------    -----      ----- -----   ------     -- -----------
   1111      42   107184      73588   609    11.89   6608 powershell
```

Each item is a complete object, so assuming you know the index number you can do things with it:

```
PS C:\> $a[0]*2
84
PS C:\> $a[1].Length
4
PS C:\> $a[-1].path
C:\WINDOWS\system32\WindowsPowerShell\v1.0\powershell.exe
```

Thus the reference to `$a[-1]` is a process object that allows you to retrieve the path property.

Measuring the number of items in an array is usually simple using the `Count` or `Length` property. Technically `Length` is the property of the .NET array object and `Count` is an alias created by PowerShell. `Count` is usually easier to remember. In PowerShell 3 and 4, an array with zero or one element will return a value for Count. Earlier versions didn't.

```
PS C:\> $a.count
4
```

Sometimes, though, you want to start with an empty array and add items to it. First, define the empty array:

```
PS C:\> $myarray=@()
```

To add an item to the array, use the += operator:

```
PS C:\> $myarray+="Don"
PS C:\> $myarray+="Jeff"
PS C:\> $myarray+="Richard"
PS C:\> $myarray.count
3
PS C:\> $myarray
Don
Jeff
Richard
```

Unfortunately, removing an item isn't as simple:

```
PS C:\> $myarray-="Jeff"
Method invocation failed because [System.Object[]] doesn't contain a method
  named 'op_Subtraction'.
At line:1 char:1
+ $myarray-="Jeff"
+ ~~~~~~~~~~~~~~~~~
    + CategoryInfo          : InvalidOperation: (op_Subtraction:String) [],
      RuntimeException
    + FullyQualifiedErrorId : MethodNotFound
```

Instead you need to re-create the array using only the items you wish to keep:

```
PS C:\> $myarray=$myarray | where {$_ -notmatch "Jeff"}
PS C:\> $myarray
Don
Richard
```

So far the arrays you've seen have all been a single list (think of a column or data). You can create arrays of any objects, including other arrays. It's also possible to have arrays with multiple, or even variable numbers of, columns, although this is a technique we haven't seen used by many administrators. Arrays can be a powerful tool, and you'll use them more than you realize.

16.5 *Hash tables and ordered hash tables*

Hash tables (which you'll also see called hash tables, associative arrays, or dictionaries) are a special kind of array. These *must* be created using the @ operator, although they're created within curly brackets rather than parentheses—and those brackets are also mandatory. Within the brackets, you create one or more *key-value pairs*, separated by semicolons. The keys and values can be anything you like:

```
PS C:\> @{name='DonJ';
>> samAccountName='DonJ';
>> department='IT'
>> title='CTO';
>> city='Las Vegas'}
>>

Name                      Value
----                      -----
samAccountName            DonJ
name                      DonJ
department                IT
city                      Las Vegas
title                     CTO
```

> **NOTE** As you can see in that example, the semicolon is one of the characters that PowerShell knows must be followed by something else. By pressing Enter after one, you made PowerShell enter a multiline prompt mode. Technically, PowerShell will recognize that the command is incomplete and provide the nested prompts even without the semicolon. You could've easily typed the entire hash table on a single line, but doing it this way makes it a bit easier to read in the book. (If we'd elected to use a single line, then the semicolon would be required between hash table entries. For the sake of consistency, you may wish to always use the semicolon.) Finally, you ended that by completing the structure's closing curly bracket, pressing Enter, and pressing Enter on a blank line.

The key is usually a string (or integer, though we don't see that used much), and we recommend avoiding spaces if you can. You'll see why in a bit. The next thing about hash tables is that they're distinct objects themselves. Simple arrays like the ones we looked at earlier don't have a type per se; their contents do. But hash tables are different. For example, if you'd assigned that hash table to a variable, you could've accessed its individual elements easily:

```
PS C:\> $user = @{name='DonJ';
>> samAccountName='DonJ';
>> department='IT';
>> title='CTO';
>> city='Las Vegas'}
>>
PS C:\> $user.department
IT
PS C:\> $user.title
CTO
```

This is why we recommend no spaces in the key name. If you pipe $user to Get-Member, you can see that this is a new type of object, a System.Collections.Hashtable:

```
PS C:\> $user | get-member

    TypeName: System.Collections.Hashtable
Name              MemberType            Definition
----              ----------            ----------
Add               Method                System.Void Add(System.Object ke...
Clear             Method                System.Void Clear()
Clone             Method                System.Object Clone()
Contains          Method                bool Contains(System.Object key)
ContainsKey       Method                bool ContainsKey(System.Object key)
ContainsValue     Method                bool ContainsValue(System.Object...
CopyTo            Method                System.Void CopyTo(array array, ...
Equals            Method                bool Equals(System.Object obj)
GetEnumerator     Method                System.Collections.IDictionaryEn...
GetHashCode       Method                int GetHashCode()
GetObjectData     Method                System.Void GetObjectData(System...
GetType           Method                type GetType()
OnDeserialization Method                System.Void OnDeserialization(Sy...
Remove            Method                System.Void Remove(System.Object...
ToString          Method                string ToString()
Item              ParameterizedProperty System.Object Item(System.Object...
Count             Property              int Count {get;}
IsFixedSize       Property              bool IsFixedSize {get;}
IsReadOnly        Property              bool IsReadOnly {get;}
IsSynchronized    Property              bool IsSynchronized {get;}
Keys              Property              System.Collections.ICollection K...
SyncRoot          Property              System.Object SyncRoot {get;}
Values            Property              System.Collections.ICollection V...
```

Each value is its own type:

```
PS C:\> $user.title.getType().Name
String
```

Because the hash table is its own object, there's a bit more you can do with it. You might want to list all the keys:

```
PS C:\> $user.keys
title
department
name
city
samAccountName
```

The Count property returns the number of items in the hash table. Just to be inconsistent, hash tables don't respond to using Length:

```
PS C:\> $user.count
5
```

Or perhaps you might want to list all the values:

```
PS C:\> $user.values
CTO
```

```
IT
DonJ
Las Vegas
DonJ
```

Managing the hash table members is also considerably easier. The object has methods for adding and removing members. Be aware that each key must be unique, so you can't add another key called Name with a different value. You could use the `Contains-Key()` method to test before invoking the `Add()` method:

```
PS C:\> if (-Not $user.containsKey("EmployeeNumber")) {
>> $user.Add("EmployeeNumber",11805)
>> }
>>
```

In this command you use the `-Not` operator to reverse the result of the `Contains-Key()` method so that if the expression is true, you'll add a new entry. As you can see, it worked:

```
PS C:\> $user.EmployeeNumber
11805
```

The `Add()` method needs the name of the key and the value, separated by a comma. It's even easier to remove an item:

```
PS C:\> $user.Remove("employeenumber")
```

The effect is immediate. And as with arrays, you can create an empty hash table and add elements to it as needed. The items don't even have to be all of the same type. For example, you might start like this:

```
PS C:\> $hash=@{}
PS C:\> $hash.Add("Computername",$env:computername)
```

Later, you gather additional data and add to the hash table:

```
PS C:\> $running=Get-Service | where Status -eq "running" | measure
PS C:\> $hash.Add("Running",$running.count)
PS C:\> $os=Get-WmiObject -Class Win32_operatingsystem
PS C:\> $hash.Add("OS",$os)
PS C:\> $time=Get-Date -DisplayHint time
PS C:\> $hash.Add("Time",$time)
```

Here's what the hash table looks like now:

```
PS C:\> $hash
Name                        Value
----                        -----
Time                        12/24/2013 12:07:40 PM
Computername                CLIENT2
Running                     65
OS                          \\CLIENT2\root\cimv2:Win32_OperatingSystem=@
```

You have different types of objects that might even be nested objects. This can lead to some handy results:

```
PS C:\> $hash.os
SystemDirectory : C:\Windows\system32
Organization    :
BuildNumber     : 7601
RegisteredUser  : LocalAdmin
SerialNumber    : 00426-065-0389393-86517
Version         : 6.1.7601
PS C:\> $hash.os.caption
Microsoft Windows 7 Ultimate
```

Because hash tables are a convenient way to organize data, you might want to try nesting hash tables:

```
PS C:\> "coredc01","client2" | foreach -begin {
>>   $comphash=@{}
>> } -process {
>>   $svc=Get-Service -ComputerName $_
>>   $proc=get-process -comp $_
>>   $cs=Get-WmiObject -Class Win32_computersystem ComputerName $psitem
>>   $nest=@{Computername=$cs.Name;
>>   Services=$svc;Processes=$proc;
>>   ComputerSystem=$cs
>>   }
>>   $comphash.Add($($cs.Name),$nest)
>> }
>>
```

This block of code takes a few names and pipes them to ForEach-Object.

> **TIP** Remember that you can interchange $_ and $psitem to represent the object on the pipeline.

In the begin script block, you define an empty hash table. In the process script block, a variety of system information is gathered from each computer and put into its own hash table, $nest. At the end, each nested hash table is added to the master hash table. Confused? Here's what you end up with:

```
PS C:\> $comphash
Name                      Value
----                      -----
CLIENT2                   {ComputerSystem, Computername, Services, Proc...
COREDC01                  {ComputerSystem, Computername, Services, Proc...
```

This offers some intriguing possibilities:

```
PS C:\> $comphash.COREDC01
Name                      Value
----                      -----
ComputerSystem            \\COREDC01\root\cimv2:Win32_ComputerSyste...
Computername              COREDC01
Services                  {AdtAgent, ADWS, AeLookupSvc, AppHostSvc...}
Processes                 {System.Diagnostics.Process (conhost), System...
```

```
PS C:\> $comphash.COREDC01.processes | select -first 3
Handles  NPM(K)    PM(K)      WS(K) VM(M)   CPU(s)     Id ProcessName
-------  ------    -----      ----- -----   ------     -- -----------
     32       5     828       2668    22           1480 conhost
    181      21    7544      13960    79           3584 cscript
    545      13    2280       1888    45            300 csrss
PS C:\> ($comphash.COREDC01.ComputerSystem).TotalPhysicalMemory
536403968
```

By using a hash table, you can explore a lot of information without having to rerun commands.

16.5.1 Ordered hash tables

One problem with hash tables is that the order of the elements isn't preserved. Consider a simple hash table:

```
$hash1 = @{
 first = 1;
 second = 2;
 third = 3
}
$hash1
```

This code produces the following output:

```
Name                     Value
----                     -----
second                   2
first                    1
third                    3
```

The order of the elements appears to be random. If you're using the hash table as a lookup device, for instance, this won't matter. But if you're using the hash table to create a new object, it may. A standard technique to create a new object looks like this:

```
$hash1 = @{
 first = 1;
 second = 2;
 third = 3
}
$test = New-Object -TypeName PSObject -Property $hash1
$test | Format-Table -AutoSize
```

But the order of the properties as you defined them isn't preserved:

```
second first third
------ ----- -----
     2     1     3
```

In most cases, this isn't a real issue, but we know of PowerShell users who object to the property order not being preserved. Okay, we'll be honest: They moan a lot!

With PowerShell v3 and v4, you can create a hash table and preserve the order of the elements:

```
$hash2 = [ordered]@{
 first = 1;
 second = 2;
 third = 3
}
$hash2
```

All you've done here is add the `[ordered]` attribute to the hash table definition. A standard hash table is a `System.Collections.Hashtable` object, but using `[ordered]` creates a `System.Collections.Specialized.OrderedDictionary` object.

Now when you create an object, you can use an ordered hash table:

```
$hash2 = [ordered]@{
 first = 1;
 second = 2;
 third = 3
}
$test2 = New-Object -TypeName PSObject -Property $hash2
$test2 | Format-Table -AutoSize
```

This results in the order of the defined properties being preserved:

```
first second third
----- ------ -----
    1      2     3
```

16.5.2   *Common uses for hash tables*

We've shown you how the `Select-Object`, `Format-Table`, and `Format-List` cmdlets use hash tables to attach custom properties, table columns, and list entries to objects. In the case of those cmdlets, the hash tables must follow a specific form that the cmdlets have been programmed to look for: The keys must be "l" or "label" or "n" or "name," along with "e" or "expression", and so forth. But these are requirements of those particular cmdlets, not of hash tables in general. In other words, we as humans have to construct the hash tables in a specific way, because those cmdlets have been designed to look for specific keys.

16.5.3   *Defining default parameter values*

Hash tables find another use in PowerShell v3 and v4 with the ability to define default parameter values. For example, let's say you commonly run cmdlets like `Invoke-Command` that have a `-Credential` parameter, and you want to always specify a particular credential. Rather than having to type the parameter and provide a value every single time you run the cmdlet, you can define your credential as a default:

```
PS C:\> $cred = Get-Credential COMPANY\Administrator
PS C:\> $PSDefaultParameterValues.Add("Invoke-Command:Credential",$cred)
```

`$PSDefaultParameterValues` is a built-in PowerShell variable, and it's a specialized hash table. In this example, you use its `Add()` method to add a new key-value pair. Doing so lets you continually add more items to it, without overwriting what was already there. You can see that the key added here takes a special form, `cmdlet:parameter`, where `cmdlet` is the cmdlet or advanced function you want to define a default for and `parameter` is the parameter you're defining a default for. The value of the hash table item is whatever you want the default parameter value to be—in this case, the credential you created and stored in `$cred`.

You could even use a wildcard to create a default for all cmdlets that use the `-Credential` parameter. This time, you'll completely redefine `$PSDefaultParameterValues`, overwriting whatever else you've put in there with this new setting:

```
PS C:\> $PSDefaultParameterValues = @{"*:Credential"=$cred}
```

This is a great feature, although it can be a bit cumbersome to use—you'll see more on default parameters in chapter 18. `$PSDefaultParameterValues` starts out empty each time you open a new shell window; if you want to define a "persistent" default, the only way to do so is to put the definition into a PowerShell profile script. That way, your definition is re-created each time you open a new shell. You can read more about default parameter values by running `help about_parameters_default_values` in the shell.

16.6 *Script blocks*

They might seem like a funny thing to lump into this chapter, but like variables, arrays, and hash tables, script blocks are a fundamental element in PowerShell scripting. They're key to several common commands, too, and you've been using them already.

A script block is essentially any PowerShell command, or series of commands, contained within curly brackets, or {}. Anything in curly brackets is usually a script block of some kind, with the sole exception of hash tables (which also use curly brackets in their structure). You've used a script block already:

```
PS C:\> Get-Service | Where { $_.Status -eq 'Running' }
```

In that example, you used a special kind of script block called a filter script, providing it to the `-FilterScript` parameter of the `Where-Object` cmdlet. The only thing that makes it special is the fact that the cmdlet expects the entire block to result in `True` or `False`, thus making it a filter script instead of a plain-old script block. You also used script blocks with `Invoke-Command`, in chapter 10, and with the `ForEach-Object` cmdlet, and in several other cases.

You can create a script block right from the command line and store the entire thing in a variable. In this example, notice how PowerShell's prompt changes after you press Enter for the first time. It does this because you're still "inside" the script block, and it'll continue to use that prompt until you close the script block and press Enter on a blank line.

```
PS C:\> $block = {
>> Import-Module ServerManager
>> Get-WindowsFeature | Where { $_.Installed } |
```

```
>> Select Name,DisplayName,Description |
>> ConvertTo-HTML
>> }
>>
```

Now you have the script block stored in the variable `$block` and you can execute it by using PowerShell's invocation operator and the variable:

```
PS C:\> &$block | Out-File installed.html
```

In the script block you defined, notice that it ends in `ConvertTo-HTML`, meaning the result of the script block is a bunch of HTML being placed into the pipeline. When you invoke the block, you pipe that output to `Out-File`, thus saving the HTML into a file. You could also use the variable `$block` anywhere a script block is required, such as with `Invoke-Command`:

```
PS C:\> Invoke-Command -ScriptBlock $block -ComputerName win8 |
➥ Out-File InstalledFeatures.html
```

Here, you're asking a remote machine to execute the script block. The resulting HTML is transmitted back to your computer and placed into the pipeline; you pipe it to `Out-File` to save the HTML into a file.

Script blocks can be parameterized, too. For example, create another script block that displays all processes whose names start with a particular character or characters:

```
PS C:\> $procbloc = {
>> param([string]$name)
>> Get-Process -Name $name
>> }
>>
```

The `param()` section defines a comma-delimited list of parameters; in this case, you've included only a single parameter. It's just a variable that you create. When you run the script block, pass a value to the parameter as follows:

```
PS C:\> &$procbloc svc*

Handles   NPM(K)    PM(K)      WS(K) VM(M)    CPU(s)     Id ProcessName
-------   ------    -----      ----- -----    ------     -- -----------
    481       36     9048      11984    60      1.00    348 svchost
    301       12     2124       7512    36      1.17    600 svchost
    295       14     2572       5656    27      1.89    636 svchost
    392       15    18992      21248    56      3.02    728 svchost
   1289       43    19312      33964   129     41.09    764 svchost
    420       24     5768      11488    98      1.20    788 svchost
    712       45    19932      24076  1394     10.41    924 svchost
     45        4      508       2340    13      0.02   1248 svchost
    213       18    10076       9104  1375      0.13   1296 svchost
     71        6      804       3560    28      0.00   1728 svchost
```

This passed the value svc* into the parameter `$name`, which you then pass to the `-Name` parameter of `Get-Process`. You can see that script blocks are flexible; you'll see a lot more of them, and more of what they can do, as you read about other topics in this book.

16.7 *Summary*

Variables are one of the core elements of PowerShell that you'll find yourself using all of the time. They're easy to work with, although some of the specific details and behaviors that we covered in this chapter represent some of the biggest "gotchas" that newcomers stumble into when they first start using the shell. Hopefully, by knowing a bit more about them, you'll avoid those pitfalls and be able to make better use of variables.

PowerShell security

Security is important in any computer software, and PowerShell is no exception. That said, you may have some confusion about what PowerShell's security is meant to accomplish. We'll clear that up in this chapter.

17.1 PowerShell security goals

Let's start by defining exactly what PowerShell's security is meant to accomplish and outlining a few things that it's explicitly *not* intended to provide.

PowerShell's only security goal is to prevent an *uninformed* user from *unintentionally* executing scripts. That's it. The goal is to try to stop PowerShell from becoming an easy source for malicious scripts, as VBScript was back in the days of the "Melissa" and "I Love You" viruses. Keep in mind that PowerShell is security neutral, meaning that it neither adds to nor takes away from the existing security of the Windows operating system. In other words, if you have permission to delete users in Active Directory, PowerShell will let you do so—as will many other tools that have nothing to do with PowerShell. One reason that PowerShell doesn't attempt to become a security gateway is because it's almost never the only way in which you can do something. It makes no sense for PowerShell to act as a security system when it's so easily bypassed by simply choosing to use other tools. If you're concerned about your users using PowerShell to, say, delete every user in Active Directory, we can give you an easy fix: Don't give them the permissions they'd need to do that. That way, they won't be able to use PowerShell *or any other tool* to create that kind of havoc.

PowerShell is also *not* intended to stop an *informed* user from *intentionally* doing something stupid or dangerous. It's like users having the keys to a nuclear missile: If they deliberately turn the key because they possess the necessary privilege or authority, lift the cover over the "fire" switch, and press the button, well, that's hardly an accidental series of events, is it? If you don't trust users to not do something stupid on purpose, they shouldn't be in the missile silo in the first place. PowerShell is no different. If an administrator attempts to stop a mission-critical service, and they have the necessary rights and privileges, PowerShell won't stop them, whether or not they're using a script. The script means they can screw up faster with less typing. The bottom line is, don't expect PowerShell to do your job when it comes to security.

17.2 PowerShell security mechanisms

So what exactly does PowerShell do to accomplish its security goals? Three levels of protection exist, each designed to thwart a particular type of attack that's commonly targeted against uninformed users. To be clear, when we talk about uninformed users, we're referring to someone lacking the necessary skills or experience to manage a modern Windows-based computer. This could be an end user or your summer intern.

PowerShell's security mechanisms are layered and enabled by default out of the box. Some of them you can modify. But be warned: If *you* turn off these mechanisms and are burned by a malicious event, the blame is on *you*. As a general rule, PowerShell security is weakened only by changes you make. And although we understand that some of these mechanisms may require extra work on your part, don't trade security for convenience. With experience you'll find it's not that difficult.

17.2.1 Script execution requires a path

To begin with, PowerShell never searches the current directory for a script. So, if you just run Dir, PowerShell will look to see if there's a command by that name, then an alias by that name, and then it will stop. If there happens to be a script named Dir.ps1 in the current folder, PowerShell won't execute it. So, whenever you see a command that's not prefixed by a directory path, you can be sure it's a command being run out of memory and not a script.

Script execution extends to other scripts as well such as batch files or VBScript. If you had a script in the current directory called Dir.bat, you'd ensure it too wouldn't be executed simply by typing DIR.bat.

Windows search path

PowerShell will execute scripts that are on the Windows search path. If you create a script called test3.ps1, copy it into C:\Windows, and then type `test3` at the Power-Shell prompt, the script will execute. The full path to the script isn't needed.

You can view the search path by typing this:

```
$env:path
```

A better view of the contents is supplied by using this:

```
$env:path -split ";"
```

This command will display one folder per line to make it easier to read.

If you want to add another folder to the Windows search path specifically for your PowerShell scripts, put a line like the following into your PowerShell profile:

```
$env:Path = "C:\Scripts\;" + $env:Path
```

The moral of the story is to be careful where you store your scripts so that you don't inadvertently make it easier to run code by accident.

To run a script, you have to provide a path to it. That can be a complete absolute path like C:\Scripts\MyScript.ps1, or if you're in the folder where the script lives, you might just use a simple relative path like .\MyScript.ps1. You don't need to include the file-name extension; running `.\MyScript` from the script's folder will also run the script. But if there's a chance you might have two scripts with the same name, perhaps a Power-Shell and VBScript, then go ahead and use the extension. Take advantage of tab expansion and you don't have to type that much. Start typing the path and the first part of the script name and then press Tab. PowerShell will expand the name. Keep pressing Tab until you find the script you want. Using this technique you'll find there's no misunderstanding about what command you intend to execute.

Whenever you see a path in front of a command name, you know it's a script being run from disk and not an internal command being run from memory. So if someone tries to get you to run `.\dir`, you'll know it's a script named Dir.ps1, not the internal `Dir` alias to the `Get-ChildItem` command. The whole point of this is to prevent command hijacking—unintentionally executing a malicious script with the same name as a common command.

If by chance you have scripts like Dir.bat or Dir.vbs in the same folder, they won't run unless you specify the full name with the extension. Given this, we hope you'll use common sense and not name your script files using command names like `DIR`.

17.2.2 *Filename extension associations*

PowerShell defines a number of filename extensions for the various files it uses. This list shows most of the ones you are likely to come across:

- .PS1—Script file
- .PSM1—Script module
- .PSD1—Module manifest
- .PS1XML—XML file, usually view and type extension definitions
- .PSC1—Console file
- .PSSC—PowerShell session configuration file
- .CDXML—Cmdlet definition file (PowerShell v3 or 4 only)

NOTE   The "1" in these filename extensions indicates that they rely on version 1 of PowerShell's language engine. That's the same engine included in versions 1, 2, 3, 4, and 5 of PowerShell. A script written for PowerShell v1 is compatible with PowerShell v4 primarily because both versions use the same language engine. Differences exist between the PowerShell versions, so a script written using new functionality from v5 will fail if run in v1. You can think of the language engine as a subcomponent of PowerShell. This is also why versions 1, 2, 3, and 4 of PowerShell are installed in a folder named v1.0.

By default, *none* of these filename extensions are associated with PowerShell.exe, and they're not registered with Windows as executable file types. Simply put, that means you can't just double-click a script to run it. Out of the box, double-clicking one of these files will open them for editing, usually in Notepad. But that's just the default, and it can certainly be changed. Installing third-party script editors, for example, may modify a filename extension so that it opens in that editor. You may or not want that behavior, so pay close attention when installing PowerShell-related software; the setting to stop the editor from grabbing the file association is often hard to find.

TIP   We see a lot questions in forums along the lines of "How can I run a PowerShell script when I double-click it?" The questioner is thinking ease of use rather than security. We *always* advise that this is something you shouldn't change. This is an area where we practice what we preach—we don't enable running a PowerShell file by double clicking it, *ever*!

The goal of this security mechanism is to keep users from getting emails with a "Postcard_from_Mom.ps1" file attachment, double-clicking the attachment, and running a potentially malicious script. The user could certainly save the file, open PowerShell, and run the script from disk—but that's hardly an *unintentional* act. Remember that PowerShell isn't designed to prevent *intentional* stupidity! Again, PowerShell will only execute what a user has permissions, privileges, and rights to perform. A script simply makes it easier.

17.3   *Execution policy*

The last, and perhaps most important, security mechanism is PowerShell's execution policy. We need to cover this in depth, but before we do so we'll explain a bit about some of its underlying technologies—including digital signatures.

17.3.1 *A digital signature crash course*

For years now, Microsoft has promoted the idea of signed software as a security mechanism. Signed software carries an encrypted bit of information called a *digital signature*. That signature contains information on the identity of the signer and also ensures that the software itself hasn't changed in any way since the signature was applied. The practical upshot of this is that a signature tells you (a) who's responsible for the software and (b) that it hasn't changed since that responsible person distributed it. Any problems with the software can therefore be blamed on that responsible party, and the ID information contained within the signature enables you to track them down.

Signatures don't prevent malware. But in a perfect world, only an extremely stupid person would apply a digital signature to a piece of malware because the *signature lets you track them down*. That's in a perfect world.

This whole business with digital signatures comes down to your trust in a process. Let's use an analogy: In the United States, driver's licenses are the primary form of identification that most people carry. Among other things, they include your birth date, and so bars and similar establishments will use them to verify your age before serving you an alcoholic beverage. In computer terms, the United States has about 52 certification authorities (CAs): each of the 50 states, along with Washington, DC, and the U.S. military (which issues photo IDs to service members and their dependents). If you're a resident of Nevada, you go to the Nevada Department of Motor Vehicles (DMV) to get your license. You're perfectly able to take that license to California and order a beer, because California *trusts* the Nevada DMV. In reality, all of the states trust each other's CAs, meaning your license is good throughout the entire country. Why is that? Well, there are obviously some legal reasons, but the reality comes down to this: The states trust each other because they all use basically the same process to verify your identity, and your age, prior to issuing you that certificate. It's not exactly that the states trust each other but that they each trust the process that they all share. If it came out in the news that one state was issuing certificates—sorry, driver's licenses—using a less-trustworthy process, then the residents of that state might not be able to order a beer in their neighboring states, because the trust would break down.

Okay, let's take that back to computers. In the world of digital security there are different classes of certificate. Each class is generally based on how bad things would be if a certificate was issued to the wrong person. A Class 1 certificate is used to encrypt email, and obtaining one isn't hard because the worst that could happen is that someone could read your email when you didn't want them to. Bad for you, but not that bad for society as a whole.

The certificates needed to apply a signature to software are of the Class 3 variety. These are issued only to organizations, not to individuals, and they're issued only after a fairly detailed process of verifying that the organization is who they say they are. CAs will often check a company's credit score through Dun & Bradstreet, check the company's business registration with their state authorities, and so forth. So if you have a certificate for Microsoft Corporation, folks can be pretty sure that you represent that corporation.

This is where the trust comes in. Certificates can be issued by a variety of commercial and private CAs; Windows is configured to have a list of CAs that it trusts. By default, Windows Vista and later have a small list of trusted CAs. It'd be easy for you to examine that list, contact each CA, find out what their verification process involves, and decide whether you trust that process. If you don't, you remove the CA from your "trusted" list, essentially saying, "I don't think you do a good job of verifying people's identities before issuing them a certificate." It's as if that state just started handing out driver's licenses with whatever you wanted printed on them—the process fails, and so the trust fails.

Assuming that your computer only trusts CAs that do a good job of identity verification, you can be sure that any digitally signed software did come from whatever organization that certificate was issued to. If the software is malicious, you can easily track down the responsible organization and take appropriate action. But if you trust a CA that doesn't do a good job of identity verification, it's entirely possible you'll get a malicious piece of software that claims, perhaps, to be from "Adobe, Inc." When you track them down (not too hard to do), you'll discover that they have no idea what you're talking about—someone must have fraudulently obtained a certificate with their name on it, because some CA that you trusted didn't do a very good job of checking that identity.

Signatures also don't prevent bad code. A signed script doesn't necessarily mean it's good PowerShell or that it's safe to run in your environment. All you know from the signature is who wrote it and that it hasn't been modified since it was signed.

17.3.2 *Understanding script signing*

At this point, it might be helpful to look at the script-signing process in a bit more detail. In order to sign a PowerShell script, you need a Class 3 code-signing certificate. For testing purposes, get your hands on a copy of the command-line tool Makecert.exe, which is usually part of Visual Studio. You can use this tool to create a self-signed certificate that's only good for your computer. But this is still a handy tool for testing PowerShell security and digital signatures.

To begin, open a PowerShell or command prompt and navigate to the directory that contains Makecert.exe. The first step is to create a local certification authority. Type the following command. You can change the CN value if you'd like.

```
.\makecert -n "CN=PowerShell Local Certificate Root" -a sha1 -eku
➥ 1.3.6.1.5.5.7.3.3 -r -sv root.pvk root.cer -ss Root -sr localMachine
```

When prompted, enter a password for the private key and then again when prompted. Now you'll create a digital signature and store it in the local certificate store. Type this command as is, changing the CN value if you wish:

```
.\makecert -pe -n "CN=PowerShell Script Signer" -ss MY -a sha1 -eku
➥ 1.3.6.1.5.5.7.3.3 -iv root.pvk -ic root.cer
```

Enter the password when prompted. You can check the CERT: PSDrive for the new certificate:

```
PS C:\> dir Cert:\CurrentUser\My -CodeSigningCert

    Directory: Microsoft.PowerShell.Security\Certificate::CurrentUser\My
Thumbprint                                  Subject
----------                                  -------
0E04B179F42F4B080B0FCC47C54C4A7FD0AD45DE   CN=PowerShell Script Signer
```

You can have multiple script-signing certificates, but generally all you need is one trusted in your domain. To sign scripts, you're going to need this certificate, so save it to a variable:

```
PS C:\> $cert=dir Cert:\CurrentUser\My -CodeSigningCert
```

To sign a script, use the `Set-AuthenticodeSignature` cmdlet, specifying a file and a certificate. This cmdlet supports `-Whatif`.

```
PS C:\scripts> Set-AuthenticodeSignature .\TestScript.ps1 -Certificate
➥ $cert -whatif
What if: Performing operation "Set-AuthenticodeSignature" on Target
"C:\scripts\TestScript.ps1".
```

Looks okay, so now do it for real:

```
PS C:\scripts> Set-AuthenticodeSignature .\TestScript.ps1 -Certificate
➥ $cert
    Directory: C:\scripts

SignerCertificate                            Status        Path
-----------------                            ------        ----
0E04B179F42F4B080B0FCC47C54C4A7FD0AD45DE    Valid         TestScript.ps1
```

You can use the `Get-AuthenticodeSignature` cmdlet to view signature status:

```
PS C:\scripts> dir *.ps1 | Get-AuthenticodeSignature | Format-Table -Auto
    Directory: C:\scripts
SignerCertificate                            Status        Path
-----------------                            ------        ----
                                             NotSigned     Backup-EventLogv2.ps1
                                             NotSigned     Backup-VM.ps1
                                             NotSigned     BackupAllEventLogs.ps1
                                             NotSigned     BalloonTip.ps1
                                             NotSigned     get-computers.ps1
                                             NotSigned     get-computers2.ps1
                                             NotSigned     get-computers3.ps1
                                             NotSigned     get-computers4.ps1
                                             NotSigned     get-computers5.ps1
0E04B179F42F4B080B0FCC47C54C4A7FD0AD45DE    Valid         TestScript.ps1
...
```

As you can see, you have a number of other files that need to be signed, so go ahead and sign them:

```
PS C:\scripts> dir *.ps1 | Set-AuthenticodeSignature -Certificate $cert
```

This will sign all PowerShell scripts in the current directory. When you sign a script, a special comment block will be appended:

```
PS C:\scripts> Get-Content .\TestScript.ps1
#requires -version 2.0
$s="Hello {0}. Are you ready for some PowerShell today?" -f $env:username
write-host $s -ForegroundColor Green

# SIG # Begin signature block
# MIIEPAYJKoZIhvcNAQcCoIIELTCCBCkCAQExCzAJBgUrDgMCGgUAMGkGCisGAQQB
# gjcCAQSgWzBZMDQGCisGAQQBgjcCAR4wJgIDAQAABBAfzDtgWUsITrck0sYpfvNR
# AgEAAgEAAgEAAgEAAgEAMCEwCQYFKw4DAhoFAAQUrwnikA6r8TeOkIS7piC+KAS1
# kgWgggJGMIICQjCCAAa+gAwIBAgIQ/xSr8g37e4hD3fK6vR/IcTAJBgUrDgMCHQUA
# MCwxKjAoBgNVBAMTIVBvd2VyU2hlbGwgTG9jYWwgQ2VydGlmaWNhdGUgUm9vdDAe
# Fw0xMjAxMTEyMTMwMTlaFw0zOTEyMzEyMzU5NTlaMCMxITAfBgNVBAMTGFBvd2Vy
# U2hlbGwgU2NyaXB0IFNpZ25lcjCBnzANBgkqhkiG9w0BAQEFAAOBjQAwgYkCgYEA
# vAqvNgzQ3VvU2VS4BwWPVzHYatVpI1ugAvy/uagppZmDoKTVIL4UiCfpP3tFWCLn
# 8r3Xfoldlcfqp0jkITU+ODJz9pH6tfS6WY+QB2GCFzXBOxj4nLsTqNYCH/G/mUHY
# iN1TtpGINOs5Akg4fWgo9xUfFSQCwY17OLMA2mEahOkCAwEAAaN2MHQwEwYDVR0l
# BAwwCgYIKwYBBQUHAwMwXQYDVR0RBBYwFIAQCWSVak4+ihZF92BFueq106EuMCwx
# KjAoBgNVBAMTIVBvd2VyU2hlbGwgTG9jYWwgQ2VydGlmaWNhdGUgUm9vdIIQqyHb
# dM1K1aFNW5MDoN5HwTAJBgUrDgMCHQUAA4GBADRtl+ccCCb+/Itds9iabZIyISDi
# nfN2mNkSnlrd5BdIorTMgonCYlQax5/htjGFeelD1T4u0iHfDhA3/xJOgd6aPNf4
# zSgqza8a8FEYVV8NCJZcyC0DXCJsllECpXvhQICR0sLd5z7eCNUF+7Gry78P6jdv
# mPDBAwYAtbp4/nzvMYIBYDCCAVwCAQEwQDAsMSowKAYDVQQDEyFQb3dlcldoZWxs
# IExvY2FsIENlcnRpZmljYXRlIFJvb3QCEP8Uq/IN+3uIQ93yur0fyHEwCQYFKw4D
# AhoFAKB4MBgGCisGAQQBgjcCAQwxCjAIoAKAAKECgAAwGQYJKoZIhvcNAQkDMQwG
# CisGAQQBgjcCAQQwHAYKKwYBBAGCNwIBCzEOMAwGCisGAQQBgjcCARUwIwYJKoZI
# hvcNAQkEMRYEFJC2WAEM4wvx98CaNLrvHK7BM4NgMA0GCSqGSIb3DQEBAQUABIGA
# tewnic/hZcuJoe22VxHDqjjLdrjyiaVuPFSYcPUpunTX3c8COeLfU6Yrq5QEGp8V
# 8wKFFFcp4o9ifSfRFxUqUV6CPZEr3udEhgiKugsYGv/GLOWAh1rSV01D3g2HuocS
# f2g1Bd0fcXfzMIOCOmzjkx7H6zRbo9+B4QdWO5yL7e8=
# SIG # End signature block
PS C:\scripts>
```

If you edit the file, even by changing a single character or space, the signature will break:

```
PS C:\scripts> Get-AuthenticodeSignature .\TestScript.ps1
    Directory: C:\scripts

SignerCertificate                        Status        Path
-----------------                        ------        ----
0E04B179F42F4B080B0FCC47C54C4A7FD0AD45DE HashMismatch  TestScript.ps1
```

The solution is to simply resign the script:

```
PS C:\scripts> Set-AuthenticodeSignature .\TestScript.ps1 -Cert $cert
```

Some editors such as SAPIEN's PowerShell Studio can be configured to automatically sign scripts whenever you save them. Reading the help file about_Signing is recommended. Now, how does all of this relate to PowerShell?

17.3.3 *The execution policy in depth*

PowerShell's execution policy can be set to one of five levels, all of which correspond to some degree of digital signature checking and script execution:

- *Restricted*—This is the out-of-the-box execution policy for client operating systems and most servers, and it means that scripts won't run. This includes scripts started locally or using PowerShell remoting. It also includes your profile scripts! The one exception is on Windows Server 2012 R2 where the default execution policy is RemoteSigned.

- *RemoteSigned*—With this policy, scripts created on the local computer will execute just fine. Scripts created from a remote computer, including network shares, will run only if they carry a digital signature, and that signature must have been made by using a certificate issued from a trusted CA. The signature must also be intact, meaning the script can't have changed one tiny bit since it was signed. Note that some applications, notably Firefox, Internet Explorer, and Outlook, place a special flag into the header of files they download. Those files are considered "remote" by PowerShell and may be blocked. We'll explain how to handle blocked files a bit later in the chapter.

- *AllSigned*—Basically the same as RemoteSigned, except that all scripts must be signed, no matter where they came from. This won't prevent a malicious but signed script from executing.

- *Unrestricted*—All scripts will run without a signature.

- *Bypass*—This shuts down PowerShell's execution policy entirely. It's mainly intended to be used by developers who are hosting PowerShell inside another application, when that application will provide its own security and PowerShell's isn't needed.

There's also a setting of Undefined, which means nothing is set for the current scope. Depending on how a PowerShell script is executed, you might end up with different execution policies in different scopes. If the setting is Undefined, generally this will have the same effect as Restricted. You can read more about the execution policy types in the help file about_Execution_Policies.

You can see the current execution policy by running `Get-ExecutionPolicy`:

```
PS C:\> Get-Executionpolicy
Restricted
```

To modify it, run `Set-ExecutionPolicy` in an elevated session and follow the prompts:

```
PS C:\> Set-ExecutionPolicy RemoteSigned
Execution Policy Change
The execution policy helps protect you from scripts that you do not trust.
Changing the execution policy might expose you to the security risks
described in the about_Execution_Policies help topic at
http://go.microsoft.com/fwlink/?LinkID=135170. Do you want to change the
execution policy?
[Y] Yes  [N] No  [S] Suspend  [?] Help (default is "Y"):
PS C:\> get-executionpolicy
RemoteSigned
```

If you prefer not to be prompted, use the –Force parameter:

```
PS C:\> Set-ExecutionPolicy AllSigned -Force
PS C:\> Get-ExecutionPolicy
AllSigned
```

The change is immediate. Note that the execution policy is stored in the HKEY_ LOCAL_MACHINE portion of the Registry, which normally means that you have to be a local Administrator to change it. We don't recommend modifying the Registry directly, but you can certainly check it with this one-line command:

```
PS C:\> Get-ItemProperty HKLM:\SOFTWARE\Microsoft\PowerShell\1\
➥ ShellIds\Microsoft.PowerShell -Name executionpolicy |
➥ select ExecutionPolicy
ExecutionPolicy
---------------
RemoteSigned
```

This is a handy command that you could use to query a remote computer using Invoke-Command or other .NET remote Registry tricks. Of course, the easiest way to check a remote computer's execution policy is to use PowerShell Remoting.

```
PS C:\> Invoke-Command {Get-ExecutionPolicy} -computer Client2
PSComputername          RunspaceID                   Value
--------------          ----------                   -----
Client2                 5b704b5c-cf6...              Restricted
```

The execution policy can also be deployed through an Active Directory Group Policy Object (GPO). When configured in that fashion, the GPO setting will override any local setting or any attempt to change it.

Finally, you can also change the execution policy for a single PowerShell session by using the –ExecutionPolicy switch of the PowerShell.exe executable:

```
C:\windows\system32>powershell -Executionpolicy allsigned
Windows PowerShell
Copyright (C) 2013 Microsoft Corporation. All rights reserved.

. : File C:\Users\Richard\Documents\WindowsPowerShell\profile.ps1 cannot be
loaded. The file C:\Users\Richard\Documents\WindowsPowerShell\profile.ps1 is
    not digitally signed. You cannot run this script on the current system.
    For more information about running scripts and setting execution policy,
    see about_Execution_Policies at http://go.microsoft.com/fwlink/
    ?LinkID=135170.
At line:1 char:3
+ . 'C:\Users\Richard\Documents\WindowsPowerShell\profile.ps1'
+   ~~~~~~~~~~~~~~~~~~~~~~~~~~~~~~~~~~~~~~~~~~~~~~~~~~~~~~~~~~~~~
    + CategoryInfo          : SecurityError: (:) [], PSSecurityException
    + FullyQualifiedErrorId : UnauthorizedAccess
PS C:\windows\system32>
```

In this example we started a new PowerShell session from the CMD prompt, specifying an AllSigned policy. We can tell it worked because the profile scripts, which aren't signed, failed to run.

> **NOTE**   If you're using a GPO to apply execution policies, you won't get an error message, but your setting also won't be applied.

PowerShell isn't intended to stop an informed user from intentionally doing anything—and adding a command-line parameter in that fashion is definitely the sign of an informed user doing something very much on purpose. If at this point you're still concerned about a savvy user getting hold of this to run scripts, then all we can ask is why haven't *you* limited their access and permissions by now? Remember, commands executed in a PowerShell script are generally no different than what a user could type interactively in a console. If users can't run a script, and they're savvy enough, there's nothing to prevent them from copying and pasting the script contents into a Power-Shell console and executing them (other than permissions and privileges).

So what's the effect of all of this? Well, it depends on the execution policy and the validity of any digital signatures. If the execution policy is anything but AllSigned, PowerShell will run any script, signed or not, even if the signature isn't valid. But with AllSigned, you'll get errors if the script isn't signed:

```
PS C:\scripts> Set-ExecutionPolicy Allsigned -Force
PS C:\scripts> .\NewScript.ps1
File C:\scripts\NewScript.ps1 cannot be loaded. The file
C:\scripts\NewScript.ps1 is not digitally signed. The script will not execute
    on the system. For more information, see about_Execution_Policies at
    http://go.microsoft.com/fwlink/?LinkID=135170.
At line:1 char:1
+ .\NewScript.ps1
+ ~~~~~~~~~~~~~~~~
    + CategoryInfo          : NotSpecified: (:) [], PSSecurityException
    + FullyQualifiedErrorId : UnauthorizedAccess
PS C:\scripts>
```

Or if the signature is invalid:

```
PS C:\scripts> .\TestScript.ps1
File C:\scripts\TestScript.ps1 cannot be loaded. The contents of file
C:\scripts\TestScript.ps1 may have been tampered because the hash of the
File does not match the hash stored in the digital signature. The script
will not execute on the system. Please see "get-help about_signing" for
more details..
At line:1 char:1
+ .\TestScript.ps1
+ ~~~~~~~~~~~~~~~~~
    + CategoryInfo          : NotSpecified: (:) [], PSSecurityException
    + FullyQualifiedErrorId : UnauthorizedAccess
PS C:\scripts>
```

Don't ignore these error messages. They're telling you something important, which is why you might want to use an AllSigned policy. The solution, after verifying the file, is to resign it:

```
PS C:\scripts> Set-AuthenticodeSignature .\TestScript.ps1 -Cert $cert
PS C:\scripts> .\TestScript.ps1
Do you want to run software from this untrusted publisher?
```

```
File C:\scripts\TestScript.ps1 is published by CN=PowerShell Script Signer
And is not trusted on your system. Only run scripts from trusted publishers.
[V] Never run  [D] Do not run  [R] Run once  [A] Always run  [?] Help
(default is "D"):r
Hello Administrator. Are you ready for some PowerShell today?
PS C:\scripts>
```

Because in this example you're using a self-signed certificate, you get a warning about the publisher. But because you recognize the publisher, you can go ahead and run the script. Oh, and notice that you had to specify the path to the script file, even though you were in the same directory?

To sum up these mechanisms, if you want to execute a PowerShell script you must have an appropriate execution policy. If you're using digital signatures, the signature must be valid. Then, to execute the script you need to specify the script path.

17.4 *Blocked files*

On a related note, you'll also run into issues if you try to run a script that you've downloaded from the internet. On a Windows 8.1 desktop, if we try to run this downloaded script we receive an error:

```
PS C:\scripts> .\Get-CIMFile3.ps1
.\Get-CIMFile3.ps1 : File C:\scripts\Get-CIMFile3.ps1 cannot be loaded.
The file C:\scripts\Get-CIMFile3.ps1 is not digitally signed. You cannot
run this script on the current system. For more information about running
scripts and setting execution policy, see about_Execution_Policies at
http://go.microsoft.com/fwlink/?LinkID=135170.
At line:1 char:1
+ .\Get-CIMFile3.ps1
+ ~~~~~~~~~~~~~~~~~~~
    + CategoryInfo          : SecurityError: (:) [], PSSecurityException
    + FullyQualifiedErrorId : UnauthorizedAccess
```

If you download a lot of files, you might want an easy way to identify them. The Get-Item cmdlet includes the parameter –Stream, which will display any alternate stream data. Downloaded files will have a Zone.Identifier stream.

```
PS C:\scripts> dir *.ps1 | Get-Item -Stream zone.identifier
⇒   -ErrorAction SilentlyContinue | where Stream

    FileName: C:\scripts\Get-CIMFile3.ps1

Stream                Length
------                ------
Zone.Identifier           26

    FileName: C:\scripts\Get-VMMemoryReport.ps1

Stream                Length
------                ------
Zone.Identifier           26
```

This command passes all PowerShell scripts to Get-Item looking for the Zone.Identifier stream. We're setting the ErrorAction to SilentlyContinue to suppress error messages for scripts that don't have the stream. Once identified, and after we're convinced of their safety, we can unblock them:

```
PS C:\scripts> dir *.ps1 | Get-Item -Stream zone.identifier
    -ErrorAction SilentlyContinue |
    foreach { Unblock-File $_.filename }
```

If you've downloaded a set of files into a new folder so you know that all the files will be blocked, you can simplify the process:

```
Get-ChildItem -Path c:\testdata | Unblock-File
```

From this point, execution will depend on your policy.

> **NOTE** Any file downloaded through Internet Explorer will be blocked—including Word and Excel files. This technique can also be applied to those files, not just PowerShell scripts.

17.5 *The PowerShell security debate*

Microsoft has generally recommended the RemoteSigned execution policy, suggesting that it offers a good balance between security and convenience. After all, with All-Signed you have to sign every single script you run, normally using the Set-AuthenticodeSignature cmdlet to do so. What a pain in the neck! You also have to have a certificate, and those can be expensive—about $800 per year from most commercial CAs. You can also create your own local-use-only certificate using the Makecert .exe utility; run help about_signing in PowerShell to read more about that. And of course, if your organization has its own internal Public Key Infrastructure (PKI), that can be used to issue the necessary Class 3 certificates.

Other folks, including Microsoft's own Scripting Guy, suggest using Unrestricted instead. Their argument is that the execution policy provides little in the way of protection, because it's easily bypassed. That's certainly true: If you were going to deploy a piece of malware that relied on a PowerShell script, you'd do it as a piece of .NET Framework code that hosted the shell and bypassed the execution policy entirely. Attackers are informed enough to do that. The point is that PowerShell's execution policy isn't a substitute for antimalware utilities, and if you have a good antimalware utility, then the execution policy seems less useful.

Our take? We usually go for the RemoteSigned policy. We know plenty of clients who use AllSigned, and they use it as a kind of change control mechanism: Only certain administrators possess the Class 3 certificate needed to sign scripts, and so any script released to the production network must be reviewed by one of them, in compliance with the organization's change management processes. So they're using the execution policy more as a process enforcement tool than a security mechanism, which is just fine. The other advantage, which Jeff firmly believes in, is that digital signatures guarantee script integrity. If the script has been modified in any way, even by changing a single character, the signature will fail and the script won't execute. To Jeff's way of thinking, he'd rather have a script fail to execute than start running only to fail partway through because of some bit of corruption, leaving you stuck between a rock and hard place. Granted, Jeff is an old-school "belt and suspenders" kind of IT pro, but the point is that a signed script can guarantee it hasn't been modified in any fashion, either deliberately or not. And regardless of your execution policy, you must review scripts acquired elsewhere before running them and ideally only then in a controlled test environment.

> **TIP** Remember that many of the files that ship with PowerShell, such as the format files, are digitally signed by Microsoft. Don't make any changes to those files or you will have problems running PowerShell.

We'll point out one other consideration: PowerShell profile scripts. Keep in mind that these scripts are stored in your Documents folder, which you obviously have full control over. Even if you're logging on with a lesser-privileged account (in keeping with the principle of least privilege), that account by definition has full control over the Documents folder and your profile scripts. A simple piece of malware could thus modify your profile script, inserting malicious commands. The next time you run Power-Shell—which you'd likely be doing with elevated privileges—those inserted commands would run automatically. Using the AllSigned execution policy helps thwart this specific attack, because your profile would also have to be signed, and the malicious insertions would break the signature, causing an error the next time you open the shell. Now, we'll also freely admit that AllSigned provides only the barest kind of protection against this attack, and the fact is that in order for it to happen *you have to have uncaught malware on your machine*! If you have malware, your PowerShell profile is far from your biggest problem; "Once you're 0wned, you're 0wned," as the saying goes. But it's a consideration, and an illustration of the complexity of the PowerShell security debate.

17.6   *Summary*

This chapter gave you an overview of what PowerShell security is meant to accomplish and how it attempts to do so. We hope you now have a better idea of what to expect from PowerShell's security features and how you'd like to use them in your organization.

Advanced PowerShell syntax

This chapter covers

- Splatting
- Defining default parameter values
- Running external utilities
- Using subexpressions
- Using hash tables as objects

This chapter is a kind of catchall—an opportunity to share some advanced tips and tricks that you'll see other folks using. Almost everything in this chapter can be accomplished in one or more other ways (and we'll be sure to show you those as well), but it's nice to know these shorter, more concise PowerShell expert techniques. These techniques save you time by enabling you to complete your tasks quicker and more easily.

18.1 Splatting

"Splatting" sounds like something a newborn baby does, right? In reality, it's a way of wrapping up several parameters for a command and passing them to the command all at once.

For example, let's say you want to run the following command:

```
Get-WmiObject -Class Win32_LogicalDisk -ComputerName SERVER2
➡ -Filter "DriveType=3" -Credential $cred
```

Notice that in this command, you pass a variable, $cred, to the -Credential parameter (for this example, assume that you've already put a valid credential into $cred). Now, if you were doing this from the command line, splatting wouldn't save you any time. In a script, stringing all of those parameters together can make things a little hard to read. One advantage of splatting is making that command a little prettier:

```
$params = @{class='Win32_LogicalDisk'
        computername='SERVER2'
        Filter="DriveType=3"
        Credential=$cred
      }
Get-WmiObject @params
```

This code creates a variable, $params, and loads it with a hash table. In the hash table, you create a key for each parameter name and assign the desired value to each key. To run the command, you don't have to type individual parameters; instead, use the splat operator (the @ sign—being a splat operator is one of its many duties) and the name of your variable. Note that you shouldn't add the dollar sign to the variable in this instance, which is a common mistake.

> **NOTE** We're in the habit of using single quotation marks around strings in most cases, but notice that the -Filter parameter value was enclosed in double quotation marks. That's because in WMI, the filter criteria will often contain single quotes. By wrapping it in double quotes, you can include single quotes within it without any problems. When it comes to that particular parameter value, it's best to use double quotes—even when using single quotes would work fine.

There's no reason whatsoever that the hash table has to be so nicely formatted. It's obviously easier to read when it *is* nicely formatted, but PowerShell doesn't care. This code is also perfectly valid:

```
$params = @{class='Win32_LogicalDisk';computername='SERVER2';
filter="DriveType=3";credential=$cred}
Get-WmiObject @params
```

When you're working interactively with PowerShell you can use positional parameters. Okay, technically you can use them in scripts as well, but we discourage that practice because it makes the scripts harder to read and maintain. Positional parameters take the values you pass to the cmdlet and assume that you want to apply them to the parameters that are positional in nature.

Get-WmiObject has two positional parameters: Class and Property. You'd do this if using the full parameter names:

```
Get-WmiObject -Class Win32_LogicalDisk -Property Size,FreeSpace
```

If you wanted to make use of PowerShell's ability to work with positional parameters, the code would become:

```
Get-WmiObject Win32_LogicalDisk Size,FreeSpace
```

Win32_LogicalDisk is automatically assigned to the -Class parameter and Size, FreeSpace to the -Property parameter. If you pass the data to the cmdlet in the wrong order, you'll get an error:

```
PS C:\> Get-WmiObject Size,FreeSpace Win32_LogicalDisk

Get-WmiObject : A positional parameter cannot be found
that accepts argument 'System.Object[]'.
At line:1 char:1
+ Get-WmiObject  Size, FreeSpace  Win32_LogicalDisk
+ ~~~~~~~~~~~~~~~~~~~~~~~~~~~~~~~~~~~~~~~~~~~~~~~~~~~
    + CategoryInfo          : InvalidArgument: (:)
    [Get-WmiObject], ParameterBindingException
    + FullyQualifiedErrorId : PositionalParameterNotFound,
    Microsoft.PowerShell.Commands.GetWmiObjectCommand
```

You can use an array of values to splat against positional parameters:

```
PS C:\> $params = 'Win32_LogicalDisk', @('Size','FreeSpace')
PS C:\> Get-WmiObject @params
```

You have to define the multiple values for -Property as an array; otherwise, you'll get an error:

```
PS C:\> $params = 'Win32_LogicalDisk','Size','FreeSpace'
PS C:\> Get-WmiObject @params
Get-WmiObject : A positional parameter cannot be found
that accepts argument 'FreeSpace'.
At line:1 char:1
+ Get-WmiObject @params
+ ~~~~~~~~~~~~~~~~~~~~~~
    + CategoryInfo          : InvalidArgument: (:)
    [Get-WmiObject], ParameterBindingException
    + FullyQualifiedErrorId : PositionalParameterNotFound,
    Microsoft.PowerShell.Commands.GetWmiObjectCommand
```

Remember that an array is only for positional parameters, so properties of Get-WmiObject such as -Filter or -Credential can't have values passed. You can use other parameters, as you saw with hash table splatting earlier:

```
PS C:\> $params = 'Win32_LogicalDisk', @('Size','FreeSpace')
PS C:\> Get-WmiObject @params -ComputerName server02
```

We recommend that you don't use positional parameters in scripts, but they're useful when you're working interactively. Splatting's sole purpose in life isn't necessarily to make your scripts easier—but that's one thing you can use it for. Another use is to minimize typing. For example, let's say that you wanted to run that same command against a number of computers, one at a time, all from the command line (not from within a script). You're going to be retyping the same parameters over and over, so why not bundle them into a hash table for splatting?

```
$params = @{class='Win32_LogicalDisk'
            Filter="DriveType=3"
            Credential=$cred}
Get-WmiObject @params -ComputerName SERVER1
Get-WmiObject @params -ComputerName SERVER2
Get-WmiObject @params -ComputerName SERVER3
```

As you can see, it's legal to mix splatted and regular parameters, so you can bundle up a bunch of parameters that you plan to reuse into a hash table and splat them along with manually typed parameters to get whatever effect you're after. You can take this approach a step further if you remember that the -ComputerName parameter can accept multiple machine names:

```
$computers = "Server02", "Win7", "WebR201"
$params = @{class='Win32_LogicalDisk'
            filter="DriveType=3"
            credential=$cred}
Get-WmiObject @params -ComputerName $computers
```

Run Get-WmiObject three times, once for each machine using the same class, filter, and credential values that were splatted. And that's a good lead-in to defining default values!

18.2 *Defining default parameter values*

When cmdlet authors create a new cmdlet, they often define default values for some of the cmdlet's parameters. For example, when running Dir, you don't have to provide the -Path parameter because the cmdlet internally defaults to "the current path." Before PowerShell v3, the only way to override those internal defaults was to manually provide the parameter when running the command.

PowerShell v3 introduced a new technique that lets you define default values for one or more parameters of a specific command, which creates a kind of hierarchy of parameter values:

- If you manually provide a parameter and value when running the command, then whatever information you provide takes precedence.
- If you don't manually provide a value but you've defined a default value in the current shell session, then that default value kicks in.
- If you haven't manually specified a parameter or defined a default value in the current session, then any internal defaults created by the command's author will take effect.

As with splatting, you don't have to define default values for every parameter. You can define defaults for the parameters that you want and then continue to provide other parameters manually when you run the command. And as stated in the previous list, you can override your own defaults at any time by manually specifying them when you run a command. One cool trick is specifying a default –Credential parameter so that it'll kick in every time you run a command and allow you to avoid having to retype it every single time. Keep in mind that such a definition is active only for the current shell session.

Default parameter values are stored in the $PSDefaultParameterValues variable using a hash table. This variable is empty until you add something to it. The variable is also scope- and session-specific. You could define the default value in your PowerShell profile script if you wanted it to take effect every time you opened a new shell window. The hash table key is the cmdlet and parameter name separated by a colon. The value is whatever you want to use for the default parameter value. You can define a script block, which will be evaluated to produce the default value.

Let's say that you've defined a credential object for WMI connections. Create the default parameter:

```
PS C:\> $PSDefaultParameterValues=@{"Get-WmiObject:credential"=$cred}
```

Now when you run a Get-WmiObject command, this default parameter will automatically be used:

```
PS C:\> get-wmiobject win32_operatingsystem -comp coredc01

SystemDirectory : C:\Windows\system32
Organization    : MyCompany
BuildNumber     : 7600
RegisteredUser  : Administrator
SerialNumber    : 00477-001-0000421-84776
Version         : 6.1.7600
```

But you have to be careful. This default value will apply to *all* uses of Get-WmiObject, which means that local queries will fail because you can't use alternate credentials:

```
PS C:\> get-wmiobject win32_operatingsystem

Get-WmiObject : User credentials cannot be used for local connections
At line:1 char:1
+ gwmi win32_operatingsystem
+ ~~~~~~~~~~~~~~~~~~~~~~~~~~~
    + CategoryInfo          : InvalidOperation: (:) [Get-WmiObject],
                              ManagementException
    + FullyQualifiedErrorId : GetWMIManagementException,Microsoft.PowerShell
                              .Commands.GetWmiObjectCommand
```

Perhaps a more likely scenario is a hash table, like this:

```
$PSDefaultParameterValues=@{"Get-WmiObject:class"="Win32_OperatingSystem";
"Get-WmiObject:enableAllPrivileges"=$True;
"Get-WmiObject:Authentication"="PacketPrivacy"}
```

Now whenever you run Get-WmiObject, unless you specify otherwise, the default parameter values are automatically included in the command:

```
PS C:\> Get-WmiObject -comp coredc01

SystemDirectory : C:\Windows\system32
Organization    : MyCompany
```

```
BuildNumber    : 7600
RegisteredUser : Administrator
SerialNumber   : 00477-001-0000421-84776
Version        : 6.1.7600
PS C:\> Get-WmiObject -comp coredc01 -Class Win32_LogicalDisk `
>> -Filter "Drivetype=3"
>>

DeviceID     : C:
DriveType    : 3
ProviderName :
FreeSpace    : 5384888320
Size         : 12777943040
VolumeName   :
```

The $PSDefaultParameterValues variable exists for as long as your PowerShell session is running. You can check it at any time:

```
PS C:\> $PSDefaultParameterValues

Name                           Value
----                           -----
Get-WmiObject:class            Win32_OperatingSystem
Get-WmiObject:Authentication   PacketPrivacy
Get-WmiObject:enableAllPriv... True
```

You can add definitions:

```
PS C:\> $PSDefaultParameterValues.Add("Get-ChildItem:Force",$True)
PS C:\> $PSDefaultParameterValues

Name                           Value
----                           -----
Get-WmiObject:class            Win32_OperatingSystem
Get-WmiObject:Authentication   PacketPrivacy
Get-WmiObject:enableAllPriv... True
Get-ChildItem:Force            True
```

A new default parameter has been added for Get-ChildItem that sets the -Force parameter to True, which will now display all hidden and system files by default:

```
PS C:\> dir

    Directory: C:\
Mode            LastWriteTime        Length Name
----            -------------        ------ ----
d--hs      2/16/2013   3:54 PM              $Recycle.Bin
d--hs      7/14/2009   1:08 AM              Documents and Settings
d----     12/7/2013    2:02 PM              Help
d----      7/13/2009  11:20 PM              PerfLogs
d-r--      3/22/2013  10:08 PM              Program Files
d-r--     12/2/2013    3:19 PM              Program Files (x86)
d--h-     12/2/2013    3:07 PM              ProgramData
d--hs      8/21/2009   1:08 PM              Recovery
d----      1/12/2012  10:42 AM              scripts
d--hs     12/1/2013    8:31 PM              System Volume Information
d----      3/24/2013  12:03 PM              Temp
```

```
d----        12/12/2013    2:22 PM           test
d-r--         12/2/2013    9:09 AM           Users
d----        12/29/2013    3:31 PM           Windows
-a---        12/12/2013    8:51 AM      3688 myprocs.csv
-a---         12/2/2013    6:00 AM      4168 temp.txt
```

Notice that this command works even though it contained an alias, DIR.

Here's another useful example. The Format-Wide cmdlet displays output in columns, usually based on the object's name or some other key value. This setup usually results in two columns. The cmdlet has a -Columns parameter, so let's give it a default value of 3. Add it to the existing variable:

```
PS C:\> $PSDefaultParameterValues.Add("Format-Wide:Column",3)
```

Running the command will automatically use the default parameter value:

```
PS C:\> dir | fw

    Directory: C:\
[$Recycle.Bin]            [Documents and Settings]    [Help]
[PerfLogs]                [Program Files]             [Program Files (x86)]
[ProgramData]             [Recovery]                  [scripts]
[System Volume Informat... [Temp]                     [test]
[Users]                   [Windows]                   myprocs.csv
temp.txt
```

If you want to modify this value, you can do so as you would for any other hash table value. The trick is including quotes around the key name because of the colon. Here's what you have now:

```
PS C:\> $PSDefaultParameterValues."Format-Wide:Column"
3
```

Let's assign a new value and test it out:

```
PS C:\> $PSDefaultParameterValues."Format-Wide:Column"=4
PS C:\> Get-Process | where {$_.ws -gt 10mb} | Format-Wide

explorer            powershell           powershell_ise        svchost
svchost
```

Don't forget that you can specify a different value to override the default preference:

```
PS C:\> Get-Process | where {$_.ws -gt 10mb} | Format-Wide -col 5

explorer         powershell        powershell_ise   svchost        svchost
```

Removing a default value is just as easy:

```
PS> $PSDefaultParameterValues.Remove("Format-Wide:Column")
PS> $PSDefaultParameterValues

Name                        Value
----                        -----
Get-WmiObject:enableAllPriv... True
Get-WmiObject:class         Win32_OperatingSystem
Get-WmiObject:Authentication PacketPrivacy
Get-ChildItem:Force         True
```

One thing to be aware of is that the $PSDefaultParameterValues variable contents can be overwritten with a command such as the following:

```
PS> $PSDefaultParameterValues=@{
>> "Format-Wide:Column"=4
>> "Get-WmiObject:Filter"="DriveType=3"
>> }
>>
PS> $PSDefaultParameterValues

Name                             Value
----                             -----
Format-Wide:Column               4
Get-WmiObject:Filter             DriveType=3
```

Be sure to use the Add and Remove methods to modify your default values; otherwise, your results may not be quite what you expected. $PSDefaultParameterValues is a great feature, but beware: It's easy to get in the habit of assuming that certain parameters will always be set. If you begin writing scripts with those same assumptions, you must include or define the $PSDefaultParameterValues variable; if you don't, your script might fail or produce incomplete results.

18.3 *Running external utilities*

As you work with PowerShell, you'll doubtless run into situations in which you need to accomplish something that you know can be done with an old-fashioned command-line utility but that might not be directly possible using a native PowerShell cmdlet. Mapping a network drive is a good example: The old NET USE command can do it, but there's nothing immediately obvious in PowerShell v2.

> **NOTE** The -Persist parameter introduced in PowerShell v3 enables you to map persistent network drives. As with any mapping of drives, just because you can doesn't mean you should.

That's fine—use the old-style command! In many cases, Microsoft has assigned an extremely low priority to creating PowerShell cmdlets when there's an existing method that already works and can be used from within PowerShell, and for the most part, PowerShell is good at running external or legacy commands.

Under the hood, PowerShell opens an instance of Cmd.exe, passes it the command you've entered, lets the command run there, and then captures the result as text. Each line of text is placed into PowerShell's pipeline as a String object. If necessary, you could pipe those String objects to another cmdlet, such as Select-String, to parse the strings or take advantage of other PowerShell scripting techniques.

Ideally, you should take results from external tools and turn them into objects that you can pass on to other cmdlets in the PowerShell pipeline. Several techniques might work, depending on the command you're running.

First, see whether the command produces CSV text. For example, the Driverquery.exe command-line tool has a parameter that formats the output as CSV, which is great because PowerShell happens to have a cmdlet that will convert CSV input to objects:

```
PS C:\> $d=driverquery /fo csv | ConvertFrom-Csv
PS C:\> $d

Module Name          Display Name        Driver Type      Link Date
-----------          ------------        -----------      ---------
1394ohci             1394 OHCI Compli... Kernel           11/20/2010 5:44:...
ACPI                 Microsoft ACPI D... Kernel           11/20/2010 4:19:...
AcpiPmi              ACPI Power Meter... Kernel           11/20/2010 4:30:...
adp94xx              adp94xx             Kernel           12/5/2008 6:54:4...
...
```

Because you have objects written to the pipeline, you can use other PowerShell cmdlets:

```
PS C:\> $d | Where {$_."Driver Type" -notmatch "Kernel"} |
sort @{expression={$_."Link date" -as [datetime]}} -desc |
Select -first 5 -prop "Display Name","Driver Type","Link Date"

Display Name              Driver Type            Link Date
------------              -----------            ---------
VirtualBox Shared Folders File System            12/19/2011 7:53:53 AM
SMB 1.x MiniRedirector    File System            7/8/2011 10:46:28 PM
Server SMB 1.xxx Driver   File System            4/28/2011 11:06:06 PM
Server SMB 2.xxx Driver   File System            4/28/2011 11:05:46 PM
srvnet                    File System            4/28/2011 11:05:35 PM
```

You should watch out for a few things. First, you might end up with property names that have spaces, which is why you must enclose them in quotes:

```
Where {$_."Driver Type" -notmatch "Kernel"}
```

Sometimes the values have extra spaces, in which case using an operator such as -eq might not work—hence the –NotMatch regular expression operator. Finally, everything is treated as a string, so if you want to use a particular value as a particular type, you may need to use a hash table, as shown earlier, to sort on the Link Date property:

```
sort @{expression={$_."Link date" -as [datetime]}} -desc
```

Otherwise, the property would've been sorted as a string, which wouldn't produce the correct results.

You'll often need to parse output using a combination of PowerShell techniques such as the Split operator and regular expressions. Here's how to take the results of the nbtstat command and turn them into PowerShell objects. Here's the original command:

```
PS C:\> nbtstat -n

Local Area Connection 2:
Node IpAddress: [172.16.10.129] Scope Id: []
              NetBIOS Local Name Table

       Name               Type         Status
    ---------------------------------------------
       CLIENT2        <00>  UNIQUE     Registered
       MYCOMPANY      <00>  GROUP      Registered
       CLIENT2        <20>  UNIQUE     Registered
       MYCOMPANY      <1E>  GROUP      Registered
       MYCOMPANY      <1D>  UNIQUE     Registered
       ..__MSBROWSE__. <01>  GROUP     Registered
```

You might want to turn the name table results into objects but also to ignore the MSBROWSE entry. The first step is to parse out all the irrelevant lines:

```
$data=nbtstat /n | Select-String "<" | where {$_ -notmatch "__MSBROWSE__"}
```

This command should leave only the lines that have a <> in the text. Next, take each line and clean it up:

```
$lines=$data | foreach {$_.Line.Trim()}
```

When writing this example, we took the extra step of trimming empty spaces from the beginning and end of each line. Now it's time to split each line into an array using whitespace as the delimiter. One approach is to use a regular expression pattern to indicate one or more spaces. After each line is turned into an array, you can define a "property" name for each array element in a hash table:

```
$lines | foreach {
 $temp=$_ -split "\s+"
 $phash=@{
 Name=$temp[0]
 NbtCode=$temp[1]
 Type=$temp[2]
 Status=$temp[3]
 }
```

As each line is written to the pipeline, all that remains is to write a new object to the pipeline:

```
New-Object -TypeName PSObject -Property $phash
```

Alternatively, you can use a hash table as an object. We'll discuss this topic a bit more later in the chapter. The following listing shows all of this code wrapped into a simple function.

Listing 18.1 Get-NBTName.ps1

```
#requires -version 3.0
Function Get-NBTName {
$data=nbtstat /n | Select-String "<" | where {$_ -notmatch "__MSBROWSE__"}

#trim each line
$lines=$data | foreach { $_.Line.Trim()}
#split each line at the space into an array and add
#each element to a hash table
$lines | foreach {
 $temp=$_ -split "\s+"
 #create an object from the hash table
 [PSCustomObject]@{
 Name=$temp[0]
 NbtCode=$temp[1]
 Type=$temp[2]
 Status=$temp[3]
 }
}
} #end function
```

Here's the result in a PowerShell expression:

```
PS C:\> Get-NBTName | sort type | Format-Table -Autosize

Name       NbtCode Type   Status
----       ------- ----   ------
MYCOMPANY  <1E>    GROUP  Registered
MYCOMPANY  <00>    GROUP  Registered
MYCOMPANY  <1D>    UNIQUE Registered
CLIENT2    <00>    UNIQUE Registered
CLIENT2    <20>    UNIQUE Registered
```

The final technique to be demonstrated here is how to handle output that's grouped. For example, you might run a command such as the following:

```
PS C:\> whoami /groups /fo list

GROUP INFORMATION
-----------------
Group Name: Everyone
Type:       Well-known group
SID:        S-1-1-0
Attributes: Mandatory group, Enabled by default, Enabled group
Group Name: BUILTIN\Users
Type:       Alias
SID:        S-1-5-32-545
Attributes: Mandatory group, Enabled by default, Enabled group
...
```

To convert this command into PowerShell, turn each group of four lines into an object with properties of GroupName, Type, SID, and Attributes. We recommend using property names without spaces. The first step is to save only the text that you want to work with, so skip the first few lines and strip out any empty lines:

```
whoami /groups /fo list | Select -Skip 4 | Where {$_}
```

Next, take what's left and pipe it to the ForEach-Object cmdlet. Use a Begin script block to initialize a few variables:

```
foreach-object -Begin {$i=0; $hash=@{}}
```

In the Process script block, keep track of the number of lines that have been processed. When $i is equal to 4, you can write a new object to the pipeline and reset the counter:

```
-Process {
   if ($i -ge 4) {
       #turn the hash table into an object
       [PSCustomObject]$hash
       $hash.Clear()
       $i=0
   }
```

If the counter is less than 4, split each line into an array using the colon as the delimiter. The first element of the array is added as the key to the hash table, replacing any spaces with nothing. The second array element is added as the value, trimmed of extra leading or trailing spaces:

```
$data=$_ -split ":"
$hash.Add($data[0].Replace(" ",""),$data[1].Trim())
$i++
```

This process repeats until $i equals 4, at which point a new object is written to the pipeline. The next listing provides the finished script.

Listing 18.2 Get-WhoamiGroups.ps1

```
#Requires -version 3.0
whoami /groups /fo list | Select -Skip 4 | Where {$_} |
 foreach-object -Begin {$i=0; $hash=@{}} -Process {
   if ($i -ge 4) {
       #turn the hash table into an object
       [PSCustomObject]$hash
       $hash.Clear()
       $i=0
   }
   else {
       $data=$_ -split ":"
       $hash.Add($data[0].Replace(" ",""),$data[1].Trim())
       $i++
   }
 }
```

Here's a sample of the final result in a PowerShell expression:

```
PS C:\> S:\Get-WhoamiGroups.ps1 | where {$_.type -eq "Group"} |
>> Select GroupName  | sort GroupName

GroupName
---------
MYCOMPANY\AlphaGroup
MYCOMPANY\Denied RODC Password Replication Group
MYCOMPANY\Domain Admins
MYCOMPANY\Exchange Organization Administrators
MYCOMPANY\Exchange Public Folder Administrators
MYCOMPANY\Exchange Recipient Administrators
MYCOMPANY\Group Policy Creator Owners
MYCOMPANY\LocalAdmins
MYCOMPANY\SalesUsers
MYCOMPANY\Schema Admins
MYCOMPANY\SCOM Ops Manager Admins
MYCOMPANY\Test Rollup
```

These examples are by no means the only way you could accomplish these tasks, but they demonstrate some of the techniques you might use.

We hope you caught our little caveat at the beginning of this section: "*For the most part*, PowerShell is good at running external commands." Sometimes it isn't so good—usually when the external command has its own complicated set of command-line parameters.

In such cases, PowerShell sometimes hiccups and gets confused about what it's supposed to be passing to Cmd.exe and what it's supposed to be handling itself.

> **TIP** PowerShell v3 introduced a new command-line parser feature. You can add the `--%` sequence anywhere in the command line, and PowerShell won't try to parse the remainder of that line. But be aware that it's not infallible, which is why we're showing you this approach.

The result is usually a screenful of error messages. There are some tricks you can use, though, to see what PowerShell is trying to do under the hood and to help it do the right thing.

At one time or another, you've probably done something like this:

```
PS C:\> ping 127.0.0.1 -n 1

Pinging 127.0.0.1 with 32 bytes of data:
Reply from 127.0.0.1: bytes=32 time<1ms TTL=128
```

What if you want to use some variables with that?

```
PS C:\> $pn = "-n 1"
PS C:\> $addr = "127.0.0.1"
PS C:\> ping $addr $pn

Value must be supplied for option -n 1.
```

You can't combine the variables, either:

```
PS C:\> ping "$addr $pn"

Ping request could not find host 127.0.0.1 -n 1. Please check the name and
try again.
```

Though awkward, this approach will work:

```
PS C:\> ping $addr
```

As will this approach:

```
PS C:\> cmd /c "ping $addr $pn"
```

You need to investigate what's happening with the arguments being passed to ping. PowerShell has a tokenizer (it reads the command you type, or run in your script, and works out what to do with them). You can feed this problem child to the tokenizer and see what it tells you. There's a lot of output, so it's been truncated here using `Format-Table` to control the display:

```
PS C:\> [management.automation.psparser]::Tokenize("ping $addr $pn",
⇨ [ref]$null) | ft Content, Type -a

Content            Type
-------            ----
ping               Command
127.0.0.1   CommandArgument
-n          CommandParameter
1                  Number
```

Four arguments are returned. First is ping itself, then the IP address, and finally the -n parameter and its argument. This output implies that PowerShell isn't interpreting the argument (1) for the parameter (-n) correctly; this result agrees with the error messages. So how can you get this approach to work?

You need to be able to pass the variables to ping and have the whole string run as a single expression. One way to achieve this is to use the Invoke-Expression cmdlet as follows:

```
PS C:\> Invoke-Expression "ping $addr $pn"

Pinging 127.0.0.1 with 32 bytes of data:
Reply from 127.0.0.1: bytes=32 time<1ms TTL=128
Ping statistics for 127.0.0.1:
    Packets: Sent = 1, Received = 1, Lost = 0 (0% loss),
Approximate round trip times in milli-seconds:
    Minimum = 0ms, Maximum = 0ms, Average = 0ms
```

18.4 *Expressions in quotes: $($cool)*

This example is a handy little bit of syntax that you'll see all over people's blogs, in books, and so on—but if they don't explain what it's doing, it can be downright confusing.

One thing not covered elsewhere in this book is the trick you can do with variables that are placed inside double quotes. Check out this example:

```
PS C:\> $a = 'World'
PS C:\> $b1 = 'Hello, $a'
PS C:\> $b2 = "Hello, $a"
PS C:\> $b1
Hello, $a
PS C:\> $b2
Hello, World
```

As you can see, inside double quotes PowerShell scans for the $ symbol (the dollar sign). PowerShell assumes that what follows the dollar sign is a variable name and replaces the variable with its contents. So there's rarely a need to concatenate strings—you can stick variables directly inside double quotes.

Here's a more practical example. Let's keep it simple by loading numeric values into variables and then performing some math on them so that you can display the result in a human-readable phrase:

```
$freespace = 560
$size = 1000
$freepct = 100 - (($freespace / $size) * 100)
Write-Host "There is $freepct% free space"
```

There's nothing wrong with this approach, except perhaps that a third variable was created to hold the result. That's a variable PowerShell now has to keep track of, set aside memory for, and so on. It's no big deal, but it isn't strictly necessary, either. Please note the percent sign used here: When PowerShell is doing its variable-replacement trick inside double quotes, it looks for the dollar sign. It then scans until it finds a character that isn't legal inside a variable name, such as whitespace or—in this case—the percent sign. So, in this example, PowerShell knows that `$freepct` is the variable name. That means you couldn't stick the math formula into the double quotes—you wouldn't get the intended output at all. What you can do, though, is this:

```
$freespace = 560
$size = 1000
Write-Host "There is $(100 - (($freespace / $size) * 100))% free space"
```

Here, the entire mathematical expression is placed inside a `$()` construct, shown in boldface here for emphasis. PowerShell knows that when it sees a dollar sign immediately followed by an open parenthesis it isn't looking at a variable name but instead at a complete expression. Inside those parentheses, you can put almost anything that PowerShell can execute. It'll evaluate the contents of the parentheses and replace the entire `$()` expression with its results. You avoid creating a new variable, and you still get the intended result.

You'll most often see this approach used with object properties. For example, suppose you have a variable `$service` that contains a single service. If you want to try this out on your own, run the following command:

```
$service = Get-Service | Select -first 1
```

This command won't work:

```
$service = Get-Service | Select -first 1
Write-Host "Service name is $service.name" -ForegroundColor Green
```

A period isn't a valid character in a variable name, so PowerShell will treat `$service` as a variable and treat `.name` as a literal string. The result will be something like "Service name is System.ServiceProcess.ServiceController.name," which isn't what was intended. But using the `$()` trick works:

```
$service = Get-Service | Select -first 1
Write-Host "Service name is $($service.name)" -foregroundcolor Green
```

In this code, the expression `$service.name` is enclosed in the special `$()` construct so that PowerShell will evaluate the entire expression and replace it with the result. You should see something like "Service name is ADWS" or whatever the name of the first service on your system happens to be. These subexpressions are handy when you're working in the console, where the emphasis is on efficiency and brevity.

18.5 *Parentheticals as objects*

This trick relies on the same basic premise as the previous one: When PowerShell sees a parenthetical expression, it executes the contents and then effectively replaces the entire expression with its results. This is an incredibly useful behavior, but you may see folks using it in ways that are, at first, a bit confusing to read. For example, can you make sense of this example?

```
(Get-Process -name conhost | Select -first 1).id
```

The result, on our system, is 1132—the ID of the first process named `conhost`. As in algebra, you start by executing the parentheses first. So, inside parentheses is this command:

```
Get-Process -name conhost | Select -first 1
```

Running that command entirely on its own, you can see that it returns a single process at most. That process has properties such as `Name`, `ID`, and so on. In your head, you should read the entire parenthetical expression as representing a single process. To avoid displaying the entire process, follow the process with a period, which tells Power-Shell that you want to access a piece of the object (remember: in math a period comes before the fractional portion of a number, so you can think of the period as coming before a portion of the object). Follow the period with the piece of the object you want, which in this example is its `ID` property, so that's what was displayed.

A longer form of this same command might look like this:

```
$proc = Get-Process -name conhost | Select -first 1
$proc.id
```

That form has exactly the same effect, although an intermediate variable was created to hold the original result. Using the parenthetical expression eliminates the need for the middleman variable that's helpful at the command line, but in a script there's no penalty for taking the extra step to create the variable. It'll make your code easier to read, debug, and maintain.

18.6 Increasing the format enumeration limit

Here's something you may have come across and been a little frustrated by. Consider a command like this:

```
PS C:\> Get-Module Microsoft.PowerShell.Utility

ModuleType Name                                ExportedCommands
---------- ----                                ----------------
Manifest   Microsoft.PowerShell.Utility        {Add-Member, Add-Type, Cl...
```

The braces under `ExportedCommands` indicate a collection. You might try this command next:

```
PS C:\> Get-Module Microsoft.PowerShell.Utility | select ExportedCommands

ExportedCommands
----------------
{[Add-Member, Add-Member], [Add-Type, Add-Type], [Clear-Variable, Clear-...
```

One way around this issue to see more entries is to use one of our earlier parentheticals as objects tips in section 18.5:

```
PS C:\> (Get-Module Microsoft.PowerShell.Utility).ExportedCommands
```

Alternatively, you could try

```
Get-Module Microsoft.PowerShell.Utility | select -ExpandProperty
➥ ExportedCommands
```

Sure, these commands work if that's all you want to see. Here's one more variation on the problem:

```
PS C:\> Get-Module Microsoft.PowerShell.Utility | Select Name,
➥ ExportedCommands | Format-List

Name             : Microsoft.PowerShell.Utility
ExportedCommands : {[Add-Member, Add-Member], [Add-Type, Add-Type],
                   [Clear-Variable, Clear-Variable], [Compare-Object,
                   Compare-Object]...}
```

Clearly, there are more than four commands. Wouldn't you like to see a bit more? You need to modify the `$FormatEnumerationLimit` variable, which has a default value of 4, to accomplish this:

```
PS C:\> $FormatEnumerationLimit
4
PS C:\> $FormatEnumerationLimit=8
```

See what happens:

```
PS C:\> get-module Microsoft.PowerShell.Utility | Select
➥ Name,ExportedCommands | format-list

Name             : Microsoft.PowerShell.Utility
ExportedCommands : {[Add-Member, Add-Member], [Add-Type, Add-Type],
                   [Clear-Variable, Clear-Variable], [Compare-Object,
                   Compare-Object], [ConvertFrom-Csv, ConvertFrom-Csv],
                   [ConvertFrom-Json, ConvertFrom-Json],
                   [ConvertFrom-StringData, ConvertFrom-StringData],
                   [ConvertTo-Csv, ConvertTo-Csv]...}
```

Now you'll get more enumerated items. If you set the variable to a value of –1, Power-Shell will return all enumerated values. If you want to take advantage of this, add a line in your PowerShell profile to modify this variable. If you do modify this variable in your profile, be aware that it'll apply to all format enumerations. Some of these can get quite large and could swamp your display, making it difficult to pick out other information.

18.7   *Hash tables as objects*

A feature introduced in PowerShell v3 gives you the ability to turn hash tables into objects. In v2, you could use a hash table of property values with the `New-Object` cmdlet:

```
$obj=New-Object psobject -Property @{
Name="PowerShell"
Computername=$env:computername
Memory=(Get-WmiObject Win32_OperatingSystem).TotalVisibleMemorySize/1kb
}
```

In PowerShell v3 and later, you can create an object of a known type:

```
PS C:\>[Microsoft.Management.Infrastructure.Options.
➥ DComSessionOptions]$co= @{PacketPrivacy=$True;
➥ PacketIntegrity=$True;Impersonation=
➥ "Impersonate"}
PS C:\> $co
```

```
PacketPrivacy   : True
PacketIntegrity : True
Impersonation   : Impersonate
Timeout         : 00:00:00
Culture         : en-US
UICulture       : en-US
```

You can use this object in an expression as follows:

```
PS C:\scripts> $cs=New-CIMsession coredc01 -SessionOption $co
```

The type you use must have a default Null constructor (no arguments are needed, or the arguments have default values). In this example, you could as easily have created the $co variable using the New-CIMSessionOption cmdlet, so perhaps this example doesn't help that much.

You can also use this technique to create your own custom objects:

```
$obj=[PSCustomObject]@{
 Name="PowerShell"
 Computername=$env:computername
 Memory=(Get-WmiObject Win32_OperatingSystem).TotalVisibleMemorySize/1kb
}
```

Looking at this in the shell yields a typical object:

```
PS C:\> $obj
Name                      Computername                Memory
----                      ------------                ------
PowerShell                CLIENT2                     1023.5546875
```

This is the same result you'd get with New-Object and a hash table of property values. But using the hash table as an object does have a few advantages:

- It might save a little bit of typing.
- It's better with regard to performance.
- Properties are written to the pipeline in the order defined—basically the same as an [ordered] hash table.

As a final example, consider the following code:

```
[System.Management.ManagementScope]$scope = @{
  Path = "\\webr201\root\WebAdministration"
  Options = [System.Management.ConnectionOptions]@{
     Authentication = [System.Management.AuthenticationLevel]::PacketPrivacy
  }
}
[System.Management.ManagementClass]$website = @{
  Scope = $scope
  Path = [System.Management.ManagementPath]@{
    ClassName = "Site"
  }
  Options = [System.Management.ObjectGetOptions]@{}
 }
[System.Management.ManagementClass]$bind = @{
  Scope = $scope
```

```
    Path = [System.Management.ManagementPath]@{
      ClassName = "BindingElement"
    }
    Options = [System.Management.ObjectGetOptions]@{}
  }
$BInstance = $bind.CreateInstance()
$Binstance.BindingInformation = "*:80:HTasO.manticore.org"
$BInstance.Protocol = "http"
$website.Create("HTasO", $Binstance, "c:\HTasO", $true)
```

This example uses the System.Management .NET classes to wrap WMI calls to a web server, \\webr201. The IIS WMI provider requires the Packet Privacy level of DCOM authentication. In PowerShell v2, use .NET code or Remoting to use the IIS provider remotely. This requirement changed in PowerShell v3, as is discussed in chapter 39. For now, you can simplify (yes, this is simplified) the code using hash tables as objects.

The code starts by defining the WMI scope, which includes the namespace and the authentication level; notice that the hash tables are nested. The Site and Binding-Element objects are created. The scope information is used in both objects, which is why it's defined first. The site binding information is set and then the site is created.

Using hash tables as objects does make working directly with .NET classes easier but is also an advanced technique that you should probably wait to use until you've gained some experience with PowerShell.

18.8   *Summary*

Our goal in this chapter was to introduce you to some of the advanced tricks and techniques that you'll often see people using—and that we expect you'll want to use yourself, now that you've seen them. These tricks are ones that didn't fit in neatly elsewhere in the book and that tend to confuse newcomers to PowerShell at first. Now they won't trip you up!

Part 3

PowerShell scripting and automation

The chapters in this part of the book have a single goal: repeatability. Using PowerShell's scripting language, along with associated technologies like workflow, you can begin to create reusable tools that automate key tasks and processes in your environment.

PowerShell's scripting language

19

This chapter covers

- Logical conditions
- Loops
- Branching
- Code formatting

Although we firmly maintain that PowerShell isn't a scripting language, it does—like many command-line shells—*contain* a scripting language. This language can prove useful when you want to automate complex, multipart processes that may require different actions to be taken for different scenarios. PowerShell's language is definitely simple, consisting of less than two dozen commands usually referred to as *keywords*, but it's more than adequate for most jobs.

> **NOTE** The list of keywords, plus their definitions and references to more information, can be found in the help file about_Language_Keywords.

The ability to use cmdlets, functions, and .NET negates the pure language deficiencies. The language's syntax is loosely modeled on C#, which lends it a strong resemblance to other C-based languages such as PHP, C++, and Java.

19.1   Defining conditions

As with most languages, the heart of PowerShell's scripting capabilities is based on *conditions*. You define a condition that keeps a loop repeating or define a condition that causes your script to execute some particular command that it'd otherwise ignore.

The conditions you specify will usually be contained within parentheses and will often use PowerShell's various comparison operators to achieve either a True or False result. Referred to as *Boolean values*, these True/False results tell PowerShell's various scripting language elements whether to take some action, keep executing a command, and so on.

For example, all of the following conditions—*expressions* is the proper term for them—evaluate to True, which in PowerShell is represented with the built-in variable $True:

```
(5 -eq 5)
((5 -gt 0) -or (10 -lt 100))
('this' -like '*hi*')
```

All of the following conditions evaluate to False, which PowerShell represents by using $False:

```
(5 -lt 1)
((5 -gt 0) -and (10 -gt 100))
('this' -notlike '*hi*')
```

As you dive into PowerShell's scripting language, the punctuation becomes pretty important. For now, keep in mind that we're not using parentheses in a new way here. All of these expressions evaluate to either True or False; PowerShell executes the expressions first because they're contained in parentheses (remember your algebra lessons!). The resulting True or False is then utilized by the scripting keyword to loop, branch, and so on.

19.2   Loops: For, Do, While, Until

PowerShell supports several types of loop. All of these loop constructs share a single purpose: to continue executing one or more commands until some expression is either True or False. These loops differ only in how they achieve that purpose. The choice of loop is important, because some loops will execute once even if the conditions are immediately met and others will skip the loop entirely. You may want one or the other behavior to occur depending on your processing scenario.

19.2.1   The For loop

The For loop is the simplest and is designed to execute one or more commands a specific number of times. Here's the basic syntax:

```
For (starting-state ; repeat-condition ; iteration-action) {
    Do something
}
```

The For loop is unusual in that it doesn't take a single expression within parentheses, which is what—as you'll see—the other loops use. Instead, its parentheses contain three distinct components, separated by semicolons:

- `starting-state`, which is where you usually define a variable and assign it a starting value.
- `repeat-condition`, which is where you usually compare that variable to a given value. As long as your comparison is `True`, the loop will repeat again.
- `iteration-action`, which is some action that PowerShell takes after executing the loop each time. This is where you usually increment or decrement the variable. The change doesn't have to be an increment of 1. The counter can be incremented by 2, –3, or whatever you need.

This loop is a lot easier to see in an example:

```
For ($i=0; $i -lt 10; $i++) {
  Write-Host $i
}
```

This code will output the numbers 0, 1, 2, 3, 4, 5, 6, 7, 8, and 9. After outputting 9, the `iteration-action` will be executed again, incrementing `$i` to 10. At that point, `$i` is no longer less than 10, so the `repeat-condition` will return `False` and the loop won't execute an 11th time.

In the ISE or in scripts it's possible—and legal in PowerShell—to put the conditions on multiple lines separated by carriage returns:

```
For (
$i=0
$i -lt 10
$i++) {
  Write-Host $i
}
```

The results are identical to those obtained in the previous example. The drawback to this approach is that the code can't be copied out and run in the console as easily; it's also not as easy to read and understand. Using the form with semicolons is a better approach when you're working interactively, which is also the way you're most likely to find it in shared scripts and published material.

The starting value of the counter can be set outside the condition expression:

```
$i=0
For ($i; $i -lt 10; $i++) {
  Write-Host $i
}
```

But be careful, because if the condition is met, the loop won't execute. This next example doesn't produce any output because the condition is tested at the top of the loop and immediately produces a value of `False`:

```
$i=10
For ($i; $i -lt 10; $i++) {
  Write-Host $i
}
```

Note that it's perfectly legal to change the value of the variable—such as $i in our example—within the loop. If doing so results in the repeat-condition being False at the end of the loop iteration, then the loop won't execute again.

Loop counters

Have you ever wondered why $i is used for the counter in examples of For loops?

It goes all the way back to mainframe days and the FORTRAN language. FORTRAN was one of the first computer languages that was readable—that wasn't binary or assembler-level code. Any variable starting with the letters I–N was by default treated as an integer. Simple counters were defined as I, J, K, and so on.

The concept stuck across the industry, and we now use $i as our counter in PowerShell.

19.2.2   *The other loops*

The other three keywords you'll see used in simple conditional loops are Do, While, and Until. These are designed to execute until some condition is True or False, although unlike For, these constructs don't take care of changing that condition for you. The following listing shows the three forms you can use.

Listing 19.1   Loops

```
$i = 0
Do {                       ⟵— Do-While loop
  $i
  $i++
} While ($i -lt 10)

$i = 0
Do {                       ⟵— Do-Until loop
  $i
  $i++
} Until ($i -eq 10)

$i = 0
While ($i -lt 10) {        ⟵— While loop
  $i
  $i++
}
```

NOTE   Although it's legal to use the While keyword at the beginning of the loop or, in combination with Do, at the end of the loop, it isn't legal to use Until that way. The Until keyword can be used only at the end of a loop, with Do at the beginning of that loop.

For each of these loops, we've set a starting condition of 0 for the variable $i. Within each loop, we increment $i by 1. The loops' expressions determine how many times each will execute. Some important details:

- In the Do-While loop, the commands in the loop will always execute at least one time because the condition isn't checked until the end. They'll continue executing as long as the While expression—that is, $i is less than 10—results in True.
- With the Do-Until loop, the contents of the loop will also execute at least one time. It isn't until the end of the loop that the Until keyword is checked, causing the loop to repeat if the expression is False.
- The While loop is different in that the contents of the loop aren't guaranteed to execute at all. They'll execute only if the While expression is True to begin with (we made sure it would be by setting $i = 0 in advance), and the loop will continue to execute while that expression results in True.

Try changing the starting values of $i to see how the loop structures respond.

> **TIP** The key lesson with loops is that if the condition is tested at the end of the loop, that loop will execute at least once. If the test is at the start of the loop, there are no guarantees that the loop will execute at all. The appropriate structure to use depends on the condition you're checking.

19.3 *ForEach*

This scripting construct has the exact same purpose as the ForEach-Object cmdlet. That cmdlet has an alias, ForEach, which is easy to confuse with the ForEach scripting construct because—well, because they have the exact same name. PowerShell looks at the context of the command line to figure out if you mean "foreach" as an alias or as a scripting keyword. Here's an example of both the cmdlet and the scripting construct being used to do the exact same thing:

```
Get-Service –name B* | ForEach { $_.Pause() }
$services = Get-Service –name B*
ForEach ($service in $services) {
  $service.Pause()
}
```

Here are the details of how this scripting construct works:

- You provide two variables, separated by the keyword In, within parentheses. The second variable is expected to hold one or more objects that you populate in advance. The first variable is one that you make up; it must contain one of those objects at a time. If you come from a VBScript background, this sort of thing should look familiar.
- It's common practice to give the second variable a plural name and the first one the singular version of that plural name. This convention isn't required, though. You could've put ForEach ($fred in $rockville), and provided that $rockville

contained some objects, PowerShell would've been happy. But stick to giving variables meaningful names and you'll be much happier.

- PowerShell automatically takes one object at a time from the second variable and puts it into the first. Then, within the construct, you use the first variable to refer to that one object and do something with it. In the example, you executed its Pause method. Don't use $_ within the scripting construct as you do with the ForEach-Object cmdlet.

Someday, you might be unsure whether you should be using the cmdlet or the scripting construct. In theory, the cmdlet approach—piping something to ForEach-Object—could use less overall memory in some situations. But we've also seen the cmdlet approach run considerably slower with some large sets of objects. Your mileage may vary. If the processing in the loop is complex, especially if multiple pipelines are involved (using $_ or $psitem to indicate the object on the pipeline), it may be less confusing to use the keyword to differentiate the pipelines.

You also might consider your overall need, especially if you wanted to pipe to another cmdlet or function:

```
PS C:\> foreach ($service in $services) {
>>    $service | select Name,DisplayName,Status
>>} | Sort Status
>>

An empty pipe element is not allowed.
At line:3 char:4
+ } | <<<<  Sort Status
    + CategoryInfo          : ParserError: (:) [],
    ParentContainsErrorRecordException
    + FullyQualifiedErrorId : EmptyPipeElement
```

PowerShell complains because there's nothing to come out the other side for the ForEach construct. But something like this example will work:

```
PS C:\> $services | foreach {
>>     $_ | select Name,DisplayName,Status
>> } | Sort Status
>>

Name                    DisplayName                    Status
----                    -----------                    ------
Browser                 Computer Browser               Stopped
BDESVC                  BitLocker Drive Encrypt...     Stopped
bthserv                 Bluetooth Support Service      Running
BFE                     Base Filtering Engine          Running
BITS                    Background Intelligent ...     Running
```

Another common consideration is whether you'll need to reference the collection of objects just once or multiple times—if you need access to the collection several times, it may be more efficient to use the script construct so that you don't incur the overhead of refreshing the data. The last point to make is that many of the scripts you'll find on the web are conversions from VBScript, which had to use this approach of iterating over a collection of objects. It's always worthwhile to stop and think for a second in order to determine the best approach to solve *your* problem.

What we'll commit to is this: Don't use *either* approach if you don't have to. For example, our service-pausing example would be much better written this way:

```
Get-Service -name B* | Suspend-Service
```

And our sort example is better written like this:

```
Get-Service b* | Sort Status | select Name,DisplayName,Status
```

If you don't have to manually enumerate through objects, don't. Using ForEach—either the cmdlet/alias or the scripting construct—is sometimes an indication that you're doing something you shouldn't be doing. That's not true in *all* cases—but it's worth considering each usage to make sure you're not doing something that PowerShell would be willing to do for you. But don't get hung up on this issue; many cmdlets don't accept pipeline input on the parameters you may need to use, so ForEach becomes a necessity. It's sometimes more important to get the job done than to track down the ultimate right way of doing something.

This is also a good time for us to remind you of the power of parentheses. We sort of fibbed when we said that the ForEach scripting construct requires two variables. Technically, it needs only one—the first one. The second position must contain a collection of objects, which can be either in a variable—as in our examples so far—or from the result of a parenthetical expression, like this:

```
foreach ($service in (Get-Service -name B*)) {
  $service.pause()
}
```

This version is a bit harder to read, perhaps, but it's also totally legal and a means of eliminating the need to store the results of the Get-Service command in a variable before working with those results. The inner parentheses (remember your algebra) are evaluated first and produce a collection of service objects that are iterated over.

19.4　*Break and Continue*

You can use two special keywords—Break and Continue—within the contents of a loop, that is, within the curly bracketed section of a loop:

- Break will exit the loop immediately. It exits only one level. For example, if you have Loop A nested within Loop B and the contents of Loop B include Break, then Loop B will exit but Loop A will continue executing. Break has no effect on the If construct, but it does have an effect on the Switch construct, as you'll see shortly.
- Continue will immediately skip to the end of the current loop and decide (based on how the loop was written) whether to execute another iteration.

These keywords are useful for prematurely exiting a loop, either if you've determined that there's no need to continue executing or to skip over a bunch of code and get to the next iteration.

For example, suppose you've retrieved a bunch of Active Directory user objects and put them into the variable $users. You want to check their Department property, and if it's "Accounting," you want to disable the account (hah, that'll teach those bean counters). Once you've done that to five accounts, though, you don't want to do any more (no sense in upsetting too many folks). You also don't want to disable any account that has a "Title" attribute of "CFO" (you're mean, not stupid). Here's one way to do that (again assuming that $users is already populated):

```
$disabled = 0
ForEach ($user in $users) {
  If ($user.department -eq 'accounting') {
    If ($user.title -eq 'cfo' {
      Continue
    }
    $user | Disable-ADAccount
    $disabled++
  }
  If ($disabled -eq 5) {
    Break
  }
}
```

Granted, this might not be the most efficient way to code this particular task, but it's a good example of how Continue and Break work. If the current user's title is "CFO," Continue will skip to the end of the ForEach loop—bypassing your disabling and everything else and continuing on with the next potential victim. Once $disabled equals 5, you'll just abort, exiting the ForEach loop entirely.

19.5   If . . . ElseIf . . . Else

Enough about loops for a moment. Let's look now at a logical construct, which is used to evaluate one or more expressions and execute some commands if those expressions are True. Here's the most complex form of the construct:

```
If ($this -eq $that) {
  Get-Service
} ElseIf ($those -gt $these) {
  Get-Process
} ElseIf ($him -eq $her) {
  Get-EventLog -LogName Security
} Else {
  Restart-Computer -ComputerName localhost
}
```

Here are the important details:

- The If keyword is mandatory, as is the curly bracketed section following it. The other sections—the two ElseIf sections and the Else section—are optional.
- You can have as many ElseIf sections as you want.

- You can have an Else section regardless of whether there are any ElseIf sections.
- Only the first section whose expression results in True will execute. For example, if $this equals $that, Get-Service will run and the entire remainder of the construct will be disregarded.

You can put anything you like inside the parentheses, provided that it evaluates to True or False. That said, you won't always need to make a comparison. For example, suppose you have a variable, $mood, that contains an object. That object has a property, Good, that contains either True or False. Given that supposition, the following code is completely legal:

```
If ($mood.Good) {
  Get-Service
} else {
  Restart-Computer -computername localhost
}
```

The entire contents of the parentheses will evaluate to True or False because that's what the Good property will contain—there's no need to do this:

```
If ($mood.Good -eq $True) {
  Get-Service
} else {
  Restart-Computer -computername localhost
}
```

That example is completely legal, though, and PowerShell will treat these two exactly the same. It's unusual to see an explicit comparison to $True or $False—don't expect to see experienced folks doing that. This holds true for the conditions in Do-While, Do-Until, and While loops as well.

A common use for this technique is testing connectivity to a remote machine. This code

```
$computer = "server02"
Test-Connection -ComputerName $computer -Count 1 -Quiet
```

will return True or False. So the test becomes

```
$computer = "server02"
If (Test-Connection -ComputerName $computer -Count 1 -Quiet){
  #do something to that machine
}
```

A final point to make on If is that the comparison expression can be made up of multiple components to produce a more complex test. At this point, you need to bring in the logical operators -and and -or to help you with this processing:

```
$procs = Get-Process | select Name, Handles, WS
foreach ($proc in $procs){
 if (($proc.Handles -gt 200) -and ($proc.WS -gt 50000000)) {
  $proc
 }
}
```

```
"`n`n`n"
foreach ($proc in $procs){
 if (($proc.Handles -gt 200) -or ($proc.WS -gt 50000000)) {
  $proc
 }
}
```

The variable $procs is used to hold the process information. You use foreach to iterate over the collection of processes twice. Constructing the code in this way ensures that you have the same data each time you perform some processing.

In the first foreach, you test to determine whether the Handles property is greater than 200 and that the WS property is greater than 50,000,000 (these are arbitrary values). If both of these conditions are True, you output the details. In the second case, you output the details if either Handles is greater than 200 or WS is greater than 50,000,000—only one of them has to be True. The `n`n`n throws three blank lines to break the display and show the two sets of output. Notice that we put parentheses around each condition. You don't have to do this, but we recommend you do so because it makes the code easier to read and, more importantly, easier to debug if you have problems.

19.6   *Switch*

The Switch construct is a bit like a really big list of If...ElseIf statements that all compare one specific thing to a bunch of possible values. For example, let's say you have a printer object of some kind stored in the variable $printer. That object has a Status property, which contains a number. You want to translate that number to an English equivalent, perhaps for display to an end user. You want the translated status to go into the variable $status. One way to do that might be like this (we're totally making up what these numbers mean—this is just an example):

```
If ($printer.status -eq 0) {
  $status = "OK"
} elseif ($printer.status -eq 1) {
  $status = "Out of Paper"
} elseif ($printer.status -eq 2) {
  $status = "Out of Ink"
} elseif ($printer.status -eq 3) {
  $status = "Input tray jammed"
} elseif ($printer.status -eq 4) {
  $status = "Output tray jammed"
} elseif ($printer.status -eq 5) {
  $status = "Cover open"
} elseif ($printer.status -eq 6) {
  $status = "Printer Offline"
} elseif ($printer.status -eq 7) {
  $status = "Printer on Fire!!!"
} else {
  $status = "Unknown"
}
```

There's nothing wrong whatsoever with that approach, but the `Switch` construct offers a more visually efficient way (that also involves less typing and is easier to maintain) of doing the same thing:

```
Switch ($printer.status) {
  0 {$status = "OK"}
  1 {$status = "Out of paper"}
  2 {$status = "Out of Ink"}
  3 {$status = "Input tray jammed"}
  4 {$status = "Output tray jammed"}
  5 {$status = "Cover open"}
  6 {$status = "Printer Offline"}
  7 {$status = "Printer on Fire!!"}
  Default {$status = "Unknown"}
```

The details:

- The `Switch` statement's parentheses don't contain a comparison; instead, they contain the thing you want to examine. In this case it's the `$printer.status` property.
- The following statements each contain one possible value, along with a block that says what to do if the thing being examined matches that value.
- The `Default` block is executed if none of the other statements match. We recommend that you always have a `Default` block, even if it exists only to catch errors.
- Unlike `If...ElseIf...Else`, *every* single possible value statement that matches will execute.

That last point might seem redundant. After all, `$printer.status` isn't going to be both 0 and 7 at the same time, right? Well, this is where some of `Switch`'s interesting variations come into play. Let's suppose instead that you're looking at a server name, contained in `$servername`. You want to display a different message based on what kind of server it is. If the server name contains "DC," for example, then it's a domain controller; if it contains "LAS," then it's located in Las Vegas. Obviously, multiple conditions could be true, and you might want to do a wildcard match:

```
$message = ""
Switch -wildcard ($servername) {
  "DC*" {
    $message += "Domain Controller"
  }
  "FS*" {
    $message += "File Server"
  }
  "*LAS" {
    $message += " Las Vegas"
  }
  "*LAX" {
    $message += " Los Angeles"
  }
}
```

Because of the way you've positioned the wildcard character (*), you're expecting the server role (DC or FS) at the beginning of the name and the location (LAS or LAX) at the end. So if $servername contains "DC01LAS", then $message will contain "Domain Controller Las Vegas".

There might be times when multiple matches are possible but you don't want them all to execute. In that case, just add the Break keyword to the appropriate spot. Once you do so, the Switch construct will exit entirely. For example, suppose you don't care about a domain controller's location but you do care about a file server. You might make the following modification:

```
$message = ""
Switch -wildcard ($servername) {
  "DC*" {
    $message += "Domain Controller"
    break
  }
  "FS*" {
    $message += "File Server"
  }
  "*LAS" {
    $message += " Las Vegas"
  }
  "*LAX" {
    $message += " Los Angeles"
  }
}
```

$message might contain "Domain Controller" or "File Server Las Vegas", but it'd never contain "Domain Controller Las Vegas".

The conditions we've seen so far in the Switch construct have simple, direct comparisons. It's also possible to build some logic into the comparison, for instance:

```
foreach ($proc in (Get-Process)){
switch ($proc.Handles){
  {$_ -gt 1500}{Write-Host "$($proc.Name) has very high handle count"
               break }
  {$_ -gt 1200}{Write-Host "$($proc.Name) has high handle count"
               break }
  {$_ -gt  800}{Write-Host "$($proc.Name) has medium-high handle count"
               break }
  {$_ -gt  500}{Write-Host "$($proc.Name) has medium handle count"
               break }
  {$_ -gt  250}{Write-Host "$($proc.Name) has low handle count"
               break }
  {$_ -lt  100}{Write-Host "$($proc.Name) has very low  handle count"
               break }
}
}
```

The code iterates through the set of processes and determines whether the Handles property meets one of the criteria. The logic for the test is a script block in curly braces {}. The important point is that $_ is used to represent the value of $proc.Handles in the tests. Using `break` is imperative in these scenarios, because a process that has more than 1,500 handles also has more than 1,200. This way, you only get the highest result as you test from high to low, and you use `break` to jump out of the testing once you have a match. It was a deliberate decision to not put a `default` block on this example.

Switch has four total options:

- -`Wildcard`, which you've seen and which tells `Switch` that its possible matches include wildcard characters.
- -`CaseSensitive`, which forces string comparisons to be case sensitive (usually they're case insensitive).
- -`RegEx`, which tells `Switch` that the potential matches are regular expressions, and whatever's being compared will be evaluated against those regular expressions as if you were using the -`match` operator.
- -`Exact`, which disables -`Wildcard` and -`RegEx` and forces string matches to be exact. Ignored for nonstring comparisons.

19.7 *Mastering the punctuation*

With those scripting constructs out of the way, let's take a brief tangent to examine the specifics of script construct formatting.

First, PowerShell is a little picky about the placement of the parenthetical bit in relation to the scripting keyword: You should always leave a space between the keyword and the opening parentheses, and it's considered a good practice to leave only one space. You should also leave a space or a carriage return between the closing parenthesis and the opening curly bracket. You don't have to leave a space after the opening parenthesis or before the closing parenthesis—but it doesn't hurt to do so, and the extra whitespace can make your scripts a bit easier on the eyes.

PowerShell isn't at all picky about the location of the curly brackets. As long as nothing but whitespace comes between the closing parentheses and the opening curly bracket, you're all set. But all the cool kids will make fun of you if you don't take the time to make your script easy to read. There are two generally accepted ways of formatting the curly brackets:

```
For ($i=0; $i -lt 10; $i++) {
  Write-Host $i
}
For ($i=0; $i -lt 10; $i++)
{
  Write-Host $i
}
```

The only difference is where the opening curly bracket is placed. In the first example, it's just after the closing parenthesis (with a not required but good-looking space in between them). In the second example, it's on a line by itself. In both cases, the contents of the curly brackets are indented—usually with a tab character or four spaces (we sometimes use fewer in this book just to help longer lines fit on the page). The closing curly bracket in both examples is indented to the same level as the scripting keyword, which in this case is For. In the second example, the opening curly bracket is indented to that level as well.

This may seem like incredible nitpicking, but it isn't. Consider the following example:

```
For ($i=0;$i -lt 9;$i++){
Write-Host $i
For ($x=10;$i -gt 5;$i--){
If ($x -eq $i) { break }}}}
```

Try to run that example and you'll get an error message. The error doesn't specifically come from the formatting—PowerShell doesn't care about how visually appealing a script is—but the error is a lot harder to spot because of the formatting. Let's look at the same example, this time with proper formatting:

```
For ( $i=0; $i -lt 9; $i++){
  Write-Host $i
  For ( $x=10; $i -gt 5; $i--){
    If ($x -eq $i) {
      break
    }
  }
}}
```

Wait, what's that extra closing brace (}) doing at the end? That's the error! It's a lot easier to see now, because the opening and closing braces are much more visually balanced. You can see that the last line starts with a closing brace and its indentation level of zero matches it with the scripting keyword—For—that's indented to that same level. There's already a closing brace for the second For, and for the If, and those are clearly identifiable by their indentation levels. The extra brace is just that—extra—and removing it will make the code run without error. The version of ISE in Power-Shell v3 and v4 will attempt to show you any mismatches between opening and closing braces, parentheses, and brackets. The visual clue is a little hard to spot; it's a wiggly underline where the editor thinks the problem lies. Other editors such as PowerShell Plus or PowerGUI have similar mechanisms to aid correct code construction.

> **TIP** If your code gets complex with lots of opening and closing braces, put a comment by the closing brace to remind you which construct it's closing, like this:
>
> ```
>     #your code...
> } #close ForEach computer
> ```

We're not going to go so far as to suggest that bad things will happen if you don't format your code neatly. But sometimes strange things happen, and you certainly don't want to be the one to blame, do you? What's more, if you ever run into trouble and end up having to ask someone else for help, you'll find the PowerShell community a lot more willing to help if they can make sense of your code—and proper formatting helps.

TIP Many commercial script editors, including some free ones as well as paid offerings, provide features that can reformat your code. Such features usually indent the contents of curly brackets properly, and this is a great way to beautify some ugly chunk of code that you've pulled off of the internet. We also recommend that if you're developing PowerShell scripts and modules as part of a team, you develop a standardized formatting style to ensure uniformity.

19.8 Summary

PowerShell's scripting language is a sort of glue. By itself, it isn't very useful. Combined with some useful materials, such as commands that do actual work, this glue becomes very powerful. With it, a handful of commands can be turned into complex, automated processes that make decisions, repeat specific actions, and more. It's almost impossible to write a script of any complexity without needing some of these constructs. It may not mean you're programming, exactly, but it's as close as most folks get within PowerShell.

Basic scripts and functions

20

This chapter covers

- Scripting execution scopes
- Parameterizing your script
- Outputting scripts
- Filtering scripts
- Converting a script to a function

You can accomplish many tasks in PowerShell by typing a command and pressing Enter in the shell console. We expect that most IT pros will start using PowerShell this way and will continue to do so most of the time. Eventually, you'll probably get tired of typing the same thing over and over and want to make it more easily repeatable. Or you hand off a task to someone else and need to make sure that it's done exactly as planned. That's where scripts come in—and it's also where functions come in.

20.1 Script or function?

Suppose you have some task, perhaps one requiring a handful of commands in order to complete. A script is a convenient way of packaging those commands together. Rather than typing the commands manually, you paste them into a script and PowerShell runs them in order whenever you run that script. Following best practices, you'd give that script a cmdlet-like name, such as `Set-ServerConfiguration.ps1` or `Get-ClientInventory.ps1`. Think of a script as a "canned" PowerShell session. Instead of manually typing 10 or 100 commands, you put the same commands in a script and execute the script like a twenty-first-century batch file.

There may come a time when you assemble a collection of such scripts, particularly scripts that contain commands that you want to use *within* other scripts. For example, you might write a script that checks to see whether a given server is online and responding—a task you might want to complete before trying to connect to the server to perform some management activity. Or you might write a script that saves information to a log file—you can certainly imagine how useful that could be in a wide variety of other scripts. When you reach that point, you'll be ready to start turning your scripts into functions. A *function* is a wrapper around a set of commands, created in such a way that multiple functions can be listed within a single script file. That way, you can use all of your so-called utility functions more easily, simply by loading their script into memory first. Eventually, you'll be creating modules that are autoloaded by PowerShell when you start a session; we'll cover that in chapter 25.

In this chapter, we're going to start by doing everything in a script first. At the end, we'll show you how to take what you've done and turn your PowerShell commands into a function with just a couple of extra lines of code. We'll also show you how to run the function once you've created it.

20.2 Execution lifecycle and scope

The first thing to remember about scripts is that they generally run with their own scope. We'll discuss that in more detail in chapter 22, but for now you should understand that when you do certain things within a script, those things automatically disappear when the script is finished:

- Creating a new PSDrive
- Creating new variables or assigning values to variables (which implicitly creates the variables)
- Defining new aliases
- Defining functions (which we'll get to toward the end of this chapter)

Variables can be especially tricky. If you attempt to access the contents of a variable that hasn't yet been created and assigned a value, PowerShell will look to see whether that variable exists in the shell itself. If it does, that's what your script will be reading—although if you change that variable, your script will essentially be creating a new variable with the same name. It gets confusing. We do have a complete discussion of this "scope" concept in chapter 22; for now, we're going to follow best practices and avoid the problem entirely by never attempting to use a variable that hasn't first been created and given a value inside our script.

20.3   *Starting point: a command*

You don't often sit down and just start creating scripts. Usually, you start with a problem you want to solve. The first step is to experiment with running commands in the shell console. The benefit of this approach is that you can type something, press Enter, and immediately see the results. If you don't like those results, you can press the up arrow on your keyboard, modify the command, and try again. Once the command is working perfectly, you're ready to move it into a script. For this chapter, let's start with the following command:

```
Get-WmiObject -Class Win32_LogicalDisk -Filter "DriveType=3"
➥ -ComputerName SERVER2 |
Select-Object -Property DeviceID,@{Name='ComputerName';
➥ Expression={$_.PSComputerName}},Size,FreeSpace
```

This command uses WMI to retrieve all instances of the Win32_LogicalDisk class from a given computer. It limits the results to drives having a DriveType of 3, which specifies local, fixed disks.

> **NOTE** PSComputerName is a property introduced in PowerShell v3 to store the name of the remote computer against which the command was run. You can use the __Server property if you prefer. We recommend using PSComputer-Name because it's easier to understand and for consistency (__Server isn't available on the CIM cmdlets). Otherwise, you have to check each class and see if it has another property that'll return the computer name.

The command then displays the drive letter, the computer's name, the drives' sizes, and the drives' free space. Both space attributes are given in bytes.

20.4   **Accepting input**

The first thing you'll notice about our command is that it has some hardcoded values—the computer name is the most obvious one, and the filter to retrieve only fixed local disks is another. You can imagine pasting this into a script, giving it to some less-technical colleague, and saying, "Look, if you need to run this script, you have to open it up and edit the computer name first. Don't change anything else, though, or you'll mess it up." That's sure to work out fine, right? Sure—and you'll probably get a phone call from a confused technician every time it's run.

   It'd be far better to define a way for the users to provide these pieces of information in a controlled, manageable way so that they don't ever need to even open the script file, let alone edit it. In a PowerShell cmdlet, that "defined way" is a parameter—so that's what you'll do for this script, too.

> **TIP** You'll see many scripts that prompt the user for input. *Don't* follow that pattern. As you'll see, using parameters gives the best overall experience.

The following listing shows the modified script.

Listing 20.1   Get-DiskInfo.ps1

```
Param(
     [string]$ComputerName,          Defining
     [int]$driveType = 3            parameters
)
Get-WmiObject –Class Win32_LogicalDisk –Filter "DriveType=$driveType"   ←  Using $driveType
              –ComputerName $ComputerName |
Select-Object –Property DeviceID,                                        ←  Using $Computer-Name
@{Name='ComputerName'; Expression={$_.PSComputerName}}, Size, FreeSpace
```

Here's what listing 20.1 does:

- At the top of the script, you define a `Param()` section. This section must use parentheses—given PowerShell's other syntax, it can be tempting to use braces, but here they'll cause an error message.
- You don't have to put each parameter on its own line, but your script is a lot easier to read if you do.
- Each parameter is separated by a comma—that's why there's a comma after the first parameter.
- You don't have to declare a data type for each parameter, but it's good practice to do so. In the example, `$ComputerName` is set to be a `[string]` and `$drive-Type` is an `[int]`—shorthand for the .NET classes `System.String` and `System.Int32`, respectively.
- Within your script, the parameters act as regular variables, and you can see where listing 20.1 inserted them in place of the hardcoded values.
- PowerShell doesn't care about capitalization, but it'll preserve whatever you type when it comes to parameters. That's why the example uses the neater-looking `$ComputerName` and `$driveType` instead of `$computername` and `$drivetype`.
- The fact that the `$ComputerName` variable is being given to the `-Computer-Name` parameter is sort of a coincidence. You could've called the script's parameter `$fred` and run `Get-WmiObject` with `-ComputerName $fred`. But all PowerShell commands that accept a computer name do so using a `-Computer-Name` parameter, and to be consistent with that convention, listing 20.1 uses `$ComputerName`.
- Listing 20.1 provides a default value for `$driveType` so that someone can run this script without specifying a drive type. Adding safe default values is good practice. Right now, if users forget to specify `$ComputerName`, the script will fail with an error. That's something you'll correct in chapter 24.

Running a script with these parameters looks a lot like running a native PowerShell command. Because it's a script, you have to provide a path to it, which is the only thing that makes it look different than a cmdlet:

```
PS C:\> C:Scripts\Get-DiskInfo -ComputerName SERVER2
```

Notice that you didn't specify a -driveType parameter, but this approach will work fine. You can also provide values positionally, specifying them in the same order in which the parameters are defined:

```
PS C:\> C:Scripts\Get-DiskInfo SERVER2 3
```

Here the -driveType parameter value, 3, is included, but not the actual parameter name. It'll work fine. You could also truncate parameter names, just as you can do with any PowerShell command:

```
PS C:\> C:Scripts\Get-DiskInfo -comp SERVER2 -drive 3
```

If parameters are truncated, the abbreviation must be capable of being resolved unambiguously from the script's parameters. Tab completion works for script (or function) parameter names, so abbreviation can be easily avoided without any extra typing.

The end result is a script that looks, feels, and works a lot like a native PowerShell cmdlet.

20.5   *Creating output*

If you run the script from listing 20.1 and provide a valid computer name, you'll notice that it produces output just fine. So why take up pages with a discussion of creating output?

PowerShell can do a lot of work for you, and it's easy to just let it do so without thinking about what's going on under the hood. Yet whenever something's happening under the hood, you do need to be aware of it so that you can figure out whether it's going to mess up your work.

So here's the deal: *Anything that gets written to the pipeline within a script becomes the output for that script.* Simple rule with potentially complex results. The example script ran Get-WmiObject and piped its output to Select-Object. You didn't pipe Select-Object to anything, but whatever it produced was written to the pipeline nonetheless. If you'd run that same command from the command line, the contents of the pipeline would've been invisibly forwarded to Out-Default, formatted, and then displayed on the screen—probably as a table, given that you're selecting only a few properties. But you weren't running that command from the command line—it was run from within a script. That means the output of the script was whatever was put into the pipeline.

In a simple example, this distinction is irrelevant. Consider the output when running the commands from the command line (using "localhost" as the computer name this time):

```
PS C:\> Get-WmiObject -Class Win32_LogicalDisk -Filter "drivetype=3" `
>>    -ComputerName localhost |
>> Select-Object -Property DeviceID,
>> @{name='ComputerName';expression={$_.PSComputerName}},Size,FreeSpace
>>

DeviceID            ComputerName            Size          FreeSpace
--------            ------------            ----          ---------
C:                  WIN-KNBA0R0TM23         42842714112   32461271040
```

Here's the script and its output:

```
PS C:\> .\Get-DiskInfo.ps1 -computerName localhost

DeviceID            ComputerName                     Size        FreeSpace
--------            ------------                     ----        ---------
C:                  WIN-KNBA0R0TM23             42842714112     32461238272
```

Looks the same, right? At least apart from some free space that has mysteriously gone missing—probably a temp file or something. Anyway, it produces the same basic output. The difference is that you can pipe the output of your script to something else:

```
PS C:\> .\Get-DiskInfo.ps1 -computerName localhost |
>> Where { $_.FreeSpace -gt 500 } |
>> Format-List -Property *
>>

DeviceID     : C:
ComputerName : WIN-KNBA0R0TM23
Size         : 42842714112
FreeSpace    : 32461238272
```

The example piped the output of the script to `Where-Object` and then to `Format-List`, changing the output. This result may seem obvious to you, but it impresses the heck out of us! Basically, this little script is behaving exactly like a real PowerShell command. You don't need to know anything about the black magic that's happening inside: You give it a computer name and optionally a drive type, and it produces objects. Those objects go into the pipeline and can be piped to any other command to further refine the output to what you need.

So that's Rule #1 of Script Output: If you run a command and don't capture its output into a variable, then the output of that command goes into the pipeline and becomes the output of the script. Of course, having one rule implies there are others. What if you don't want the output of a command to be the output of your script? Consider the following listing.

Listing 20.2 Test-Connectivity.ps1

```
param(
    [string]$ComputerName
)
$status = Test-Connection -ComputerName $Computername -count 1
if ($status.statuscode -eq 0) {
    Write-Output $True
} else {
    Write-Output $False
}
```

We wrote the script in listing 20.2 to test whether a given computer name responds to a network ping. Here are a couple of usage examples:

```
PS C:\> .\Test-Connectivity.ps1 -computerName localhost
True
PS C:\> .\Test-Connectivity.ps1 -computerName notonline
False
```

Okay, let's ignore for the moment the fact that the `Test-Connection` cmdlet can do this when you use its `-Quiet` switch. We're trying to teach you something. The point is that you can use `Write-Output` to manually put a piece of information—such as `$True` or `$False`—into the pipeline within a script and that'll become the script's output. You don't have to output only whatever a command produces; you can also output custom data. We're going to get a lot more robust with what can be output in the next chapter. But that leads to Rule #2 of Script Output: Whatever you put into the pipeline by using `Write-Output` will also become the output of your script.

First, a warning: Whatever you choose to be the output of your script must be a *single kind of thing*. For example, listing 20.1 produced a WMI `Win32_LogicalDisk` object. Listing 20.2 produced a Boolean value. You should never have a script producing more than one kind of thing—PowerShell's system for dealing with and formatting output can get a little wonky if you do that. For example, try running the code in the next listing.

Listing 20.3   Bad-Idea.ps1

```
Get-Service
Get-Process
Get-Service
```

The script in listing 20.3 produces two kinds of output: services and processes. PowerShell does its best to format the results, but they're not as pretty as individually running `Get-Service` and `Get-Process`. When you run the two commands independently from the command line, each gets its own pipeline, and PowerShell can deal with the results of each independently. Run them as part of a script, as you did in listing 20.3, and two types of objects get jammed into the same pipeline. That's a poor practice and one that PowerShell isn't always going to deal with gracefully or beautifully. That's Rule #3 of Script Output: Output one kind of object, and one kind only.

20.6   "Filtering" scripts

By this point in the book, you should be familiar with the `Where-Object` cmdlet. Its main purpose in life is to accept some criteria or comparison from you and then remove any piped-in objects that don't meet those criteria or result in a true comparison, for example:

```
Get-WmiObject –Class Win32_Service |
Where {$_.StartMode -eq 'Auto' –and $_.State –ne 'Running' }
```

This code displays all services that should be running but aren't. The activity happening here is *filtering*; in a more general sense, a filter gets a bunch of objects piped in, does something with each one (such as examining them), and then pipes out all or some subset of them to the pipeline. PowerShell provides a straightforward way to give your scripts this capability.

NOTE PowerShell's syntax includes the keyword `filter`, which is a special type of language construct. It's a holdover from PowerShell v1. The construct we're about to show you, a *filtering script*, supersedes those older constructs. We'll show you how to use filter in section 20.8 but keep in mind it's not an approach that we recommend.

Here's the basic layout for a filtering script. This example doesn't do anything; it's just a template that we'll work from:

```
Param()
BEGIN {}
PROCESS {}
END {}
```

What you have here is the `Param()` block, in which you can define any input parameters that your script needs. There's one parameter that'll get created automatically: the special `$_` placeholder that contains pipeline input. More on that in a moment—just know for now that you don't need to define it in the `Param()` block.

Next up is the `BEGIN` block. This is a script block, recognizable by its braces. Those tell you that it can be filled with PowerShell commands, and in this case those commands will be the first ones the script executes when it's run. The `BEGIN` block is executed only once, at the time the first object is piped into the script.

After that is the `PROCESS` block, which is also a script block and is also capable of containing commands. This block is executed one time for each pipeline object that was piped into the script. So, if you pipe in 10 things, the `PROCESS` block will execute 10 times. Within the `PROCESS` block, the `$_` placeholder will contain the current pipeline object. There's no need to use a scripting construct such as `ForEach` to enumerate across a group of objects, because the `PROCESS` block is essentially doing that for you.

Once the `PROCESS` block has run for all of the piped-in objects, the `END` block will run last—but only once. It's a script block, so it can contain commands.

PowerShell is perfectly happy to have an empty `BEGIN`, `PROCESS`, or `END` block—or even all three, although that'd make no sense. You can also omit any blocks that you don't need, but we like leaving in an empty `BEGIN` block (for example) rather than omitting it, for visual completeness.

Let's create another example. Suppose you plan to get a group of `Win32_Logical-Disk` objects by using WMI. You'll use a WMI filter to get only local fixed disks, but from there you want to keep only those disks that have less than 20% free space. You could absolutely do that in a `Where-Object` cmdlet, like so:

```
Get-WmiObject -Class Win32_LogicalDisk -Filter "drivetype=3" |
Where-Object {$_.FreeSpace / $_.Size -lt .2 }
```

But you could also build that into a simple filtering script. The following listing shows the Where-LowFreeSpace.ps1 script. Note that we've added a parameter for the desired amount of free space, making the script a bit more flexible.

Listing 20.4   Where-LowFreeSpace.ps1

```
Param(
  [int]$PercentFreeSpace
)
BEGIN {}
PROCESS {

  If ((100 * ($_.FreeSpace / $_.Size) -lt $PercentFreeSpace)) {
    Write-Output $_
  }
}
END {}
```

> Using $_
> placeholder

Run the script in listing 20.4 as follows:

```
Get-WmiObject -Class Win32_LogicalDisk -Filter "drivetype=3" |
C:\Where-LowFreeSpace -percentfreeSpace 20
```

Look at that carefully so that you're sure you understand what it's doing. The `Param()` block defines the `$PercentFreeSpace` parameter, which was set to 20 when the script was run earlier. The `Get-WmiObject` command produced an unknown number of disk objects, all of which were piped into your script. The `BEGIN` block ran first but contained no commands.

The `PROCESS` block then ran with the first disk stored in the `$_` placeholder. Let's say it had 758,372,928 bytes total size and 4,647,383 bytes of free space. So that's 4,647,383/758,372,928, or 0.0061. Multiplied times 100, that's 0.61, meaning you have 0.61% free space. That's not much. It's less than 20, so the `If` construct will use `Write-Output` to write that same disk out to the pipeline. This is truly a filtering script in the purest sense of the word, because it's applying some criteria to determine what stays in the pipeline and what gets filtered out.

You can do a lot more with these kinds of scripts than removing data from the pipeline. For example, imagine piping in a bunch of new usernames and having the script create accounts, set up home directories, enable mailboxes, and much more. We're going to save a more complex example, because once you see the more advanced possibilities, it's more likely that you'll want to use them within a function.

20.7   *Moving to a function*

There are a lot of benefits to moving your script code into a function, and doing so is easy. Take a look at this next listing, in which the script from listing 20.4 is converted into a function.

Listing 20.5   Creating a function in Tools.ps1

```
Function Where-LowFreeSpace {
  Param(
    [int]$FreeSpace
  )
  BEGIN {}
```

```
PROCESS {
  If ((100 * ($_.FreeSpace / $_.Size) -lt $FreeSpace)) {
    Write-Output $_
  }
}
END {}
}
```

Listing 20.5 wraps the contents of the preceding script with a `Function` keyword, defines a name for the function (this listing reuses the same name it had when it was just a script), and encloses the contents of the script in braces. Presto, a function!

If you run the script—which is called Tools.ps1—some neat things happen:

- PowerShell sees the function declaration and loads the function into memory for later use. It creates an entry in the Function: drive that lets it remember the function's name, parameters, and contents.
- When you try to use the function, PowerShell will tab-complete its name and parameter names for you.
- You can define multiple functions inside the Tools.ps1 script, and PowerShell will remember them all.

But there's a downside. Because the function lives within a script, you have to remember what we said at the outset of this chapter about scripts: They have their own scope. Anything defined in a script goes away after the script is done. Because the only thing in your script is that function, running the script simply defines that function—and then the script is completed, so the function definition is erased. The net effect is zero.

There's a trick to resolve this, called *dot sourcing*. It looks like this:

```
PS C:>. C:\Tools.ps1
```

By starting the command with a period, then a space, then the path and name of your script, you run the script without creating a new scope. Anything created inside the script will continue to exist after the script is done. Now, the entry for `Where-LowFreeSpace` still exists in the shell's Function: drive, meaning that you've basically added your own command to the shell! It'll go away when you close the shell, of course, but you can always re–dot-source the script to get it back. Once the function is loaded, you can use it like any other PowerShell command:

```
Get-WmiObject -Class Win32_LogicalDisk -Filter "drivetype=3" |
Where-Lowfreespace -FreeSpace 20
```

You could also dot-source a script inside another script, for example:

1. Run ScriptA.ps1 normally, which creates a scope around it, so whatever it defines will go away when the script completes.
2. Inside ScriptA, dot-source Tools.ps1. Tools doesn't get its own scope; instead, anything it creates will be defined in the calling scope—that is, inside ScriptA. So it will look as if everything in Tools.ps1 had simply been copied and pasted into ScriptA.ps1.

3 ScriptA.ps1 can now use any function from Tools.ps1.

4 When ScriptA.ps1 completes, its scope is cleaned up, including everything that
   was dot-sourced from Tools.ps1.

This is a handy trick. It's a lot like the "include" capabilities that programming languages have. But in the end, it's a bit of a hack. The bottom line is that we don't do
this very often, because there are better, more manageable, and less confusing ways to
accomplish everything we've done here. We're working up to that method, and you'll
see it in chapter 25 when we discuss script modules.

20.8 *Filter construct*

The Filter construct was introduced in PowerShell v1. A Filter is best regarded as
a specialized function. It was useful in those days because it enabled you to write a
function-like construct that could be used on the pipeline. A standard function, unlike
a filter, blocks the pipeline until it has completed.

The introduction of advanced functions in PowerShell v2 gives you a much better
approach (see chapter 24). You won't see much use of Filter these days, but just in
case you need it this is how it works.

There are two things you need to remember about Filters:

1 They're designed to run once for each object on the pipeline

2 A Filter looks like a Function but all the statements are in a PROCESS block.
   You can't use BEGIN or END blocks in a Filter.

As a demonstration, we'll take the Where-LowFreeSpace function and turn it into a
Filter (listing 20.6).

Listing 20.6 Creating a filter

```
Filter Where-LowFreeSpace {
Param(
  [int]$FreeSpace
)
 If ((100 * ($_.FreeSpace / $_.Size) -lt $FreeSpace)) {
    Write-Output $_
 }
}

Get-WmiObject -Class Win32_LogicalDisk | Where-LowFreeSpace -FreeSpace 75
```

The code inside the Filter construct runs once for each object on the pipeline; it's a
PROCESS block, as previously stated. You can use the PROCESS{} syntax if you want, but
it's not necessary.

You could write this code as:

```
$FreeSpace = 75

Get-WmiObject -Class Win32_LogicalDisk |
foreach {
  If ((100 * ($_.FreeSpace / $_.Size) -lt $FreeSpace)) {
```

```
    Write-Output $_
  }
}
```

The code you put into a `Foreach-Object` `PROCESS` block is in effect an anonymous `Filter`. There's a small amount of information, plus another example, in the about_ Functions help file. We recommend you use advanced functions rather than filters.

20.9 *Summary*

Scripts and functions are the basis for creating complex, repeatable automations in your environment. In this chapter, we've touched on the basics—but almost everything we've shown you here needs some refinement. We'll continue doing that over the next few chapters so that you can build scripts and functions that are truly consistent with PowerShell's overall philosophy and operational techniques.

As a reference, we'll repeat our Scripting Output Rules:

- Rule #1: If you run a command and don't capture its output into a variable, then the output of that command goes into the pipeline and becomes the output of the script.
- Rule #2: Whatever you put into the pipeline by using `Write-Output` will also become the output of your script.
- Rule #3: Output one kind of object, and one kind only.

Remember these three rules when you're creating your scripts and you'll minimize problems with your output.

Creating objects for output

This chapter covers
- "Objectifying" your output
- Creating custom objects
- Working with collections of properties

In the previous chapter, we showed you how to create a simple script and turn it into a function. We emphasized the need for scripts and functions to output only one kind of thing, and in those simple examples you found it easy to comply because you were running only a single command. But you're doubtless going to come across situations where you need to run multiple commands, combine pieces of their output, and use that as the output of your script or function. This chapter will show you how: The goal is to create a custom object that consolidates the information you need and then output it from your script or function. Richard remembers being asked at a conference session if PowerShell had a command that worked in a similar way to the Union command in SQL. This chapter is the closest you'll get with PowerShell because you're working with objects.

344

21.1   *Why output objects?*

Objects are the only thing a script (or function; from here out you can assume that everything we say applies to both scripts and functions) can output. You may only need to output a simple Boolean `True`/`False` value, but in PowerShell that's a Boolean object. A date and a time? Object. A simple string of characters? Object. More complex data, like the details of a process or a service, are all represented as objects.

> **NOTE**   We still see lots of people outputting text from their scripts. Simple word of advice. *Don't.* You should always output objects. If you output text in a script, get stuck and ask for help in the forums—expect to be told about outputting objects.

Objects, for our purposes, are just a kind of data structure that PowerShell understands and can work with. Developers probably won't like that definition, so it's probably best if we don't tell them.

Creating a custom object allows you to follow the main rule of scripts (and functions), which is to output only one kind of thing—for example, multiple calls to WMI to access several classes. When you need to output information that comes from multiple places, you can create a custom object to hold that information so that your script is outputting just one kind of thing—that custom object. The alternative is to accept that your script is for reporting purposes only and that you won't ever want to do anything else with the output. This is only acceptable in restricted circumstances, and even Richard is moving away from the concept.

We're going to start with the four commands shown in listing 21.1. Each retrieves a different piece of data from a computer (we'll stick with localhost for this example because it's easy and should work on any computer).

> **TIP**   If you're creating functions that have a computer name as a parameter, use `$env:COMPUTERNAME` as the default rather than localhost or ".". There are a few occasions where the actual name of the machine is required, which you can access through the environment variable and save extra steps in your code.

You don't want to output all that information, though, so store the retrieved data in a variable. That way, it'll be easier to extract the pieces you do want. Listing 21.1 has the four commands—keep in mind that running this as is won't produce any output because you're storing the objects produced by these commands in variables but you're not outputting those variables.

Listing 21.1   Starting commands

```
$os = Get-WmiObject -Class Win32_OperatingSystem -comp localhost
$cs = Get-WmiObject -Class Win32_ComputerSystem -comp localhost
$bios = Get-WmiObject -Class Win32_BIOS -comp localhost
$proc = Get-WmiObject -Class Win32_Processor -comp localhost |
Select -First 1
```

The last of our four commands is slightly different. Although the first three are retrieving things that, by definition, exist only once per computer (operating system, computer system, and BIOS), the last one is retrieving something that a computer often has more than one of (processors). Because all processors in a system will be the same, you've elected to just retrieve the first one by piping the command to `Select-Object -First 1`. Windows Server 2003 and Windows XP will return one instance of the `Win32_Processor` class per core, so be aware that the results of using that class will vary depending on operating system version.

> **NOTE** There's a hotfix available to resolve this issue for Windows Server 2003 at http://support.microsoft.com/kb/932370—though given the limited time left in the support lifecycle for these products, it may not be worthwhile applying it.

That way, each of our four variables has just one object. That's important for the next technique we'll cover. Generally, you'll want to have your variables contain just one thing if possible.

> **TIP** In PowerShell v3 and v4 you have the option to use the Common Information Model (CIM) cmdlets in place of the WMI cmdlets. The choice of which to use doesn't affect the discussion in this chapter. Alternative listings using the CIM cmdlets will be available in the code download.

With your four variables populated, you're ready to begin putting them in a custom object.

21.2 Syntax for creating custom objects

We've often said that there are always multiple ways to do anything in PowerShell, and that's certainly true for custom objects. We'll show you all the major ways because you're likely to run into them in the wild, and we want you to be able to recognize them and use them when you do.

21.2.1 Technique 1: using a hash table

Let's start with the way that we prefer ourselves. Call it the *official* way, if you like: We use it because it's concise, fairly easy to read, and gets the job done. It's in listing 21.2.

> **NOTE** In each of the upcoming listings, we'll repeat the four original commands from listing 21.1. That way, each of these is a complete, stand-alone example that you can run to see the results.

Listing 21.2 Creating objects using a hash table

```
$os = Get-WmiObject -Class Win32_OperatingSystem -comp localhost
$cs = Get-WmiObject -Class Win32_ComputerSystem -comp localhost
$bios = Get-WmiObject -Class Win32_BIOS -comp localhost
$proc = Get-WmiObject -Class Win32_Processor -comp localhost |
Select -First 1
```

```
$props = @{OSVersion=$os.version
           Model=$cs.model
           Manufacturer=$cs.manufacturer
           BIOSSerial=$bios.serialnumber
           ComputerName=$os.CSName
           OSArchitecture=$os.osarchitecture
           ProcArchitecture=$proc.addresswidth}
$obj = New-Object -TypeName PSObject -Property $props
Write-Output $obj
```

Run the code in listing 21.2 and you'll see something like this:

```
Manufacturer      : Microsoft Corporation
OSVersion         : 6.3.9600
OSArchitecture    : 64-bit
BIOSSerial        : 036685734653
ComputerName      : RSSURFACEPRO2
Model             : Surface Pro 2
ProcArchitecture  : 64
```

Because your output included more than four properties, PowerShell chose a list-style layout; you could've run `Write-Output $obj | Format-Table` to force a table-style layout, but the point is that you've created a single, consolidated object by combining information from four different places. You did that by creating a hash table, in which your desired property names were the keys and the contents of those properties were the values. That's what each of these lines did:

```
Manufacturer=$cs.manufacturer
```

If you put the hash table entries all on one line, you'll need to separate each property with a semicolon. If you put each property on a separate line, you don't need the semicolon, which makes things a little easier to read. The bracketed structure was preceded by an @ sign—telling PowerShell that this is a hash table—and then assigned to the variable $props so that you could easily pass it to the -Property parameter of New-Object. The object type—PSObject—is one provided by PowerShell specifically for this purpose. As an aside, CSName is a WMI property that's available on the objects returned by Win32_OperatingSystem using both Get-WmiObject and Get-CimInstance.

> **TIP** The property __SERVER and other system variables aren't available when using the CIM cmdlets, so we recommend that you don't use them in your scripts. That way, changing to using the CIM cmdlets will be easier if you decide to do so.

The benefit of this approach is that it's easy to build a hash table *on the fly* and create as many custom objects as you need. You'll also notice that the hash table output isn't in the same order in which it was defined. One solution is to create a custom type and format extension, which we cover elsewhere in the book. Or in PowerShell v3 and v4, you can create an ordered hash table:

```
$props = [ordered]@{ OSVersion=$os.version
         Model=$cs.model
```

```
Manufacturer=$cs.manufacturer
BIOSSerial=$bios.serialnumber
ComputerName=$os.CSName
OSArchitecture=$os.osarchitecture
ProcArchitecture=$proc.addresswidth}
```

Everything else is the same, but now the object will be displayed with the properties in entered order. If you pipe $obj to Get-Member, you'll see that the type is a PS-CustomObject.

> **NOTE** PowerShell doesn't by default keep track of the order of items in the hash table. That's why, when you see the final output object, its properties aren't in the same order in which you put them in. Beginning with Power-Shell v3, you can remedy that by preceding the hash table declaration with the [ordered] attribute as you did earlier. This creates an ordered dictionary (or ordered hash table, if you prefer) and maintains the order of the items.

21.2.2 *Technique 2: using Select-Object*

This next technique was a favorite in PowerShell v1, and you still see people using it quite a bit. We don't like it as much as Technique 1 because it can be a bit harder to read. The following listing shows the technique, where you're basically creating an object that has a bunch of blank properties and then filling in those properties' values in subsequent steps.

> **Listing 21.3   Creating objects using `Select-Object`**

```
$os = Get-WmiObject -Class Win32_OperatingSystem -comp localhost
$cs = Get-WmiObject -Class Win32_ComputerSystem -comp localhost
$bios = Get-WmiObject -Class Win32_BIOS -comp localhost
$proc = Get-WmiObject -Class Win32_Processor -comp localhost |
Select -First 1
$obj = 1 | Select-Object ComputerName,OSVersion,OSArchitecture,
           ProcArchitecture,Model,Manufacturer,BIOSSerial
$obj.ComputerName = $os.CSName
$obj.OSVersion = $os.version
$obj.OSArchitecture = $os.osarchitecture
$obj.ProcArchitecture = $proc.addresswidth
$obj.BIOSSerial = $bios.serialnumber
$obj.Model = $cs.model
$obj.Manufacturer = $cs.manufacturer
Write-Output $obj
```

Note that in listing 21.3 the initial $obj = 1 is essentially bogus; the value 1 won't ever be seen.

> **TIP** You'll see many examples where an empty string is used as the starting point: $obj = "" | select .... The same comments apply.

It's just a way to define $obj as an object so that there's something in the pipeline to pass to Select-Object, which does all the work.

There's a potential drawback with this approach. If you pipe `$obj` to `Get-Member`, look at the result:

```
PS C:\> $obj | Get-Member

    TypeName: Selected.System.Int32
Name               MemberType   Definition
----               ----------   ----------
Equals             Method       bool Equals(System.Object obj)
GetHashCode        Method       int GetHashCode()
GetType            Method       type GetType()
ToString           Method       string ToString()
BIOSSerial         NoteProperty System.String BIOSSerial=
ComputerName       NoteProperty System.String ComputerName= WIN-KNBA0R0TM23
Manufacturer       NoteProperty System.String Manufacturer= VMware, Inc.
Model              NoteProperty System.String Model= VMware Virtual Platform
OSArchitecture     NoteProperty System.String OSArchitecture= 64-bit
OSVersion          NoteProperty System.String OSVersion= 6.1.7601
ProcArchitecture NoteProperty System.UInt16 ProcArchitecture=64
```

Sure the properties are okay, but the `typename` could lead to problems, or even just confusion, depending on what else you might want to do with this object. We recommend avoiding this technique.

21.2.3 Technique 3: using Add-Member

This technique is what we think of as the formal technique for creating a custom object. Under the hood, this is what happens (more or less) with all the other techniques, so this is a *fully spelled-out* kind of approach. This approach is more computationally expensive, meaning it's slower, so you don't often see folks using it in the real world. Again, this was a more common approach in PowerShell v1. There are two variations, and the following listing has the first.

> **Listing 21.4 Creating objects using `Add-Member`**

```
$os = Get-WmiObject -Class Win32_OperatingSystem -comp localhost
$cs = Get-WmiObject -Class Win32_ComputerSystem -comp localhost
$bios = Get-WmiObject -Class Win32_BIOS -comp localhost
$proc = Get-WmiObject -Class Win32_Processor -comp localhost |
Select -First 1
$obj = New-Object -TypeName PSObject
$obj | Add-Member NoteProperty ComputerName $os.CSName
$obj | Add-Member NoteProperty OSVersion $os.version
$obj | Add-Member NoteProperty OSArchitecture $os.osarchitecture
$obj | Add-Member NoteProperty ProcArchitecture $proc.addresswidth
$obj | Add-Member NoteProperty BIOSSerial $bios.serialnumber
$obj | Add-Member NoteProperty Model $cs.model
$obj | Add-Member NoteProperty Manufacturer $cs.manufacturer
Write-Output $obj
```

With the technique shown in listing 21.4, you're still creating a `PSObject` but you're adding one property to it at a time. Each time, you add a `NoteProperty`, which is the type of property that just contains a static value. That's exactly what the previous techniques did, but they sort of did it implicitly, under the hood, whereas you're spelling it out here.

We're using positional parameters to reduce the amount of code displayed in the listing. Each of the Add-Member statements looks like this when expanded:

```
Add-Member -MemberType NoteProperty -Name ComputerName -Value $os.CSName
```

The variation on this technique is to use the –PassThru (abbreviated to –pass in listing 21.5) parameter of Add-Member. Doing so puts the modified object back into the pipeline, so you can pipe it right to the next Add-Member. The next listing shows this variation, which produces the same result in the same amount of time.

Listing 21.5   Creating objects using Add-Member with -Passthru

```
$os = Get-WmiObject -Class Win32_OperatingSystem -comp localhost
$cs = Get-WmiObject -Class Win32_ComputerSystem -comp localhost
$bios = Get-WmiObject -Class Win32_BIOS -comp localhost
$proc = Get-WmiObject -Class Win32_Processor -comp localhost |
Select -First 1
$obj = New-Object -TypeName PSObject
$obj | Add-Member NoteProperty ComputerName $os.CSName -pass |
 Add-Member NoteProperty OSVersion $os.version -pass |
 Add-Member NoteProperty OSArchitecture $os.osarchitecture -Pass |
 Add-Member NoteProperty ProcArchitecture $proc.addresswidth -pass |
 Add-Member NoteProperty BIOSSerial $bios.serialnumber -pass |
 Add-Member NoteProperty Model $cs.model -pass |
 Add-Member NoteProperty Manufacturer $cs.manufacturer
Write-Output $obj
```

You'll see this approach in the wild, and, in fact, from an instruction perspective, it's a great technique because it's much clearer what's happening. This technique doesn't use any syntactic shortcuts, so it's a bit easier to follow each step of the process.

21.2.4 *Technique 4: using a Type declaration*

This one is a variation of our Technique 1, and it's only valid in PowerShell v3 or v4. You're going to start with the same hash table of properties. This technique provides a more compact means of creating the new object and assigning the properties, as shown in the following listing.

Listing 21.6   Creating objects using a Type declaration

```
$os = Get-WmiObject -Class Win32_OperatingSystem -comp localhost
$cs = Get-WmiObject -Class Win32_ComputerSystem -comp localhost
$bios = Get-WmiObject -Class Win32_BIOS -comp localhost
$proc = Get-WmiObject -Class Win32_Processor -comp localhost |
Select -First 1
$obj = [pscustomobject]@{OSVersion=$os.version
        Model=$cs.model
        Manufacturer=$cs.manufacturer
        BIOSSerial=$bios.serialnumber
        ComputerName=$os.CSName
```

```
            OSArchitecture=$os.osarchitecture
            ProcArchitecture=$proc.addresswidth
            }
Write-Output $obj
```

You could've continued to put the hash table into the $props variable and used that to create the new object, but there's a neat trick about this technique in that it preserves the insertion order of the properties just as if you'd used [ordered].

> **NOTE** The type that we're using is PSCustomObject. This is a placeholder for the PSObject type we used in Technique 1. You have to use PSCustomObject because in .NET terms you're using the PSObject constructor with no parameters. Don't try to shorten the code by substituting PSObject for PSCustom-Object—you won't get the results you expect.

You may have noticed with all of the previous techniques that the properties came out listed in a different order than the order you used to add them. In Technique 1, for example, you didn't add ComputerName first, but it wound up being listed first for some reason. In many instances, you won't care—PowerShell can work with properties in any order. Technique 4, however, preserves that order for times when you do care.

21.2.5 Technique 5: creating a new class

There's one more technique you can use. It isn't used much but it provides some advantages if the object will be placed on the pipeline for further processing. It can be classified as an advanced technique—not all IT pros will want to delve this far into .NET, but it's available as an option (see the following listing).

Listing 21.7 Creating objects using a new class

```
$source=@"
public class MyObject
{
  public string ComputerName {get; set;}
  public string Model {get; set;}
  public string Manufacturer {get; set;}
  public string BIOSSerial {get; set;}
  public string OSArchitecture {get; set;}
  public string OSVersion {get; set;}
  public string ProcArchitecture {get; set;}
}
"@
Add-Type -TypeDefinition $source -Language CSharpversion3
$os = Get-WmiObject -Class Win32_OperatingSystem -comp localhost
$cs = Get-WmiObject -Class Win32_ComputerSystem -comp localhost
$bios = Get-WmiObject -Class Win32_BIOS -comp localhost
$proc = Get-WmiObject -Class Win32_Processor -comp localhost |
Select -First 1
$props = @{OSVersion=$os.version
          Model=$cs.model
          Manufacturer=$cs.manufacturer
          BIOSSerial=$bios.serialnumber
```

```
            ComputerName=$os.CSName
            OSArchitecture=$os.osarchitecture
            ProcArchitecture=$proc.addresswidth}
$obj = New-Object -TypeName MyObject -Property $props
Write-Output $obj
```

The script in listing 21.7 starts by creating a PowerShell here-string that holds the C#
code to define the class. The class has a name, MyObject, and makes a number of
statements defining the properties. In this example, the properties are all strings, but
a mixture of types is allowed. And even though we don't expect to set any values on
the object, the class definition requires both GET and SET accessors; otherwise, Power-
Shell will throw an exception.

Add-Type is used to compile the class, which can then be used in place of PSObject
when you create an object with New-Object. The object's properties can be supplied
using the technique shown here or in listing 21.6:

```
$obj = [MyObject]@{OSVersion=$os.version
            Model=$cs.model
            Manufacturer=$cs.manufacturer
            BIOSSerial=$bios.serialnumber
            ComputerName=$os.CSName
            OSArchitecture=$os.osarchitecture
            ProcArchitecture=$proc.addresswidth}
```

It's worth testing $obj with Get-Member:

```
PS C:\> $obj | get-member


    TypeName: MyObject

Name            MemberType Definition
----            ---------- ----------
Equals          Method     bool Equals(System.Object obj)
GetHashCode     Method     int GetHashCode()
GetType         Method     type GetType()
ToString        Method     string ToString()
BIOSSerial      Property   string BIOSSerial {get;set;}
ComputerName    Property   string ComputerName {get;set;}
Manufacturer    Property   string Manufacturer {get;set;}
Model           Property   string Model {get;set;}
OSArchitecture  Property   string OSArchitecture {get;set;}
OSVersion       Property   string OSVersion {get;set;}
ProcArchitecture Property  string ProcArchitecture {get;set;}
```

This technique is a little more complicated, but its advantage is that the individual
properties on the object are typed. If you define a property as an integer and try to put
a string into it, an error will be thrown.

21.2.6 *What's the difference?*

Other than readability, the amount of typing required, and the preservation of the properties' order, these techniques are all essentially the same. A few subtle differences do
exist. Technique 1, our hash table approach, is generally the fastest, especially when

you're working with multiple output objects. Technique 2 is a bit slower, and Technique 3 can be significantly slower. There's a good write-up at http://learn-powershell.net/2010/09/19/custom-powershell-objects-and-performance/ from PowerShell MVP Boe Prox, which compares the speeds of these three techniques across 10 objects, and the Add-Member technique (our Technique 3) is something like 10 times slower. So it's worth choosing a quicker technique, and our Technique 1, which we also feel is concise and readable, was the speed winner. We haven't tested the speed of Technique 4, which was new in PowerShell v3, to the same extent that Boe did with the other techniques, but our tests indicate that Technique 4 is about 10% faster than Technique 1. Technique 5 should be reserved for the occasions when data typing of the properties is essential.

21.3 Complex objects: collections as properties

Earlier in this chapter, in the discussion of listing 21.1, we pointed out the use of Select-Object –first 1 to ensure you only get one processor back from the WMI query. What about instances where you might get multiple objects, and where you explicitly need to keep each one of them, because they're each different? Getting user accounts is a good example of that. You can certainly create a custom object that has multiple child objects. Essentially, you first construct a variable that contains each of those objects and then append it to a second, top-level object that will be your final output. This is a lot easier to see than to talk about, so let's go right to the next listing.

Listing 21.8 Working with multiple objects

```
$os = Get-WmiObject -Class Win32_OperatingSystem
$users = Get-WmiObject -Class Win32_UserAccount
$disks = Get-WmiObject -Class Win32_LogicalDisk -filter "drivetype=3"    ❷ Enumerate
$diskObjs = @()                                                              disks
foreach ($disk in $disks) {
    $props = @{Drive=$disk.DeviceID
               Space=$disk.Size
               FreeSpace=$disk.FreeSpace}
    $diskObj = New-Object -TypeName PSObject -Property $props
    $diskObjs += $diskObj
}
$userObjs = @()
foreach ($user in $users) {
    $props = @{UserName=$user.Name
               UserSID=$user.SID}
    $userObj = New-Object -TypeName PSObject -Property $props
    $userObjs += $userObj
}
$props = @{ComputerName=$os.CSName
           OSVersion=$os.version
           SPVersion=$os.servicepackmajorversion
           Disks=$diskObjs

           Users=$userObjs
          }
```

Empty ❶ **array**

❸ **Set up single disk object**

❹ **Create disk object**

❺ **Append to array**

❻ **Repeat for users**

❼ **Add users and disks**

```
$obj = New-Object -TypeName PSObject -Property $props
Write-Output $obj                                          ◁──❽  Output to pipeline
```

The script begins by retrieving information into variables, just as you've done in prior examples. This time, you're getting disks and users, which may well have multiple objects on any given machine. You're not limiting this to the first one of each; you're grabbing whatever's present on the machine. The fun starts when you create an empty array to hold all your custom disk objects ❶. You then enumerate through the disks, one at a time ❷. Each time through, you set up a hash table for the properties you want to display for a disk ❸, and then you create the disk object using those properties ❹. At the end of the iteration, you append that disk object to your originally empty array ❺. Once you've made it through all the disks, you repeat the same basic process for the users ❻.

Once that's all done, you create your final output object. It includes information from the operating system but also the collections of user and disk objects you just created ❼. That final object is output to the pipeline ❽. The result looks something like this:

```
Users       : {@{UserSID=S-1-5-21-29812541-3325070801-1520984716-500
              ; UserName=Administrator}, @{UserSID=S-1-5-21-29812541
              -3325070801-1520984716-501; UserName=Guest}, @{UserSID
              =S-1-5-21-29812541-3325070801-1520984716-502; UserName
              =krbtgt}, @{UserSID=S-1-5-21-29812541-3325070801-15209
              84716-1103; UserName=rhondah}}
OSVersion   : 6.1.7601
Disks       : {@{Space=42842714112; Drive=C:; FreeSpace=32443473920}
              }
ComputerName : WIN-KNBA0R0TM23
SPVersion    : 1
```

What you're seeing in the Disks and Users properties is PowerShell's way of displaying properties that have multiple subobjects as their contents. Each of your disks and users is being displayed as a hash table of property=value entries. If there are a number of accounts on the system, you may see "..." in the users display. This is because PowerShell will only show the first four values in a collection by default. You can change this by modifying the value contained in the $FormatEnumeration-Limit variable.

You can use Select-Object to extract just one of those properties' children in a more sensible fashion:

```
PS C:\> .\multitest.ps1 | select -expand users

UserSID                          UserName
-------                          --------
S-1-5-21-29812541-3325070801-15... Administrator
S-1-5-21-29812541-3325070801-15... Guest
S-1-5-21-29812541-3325070801-15... krbtgt
S-1-5-21-29812541-3325070801-15... rhondah
```

So this is how you can create, and ultimately access, a complex hierarchy of data by using a single output object type. This is also—finally—a good time to show you a potential use for the Format-Custom cmdlet. Check this out:

```
PS C:\> .\multitest.ps1 | format-custom

class PSCustomObject
{
  Users =
    [
      class PSCustomObject
      {
        UserSID = S-1-5-21-29812541-3325070801-1520984716-500
        UserName = Administrator
      }
      class PSCustomObject
      {
        UserSID = S-1-5-21-29812541-3325070801-1520984716-501
        UserName = Guest
      }
      class PSCustomObject
      {
        UserSID = S-1-5-21-29812541-3325070801-1520984716-502
        UserName = krbtgt
      }
      class PSCustomObject
      {
        UserSID = S-1-5-21-29812541-3325070801-1520984716-1103
        UserName = rhondah
      }
    ]
  OSVersion = 6.1.7601
  Disks =
    [
      class PSCustomObject
      {
        Space = 42842714112
        Drive = C:
        FreeSpace = 32442359808
      }
    ]

  ComputerName = WIN-KNBA0R0TM23
  SPVersion = 1
}
```

Given a bunch of objects, Format-Custom will attempt to display their properties. When it runs across a property that itself contains subobjects, it'll attempt to break those down. Parameters let you specify how deeply it'll attempt to do this within a nested hierarchy of objects. Format-Custom is covered in more detail in chapter 9.

21.4 Applying a type name to custom objects

The custom objects you've created so far are all of a generic type. You can test that by piping any of them to Get-Member:

```
PS C:\> .\multitest.ps1 | get-member


    TypeName: System.Management.Automation.PSCustomObject

Name         MemberType   Definition
----         ----------   ----------
Equals       Method       bool Equals(System.Object obj)
GetHashCode  Method       int GetHashCode()
GetType      Method       type GetType()
ToString     Method       string ToString()
ComputerName NoteProperty System.String ComputerName=WIN-KNBA0R0TM23
Disks        NoteProperty System.Object[] Disks=System.Object[]
OSVersion    NoteProperty System.String OSVersion=6.1.7601
SPVersion    NoteProperty System.UInt16 SPVersion=1
Users        NoteProperty System.Object[] Users=System.Object[]
```

There's nothing wrong with all of these objects having the same type, unless you want to apply a custom format view or a custom type extension (something we cover in upcoming chapters). Those custom extensions require an object to have a unique name so that PowerShell can identify the object and apply the extension appropriately. Giving one of your objects a custom name is easy—just do so before outputting it to the command line. We'll revise listing 21.6, as shown in listing 21.9, to add a custom type name. This technique isn't needed if the syntax from listing 21.7 is used because you define a type name when creating the class.

Listing 21.9 Adding a type name to custom objects

```
$os = Get-WmiObject -Class Win32_OperatingSystem
$users = Get-WmiObject -Class Win32_UserAccount
$disks = Get-WmiObject -Class Win32_LogicalDisk -filter "drivetype=3"
$diskObjs = @()
foreach ($disk in $disks) {
    $props = @{Drive=$disk.DeviceID
               Space=$disk.Size
               FreeSpace=$disk.FreeSpace}
    $diskObj = New-Object -TypeName PSObject -Property $props
    $diskObjs = $diskObjs + $diskObj
}

$userObjs = @()
foreach ($user in $users) {
    $props = @{UserName=$user.Name
               UserSID=$user.SID}
    $userObj = New-Object -TypeName PSObject -Property $props
    $userObjs = $userObjs + $userObj
}
$props = @{ComputerName=$os.CSName
           OSVersion=$os.version
           SPVersion=$os.servicepackmajorversion
```

```
            Disks=$diskObjs
            Users=$userObjs}
$obj = New-Object -TypeName PSObject -Property $props          Adding custom
$obj.PSObject.TypeNames.Insert(0,'My.Awesome.Type')   <───┐   type name
Write-Output $obj
```

The script in listing 21.9 produces the following output when piped to Get-Member:

```
PS C:\> .\multitest.ps1 | get-member

   TypeName: My.Awesome.Type

Name         MemberType   Definition
----         ----------   ----------
Equals       Method       bool Equals(System.Object obj)
GetHashCode  Method       int GetHashCode()
GetType      Method       type GetType()
ToString     Method       string ToString()
ComputerName NoteProperty System.String ComputerName=WIN-KNBA0R0TM23
Disks        NoteProperty System.Object[] Disks=System.Object[]
OSVersion    NoteProperty System.String OSVersion=6.1.7601
SPVersion    NoteProperty System.UInt16 SPVersion=1
Users        NoteProperty System.Object[] Users=System.Object[]
```

As you can see, the custom type name was applied and is reflected in the output. Your only real concern with custom type names is that they not overlap with any other type names that might be running around inside the shell. The easiest way to ensure that uniqueness is to use a standard naming convention, within your organization, for custom type names. For example, a type name like Contoso.PowerShell.UserInfo is unique, describes the kind of information that the object holds, and is unlikely to interfere with anyone else's efforts. We'll show you how to put that custom type name to use in chapters 26 and 27.

21.5 So, why bother?

This may seem like an awful lot of trouble. Let's skip back to our first complete example, in listing 21.2, and redo it in the way that a lot of PowerShell newcomers would do. The following listing shows this approach, which we consider substandard, and we'll explain why in a moment.

Listing 21.10 Multiple objects

```
Get-WmiObject -Class Win32_OperatingSystem -comp localhost |
Select CSName,Version,OSArchitecture

Get-WmiObject -Class Win32_ComputerSystem -comp localhost |
Select Model,Manufacturer

Get-WmiObject -Class Win32_BIOS -comp localhost |
Select SerialNumber

Get-WmiObject -Class Win32_Processor -comp localhost |
Select -First 1 -property AddressWidth
```

Here's what this script gets you:

```
PS C:\> .\NoObjects.ps1

CSName                Version            OSArchitecture
------                -------            --------------
WIN-KNBA0R0TM23       6.1.7601           64-bit
```

Um, wait—where's all of the other information? The problem is that this script violates a primary PowerShell law because it's outputting multiple kinds of objects. There's an operating system object first, then a computer system object, then a BIOS object, then a processor object. We explained in the previous chapter that PowerShell doesn't deal well with that situation. PowerShell sees the first object and tries to format it and then gets lost because all this other stuff comes down the pipe. So, this is a bad approach. Most folks' second attempt will look like the next listing.

Listing 21.11   Outputting text

```
$os = Get-WmiObject -Class Win32_OperatingSystem -comp localhost |
Select CSName,Version,OSArchitecture

$cs = Get-WmiObject -Class Win32_ComputerSystem -comp localhost |
Select Model,Manufacturer

$bios = Get-WmiObject -Class Win32_BIOS -comp localhost |
Select SerialNumber

$proc = Get-WmiObject -Class Win32_Processor -comp localhost |
Select -first 1 -property AddressWidth
Write-Host "            Name: $($os.CSName)"
Write-Host "      OS Version: $($os.version)"
Write-Host "           Model: $($cs.model)"
Write-Host "  OS Architecture: $($os.osarchitecture)"
Write-Host "     Manufacturer: $($cs.manufacturer)"
Write-Host "Proc Architecture: $($proc.addresswidth)"
Write-Host "      BIOS Serial: $($bios.serialnumber)"
```

Here's what you get when you run listing 21.11:

```
PS C:\> .\OutputText.ps1
            Name: RSSURFACEPRO2
      OS Version: 6.3.9600
           Model: Surface Pro 2
  OS Architecture: 64-bit
     Manufacturer: Microsoft Corporation
Proc Architecture: 64
      BIOS Serial: 036685734653
```

Look at all of the care that went into formatting that! Everything all lined up and pretty. Too bad it's a waste of time. Try to reuse that information in any way whatsoever, and it'll fail. None of the following will do anything useful at all:

- .\OutputText.ps1 | ConvertTo-HTML | Out-File inventory.html
- .\OutputText.ps1 | Export-CSV inventory.csv
- .\OutputTest.ps1 | Export-CliXML inventory.xml

This is the problem with a script that simply outputs text. And whether you output formatted text via `Write-Host` or `Write-Output` doesn't matter; it's still just text. PowerShell wants the structured data offered by an object, and that's why the techniques in this chapter are so important.

If we haven't stressed this enough, we'll leave you with one more code example where you can create your own object out of just about anything.

Listing 21.12   Creating your own custom object

```
$computername=$env:computername
$prop=[ordered]@{Computername=$Computername}
$os=Get-WmiObject Win32_OperatingSystem -Property Caption,LastBootUpTime `
-ComputerName $computername
$boot=$os.ConvertToDateTime($os.LastBootuptime)
$prop.Add("OS",$os.Caption)
$prop.Add("Boot",$boot)
$prop.Add("Uptime",(Get-Date)-$boot)

$running=Get-Service -ComputerName $computername |
Where status -eq "Running"
$prop.Add("RunningServices",$Running)
$cdrive=Get-WMIObject win32_logicaldisk -filter "DeviceID='c:'" `
-computername $computername
$prop.Add("C_SizeGB",($cdrive.Size/1GB -as [int]))
$prop.Add("C_FreeGB",($cdrive.FreeSpace/1GB))
$obj=New-Object -TypeName PSObject -Property $prop
$obj.PSObject.TypeNames.Insert(0,"MyInventory")
Write-Output $obj
```

In this example you're getting information from a variety of sources and building a custom object. Here's the sample output:

```
Computername    : RSSURFACEPRO2
OS              : Microsoft Windows 8.1 Pro
Boot            : 27/01/2014 17:27:00
Uptime          : 6.22:30:22.8385355
RunningServices : {AdobeARMservice, Appinfo, AppMgmt, AudioEndpointBuilder...}
C_SizeGB        : 232
C_FreeGB        : 162.906734466553
```

Here, the `RunningServices` property is a collection of service objects. You didn't need to use the `ForEach` technique as you did in listing 21.8. The `$Running` variable simply becomes the value of the custom property.

Listing 21.12 is the type of code you'll want to turn into a function where you can pass a collection of computer names. The output is an object, written to the pipeline, which you can see on the screen, convert to HTML, export to a CSV file, or do just about anything else you can think of to. The bottom line is, think *objects in the pipeline.*

21.6   *Summary*

Creating output is possibly the most important thing many scripts and functions will do, and creating that output so that it can work with PowerShell's other functionality is crucial to making a well-behaved, flexible, consistent unit of automation. Custom objects are the key, and by making them properly you'll be assured of an overall consistent PowerShell environment.

22

Scope

Scope is one of the most confusing things about PowerShell when you're a newcomer, and even experienced gurus get tripped up by it from time to time. If you're just using the shell as a shell—meaning you're running commands and seeing the results onscreen—then scope won't affect your life much. It's when you start writing scripts, functions, and modules that scope comes into play.

22.1 Understanding scope

Scope is a form of *containerization*. Certain elements in PowerShell are considered *scoped elements*, and when you create one it exists only within the container, or scope, in which you created it. Generally speaking, it can only be used from within that scope as well. There are obviously a lot of rules and caveats around this, but we're going to start with the basics and general realities and then diverge from there.

Take a look at figure 22.1, which illustrates the relationship between different kinds of scope.

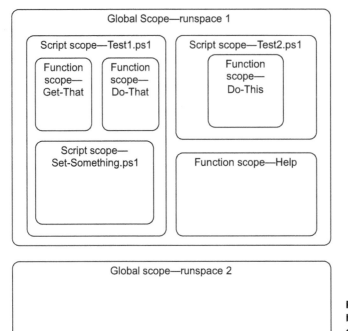

Figure 22.1 Scopes can have both child and parent scopes, creating a hierarchical relationship.

There are three main types of scope in PowerShell. They all do exactly the same thing—the names just reflect the ways in which these scopes are created.

- A *global* scope is created when you start a new PowerShell session, such as opening a new console window. PowerShell refers to a shell instance as a *runspace*. With the normal console application, you can only have one runspace, so an *instance of the shell* equals *one runspace*. But other hosting applications can have multiple runspaces within the same application. In the PowerShell ISE, for example, you can select New PowerShell Tab from the File menu and in doing so create an additional runspace within the same application window. Because it's possible to have multiple runspaces active at the same time, such as when you open two console windows side by side, you can have multiple global scopes. A session created on another machine using PowerShell remoting has its own global scope that's totally independent of the scope from which the session was created.

- A *script* scope is created whenever PowerShell runs a new script (with one exception, called dot sourcing, which we cover later in this chapter). As illustrated in figure 22.1, a script can run another script, and the second one (Set-Something.ps1 in the illustration) gets its own scope.

- A *function* scope is created whenever you define a function. Functions can be defined within the shell itself (meaning within the global scope), or within a script, or even within another function.

Using scope

PowerShell v3 introduced another level of scope called *using*. It doesn't fit into the hierarchical model described in figure 22.1, and the rules laid down in this chapter don't apply, because it's designed to be used in situations where you want to access a local variable in a remote session. The definition from the help file about_scopes is:

> *Using is a special scope modifier that identifies a local variable in a remote command. By default, variables in remote commands are assumed to be defined in the remote session.*

More on using can be found in about_Remote_Variables. It's used like this:

```
PS C:\> $s = New-PSSession -ComputerName W12Standard
PS C:\> $dt = 3
PS C:\> Invoke-Command -Session $s -ScriptBlock {Get-WmiObject -Class
➥ Win32_LogicalDisk -Filter "DriveType=$dt"}

Invalid query "select * from Win32_LogicalDisk where DriveType="
    + CategoryInfo          : InvalidArgument: (:)
[Get-WmiObject], ManagementException
    + FullyQualifiedErrorId : GetWMIManagementException,
Microsoft.PowerShell.Commands.GetWmiObjectCommand
    + PSComputerName        : W12Standard
PS C:\> Invoke-Command -Session $s -ScriptBlock {Get-WmiObject -Class
➥ Win32_LogicalDisk -Filter "DriveType=$Using:dt"}

DeviceID      : C:
DriveType     : 3
ProviderName  :
FreeSpace     : 126600425472
Size          : 135994011648
VolumeName    :
PSComputerName : W12Standard
```

Create a remoting session to another machine and define a local variable. If you try to use that variable (which is local) in the remote session, you'll get the error shown in the first command, but if you employ the using scope, it works.

In PowerShell v2, you could do this:

```
PS C:\> Invoke-Command -Session $s -ScriptBlock {param($d) Get-
➥ WmiObject -Class Win32_LogicalDisk -Filter "DriveType=$d" }
➥ -ArgumentList $dt
```

Using is a valuable addition to your toolbox when you're working with remote machines.

As you can see in figure 22.1, the global, script, and function scopes create a hierarchy: The global scope is always at the top. That contains one or more function scripts (PowerShell's Help command is actually a function, not an alias, which is defined in the global scope). The global scope will also contain a script scope whenever you run a script. A script or function can create additional scopes by containing functions or running other scripts.

When one scope hosts another, such as when our Test1.ps1 ran Set-Something.ps1 in figure 22.1, the higher-level scope is referred to as a *parent* and the newly created scope as a *child*. So, in our illustration, Test1.ps1, Test2.ps1, and the Help function are all *children* of the global scope. They all refer to the global scope as their *parent*. A child, such as Test2.ps1, can also be a parent to its own children, which in our illustration is the function Do-This.

As we mentioned earlier, scope is only important in relation to scoped elements. The following elements of PowerShell are scoped:

- PSDrives
- Variables
- Functions
- Aliases

Here are the general rules for scope, along with some examples for each:

- When you create a new scoped element, it exists only within the current scope. That is, if Test1.ps1 defines a new alias named "Fred," that alias won't be available in the global scope. Parent scopes can never see anything in a child scope.
- If you try to access an element that doesn't exist in the current scope, Power-Shell will go up the scope relationships from child to parent to see if that item exists somewhere else. For example, let's say the Set-Something.ps1 function runs Dir, which is an alias to Get-ChildItem. Assuming Set-Something.ps1 didn't define Dir as an alias, PowerShell would look to see if it was defined in the parent scope, Test1.ps1. Assuming it was also not defined there, PowerShell would look to the next parent, which is the global scope. The alias is definitely defined there, and so it'd run normally.
- You're allowed to create a scoped element whose name conflicts with a parent scope's definition. In other words, Test1.ps1 could create a new alias named Dir that pointed to the Get-WmiObject cmdlet. From then on, until the script finished running, executing Dir would run Get-WmiObject, not Get-ChildItem. In effect, the child scope's local definition would prevent PowerShell from going up to the parent scope to find the normal definition of Dir.
- When a scope is finished, everything in it, including all child scopes, is destroyed and removed from memory. Assume Set-Something created a variable named $x. Once Test1.ps1 finished running, that $x—and everything else defined by Test1.ps1 or one of its children—would go away.

NOTE   Our example of redefining the Dir alias is strictly theoretical. In practice, PowerShell's creators have made it more or less impossible to overwrite the built-in aliases. We'll use a more practical example in the next section of this chapter.

We're going to cover plenty of examples of these behaviors, because we realize they can be a little confusing. But we have one more thing to point out: Plenty of PowerShell elements are not scoped. For example, if Test1.ps1 were to load a module by using the `Import-Module` cmdlet, that module would remain loaded even after the script finished running. That's because modules aren't scoped elements: Messing with them in any way affects the entire runspace, or global scope.

22.2 Observing scope in action

Perhaps the easiest way to understand scope's general rules is to see them in action. To do that, you'll start by creating a little demonstration script, shown in the following listing.

Listing 22.1   Scope demonstration script, test.ps1

```
function Do-This {
    Write-Host "Inside the function" –Foreground Green
    Write-Host "Variable contains '$variable'" –Foreground Green
    $variable = 'Function'
    Write-Host "Variable now contains '$variable'" –Foreground Green
    Gw -Class Win32_BIOS
}

Write-Host "Inside the script" –Foreground Red
$variable = "Script"
Write-Host "Variable now contains '$variable'" –Foreground Red
New-Alias -Name gw -Value Get-WmiObject -Force
Gw -Class Win32_ComputerSystem
Do-This
Write-Host "Back in the script" –Foreground Red
Write-Host "Variable contains '$variable'" –Foreground Red
Write-Host "Done with the script" –Foreground Red
```

Save the script as `C:\Test.ps1`. Then, open a brand-new PowerShell console window (just to make sure you're starting fresh) and run the script. Here are the results:

```
PS C:\> ./test
Inside the script
Variable now contains 'Script'
Domain              : company.pri
Manufacturer        : VMware, Inc.
Model               : VMware Virtual Platform
Name                : WIN-KNBA0R0TM23
PrimaryOwnerName    : Windows User
TotalPhysicalMemory : 1073209344
Inside the function
Variable contains 'Script'
Variable now contains 'Function'
SMBIOSBIOSVersion : 6.00
Manufacturer      : Phoenix Technologies LTD
Name              : PhoenixBIOS 4.0 Release 6.0
SerialNumber      : VMware-56 4d 47 10 6b f6 d7
                    9e 4b
Version           : INTEL  - 6040000
Back in the script
Variable contains 'Script'
```

```
Done with the script
PS C:\> gw -class win32_operatingsystem
The term 'gw' is not recognized as the name of a cmdlet, function,
script file, or operable program. Check the spelling of the name, or if
 a path was included, verify that the path is correct and try again.
At line:1 char:3
+ gw <<<<  -class win32_operatingsystem
    + CategoryInfo          : ObjectNotFound: (gw:String) [], Comman
  dNotFoundException
    + FullyQualifiedErrorId : CommandNotFoundException
```

Note that the script used a foreground color with Write-Host to make it clear when scope changes. Let's walk through exactly what happened, step by step:

1 You run the script.

2 The first executable line of the script displays "Inside the script."

3 The next line of the script puts Script inside $variable. The $variable element hasn't been seen before, so PowerShell creates it within this scope.

4 The next line displays the contents of the variable, resulting in Variable now contains 'Script'—all good so far.

5 The script defines an alias, Gw, that points to Get-WmiObject. This alias is created within the script's own scope.

6 The script runs its Gw alias, creating some output in the shell.

7 Now the script executes the Do-This function, which is located within the script. We're now in scope #3: Scope #1 is the global scope, scope #2 is the Test.ps1 script, and the third scope is the interior of the Do-This function.

8 The function starts by displaying Inside the function, just so you know where you're at.

9 The function attempts to display the contents of $variable. But $variable hasn't been created inside this scope. So the shell goes up a level to the first parent and finds that $variable was defined there. So the shell displays Variable contains 'script' and moves on.

10 The function now puts Function inside $variable. This creates a new element called $variable inside the current scope. The $variable owned by the parent isn't affected!

11 Next, the function displays Variable now contains 'Function', which is true because $variable now exists inside the local scope and contains Function.

12 Now the function tries to use the Gw alias. It doesn't exist in this scope, so again the shell goes up to the parent. The alias exists there, and so the command runs successfully. You can see the output with a bit of information about the computer's BIOS.

13 The function exits and its scope is destroyed. The script displays Back in the script.

14 The script displays Variable contains 'Script', which is true because $variable exists in the script scope, and in this scope it does contain Script. It was never changed by what the function did.

15 Finally, the script displays Done with the script.

16 The script finishes, and its scope is destroyed. Back in the shell, you attempt to use the Gw alias and find that it won't work. The alias was never defined in the global scope, so you can't use it here. There's no parent to the global scope, so the shell has nowhere *up* to go and find the alias.

That's a good look at the basics of scope. Just remember the rules we outlined earlier, and you'll usually be okay. Now for the creative stuff!

22.3   Dot sourcing

As you'll recall from chapter 20, *dot sourcing* is a technique in PowerShell that lets you run a script without first creating a new scope for it. In other words, rather than creating a container in which to run the script, PowerShell runs it inside the current scope. The practical upshot of this is that anything created within the script *continues to exist after the script is finished.* Let's use our Test.ps1 demonstration from listing 22.1 again. Again open a brand-new PowerShell console window and run the following:

```
PS C:\> . .\test.ps1                              ◁──┐  Dot-sourced
Inside the script                                     │  script
Variable now contains 'Script'
Domain               : company.pri
Manufacturer         : VMware, Inc.
Model                : VMware Virtual Platform
Name                 : WIN-KNBA0R0TM23
PrimaryOwnerName     : Windows User
TotalPhysicalMemory  : 1073209344

Inside the function
Variable contains 'Script'
Variable now contains 'Function'
SMBIOSBIOSVersion : 6.00
Manufacturer      : Phoenix Technologies LTD
Name              : PhoenixBIOS 4.0 Release 6.0
SerialNumber      : VMware-56 4d 47 10 6b f6 d7 bc-a3 d6 b1 99 a2 6f
                    9e 4b
Version           : INTEL  - 6040000

Back in the script
Variable contains 'Script'
Done with the script
PS C:\> $variable                              ┐  Script's elements
Script                                         │  still exist
PS C:\> gw -class win32_operatingsystem
SystemDirectory : C:\Windows\system32
Organization    :
BuildNumber     : 7601
RegisteredUser  : Windows User
SerialNumber    : 55041-507-0078841-84800
Version         : 6.1.7601
```

```
PS C:\> Do-This
Inside the function                          ◁─┐  Function
Variable contains 'Script'                      │  still exists
Variable now contains 'Function'
SMBIOSBIOSVersion : 6.00
Manufacturer      : Phoenix Technologies LTD
Name              : PhoenixBIOS 4.0 Release 6.0
SerialNumber      : VMware-56 4d 47 10 6b f6 d7 bc-a3 d6 b1 99 a2 6f
                    9e 4b
Version           : INTEL  - 6040000
PS C:\> $variable
Script
```

To dot-source the script, you type a period, followed by a space, and then the path and filename of the script. The script's output looks exactly the same as it did last time. But when the script finishes, you're able to display the contents of $variable, and you're able to use the Gw alias. That's because you've essentially created those items within the global scope! The script was never given a scope of its own, so everything it did technically happened inside the global scope. When the script finishes running, the global scope continues to exist, and so those two elements remain accessible.

Even the Do-This function continued to be accessible. That's because it was defined within the script. But the script didn't have its own scope, so Do-This was technically defined into the global scope. That means it continues to exist after the script has finished running. All the regular scope rules still apply, though: When Do-This runs, it creates its own $variable and puts Function inside it. Once the function completes, its scope is destroyed. At the global scope, $variable still contains Script, as shown in the output. The dot sourcing only prevented a scope from being created for the script; it didn't stop any other scope rules, such as the function getting its own scope, from operating.

Some folks will use dot sourcing as a way of including a library script inside another script they want to run. For example, they'll put a bunch of functions, and nothing else, into a script, perhaps naming it Library.ps1. Then, inside all their other scripts, they'll dot-source Library.ps1. Doing so makes all of the functions from Library.ps1 available inside the other scripts. That was the only way to accomplish such a thing in PowerShell v1; in v2 and later, that library should be written as a script module and loaded by running Import-Module. That way, it (and its contents) can be easily removed by running Remove-Module. You also save the overhead of continually loading the library of functions.

> **TIP** Dot sourcing is great when developing scripts. If you're having problems working out how to do something, run your script using dot sourcing and you'll have all your variables and functions available. You can experiment at the command line to get the code working and copy the working code into your script.

22.4 *Manipulating cross-scope elements*

Our general rules from earlier in this chapter boil down to two important basics:

- A parent can never see or change scoped elements that exist within a child. We're not going to budge on this one—it's always true and there's no way around it.
- A child scope can read items from its parent, but it can't change them. If a child scope tries to change an element from its parent, it winds up creating a new element, having the same name, inside its own local scope.

That second rule is the one that we're now going to mess with. To do that we're going to create a slightly simpler demonstration script that only manipulates variables. These same rules apply to other scoped elements, such as aliases and PSDrives, but variables are the easiest to observe in action. The following listing contains our simplified example script, which should be saved as `test2.ps1`.

Listing 22.2 Demonstrating cross-scope activities

```
function Do-That {
    Write-Host "Inside Do-That `$var is '$var'"
    $var = 3
    Write-Host "Now, inside Do-That `$var is '$var'"
}

Write-Host "Inside Test2 `$var is '$var'"
$var = 2
Write-Host "Now, inside Test2 `$var is '$var'"
Do-That
Write-Host "Back inside Test2 `$var is '$var'"
```

As before, open a fresh PowerShell console window to try this out. Begin by setting $var to something in the global scope, running the script, and then checking the contents of $var. Here's what happens:

```
PS C:\> $var = 1
PS C:\> .\test2.ps1
Inside Test2 $var is '1'
Now, inside Test2 $var is '2'
Inside Do-That $var is '2'
Now, inside Do-That $var is '3'
Back inside Test2 $var is '2'PS C:\> $var
1
PS C:\>
```

This is exactly the same behavior that we demonstrated before. At the beginning of each new scope, $var doesn't exist. When the scope tries to access it, PowerShell pops up a level to that scope's parent. So at the beginning of the script, the value 1 is coming from your global scope $var; at the beginning of the function, the value of 2 is coming from the script. Each scope then sets its own value for the variable, which in essence creates a new variable that happens to have the same name as a variable in the parent scope. The scopes' use of $var doesn't in any way change their parent scopes' definition of the variable: You can see after the script runs that $var remains 1 in the global scope.

Now let's change up the rules a bit. You'll use PowerShell's variable cmdlets to do this, resulting in the script shown in the next listing.

Listing 22.3   Test2.ps1, which now uses cmdlets to modify out-of-scope elements

```
function Do-That {
    Write-Host "Inside Do-That `$var is '$var'"
    Set-Variable -Name var -Value 3 -Scope 2
    Write-Host "Now, inside Do-That `$var is '$var'"
}

Write-Host "Inside Test2 `$var is '$var'"
Set-Variable -Name var -Value 2 -Scope 1
Write-Host "Now, inside Test2 `$var is '$var'"
Do-That
Write-Host "Back inside Test2 `$var is '$var'"
```

Here are the results of running the script in listing 22.3 in a brand-new console window:

```
PS C:\> $var = 1
PS C:\> .\test2.ps1
Inside Test2 $var is '1'
Now, inside Test2 $var is '2'
Inside Do-That $var is '2'
Now, inside Do-That $var is '3'
Back inside Test2 $var is '3'
PS C:\> $var
3
PS C:\>
```

Unlike the previous example, in this case there's only one copy of $var running around, and it's the one in the global scope. The various -Variable cmdlets, including Set-Variable, all have a -Scope parameter. This parameter lets you explicitly modify an element in a higher-level scope. The parameter accepts a number, and 0 means *do it in my local scope*, which is the default behavior if you don't use -Scope at all. A value of 1 means *do this in my parent's scope*, a value of 2 means *do it in my parent's parent's scope* (which you could call *my grandparent's scope*, but that might be taking the family analogy a bit too far).

So when the function ran this:

```
Set-Variable -Name var -Value 3 -Scope 2
```

it was telling the shell to "modify the contents of $var, placing a 3 into the variable. But don't do this locally. Go up two levels, to my parent's parent, and make the change there." Because the function was three levels down—global, script, function—this resulted in the global scope's copy of $var being modified.

It can be tough to keep track of scopes by number like that. For example, let's say you wrote another script, test3.ps1, as shown here.

```
C:\test2.ps1
```

Now, open a fresh shell console and try this:

```
PS C:\> $var = 1
PS C:\> ./test3
Inside Test2 $var is '1'
Now, inside Test2 $var is '2'
Inside Do-That $var is '2'
Now, inside Do-That $var is '3'
Back inside Test2 $var is '3'
PS C:\> $var
1
```

You get different results. At the end of everything, $var continues to contain 1 in the global scope. That's because Test3.ps1 created its own scope, which was a child of the global. When the function modified the variable, it went *up* two levels (that's what -Scope 2 means). Up one level is Test2.ps1, and up a second level is Test3.ps1. So the function modified $var in Test3.ps1 rather than in the global scope.

To help get more predictable results, you can refer to specific scopes by name instead of by numbers. The following listing contains a modified Test2.ps1.

```
function Do-That {
    Write-Host "Inside Do-That `$var is '$var'"
    Set-Variable -Name var -Value 3 -Scope global
    Write-Host "Now, inside Do-That `$var is '$var'"
}
Write-Host "Inside Test2 `$var is '$var'"
Set-Variable -Name var -Value 2 -Scope global
Write-Host "Now, inside Test2 `$var is '$var'"
Do-That
Write-Host "Back inside Test2 `$var is '$var'"
```

Now let's go run Test3.ps1, from listing 22.4, again:

```
PS C:\> $var = 1
PS C:\> .\test3.ps1
Inside Test2 $var is '1'
Now, inside Test2 $var is '2'
Inside Do-That $var is '2'
Now, inside Do-That $var is '3'
Back inside Test2 $var is '3'
PS C:\> $var
3
```

Now the global scope's $var has again been modified, because Test2.ps1 referred specifically to the global scope by name, rather than by trying to count up a certain number of levels. This is an absolute scope reference, meaning no matter how deeply nested the `Set-Variable` command becomes, it'll always modify the global scope when `-Scope global` is specified.

You can refer to a few scopes by name:

- *Global* always refers to the global scope.
- *Local* always refers to the current scope and is the default.
- *Script* refers to the nearest script scope upward in the hierarchy.

If you can accomplish what you need by using a named scope in that fashion, then you don't even have to use a `-Variable` cmdlet. PowerShell recognizes a shortcut syntax that can be used directly with variable names:

- `$global:var` will always refer to the variable `$var` in the global scope.
- `$local:var` will always refer to the variable `$var` in the current scope.
- `$script:var` will always refer to the variable `$var` in the next script scope that's upward in the hierarchy.

As a best practice, assiduously avoid messing with any scopes that aren't your own. For example, don't rely on the global scope containing information that you need, because you don't know what else might be playing with the global scope and possibly messing you up and causing bugs in your script. We see people use higher-scope variables as a way of passing information between two scripts, or between two functions, or something else. As a rule, that's a bad idea. It can create complex debugging situations, along with other troubles. It can also cause your script to conflict with other people's scripts, if those other people are also relying on higher-scope variables and information. As a rule, you should only mess with things in the local scope. To pass information between scopes, rely on parameters for input and the pipeline for output. We cover all of that in upcoming chapters.

22.5 *Being private*

There's one more scope we have to cover, and that's the private scope. When you create a scoped item and give it a scope of private, it exists only inside the current, local scope. As always, it can't be seen by the current scope's parent—that's always impossible. But unlike other elements, a private element also can't be seen by a scope's children.

For example, suppose a script creates a variable like this:

```
$private:computername = 'SERVER1'
```

Normally, any functions contained within that script—its children—would be able to access the contents of `$computername`. Not in this case. To them, `$computername` will appear to be undefined. They're welcome to create their own copy of `$computername`, of course, but they can't see the parent's. But if a child scope explicitly tried to access `$private:computername`, it'd be able to do so.

22.6 *Being strict*

We discussed the Set-StrictMode cmdlet in chapter 16. Because this cmdlet ties in so closely with scope, we'll cover it in a bit more detail here. Let's first see it in normal operation: You set a global scope variable named $check and then write a script named Strict.ps1, which contains one line that displays the contents of $check, as shown in the next listing.

Listing 22.6 Strict.ps1

```
$check
```

Now let's see what happens with the various strict modes:

```
PS C:\> $check = 'Please'
PS C:\> Set-StrictMode -Off
PS C:\> ./strict
Please
PS C:\> Set-StrictMode -Version 1
PS C:\> ./strict
Please
PS C:\> Set-StrictMode -Version 2
PS C:\> ./strict
Please
PS C:\> Set-StrictMode -Version 3
PS C:\> ./strict
Please
PS C:\> Set-StrictMode -Version 4
PS C:\> ./strict
Please
PS C:\>
```

That's the same behavior you've seen throughout this chapter: In all three modes, with strict set to Off, version 1, version 2, version 3, or version 4, the script's scope is able to go up the scope hierarchy to access the global $check variable. Now modify Strict.ps1, as shown in the following listing, to display a variable that hasn't been created in the global scope (or anywhere else).

Listing 22.7 Modifying Strict.ps1

```
$peace
```

Now try running that script in the different strict modes:

```
PS C:\> Set-StrictMode -Off
PS C:\> ./strict
PS C:\> Set-StrictMode -Version 1
PS C:\> ./strict
The variable '$peace' cannot be retrieved because it has not been set.
At C:\Test\strict.ps1:1 char:1
+ $peace
+ ~~~~~~
    + CategoryInfo          : InvalidOperation: (peace:String) [],
                              RuntimeException
    + FullyQualifiedErrorId : VariableIsUndefined
```

```
PS C:\> Set-StrictMode -Version 2
PS C:\> ./strict
The variable '$peace' cannot be retrieved because it has not been set.
At C:\Test\strict.ps1:1 char:1
+ $peace
+ ~~~~~~
    + CategoryInfo          : InvalidOperation: (peace:String) [],
                              RuntimeException
    + FullyQualifiedErrorId : VariableIsUndefined

PS C:\> Set-StrictMode -Version 3
PS C:\> ./strict
The variable '$peace' cannot be retrieved because it has not been set.
At C:\Test\strict.ps1:1 char:1
+ $peace
+ ~~~~~~
    + CategoryInfo          : InvalidOperation: (peace:String) [],
                              RuntimeException
    + FullyQualifiedErrorId : VariableIsUndefined

PS C:\> Set-StrictMode -Version 4
PS C:\> ./strict
The variable '$peace' cannot be retrieved because it has not been set.
At C:\Test\strict.ps1:1 char:1
+ $peace
+ ~~~~~~
    + CategoryInfo          : InvalidOperation: (peace:String) [],
                              RuntimeException
    + FullyQualifiedErrorId : VariableIsUndefined
```

As you can see, with strict off, the $peace variable has a default value of $null. With any of the strict modes engaged, trying to use an undefined variable—undefined both in the local scope and in any parent scope—is an illegal operation, resulting in an error.

Some subtle differences exist between version 1 and 2 (and 3) strict mode. There doesn't appear to be any difference between using version 2, version 3, or version 4 with Set-StrictMode. Table 22.1 sums up the major differences.

Table 22.1 Differences between Set-StrictMode versions

	Strict off	Strict v1	Strict v2, v3, and v4
Uninitialized variable	Variable presumed to be empty	Illegal	Illegal
Uninitialized variable referenced from within a double-quoted string	Variable presumed to be empty	Variable presumed to be empty	Illegal
References to nonexistent properties of an object	Property value presumed to be empty	Property value presumed to be empty	Illegal
Calls to functions that enclose parameters in parentheses, as a method would	Allowed	Allowed	Illegal

Table 22.1 Differences between `Set-StrictMode` versions *(continued)*

	Strict off	Strict v1	Strict v2, v3, and v4
Variables with no name, such as ${}	Allowed	Allowed	Illegal

As you can see, the higher strict versions (you can always select the most recent by running `Set-StrictMode -Version latest`) offers the best protection against common mistakes that can often lead to extensive, difficult debugging sessions.

If you try to set strict mode to a version that doesn't exist, an error will be generated:

```
PS C:\> Set-StrictMode -Version 5
Set-StrictMode : Cannot validate argument on parameter 'Version'. The "5.0"
    argument does not contain a valid Windows PowerShell version. Supply a
    valid version number and then try the command again.
At line:1 char:25
+ Set-StrictMode -Version 5
+                         ~
    + CategoryInfo          : InvalidData: (:) [Set-StrictMode],
                              ParameterBindingValidationException
    + FullyQualifiedErrorId : ParameterArgumentValidationError,Microsoft
                              .PowerShell.Commands.SetStrictModeCommand
```

Although the default strict mode is `Off`, we recommend setting it to `Latest` whenever you're beginning work on a new script or function.

22.7 Summary

As we mentioned at the outset of this chapter, scope can be a complex topic. Our usual recommendation is to avoid dealing with it as much as possible: Don't use variables and other scoped elements until you've given them an explicit value within the current scope. Don't mess with out-of-scope elements. That's the easiest way to keep out of trouble.

PowerShell workflows

Workflows are an important new feature that was introduced in PowerShell v3. They're an incredibly rich, complex technology that we can't possibly cover comprehensively in this chapter—they deserve their own book. But they *are* a type of tool you can create and make great use of, which is why we want to include this chapter as an introduction to them.

We view workflows as a hardcore programming topic, and that's another reason we won't try to give them full coverage in this chapter. Instead, we're going to skim them lightly, showing you enough to create a basic workflow on your own, and we'll continue to assume that you're an administrator and not a professional developer. You have plenty of time to explore on your own, using this chapter as your starting point.

23.1 *Workflow overview*

Workflows are a type of PowerShell command, just as cmdlets and functions are types of commands. In fact, one of the easiest ways to understand workflows is to contrast them with their closest cousin: functions.

Functions are declared with the `function` keyword, as you've seen several times in earlier chapters; workflows are declared with the `workflow` keyword. Functions are executed by PowerShell itself; workflows are translated to the .NET Framework's Windows Workflow Foundation (WWF) and executed by WWF external to Power-Shell. Both functions and workflows execute a given set of commands in a specific sequence, but workflows—thanks to WWF—include detailed logging and tracking of each and include the ability to retry steps that fail because of an intermittent network hiccup, for example, or some other transitory issue. Functions do one thing at a time; workflows can do one thing at multiple times—they can do parallel multitasking. Functions start, run, and finish; a workflow can pause, stop, and restart. If you turn off your computer in the middle of a function, the function is lost; if you do so as a workflow is running, the workflow can potentially be recovered and resumed automatically.

> **NOTE** Probably the most important take away from this chapter is that although workflows are written using a PowerShell-like syntax, they aren't PowerShell. As we said earlier, workflows translate to the WWF engine and execute externally to PowerShell.

Table 23.1 illustrates some of the differences between a function and a workflow.

Table 23.1 Function or workflow

Function	Workflow
Executed by PowerShell	Executed by workflow engine
Logging and retry attempts through complicated coding	Logging and retry attempts part of the workflow engine
Single action processing	Supports parallelism
Run to completion	Can run, pause, and restart
Data loss possible during network problems	Data can persist during network problems
Full language set and syntax	Limited language set and syntax
Run cmdlets	Run activities

Workflow is incorporated into the shell by PSWorkflow; that module extends Power-Shell to understand workflows and to execute them properly. The module is auto-loaded when you define a workflow in either the console or the PowerShell ISE.

TIP We don't recommend executing PowerShell workflows from the ISE. You'd experience problems, especially when a remote machine is rebooting and you're expecting the workflow to wait on the reboot.

Workflows are exposed as commands, meaning you execute them just like any other PowerShell commands. For example, if you created a workflow named Do-Something, you'd just run Do-Something to execute it or Do-Something -AsJob to run it in Power-Shell's background job system. Executing a workflow as a job is cool, because you can then use the standard Job cmdlets (like Get-Job and Receive-Job) to manage them. There are also Suspend-Job and Resume-Job commands to pause and resume a workflow job—these cmdlets only work with workflow-related jobs. They won't work on standard background jobs or WMI jobs, for instance.

NOTE Most of the workflow samples in this chapter are designed to illustrate concepts and not intended as practical, production-worthy workflows. Also, when it comes to naming your workflows you should keep to the standard verb-noun naming convention, even though we didn't always do so in this chapter. Take this chapter as an example of "Do as I say, not as I do."

23.2   *Workflow basics*

A workflow is a set of commands, technically known as *activities*, which you want to execute to fulfill a larger IT task. For example, you might have a checklist of tasks when building a new server:

1   Create a standard folder hierarchy.
2   Add standard Windows roles and features.
3   Configure event log settings.
4   Configure key services.
5   Configure the page file.
6   Reboot.
7   Create a baseline XML configuration report.

You can construct a workflow of PowerShell expressions to complete these tasks and execute it against any number of remote computers. Workflows are intended for a chain of long-running, unattended tasks that's robust enough to survive network interruptions and persistent enough to survive reboots—something they accomplish by saving their status to disk in a process called *checkpointing*. Workflows are designed for performance and scalability through connection pooling, parallel command execution, and connection throttling. Workflows can even be suspended and restarted. If you think of PowerShell as a management engine for servers in a cloud, this workflow concept begins to make a lot of sense.

Workflows have been around for quite a while as part of the .NET Framework and received a major overhaul in version 4.0. In the past, you needed to use Visual Studio to build and deploy a workflow in a complex XAML file format, which limited who had access to this technology. But with PowerShell v3 and later, any IT pro can create a workflow using PowerShell commands. You don't have to be a developer and you don't need Visual Studio.

> **NOTE** The whole point of PowerShell workflow is to give an IT pro the tools to build workflows without developing something in Visual Studio. You should approach PowerShell workflows as "wrappers" for the underlying workflow engine. These wrappers attempt to simplify much of the underlying complexity. If you're a .NET developer, you'll most likely continue creating workflows as you have in the past. This chapter is targeted at the IT pro looking to get started with workflows and leverage their PowerShell skills.

A workflow looks a lot like a PowerShell function:

```
Workflow DeployServer {
    #my workflow commands
}
```

But don't think you can simply take a function and change it to a workflow. Not only are there a substantial number of significant technical differences, there's a paradigm shift you need to adopt.

In the past, you'd run scripts or functions interactively to manage servers and desktops in your environment. Long-running tasks could be thrown into a background task. Or you might've leveraged PowerShell Remoting to distribute the workload. But typically everything came back to the machine that launched the command. With workflow, the idea is to provide a command framework to one or more remote computers and then *let it go*. Although you can run workflows locally, the intent is that you'll be managing remote computers, providing a set of instructions that they can execute on their own.

23.2.1 Common parameters for workflows

Just by using the workflow keyword, you give your workflow command a large set of built-in common parameters. We're not going to provide an extensive list, but here are some of the more interesting ones (and you can consult PowerShell's about_WorkflowCommonParameters documentation for the complete list):

- -PSComputerName—A list of computers to execute the workflow on
- -PSParameterCollection—A list of hash tables that specify different parameter values for each target computer, enabling the workflow to have variable behavior on a per-machine basis
- -PSCredential—The credential to be used to execute the workflow
- -PSPersist—Forces the workflow to save ("checkpoint") the workflow data and state after executing each step (we'll show you how you can also do this manually)

In addition, there are a variety of parameters that let you specify remote connectivity options, such as -PSPort, -PSUseSSL, -PSSessionOption, and so on; these correspond to the similarly named parameters of remoting commands like Invoke-Command and New-PSSession.

The values passed to these parameters are accessible as values within the workflow. For example, a workflow can access `$PSComputerName` to get the name of the computer that particular instance of the workflow is executing against right then.

23.2.2 *Activities and stateless execution*

Workflow is built around the concept of *activities*. Each PowerShell command that you run within a workflow is a single, stand-alone activity. It may look like a cmdlet and have the same name and (mainly) the same set of parameters (see about_Activity-CommonParameters), but when you create a workflow you're dealing with a workflow activity, not a PowerShell cmdlet. This is the source of a lot of the confusion around workflows that we mentioned earlier.

So the big thing to get used to in a workflow is that each command, or activity, executes entirely on its own. Because a workflow can be interrupted and later resumed, each command has to assume that it's running in a completely fresh, brand-new environment. That means variables created by one command can't be used by the next command—which can get a bit difficult to keep track of, especially if you're accustomed to traditional PowerShell functions, which don't work that way at all. Workflow does support an `InlineScript` block, which will execute all commands inside the block within a single PowerShell session. Everything within the block is, essentially, a stand-alone mini-script.

Now, this isn't to say that variables don't work at all—that'd be pretty pointless. For example, consider the script in the following listing.

Listing 23.1 Example workflow with variables

```
workflow Test-Workflow {
    $a = 1
    $a
    $a++
    $a
    $b = $a + 2
    $b
}
Test-Workflow
```

Run the code in listing 23.1, and you should see the output 1, 2, and 4, with each number on its own line. That's the expected output, and seeing that will help you verify that the workflow is operating on your system. Now try the example in the next listing.

Listing 23.2 Example workflow that won't work properly

```
workflow Test-Workflow {
    $obj = New-Object -TypeName PSObject
    $obj | Add-Member -MemberType NoteProperty `
                      -Name ExampleProperty `
                      -Value 'Hello!'
    $obj | Get-Member
}
Test-Workflow
```

The script in listing 23.2 doesn't produce the intended results, in that the object in `$obj` won't have an `ExampleProperty` property containing "Hello!" That's because `Add-Member` runs in its own space, and its modification to `$obj` doesn't persist to the third command in the workflow. To make this work, you could wrap the entire set of commands as an `InlineScript`, forcing them to all execute at the same time, within a single PowerShell instance. Our next listing shows this example.

Listing 23.3 Example workflow using `InlineScript`

```
workflow Test-Workflow {
    InlineScript {
        $obj = New-Object -TypeName PSObject
        $obj | Add-Member -MemberType NoteProperty `
                          -Name ExampleProperty `
                          -Value 'Hello!'
        $obj | Get-Member
    }
}
Test-Workflow
```

Try each of these three examples and compare their results. Workflows do take a bit of getting used to, and these simple examples will help you to grasp the main differences in workflows.

23.2.3 Persisting state

The state of a workflow consists of its current output, the task that it's currently executing, and other information. It's important that you help a workflow maintain this state, especially when kicking off a long-running command that might be executed. To do so, run the `Checkpoint-Workflow` command (or the `Persist` workflow activity). You can force this to happen after every single command is executed by running the workflow with the `-PSPersist` switch. State information is saved to disk by WWF so that the workflow can be resumed after a power failure or other problem or if you intentionally need to pause the workflow.

23.2.4 Suspending and resuming workflows

A workflow can suspend itself by running `Suspend-Workflow` within the workflow. You might do this, for example, if you're about to run some high-workload command that can only be run during a maintenance window. Before running the command, you check the time, and if you're not in the window, you suspend the workflow. Someone would need to manually resume the workflow (or schedule the resumption in Task Scheduler) by running `Resume-Job` and providing the necessary job ID.

23.2.5 Workflow limitations

Workflows are intended, by design, to run without any user interaction, usually via a workflow Remoting session. As a result, they're configured to allow only a subset of the full PowerShell language. Technically, you're executing a series of workflow *actions* that happen to look like cmdlets, which leads to some limitations and "gotchas" that you must be aware of when creating a workflow.

> **NOTE** When you write a workflow, you use PowerShell commands and scripts that look familiar. But when the workflow is executed, PowerShell must translate all of them to a language understood by WWF, which runs the workflow. So only those things that can be translated to WWF can be used within a workflow.

First and foremost, all objects and data must be *serializable* or your workflow will fail. In other words, if a command can't return the data as serialized XML, it can't be used in a workflow. One good test to see if a command's output is serializable is to see if the command fails when run through Invoke-Command. If it does, it'll most likely also fail when used within a workflow.

Workflows can be designed to use cmdlet binding and parameters, but within the workflow you must use full command and parameter names. Positional parameters aren't allowed in PowerShell v3, for example:

```
PS C:\> Workflow Test { Param([string]$path) dir $path }
At line:1 char:42
+ Workflow Test { Param([string]$path) dir $path }
+                                          ~~~~~
Positional parameters are not supported in a Windows PowerShell Workflow.
To invoke this command, use explicit
parameter names with all values. For example: "Command -Parameter
 <value>".
    + CategoryInfo          : ParserError: (:) [], ParseException
    + FullyQualifiedErrorId : PositionalParametersNotSupported
```

This code failed because it tried to use a positional parameter. Here's the correct syntax:

```
PS C:\> Workflow Test { Param([string]$path) dir -Path $path }
```

> **NOTE** The code will work as written in PowerShell v4.

As you can see, aliases are allowed, but we still recommend adhering to the best practice of using full command names. Here's a more complete, albeit simple, example:

```
Workflow Test {
Param([string]$path)
  Get-Childitem -Path path -Recurse -File |
  Measure-Object -Property length -sum -Average |
  Add-Member -MemberType NoteProperty -Name Path -Value Path -PassThru
}
```

Other limitations you might face include the following:

- Workflows don't use Begin, Process, and End script blocks. One implication of this is that you can't pipe anything into a workflow. Parameter attributes like ValueFromPipeline aren't allowed.
- Workflows don't use traps for error handling but rather use Try/Catch.

- There's no built-in event handling with a workflow. Though it's possible to build your own eventing, doing so will be a complicated task. We don't think eventing is appropriate for a workflow anyway. If you think of a workflow as a chain of activities, eventing doesn't play a role.

- PowerShell workflows aren't designed to be interactive. As such, you can't use `Write-Host` commands. You won't get an error until you try to run a workflow that uses it, although you can use `Write-Verbose` and `Write-Progress`. This also means you generally can't use `Read-Host` either. Think of workflows as system-run and isolated scripts.

- Workflows can't use comment-based help like advanced functions. You can include as much internal documentation as you like with comment blocks, but you can't do formal help like you would with advanced functions. If you need to include help, you'll need to create an external help file using the Microsoft Assistance Markup Language (MAML) format.

You'll also need to be careful about what you use for variable names because there are more restrictions. As a rule of thumb, any keyword in VB.NET isn't allowed as a variable name. But hopefully you won't have to worry too much about this. If you use a "bad" variable name, the workflow will fail with an error like this:

```
The workflow 'ParamDemo' could not be started: The following errors were
encountered while processing the workflow tree:
'DynamicActivity': The private implementation of activity '1:
DynamicActivity'
has the following validation error:   Compiler error(s) encountered
processing
expression "end".
Expression expected.
At line:327 char:21
+                     throw (New-Object
System.Management.Automation.ErrorRecord $ ...
+ ~~~~~~~~~~~~~~~~~~~~~~~~~~~~~~~~~~~~~~~~~~~~~~~~~~~~~~~~~~~~~~~~~~~~~~~~~
    + CategoryInfo          : InvalidArgument: (System.Manageme...etersDic
                              tionary:PSBoundParametersDictionary) [],
                              RuntimeException
    + FullyQualifiedErrorId : StartWorkflow.InvalidArgument
```

The error message, which we've boldfaced, states where the error occurred. This says you can't use $end as a variable name. A simple rename and perhaps a find and replace are all that's required.

A number of cmdlets aren't appropriate or even legal when used in a workflow. The most likely commands to avoid, or those that will throw an exception when you try to invoke the workflow, are as follows:

Add-History	Add-PSSnapin	Clear-History	Clear-Variable
Complete-Transaction	Connect-PSSession	Debug-Process	Disable-PSBreakpoint
Disconnect-PSSession	Enable-PSBreakpoint	Enter-PSSession	Exit-PSSession

Export-Alias	Export-Console	Export-ModuleMember	Export-PSSession
Format-Custom	Format-List	Format-Table	Format-Wide
Get-Alias	Get-CimSession	Get-ControlPanelItem	Get-Credential
Get-FormatData	Get-History	Get-PSBreakpoint	Get-PSCallStack
Get-PSSnapin	Get-Transaction	Get-Variable	Import-Alias
Import-PSSession	Invoke-Command	Invoke-History	New-Alias
New-Module	New-Object	New-PSDrive	New-PSSession
New-PSSession-ConfigurationFile	New-PSSessionOption	New-Variable	Out-Default
Out-GridView	Out-Host	Out-Null	Pop-Location
Push-Location	Read-Host	Receive-PSSession	Register-CimIndicationEvent
Remove-CimSession	Remove-PSBreakpoint	Remove-PSDrive	Remove-PSSnapin
Remove-TypeData	Remove-Variable	Set-Alias	Set-Location
Set-PSBreakpoint	Set-PSDebug	Set-StrictMode	Set-Variable
Show-Command	Show-ControlPanelItem	Show-EventLog	Start-Transaction
Trace-Command	Undo-Transaction	Update-FormatData	Update-TypeData
Use-Transaction	Write-Host		

> **NOTE** Even though the commands in this list should be avoided, it may be possible to use some of them within an InlineScript block.

In addition, for performance purposes, some cmdlets execute only locally in a workflow. That said, you might be able to execute them remotely using an InlineScript activity, which we'll cover later in the chapter. The following commands are always executed locally:

Add-Member	Compare-Object	ConvertFrom-CSV
ConvertFrom-Json	ConvertFrom-StringData	Convert-Path
ConvertTo-CSV	ConvertTo-HTML	ConvertTo-Json
ConvertTo-XML	Foreach-Object	Get-Host
Get-Member	Get-Random	Get-Unique
Group-Object	Measure-Command	Measure-Object
New-PSSessionOption	New-PSTransportOption	New-TimeSpan
Out-Default	Out-Host	Out-Null
Out-String	Select-Object	Sort-Object
Update-List	Where-Object	Write-Debug
Write-Error	Write-Host	Write-Output
Write-Progress	Write-Verbose	Write-Warning

Finally, workflow activities typically run isolated. You should minimize sharing variables across activities. This also means you have to pay close attention to scope. Don't assume PowerShell will "find" a variable as it does in a normal script or function. There are some specific rules regarding scope that we'll cover later in the chapter.

Workflows will take a bit more planning than a normal PowerShell script or function. We mentioned it earlier, but don't try to take an existing function and slap on the Workflow keyword. Even if it runs without error, you most likely aren't taking advantage of some cool features.

23.2.6 *Parallelism*

WWF is designed to execute tasks in parallel, and PowerShell exposes that capability through a modified ForEach scripting construct and a new Parallel construct. They work a bit differently.

With Parallel, the commands inside the construct can run in any order. Within the Parallel block, you can use the Sequence keyword to surround a set of commands that must be executed in order. That batch of commands may begin executing at any point, for example:

```
Workflow Test-Workflow {
    "This will run first"
    parallel {
        "Command 1"
        "Command 2"
        sequence {
            "Command A"
            "Command B"
        }
    }
}
```

The output here might be

```
"This will run first"
Command 1
Command A
Command B
Command 2
```

"Command B" will always come after "Command A," but "Command A" might come first, second, or third—there's no guarantee. The commands actually execute at the same time, meaning "Command 1," "Command 2," and the sequence may all kick off at once, which is what makes the output somewhat nondeterministic. This technique is useful for when you have several tasks to complete, don't care about the order in which they run, and want them to finish as quickly as possible.

The parallelized ForEach is somewhat different. In this situation you can execute a set of activities in parallel for every object in a collection of objects. Here's what it looks like:

```
Workflow Test-Workflow {
  Param ([string[]]$computername)
    Foreach -parallel ($computer in $computerName) {
```

```
        Do-Something -PScomputerName $computer
    }
}
```

Here, WWF may launch multiple simultaneous Do-Something commands, each targeting a different computer. Execution should be roughly in whatever order the computers are stored in $ComputerName, although because of varying execution times the order of the results is nondeterministic.

NOTE   The -Parallel parameter for ForEach is valid only in a workflow.

Here's an example that might make this concept easier to visualize. We have a simple workflow that writes a number multiplied by 2:

```
Workflow Demo-ForEachParallel {

foreach -parallel ($i in (1..20)) {

 Write-Verbose -message "$((Get-Date).TimeOfDay) $i * 2 = $($i*2)"
 Start-Sleep -seconds (Get-Random -Minimum 1 -Maximum 5)
}

}
```

We inserted a random sleep command to simulate the workflow actually doing something. This is what you can expect when you run it:

```
PS C:\> Demo-ForEachParallel -Verbose
VERBOSE: [localhost]:14:17:32.2171668 20 * 2 = 40
VERBOSE: [localhost]:14:17:32.2251678 19 * 2 = 38
VERBOSE: [localhost]:14:17:32.2301687 18 * 2 = 36
VERBOSE: [localhost]:14:17:32.2351650 17 * 2 = 34
VERBOSE: [localhost]:14:17:32.2401696 16 * 2 = 32
VERBOSE: [localhost]:14:17:32.2451692 15 * 2 = 30
VERBOSE: [localhost]:14:17:32.2512203 14 * 2 = 28
VERBOSE: [localhost]:14:17:32.2651769 13 * 2 = 26
VERBOSE: [localhost]:14:17:32.2711768 12 * 2 = 24
VERBOSE: [localhost]:14:17:32.2761756 11 * 2 = 22
VERBOSE: [localhost]:14:17:32.2811816 10 * 2 = 20
VERBOSE: [localhost]:14:17:32.2861792 9 * 2 = 18
VERBOSE: [localhost]:14:17:32.3001807 8 * 2 = 16
VERBOSE: [localhost]:14:17:32.3061793 7 * 2 = 14
VERBOSE: [localhost]:14:17:32.3101798 6 * 2 = 12
VERBOSE: [localhost]:14:17:32.3151774 5 * 2 = 10
VERBOSE: [localhost]:14:17:32.3201788 4 * 2 = 8
VERBOSE: [localhost]:14:17:32.3441826 2 * 2 = 4
VERBOSE: [localhost]:14:17:32.3401815 3 * 2 = 6
VERBOSE: [localhost]:14:17:32.3491854 1 * 2 = 2
```

From the timestamp you can see that all 20 numbers were processed essentially at the same time. But there may be situations where you want to process in parallel but in a more controlled manner. Starting with PowerShell v4, you can throttle this activity. Here's a revised version of the demo workflow.

```
Workflow Demo-ForEachThrottle {

foreach -parallel -throttlelimit 4 ($i in (1..20)) {

 write-verbose -message "$((Get-Date).TimeOfDay) $i * 2 = $($i*2)"
 Start-Sleep -seconds (Get-Random -Minimum 1 -Maximum 5)
}

}
```

We boldfaced the one change. Now, PowerShell will process the collection of numbers in batches of 4.

```
PS C:\> Demo-ForeachThrottle -Verbose
VERBOSE: [localhost]:14:21:42.3276999 4 * 2 = 8
VERBOSE: [localhost]:14:21:42.4256579 3 * 2 = 6
VERBOSE: [localhost]:14:21:42.4407110 2 * 2 = 4
VERBOSE: [localhost]:14:21:42.4506479 1 * 2 = 2
VERBOSE: [localhost]:14:21:44.4668354 5 * 2 = 10
VERBOSE: [localhost]:14:21:46.4700108 6 * 2 = 12
VERBOSE: [localhost]:14:21:46.4800734 7 * 2 = 14
VERBOSE: [localhost]:14:21:46.5170116 8 * 2 = 16
VERBOSE: [localhost]:14:21:47.5061695 9 * 2 = 18
VERBOSE: [localhost]:14:21:47.5471064 10 * 2 = 20
VERBOSE: [localhost]:14:21:50.5174319 11 * 2 = 22
VERBOSE: [localhost]:14:21:50.5723722 12 * 2 = 24
VERBOSE: [localhost]:14:21:50.5823687 13 * 2 = 26
VERBOSE: [localhost]:14:21:51.5665379 14 * 2 = 28
VERBOSE: [localhost]:14:21:52.5856140 15 * 2 = 30
VERBOSE: [localhost]:14:21:53.5356970 16 * 2 = 32
VERBOSE: [localhost]:14:21:54.6407847 17 * 2 = 34
VERBOSE: [localhost]:14:21:54.6517802 18 * 2 = 36
VERBOSE: [localhost]:14:21:54.6608001 19 * 2 = 38
VERBOSE: [localhost]:14:21:55.6838838 20 * 2 = 40
```

Again, the timestamps should make it clear four numbers were processed at any one time.

23.3   *General workflow design strategy*

It's important to understand that the entire contents of the workflow get translated into WWF's own language, which only understands "activities." With the exception of a few commands listed in section 23.2.5, Microsoft has provided WWF activities that correspond to most of the core PowerShell cmdlets. That means most of PowerShell's built-in commands—the ones available before any modules have been imported—work fine.

That isn't the case with add-in modules, though. Further, because each workflow activity executes in a self-contained space, you can't even use Import-Module by itself in a workflow. You'd basically import a module, but it'd go away by the time you tried to run any of the module's commands.

The solution is to think of a workflow as a high-level task coordination mechanism. You're likely to have a number of InlineScript blocks within a workflow, because the contents of those blocks execute as a single unit, in a single PowerShell session. Within an `InlineScript`, you can import a module and then run its commands. Each `Inline-Script` block that you include runs independently, so think of each one as a stand-alone script file of sorts: Each should perform whatever setup tasks are necessary for it to run successfully. You'll see an example of this approach later in this chapter.

23.4   *Example workflow scenario*

For an example scenario, let's pretend you have a new in-house corporate application update that needs to be deployed. You've already taken care of getting the necessary executables deployed to your client computers, but the developers neglected to make a few critical configuration changes as part of the installer. It's up to you to make those changes. You need to do the following:

- Add an HKEY_LOCAL_MACHINE\SOFTWARE\Company\LOBApp\Settings Registry key, adding the setting `Rebuild` with a value of 0 (zero).
- Register a new PowerShell Remoting endpoint (or "session configuration") named LOBApp. There's already a local session configuration file stored on each computer that defines this endpoint's capabilities; the file should be in C:\C-orpApps\LOBApp\LOBApp.pssc.
- Set the service named LOBApp to start automatically, and ensure that the service is started.
- Run `Set-LOBRebuildMode –Mode 1`. That command is located in a module named LOBAppTools, which is already deployed to the client computers.

None of these steps need to be done in any particular order. Keep in mind that the contents of your workflow are intended to be remoted, so you can assume that everything you're doing is running "locally," and they'll be deployed to the remote computers and executed there.

> **WARNING** Don't try the following workflow now because we're using made-up stuff in the example, and you won't be able to follow along.

23.5   *Writing the workflow*

The following listing shows the workflow to accomplish this example scenario.

Listing 23.4   A sample workflow

```
workflow Set-LOBAppConfiguration {
    parallel {
        InlineScript {
          New-Item -Path HKLM:\SOFTWARE\Company\LOBApp\Settings
          New-ItemProperty -Path HKLM:\SOFTWARE\Company\LOBApp\Settings `
                      -Name Rebuild `
                      -Value 0
        }
        InlineScript {
          Set-Service -Name LOBApp -StartupType Automatic
          Start-Service -Name LOBApp
        }
```

```
                InlineScript {
                  Register-PSSessionConfiguration `
                     -Path C:\CorpApps\LOBApp\LOBApp.pscc `
                     -Name LOBApp
                }
                InlineScript {
                  Import-Module LOBAppTools
                  Set-LOBRebuildMode -Mode 1
                }
          }
    }
```

You can see that listing 23.4 follows the general strategy of breaking each distinct task into its own `InlineScript` block, allowing each block to execute independently and in this workflow simultaneously in parallel. Each script block can assume it's accessing local resources, because the contents of the workflow will be remoted out to whatever machines you target. Run it like so:

```
PS C:\> Set-LOBAppConfiguration –PSComputerName one,two,three
```

This code runs the workflow on computers named "ONE," "TWO," and "THREE." `InlineScript` is probably one of the techniques you'll use most in workflows, and we're going to give it more coverage later in this chapter.

23.6 *Workflows vs. functions*

We pointed this out earlier in the chapter, but it bears repeating: Workflows seem so similar to functions that it can be tempting to assume they're just a fancy kind of function. In many respects, it's safe to think of them that way, which is one of their most appealing aspects! After all, if you already know a lot about functions, you can move that knowledge right into workflows with little additional learning. That said, a few major differences exist. Specifically, workflows don't permit any of the following things that are legal in functions:

> **NOTE** We know we've listed some of these restrictions earlier, but we want to outline them again because we've found that they cause confusion in workflows. This is also a good place for us to consolidate the various differences into a comprehensive list.

- You can't use the `BEGIN`, `PROCESS`, and `END` script blocks that we've been using in our advanced functions.
- You can't use subexpressions, like `$myvar = "$($service.name)"`, although you can use them in a cmdlet or pipelined expression as we did earlier. This restriction is lifted in PowerShell v4.
- You can't access drive-qualified variables like `$env:computername`; use `Get-Content ENV:ComputerName` instead. This restriction is lifted in PowerShell v4.
- Variable names may only contain letters, digits, -, and _.
- You can't execute methods of objects. This is tricky, but there's a good reason: To execute a method, you need a live object. If the workflow resumes from

interruption, all you'll have is a persisted, deserialized object, which has no methods. If you create an object within an `InlineScript` block, you can execute its methods within that block, because the block ensures that the commands all execute together.

- You can't assign values to object properties—again, doing so assumes a live object, which you won't necessarily have.
- You can't dot-source scripts or use the invocation (`&`) operator.
- Advanced function parameter validation (like `Mandatory` and other attributes we've used) aren't supported on workflows that are contained within other workflows. Technically, they're not allowed at all, but PowerShell "fakes it" for the outermost workflow. Our recommendation is to not try to use them.
- Positional parameters aren't permitted on commands within a PowerShell v3 workflow (the restriction is lifted in PowerShell v4). This forces you to follow what you should be doing anyway and list the parameter name for every parameter you use. This means `Dir C:\` won't work, but `Dir -Path C:\` will.
- The old trap error-handling statement isn't supported. Use `Try...Catch...Finally` instead.
- The `Switch` statement doesn't work the same within a workflow; we recommend not using it at all in a workflow.
- Workflows can't use comment-based help. If you want to include help for a workflow command, you must create an external XML file in the appropriate MAML format; we won't be covering that topic in this book.
- Within a workflow, you can't change the value of a variable that has already been defined in a parent scope. In a normal PowerShell function, doing so creates a new local-scope variable of the same name; in a workflow, you get an error. PowerShell adds a new `$workflow` scope identifier to provide access to a workflow's scope from any child scope. For example, `$workflow:myvar` will provide access to the `$myvar` variable defined in the workflow scope. This syntax is mandatory for any child scope; were one of them to try to modify `$myvar` without specifying `$workflow:myvar`, it would get an error.

NOTE   This isn't a comprehensive list of things that are legal in a function but not in a workflow, but the list does cover every function-related thing we've shown you in this book (including stuff in upcoming chapters).

Again, most of these restrictions come from the fact that a workflow is eventually translated into an external language usable by WWF, meaning a workflow can't contain anything for which there's no WWF equivalent.

23.7 *Specific workflow techniques*

Although we've touched on a couple of these already, we want to cover these techniques in more depth because we think you're going to be using them a lot.

23.7.1 Sequences

A workflow is intended for a series of potentially long-running tasks. You may need to do step A, then B, then C and in that order. One way to guarantee that order is to use a sequence in your workflow. A sequence is a self-contained script block. The script block must finish before any other sequences are executed. The next listing is a sample workflow that illustrates this concept.

Listing 23.5   Workflow sequences

```
Workflow DemoSequence {
write-verbose -message ("{0} starting" -f (Get-Date).TimeofDay)
$a=10
$b=1
"Variables Pre-Sequence"
"`$a = $a"
"`$b = $b"
"`$c = $c"
    Sequence {
        "{0} sequence 1" -f (Get-Date).TimeOfDay
        $workflow:a++
        $c=1
        start-sleep -seconds 1
    }
    Sequence {
        "{0} sequence 2" -f (Get-Date).TimeofDay
        $workflow:a++
        $workflow:b=100
        $c++
        start-sleep -seconds 1
    }
    Sequence {
        "{0} sequence 3" -f (Get-Date).TimeofDay
        $workflow:a++
        $workflow:b*=2
        $c++
        start-sleep -seconds 1
    }
"Variables Post-Sequence"
 "`$a = $a"
 "`$b = $b"
 "`$c = $c"
write-verbose -Message ("{0} ending" -f (Get-Date).TimeOfDay)
}
```

Let's run listing 23.5 so you can see how it behaves:

```
PS C:\> demosequence -Verbose

VERBOSE: [localhost]:08:12:12.5756488 starting
Variables Pre-Sequence
$a = 10
$b = 1
$c =
08:12:12.8564498 sequence 1
```

```
08:12:14.1668659 sequence 2
08:12:15.2744786 sequence 3
Variables Post-Sequence
$a = 13
$b = 200
$c =
VERBOSE: [localhost]:08:12:16.5224938 ending
```

The workflow writes the starting values for variables a, b, and c. Each sequence modifies these variables in a different way. Sometimes a new value is assigned directly; other times a value is assigned the $workflow: prefix to illustrate the effect of scope in a workflow. We've also added a brief sleep statement so that you can see from the time stamp that the workflow runs in sequence.

Sequences should be self-contained. It's possible to reference variables outside the sequence scope, but you must include the $workflow: prefix. We've boldfaced those variables in the listing. The $workflow: prefix allows you to modify variables a and b in each sequence. We left variable c alone, and as you can see from the output, the workflow never picked up the value for $c from the last sequence. In other words, the variables set in sequences are scope-specific unless you use the $workflow: prefix, which acts in much the same way as $global: would in a regular script or function.

You can nest sequences within sequences as well as the other syntax elements we'll be covering in this chapter.

23.7.2   *InlineScript*

Another option you might want to use is InlineScript. This script block is essentially just an Invoke-Command sequence that runs out-of-process in relation to the rest of the workflow, but depending on how you need to use parameters and variables, you might find it helpful. Listing 23.6 shows a simple workflow using InlineScript. As we've stated before, this is a useful tool within workflows, because in most cases it lets you include any PowerShell commands—not just those that can be translated to WWF—inside a workflow. You'll also need to use InlineScript if you want to call external PowerShell scripts or use a .NET class or method. Each InlineScript is executed as a single unit: It's transmitted to the target computer and executed, and the results are sent via XML back to the initiating machine.

Listing 23.6   Demo of InlineScript

```
Workflow Get-ARPCache {
$data = InlineScript {
  $results = arp -a | where {$_ -match 'dynamic'}
  [regex]$rxip="(\d{1,3}\.){3}\d{1,3}"
  [regex]$rxmac="(\w{2}-){5}\w{2}"
  foreach ($line in $results) {
    [pscustomobject] [ordered]@{
    IP=$rxip.Match($line).Value
    MAC=$rxmac.Match($line).Value
    }
  } #foreach
```

```
} #inlinescript
$data | Sort-Object -Property IP
} #workflow
```

This workflow is designed to get the `ARPCache` and turn the results into custom objects. Because the workflow needs to use a .NET method like `Match`, these commands should be placed in an `InlineScript` block. This is a completely self-contained unit that writes results to the pipeline. The workflow saves this output to `$data`. Then at the end of the workflow, `$data` is sorted on the `IP` property.

This example doesn't try to access data outside of the script block via variables, but often you might need to do just that. As we've shown in a few examples earlier, you handle variable scope in `InlineScript` with `$using`. The next listing illustrates this concept.

Listing 23.7　`InlineScript` with `$using`

```
Workflow DemoNotUsing {
Param([string]$log="System",[int]$newest=10)
#creating a variable within the workflow
$source="Service Control Manager"
Write-verbose -message "Log parameter is $log"
Write-Verbose -message "Source is $source"
InlineScript {
    <#
    What happens when we try to access
    out of scope variables?
    #>
    "Getting newest {0} logs from {1} on {2}" -f $newest,$log,$pscomputername
    get-eventlog -LogName $log -Newest $newest -Source $source
 } #inlinescript
 Write-verbose -message "Ending workflow"
} #close workflow
```

In a traditional PowerShell function you might think this code would work with no problem. The workflow can access variables `$log` and `$source` at the beginning. But within `InlineScript` is a totally new scope, and PowerShell *doesn't* look outside the scope for the variables as you might expect, so this workflow will fail.

```
PS C:\> DemoNotUsing -log application –Verbose

VERBOSE: [localhost]:Log parameter is application
VERBOSE: [localhost]:Source is Service Control Manager
Getting newest  logs from  on localhost
Get-EventLog : Cannot bind argument to parameter 'LogName' because it is
null.
At DemoNotUsing:7 char:7
+
    + CategoryInfo          : InvalidData: (:) [Get-EventLog],
ParameterBindingValidationException
    + FullyQualifiedErrorId :
ParameterArgumentValidationErrorNullNotAllowed,Microsoft.P
   owerShell.Commands.GetEventLogCommand
    + PSComputerName        : [localhost]
VERBOSE: [localhost]:Ending workflow
```

The solution is to use the $using variable prefix introduced in PowerShell v3. This tells PowerShell to use the variable from the current scope—that is, the workflow. The following listing shows a revised version. We've boldfaced the changes.

Listing 23.8   Revised `InlineScript` with $using

```
Workflow DemoUsing {
Param([string]$log="System",[int]$newest=10)
#creating a variable within the workflow
$source="Service Control Manager"
Write-verbose -message "Log parameter is $log"
Write-Verbose -message "Source is $source"
InlineScript {
    <#
    this is the way to access out of scope variables.
    #>
    "Getting newest {0} logs from {1} on {2}" -f $using:newest,$using:log,
$pscomputername
    get-eventlog -LogName $using:log -Newest $using:newest `
-Source $using:source
 } #inlinescript
} #close workflow
```

Now watch what happens when you run the workflow in listing 23.8:

```
PS C:\> DemoUsing -log system -Verbose

VERBOSE: [localhost]:Log parameter is system
VERBOSE: [localhost]:Source is Service Control Manager
Getting newest 10 logs from system on localhost
   Index Time          EntryType   Source              InstanceID Message
   ----- ----          ---------   ------              ---------- -------
     948 Jun 10 15:54  Information Service Contro...    3221232498 The fol...
     911 Jun 10 07:22  Information Service Contro...    3221232498 The fol...
     852 Jun 07 13:44  Information Service Contro...    3221232498 The fol...
     820 Jun 07 13:35  Information Service Contro...    1073748869 A servi...
     806 Jun 07 09:28  Information Service Contro...    1073748864 The sta...
     803 Jun 07 08:25  Information Service Contro...    1073748864 The sta...
     791 Jun 06 13:04  Information Service Contro...    1073748864 The sta...
     787 Jun 06 11:58  Information Service Contro...    1073748864 The sta...
     760 Jun 04 12:55  Information Service Contro...    1073748864 The sta...
     752 Jun 04 10:52  Information Service Contro...    3221232498 The fol...
```

NOTE   For the sake of our demonstration, we hardcoded the variable $source, which will only work with the system event log.

When PowerShell encountered $using, it looked for a variable in the current scope, and thus everything worked as planned. You can't use the $workflow prefix in an `InlineScript` block. You must use $using.

You're able to use `InlineScript` to execute commands that won't run anywhere else in a workflow. But you should still use full command and parameter names as a best practice.

23.8 Running a workflow

Workflows are loaded into PowerShell the same as functions—that is, by dot-sourcing a script file. Starting with PowerShell v3, a workflow is a new command type, which means you can use `Get-Command` to list them:

```
Get-Command –commandtype workflow
```

You run a workflow like any other cmdlet or function. You've done that in some of the examples earlier. You can pass parameters and take advantage of tab completion for parameter names, even automatic parameters like `PSComputername`. One thing you aren't likely to do is save the results to a variable. Typically you'll be using workflows for unattended and configuration-related tasks where you aren't expecting any output. You might also want to set up a workflow as a scheduled job.

Because workflows are designed for robustness and to survive temporary interruptions like reboots or network glitches, running workflows offers a few intriguing options. Often, these features we're going to discuss work together.

23.8.1 Workflow jobs

Normally you can just run a workflow interactively and hope for the best. But you can also run a workflow as a background job, which offers a number of advantages such as suspending and restarting the job. You don't have to add any extra code to your workflow. In PowerShell v3 the job infrastructure was enhanced to work with the new job type. All you need to do is run your workflow with the `-AsJob` parameter:

```
PS C:\> MyWorkflow –pscomputername server01,server02 –AsJob
```

PowerShell will automatically import the `PSWorkflow` module, which adds the necessary type information to manage the job with the Job cmdlets.

23.8.2 Suspending and restarting a workflow

If you start your workflow as a job, you can suspend and resume it at any time. Here's a quick demonstration with an ad hoc workflow:

```
PS C:\> workflow Test-MyWorkflow {
>> get-service -name w*
>> start-sleep -seconds 20
>> get-process -name powershell*
>> }
>>
PS C:\> Test-MyWorkflow -asjob

Id  Name  PSJobTypeName   State     HasMoreData   Location   Command
--  ----  -------------   -----     -----------   --------   -------
2   Job2  PSWorkflowJob   Running   True          localhost  Test-MyWo...
```

If you're fast enough, you can suspend or pause this job with the `Suspend-Job` cmdlet introduced alongside workflows in PowerShell v3:

```
PS C:\> Suspend-Job 2

Id   Name   PSJobTypeName   State       HasMoreData   Location   Command
--   ----   -------------   -----       -----------   --------   -------
2    Job2   PSWorkflowJob   Suspending  True          localhost  Test-MyW...
```

Starting in PowerShell v4 you can also have your workflow automatically suspend on a terminating error. Here's a sample workflow to illustrate this concept:

```
Workflow Demo-Problem {

Param([string]$Path)

Write-Verbose -Message $((Get-Date).TimeOfDay) Starting $workflowcommandname"

Try {
$files = Get-ChildItem -Path $Path -File -ErrorAction Stop
}
Catch {
 #left blank
}

$files | Measure-Object -Property length -Sum
}
```

When you run the workflow, use the new Suspend value for the –ErrorAction parameter:

```
PS C:\> demo-problem c:\foo -ErrorAction Suspend
The running command stopped because the preference variable
"ErrorActionPreference" or common parameter is set to Stop: Cannot
find path 'C:\foo' because it does not exist.
    + CategoryInfo          : InvalidResult: (:) [],
ActionPreferenceStopException
    + FullyQualifiedErrorId : ActivityActionFailed
    + PSComputerName        : [localhost]

Id    Name    PSJobTypeName   State       HasMoreData   Location   Command
--    ----    -------------   -----       -----------   --------   -------
116   Job116  PSWorkflowJob   Suspended   True          localhost  demo-...
```

The assumption is that you can correct whatever caused the problem and interrupted the workflow.

No matter how your workflow is suspended, when you're ready to resume simply call the Resume-Job cmdlet:

```
PS C:\> Resume-Job 2
```

Receiving the results, assuming something was written to the pipeline, is no different than any other job:

```
PS C:\> Receive-Job 2
```

If you prefer to give your job a name, do so when you launch the workflow:

```
PS C:\> Test-MyWorkflow -asjob -JobName Demo
```

Everything else remains the same.

You can also suspend a workflow from within by using the `Suspend-Workflow` activity. When you invoke this activity, a job will automatically be created. You don't have to use –AsJob.

```
PS C:\> workflow Test-MyWorkflowSuspend {
>> $s=get-service -name w*
>> suspend-workflow
>> "resuming"
>> $p=get-process -name Powershell*
>> $s
>> $p
>> }
>>
PS C:\> Test-MyWorkflowSuspend

Id  Name   PSJobTypeName   State      HasMoreData   Location    Command
--  ----   -------------   -----      -----------   --------    -------
8   Job8   PSWorkflowJob   Suspended  True          localhost   Test-MyWor...
```

This job will remain even if you reboot the computer. You can get the same job in a new PowerShell session, provided you remember to reimport the PSWorkflow module in PowerShell v3 (PowerShell v4 will autoload the module) and are using the same credentials and elevation of privileges. If you don't, you can't "see" the job. Here's the session after you reboot the computer:

```
PS C:\> get-job Job8

Id  Name   PSJobTypeName   State      HasMoreData  Location  Command
--  ----   -------------   -----      -----------  --------  -------
6   Job8   PSWorkflowJob   Suspended  True         localhost Test-MyWorkfl...
```

Notice that you used the job name. In the new session, the job ID numbers can change. But this is in fact the job you suspended, so now you can resume it:

```
PS C:\> Resume-Job Job8
```

Once it's completed, you can receive the results like any other job.

23.8.3 *Workflow credentials*

When running workflows against remote computers, PowerShell will use your current credentials, which must have administrative rights on the remote computer. You can specify alternate credentials when invoking the workflow using the ubiquitous `PSCredential` parameter:

```
PS C:\> Configure-Desktop -pscomputername Desk1,Desk2,Desk3 -pscredential
➡   mydomain\administrator
```

You don't have to include any code to handle the parameter or its value. It just works. This means you should be able to use workflows even in a workgroup environment, assuming you have taken steps to configure PowerShell Remoting for a workgroup, such as updating the `TrustedHosts` value.

You can use a credential object created with `Get-Credential` as an alternative. If you just supply the username, you'll be prompted for the password.

23.9   *A practical example*

Many of the examples in this chapter have been simple and far from practical. Our goal is to illustrate some complex concepts with simple commands. The workflow in our next listing is one that you should be able to try on your own in a nonproduction environment.

Listing 23.9   A practical workflow

```
#requires -version 3.0
Workflow New-ServerConfiguration {
Param()
Write-Verbose -Message "Starting $($workflowcommandname)"
#services to be configured
$autoservices = @("wuauserv","spooler","w32Time","MpsSvc","RemoteRegistry")
$disabledServices = @("PeerDistSvc","browser","fax","efs")
#folders to be created
$folders="C:\Work","C:\Company\Logs","C:\Company\Reports","C:\Scripts"
Parallel {
#these commands can happen in parallel since there are no
#dependencies
    Sequence {
        #Create new folder structure
        Write-Verbose -message "Creating default folders"
        foreach ($folder in $Workflow:folders) {
          Write-verbose -Message "Testing $folder"
          if (-Not (Test-Path -Path $folder)) {
            Write-Verbose -Message "Creating $folder"
            New-Item -Path $folder -ItemType Directory
          }
          else {
            Write-Verbose -Message "$folder already exists"
          }
        } #foreach
    } #sequence
    #Configure auto start service settings
    foreach -parallel ($service in $workflow:autoservices) {
        Write-Verbose -Message "Configuring autostart on $service"
        Set-Service -Name $service -StartupType Automatic
    } #foreach
    #Configure disabled service settings
    foreach -parallel ($service in $workflow:disabledServices) {
        Write-Verbose -Message "Configuring Disable on $service"
        Set-Service -Name $service -StartupType Disabled
    } #foreach
} #parallel
#reboot and wait. This only works on remote computers
Write-Verbose -message "Rebooting $pscomputername"
Restart-Computer -Force -Wait
Write-Verbose -Message "Auditing service configuration"
InlineScript {
    <#
      get services that were configured and export current configuration
      to an xml file. Running this in an inline script to avoid remoting
```

❶ Create list of folders

❷ Set services to autostart

❸ Set services to be disabled

❹ Reboot computer

❺ Create XML report for services

```
      artifacts in the exported output.
    #>
    $using:autoservices+$using:disabledServices | ForEach-Object -process {
      Get-WmiObject -class win32_service -filter "name='$_'"
      } | Select-Object -Property Name,StartMode,State,StartName |
      Export-Clixml -Path C:\Company\Logs\ServiceAudit.xml
}
Write-Verbose -Message "Ending $($workflowcommandname)"
} #close Workflow
```

The workflow in listing 23.9 is designed to automate some tasks you might otherwise manually perform when configuring a new system. Here you want to create some default local folders and configure some services. The tasks ❶, ❷, and ❸ have no dependencies, which means they can take place in parallel. But notice that in ❷ and ❸ you're using another nested parallel structure with Foreach. Some services you're setting to autostart and some to be disabled, but you can set each group of services simultaneously! You're not using -parallel with Foreach in ❶ because you want to test and create each folder sequentially.

After all the parallel tasks are completed, the workflow reboots the computer ❹ and waits for it to come back on the network. This won't work if you run the workflow against the local host. You can only wait for reboots on remote computers. When a connection can be made again, the workflow ends by joining the array of service names together and creating an XML report ❺ using service information gathered from WMI.

You can run the workflow against a remote computer like this:

```
PS C:\> New-ServerConfiguration -verbose -PSComputerName novo8

VERBOSE: [novo8]:Starting New-ServerConfiguration
VERBOSE: [novo8]:Creating default folders
VERBOSE: [novo8]:Configuring autostart on RemoteRegistry
VERBOSE: [novo8]:Configuring autostart on MpsSvc
VERBOSE: [novo8]:Configuring autostart on w32Time
VERBOSE: [novo8]:Configuring autostart on spooler
...
```

Notice that there's no code within the workflow for handling Remoting or the remote computer name. Workflows implicitly use PowerShell Remoting. When you specify a computer name, a Remoting connection is made to the workflow endpoint and the workflow actions are executed.

Developing a workflow takes time, patience, and testing. Before you sit down to write one, ask yourself if it's the right solution to your problem. Even the workflow you just saw could've been written as a traditional script or function, as long as you didn't need the reboot.

When writing workflows, start simple and spend time learning how to use the various workflow elements like Parallel and InlineScript.

23.10 *Invoke-AsWorkflow*

Two workflow-related modules are available in PowerShell v3 and v4:

```
PS C:\> Get-Command *workflow* | format-table –AutoSize

CommandType Name                                ModuleName
----------- ----                                ----------
Function    New-PSWorkflowSession               PSWorkflow
Cmdlet      New-PSWorkflowExecutionOption       PSWorkflow
Workflow    Invoke-AsWorkflow                   PSWorkflowUtility
```

The PSWorkflowUtility module is interesting because it consists of a single workflow: `Invoke-AsWorkflow`. Let's examine the syntax of `Invoke-AsWorkflow`:

```
PS> Get-Command Invoke-AsWorkflow –Syntax

Invoke-AsWorkflow [-CommandName <string>] [-Parameter <hashtable>]
[<WorkflowCommonParameters>] [<CommonParameters>]
Invoke-AsWorkflow [-Expression <string>] [<WorkflowCommonParameters>]
    <CommonParameters>]
```

Supplying a command name, with or without parameters, causes the command to be run as an `InlineScript` within the workflow. If an expression is supplied, then `Invoke-Expression` is run.

What sort of commands can you pass to `Invoke-AsWorkflow`?

According to the help file, "The `Invoke-AsWorkflow` workflow runs any command or expression as a workflow. These workflows use the standard workflow semantics, have all workflow common parameters, and have all benefits of workflows, including the ability to stop, resume, and recover." This includes cmdlets, cmdlets with parameters, expressions, advanced functions (if you import them as a module), and even scripts.

Using a cmdlet is straightforward:

```
PS C:\> Invoke-AsWorkflow -CommandName Get-Process
```

If you need to pass parameters to the command, use a hash table of parameter names and values. Here are some examples:

```
PS C:\> Invoke-AsWorkflow -CommandName Get-Process -Parameter
➥ @{Name="PowerShell"}
PS C:\> Invoke-AsWorkflow -CommandName Get-Eventlog -Parameter
➥ @{Logname='System';Newest=10;EntryType='Error'}
```

The option to use an expression enables command-line tools to be run:

```
PS C:\> Invoke-AsWorkflow -Expression "ipconfig /all" -AsJob
```

Though the help file doesn't explicitly mention them, `Invoke-AsWorkflow` supports the workflow parameters, including `–AsJob`, that you've already seen.

If you create a simple advanced function like this:

```
function testfunction28 {
[CmdletBinding()]
param (
 [string]$name
)
Get-Process -Name $name
}
```

the function should be saved as a PSM1 file. In our example, we called the module Test and saved it in the usual module location. The module can be imported and run as follows:

```
Import-Module Test
Get-Command -Module test
Invoke-AsWorkflow -CommandName testfunction28 `
-Parameter @{Name="powershell"} –pscomputername $computers
```

The rules we discussed earlier regarding the use of and restrictions on the Inline-Script elements still apply. If you need to run a script, you must supply the full path to the script file even if it's in the current folder:

```
Invoke-AsWorkflow -CommandName C:\scripts\Miscellaneous\get-names.ps1
```

A command like this will fail:

```
Invoke-AsWorkflow -CommandName .\get-names.ps1
```

Using Invoke-AsWorkFlow is great for a "quick and dirty" workflow solution where you want to leverage an existing script or carefully constructed one-liner.

23.11 *PSWorkflowSession*

Moving on to the PSWorkflow module, we find two cmdlets:

- New-PSWorkflowSession
- New-PSWorkflowExecutionOption

These can be used together in a similar manner to the Remoting or CIM cmdlets used to configure sessions. The options are similar, but not necessarily identical, across all Remoting approaches. We suggest reviewing the help files for information on the options you can use.

Using workflow sessions is similar to Remoting sessions, but you must remember that the commands are running on the remote machine. That means that you have to import the module containing your workflow into your remote session. Here's an example of using a workflow session:

```
$w1 = New-PSWorkflowSession -ComputerName "dc02", "server02", "w12standard"
```

A `PSWorkflowSession` object is created that spans a number of computers. This session isn't much different than other Remoting sessions except that it's designed specifically to execute workflows. You can enter the session interactively, but most likely you'll use `Invoke-Command`.

First, you need a script block to run with your workflow:

```
$sb ={
workflow Get-OS {
 Get-WmiObject -Class Win32_OperatingSystem  |
 Select-Object -Property Caption
}
Get-OS
}
```

You'll most likely have modules with your workflows that need to be be imported into the session. All that remains is to invoke the script block in the workflow session:

```
Invoke-Command -Session $w1 -ScriptBlock $sb
```

TIP   Be sure you include the command to run the script block!

`Invoke-Command` is used to run the workflow script block against the computers defined in the session. When you execute the workflow, you can use any of the workflow parameters you need, such as `-AsJob`. Remember, though, that everything is running within the session. But you can disconnect and reconnect like any other PowerShell Remoting session.

An alternative is to create the endpoint locally:

```
$wf = New-PSWorkflowSession
```

Then continue as before, perhaps importing a module with your workflows:

```
Invoke-Command -Session $wf -ScriptBlock {Import-module MyWorkflows}
```

Finally, execute the workflow within the session connecting to remote systems as necessary:

```
Invoke-Command -Session $wf -ScriptBlock {Set-Config –pscomputername
  $using:servers –pscredential $using:cred }
```

This command assumes you've previously defined an array of computer names and a saved administrative credential. Whether you run the workflows via a local or remote endpoint might depend on what the workflow does, whether you're running as a job, how many machines you need to manage, and whether you might need to disconnect and reconnect, among other considerations.

We've said repeatedly that PowerShell workflow isn't simply another way to script. It requires a new paradigm for many IT pros. In many cases it may be easier to use the Remoting capabilities of the individual cmdlets rather than creating a workflow.

23.12 Troubleshooting a workflow

Because workflows tend to run unattended, troubleshooting or debugging can be problematic. Here's a short list of suggestions:

- We hope it goes without saying, but try to avoid problems in the first place by manually testing and verifying the individual steps in an interactive session.
- Test parts of your workflow using Invoke-AsWorkflow. Yes, the code will run in essentially an InlineScript block, but you can use all the other workflow parameters and it'll also verify that you can access the workflow endpoint on remote computers.
- Include Write-Verbose statements to indicate workflow progress and state.
- Verify that the remote computers are running PowerShell v3 or v4, with Test-WSMan.
- If using syntax elements like InlineScript or Sequence, make sure each script block can execute independently. Watch your scope!

As a last resort, you can turn to tracing in the PSDiagnostics module. When you run a workflow, because it uses WSMAN you can trace its calls. First, turn on tracing:

```
PS C:\> Enable-PSWSManCombinedTrace
```

Next, run your workflow to either completion or error:

```
PS C:\> get-data -pscomputername novo8
```

At this point disable tracing:

```
PS C:\> Disable-PSWSManCombinedTrace
```

All of the trace information is stored in a Windows event log file, pstrace.etl, which can be found under $pshome\Traces\. Use Get-WinEvent to retrieve the data:

```
PS C:\> Get-WinEvent -Path $pshome\traces\PSTrace.etl -oldest | format-
    table TimeCreated,LevelDisplayname,Message -wrap -auto | more
```

Because there will be a lot of data, you might prefer to direct results to Out-Gridview:

```
PS C:\> Get-WinEvent -Path $pshome\traces\PSTrace.etl -oldest | Select
    TimeCreated,LevelDisplayname,Message | out-gridview
```

You can see the result in figure 23.1.

We're not implying it'll be easy to figure out what the trace information is trying to tell you, but it's a start.

Support for debugging workflows using the standard debugging techniques explained in chapter 31 was introduced in PowerShell v4.

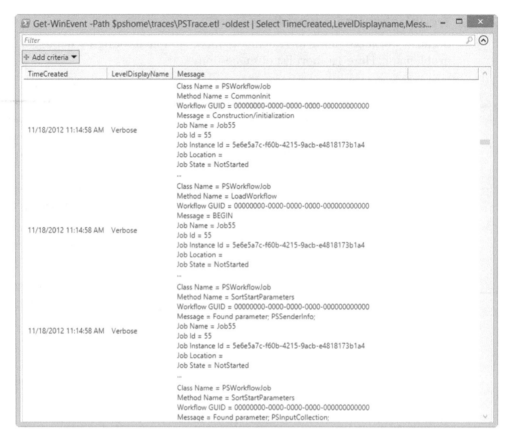

Figure 23.1   Trace information in `Out-GridView`

23.13 Summary

In this chapter we provided an overview of workflows and how they differ from Power-Shell scripts. Workflows have a lot of configuration parameters available, and this chapter explored the most important. One big advantage of workflows is their ability to be stopped and restarted—which also includes surviving reboots. Workflows are made more powerful by being integrated with the PowerShell job engine. We provided an example workflow and a look at using the workflow-related cmdlets.

This chapter has only scratched the surface. The capabilities are so new they haven't been fully explored by the PowerShell community. Expect the use of workflows to be a major area of productivity gain over the life of PowerShell v3 and later versions.

PowerShell workflows aren't the answer to all of your problems, but in the right place—when you need to perform robust, parallel, long-running tasks—they're a boon. Many IT pros have avoided workflows through a misguided sense of them being too hard to follow. Work through the examples in this chapter, as well as the series of articles

Richard did for the Scripting Guy blog (the first one is at http://blogs.technet.com/
b/heyscriptingguy/archive/2012/12/26/powershell-workflows-the-basics.aspx, with the
rest following at approximately weekly intervals) and you'll be well on the way to mastering PowerShell workflows.

Advanced syntax
for scripts and functions

24

This chapter covers

- Using advanced parameters
- Aliasing parameters
- Validating parameter input
- Using parameter sets
- Using common parameters

This is the chapter we've been waiting to get to. In it, we're going to take almost everything from the prior chapters—writing scripts and functions, creating objects as output, using scope, and more—to the next level. In our minds, the advanced syntax we'll cover in this chapter is something every script or function should eventually use. You'll get an amazing amount of additional functionality and capability almost entirely *for free*, simply by giving PowerShell a few extra keywords here and there.

The type of script and function you're going to build in this chapter is called an *advanced script* or *advanced function*, although many folks like to refer to them as *script cmdlets*, which was their first name during the PowerShell v2 beta process. As the name implies, you'll be able to build something that looks, smells, feels, and tastes almost exactly like a real, native PowerShell cmdlet—and you won't need a copy of Visual Studio to do it!

24.1 Starting point

To begin with, everything we'll show you in this chapter will work fine in either a script or a function. But it's most common to see these techniques used in a function, because you can stack multiple functions into a single file to create a library of reusable tools—a PowerShell script module, as you'll see in the next chapter. With that in mind, we'll demonstrate these advanced techniques in functions. Just keep in mind that, if you wanted, you could do all of the same syntax tricks in a plain script.

> **TIP** After a while the collection of scripts that you build up becomes unmanageable. Creating functions and loading them as modules makes your code management a bit easier. You can also add and remove functionality from your PowerShell session as you need it. In PowerShell v3 and v4, modules are autoloaded when you start a PowerShell session—which is another great reason to go that route.

Our first listing shows your starting point: a plain function that runs a couple of commands and outputs a single, consolidated object. You'll notice that we've used an ordered hash table for the properties; we discussed ordered hash tables in chapter 16 if you need a refresher. You'll be building on this code as we go.

Listing 24.1 Your starting point for advanced function syntax

```
function Get-SystemInfo {
    $os = Get-WmiObject -Class Win32_OperatingSystem -ComputerName localhost
    $cs = Get-WmiObject -Class Win32_ComputerSystem -ComputerName localhost
    $props = [ordered]@{
        OSVersion = $os.version
        Model = $cs.model
        Manufacturer = $cs.manufacturer
        ComputerName = $os.PSComputerName
        OSArchitecture = $os.osarchitecture
    }
    $obj = New-Object -TypeName PSObject -Property $props
    Write-Output $obj
}
```

With that basic starting point in mind, let's tackle parameters first.

24.2 Advanced parameters

We've already shown you how to build a `Param()` block to define input parameters. You'll use that same technique, but you'll add just a bit more framework to it in the next listing. You can read more about this technique in the shell's about_Functions_Advanced_Parameters help topic, but we'll walk you through the general approach.

Listing 24.2 Adding parameters

```
function Get-SystemInfo {
    [CmdletBinding()]          ◁——❶ CmdletBinding
    param(
```

```
    [Parameter(Mandatory=$True)] [string]$computerName
)
$os = Get-WmiObject -Class Win32_OperatingSystem `
-ComputerName $computerName

$cs = Get-WmiObject -Class Win32_ComputerSystem `
-ComputerName $computerName

$props = [ordered]@{
  OSVersion = $os.version
  Model = $cs.model
  Manufacturer = $cs.manufacturer
  ComputerName = $os.PSComputerName
  OSArchitecture = $os.osarchitecture
}
$obj = New-Object -TypeName PSObject -Property $props
Write-Output $obj
}
```

**Parameter
attribute**

In listing 24.2, you precede the Param() block with a [CmdletBinding()] decorator ❶;
see the about_Functions_CmdletBindingAttribute help topic. That activates a certain
feature set, such as the –Verbose and –Debug parameters you're going to rely on for
the remainder of this chapter. Now, although PowerShell will detect your use of
some of those features and allow them even without [CmdletBinding()], other features require it, and as a best practice you should include it in all your scripts or
functions that use any of the techniques we're presenting in this chapter. One feature the [CmdletBinding()] decorator enables is the [Parameter()] decorator ❷,
and you can see that listing 24.2 includes a Mandatory=$True attribute within that.
The Mandatory attribute forces PowerShell to prompt you for a value for any parameter marked as such.

> **NOTE**   In PowerShell v3 and v4, you don't have to type Mandatory=$True. You
> can just use Mandatory. We prefer the full syntax because it's much clearer to
> new PowerShell users.

The parameter list is still comma-separated, meaning that if you had a second parameter you'd need to put a comma after $computerName. After that comma you could put
another [Parameter()] decorator for the second parameter. It might end up looking
something like this:

```
[CmdletBinding()]
Param(
  [Parameter()] [string]$one,
  [Parameter()] [int]$two,
  [Parameter()] $three
)
```

Whenever possible, you should specify a data type for your parameters, as you've
done with $computerName. Doing so provides another level of error checking for
free; for instance, if you define the parameter as an integer and input a string, you'll

get an error. This simple function takes two integers as parameters and multiplies them together:

```
function test-typecheck {
param (
 [int]$a,
 [int]$b
)
$a * $b
}
```

If you supply two integers, everything works:

```
PS C:\> test-typecheck -a 4 -b 5
20
```

But if you put in the wrong sort of data, you'll get an error:

```
PS C:\> test-typecheck -a 4 -b "blue"
test-typecheck : Cannot process argument transformation
on parameter 'b'. Cannot convert value "blue" to type
"System.Int32". Error: "Input string was not in a correct format."
At line:1 char:24
+ test-typecheck -a 4 -b "blue"
+                       ~~~~~~
    + CategoryInfo          : InvalidData: (:)
[test-typecheck],
ParameterBindingArgumentTransformationException
    + FullyQualifiedErrorId : ParameterArgumentTransformationError,
test-typecheck
```

Defining a type for the parameter input data won't protect you from entering incorrect values as long as they're the right type. It also doesn't mean PowerShell can implicitly convert your input to the required type, but defining a type is a useful test for no real effort.

> **TIP** If you don't know the type to use, put an example through `Get-Member` and the full type name will be displayed.

Your parameter names should also, whenever appropriate, be consistent with the parameter names used by native PowerShell commands—$computerName rather than $host, for example, or $FilePath rather than something like $filespec. Again, this isn't compulsory, but it makes your functions blend seamlessly into the PowerShell ecosystem.

Within the [Parameter()] decorator, you specify a number of attributes that tell PowerShell more about each parameter. In many cases, these attributes tell PowerShell to do extra work on your behalf, which is nice. Here's a list:

- Mandatory=$True—Indicates that the parameter isn't optional and must be specified. If someone runs your function and doesn't supply this parameter, PowerShell will prompt for it—with no extra coding on your part needed to make that happen. If you make a parameter mandatory, any default values you code will be ignored.

- `ValueFromPipeline=$True`—Enables the parameter to accept pipeline input of the same type (in other words, ByValue). You must specify a data type, such as `[string]`, so that PowerShell knows what input types to attach. You can have only one parameter accept pipeline input for a given type. So, if you specify `ValueFromPipeline` for one `[string]` parameter, you can't do so for a second `[string]` parameter. You could have a parameter of another type, such as `[int]`, that could accept input by type.

- `ValueFromPipelineByPropertyName=$True`—Enables By-Property-Name pipeline input for the parameter. So, if the parameter is named `$computerName`, it'll grab the values from the `ComputerName` property of whatever objects are piped in. If piped-in objects don't have a `ComputerName` property (in this example), the parameter would be left empty.

- `Position=x`—Tells PowerShell that this parameter can accept values positionally. In other words, rather than providing the parameter name, a user has to provide the necessary values in the indicated order. You should specify only one parameter per position. For example, only one parameter will be at position 0, one will be at position 1, and so on. Parameters that don't have a position number specified can be used only if the user provides the parameter name.

There are other attributes you can specify, such as `HelpMessage`, which are described in PowerShell's help file, but you'll use the preceding ones most often. Next, you're going to modify your parameter to accept input from the pipeline both `ByValue` and `ByPropertyName`. Listing 24.3 shows the modification; also notice that we've hit Enter a few times to break up the lines and make them more readable. This is perfectly legal, and it's how many people routinely format this kind of parameter. Also notice that we're changing the data type from `[string]` to `[string[]]`, indicating that it can accept multiple values when used as a parameter rather than on the pipeline.

Listing 24.3 Adding information to the parameter

```
function Get-SystemInfo {
  [CmdletBinding()]
  param(
    [Parameter(Mandatory=$True,
               ValueFromPipeline=$True,
               ValueFromPipelineByPropertyName=$True)]
    [string[]]$computerName
  )
  $os = Get-WmiObject -Class Win32_OperatingSystem `
  -ComputerName $computerName

  $cs = Get-WmiObject -Class Win32_ComputerSystem `
  -ComputerName $computerName

  $props = [ordered]@{
    OSVersion = $os.version
    Model = $cs.model
    Manufacturer = $cs.manufacturer
```

```
    ComputerName = $os.PSComputerName
    OSArchitecture = $os.osarchitecture
  }
  $obj = New-Object -TypeName PSObject -Property $props
  Write-Output $obj
}
```

At this point, your function is technically broken. You've rigged it to accept pipeline input, but you haven't modified it to handle that input properly. You have two situations to deal with: one where input comes in via the parameter and another where input comes in via the pipeline. For example, the function could be run in any of several ways. Here's one:

```
Get-Content names.txt | Get-SystemInfo
```

With the preceding example, you're reading in strings (one computer name per line is assumed in names.txt) and piping them to Get-SystemInfo.

```
Get-ADComputer -Filter * |
Select-Object @{n='ComputerName';e={$_.Name}} |
Get-SystemInfo
```

In this code, objects are being given a ComputerName property with values from the original Name property and are then being piped into the Get-SystemInfo function. Both of the preceding examples are using pipeline input; the next two use parameter input:

```
Get-SystemInfo -computerName SERVER2
```

Obviously, the preceding just passes in a single computer name.

```
Get-SystemInfo -computerName (Get-Content names.txt)
```

The previous code passes in one or more names. PowerShell executes the function somewhat differently in each situation. The next listing shows the modifications you need to make and walks you through the execution sequence for either of the pipeline input examples.

Listing 24.4   AdvancedFunction.ps1: pipeline input sequence

```
function Get-SystemInfo {
  [CmdletBinding()]
  param(
    [Parameter(Mandatory=$True,
               ValueFromPipeline=$True,
               ValueFromPipelineByPropertyName=$True)]
    [string[]]$computerName
  )
  BEGIN {}
  PROCESS {                                              ❶ PROCESS block
    foreach ($computer in $computername) {               ❷ ForEach
                                                           enumeration
```

```
    $os = Get-WmiObject -Class Win32_OperatingSystem `
    -ComputerName $computer
    $cs = Get-WmiObject -Class Win32_ComputerSystem `
    -ComputerName $computer

    $props = [ordered]@{
      OSVersion = $os.version
      Model = $cs.model
      Manufacturer = $cs.manufacturer
      ComputerName = $os.PSComputerName
      OSArchitecture = $os.osarchitecture
    }

    $obj = New-Object -TypeName PSObject -Property $props
    Write-Output $obj
   }
  }
  END {}
}
```

3 Using $computer

When the function is called with pipeline input, PowerShell first looks for and executes a BEGIN block. Yours is empty, so it moves on to the PROCESS block ❶. This is executed one time for each object that was piped in, and a single piped-in object at a time is placed in the $computerName parameter. You're using a ForEach block ❷ to enumerate the contents of $computerName, which is technically redundant because it'll only ever contain one object. But ForEach is capable of enumerating one thing, so your computer name goes into the $computer variable ❸, which is what you use for the remainder of the script.

The procedure is somewhat different when the -computerName parameter is used instead of pipeline input. In that case, the entire value or set of values given to -computerName is placed into the $computerName variable. BEGIN, PROCESS, and END are still executed, but only one time apiece. That means your ForEach loop isn't redundant—you need it to enumerate whatever was passed to $computerName. By using both a PROCESS block and the ForEach loop, you've enabled both parameter input and pipeline input for your function:

```
PS C:\> get-systeminfo "serenity","quark"
ComputerName   : SERENITY
Manufacturer   : TOSHIBA
OSVersion      : 6.1.7601
OSArchitecture : 64-bit
Model          : Qosmio X505
ComputerName   : QUARK
Manufacturer   : LENOVO
OSVersion      : 6.1.7601
OSArchitecture : 32-bit
Model          : S10-3

"serenity","quark" | get-systeminfo
ComputerName   : SERENITY
Manufacturer   : TOSHIBA
OSVersion      : 6.1.7601
```

```
OSArchitecture : 64-bit
Model          : Qosmio X505
ComputerName   : QUARK
Manufacturer   : LENOVO
OSVersion      : 6.1.7601
OSArchitecture : 32-bit
Model          : S10-3
```

See? It works both ways.

24.3　*Variations on parameter inputs*

You can run into quite a lot of variations, and different ways of handling them, when you combine parameter and pipeline input.

First, specifying a parameter always manually overrides pipeline input to it. In the following example, assume that names.txt contains 10 names:

```
Get-Content names.txt | Get-SystemInfo –computername localhost
```

Your function will run only once, against localhost. PowerShell won't *combine* the pipeline and parameter input; it'll simply disregard the pipeline input in favor of the parameter input.

In instances where you have pipeline- and non-pipeline-enabled parameters, you can have both pipeline and parameter input. For example, here's an incomplete function to illustrate:

```
function Do-Something {
  [CmdletBinding()]
  Param(
    [Parameter(ValueFromPipeline=$True}] [string[]]$one,
    [Parameter(Mandatory=$True)] [string]$two
  )
  PROCESS {
    ForEach ($thing in $one) {
      Write-Host $thing
    }
  }
}
```

There's no useful code within this function; we're just showing how it'd work. Assuming you ran it like this:

```
Do-Something –one a,b,c –two something
```

the PROCESS block would execute only once. The ForEach loop would execute three times, because $one contains three objects, so $thing would contain a on the first iteration, then b, then c. $two would contain something throughout the entire function. Now assume you ran the same function like this:

```
'a','b','c' | Do-Something –two wow
```

The piped-in strings would be bound to $one because it accepts pipeline input ByValue for the type String. The PROCESS block would execute three times because three objects were piped in. The first time PROCESS executes, $one will contain a, and after that it'd contain b and then c. Each of those times, the ForEach block would execute once, basically transferring the current contents of $one into the variable $thing. The $two parameter would contain wow for the entire time.

It's also important to note that when a parameter receives input from the pipeline, that variable won't exist within the function's BEGIN block. That's because Power-Shell doesn't internally create and populate the parameter variable until it reaches the PROCESS block, at which point the variable will contain only a single piped-in object at a time.

24.4 Parameter aliases

Sometimes, the consistent name you choose for a parameter might not be the one you prefer to use most often. Some folks might prefer –host instead of –computer-Name, for example. PowerShell enables you to create an alias for parameters, as shown in this listing.

Listing 24.5 Specifying parameter aliases

```
function Get-SystemInfo {
  [CmdletBinding()]
  param(
    [Parameter(Mandatory=$True,
               ValueFromPipeline=$True,
               ValueFromPipelineByPropertyName=$True)]        Parameter
    [Alias('hostname')]                                    ⟵┘ alias
    [string[]]$computerName
  )
  BEGIN {}
  PROCESS {
    foreach ($computer in $computername) {
      $os = Get-WmiObject -Class Win32_OperatingSystem `
      -ComputerName $computer

      $cs = Get-WmiObject -Class Win32_ComputerSystem `
      -ComputerName $computer

      $props = [ordered]@{
        OSVersion = $os.version
        Model = $cs.model
        Manufacturer = $cs.manufacturer
        ComputerName = $os.PSComputerName
        OSArchitecture = $os.osarchitecture
      }

      $obj = New-Object -TypeName PSObject -Property $props
      Write-Output $obj
    }
  }
  END {}
}
```

Listing 24.5 used –hostname, because PowerShell's normal rules of parameter name truncation will allow –host to work as well. Note that aliases can't be used for pipeline ByPropertyName; you couldn't pipe in an object that had a hostname property and expect this parameter to grab that property's values. ByPropertyName works only with the parameter's actual name, which in this example is still computerName.

> **TIP** Notice that the alias is defined in a separate decorator. A common mistake is to try to define the alias in the parameter decorator.

Defining an alias doesn't create a different variable name, either; you'll never have $hostname within the script. Instead, it directs any value input to –hostname into the defined $computerName parameter variable:

```
PS C:\> get-systeminfo -hostname localhost | Select osversion
OSVersion
---------
6.1.7601

PS C:\> get-systeminfo -host localhost | Select osversion
OSVersion
---------
6.1.7601
```

24.5 *Parameter validation*

PowerShell can do a certain amount of data checking for you, automatically rejecting improper parameter input before any of your code even runs. This data checking is defined through an additional set of parameter decorators. The following listing shows an example, which defines the $computerName parameter to accept only between 1 and 5 values, with each value being 5 to 20 characters in length.

Listing 24.6 Adding parameter validation

```
function Get-SystemInfo {
  [CmdletBinding()]
  param(
    [Parameter(Mandatory=$True,
               ValueFromPipeline=$True,
               ValueFromPipelineByPropertyName=$True)]
    [Alias('hostname')]
    [ValidateCount(1,5)]                    ❶ Validation
    [ValidateLength(5,20)]                     decorators
    [string[]]$computerName
  )
  BEGIN {}
  PROCESS {
    foreach ($computer in $computername) {
      $os = Get-WmiObject -Class Win32_OperatingSystem `
      -ComputerName $computer

      $cs = Get-WmiObject -Class Win32_ComputerSystem `
      -ComputerName $computer
```

```
      $props = [ordered]@{
        OSVersion = $os.version
        Model = $cs.model
        Manufacturer = $cs.manufacturer
        ComputerName = $os.PSComputerName
        OSArchitecture = $os.osarchitecture
      }
      $obj = New-Object -TypeName PSObject -Property $props
      Write-Output $obj
    }
  }
  END {}
}
```

Note that you can tack on as many of these validation elements as you like, but each one goes in as a separate decorator ❶. They're usually typed on separate lines immediately preceding the variable, although it's also legal just to string the whole thing together on a single line (which is harder to read).

> **TIP** Making your code easier to read may seem trivial, but when you come back to it next year because it needs updating you'll be much happier because you spent the time making it readable. Well-formatted code will also make your life easier if you have to ask for help on the forums. People are much more inclined to help if they can read the code easily.

You can specify several other validations. For example, you might want to run a small validation script:

```
function Get-SystemInfo {
  [CmdletBinding()]
  param(
    [Parameter(Mandatory=$True,
               ValueFromPipeline=$True,
               ValueFromPipelineByPropertyName=$True)]
    [Alias('hostname')]
    [ValidateScript({Test-Connection -Computername $_ -Count 1 -Quiet})]
    [string[]]$computerName
  )
```

In the ValidateScript decorator, you can define a script block. The code should return True or False. Use $_ to indicate the parameter value. In this example, you have a short script block that's calling the Test-Connection cmdlet using the –Quiet parameter. If this fails, the script block will return False, validation will fail, and PowerShell will throw an exception.

Another common validation is to test for a predefined value. Let's say you were writing a function to query an event log but you wanted to make sure the person running the command entered the right log name. You could do something like this:

```
function get-log {
Param (
    [ValidateSet("Security","System","Application")]
```

```
      [string] $Logname
  )
 Get-EventLog -LogName $Logname
}
```

If anything other than a value in the set is specified, PowerShell will complain. It'll also tell the user the members of the set:

```
PS C:\> get-log -Logname Ssytem
get-log : Cannot validate argument on parameter 'Logname'.
The argument "Ssytem" does not belong to the set
    "Security,System,Application"
specified by the ValidateSet attribute. Supply an argument
that is in the set and then try the command again.
At line:1 char:18
+ get-log -Logname Ssytem
+                 ~~~~~~
    + CategoryInfo          :
InvalidData: (:) [get-log],
ParameterBindingValidationException
    + FullyQualifiedErrorId :
ParameterArgumentValidationError,get-log
```

The last validation test is a pattern test using a regular expression pattern:

```
Param (
[ValidatePattern("\w+\\\w+")]
    [string] $Username
)
```

In this example you want to validate that any value for -Username be in the format domain\username. This tests only whether the credential looks right, not that it's valid.

There are a few other validation decorators you can use. You've seen how to validate against a set of values—it's also possible to validate against a range of values. As an example, consider the Win32_LogicalDisk class. It has a DriveType property that can take values from 0 (Unknown) to 6 (RAM disk). You'll probably be most interested in the range 1–5, which covers local and network disks together with CDs.

```
function get-disk {
param (
  [Parameter(Mandatory=$True)]
  [ValidateRange(1,5)]
  [uint32] $drivetype,

  [string] $computername="$env:COMPUTERNAME"
)
Get-WmiObject -Class Win32_LogicalDisk `
-Filter "DriveType = $drivetype" `
-ComputerName $computername |
select DeviceID,
@{N="PercentFree"; E={[math]::Round((($_.FreeSpace / $_.Size) * 100), 2)}}
}
```

The function can be used like this:

```
get-disk -drivetype 3 | Format-Table -AutoSize
DeviceID PercentFree
-------- -----------
C:             69.69
```

If you supply a value for $drivetype that's outside of the range 1–5, an error will be thrown and you'll be told you're below the minimum or above the maximum value. The default value you've put on the $computername variable supplies the name of the local machine. A few cmdlets won't accept "." or localhost as values for computer names. Using the environment variable steps around that problem.

Calculations involving disk or file sizes often result in a lot of decimal places being shown. You don't always need that level of precision, so rounding to two decimal places is usually enough. One way to achieve that is to use the System.Math class's Round method, as shown in the preceding code.

Variables can be set to null or, in the case of strings, to being empty. These situations can cause an error because, for example, you can't have a computer with a name of $null! Two validation decorators exist to catch this problem:

- [ValidateNotNull()]
- [ValidateNotNullOrEmpty()]

We tend to use [ValidateNotNullorEmpty()] because it covers both situations. Use [ValidateNotNull()] if you just want to test for a null value:

```
function get-disk {
[CmdletBinding()]
param (
 [Parameter(Mandatory=$True)]
 [ValidateRange(1,5)]
 [uint32]$drivetype,
 [ValidateNotNullorEmpty()]
 [string]$computername
)
Get-WmiObject -Class Win32_LogicalDisk `
-Filter "DriveType = $drivetype" `
-ComputerName $computername |
select DeviceID,
@{N="PercentFree"; E={[math]::Round((($_.FreeSpace / $_.Size) * 100), 2)}}
}
```

The function can be tested like this:

```
$comp = $null
get-disk -drivetype 3 -computername $comp -Debug | Format-Table -AutoSize
$comp = ""
get-disk -drivetype 3 -computername $comp -Debug | Format-Table -AutoSize
```

You've seen that parameters marked as mandatory will prompt for a value if you don't supply one. There's a way to override that behavior using parameter decorators. You have three options:

- [AllowNull()]
- [AllowEmptyString()]
- [AllowEmptyCollection()]

The following function demonstrates how these parameter decorators can be used:

```
function get-disk {
[CmdletBinding()]
param (
 [Parameter(Mandatory=$True)]
 [ValidateRange(1,5)]
 [uint32]$drivetype,

[Parameter(Mandatory=$True)]
 [AllowNull()]
 [AllowEmptyString()]
 [string]$computername
)
if ($computername -eq $null -or $computername -eq ""){
  $computername="$env:COMPUTERNAME"
}
Write-Debug $computername
Get-WmiObject -Class Win32_LogicalDisk  -Filter "DriveType = $drivetype"
-ComputerName $computername |
select DeviceID,
@{N="PercentFree"; E={ [math]::Round((($_.FreeSpace / $_.Size) * 100), 2)}}
}
```

In this example you've kept the validation on drive type and made the $computername parameter mandatory. The two decorators allow a null value or an empty string to be passed into the function as the computer name. This can sometimes occur if you're using those values to initialize a string. You can test the code like this:

```
$comp = $null
get-disk -drivetype 3 -computername $comp -Debug | Format-Table -AutoSize

$comp = ""
get-disk -drivetype 3 -computername $comp -Debug | Format-Table -AutoSize
```

You did force the local computer name to be selected if the $computername variable is null or an empty string. Either of these cases would cause Get-WmiObject to fail.

Note that PowerShell runs all of the validations you specify; if any one of them fails, your function will quit immediately with a descriptive error message:

```
PS C:\> get-systeminfo sys
Get-SystemInfo : Cannot validate argument on parameter 'computerName'. The
 number of characters (3) in the argument is too small. Specify an
argument whose length is greater than or equal to "5" and then try the
 command again.
At line:1 char:15
+ get-systeminfo <<<<  sys
    + CategoryInfo          : InvalidData: (:)
[Get-SystemInfo], ParameterBindingValidationException
    + FullyQualifiedErrorId : ParameterArgumentValidationError,Get-SystemInfo
```

No further validations will be performed once an error has occurred. Even with all of these validation options, you might still need to add more tests or error handling to accommodate potentially bad values.

> **NOTE** Jeff posted a number of articles on these validation techniques on his blog. He then turned the articles into a collection of About help topics and packaged them in a PowerShell module. You can visit http://jdhitsolutions .com/blog/2012/05/introducing-the-scriptinghelp-powershell-module/ to learn more.

24.6   *Parameter sets*

Many PowerShell commands support multiple parameter sets. Look at the help for `Get-WmiObject`, for example, and you'll see a good example of multiple parameter sets. The important thing to remember is that once you start creating parameter sets, each `parameterset` must have a parameter that's a member of no other `parameter-set`; otherwise PowerShell can't unambiguously resolve the `parameterset` to use. A parameter that isn't explicitly in any `parametersets` is counted as being in all of them. When users run your function, they can only use the parameters from a given set (or any *belongs to all sets* parameters) at a time. For example, here's the parameter declaration portion of a function:

```
Function Get-Stuff {
  [CmdletBinding()]
  Param(
    [Parameter(ParameterSetName='Fred')][string]$one,
    [Parameter(ParameterSetName='Fred')][string]$two,
    [Parameter(ParameterSetName='Wilma')][string]$buckle,
    [Parameter(ParameterSetName='Wilma')][string]$my,
    [Parameter(ParameterSetName='Wilma')][string]$shoe,

    [Parameter(ParameterSetName='Dino')][string]$bag,
    [Parameter(ParameterSetName='Dino')][string]$sack,

    [Parameter()][string]$peach,
    [Parameter()][string]$apple
  )
}
```

The actual parameter set names are completely made up and for the most part are invisible to users of the function. They exist only as grouping identifiers. Any of the following would be legal ways to run this function:

- `Get-Stuff -one 'see' -two 'here' -peach 'certainly'`
- `Get-Stuff -buckle 'brass' -shoe 'leather' -apple 'mcintosh'`
- `Get-Stuff -bag 'leather' -sack 'paper'`

These are legal because no single command uses parameters that are from multiple sets, except one of the two *doesn't belong to any set* parameters, which can be used anywhere. The following would all be illegal:

- `Get-Stuff -my 'belong' -bag 'leather'`
- `Get-Stuff -one 'here' -two 'there' -buckle 'copper'`
- `Get-Stuff -apple 'yes' -peach 'yes'`

Those are illegal because they combine parameters from different named parameter sets. The third one may seem odd to be illegal, but because the two parameters are members of all three `parametersets`, PowerShell doesn't know which one you want to use. In addition, you can't define a parameter more than once. For example, you couldn't create a second parameter named $one and assign it to the `Wilma` parameter set; you've already defined $one and can't create a second instance of it. Doing so will result in an error. But you can make a parameter a member of multiple `parametersets`:

```
[Parameter(ParameterSetName='Fred')]
[Parameter(ParameterSetName='Wilma')]
[string]$house
```

And the function would be called as

```
Get-Stuff -one 'see' -house 'his'
Get-Stuff -my 'see' -house 'hers'
```

There may be situations where you want to specify a default parameter set name. To accomplish this, make a small adjustment to the `cmdletbinding` attribute:

```
[CmdletBinding(DefaultParameterSetName="Wilma")]
```

If you've provided some default parameter values for the Fred set, this simplifies things for the admin running the script. You can see your parameter sets by using `Get-Help`:

```
PS C:\> help get-stuff
Get-Stuff [-buckle <String>] [-my <String>] [-shoe <String>]
[-peach <String>] [-apple <String>] [-Verbose] [-Debug]
[-ErrorAction <ActionPreference>] [-WarningAction <ActionPreference>]
[-ErrorVariable <String>] [-WarningVariable <String>]
[-OutVariable <String>] [-OutBuffer <Int32>]

Get-Stuff [-one <String>] [-two <String>] [-peach <String>]
[-apple <String>] [-Verbose] [-Debug] [-ErrorAction <ActionPreference>]
[-WarningAction <ActionPreference>] [-ErrorVariable <String>]
[-WarningVariable <String>] [-OutVariable <String>] [-OutBuffer <Int32>]

Get-Stuff [-bag <String>] [-sack <String>] [-peach <String>]
[-apple <String>] [-Verbose] [-Debug] [-ErrorAction <ActionPreference>]
[-WarningAction <ActionPreference>] [-ErrorVariable <String>]
[-WarningVariable <String>] [-OutVariable <String>] [-OutBuffer <Int32>]
```

The output is limited because you haven't added any comment-based help, but you can see there are three ways to run `Get-Stuff`. Also notice that the first syntax example corresponds with the default parameter set.

24.7   *WhatIf and Confirm parameters*

PowerShell supplies a huge amount of power to the administrator, and with great power comes the opportunity to make great mistakes. Look at this snippet:

```
Get-Service s* | Stop-Service
```

Would you run that on your server? Do you know what it could do? We guess that the answer to both questions is no, but it's easy to discover the answer to the second question. You can use

```
Get-Service s* | Stop-Service -WhatIf
```

The result will be a lot of messages of the form

```
What if: Performing operation "Stop-Service" on Target
"Security Accounts Manager (SamSs)".
```

All well-written cmdlets that have the potential to modify your system should have a `-WhatIf` parameter. They should also have a `-Confirm` parameter so you can prompt for confirmation before performing the action:

```
Get-Service s* | Stop-Service -Confirm
Confirm
Are you sure you want to perform this action?
Performing operation "Stop-Service" on Target "Security Accounts Manager
(SamSs)".
[Y] Yes  [A] Yes to All  [N] No  [L] No to All  [S] Suspend  [?] Help
(default is "Y"): L
```

Would you like to be able to add that functionality to your functions? Well, that's just what we're going to show you in this section.

The key to adding `-WhatIf` and `-Confirm` parameters to your functions is the `[CmdletBinding()]` decorator. All you have to do is add `SupportsShouldProcess=$True` and `ConfirmImpact="Medium"` in the parentheses and do a bit of clever stuff in the body of the function, as demonstrated in listing 24.7. We'll use WMI as an example and show you how to add the `-Confirm` and `-Whatif` parameters to the `Win32_Process` class—remember that methods on WMI classes just perform their actions; you normally don't get the opportunity to test what they'll do or prompt for confirmation to proceed. `Invoke-WmiMethod` does have `-Confirm` and `-Whatif` parameters, but it involves more work on your part if you try to use them in the function.

> **Listing 24.7   Adding WhatIf and Confirm parameters**

```
function stop-wmiprocess{
[CmdletBinding(SupportsShouldProcess=$True,
   ConfirmImpact="Medium" )]
param (
[parameter(Mandatory=$True)]
  [string]$name
)
```

① **Add functionality**

```
if ($psCmdlet.ShouldProcess("$name", "Stop Process")) {       ←┐   Testing
    Get-WmiObject -Class Win32_Process -Filter "Name = '$name'" |  ❷  WhatIf
    Invoke-WmiMethod -Name Terminate
    }
}
```

The `[CmdletBinding()]` decorator has `SupportsShouldProcess=$True` and `Confirm-Impact="Medium"` added ❶. The first one adds the parameters, and the second works with the `$ConfirmPreference` setting to determine if confirmation is automatically triggered. If the `ConfirmImpact` setting is the same or higher than the setting in the `$ConfirmPreference` variable, then confirmation is automatically requested.

$psCmdlet represents the cmdlet or advanced function that's being run. You use its `ShouldProcess()` method ❷ to control the parameter's action. If either `-Whatif` or `-Confirm` is used, the method kicks in and uses the message `Stop Process` to tell you what it's doing to the object $name, as can be seen in these examples:

```
PS C:\> stop-wmiprocess -name notepad.exe -WhatIf
What if: Performing operation "Stop Process" on Target "notepad.exe".

PS C:\> stop-wmiprocess -name notepad.exe -Confirm
Confirm
Are you sure you want to perform this action?
Performing operation "Stop Process" on Target "notepad.exe".
[Y] Yes  [A] Yes to All  [N] No  [L] No to All  [S] Suspend  [?] Help
(default is "Y"): n
```

If the parameters aren't used, the WMI cmdlets are called and notepad.exe is terminated. This is a huge amount of functionality for little effort, and the advanced function toolbox isn't empty yet.

24.8   *Verbose output*

This final trick is one we like to use a lot. You can technically use it in any script or function, but it works especially smoothly in combination with the `[CmdletBinding()]` directive.

Here's the situation: Administrators often write long, complex scripts, and they get a bit nervous about whether they're working properly. Nobody likes to run a command and have it just sit there. So, to give themselves some assurances that things are going well—and to make any eventual troubleshooting a bit easier—they'll add what we call *progress* information. The next listing shows what this often looks like.

Listing 24.8   Adding progress information to a function

```
function Get-SystemInfo {
  [CmdletBinding()]
  param(
    [Parameter(Mandatory=$True,
               ValueFromPipeline=$True,
               ValueFromPipelineByPropertyName=$True)]
    [string[]]$computerName
  )
```

```
  BEGIN {}
  PROCESS {
    foreach ($computer in $computername) {
      Write-Host "Connecting to $computer"
      $os = Get-WmiObject -Class Win32_OperatingSystem `
      -ComputerName $computer

      $cs = Get-WmiObject -Class Win32_ComputerSystem `
      -ComputerName $computer

      Write-Host "Connection done, building object"

      $props = [ordered]@{
        OSVersion = $os.version
        Model = $cs.model
        Manufacturer = $cs.manufacturer
        ComputerName = $os.PSComputerName
        OSArchitecture = $os.osarchitecture
      }

      $obj = New-Object -TypeName PSObject -Property $props
      Write-Host "Object done, OS ver is $($os.version)"
      Write-Output $obj
    }
  }
  END {}
}
```

❶ Progress output

The example in listing 24.8 uses `Write-Host` to create the progress output ❶. When run, it looks something like this:

```
PS C:\> C:\CustomObjects.ps1
Connecting to localhost
Connection done, building object
Object done, OS ver is 6.1.7601

ComputerName   : localhost
Manufacturer   : VMware, Inc.
OSVersion      : 6.1.7601
OSArchitecture : 64-bit
Model          : VMware Virtual Platform
```

That's all well and good, but we hate it (well, some of us more than others). It breaks one of our primary rules: to avoid using `Write-Host`. Our main problem with it is that it messes up the script's normal output and there's no way to shut it off, short of going back through the script, one line at a time, and either removing or commenting out the `Write-Host` commands. Fortunately, there's a much better way, and it's easy to use. The following listing shows the right way to create this kind of progress output, which PowerShell would refer to as *verbose* output.

Listing 24.9   The right way to show verbose output

```
function Get-SystemInfo {
  [CmdletBinding()]
  param(
```

```
        [Parameter(Mandatory=$True,
                    ValueFromPipeline=$True,
                    ValueFromPipelineByPropertyName=$True)]
        [string[]]$computerName
    )
    BEGIN {}
    PROCESS {
        foreach ($computer in $computername) {
            Write-Verbose "Connecting to $computer"
            $os = Get-WmiObject -class Win32_OperatingSystem `
            -ComputerName $computer

            $cs = Get-WmiObject -class Win32_ComputerSystem `
            -ComputerName $computer

            Write-Verbose "Connection done, building object"

            $props = [ordered]@{
                OSVersion = $os.version
                Model = $cs.model
                Manufacturer = $cs.manufacturer
                ComputerName = $os.PSComputerName
                OSArchitecture = $os.osarchitecture
            }

            $obj = New-Object -TypeName PSObject -Property $props
            Write-Verbose "Object done, OS ver is $($os.version)"
            Write-Output $obj
        }
    }
    END {}
}
```

All listing 24.9 does is replace Write-Host with Write-Verbose. Run the script again, this time with a couple of computer names, and you get this:

```
PS C:\> Get-SystemInfo -computerName localhost,WIN-KNBA0R0TM23
ComputerName   : localhost
Manufacturer   : VMware, Inc.
OSVersion      : 6.1.7601
OSArchitecture : 64-bit
Model          : VMware Virtual Platform

ComputerName   : WIN-KNBA0R0TM23
Manufacturer   : VMware, Inc.
OSVersion      : 6.1.7601
OSArchitecture : 64-bit
Model          : VMware Virtual Platform
```

Hey, wait! Where's the output? It's suppressed, which means your script output looks nice, clean, and uninterrupted. If you need that progress information, you just have to turn it on by adding the -Verbose switch to your command. The [CmdletBinding()] element adds the -Verbose switch to your function automatically; you don't have to code it. You just have to use Write-Verbose, and the switch will turn that output on:

```
PS C:\> Get-SystemInfo -computerName localhost,WIN-KNBA0R0TM23 -Verbose
VERBOSE: Connecting to localhost
```

```
VERBOSE: Connection done, building object
VERBOSE: Object done, OS ver is 6.1.7601
ComputerName   : localhost
Manufacturer   : VMware, Inc.
OSVersion      : 6.1.7601
OSArchitecture : 64-bit
Model          : VMware Virtual Platform
VERBOSE: Connecting to WIN-KNBA0R0TM23
VERBOSE: Connection done, building object
VERBOSE: Object done, OS ver is 6.1.7601
ComputerName   : WIN-KNBA0R0TM23
Manufacturer   : VMware, Inc.
OSVersion      : 6.1.7601
OSArchitecture : 64-bit
Model          : VMware Virtual Platform
```

In the shell, that verbose output is even given an alternate color, making it easy to visually distinguish from the primary script output. Finished looking at it? Just run the function again without the –Verbose switch, and the output is suppressed again. As an additional bonus, the strings in the Write-Verbose calls can be used as comments to document your code.

24.9 *Summary*

We've covered a lot of ground, and these are all practical, useful tricks for you to use. As we said at the outset of this chapter, the extra work that PowerShell does on your behalf in terms of validation, along with the ability to make your scripts and functions look and work more like real PowerShell cmdlets, is worth the minor additional effort in using these syntactic techniques. We think every script or function should strive to implement these features—and as we've shown you, there's not much extra work involved in doing so.

25

Script modules
and manifest modules

This chapter covers

- Turning a PowerShell script into a module
- Exporting module members
- Using a module manifest
- Working with dynamic modules

In previous chapters, we've shown you how to build a script—or, more likely, a function—that works much like a native PowerShell cmdlet. In this chapter, we're going to show you how to package multiple functions together into a distributable form that can be loaded into, and unloaded from, the shell. You've almost certainly used these *modules* before, perhaps loading the ActiveDirectory module. The only difference in what you'll build now is that you'll work entirely in PowerShell's scripting language, whereas many of the modules you've used to this point will have been written in Visual Studio. PowerShell v3 introduced the ability to create CDXML modules—a WMI class wrapped in XML. These are covered in chapter 39. The module manifest techniques shown later in this chapter can also be applied to CDXML modules.

> **NOTE** We covered modules more extensively in chapter 5. If you need a refresher on how to load or unload modules, please refer back to that chapter.

25.1 *Making a script module*

Listing 25.1 shows a complete script that contains a single function. This is a repeat of a function that you built in an earlier chapter; you'll use it as a starting point. Remember that you can easily add as many functions to this script as you want to—we're sticking with a single function to keep things easy to read.

Listing 25.1   MyModule.ps1

```
function Get-DiskInfo {
  [CmdletBinding()]
  param(
    [Parameter(Mandatory=$True,
               ValueFromPipeline=$True,
               ValueFromPipelineByPropertyName=$True)]
    [string[]]$computerName,
    [Parameter(Mandatory=$True)]
    [ValidateRange(10,90)]
    [int]$threshold
  )
  BEGIN {}
  PROCESS {
    foreach ($computer in $computername) {
      $params = @{computername=$computer
                  filter="drivetype=3"
                  class="win32_logicaldisk"}
      $disks = Get-WmiObject @params
      foreach ($disk in $disks) {
        $danger = $False
        if ($disk.freespace / $disk.size * 100 -le $threshold) {
          $danger = $True
        }
        $props = @{ComputerName=$computer
                   Size=$disk.size / 1GB -as [int]
                   Free = $disk.freespace / 1GB -as [int]
                   Danger=$danger}
        $obj = New-Object -TypeName PSObject -Property $props
        $obj
      }
    }
  }
  END {}
}
```

To run the function in listing 25.1, all you have to do is dot-source the script file. It'd be easier to import a module, and making this script into a script module is incredibly easy: Just change the .ps1 filename extension to .psm1. That's it.

To make this behave more like a regular PowerShell module, you should put it into one of the folders that PowerShell automatically searches when you list or load modules. Those places are defined in the system-wide PSModulePath environment variable:

```
PS C:\> $env:psmodulepath
C:\Users\Richard\Documents\WindowsPowerShell\Modules;C:\Program Files\WindowsPo
werShell\Modules;C:\windows\system32\WindowsPowerShell\v1.0\Modules\
```

To make the display a bit easier to identify all the paths, use the `-split` operator:

```
PS C:\> $env:psmodulepath -split ";"
C:\Users\Richard\Documents\WindowsPowerShell\Modules
C:\Program Files\WindowsPowerShell\Modules
C:\windows\system32\WindowsPowerShell\v1.0\Modules\
```

> **NOTE** It should probably go without saying—but we'll say it anyway: Your modules should go in the Documents location, not in the System32 location. System32 is generally reserved for modules distributed by Microsoft. Windows security will also make it more difficult to change modules in the System32 location. The Program Files location is used for modules you need for configurations managed in Desired State Configuration, as explained in chapter 41.

Depending on what other applications you've installed, your path may be different. What we're showing here is the default. Keep in mind that this environment variable is accessible from within PowerShell, but it's defined globally in Windows (%PSMODULE-PATH%). You could add more locations to this variable by appending a semicolon and the additional path. It's also possible to prepend another location. If you're creating a lot of modules, it's probably better to prepend because your development area will be scanned for the module first. It's perfectly legal to list a Universal Naming Convention (UNC) path here also so that you can use a file server to store your modules. Because a UNC might be interpreted as an internet location, you might need to sign your modules or modify your execution policy to allow them to run. You can also put a line like this in your profile to make the extra locations a permanent addition to your Power-Shell environment:

```
$env:PSModulePath = "C:\Scripts\Modules;" + $env:PSModulePath
```

> **WARNING** The location and naming conventions for modules are what trips up almost everyone at first. Read the following instructions carefully.

Within one of the paths listed in `PSModulePath`, you must create a folder for your module. The folder name will become the module name, and it should contain only letters and numbers. Avoid spaces, punctuation, and so on. Save your script module within that folder, giving it the exact same filename as the folder, plus the .psm1 filename extension.

For example, if you've decided to name your module MyModule, then you might save it as \My Documents\WindowsPowerShell\Modules\MyModule\MyModule.psm1. It's very, very important that the folder name—MyModule—and the filename—MyModule .psm1—match exactly. Otherwise, PowerShell won't be able to find the module.

> **WARNING** The latest versions of Windows use a Documents library, which consists of two locations: a Shared Documents folder and a My Documents folder. `PSModulePath` only refers to the My Documents location. If you're creating the necessary folders by using Windows File Explorer, make sure you're in My Documents and not Shared Documents.

That's all you have to do. With the module file saved in the correct location, you can run `Import-Module MyModule` (assuming you stuck with `MyModule` as the module name and used that name for the folder and filename) to load the module; `Remove-Module MyModule` will unload it. Of course, you don't have to keep your module in one of the locations listed in `PSModulePath`; you can store it anywhere. If you store it elsewhere, provide the path and filename to `Import-Module`, such as `Import-Module C:\Mine\MyModule.psm1`.

> **NOTE** The command autodiscovery feature in PowerShell v3 and v4 will work only if you store your module in one of the locations listed in `PSModulePath`.

It may be beneficial to keep the module in another location during development, especially if you're running later versions of PowerShell and leave the autodiscovery function switched on.

A .psm1 file can contain a number of item types:

- Functions, as discussed earlier
- Other calls to `Import-Module`
- Dot-sourced PowerShell scripts to run PowerShell scripts (usually in the same folder) that each contain one or more functions

One file or many files?

You can create your module with a single PSM1 file. The advantages of doing this are that you have everything in one place and you can unload the functions when you're finished with working with the module.

The alternative is to have a number of scripts that contain your functions and dot-source them in the PSM1 file. Each script would have a line like this in the PSM1 file:

```
. $psScriptRoot\FileFunctions.ps1
```

`$psScriptRoot` is a PowerShell automatic variable that contains the directory from which a script is being run.

The advantage of this approach, especially if you have a large amount of code, is that it becomes easier to maintain. The disadvantage is that the functions don't unload when you call `Remove-Module`.

Which should you use? As always, it's your call depending on your preferences and how you want to work.

> **TIP** In PowerShell v2, `$psScriptRoot` was only available in PSM1 files. In PowerShell v3 and v4, you can use it in all scripts.

25.2 *Exporting module members*

When you import, or load, a script module into memory, PowerShell runs the PSM1 file within the global scope. That means any functions defined within the module become visible to the entire shell. You can import a module and then get a directory listing of PowerShell's Function: drive to see the module's functions, or you can use Get-Command. That's often the exact behavior you'll want; sometimes, though, you might want certain things within the module to remain hidden, or *private*.

For example, take a look at listing 25.2. Here, you're adding a small utility function. This function does something useful, but you don't want anyone to see or use it. You plan to use it from within some of the module's other functions, but you haven't taken the time to make it fit for public consumption. It has a nonstandard name, it defines its parameters in the simplest possible manner, and so on. Alternatively, it may be a function that's used only in the middle of a process and it doesn't make sense for it to be accessed outside of that context.

Listing 25.2 MyModule.psm1, revised

```
function utilPingWMI {
  param([string]$computername)
  Test-Connection -ComputerName $computername -Count 1 -Quiet
  }
function Get-DiskInfo {
  [CmdletBinding()]
  param(
    [Parameter(Mandatory=$True,
               ValueFromPipeline=$True,
               ValueFromPipelineByPropertyName=$True)]
    [string[]]$computerName,
    [Parameter(Mandatory=$True)]
    [ValidateRange(10,90)]
    [int]$threshold
  )
  BEGIN {}
  PROCESS {
    foreach ($computer in $computername) {
      $params = @{computername=$computer
                  filter="drivetype=3"
                  class="win32_logicaldisk"}
      if (utilPingWMI $computer ){
       $disks = Get-WmiObject @params
       foreach ($disk in $disks) {
         $danger = $False
         if ($disk.freespace / $disk.size * 100 -le $threshold) {
           $danger = $True
         }
         $props = @{ComputerName=$computer
                    Size=$disk.size / 1GB -as [int]
                    Free = $disk.freespace / 1GB -as [int]
                    Danger=$danger}
         $obj = New-Object -TypeName PSObject -Property $props
         $obj
       }
     }
      else {
          write-Warning "Could not contact $computer"
```

```
          }
        }
     }
     END {}
  }
```

By default, when users load that module into the shell, the `utilPingWMI` function will be visible in the Function: drive and they'll be able to call the function themselves. That's not what you want, so you'll make use of a cmdlet called `Export-ModuleMember`. This cmdlet tells the shell exactly which pieces of your module you want made visible to the public; everything else will remain private.

This sometimes confuses folks, so here are the rules to remember:

- If you don't use `Export-ModuleMember` at all, all functions in your script module become publicly visible. This includes functions, aliases, and any variables you define in the script. Variables and aliases aren't made visible.

- If you use `Export-ModuleMember`, only the things you explicitly export, or make public, will be publicly visible. Everything else will be private. Private means that non-exported elements can be *seen* by anything in the module's PSM1 file but not by anything external to that file.

This sometimes confusing behavior was designed by Microsoft as an ease-of-use feature. The idea is that, if you do nothing, the module will do something. If you want to get more sophisticated and start hiding stuff, the shell will shift modes and expose only what you tell it to.

We mentioned aliases and variables in the rules, and you can be pretty clever in how you use those. Our next listing shows a new MyModule.psm1, which has several public and private elements.

Listing 25.3 MyModule.psm1, using `Export-ModuleMember`

```
[string]$MMLogfile = 'C:\ErrorLog.txt'
[int]$_counter = 0
function utilPingWMI {
  param([string]$computername)
  Test-Connection -ComputerName $computername -Count 1 -Quiet

}
function Get-MMDiskInfo {
  [CmdletBinding()]
  param(
    [Parameter(Mandatory=$True,
               ValueFromPipeline=$True,
               ValueFromPipelineByPropertyName=$True)]
    [string[]]$computerName,
    [Parameter(Mandatory=$True)]
    [ValidateRange(10,90)]
    [int]$threshold
  )
```

Annotations:
- **Define public variable** → points to `[string]$MMLogfile = 'C:\ErrorLog.txt'`
- **Define private variable** → points to `[int]$_counter = 0`
- **Define private function**
- **Rename public function** → points to `function Get-MMDiskInfo {`

```
BEGIN {}
PROCESS {
  foreach ($computer in $computername) {
    $params = @{computername=$computer
               filter="drivetype=3"
               class="win32_logicaldisk"}
    if (utilPingWMI $computer ){
      $disks = Get-WmiObject @params
      foreach ($disk in $disks) {
        $danger = $False
        if ($disk.freespace / $disk.size * 100 -le $threshold) {
          $danger = $True
        }
        $props = @{ComputerName=$computer
                  Size=$disk.size / 1GB -as [int]
                  Free = $disk.freespace / 1GB -as [int]
                  Danger=$danger}
        $obj = New-Object -TypeName PSObject -Property $props
        $obj
      }
    }
    else {
        write-Warning "Could not contact $computer"
    }
  }
}
END {}
}
New-Alias -Name gdi -Value Get-MMDiskInfo
Export-ModuleMember -Function Get-MMDiskInfo
Export-ModuleMember -Variable MMLogfile
Export-ModuleMember -Alias gdi
```

⟵┐ **Define public alias**

Make items public

Let's cover a few specifics about what you're doing in listing 25.3:

- You defined two variables, one of which you'll make public. You're using the prefix MM for public items, which will help ensure that they don't conflict with something that another module is making public or that's already built into the shell.

- In keeping with the nonconflict theory, you're renaming your function to Get-MMDiskInfo. In PowerShell v3 and v4, you can also use the -Prefix parameter to dynamically set the prefix at time of import into the shell, meaning you don't need to modify your code. If you use the -Prefix parameter in PowerShell v4, the ExportedCommands property of the module shows the commands in the module with the prefix applied. When you run commands using the Module-Name\CommandName syntax, you must use the prefix.

- PowerShell doesn't know what will be public or private until the very end, when you start issuing Export-ModuleMember commands. That's where everything you export officially becomes public and everything else remains private. Remember that *remaining private* isn't the default; it only becomes the default once you start using Export-ModuleMember to explicitly make things public.

- The alias you created and exported, `gdi`, will enable someone who loads your module to run `gdi` in order to run the `Get-MMDiskInfo` function. That alias will vanish if they remove your module from the shell's memory.
- You give the private variable a name that starts with an underscore, `$_counter`, as a visual reminder to yourself that the variable isn't public. That variable can safely be used within any of the functions that your PSM1 file contains, but it won't be visible anywhere else.

With a clever plan, you can create complex modules that contain internal functions and variables and that expose just your intended aliases, functions, and variables to the public.

25.3   *Making a module manifest*

One of the downsides of a script module is that you're limited to a single PSM1 file. There might well be instances where you need to work with a greater number of files, and that's where a *module manifest* comes into play. A manifest is essentially a text file that uses special formatting to tell PowerShell what files are included in your module—an inventory of sorts. Module manifests have the same name as your module; if your module folder is MyModule, then the manifest file must be named MyModule.psd1.

When PowerShell loads a module by name—such as when you run `Import-Module MyModule`—it looks for a PSD1 file first. If it doesn't find one, it'll then look for a DLL file and then a PSM1 file. So normally, if you want to provide a manifest, saving one with the proper filename is enough to get PowerShell to use it.

You can create a new manifest by using the `New-ModuleManifest` cmdlet. It has several parameters that we'll need to cover, so let's start with the ones that are mandatory. There are two things you should keep in mind when using these:

- Parameters we identify as *skippable* can be given an empty string for their value, and the resulting manifest will function properly. You still have to specify the parameter or the cmdlet will prompt you for it, but you don't have to provide a value other than an empty string.
- Parameters we identify as *multivalued* can accept a comma-separated list of values.

Here are the parameters you must specify when running the cmdlet:

- `Author`—The module's author. Skippable.
- `CompanyName`—The name of the company that produces the module. Skippable.
- `Copyright`—A copyright notice for the module. Skippable.
- `Description`—A textual description of the module. Skippable.
- `FileList`—A list of files contained within the module, intended for informational purposes only. Multivalued.
- `FormatsToProcess`—A list of .format.ps1xml files that provide formatting instructions for the module. Skippable and multivalued.

- `ModuleToProcess`—The primary module, usually a PSM1 file with a script module, that should be loaded first.
- `Path`—The path and filename of the final manifest file, which must be given a .psd1 filename extension.
- `RequiredAssemblies`—A list of .NET Framework assemblies that the module needs to run. Skippable and multivalued.
- `TypesToProcess`—A list of PS1XML files that provide type extension instructions for the module. Skippable and multivalued.

NOTE Two of these parameters, -TypesToProcess and –FormatsToProcess, will make more sense after we've covered custom format views and custom type extensions in upcoming chapters.

There are also a few optional parameters you may find useful. Three of these control what's made public from the module:

- `AliasesToExport`
- `FunctionsToExport`
- `VariablesToExport`

These all default to *, which means the elements exported by the module will in fact be exported and made public. These don't override your use of `Export-ModuleMember` within the PSM1 file; rather, they overlay it. In order for a function, variable, or alias to be public, it must meet both of these criteria:

- It must be exported by using `Export-ModuleMember` or be contained in a module that doesn't use `Export-ModuleMember` at all.
- It must be listed on the appropriate Module manifest parameter, or the parameter must not be specified, or the parameter must be specified with a value of * (which is the default).

These parameters all support wildcards; -AliasesToExport b* would export all aliases starting with the letter "b" that had also been exported within the PSM1 file.

Here are a few more optional parameters you may find useful:

- `ModuleList`—This is an information-only list of modules contained within the module.
- `ModuleVersion`—This defaults to 1.0 and is for informational purposes only.
- `NestedModules`—This is a multivalued list of additional modules that must be loaded into memory in order for the root module to work. You can use it instead of adding `Import-Module` commands at the top of your PSM1 file.
- `ScriptsToProcess`—This is a multivalued list of PS1 files that should be run when the module is loaded.
- `DefaultCommandPrefix`—New in PowerShell v4, this parameter specifies a prefix that's prepended to the nouns of all functions in the module. The `Exported-Commands` property of the module will use the prefix. If you use the module

qualified syntax, ModuleName\CommandName, the command names must include the prefix.

It's a lot of information to provide, but the cmdlet lets you create complex, multifile modules that can be loaded in a single step.

25.4 *Creating dynamic modules*

Before we leave the world of modules and script blocks, let's look at an interesting way of creating dynamic modules using the New-Module cmdlet. A dynamic module is a collection of code that exists in memory only; nothing is written to disk. Frankly, this is something most IT pros won't need very often, but it offers some intriguing possibilities.

One possibility is to use a dynamic module to copy a function from one computer to another without writing anything to disk. There are a few moving pieces, so we'll go through this process step by step.

Say on your machine you have a few functions loaded into the shell that you want to execute on a remote machine. You begin by creating a string that contains the function code, separated by a semicolon to indicate a new command:

```
$command=""
$command="Function Get-Mac { $((get-command get-mac).Definition)} ;"
$command+="Function Get-Uptime { $((get-command get-uptime).Definition)}"
```

The variable $command now contains two functions separated by a semicolon. Next, you push these functions to a remote machine. You're going to use a session so you can run several commands. It's possible to do everything with one command using Invoke-Command, but you want to make this easier to follow:

```
$sess=New-PSSession -ComputerName Quark
```

With the session in place you'll create a dynamic module on the remote computer:

```
invoke-command {
 Param ($commandText)
 $sb=[scriptblock]::Create($commandText)
 $mod=New-Module -scriptblock $sb
 $mod | import-module} -session $sess -argumentlist $command
```

The script block you're invoking accepts a parameter, $commandText. You'll create a script block from it using the Create() method of the [scriptblock] type accelerator. This new script block is then used by New-Module to create a dynamic module. It isn't necessary, but you'll explicitly import the module so you can see it, if you want, with Get-Module. The end result, though, is that the functions from $command are now loaded in memory on the remote computer and you can execute them:

```
invoke-command {get-uptime} -session $sess
```

When the session ends, the dynamic module ends and nothing ever touches the filesystem. You can take this concept even further and copy a script-based module from the local machine to a dynamic module on a remote machine, as shown in the following listing.

Listing 25.4 Copying a module to a remote computer

```
$module="FileSystem"
 Import-Module $module
 Get-Command -Module $module -CommandType Function |
 ForEach -begin { $commands=""} -Process {
   $commands+="Function $($_.Name) { $($_.Definition) } ;"
 } -end { $commands+="Export-ModuleMember -function *" }
#create a dynamic module on the remote machine
invoke-command {
 Param ($commandText)
$sb=[scriptblock]::Create($commandText)
$mod=New-Module -scriptblock $sb
$mod | import-module
 } -session $sess -argumentList $commands
```

The code in listing 25.4 is similar to what you did earlier with the exception of piping the module functions to `ForEach-Object` to build the command string.

The other interesting use of `New-Module` is to create a custom object. There are easier ways to create custom objects, but in the interest of completeness we felt we should at least offer a quick glimpse at this technique.

First, define a script block with a number of functions. These will become the custom object's methods so you don't need to adhere to typical naming conventions; it's probably better if you don't.

```
$sb={
Function GetBootTime {
$os=get-wmiobject win32_operatingsystem
$os.ConvertToDateTime($os.LastBootUpTime)
}
Function GetCDrive {
get-wmiobject win32_logicaldisk -filter "deviceid='c:'"
}
Function ClearTemp {
Param($path=$env:temp)
Write-Host "Checking $path" -foreground Cyan
dir -path $path -recurse | Where {$_.LastWriteTime -ge (GetBootTime)} |
Remove-item -Recurse
}
}
```

Next, create a dynamic module, but this time create a custom object:

```
PS C:\> $co=new-module -ScriptBlock $sb -AsCustomObject
PS C:\> $co | get-member

   TypeName: System.Management.Automation.PSCustomObject

Name          MemberType   Definition
----          ----------   ----------
Equals        Method       bool Equals(System.Object obj)
GetHashCode   Method       int GetHashCode()
GetType       Method       type GetType()
ToString      Method       string ToString()
```

```
ClearTemp    ScriptMethod System.Object ClearTemp();
GetBootTime  ScriptMethod System.Object GetBootTime();
GetCDrive    ScriptMethod System.Object GetCDrive();
```

The module functions become methods that you can execute like any other method:

```
PS C:\> $co.GetCDrive()

DeviceID     : C:
DriveType    : 3
ProviderName :
FreeSpace    : 124712972288
Size         : 201504845824
VolumeName   :
```

Using a dynamic module like this is a terrific way of creating an object that can do something without much effort. Again, this isn't something we think most people will need on a regular basis, but it might come in handy for those special situations or when you feel like showing off your PowerShell ninja skills.

25.5 *Summary*

Modules are a powerful and convenient way to distribute sets of related functionality. If you build a module manifest, your modules can even consist of multiple files, including type extensions and custom formatting views, which we'll be covering in chapters 26 and 27.

Custom formatting views

This chapter covers

- Changing object type names
- Creating view types
- Loading view types
- Using named views

One of the biggest features of PowerShell's formatting system is its ability to use predefined layouts, or views, to display specific types of objects. When you run a cmdlet like `Get-Process` or `Get-Service`, the display you see by default is controlled by a set of predefined views that Microsoft provides along with PowerShell. The default display is a best guess at what you're most likely to want to see. Those guesses don't always work out:

```
PS C:\> Get-WmiObject -Class Win32_OperatingSystem

SystemDirectory : C:\windows\system32
Organization    :
BuildNumber     : 9600
RegisteredUser  : richard_siddaway@hotmail.com
SerialNumber    : 00258-70157-84935-AAOEM
Version         : 6.3.9600
```

What you need to do is select the data you want:

```
PS C:\> Get-WmiObject -Class Win32_OperatingSystem |
⮡ select PSComputerName, Caption, ServicePackMajorVersion,
⮡ SystemDirectory, OSArchitecture

PSComputerName           : RSSURFACEPRO2
Caption                  : Microsoft Windows 8.1 Pro
ServicePackMajorVersion  : 0
SystemDirectory          : C:\windows\system32
OSArchitecture           : 64-bit
```

You can also create your own predefined views, either to override the ones Microsoft provides or to provide default formatting for custom objects that you create.

> **TIP**   If you don't see the data you want, or expect, when running a new Power-Shell cmdlet, always try piping into `Format-List *` to see if there's more.

26.1   *Object type names*

The first thing to remember is that PowerShell applies views based on the type name of the object being formatted. You can see an object's type name by piping one or more instances of the object to `Get-Member`:

```
PS C:\> Get-Process | Get-Member

   TypeName: System.Diagnostics.Process
...
```

Or try this to get just the type name:

```
PS C:\> get-process | get-member| select TypeName -unique

TypeName
--------
System.Diagnostics.Process
```

You'll find that most objects produced by a PowerShell Get cmdlet have a unique type name. But objects you produce yourself by running `New-Object -TypeName PSObject` don't have a unique type name—they're a generic `PSObject`, so you can't apply a formatting view to them.

PSObject and PSCustomObject

When you use `PSObject` to create a new object, for instance:

```
$obj = New-Object -TypeName PSObject -Property @{a=1; c=2}
```

the .NET class you're using to give the object's full type name is `System.Management.Automation.PSObject`. Because PowerShell loads the `System.Management.Automation` namespace, you can abbreviate to just `PSObject`. You may see references to the full name in scripts from the internet, but many people just use `PSObject` as the type name.

> **(continued)**
>
> You'll notice the following when you pass an object you've created through Get-Member:
>
> ```
> PS C:\> $c | Get-Member
>    TypeName: System.Management.Automation.PSCustomObject
> ```
>
> Don't panic—nothing's gone wrong. PSCustomObject is a placeholder, or base type, that's used when you create a PSObject using the constructor (which has no parameters).
>
> Some people prefer to use PSCustomObject directly and you may see code like this:
>
> ```
> $obj2 = New-Object -TypeName PSCustomObject -Property @{a=1; c=2}
> ```
>
> In reality it doesn't matter whether you use PSObject or PSCustomObject, but we recommend PSObject because doing so involves less typing.

If your goal is to apply a view to an object you've created in that fashion, you must first give the object a unique type name:

```
PS C:\> $obj = New-Object -TypeName PSObject
PS C:\> $obj.PSObject.TypeNames.Insert(0,'My.Custom.Object')
```

In this example, My.Custom.Object is the custom type name. The TypeNames property is an array of names, and your command says to insert a new value at the beginning of the array:

```
PS C:\> $obj.PSObject.TypeNames
My.Custom.Object
System.Management.Automation.PSCustomObject
System.Object
```

You may also see scripts that define the custom type like this:

```
PS C:\> $obj.PSObject.TypeNames.[0]='My.Custom.Object'
```

Either is perfectly valid. But in any case, before you proceed make sure you're clear on the object type name that you want to apply formatting to!

26.2   *Getting view templates*

The syntax of the XML files that define views isn't well documented, so it's often easiest to use one of Microsoft's files as a starting point. You'll find them in PowerShell's installation folder:

```
PS C:\> cd $pshome
PS C:\Windows\System32\WindowsPowerShell\v1.0> dir *.format.ps1xml

    Directory: C:\Windows\System32\WindowsPowerShell\v1.0

Mode                LastWriteTime     Length Name
----                -------------     ------ ----
-a---        18/06/2013     15:50      27338 Certificate.format.ps1xml
-a---        18/06/2013     15:50      27106 Diagnostics.Format.ps1xml
```

```
-a---        18/06/2013      15:50       147702 DotNetTypes.format.ps1xml
-a---        18/06/2013      15:50        14502 Event.Format.ps1xml
-a---        18/06/2013      15:50        21293 FileSystem.format.ps1xml
-a---        18/06/2013      15:50       287938 Help.format.ps1xml
-a---        18/06/2013      15:50        97880 HelpV3.format.ps1xml
-a---        18/06/2013      19:30       105230 PowerShellCore.format.ps1xml
-a---        18/06/2013      15:50        18612 PowerShellTrace.format.ps1xml
-a---        18/06/2013      15:50        13659 Registry.format.ps1xml
-a---        18/06/2013      15:50        17731 WSMan.Format.ps1xml
```

WARNING   Do not, *under any circumstances*, modify these files in any way. They're signed using a Microsoft digital signature and must remain unchanged. Even an extra space, tab, or carriage return can render them useless. Be careful to open them, copy what you need to the Clipboard, and then close the file without saving any changes.

For the examples in this chapter, we used DotNetTypes.format.ps1xml as our starting point, copying and pasting the appropriate parts. An alternative approach is to use Export-FormatData:

```
Get-FormatData -TypeName System.Diagnostics.Process |
Export-FormatData -Path f1.xml
```

You'll need to run the resultant XML through a routine to *pretty print*, but it's safe and removes the risk of damaging the format files.

26.3   *Starting a view file*

View files can be edited in any text editor, including the PowerShell ISE, Notepad, or whatever you like. XML-specific editors can make the files easier to work with, but keep in mind that there are currently no public XML schema definitions (XSD or DTD files) that a dedicated XML editor can use to validate your file.

The following listing shows the content that an empty view file will have. Save this as C:\Test.format.ps1xml; you'll find it easier to keep files in progress in a folder that has a short path, because you'll be typing it a lot.

Listing 26.1   Starting Test.format.ps1xml

```
<?xml version="1.0" encoding="utf-8" ?>
<Configuration>
    <ViewDefinitions>
    </ViewDefinitions>
</Configuration>
```

WARNING   Unlike most of PowerShell, these XML files are case sensitive. That's one reason we rely so heavily on copying and pasting—it's easier to not make mistakes that way.

Once you have that starting point, you can add specific view definitions between the <ViewDefinitions> and </ViewDefinitions> XML tags. In other words, the three examples we're about to walk through can all be pasted in between those two tags.

26.4   Adding view types

PowerShell supports four distinct view types: Table, List, Wide, and Custom. We won't be covering the Custom type; it's extremely complex and not publicly documented. You can see an example in the Microsoft-provided Help.format.ps1xml file, and you're welcome to play with it on your own if you like. Please share any discoveries relating to Custom type with the wider PowerShell community.

For the following examples, you're going to create a custom object having five properties. The next listing shows the code that creates that object.

Listing 26.2   FormatTest.ps1

```
function Get-Info {
    param([string]$computername=$env:COMPUTERNAME)
    $os = Get-WmiObject -Class Win32_OperatingSystem -comp $computername
    $cs = Get-WmiObject -Class Win32_ComputerSystem -comp $computername
    $props = @{'ComputerName'=$os.csname;
               'OSVersion'=$os.version;
               'SPVersion'=$os.servicepackmajorversion;
               'Model'=$cs.model;
               'Mfgr'=$cs.manufacturer}
    $obj = New-Object -TypeName PSObject -Property $props
    $obj.PSObject.TypeNames.Insert(0,'Custom.Info')
    Write-Output $obj
}
Get-Info | Format-Table -Autosize
Get-Info | Format-List
Get-Info | Format-Wide
```

When you run the script in listing 26.2, the `Get-Info` function is run each time, and each time it's passed to a different formatting cmdlet. In the following examples, you'll develop the Table, List, and Wide views that you want to be displayed when those formatting cmdlets run.

TABLE VIEWS

We'll start with Table views, because they're the most complex. Listing 26.3 shows our example. Take a look, and then we'll explain what's going on. Remember that this entire block of XML represents a single view definition and would be pasted between the `<ViewDefinitions>` and `</ViewDefinitions>` XML tags in your view file.

Listing 26.3   Example Table view

```
<View>
    <Name>MyCustomInfoTable</Name>              ⟵┘ View name
    <ViewSelectedBy>
        <TypeName>Custom.Info</TypeName>        ⟵┐ Object type
    </ViewSelectedBy>                               │ name
    <TableControl>
        <TableHeaders>
            <TableColumnHeader>
                <Label>OS Ver</Label>           │ Column header
                <Width>9</Width>                │ definitions
```

```
            </TableColumnHeader>
            <TableColumnHeader>
                <Label>SP Ver</Label>                      ⎫
                <Width>9</Width>                           ⎬  Column header
                <Alignment>Right</Alignment>               ⎭  definitions
            </TableColumnHeader>
        <TableColumnHeader/>                               ←⎤ Empty column
        </TableHeaders>                                    ⎦ header
      <TableRowEntries>
          <TableRowEntry>
              <TableColumnItems>
                  <TableColumnItem>
                      <PropertyName>OSVersion</PropertyName>
                  </TableColumnItem>
                  <TableColumnItem>
                      <PropertyName>SPVersion</PropertyName>
                  </TableColumnItem>
                  <TableColumnItem>
                      <PropertyName>ComputerName</PropertyName>
                  </TableColumnItem>
              </TableColumnItems>
          </TableRowEntry>
      </TableRowEntries>
    </TableControl>
  </View>
```

Column data definitions (label for the block above)

Pay attention to the following specifics:

- The entire section of column header definitions is optional. You can omit `<TableHeaders>` and `</TableHeaders>` and everything in between them. If you do, the names of the properties you choose will be used as column headers.
- If you decide to define column headers, you must have the same number of headers as you'll have columns in the table. But you can have an *empty* column header tag of just `<TableColumnHeader />`, which will force that column to just use its property name.
- The data definitions indicate which properties' values will be displayed on the rows of the table. The number of properties defines the number of columns in the table.

LIST VIEWS

List views are simpler than Table views. The following listing is an example of a List view. Remember that this entire block of XML represents a single view definition and would be pasted between the `<ViewDefinitions>` and `</ViewDefinitions>` XML tags in your view file.

Listing 26.4   Example List view

```
<View>
    <Name>MyCustomInfoList</Name>                          ←⎦ View name
    <ViewSelectedBy>
        <TypeName>Custom.Info</TypeName>                   ←⎤ Object type
    </ViewSelectedBy>                                      ⎦ name
```

```
                <ListControl>
                    <ListEntries>
                        <ListEntry>
                            <ListItems>
                                <ListItem>
                                    <PropertyName>OSVersion</PropertyName>
                                </ListItem>
                                <ListItem>
                                    <PropertyName>SPVersion</PropertyName>
                                </ListItem>
                                <ListItem>
                                    <PropertyName>Mfgr</PropertyName>
                                </ListItem>
                            </ListItems>
                        </ListEntry>
                    </ListEntries>
                </ListControl>
            </View>
```

Where the brace marks **Properties included in list** against the `<ListItems>` block.

Listing 26.4 includes only three properties in its list: `OSVersion`, `SPVersion`, and `Mfgr`. You refer to these properties by the same names you gave them when you created the custom object. Your own List views can have as many properties as you like.

WIDE VIEWS

Wide views are unique in that they only display one property, so they're simple to create, as the following listing demonstrates. Again, this entire block of XML represents a single view definition and would be pasted between the `<ViewDefinitions>` and `</ViewDefinitions>` XML tags in your view file.

Listing 26.5 Example Wide view

```
        <View>
            <Name>MyCustomInfoWide</Name>                      ⟵ View name
            <ViewSelectedBy>
                <TypeName>Custom.Info</TypeName>               ⟵ Object type name
            </ViewSelectedBy>
            <WideControl>
                <WideEntries>
                    <WideEntry>
                        <WideItem>
                            <PropertyName>ComputerName</PropertyName>  ⟵ Property to display
                        </WideItem>
                    </WideEntry>
                </WideEntries>
            </WideControl>
        </View>
```

26.5 *Importing view data*

Before we continue, run the test script and see what its normal output—without the custom views you've created—would look like:

```
Mfgr                   ComputerName SPVersion Model       OSVersion
----                   ------------ --------- -----       ---------
Microsoft Corporation RSSURFACEPRO2         0 Surface Pro 2 6.3.9600
```

```
Mfgr         : Microsoft Corporation
ComputerName : RSSURFACEPRO2
SPVersion    : 0
Model        : Surface Pro 2
OSVersion    : 6.3.9600

RSSURFACEPRO2
```

There you can see the default Table, List, and Wide views. Our next listing shows the completed formatting file, with all three of the custom views pasted in.

Listing 26.6   Final Test.format.ps1xml

```xml
<?xml version="1.0" encoding="utf-8" ?>
<Configuration>
    <ViewDefinitions>
 <View>
            <Name>MyCustomInfoTable</Name>
            <ViewSelectedBy>
                <TypeName>Custom.Info</TypeName>
            </ViewSelectedBy>
            <TableControl>
                <TableHeaders>
                    <TableColumnHeader>
                        <Label>OS Ver</Label>
                        <Width>9</Width>
                    </TableColumnHeader>
                    <TableColumnHeader>
                        <Label>SP Ver</Label>
                        <Width>9</Width>
                        <Alignment>Right</Alignment>
                    </TableColumnHeader>
                  <TableColumnHeader/>
                </TableHeaders>
              <TableRowEntries>
                  <TableRowEntry>
                      <TableColumnItems>
                          <TableColumnItem>
                              <PropertyName>OSVersion</PropertyName>
                          </TableColumnItem>
                          <TableColumnItem>
                              <PropertyName>SPVersion</PropertyName>
                          </TableColumnItem>
                          <TableColumnItem>
                              <PropertyName>ComputerName</PropertyName>
                          </TableColumnItem>
                      </TableColumnItems>
                  </TableRowEntry>
              </TableRowEntries>
            </TableControl>
        </View>
        <View>
            <Name>MyCustomInfoList</Name>
            <ViewSelectedBy>
                <TypeName>Custom.Info</TypeName>
            </ViewSelectedBy>
```

```
                <ListControl>
                    <ListEntries>
                        <ListEntry>
                            <ListItems>
                                <ListItem>
                                    <PropertyName>OSVersion</PropertyName>
                                </ListItem>
                                <ListItem>
                                    <PropertyName>SPVersion</PropertyName>
                                </ListItem>
                                <ListItem>
                                    <PropertyName>Mfgr</PropertyName>
                                </ListItem>
                            </ListItems>
                        </ListEntry>
                    </ListEntries>
                </ListControl>
            </View>
            <View>
                <Name>MyCustomInfoWide</Name>
                <ViewSelectedBy>
                    <TypeName>Custom.Info</TypeName>
                </ViewSelectedBy>
                <WideControl>
                    <WideEntries>
                        <WideEntry>
                            <WideItem>
                                <PropertyName>ComputerName</PropertyName>
                            </WideItem>
                        </WideEntry>
                    </WideEntries>
                </WideControl>
            </View>
        </ViewDefinitions>
</Configuration>
```

You'll need to load that view file into each new shell session in which you want those views to be displayed. To do that, run the `Update-FormatData` cmdlet. It has two parameters to specify a file path, and you must specify one of them but not both. Which you use makes a difference only if you're providing a view for an object type that already has a view loaded into memory, such as one of the object types for which Microsoft provides a default view. Here are your choices:

- -AppendPath loads the specified view file into the end of memory. That means it won't override any views that are already in memory for the same object type.
- -PrependPath loads the specified view file into the beginning of memory. That means it'll override any existing views for the same object type.

Here's what happens when you load the custom view file and rerun your test script:

```
PS C:\> Update-FormatData -AppendPath .\test.format.ps1xml
PS C:\> ./formattest
```

```
OS Ver    SP Ver ComputerName
------    ------ ------------
6.3.9600       0 RSSURFACEPRO2

OSVersion : 6.3.9600
SPVersion : 0
Mfgr      : Microsoft Corporation

RSSURFACEPRO2
```

You can see that all three views—Table, List, and Wide—were used. The Wide view isn't any different than when you ran this earlier, because the Wide view was already selecting, on its own, the same property, ComputerName, that you specified in your XML file.

26.6   *Using named views*

So far you've given each of your views a name in their XML definitions. Although there's no easy way to get PowerShell to list all of the available views by name for a given object type, you can open the XML files and figure out what view names are available. The difficulty level is raised because views for a particular type aren't necessarily grouped.

If you're prepared to experiment a little, you can use something like this to match the view names against the type:

```
$data = @()
$file = "DotNetTypes.format.ps1xml"
$names = Select-Xml -Path $pshome\$file -XPath "Configuration/
    ViewDefinitions/View/Name" |
select -expand  Node |
select -ExpandProperty "#text"
$types = Select-Xml -Path $pshome\$file -XPath "Configuration/
    ViewDefinitions/View/ViewSelectedBy" |
select -expand Node |
select -ExpandProperty TypeName
If ($names.Count -eq $types.Count){
  for ($i=0; $i -le ($names.Count -1); $i++){
    $data += New-Object -TypeName PSobject -Property @{
     Name = $($names[$i])
     TypeName = $($types[$i])
    }
  }
}
else {
 Throw "Error - mismatch between number of names and types"
}
$data | sort TypeName | select Name, TypeName
```

Use Select-XML to find the Name and TypeName nodes. Loop through the results and combine them into a single object for each view, sort, and output. The (abridged) results look like this:

```
Name                     TypeName
----                     --------
process                  System.Diagnostics.Process
```

```
StartTime                    System.Diagnostics.Process
Priority                     System.Diagnostics.Process
process                      System.Diagnostics.Process
ProcessWithUserName          System.Diagnostics.Process#IncludeUserName
```

The last one in the list is for the `-IncludeUserName` parameter that PowerShell v4 introduced. To see this parameter in action, compare the following code and the change to the output:

```
PS C:\> Get-Process powershell

Handles  NPM(K)    PM(K)     WS(K) VM(M)   CPU(s)     Id ProcessName
-------  ------    -----     ----- -----   ------     -- -----------
    662      28    85832     94488   626     0.89   3216 powershell

PS> Get-Process powershell -IncludeUserName

Handles     WS(K) VM(M)   CPU(s)     Id UserName          ProcessName
-------     ----- -----   ------     -- --------          -----------
    428     96204   626     1.11   3216 RSSURFACEPRO2\... powershell
```

When multiple views are available for an object type, PowerShell displays the first one in memory, which is why the `-AppendPath` and `-PrependPath` parameters of `Update-FormatData` are so important. But all the formatting cmdlets have a `-View` parameter that accepts the name of a specific view. Provided the view type matches the formatting cmdlet you used and the type of object being displayed, this parameter will force the shell to use the named view instead of the first one in memory.

For example, Microsoft provides multiple views for the `System.Diagnostics.Process` objects produced by `Get-Process`. You'd never know it unless you explored the DotNetTypes.format.ps1xml file, as shown earlier, but it's true! The second one, which you'd normally never see because it isn't the first one, is named `Priority`. Take a look at the output of the normal view:

```
PS C:\> Get-Process

Handles  NPM(K)    PM(K)     WS(K) VM(M)   CPU(s)     Id ProcessName
-------  ------    -----     ----- -----   ------     -- -----------
     39       6     2012      4348    57     7.69    928 conhost
     30       4      844      1400    41     0.00   2176 conhost
     33       5      968      3164    46     0.02   2964 conhost
    558      11     2072      2796    43     0.44    328 csrss
    221      14    10020      8428    54    16.07    368 csrss
    307      30    17804     17012   351    28.97   1292 dfsrs
```

Now compare the output of the normal view with the output displayed by this alternate, named view:

```
PS C:\> Get-Process | Format-table -view priority

   PriorityClass: Normal
ProcessName                    Id  HandleCount    WorkingSet
-----------                    --  -----------    ----------
conhost                       928           39       4452352
conhost                      2176           30       1433600
conhost                      2964           33       3239936
```

```
csrss                           328            562        2863104
csrss                           368            226        8630272
dfsrs                          1292            307       17420288
dfssvc                         1464            122        4354048
dllhost                        1096            197        6701056
dns                            1328           5163       58880000
    PriorityClass: High
ProcessName                      Id    HandleCount      WorkingSet
-----------                      --    -----------      ----------
vmtoolsd                       1540            259       12238848
    PriorityClass: Normal
ProcessName                      Id    HandleCount      WorkingSet
-----------                      --    -----------      ----------
VMwareTray                     1784             64        5619712
    PriorityClass: High
ProcessName                      Id    HandleCount      WorkingSet
-----------                      --    -----------      ----------
wininit                         376             77        2289664
winlogon                        412             98        2527232
```

We'll leave exploring the StartTime view to you. Because PowerShell doesn't provide a way of discovering these alternate, named views, they're of limited use. But the functionality is there if you choose to use it. Obviously, if you choose to create multiple named views yourself, then you'll at least be aware they exist and can use them!

26.7   *Going further*

In this chapter, we've focused on views that display specific object properties. It's also possible to create view definitions that execute code, such as a table column that provides specific formatting for a numeric value. We find that administrators don't need to do that all too often; that capability is primarily useful when you're displaying an object created by someone else's code, such as a .NET Framework class. In those cases, you can't modify the object itself; you can modify only what's displayed, and so things like *script properties* become useful. But with a custom object like the one you created for this chapter's examples, you can put whatever you want into the properties, so it's usually better to initially populate your object properties with exactly what you want and then let the view definition control things like column headers and widths.

Note that you can also define dynamic properties using a type extension file, which we cover in a chapter 27. Our preference is to let views worry solely about visual formatting and to keep any code—like script properties—contained within type files. With that in mind, we cover script properties in chapter 27.

26.8   *Summary*

Custom views are a powerful technique for creating great-looking output by default. Because you have to load the view files manually in each new shell session, their use might seem limited to you. But once we start talking more about advanced functions in chapter 32, you'll see how useful these can be together.

Custom type extensions

This chapter covers

- Using PowerShell's Extensible Type System
- Creating custom type extensions
- Importing custom type extensions
- Creating custom type extensions dynamically

Windows PowerShell includes a feature known as the Extensible Type System (ETS). A *type*, in PowerShell's world, is a data structure that describes what a type of data looks like, as well as what capabilities that type of data has. For example, there's a type that represents a Windows service. The type says that a service has a name, a description, a status, and other properties. The type also says that a service has methods enabling you to stop the service, start it, pause it, resume it, and so on.

Types are generally born within the .NET Framework that lies underneath PowerShell.

> **WARNING** The objects returned by PowerShell aren't necessarily pure .NET objects. In many cases the PowerShell wrapper will add, or hide, properties and methods. Use the options on the -View parameter of Get-Member to determine the modifications that have been performed.

So, the properties and methods—collectively, the *members*—of a type are defined in the Framework and carried up through PowerShell to you. You can visit http://msdn.microsoft.com/en-us/library/system.serviceprocess.servicecontroller.aspx to see Microsoft's .NET Framework documentation for a service, and you'll see its properties, methods, and so on.

27.1 What are type extensions?

PowerShell has the ability to extend a type, adding more members to it. In most cases, these *type extensions* are intended to make the type easier to use or more consistent. For example, most types in the .NET Framework include a `Name` property, and Power-Shell relies on that for several tasks. When you use `Format-Wide`, for example, it defaults to displaying a type's `Name` property. But services don't have a `Name` property—for some reason, they were given a `ServiceName` property. That makes a service more difficult to use because it isn't consistent with the rest of the Framework. So, Power-Shell extends the service type, adding a `Name` property. Technically, it's an *AliasProperty* because it simply points to the existing `ServiceName` property. But it helps make the type more consistent.

PowerShell can add a number of extensions to a type:

- `DefaultDisplayPropertySet`—For types that don't have a defined default view, the `DefaultDisplayPropertySet` tells PowerShell which of a type's properties to display by default. If this set includes more than four properties, they'll be displayed as a list; otherwise, PowerShell uses a table. Run `Get-WmiObject –Class Win32_OperatingSystem` to see a `DefaultDisplayPropertySet` in action.

NOTE   Technically, `DefaultDisplayPropertySet` is a kind of extension called a `PropertySet`. You can create other `PropertySet` extensions apart from a `DefaultDisplayPropertySet`. Practically speaking, there's little reason to do so. Microsoft originally had plans for other kinds of `PropertySet` extensions, but those were never implemented.

- `AliasProperty`—This extension points to another property. It doesn't *rename* the original property because the original also remains accessible; it simply provides access to the property under an alternate name. Usually the alias is something that makes more sense to you, like `Name` instead of `ServiceName`. Or it can be a shortcut, like `VM` instead of `VirtualMemorySize`.
- `NoteProperty`—This extension adds a property that contains static—that is, unchanging—information. You don't see these used a lot in predefined type extensions because you don't often want to add an unchanging piece of information to a type. You'll mainly see `NoteProperty` used for dynamically generated types, such as the types created by a command like `Get-Service | Select-Object –property Name`. You'll also see this used when creating your own custom objects.
- `ScriptProperty`—This extension adds a property whose value is determined dynamically by an embedded PowerShell script. In other words, when you

access the property, a short PowerShell script will run to produce the property's value. Microsoft uses these a lot, especially to provide easy access to some piece of data that's otherwise a bit buried. For example, when you run `Get-Process`, the output objects will include several `ScriptPropertys`. These provide access to information about a process that would otherwise be difficult to retrieve.

- `ScriptMethod`—This extension is similar to a `ScriptProperty`: When you execute a `ScriptMethod`, an embedded PowerShell script runs to take whatever action the method provides.
- `CodeMethod`—This extension executes a static method of a .NET Framework class. A *static method* is one that can be executed without creating an instance of the class. The `Math` class, for example, has a number of static methods that perform various mathematical operations.
- `CodeProperty`—This extension accesses a static property of a .NET Framework class.

In this book, we'll focus primarily on the extensions that get the most use by administrators: We'll show you how to create a `DefaultDisplayPropertySet`, an `AliasProperty`, a `ScriptProperty`, and a `ScriptMethod`.

27.2 *Creating and loading a type extension file*

Type extensions are defined in a special kind of XML file, which usually has a .ps1xml filename extension. You can see an example of a type extension file by running these two commands:

```
PS C:\> cd $pshome
PS C:\Windows\System32\WindowsPowerShell\v1.0> notepad .\types.ps1xml
```

> **WARNING** Don't change, even in the slightest way, any of the files in PowerShell's installation folder, including types.ps1xml. These files carry a Microsoft digital signature. Altering the file will break the signature, preventing the entire file from being used. Even something as minor as an extra space or carriage return will render the file useless.

A type extension file starts off with the following XML, which you can copy from types.ps1xml:

```
<?xml version="1.0" encoding="utf-8" ?>
<Types>
</Types>
```

> **NOTE** You can use the PowerShell ISE, Notepad, or almost any text editor to create and edit type extension files.

Between the `<Types>` and `</Types>` tags is where you place your individual type extensions. Once you've created a file, you're ready to load it into PowerShell to test it. PowerShell loads only Microsoft-provided type extensions by default; when you import a module or add a PSSnapin, they can also include type extensions that PowerShell loads into memory. To load your own extensions (that aren't part of a module), you run the `Update-TypeData` cmdlet. This requires that you use either the `-PrependPath` or `-AppendPath` parameter, and both parameters accept the path and filename of your type extension XML file. Which do you choose? It depends on what you want your extensions to do.

> **NOTE**   Keep in mind that your extensions last only as long as the current shell session. Once you close the shell, your extensions are removed from memory until you reload them. So if you mess up, in the worst case close the shell and open a new shell window to start fresh. If you want the extensions to be always loaded, use `Update-TypeData` in your profile.

When PowerShell is ready to add extensions to a type, it looks at the type extensions it has loaded in memory. It scans them in the order in which they were loaded into memory, and the first one it finds that matches the type it's working with is the only one it uses. Imagine that you're providing an extension for a type that Microsoft already provided an extension for. If you load your XML file with the `-PrependPath` parameter, then your extension will be *first* in memory, so PowerShell will use it. In other words, your extensions are prepended to the ones already in memory. On the other hand, if you use `-AppendPath`, then your extension will be *last* in memory, and it won't be used if Microsoft has already provided an extension for that type. So the rules are these:

- If you're extending a type that already has an extension, prepend your extension into memory.
- If you're extending a type that doesn't already have an extension, append your extension into memory.
- If you're not sure, try prepending. You may find that some functionality of a type was being provided by a Microsoft-supplied extension, and you'll lose that functionality unless your type extension duplicates it.

> **NOTE**   It's perfectly safe to go into Microsoft's types.ps1xml file, copy things from it, and paste them into your own type extensions. That's one way of providing additional extensions while retaining the ones Microsoft created. You'd then prepend your extensions into memory.

When you run `Update-TypeData`, it'll first parse your file to see if the XML makes sense. This is where errors are most likely to creep in. Read the error carefully; it'll tell you the exact line of the file that PowerShell has a problem with. Unfortunately, you'll have to close PowerShell at this point because it won't let you try to load the same file a second time. For that reason, we tend to put our type extension files into an easy-to-reach folder like C:\ because we often have to open a shell window, load our extension, read the error, and close the shell several times before we finally get it right.

Once the type extension is working to your satisfaction, and you need it to be loaded every time you start PowerShell, you can add a command to your profile to perform the load. It's better to make the type extension part of a module and load it as required.

> **TIP** Unlike almost everything else in PowerShell, the XML files are case sensitive. `<types>` isn't the same as `<Types>`, and the former will generate an error. Be careful! If you use the PowerShell ISE, watch for IntelliSense errors regarding missing tags.

27.3 *Making type extensions*

Within the `<Types>` and `</Types>` tags of your XML file, you'll create your type extensions. We'll go through each of the major types and provide you with examples to see them in action.

All of the extensions associated with a single type, such as a process, go into a single block within the XML file. That basic block, which will always be your starting point for new extensions, looks like this:

```
<Type>
    <Name>type_name_goes_here</Name>
    <Members>
    </Members>
</Type>
```

You can see where the type name goes. This is the exact and full name of the type, as revealed by `Get-Member`. For example, run `Get-Process | Get-Member` and the first line of output will be

```
TypeName: System.Diagnostics.Process
```

That's the type name you'd put between the `<Name>` and `</Name>` tags. Remember, the tags are case sensitive! From there, all of the extensions for this type would appear between the `<Members>` and `</Members>` tags.

> **NOTE** For the four following examples, we'll focus on the Process type. This is a type already extended by Microsoft, and when you prepend your extension, you're going to essentially turn off Microsoft's extensions. That's okay. Closing and reopening the shell will put Microsoft's extensions back into place.

27.3.1 *AliasProperty*

Remember that an alias simply defines an alternate name for accessing an existing property. An `AliasProperty` extension looks like this:

```
<AliasProperty>
    <Name>PID</Name>
    <ReferencedMemberName>Id</ReferencedMemberName>
</AliasProperty>
```

You've just created a new property called PID, which will point to the underlying ID property of the process type.

27.3.2 *ScriptProperty*

A `ScriptProperty` is a value that's calculated or returned from executing a small PowerShell expression. A `ScriptProperty` extension looks like this:

```
<ScriptProperty>
    <Name>Company</Name>
    <GetScriptBlock>
      $this.Mainmodule.FileVersionInfo.CompanyName
    </GetScriptBlock>
</ScriptProperty>
```

You're adding a new property called `Company` (this extension is one of the ones Microsoft provides for the process type). It runs a script, which uses the special $this variable (see about_Automatic_Variables). That variable always refers to the current instance of the type. In other words, when you've created a process object—usually by running `Get-Process`, which creates several objects—$this will refer to a single process. Here you're using it to access the process type's native `Mainmodule.FileVersionInfo.CompanyName` property. In other words, you're not running any .NET Framework code; you're simply providing an easier way to access a deeply nested property that's already there.

27.3.3 *ScriptMethod*

A `ScriptMethod` is a method that you define in your extension. The method's *action* is coded by one or more PowerShell commands. Here's what a `ScriptMethod` looks like:

```
<ScriptMethod>
    <Name>Terminate</Name>
    <Script>
      $this.Kill()
    </Script>
</ScriptMethod>
```

This isn't a fancy `ScriptMethod`: You're simply creating a method called `Terminate()` that executes the object's `Kill()` method. *Kill* just seemed so forceful and gritty that we felt more comfortable with the softer, friendlier-sounding `Terminate()`. Your `ScriptMethods` can contain much more complicated scripts, if needed, although we'll again point out that the $this variable provides access to the current object instance.

ScriptMethod or ScriptProperty?

The difference between a `ScriptProperty` and a `ScriptMethod` can be somewhat arbitrary. Under the hood, the .NET Framework doesn't technically have properties—they're implemented as methods. So the line is blurry all the way down! Which you choose to use depends on how you plan to use whatever the extension produces.

If you plan to display information as part of the type's normal output, such as in a list or a table, you want to make a `ScriptProperty`. Like all the other properties available in PowerShell, a `ScriptProperty` can be used with Format cmdlets, with `Select-Object`, and with other cmdlets that choose rows and columns to display.

(continued)

If you're planning on filtering objects based on the contents of something, a `Script-Property` will do the job. So, if you can imagine your data being used as criteria in a `Where-Object` cmdlet, use a `ScriptProperty` to expose that data.

A `ScriptMethod` is generally used when you need to access *outside information*, such as getting data from another computer, from a database, and so on. A `Script-Method` is also a good choice when you're transforming data, such as changing the format of a date or time. You'll notice that every object produced by `Get-WmiObject`, for example, includes a couple of `ScriptMethods` for reformatting dates. The `Convert-ToDateTime` script method is useful and saves a lot of additional effort.

27.3.4 *DefaultDisplayPropertySet*

Because Microsoft once had big plans for property sets—most of which were never realized—the XML for creating a `DefaultDisplayPropertySet` is a bit more complicated than you might think necessary. A property set is a collection of properties that can be referenced by a single property name. The `DefaultDisplayPropertySet` is therefore made up of a few other properties, hence the complexity:

```
<MemberSet>
    <Name>PSStandardMembers</Name>
    <Members>
        <PropertySet>
            <Name>DefaultDisplayPropertySet</Name>
            <ReferencedProperties>
                <Name>ID</Name>
                <Name>Name</Name>
            </ReferencedProperties>
        </PropertySet>
    </Members>
</MemberSet>
```

We know, it's a lot. You're just worried about the `<Name></Name>` tag pairs that identify the properties you want displayed by default. Here, you're identifying two: `Name` and `ID`. Because that's less than five, it'll be displayed as a table. But keep in mind that PowerShell doesn't even look for a `DefaultDisplayPropertySet` unless it can't find a predefined view. In the case of the process type, there's a predefined view, which constructs the familiar multicolumn table that you see when you run `Get-Process`. As a result, your `DefaultDisplayPropertySet` won't have any effect on the shell's operation or output.

27.4 *A complete example*

Next, you'll create a short script that illustrates how these type extensions are used. This isn't how you'd normally deploy a type extension; it's preferable to load them as part of a module. In chapter 32 that's exactly what you'll do. For now, let's keep things simple and have the script load the type extension file every time you run it.

First, create the type extension file shown in listing 27.1. Save it as `OurTypes`
`.ps1xml` in your C directory. Next, create the script shown in listing 27.2, which uses the
type extension. This type extension is for a new type that you're creating in your script.

Listing 27.1   OurTypes.ps1xml

```xml
<?xml version="1.0" encoding="utf-8" ?>
<Types>
    <Type>
        <Name>OurTypes.Computer</Name>
        <Members>
            <AliasProperty>
                <Name>Host</Name>
                <ReferencedMemberName>ComputerName</ReferencedMemberName>
            </AliasProperty>
            <ScriptProperty>
                <Name>MfgModel</Name>
                <GetScriptBlock>
                  $this.Model + ' ' + $this.Manufacturer
                </GetScriptBlock>
            </ScriptProperty>
            <ScriptMethod>
                <Name>IsReachable</Name>
                <Script>
                  Test-Connection $this.computername -quiet
                </Script>
            </ScriptMethod>
            <MemberSet>
                <Name>PSStandardMembers</Name>
                <Members>
                    <PropertySet>
                        <Name>DefaultDisplayPropertySet</Name>
                        <ReferencedProperties>
                          <Name>ComputerName</Name>
                          <Name>MfgModel</Name>
                        </ReferencedProperties>
                    </PropertySet>
                </Members>
            </MemberSet>
        </Members>
    </Type>
</Types>
```

Listing 27.2   The type extension test script

```powershell
param([string]$computername)
Update-TypeData -AppendPath C:\OurTypes.ps1xml -EA SilentlyContinue
$bios = Get-WmiObject -Class Win32_BIOS -ComputerName $computername
$cs = Get-WmiObject -Class Win32_ComputerSystem -ComputerName $computername
$properties = @{ComputerName=$computername
                Manufacturer=$cs.manufacturer
                Model=$cs.model
                BIOSSerial=$bios.serialnumber}
$obj = New-Object -TypeName PSObject -Property $properties
```

```
$obj.PSObject.TypeNames.Insert(0,"OurTypes.Computer")
Write-Output $obj
```

Notice that the script in listing 27.2 uses `-EA SilentlyContinue` when it attempts to load the type extension. That's because you'll get an error if you try to load an extension that's already in memory. For this simple demonstration, you're suppressing the error.

Running your script produces the following output:

```
ComputerName                            MfgModel
------------                            --------
localhost                               VMware Virtual Platform VMware, Inc.
```

If you pipe your script's output to `Get-Member`, you'll see this:

```
    TypeName: OurTypes.Computer

Name          MemberType      Definition
----          ----------      ----------
Host          AliasProperty   Host = ComputerName
Equals        Method          bool Equals(System.Object obj)
GetHashCode   Method          int GetHashCode()
GetType       Method          type GetType()
ToString      Method          string ToString()
BIOSSerial    NoteProperty    System.String BIOSSerial=VMware-56 4d 47 10...
ComputerName  NoteProperty    System.String ComputerName=localhost
Manufacturer  NoteProperty    System.String Manufacturer=VMware, Inc.
Model         NoteProperty    System.String Model=VMware Virtual Platform
IsReachable   ScriptMethod    System.Object IsReachable();
MfgModel      ScriptProperty  System.Object MfgModel {get=$this.Model + '...
```

You can see that your `ScriptMethod` and `ScriptProperty` are both there, as well as your `AliasProperty`. Your default display only included the two properties you specified as your `DefaultDisplayPropertySet`. You can also see your `ScriptMethod` in action:

```
PS C:\> $object = ./test localhost
PS C:\> $object.IsReachable()
True
```

Now, we do have to admit to something: Given that the object produced by the script was created by that script, we could've had you add your `AliasProperty`, `Script-Property`, and `ScriptMethod` right in the script. We suppose you could've added the `DefaultDisplayPropertySet` that way too, although the syntax is pretty complicated. So why bother with the XML file? Because you may produce this same type of object in other scripts. You can also control the default data displayed by your object. By defining these type extensions in the XML file and loading that into memory, you're applying your extensions to this object type no matter where it's created. It's a much more centralized way of doing things, and it keeps your script nice and easy to read.

27.5 Updating type data dynamically

If you've made it this far into the chapter, you're probably thinking that creating custom type extensions is a lot of work. Well, it doesn't have to be. One of the reasons we went through the previous material is so that you understand how it all works. Now that you do, we'll show you some easier ways to add custom type extensions that were introduced in PowerShell v3.

Earlier we showed you how to use `Update-TypeData` to load type extensions from an XML file. But you can also use the cmdlet to define a type extension for the current PowerShell session without an XML file. You'll need to know the type name, which you can get by piping an object to `Get-Member`, the type of member (such as `Script-Property`), and a value. Here's a quick example:

```
Update-TypeData -TypeName system.io.fileinfo `
-MemberType ScriptProperty -MemberName IsScript -Value {
 $extensions=".ps1",".bat",".vbs",".cmd";
if ($this.extension -in $extensions) {$True} else {$False}
 }
```

This command is adding a `ScriptProperty` to the file object type. The name of this new member is `IsScript`. The value will be calculated for each file by testing if the file extension of the current object (`$this`) is in a defined list of script extensions. If it is, the value will be `True`.

Once it's loaded, you can run a command like this:

```
PS C:\> dir c:\work\ -file | select Name,IsScript
Name                          IsScript
----                          --------
a.xml                           False
AccessMaskConstants.ps1         True
acl-formatdemo.ps1              True
add-managemember.ps1            True
add-managemember2.ps1           True
Audit.ps1                       True
b.txt                           False
b.xml                           False
Backup-EventLog.ps1             True
Backup-EventLogv2.ps1           True
Backup-FolderToCloud.ps1        True
Backup-VM.ps1                   True
BackupAllEventLogs.ps1          True
...
```

Remember, the new property isn't part of the default display so you need to specify it.

For quick, ad hoc type extensions, this approach is handy. You can also redefine types without having to start a new PowerShell session. If your extension doesn't work the way you want, revise and add it again, but use the `-Force` parameter to overwrite the existing type extension.

You can't accomplish everything that you can in an XML file, and if you need to define multiple members, you'll need multiple commands. The following listing demonstrates how to add several new type extensions.

Listing 27.3   Adding dynamic type extensions

```
$type="System.Management.ManagementObject#root\cimv2\Win32_OperatingSystem"
Update-TypeData -TypeName $type `
-MemberType ScriptProperty -MemberName LastBoot `
-Value { $This.ConvertToDateTime($this.LastBootUpTime)}
Update-TypeData -TypeName $type `
-MemberType ScriptProperty -MemberName Installed `
-Value { $This.ConvertToDateTime($this.InstallDate)}
Update-TypeData -TypeName $type `
-MemberType AliasProperty -MemberName OperatingSystem `
-Value {Caption}
Update-TypeData -TypeName $type `
-MemberType AliasProperty -MemberName Computername `
-Value {CSName}
Update-TypeData -TypeName $type `
-MemberType AliasProperty -MemberName ServicePack `
-Value {CSDVersion}
Update-TypeData -TypeName $type `
-DefaultDisplayPropertySet
     Computername,Operatingsystem,ServicePack,OSArchitecture,
Installed,LastBoot    -Force
```

① **Define script property**
② **Define script property**
③ **Define alias property**
④ **Define alias property**
⑤ **Define alias property**
⑥ **Define default display property set**

Listing 27.3 first defines new properties (①, ②). The existing properties are formatted in the less-than-friendly WMI date time format. We like easy-to-read date times, so this listing uses the `ConvertToDateTime()` method that's part of every WMI object in Power-Shell and converts the existing value. You can't overwrite the existing value, `LastBoot-UpTime`, because you'll end up in a loop. That's why you created new properties.

You then created alias properties (③, ④, ⑤). Some WMI property names are less than meaningful. Finally, you redefined the default display property ⑥ to use the new properties. This means that when you display a `Win32_OperatingSystem` object, you'll get a new default display. You might've preferred to create a `PropertySet`, which would leave the default intact. But you can't do that dynamically. This is a situation where using an XML file would be a better solution.

You can confirm the changes by looking at an instance of `Win32_OperatingSystem` with `Get-Member`:

```
PS C:\> get-wmiobject win32_operatingsystem |
>> get-member -MemberType AliasProperty,ScriptProperty

   TypeName:
System.Management.ManagementObject#root\cimv2\Win32_OperatingSystem

Name            MemberType      Definition
----            ----------      ----------
Computername    AliasProperty   Computername = CSName
OperatingSystem AliasProperty   OperatingSystem = Caption
PSComputerName  AliasProperty   PSComputerName = __SERVER
ServicePack     AliasProperty   ServicePack = CSDVersion
Installed       ScriptProperty  System.Object Installed {get=
$This.Conve...
LastBoot        ScriptProperty  System.Object LastBoot {get=
$This.Conver...
```

And here's what it looks like in action:

```
PS C:\> get-wmiobject win32_operatingsystem

Computername    : RSSURFACEPRO2
Operatingsystem : Microsoft Windows 8.1 Pro
ServicePack     :
OSArchitecture  : 64-bit
Installed       : 05/12/2013 10:16:49
LastBoot        : 27/01/2014 17:27:00
```

These extensions will remain for the duration of the current PowerShell session.

27.6   *Get-TypeData*

Another feature introduced in PowerShell v3 is the ability to examine all of the currently installed type extensions with Get-TypeData:

```
PS C:\> get-typedata

TypeName                                    Members
--------                                    -------
System.Array                                {[Count, System.Management.Au...
System.Xml.XmlNode                          {[ToString, System.Management...
System.Xml.XmlNodeList                      {[ToString, System.Management...
System.Management.Automation.PSDriveInfo    {[Used, System.Management.Aut...
System.DirectoryServices.PropertyValu...    {[ToString, System.Management...
System.Drawing.Printing.PrintDocument       {[Name, System.Management.Aut...
System.Management.Automation.Applicat...    {[FileVersionInfo, System.Ma...
System.DateTime                             {[DateTime, System.Managemen...
System.Net.IPAddress                        {[IPAddressToString, System.M...
...
```

The output is a TypeData object. Let's look at the WMI object you modified in the previous section:

```
PS C:\> $type = 'System.Management.ManagementObject#
➥ root\cimv2\Win32_OperatingSystem'
PS C:\> Get-TypeData $type | select *

TypeName                      : System.Management.ManagementObject#root\
                                cimv2\Win32_OperatingSystem...
Members                       : {[Installed,
                                System.Management.Automation.Runspaces.
                                ScriptPropertyData],
                                [OperatingSystem,
                                System.Management.Automation.Runspaces.
                                AliasPropertyData],
                                [Computername,
                                System.Management.Automation.Runspaces.
                                AliasPropertyData],
                                [ServicePack,
                                System.Management.Automation.Runspaces.
                                AliasPropertyData]...}
TypeConverter                 :
TypeAdapter                   :
IsOverride                    : False
```

```
SerializationMethod             :
TargetTypeForDeserialization    :
SerializationDepth              : 0
DefaultDisplayProperty          :
InheritPropertySerializationSet : False
StringSerializationSource       :
DefaultDisplayPropertySet       : System.Management.Automation.Runspaces.
                                  PropertySetData
DefaultKeyPropertySet           :
PropertySerializationSet        :
```

You can see the new members you defined. You can also see the new default display property set:

```
PS C:\> Get-TypeData $type |
>> select -ExpandProperty DefaultDisplayPropertySet
>>

ReferencedProperties
--------------------
{Computername, Operatingsystem, ServicePack, OSArchitecture...}
```

27.7   Remove-TypeData

If you decide to revert your type extensions, you can use the Remove-TypeData cmdlet. This cmdlet will remove extensions from the current session regardless of whether they were loaded from an XML file or dynamically. Only the extensions in the current session, and no XML files, are deleted. Go ahead and remove the WMI extensions you've been testing:

```
PS C:\> Remove-TypeData $type
```

You can now continue in your current session and Win32_OperatingSystem instances will be displayed just as before. Well, almost. When you remove the type it also removes the default display property set, so the next time you run a command you'll get all properties. If you think you might need to revert, save the default display set first:

```
$dds = Get-TypeData $type |
select -ExpandProperty DefaultDisplayPropertySet |
select -ExpandProperty ReferencedProperties
```

Then, should you need to reset them, you can do so dynamically:

```
PS C:\> Update-TypeData -TypeName $type –DefaultDisplayPropertySet $dds
```

The only way to return to a completely default environment is to start a new PowerShell session, but if you plan ahead it might save some headaches.

27.8   Summary

Type extensions aren't something every administrator needs to worry about. They're definitely a specialized piece of PowerShell. But when you run into a situation that calls for them, it's certainly nice to know how they work. Keep in mind that those XML files are case sensitive! We usually prefer to copy and paste chunks of XML from Microsoft's types.ps1xml file and then modify our pasted parts to suit our needs. That way, we're much less likely to mess up the XML. Always, always remember *not* to modify the default PowerShell type files but create your own and use `Update-TypeData` to load them into memory either from an XML file or dynamically.

28
Data language and internationalization

This chapter covers

- Creating localized data tables
- Using PSD1 files
- Testing localized scripts

PowerShell v2 introduced a *data language* element for the shell, designed to help separate text from the functional code of a script or command. By separating text, you can make it easier to swap out alternate versions of that text. The primary use case for doing so is *localizing* a script, meaning you swap out your original language text strings for an alternate language. *Internationalization* is the act of designing your code to enable this swap-out of language-specific data.

We acknowledge up front that this is a fairly specialized feature and that few administrators will typically use it, though if you're working for a large multinational company this feature might just be a big help. We're including it to help ensure that this book is as complete as possible, but we'll keep it brief. You can find additional help in two of PowerShell's help files: about_script_internationalization and about_data_sections.

28.1   *Internationalization basics*

Internationalization is implemented through several specific features in PowerShell:

- A data section, which we'll discuss next, that contains all the text strings intended for display or other output.
- Two built-in variables, $PSCulture and $PSUICulture, that store the name of the user interface language in use by the current system. That way, you can detect the language that the current user is using in Windows. $PSCulture contains the language used for regional settings such as date, time, and currency formats, whereas $PSUICulture contains the language for user interface elements such as menus and text strings.
- ConvertFrom-StringData, a cmdlet that converts text strings into a hash table, which makes it easier to import a batch of strings in a specific language and then use them from within your script. By varying the batch that you import, you can dynamically vary what your script outputs.
- The PSD1 file type, which in addition to being used for module manifests, can be used to store language-specific strings. You provide a single PSD1 file for each language you want to support.
- Import-LocalizedData, a cmdlet that imports translated text strings for a specific language into a script.

Changes to the handling of culture

Don't assume anything about the cultures that PowerShell is running. One of us is based in the UK and in PowerShell v2 gets these results returned for $PSCulture and $PSUICulture:

```
PS C:\> $psculture
en-GB
PS C:\> $psuiculture
en-US
```

Notice that $PSCulture is what you'd expect but that the UI culture is set to US English. Additional cultural information can be found by using Get-Culture and Get-UICulture.

You should also note that in PowerShell v2 the culture can be changed, but the UI culture is dependent on the cultural version of Windows installed. This can have unintended consequences when you're trying to run a localized script.

In PowerShell v3 and v4, this changes:

```
PS C:\> $PSCulture
en-GB
PS C:\> $PSUICulture
en-GB
```

The UI culture now reflects the system settings rather than being fixed.

(continued)
Windows 8, Windows 8.1, Windows Server 2012, and Windows Server 2012 R2 have an International module that enables changes to cultural settings. You do have to restart PowerShell for the changes to take effect. We present an alternative method of temporarily changing the current culture in section 28.4. This method is great for testing multiple cultural scenarios.

We figure the best way to show you all this is to dive into a sample project and explain as we go, so that's what we'll do. We're going to start with a script (shown in listing 28.1) that's functionally very simple.

NOTE The scripts in this chapter are written on PowerShell v3 and have been tested on PowerShell v3 and v4. Don't assume backward compatibility to Power-Shell v2 on your system, especially if it uses a culture different from the ones we've used. If your machine has a culture setting different from ours, test internationalized scripts carefully because we can't test all possible combinations of settings.

Notice that the script includes several `Write-Verbose` statements that output strings of text. We'll focus on those for our internationalization efforts. For our examples, we're using Google Translate to produce non-English text strings. We hope any native speakers of our chosen languages will forgive any translation errors.

Listing 28.1 Our starting point, Tools.psm1

```
function Get-OSInfo {
    [CmdletBinding()]
    param(
        [Parameter(Mandatory=$True,ValueFromPipeline=$True)]
        [string[]]$computerName
    )
    BEGIN {
        Write-Verbose "Starting Get-OSInfo"           ◄
    }
    PROCESS {
        ForEach ($computer in $computername) {
            try {
                $connected = $True
                Write-Verbose "Attempting $computer"   ◄    Write-
                $os = Get-WmiObject -ComputerName $computer `   verbose
                                -Class Win32_OperatingSystem `   calls
                                -ErrorAction Stop
            } catch {
                $connected = $false
                Write-Verbose "Connection to $computer failed"   ◄
            }
            if ($connected) {
                Write-Verbose "Connection to $computer succeeded"  ◄
                $cs = Get-WmiObject -ComputerName $computer `
                                -Class Win32_ComputerSystem
```

```
                    $props = @{'ComputerName'=$computer;
                              'OSVersion'=$os.version;
                              'Manufacturer'=$cs.manufacturer;
                              'Model'=$cs.model}
                    $obj = New-Object -TypeName PSObject -Property $props
                    Write-Output $obj
                }
            }
        }
        END {                                                        Write-verbose
            Write-Verbose "Ending Get-OSInfo"                        calls
        }
    }
```

NOTE This listing uses the backtick (`` ` ``) character so that longer lines could be broken into multiple physical lines. If you're typing this in, be sure to include the backtick character, and make sure it's the very last thing on the line—it can't be followed by any spaces or tabs. We don't think it's the prettiest way to type code, but it makes it easier to fit it within the constraints of the printed page.

Save this script as Tools.psm1 in \Documents\WindowsPowerShell\Modules\Tools\. Doing so will enable it to be autoloaded when PowerShell starts. Alternatively, you can load it into the console by running `Import-Module tools` and test it by running `Get-OSInfo -computername $env:COMPUTERNAME`. If you're going to follow along, make sure that you can successfully complete those steps before continuing.

28.2 Adding a data section

Currently, your script has hardcoded strings—primarily the `Write-Verbose` statements, which we're going to address—but also the output object's property names. You could also localize the property names, but we're not going to ask you to do that. Generally speaking, even Microsoft doesn't translate those because other bits of code might take a dependency on the property names, and translating them would break those dependencies. If you wanted the property names to *display* with translated column names, then you could use a custom view to do that. You also can't localize any parameter help messages in comment-based help that you might've added to your scripting project.

Take a look at the next listing, where you're adding a data section to contain your default strings.

Listing 28.2 Adding a data section to Tools.psm1

```
$msgTable = Data {                                            Data section  ❶
    # culture="en-US"
    ConvertFrom-StringData @'
        attempting = Attempting
        connectionTo = Connection to
        failed = failed
        succeeded = succeeded
```

```
        starting = Starting Get-OSInfo
        ending = Ending Get-OSInfo
'@
}
function Get-OSInfo {
    [CmdletBinding()]
    param(
        [Parameter(Mandatory=$True,ValueFromPipeline=$True)]
        [string[]]$computerName
    )
    BEGIN {
        Write-Verbose $msgTable.starting
    }
    PROCESS {
        ForEach ($computer in $computername) {
            try {
                $connected = $True
                Write-Verbose "$($msgTable.attempting) $computer"
                $os = Get-WmiObject -ComputerName $computer `
                                    -Class Win32_OperatingSystem `
                                    - ErrorAction Stop
            } catch {
                $connected = $false
                Write-Verbose "$($msgTable.connectionTo) $computer
$($msgTable.failed)"
            }
            if ($connected) {
                Write-Verbose `
        "$($msgTable.connectionTo) $computer $($msgTable.succeeded)"
                $cs = Get-WmiObject -ComputerName $computer `
                                    -Class Win32_ComputerSystem
                $props = @{'ComputerName'=$computer;
                           'OSVersion'=$os.version;
                           'Manufacturer'=$cs.manufacturer;
                           'Model'=$cs.model}
                $obj = New-Object -TypeName PSObject -Property $props
                Write-Output $obj
            }
        }
    }
    END {
        Write-Verbose $msgTable.ending
    }
}
Export-ModuleMember -function "Get-OSInfo"
```

String property ❷

Export-ModuleMember ❸

In listing 28.2, you've added a data section ❶. This uses the ConvertFrom-StringData cmdlet to convert a here-string into a hash table. The end result is that you'll have a $msgTable object, with properties named connectionTo, starting, ending, and so on. The properties will contain the English-language values shown in the script. You can then use those properties ❷ whenever you want to display the associated text. Because this is a script module, it'd ordinarily make the $msgTable variable accessible to the global shell once the module is imported. You don't want that; you'd rather

$msgTable remain *internal use only* within this module. So you've also added an Export-ModuleMember call ❸. By exporting your Get-OSInfo function, everything else—that is, everything you don't explicitly export—remains private to the module and accessible only to other things within the script file.

Test the changes by removing the module, reimporting it, and then running it. Be sure to use the –Verbose switch so that you can test your localized output. Here's what it should look like:

```
PS C:\> remove-module tools
PS C:\> import-module tools
PS C:\> Get-OSInfo -computerName localhost
Manufacturer      OSVersion        ComputerName      Model
------------      ---------        ------------      -----
VMware, Inc.      6.1.7601         localhost         VMware Virtua...

PS C:\> Get-OSInfo -computerName localhost -verbose
VERBOSE: Starting Get-OSInfo
VERBOSE: Attempting localhost
VERBOSE: Connection to localhost succeeded
Manufacturer      OSVersion        ComputerName      Model
------------      ---------        ------------      -----
VMware, Inc.      6.1.7601         localhost         VMware Virtua...
VERBOSE: Ending Get-OSInfo
```

As you can see, your changes seem to be successful. Your verbose output is displaying with the correct English-language strings. Now you can move on to the next step: creating translated versions of those strings.

28.3   *Storing translated strings*

You need to set up some new text files and a directory structure to store the translated strings. Each text file will contain a copy of your data section. Begin by creating the following new directories and files:

- \Documents\WindowsPowerShell\Modules\Tools\de-DE\Tools.PSD1
- \Documents\WindowsPowerShell\Modules\Tools\es\Tools.PSD1

By doing so, you create two localized languages, German and Spanish. The "es" and "de-DE," as well as the "en-US" used in your data section, are language codes defined by Microsoft. You have to use the correct codes, so be sure to consult the list at http://msdn.microsoft.com/en-us/library/ms533052(v=vs.85).aspx. The filenames must also match the name of the module or script file that you're localizing.

With the files created, copy your ConvertFrom-StringData command from the original script into the two new PSD1 files. You'll then translate the strings. Listings 28.3 and 28.4 show the final result. As we said, you're just using Google Translate here—we're sure the results will be amusing to anyone who knows what these mean.

> **Listing 28.3   German version of Tools.PSD1**

```
ConvertFrom-StringData @'
    attempting = Versuch
```

```
        connectionTo = Der anschluss an
        failed = gescheitert
        succeeded = gelungen
        starting = Ab Get-OSInfo
        ending = Ende Get-OSInfo
'@
```

Listing 28.4 Spanish version of Tools.PSD1

```
    ConvertFrom-StringData @'
        attempting = Intentar
        connectionTo = Conexion a
        failed = fracasado
        succeeded = exito
        starting = A partir Get-OSInfo
        ending = Final Get-OSInfo
'@
```

NOTE The way in which you type the here-strings is very specific. The closing `'@` can't be indented—it must be typed in the first two characters of a line, all by itself. Read about_here_strings in PowerShell for more information on them.

You also have to move the en-US version of the data out into its own PSD1 file; otherwise, you'll see this sort of error when you try to import the module:

```
PS C:\> Import-Module tools -Force

Import-LocalizedData : Cannot find PowerShell data file
'toolsPSD1' in directory 'C:\Scripts\Modules\tools\en-US\' or
any parent culture directories.
At C:\Scripts\Modules\tools\tools.psm1:12 char:1
+ Import-LocalizedData -BindingVariable $msgTable
+ ~~~~~~~~~~~~~~~~~~~~~~~~~~~~~~~~~~~~~~~~~~~~~~~~~~
    + CategoryInfo      : ObjectNotFound: (C:\Scripts\Modu...n-
US\toolsPSD1:String) [Import-LocalizedData],
PSInvalidOperationException + FullyQualifiedErrorId :
ImportLocalizedData,
Microsoft.PowerShell.Commands.ImportLocalizedData
```

If you allow automatic loading of the module to occur (PowerShell v3 and v4), you'll get an error that looks like this:

```
Write-Verbose : Cannot bind argument to parameter 'Message' because it is null
```

But the output should be produced. There are no guarantees on cultures we haven't tested. The following listing shows the file. Save it in an en-US subfolder of your module folder.

Listing 28.5 en-US version of Tools.PSD1

```
    ConvertFrom-StringData @'
        attempting = Attempting
        connectionTo = Connection to
```

```
        failed = failed
        succeeded = succeeded
        starting = Starting Get-OSInfo
        ending = Ending Get-OSInfo
'@
```

You're not quite ready to retest the script; you must modify it to load the translated data. That's done with the `Import-LocalizedData` cmdlet, and one of the two built-in variables we mentioned earlier will play a role. The cmdlet automatically uses `$PSUICulture`'s contents to figure out which PSD1 file to import. That means it can be tricky to test on a single-language Windows installation. We've called upon our international MVP contacts, who own localized versions of Windows, to help us test this. The following listing shows the changes to Tools.psm1.

Listing 28.6   Modifying tools.psm1 to import the current language

```
Import-LocalizedData -BindingVariable msgTable         ◀─┐  Import current
function Get-OSInfo {                                    ❶ language
    [CmdletBinding()]
    param(
        [Parameter(Mandatory=$True,ValueFromPipeline=$True)]
        [string[]] $computerName
    )
    BEGIN {
        Write-Verbose $msgTable.starting
    }
    PROCESS {
        ForEach ($computer in $computername) {
            try {
                $connected = $True
                Write-Verbose "$($msgTable.attempting) $computer"
                $os = Get-WmiObject -ComputerName $computer `
                                    -Class Win32_OperatingSystem `
                                    -ErrorAction Stop
            } catch {
                $connected = $false
                Write-Verbose `
        "$($msgTable.connectionTo) $computer $($msgTable.failed)"
            }
            if ($connected) {
                Write-Verbose `
        "$($msgTable.connectionTo) $computer $($msgTable.succeeded)"
                $cs = Get-WmiObject -ComputerName $computer `
                                    -Class Win32_ComputerSystem
                $props = @{'ComputerName'=$computer;
                           'OSVersion'=$os.version;
                           'Manufacturer'=$cs.manufacturer;
                           'Model'=$cs.model}
                $obj = New-Object -TypeName PSObject -Property $props
                Write-Output $obj
            }
        }
    }
}
```

```
    END {
        Write-Verbose $msgTable.ending
    }
}
Export-ModuleMember -function "Get-OSInfo"
```

Listing 28.6 adds the `Import-LocalizedData` command ❶. Because it isn't contained in a function, it's executed when your module is loaded. The binding variable will be used to define a hash table of localized strings. Make sure you don't insert a $ in front of the variable. The neat thing about this command is that it automatically reads $PSUICulture, which we've mentioned, and looks for the PSD1 file in the appropriate subfolder. If it doesn't find the right file, it throws an error as shown.

28.4 Testing localization

Testing nonnative localization is bit more difficult. Ideally you'll want to test on a computer running the appropriate language. But there's a workaround—okay, a hack—that you can use to test localization. You can't just assign a new value to the $PSUICulture variable. You must start a temporary PowerShell thread using a new culture, as shown in the next listing.

Listing 28.7 Testing localization with Using-Culture.ps1

```
Param (
    [Parameter(Position=0,Mandatory=$True,`
    HelpMessage="Enter a new culture like de-DE")]
    [ValidateNotNullOrEmpty()]
    [System.Globalization.CultureInfo]$culture,
    [Parameter(Position=1,Mandatory=$True,`
    HelpMessage="Enter a script block or command to run.")]
    [ValidateNotNullorEmpty()]
    [scriptblock]$Scriptblock
)
Write-Verbose "Testing with culture $culture"
#save current culture values
$OldCulture = $PSCulture
$OldUICulture = $PSUICulture
#define a trap in case something goes wrong so we can revert back.
#better safe than sorry
trap
{
    [System.Threading.Thread]::CurrentThread.CurrentCulture = $OldCulture
    [System.Threading.Thread]::CurrentThread.CurrentUICulture = $OldUICulture
    Continue
}
#set the new culture
[System.Threading.Thread]::CurrentThread.CurrentCulture = $culture
[System.Threading.Thread]::CurrentThread.CurrentUICulture = $culture
#run the command
Invoke-command $ScriptBlock
#roll culture settings back
```

```
[System.Threading.Thread]::CurrentThread.CurrentCulture = $OldCulture
[System.Threading.Thread]::CurrentThread.CurrentUICulture = $OldUICulture
```

To use this test function, specify a culture and a script block of PowerShell commands to execute. The script modifies the culture of the thread and then invokes the script block. Use the following to test your module:

```
PS C:\Scripts> .\Using-Culture.ps1 de-de {import-module tools -force;
➥ get-osinfo client2 -verbose}
VERBOSE: Ab Get-OSInfo
VERBOSE: Versuch client2
VERBOSE: Der anschluss an client2 gelungen
Model               ComputerName        OSVersion        Manufacturer
-----               ------------        ---------        ------------
VirtualBox          client2             6.1.7601         innotek GmbH
VERBOSE: Ende Get-OSInfo
```

The –Force parameter is used when importing the module to ensure that the culture is refreshed correctly. It isn't necessary to run PowerShell with elevated privileges to work with cultures in this way. We do recommend that you check carefully that your settings have been put back to the correct values when you've finished.

Although we've been demonstrating using a module, you can localize individual scripts and functions as well. Jeff has done a fair amount of localization work for a client that includes many stand-alone functions. Let's look at another localization example that also demonstrates how to incorporate variables into your localized strings using the –f operator.

The following listing is the main script that contains a single function.

> **Listing 28.8 A localized function, Get-Data.ps1**

```
Import-LocalizedData -BindingVariable msgTable
Function Get-Data {
[cmdletbinding()]
Param()
Write-Verbose ($msgtable.msg3 -f (Get-Date),$myinvocation.mycommand)
Write-Host $msgtable.msg5 -foreground Magenta
$svc=Get-Service | where {$_.status -eq "running"}
Write-Host ($msgtable.msg1 -f $svc.count)
Write-Host $msgtable.msg6 -foreground Magenta
$procs=Get-Process
Write-Host ($msgtable.msg2 -f $procs.count,$env:computername)
Write-verbose ($msgtable.msg4 -f (Get-Date),$myinvocation.mycommand)
}
```

The function in listing 28.8 isn't the most groundbreaking function, but it makes a nice demonstration. Notice that you've moved the message strings to a culture-specific PSD1 file. Again, this will require a subfolder named for the appropriate culture. You're testing with en-US and de-DE (listings 28.9 and 28.10).

Listing 28.9   English Get-DataPSD1

```
#English US strings
ConvertFrom-StringData @"
MSG1= Found {0} services that are running.
MSG2= Found {0} processes on the computer {1}.
MSG3= {0} Starting command {1}
MSG4= {0} Ending command {1}
MSG5= Getting the list of services that are currently running.
MSG6= Getting all of the running processes.
"@
```

Listing 28.10   German Get-DataPSD1

```
#localized German strings
ConvertFrom-StringData @"
MSG1= Gefunden {0} Dienste, die ausgeführt.
MSG2= Gefunden {0} Prozesse auf dem Computer {1}.
MSG3= {0} Ab Befehl {1}
MSG4= {0} Ende-Befehl {1}
MSG5= Getting der Liste der Dienste, die derzeit ausgeführt werden.
MSG6= Getting alle laufenden Prozesse.
"@
```

First, run the function on a computer that uses the en-US culture:

```
PS C:\> get-data -verbose
VERBOSE: 11/25/2013 8:35:19 PM Starting command Get-Data
Getting the list of services that are currently running.
Found 67 services that are running.
Getting all of the running processes.
Found 37 processes on the computer CLIENT2.
VERBOSE: 11/25/2013 8:35:19 PM Ending command Get-Data
```

Now, test it with your Using-Culture script:

```
PS C:\Scripts> .\Using-Culture.ps1 de-de {. f:\get-data.ps1;
➡ get-data -verbose}
VERBOSE: 25.11.2013 20:37:59 Ab Befehl Get-Data
Getting der Liste der Dienste, die derzeit ausgeführt werden.
Gefunden 67 Dienste, die ausgeführt.
Getting alle laufenden Prozesse.
Gefunden 37 Prozesse auf dem Computer CLIENT2.
VERBOSE: 25.11.2013 20:37:59 Ende-Befehl Get-Data
```

Notice that the values have been inserted into the placeholders. Also notice that the date time format was affected by the change in culture.

Richard took the en-US folder and copied it as en-GB (British English). The date was displayed correctly for that culture. This shows how you can deal with minor cultural differences as well as language issues.

A bit more about data sections

The data section in a script or a PSD1 file has a strict syntax. In general, it can contain only supported cmdlets like `ConvertFrom-StringData`. It can also support PowerShell operators (except `-match`), so that you can do some logical decision making using the `If...ElseIf...Else` construct; no other scripting language constructs are permitted. You can access the `$PSCulture`, `$PSUICulture`, `$True`, `$False`, and `$Null` built-in variables but no others. You can add comments, too. There's a bit more to them, but that's the general overview of what's allowed. You're not meant to put much code in there; they're intended to separate string data from your code, not to contain a bunch *more code*.

28.5   *Summary*

We don't see a lot of cases where administrators need to write localized scripts, but we can certainly imagine them. Larger, international organizations might well want to make the effort to localize scripts, especially when the output will be shown to end users rather than other administrators. PowerShell's built-in support for handling multilanguage scripts is fairly straightforward to use, and as you've seen here it's not difficult to convert a single-language script to this multilanguage format.

Writing help

29

As you develop your own scripts and functions, or even if you dive into .NET Framework programming and create your own binary cmdlets, you'll doubtless want to include help with them. PowerShell's help system (see chapter 3) is a crucial feature for shell users, giving them the ability to discover, learn, and use commands. Without help, your functions and cmdlets become essentially invisible, unlearnable, and unusable. Fortunately, PowerShell makes it relatively easy to write your own help.

One thing we've seen in recent Scripting Games (a competition originally run by Microsoft and now hosted by PowerShell.org; see http://powershell.org/wp/the-scripting-games/ for more information) is that many people try to develop their own way of delivering help. This is a bad idea because it takes time and effort that's better spent in developing additional functionality for your organization. Use comment-based help or XML-based help as described in this chapter to provide the information your users need while minimizing the work you must do.

29.1   *Comment-based help*

The easiest way to provide help is using the shell's comment-based help feature (read about_comment_based_help in the shell for full details). This feature scans scripts, functions, and modules for specially formatted block comments, which use certain keywords to define the common sections of a help file: synopsis, description, parameters, examples, and so forth. Here's an example of a help comment block:

```
<#
.SYNOPSIS
Get-OSInfo retrieves operating system information from one or more remote
computers.
.DESCRIPTION
This command uses a CIM connection to contact remote computers, and
therefore requires that WinRM be enabled and working. Three different
CIM/WMI classes are queried, and the results are output as a single,
consolidated object.
.PARAMETER Computername
Accepts one or more computer names or IP addresses.
.PARAMETER Errorlog
Accepts the path and file name of a text file to which failed computer
names will be written.
.EXAMPLE
This example queries a single computer:
  Get-OSInfo -computerName SERVER2
.EXAMPLE
This example uses pipeline input to query all computers listed in
Names.txt. That file is expected to have one computer name per line.
  Get-Content Names.txt | Get-OSInfo
.LINK
  Get-CimInstance
#>
```

> **NOTE**   We used a block comment, which is surrounded by the <# and #> tags. It's also legal to create comment-based help with the # character at the start of each line, but we find that block comments are easier to type, edit, and read.

Some things to note about this example:

- The keywords .SYNOPSIS, .DESCRIPTION, and so forth don't need to be in uppercase, but typing them this way does help them stand out visually to someone viewing the script.
- The keywords can occur in any order, although they typically follow our example. In any event, we recommend being consistent. Unless stated otherwise each keyword can only be used once.
- Examples aren't numbered. The shell will automatically number them in the order in which they appear. Include as many examples as you'd like. You also don't need to include the shell prompt. The help system will add that automatically. We do recommend, however, adding some explanation after your code example.

- A `.PARAMETER` block should be provided for each parameter that your command exposes. Specify the parameter name after the `.PARAMETER` keyword, as in this example. The help system will pick up on whether your parameter can take pipeline input, what type of object it is, and whether it accepts arrays. But in addition to a brief description, you might want to add information on any aliases or default values.

- Under `.LINK`, add as many cross references as you'd like. These will show up under RELATED LINKS when help is displayed. Optionally, you can add a single URL to point to online help. You should only have a single URL and it must be under its own `.LINK` heading like this:

```
.LINK
   http://intranet/help/Get-OSInfo.htm
.LINK
  Get-WmiObject
  Get-CIMInstance
```

- For a minimally useful help display, include the sections we have in this example: a synopsis, longer description, parameters, and at least one example. Other keywords and sections are available, and you can find some by reading the about_comment_based_help file in the shell.

The real trick with comment-based help is in where you put it.

- For functions, the comment block can appear:
  - Immediately before the function keyword that defines the function, with no more than one blank line between the last line of the comment block and the function keyword.
  - Immediately after the function keyword and within the body of the function. This is the style we prefer and use.
  - At the very end of the function but still within the body of the function. If you use this option, be sure to leave a blank line between the closing comment and the } that closes the function.
- For scripts, the comment block can appear:
  - At the beginning of the script file, preceded only by comment lines or blank lines but not by any code or commands.
  - If the first code in the script body is a function declaration, then any help for the script itself must be followed by at least two blank lines between the last line of help and the function declaration (or the function's help).
  - At the end of the script, unless the script is signed, in which case this isn't a valid location.

NOTE Follow the rules for scripts when adding module-level help to a script module. But if your module includes a number of standalone scripts with your functions, each function can have its own comment-based help.

When your function is loaded into the shell, you should be able to run Get-Help for your command just as if it were a cmdlet. But if you have an error in your comment-based help, all you'll see is your syntax with no idea of why there's no help. Usually it's because a keyword has been misspelled or you're missing the leading period before each keyword. Sometimes the best solution is to let another set of eyes look at your script.

Finally, don't think you need to create all of your help manually. There are a number of scripts and functions you can find that will help create the help content. Jeff has a few such tools on his blog that you might find useful (http://jdhitsolutions.com/blog/2011/10/ise-scripting-geek-module/). One of the easiest ways is to use the Snippets functionality in the ISE to generate an outline advanced function complete with inline comment–based help.

29.2   *Writing About topics*

In addition to comment-based help for your scripts and functions, you can create content help files like PowerShell's About files. This is something you'd typically do with a module. In your module folder, create as many About topics as you want. Make sure the files are TXT files and include Help in the name, as shown in these examples:

```
About_MyModule.help.txt
About_Scripting_Best_Practices.help.txt
```

When your module is loaded, these files will be available as well. You can create these files with any text editor. Use this template:

```
TOPIC
    about_mymodule_content
SHORT DESCRIPTION
    A very short description or synopsis.
LONG DESCRIPTION
    Detailed content goes here
SEE ALSO
    Related cmdlet names
    Related about topics
```

Doing this is quite simple. Look to existing About topics as examples. You might also want to download the ScriptingHelp module from Jeff's blog at http://jdhitsolutions .com/blog/2012/05/introducing-the-scriptinghelp-powershell-module/, which can serve as model for creating and packaging your own About topics.

29.3   *XML-based help*

PowerShell's native help is built into XML files. These offer a few advantages over comment-based help:

- You can provide an XML file for several different languages, and PowerShell will display the correct language based on the local Windows configuration.
- You can download and update XML help files using Save-Help and Update-Help, respectively.

- XML help files can contain a somewhat higher level of detail about commands.
- CDXML-based modules (see chapter 39) can't use comment-based help, so you have to create XML-based help files.

The downside is that XML help files are a lot harder to produce. The XML format used, MAML, is complicated and doesn't leave any room for mistakes or errors. It's definitely outside the scope of this book. Still, if you want to pursue this approach, we recommend that you generate the XML files using one of two free tools:

- An InfoPath template created by a well-known PowerShell expert, James O'Neill, lets you get the basic format right using Microsoft's InfoPath tool, which you'll need to install. We've tested InfoPath 2007 and 2010 with this template. The output of InfoPath can't be used directly by PowerShell, though; you'll have to make some minor adjustments to it after saving it. You can get the template, and directions for using it, from http://blogs.technet.com/b/jamesone/archive/2009/07/24/powershell-on-line-help-a-change-you-should-make-for-v2-3-and-how-to-author-maml-help-files-for-powershell.aspx.
- If you're primarily creating help for modules, you can download a free, standalone help editor from http://blogs.msdn.com/b/powershell/archive/2011/02/24/cmdlet-help-editor-v2-0-with-module-support.aspx. Basically, you copy and paste the different help sections (synopsis, description, and so on) into the tool, and it produces a ready-to-use XML file for you. You can use the tool for standalone functions and scripts, but there's a bit more manual intervention.

If you want to use the InfoPath template, you can use a simple script like the following to make the modifications to the XML.

Listing 29.1 Creating MAML Help

```
param (
    [string]$filepath
)
$line1 = @'
<?xml version="1.0" encoding="UTF-8"?><?mso-infoPathSolution
solutionVersion="1.0.0.12" PIVersion="1.0.0.0"
href="file:///C:\Users\Jamesone\Documents\windowsPowershell\PSH-Help.xsn"
name="urn:schemas-microsoft-com:office:infopath:PSH-Help:"
productVersion="14.0.0" ?><?mso-application progid="InfoPath.Document"
versionProgid="InfoPath.Document.2"?>
<helpItems xmlns="http://msh" schema="maml"
xmlns:xsi="http://www.w3.org/2001/XMLSchema-instance"
xmlns:dev="http://schemas.microsoft.com/maml/dev/2004/10"
xmlns:command="http://schemas.microsoft.com/maml/dev/command/2004/10"
xmlns:maml="http://schemas.microsoft.com/maml/2004/10"
xmlns:my="http://schemas.microsoft.com/office/infopath/2003/myXSD/2009-07-
13T15:24:29" xmlns:xd="http://schemas.microsoft.com/office/infopath/2003"
xml:lang="en-gb">
'@
```

```
if ($filepath -eq $null){
  Throw "Help File Not given"
}
if (!(Test-Path $filepath)){
 Throw "File Not found"
}
$file = Get-Content -Path $filepath
$file[0] = $line1
$outpath = Join-Path -Path $(Split-Path -Path $filepath -Parent) `
-ChildPath $("Maml-" + (Split-Path -Path $filepath -Leaf))
Set-Content -Value $file -Path $outpath
```

This code assumes that the InfoPath file is in the same folder in which you need the MAML file created. It has the advantage of preserving the InfoPath file so that future modifications don't mean any rework.

You'll generate one XML file for each language that you want to support; each file can contain help for many different commands. XML help is intended to be used in conjunction with modules (including script modules); it isn't made to work with standalone scripts or functions. You'll need to use XML-based help for cmdlets produced using the *cmdlets over objects* functionality in PowerShell v3 and v4 (see chapter 39). So, you'll already have a folder structure for your module that might look something like this:

```
\Users\<username>\Documents\WindowsPowerShell\Modules\MyModule
```

This structure assumes your module is named MyModule. Within that folder, you'll create a subfolder for each help file language that you're providing. These folder names must use the standard Windows culture identifiers from RFC 4646. So, to support both English and German help files, you'd create folders named en-US and de-DE under the MyModule folder.

> **NOTE** A list of permitted language identifiers can be found in Appendix B of RFC 4646, at www.ietf.org/rfc/rfc4646.txt. You can see a complete list of currently registered and allowable tags at www.iana.org/assignments/language-subtag-registry.

Within the language subfolder, you'll save your XML file as MyModule-help.xml (because your module name is MyModule; if your module name were Fred, then the filename would be Fred-help.xml). You can also include an about_MyModule.txt file (or about_Fred.txt file, if your module were named Fred), which is just a simple text file that provides information about the overall module rather than about a single command in the module.

If you want your help to be updatable, your module manifest file (PSD1) needs to include a line like this:

```
HelpInfoUri=http://go.microsoft.com/fwlink/?LinkId=227015
```

The link points to the website from which the updated help can be downloaded. This isn't the same link you might use for any online version of your help.

29.4 *Summary*

Adding help is the perfect way to polish the commands you write, whether they're standalone scripts or a collection of functions in a module. Comment-based help is definitely the easiest way to go, and if you don't need to support multiple languages or updatable help there's not much reason to dive into the more complex XML format. But the XML option is there if you can't use comment-based help, need to support multiple languages, or want to provide online, updatable help to your command users.

Error handling techniques

You'll inevitably write a script that contains a command that fails. Failure is often something you can anticipate: A computer isn't online or reachable, a file can't be found, access is denied, and other similar conditions are all ones that you expect from time to time. PowerShell enables you to catch those errors and handle them in your own way. For example, you might want to log a failed computer name to a file for retrying, or you might want to write an entry to the Windows event log when access is denied. *Error handling* is the process of identifying these conditions, catching the error, and doing something about it while continuing your processes on other machines.

The point of this chapter isn't just to teach you how to *catch errors* but rather how to *handle errors gracefully*. A simple script that fails when it encounters an error is *handling* it, but not very well if it fails on the first computer of 30, which means you have to restart the script. This is especially bad news if the script ran as an overnight activity. Proper application of error handling techniques enables you to be more productive. Which do you want your script to report: "I did 299 out of 300 machines and failed on this one" or "It failed"?

30.1 *About errors and exceptions*

Let's begin by defining a few terms. These aren't necessarily official PowerShell terms, but they're useful for describing PowerShell's behavior, so we'll go ahead and use them.

   The first word is *error*. An error in PowerShell is a message that's displayed on screen when something goes wrong. By default, PowerShell displays its errors in red text on a black background (in the console host, that is; the ISE uses red text).

> **TIP** If you find the red on black difficult to read (many folks do), or if it takes you back to high school English class and red-penned essays, you can change the color. Don prefers green on black; he says it's easy to read and makes him feel like he's done something right: `$host.PrivateData.ErrorForeground-Color = 'green'` will do the trick. This resets in every new session, so add it to a profile script if you want it to be permanent.

An *exception* is a specific kind of object that results from an error. Specifically, an exception forces PowerShell to see if you've implemented some routine that should run in response to the error. With an error, you're just getting the red text; with an exception handling routine, you're getting the chance to do something about it. That's what this chapter is all about.

30.2 *Using $ErrorActionPreference and –ErrorAction*

PowerShell commands can encounter two types of error conditions: *terminating* and *nonterminating*. A terminating error is PowerShell saying, "There's no way I can possibly continue—this party is over." A nonterminating error says, "Something bad happened, but I can try to keep going." For example, suppose you ask PowerShell to retrieve some WMI information from 10 computers. Computer number five fails—perhaps it isn't online at the time. That's bad, but there's no reason PowerShell can't continue with computers six, seven, and so on—and it will, by default, because that's a nonterminating error.

   You can use a shell-wide setting in `$ErrorActionPreference`, a built-in variable (technically, a preference variable—see about_Preference_Variables for more information on preference variables) to tell a command what to do when a nonterminating error pops up. `$ErrorActionPreference` offers these four settings:

- `Inquire`—Ask the user what to do. You'll probably never do this except when debugging a command because it's pretty intrusive. With scheduled or other unattended scripts, it's totally impractical.
- `Continue`—The default setting, this tells PowerShell to display an error message and keep going.

- `SilentlyContinue`—The setting you wish your kids had, this tells PowerShell not only to keep going but to not display any error messages.
- `Stop`—This forces the nonterminating error to become a terminating exception. That means you can catch the exception and do something about it.

Unfortunately, a great many PowerShell users think it's okay to put this right at the top of their scripts:

```
$ErrorActionPreference = 'SilentlyContinue'
```

In the days of VBScript, `On Error Resume Next` had the same effect as this command. This sends us into a rage, and not a silent one. Adding this to the top of a script effectively suppresses every single error message. What's the author trying to hide here? We understand why people do this: They think, "Well, the only thing that can go wrong is the thing I don't care about, like a computer not being available, so I'll just hide the error message." The problem is that other errors can crop up, and by hiding the error message you'll have a much harder time detecting, debugging, and solving those errors. So please don't ever put that line in your scripts. In fact, you'll rarely have to mess with `$ErrorActionPreference` at all.

Every single PowerShell cmdlet supports a set of *common parameters*. Look at the help for any cmdlet and you'll see `<CommonParameters>` at the end of the parameter list. Run `help about_common_parameters` to see the list of common parameters. One of them of particular interest to us right now is `-ErrorAction`, which can be abbreviated as `-EA`. This parameter lets you specify an error action for just that command. Essentially, it's as if you set `$ErrorActionPreference` to something, ran the command, and then put `$ErrorActionPreference` back the way you found it. The parameter accepts the same four values as `$ErrorActionPreference`. Let's see them in action. This example has PowerShell attempt to display the contents of two files, one that exists and one that doesn't. Start with `Inquire`:

```
PS C:\> Get-Content -Path good.txt,bad.txt -ErrorAction Inquire
Confirm
Cannot find path 'C:\bad.txt' because it does not exist.
[Y] Yes  [A] Yes to All  [H] Halt Command  [S] Suspend  [?] Help
(default is "Y"):y
Get-Content : Cannot find path 'C:\bad.txt' because it does not exist
.
At line:1 char:12
+ Get-Content <<<<  -Path good.txt,bad.txt -ErrorAction Inquire
    + CategoryInfo          : ObjectNotFound: (C:\bad.txt:String) [G
    et-Content], ItemNotFoundException
    + FullyQualifiedErrorId : PathNotFound,Microsoft.PowerShell.Comm
    ands.GetContentCommand
This is the content from the file that exists
```

As you can see, the code prompts you to continue when it runs into the bad file. You say "Y" to continue, and it goes on to the second file, displaying its contents. Now let's look at `Continue`:

```
PS C:\> Get-Content -Path good.txt,bad.txt -ErrorAction Continue
Get-Content : Cannot find path 'C:\bad.txt' because it does not exist
.
At line:1 char:12
+ Get-Content <<<<  -Path good.txt,bad.txt -ErrorAction Continue
    + CategoryInfo          : ObjectNotFound: (C:\bad.txt:String) [G
   et-Content], ItemNotFoundException
    + FullyQualifiedErrorId : PathNotFound,Microsoft.PowerShell.Comm
   ands.GetContentCommand
This is the content from the file that exists
```

You get the same basic effect, only this time without the prompt. You get an error, followed by the content of the file that existed. Now look at SilentlyContinue:

```
PS C:\> Get-Content -Path good.txt,bad.txt -ErrorAction SilentlyContinue
This is the content from the file that exists
```

There's no error, just the content from the file that existed. Finally, we'll look at Stop:

```
PS C:\> Get-Content -Path good.txt,bad.txt -ErrorAction Stop
Get-Content : Cannot find path 'C:\bad.txt' because it does not exist
.
At line:1 char:12
+ Get-Content <<<<  -Path good.txt,bad.txt -ErrorAction Stop
    + CategoryInfo          : ObjectNotFound: (C:\bad.txt:String) [G
   et-Content], ItemNotFoundException
    + FullyQualifiedErrorId : PathNotFound,Microsoft.PowerShell.Comm
   ands.GetContentCommand
```

This error action prevents PowerShell from going on to the second file. When PowerShell hits an error, it stops, exactly as you told it to do. This generated a trappable (or catchable) exception, although you haven't put anything in place to deal with it, so you still get the error message. We'll cover handling these caught exceptions in a bit.

30.3 *Using –ErrorVariable*

Another one of the common parameters is –ErrorVariable, or –EV for short. This parameter accepts the name of a variable (remember, the name doesn't include the $ symbol), and if the command generates an error, it'll be placed into that variable. Using this parameter is a great way to see which error occurred and perhaps take different actions for different errors. The neat thing is that it'll grab the error even if you set –ErrorAction to SilentlyContinue, which suppresses the output of the error on the screen:

```
PS C:\> Get-Content good.txt,bad.txt -EA SilentlyContinue -EV oops
This is the content from the file that exists
PS C:\> $oops
Get-Content : Cannot find path 'C:\bad.txt' because it does not exist
.
At line:1 char:12
+ Get-Content <<<<  good.txt,bad.txt -EA SilentlyContinue -EV oops
    + CategoryInfo          : ObjectNotFound: (C:\bad.txt:String) [G
   et-Content], ItemNotFoundException
    + FullyQualifiedErrorId : PathNotFound,Microsoft.PowerShell.Comm
   ands.GetContentCommand
```

As you can see, this code specified oops as the variable name, and after running the command you can display the error by accessing $oops.

30.4   Using $?

The $? variable is a way to tell if your last command succeeded. PowerShell has a number of variables that it automatically creates for you. You've already met some of them and will meet more in this chapter. We recommend that you read the help file about_Automatic_Variables to discover the full suite and what you can do with them.

One such automatic variable is $?. It stores the execution status of the last operation you performed in PowerShell. The status is stored as a Boolean value and will be set to True if the operation succeeded and False if it failed. You can see the $? automatic variable in use as you try this code:

```
PS C:\> Get-Process powershell

Handles   NPM(K)     PM(K)      WS(K) VM(M)   CPU(s)      Id ProcessName
-------   ------     -----      ----- -----   ------      -- -----------
    573       45    273040     277928   778     9.84    3920 powershell

PS C:\> $?
True
```

The command succeeded so the value of $? is set to True. Now, try a command that'll fail:

```
PS C:\> Get-Pracess powershell
Get-Pracess : The term 'Get-Pracess' is not recognized as
➥ the name of a cmdlet, function, script file, or operable
➥ program. Check the spelling of the name, or if a path was
➥ included, verify that the path is correct and try again.
At line:1 char:1
+ Get-Pracess powershell
+ ~~~~~~~~~~~~
    + CategoryInfo          : ObjectNotFound:
(Get-Pracess:String) [], CommandNotFoundException
    + FullyQualifiedErrorId : CommandNotFoundException

PS C:\> $?
False
```

Get-Pracess doesn't exist so the command fails and $? is set to False. You can use $? to test an action and determine what to do next:

```
$proc = Get-Process notepad -ErrorAction SilentlyContinue
if ($?) {
  Stop-Process -InputObject $proc
}
else {
  Write-Warning -Message "Notepad not running"
}
```

An attempt is made to get the process associated with notepad.exe. If it succeeds ($? = True), the process is stopped. If the notepad process isn't running, a warning to that effect is issued.

Knowing whether or not a command worked is useful, but to take your error handling to the next level, you need to know the type of error that occurred.

30.5 *Using $Error*

In addition to using the common -ErrorVariable, which is completely optional, you can find recent exception objects in the variable $Error, which is another PowerShell automatic variable. Whenever an exception occurs, it's added to $Error. By default the variable holds the last 256 errors. The maximum number of errors is controlled by another preference variable, $MaximumHistoryCount:

```
PS C:\> $MaximumErrorCount
256
PS C:\> $MaximumErrorCount=512
```

Now this PowerShell session will keep track of the last 512 exceptions. If you want to always use this setting, put this command in your profile.

The $Error variable is an array where the first element is the most recent exception. As new exceptions occur, the new one pushes the others down the list. Once the maximum count is reached, the oldest exception is discarded. If you wanted to revisit the last error, you'd do this:

```
PS C:\> $error[0]
Get-WmiObject : Invalid class "win32_bis"
    + CategoryInfo          : InvalidType: (:) [Get-WmiObject],
      ManagementException
    + FullyQualifiedErrorId : GetWMIManagementException,
      Microsoft.PowerShell.Commands.GetWmiObjectCommand
```

We should point out that this is an object. You can pipe it to Get-Member to learn more:

```
PS C:\> $error[0] | Get-Member

    TypeName: System.Management.Automation.ErrorRecord

Name                    MemberType     Definition
----                    ----------     ----------
Equals                  Method         bool Equals(System.Object obj)
GetHashCode             Method         int GetHashCode()
GetObjectData           Method         System.Void GetObjectData(System.R...
GetType                 Method         type GetType()
ToString                Method         string ToString()
writeErrorStream        NoteProperty   System.Boolean writeErrorStream=True
CategoryInfo            Property       System.Management.Automation.ErrorC...
ErrorDetails            Property       System.Management.Automation.ErrorD...
Exception               Property       System.Exception Exception {get;}
FullyQualifiedErrorId   Property       string FullyQualifiedErrorId {get;}
InvocationInfo          Property       System.Management.Automation.Invoca...
PipelineIterationInfo   Property       System.Collections.ObjectModel.Read...
ScriptStackTrace        Property       string ScriptStackTrace {get;}
TargetObject            Property       System.Object TargetObject {get;}
PSMessageDetails        ScriptProperty System.Object PSMessageDetails {get...
```

Some of these properties are nested objects, such as `Exception`:

```
PS C:\> $error[0].exception  | Get-Member

   TypeName: System.Management.ManagementException

Name               MemberType Definition
----               ---------- ----------
Equals             Method     bool Equals(System.Object obj)
GetBaseException   Method     System.Exception GetBaseException()
GetHashCode        Method     int GetHashCode()
GetObjectData      Method     System.Void GetObjectData(System.Runtime.Ser...
GetType            Method     type GetType()
ToString           Method     string ToString()
Data               Property   System.Collections.IDictionary Data {get;}
ErrorCode          Property   System.Management.ManagementStatus ErrorCode...
ErrorInformation   Property   System.Management.ManagementBaseObject Error...
HelpLink           Property   string HelpLink {get;set;}
InnerException     Property   System.Exception InnerException {get;}
Message            Property   string Message {get;}
Source             Property   string Source {get;set;}
StackTrace         Property   string StackTrace {get;}
TargetSite         Property   System.Reflection.MethodBase TargetSite {get;}
```

When you get to trapping and catching exceptions, this object is passed to your error handler, so understanding that the exception is an object is important. For example, you might want to display the following error message:

```
PS C:\> Write-Host "Command failed with error message
$($error[0].exception.message)" -ForegroundColor Yellow
Command failed with error message Invalid class "win32_bis"
```

You can use the common –`ErrorVariable` to capture exception objects on a per-cmdlet basis or look at the `$Error` variable to work with the most recent exceptions. But ideally, especially when scripting, you'll want to handle exceptions more gracefully.

30.6   *Trap constructs*

The `Trap` construct was introduced in PowerShell v1. It's not an awesome way of handling errors, but it's the best Microsoft could get into the product and still hit their shipping deadline. It's effective but it can be confusing, especially because it wasn't documented in the help files. These days, almost everyone prefers the newer, and more versatile, `Try...Catch...Finally` construct, but because `Trap` still exists and still works, we wanted to take the time to explain.

Whenever a trappable exception occurs (meaning a terminating error, or a non-terminating one that was made terminating by the `-ErrorAction Stop` parameter), PowerShell will jump back in your script and execute a `Trap` construct if it has encountered one by then. In other words, your `Trap` construct has to be defined before the error happens; PowerShell won't *scan ahead* to look for one. For example, start with the following script.

Listing 30.1 Trap.ps1, demonstrating the use of the `Trap` construct

```
trap {
  Write-Host "Trapping..."
      "Error!" | Out-File c:\errors.txt
  continue
}
Write-Host "Starting..."
Get-Content good.txt,bad.txt -EA Stop
Write-Host "Finishing..."
```

In listing 30.1, you're using `Write-Host` mainly to give you some output to follow the flow of this; that's going to become important in a minute. Right now, running the script displays the following output:

```
PS C:\> C:\trap.ps1
Starting...
Trapping...
Finishing...
```

You can use that output to follow what happened. Once the error occurred—and you made sure to turn it into a trappable exception by specifying `-ErrorAction Stop`—PowerShell handed off control to the `Trap` construct. You ended with the `Continue` statement, which tells the shell to go back and pick up on the line after the one that caused the exception.

How you end a `Trap` construct is crucial. You have two choices:

- `Continue`—Tells the shell to stay within the same scope as the `Trap` construct and resume execution on the line that follows the command that caused the error
- `Break`—Tells the shell to exit the current scope, passing the exception up to the parent scope

This scope business is one reason why `Trap` is so complex. Consider the following listing, which revises the script significantly. You're adding a function, which is its own scope, and installing a `Trap` construct inside it.

Listing 30.2 Trap.ps1, demonstrating the flow of scope for trapping

```
trap {
  Write-Host "Trapping at script scope..."
  "Error!" | Out-File c:\script-errors.txt
  continue
}
function try-this {
  trap {
    Write-Host "Trapping at function scope..."        ❹ Handle
    "Error!" | Out-File c:\func-errors.txt               error
    continue
  }                                                   ❺ Exit trap
  Write-Host "Starting the function..."
  Get-Content good.txt,bad.txt -EA Stop        ❸ Error occurs here
```

```
    Write-Host "Ending the function..."
}                                                        ◄──   ⑥  Resume here
Write-Host "Starting the script..."                      ◄──
Try-This                                                       ①  Start execution
Write-Host "Finishing the script..."      ◄──
                                           ②  Call function
```

Finish ⑦

The script in listing 30.2 starts with the first `Write-Host` command ① because the trap and function defined earlier in the code haven't been called yet. It then calls the function ②, so execution proceeds to the `Try-This` function. An error occurs ③, so PowerShell looks for a trap within the current scope. It finds one ④ and executes it. The trap exits ⑤ with `Continue`, so the shell stays within the same scope and finishes the function ⑥. The function exits naturally, allowing the script to continue and wrap up ⑦. The `Trap` defined within the script never executes. The output looks like this:

```
Starting the script...
Starting the function...
Trapping at function scope...
Ending the function...
Finishing the script...
```

Now look at the next listing, which makes only one change, which we've boldfaced.

Listing 30.3   Trap.ps1, with one change: how the function's trap ends

```
trap {
  Write-Host "Trapping at script scope..."
  "Error!" | Out-File c:\script-errors.txt
  continue
}
function try-this {
  trap {
    Write-Host "Trapping at function scope..."
    "Error!" | Out-File c:\func-errors.txt        ①  Change to
    Break                                     ◄──     trap exit
  }
  Write-Host "Starting the function..."
  Get-Content good.txt,bad.txt -EA Stop
  Write-Host "Ending the function..."
}
Write-Host "Starting the script..."
Try-This
Write-Host "Finishing the script..."
```

All you're doing in listing 30.3 is changing the way the function's trap exits, but it's going to significantly affect the output. By changing `Continue` to `Break` ①, you're telling PowerShell to exit the function's scope and pass the error with it. That'll force the parent scope to look for a trap and execute the one it finds. The output looks like this:

```
Starting the script...
Starting the function...
Trapping at function scope...
Trapping at script scope...
Finishing the script...
```

As you can see, because you exited the function's scope, the `Ending the function` line never got to execute. The script "saw" the error as occurring on the `Try-This` line, ran its trap, and then continued with `Finishing the script....`

You can also set up multiple traps, each one designed to handle a different exception:

```
trap {
  "Other terminating error trapped"
}
trap [System.Management.Automation.CommandNotFoundException] {
  "Command error trapped"
}
```

To set this up, you'll need to know the .NET Framework class of a specific exception, such as `[System.Management.Automation.CommandNotFoundException]`. That can be tricky, and you probably won't run across this technique much, but we wanted to make sure you knew what it was in case you do see someone using it.

> **TIP** Examine any error messages carefully when developing your script. If you look at the error messages at the start of section 30.3, you'll see `ItemNot-FoundException`. The exception that has caused the error is often given in PowerShell's error messages. You can search MSDN for the full .NET class name of the exception.

Following this chain of scope, traps, and so forth can be difficult, especially when you're trying to debug a complex, multilevel script. We think you need to be aware of this technique and how it behaves, because you're likely to run across folks who still use it in the examples they write online. You'll also run across older examples that use this, and we don't think the `Trap` construct alone should put you off. But we don't recommend using this construct; the newer `Try...Catch...Finally` is much better.

30.7 *Try...Catch...Finally constructs*

PowerShell v2 introduced this new, improved error handling construct. It looks and works a lot more like the error handling constructs in high-level languages like Visual Basic and C# or other languages such as T-SQL. You build a construct with two or three parts:

- The `Try` part contains the command or commands that you think might cause an error. You have to set their `–ErrorAction` to `Stop` in order to catch the error.
- The `Catch` part runs if an error occurs within the `Try` part.
- The `Finally` part runs whether or not an error occurred.

You must have the `Try` part, and you can choose to write a `Catch`, a `Finally`, or both. You must have at least one `Catch` or `Finally` block. A simple example looks like this:

```
Try {
 Get-Content bad.txt,good.txt -EA Stop
} Catch {
 Write-Host "Uh-oh!!"
}
```

This produces the following output:

```
PS C:\> C:\test.ps1
Uh-oh!!
```

There's an important lesson here: If a command is trying to do more than one thing and one of them causes an error, the command stops. You'll be able to catch the error, but you have no way to make the command go back and pick up where it left off. In this example, trying to read Bad.txt caused an error, and so Good.txt was never even attempted. Keep in mind that your commands should try to do only one thing at a time if you think one thing might cause an error that you want to trap. For example, you can pull your filenames out into an array and then enumerate the array so that you're attempting only one file at a time:

```
$files = @('bad.txt','good.txt')
foreach ($file in $files) {
  Try {
    Get-Content $file -EA Stop
  } Catch {
    Write-Host "$file failed!!!"
  }
}
```

This produces the following output:

```
PS C:\> C:\test.ps1
bad.txt failed!!!
This is the content from the file that exists
```

That's the pattern you'll generally see people use: Try one thing at a time, Catch the error, and rely on the Foreach construct to loop back around and pick up the next thing to try. This approach will make your scripts more verbose, but the robustness and stability introduced by using Try...Catch...Finally is worth the extra effort.

Like the Trap construct, this also lets you catch specific errors. Again, we don't always see people do this a lot, but it's a good way to specify different actions for different types of errors, perhaps handling "file not found" differently than "access denied." Here's an example, from the about_try_catch_finally help file:

```
try
{
    $wc = new-object System.Net.WebClient
    $wc.DownloadFile("http://www.contoso.com/MyDoc.doc")
}
catch [System.Net.WebException],[System.IO.IOException]
{
    "Unable to download MyDoc.doc from http://www.contoso.co
}
catch
{
    "An error occurred that could not be resolved."
}
```

The first `Catch` block is catching two specific errors, a `WebException` and an `IOException`. The final `Catch` block is the *catch-all* and will catch any exceptions that haven't been caught by a previous block. When using multiple `Catch` blocks, you must ensure that the `Catch` blocks for the most specific exceptions occur *before* more generic ones. PowerShell will use the first `Catch` block it has that can process the exception that has occurred.

When an exception is caught, the exception object is piped to the `Catch` block. This means you can incorporate the object into whatever code you want to execute. The exception object can be referenced using `$_` because it's a piped object. For example, you might use this for the second script block:

```
catch
{
  $msg=("An error occurred that could not be resolved: {0}" -f
    $_.Exception.Message)
  Write-Warning $msg
  #Write the exception to a log file
  $_.Exception | Select * | Out-file myerrors.txt -append
  #Export the error to XML for later diagnosis
  $_ | Export-Clixml UnknownWebException.xml
}
```

In this version, you're referencing the exception object using `$_` to write a warning message, log some information to a text file, and export the complete exception to an XML file. Later you could reimport the file to re-create the exception object and try to figure out what went wrong.

As you can see from the preceding code, you almost always need at least one `Catch` block for every `Try`, and they must be in sequence. Code in a `Finally` block runs regardless of whether there was an error. For example, you might use a `Finally` block to clean up connections or close files. The `Finally` block is completely optional.

One of the reasons we think `Try...Catch...Finally` is better than `Trap` is because there's no jumping back and forth in your script. An error occurs, and you handle it right then and there in a linear, easy-to-follow fashion. You can use the two techniques in the same script, though. For example, you might use `Try...Catch` for the errors you can anticipate and want to handle, and use `Trap` to grab any other errors that pop up. We tend to steer clear of `Trap`, though, because it makes following the script's execution flow much more difficult.

30.8 Summary

Handling errors in PowerShell scripts can be straightforward, particularly with the newer `Try...Catch...Finally` construct. Error handling adds a level of sophistication and professionalism to your scripts, dealing with errors gracefully rather than spewing a screenful of red text in front of your script's users. When running scheduled and unattended scripts, error handling can be crucial to capturing errors (perhaps in a log file) for later review. We're not implying that writing effective error handling is easy, but it's essential if you want to create robust PowerShell tools.

31
Debugging tools and techniques

This chapter covers

- Understanding the debugging methodology
- Working with debugging cmdlets
- Using breakpoints
- Remote debugging
- Debugging workflows

Debugging is a difficult topic in any kind of computer system, and PowerShell is no exception. PowerShell provides decent tools for debugging, but those tools don't make debugging magically easier. The trick with debugging, it turns out, is having an expectation of how things are supposed to work so that you can spot the place where they stop doing so.

For example, let's say your car won't start. Do you have any idea why? Do you know what's supposed to be happening when you turn the key? If not, then you can't debug the problem. If you know that the battery needs to be charged, your foot has to be on the brake, the starter motor has to be wired up and functional, and so forth, you can start debugging by testing each of those elements individually.

All PowerShell can do is give you tools, things that you can use to check the current state of the shell, a script, or something else. PowerShell can't tell you whether or not the current state is *correct*. It's like having an electrical meter: If you don't know where to put it, how to read the output, and what the output is supposed to be and why, the tool isn't all that helpful.

Computers are no different. If Active Directory replication isn't working, you can't troubleshoot—or debug—that problem unless you know how all the little components of replication are supposed to work and how you can check them to see if they're doing so. From that perspective, PowerShell doesn't make debugging any more difficult. It just tends to highlight the fact that we've been so separated from Windows' internals by its GUI for so long that we often don't know how the product is working under the hood. PowerShell gives you great tools for checking on things, but if you don't know what to check, and don't know what it should look like when you do check, you can't troubleshoot it.

31.1　*Debugging: all about expectations*

Let's be very clear that, when it comes to a PowerShell script, you can't debug it unless you think you know what it's doing. If you're staring at a screenful of commands and haven't the slightest idea what any of it's supposed to do, you're not going to be able to debug it. If you've pasted some code from someone's internet blog and don't know what the code is supposed to do, you won't be able to fix it if it doesn't do what you want. So the starting point for any debugging process is to clearly document what your expectations are. In the process of doing so, you'll quickly identify where your knowledge is incomplete, and you can work to make it more complete.

To that end, let's start with the following listing, a script that was donated to us by a colleague. We'll use it to walk you through how you can go about this identifying-expectations process.

> **Listing 31.1　A script to debug**

```
function Get-DiskInfo {
  [CmdletBinding()]
  param(
    [Parameter(Mandatory=$True,
               ValueFromPipeline=$True,
               ValueFromPipelineByPropertyName=$True)]
    [string[]]$computerName,
    [Parameter(Mandatory=$True)]
    [ValidateRange(10,90)]
    [int]$threshold
  )
  BEGIN {}
  PROCESS {
    foreach ($computer in $computername) {
      $params = @{computername=$computer
                  filter="drivetype='fixed'"
                  class='win32_logicaldisk'}
      $disks = Get-WmiObject @params
      foreach ($disk in $disks) {
        $danger = $True
```

```
        if ($disk.freespace / $disk.capacity * 100 -le $threshold) {
          $danger = $False
        }
        $props = @{ComputerName=$computer
                   Size=$disk.capacity / 1GB -as [int]
                   Free = $disk.freespace / 1GB -as [int]
                   Danger=$danger}
        $obj = New-Object -TypeName PSObject -Property $props
        Write-Output $obj
      }
    }
  }
  END {}
}
```

NOTE   The script in listing 31.1 doesn't work as is. We know that. It's a chapter on debugging. You're going to fix it as you go.

Don't even try to run this script; we'll start by walking you through each section and documenting what we think it should do. We follow this exact process all the time, although with experience you'll start doing bits of it in your head and moving more quickly. For right now, let's take it slow. Have a pencil and blank sheet of paper ready, too—you'll need that. First up:

```
function Get-DiskInfo {
  [CmdletBinding()]
  param(
    [Parameter(Mandatory=$True,
               ValueFromPipeline=$True,
               ValueFromPipelineByPropertyName=$True)]
    [string[]]$computerName,
    [Parameter(Mandatory=$True)]
    [ValidateRange(10,90)]
    [int]$threshold
  )
  BEGIN {}
```

This section appears to be defining two parameters. They're both listed as mandatory, so you should expect to run Get-DiskInfo with both a -computerName and a -threshold parameter. Notice that -computerName accepts an array of names. At the moment you don't know whether or not that's significant. The latter appears to accept values in the range from 10 to 90. If you don't know what every single piece of information here means to PowerShell, you should look it up; it's all covered elsewhere in this book.

This section of the script ends with a BEGIN block, which is empty, so record that fact but otherwise ignore it. Here's the next hunk of code:

```
PROCESS {
  foreach ($computer in $computername) {
    $params = @{computername=$computer
                filter="drivetype='fixed'"
                class='win32_logicaldisk'}
    $disks = Get-WmiObject @params
```

This section is a PROCESS block. We expect that, when this function is given pipeline input, the PROCESS block will run once for each piped-in item. If there's no pipeline input, then this entire PROCESS block will execute once. The ForEach block will enumerate through the contents of the $computerName parameter, taking one value at a time and putting it into the $computer variable. So if you ran Get-DiskInfo -comp SERVER1,SERVER2 -thresh 20, you'd expect the $computer variable to initially contain SERVER1. Take that blank sheet of paper and your pencil, and write that down:

$computer = SERVER1

$threshold = 20

Next, this section is creating a hash table named $params. It looks like it'll contain three values, and those are being fed as parameters (via the technique called *splatting*) to the Get-WmiObject command. Two of those parameters, class and filter, are fixed, whereas the other, computerName, is variable. The -computerName parameter is being given the contents of the $computer variable. Well, we think we know what that variable contains, right? Assuming SERVER1 is a legitimate computer name on the network, let's just try running that command (if SERVER1 won't work on your network, substitute localhost, $env:COMPUTERNAME, or another valid computer name).

> **TIP** The techniques in this chapter take advantage of the fact that the same commands can be run interactively as in your script. Whenever you're in doubt about some code, try running it interactively to see what happens—it can save you lots of time.

You'll expand Get-WmiObject @params and test this part of the function by hand-coding the values and parameters:

```
PS C:\> get-wmiobject -class win32_logicaldisk -filter "drivetype=
    'fixed'" -computername localhost
Get-WmiObject : Invalid query
At line:1 char:14
+ get-wmiobject <<<<  -class win32_logicaldisk -filter "drivetype='fi
xed'" -computername localhost
    + CategoryInfo          : InvalidOperation: (:) [Get-WmiObject],
    ManagementException
    + FullyQualifiedErrorId : GetWMIManagementException,Microsoft.Po
    werShell.Commands.GetWmiObjectCommand
```

Well, there's a problem. Your expectation was that this would do something other than produce an error. But you got an error. So you have one of two things going on:

- You don't know what you're doing.
- The command is wrong.

Far too often, people tend to assume that the first possibility is true, and we beg you not to do that. Prove to yourself that you're wrong—don't just assume it. For example, in this case, your command had three parameters. Take one off—remove -computer-Name and try again:

```
PS C:\> get-wmiobject -class win32_logicaldisk -filter "drivetype=
➥ 'fixed'"
Get-WmiObject : Invalid query
At line:1 char:14
+ get-wmiobject <<<<  -class win32_logicaldisk -filter "drivetype='fi
xed'"
    + CategoryInfo          : InvalidOperation: (:) [Get-WmiObject],
    ManagementException
    + FullyQualifiedErrorId : GetWMIManagementException,Microsoft.Po
  werShell.Commands.GetWmiObjectCommand
```

Same problem. Okay, fine, put -computerName back so that you're changing only one thing at a time.

Be methodical

The most important point in the whole chapter is that when you're making changes during the debugging process, make only one change at a time so you can correctly record the outcome of that change. If you make multiple changes, you won't know which caused the change in output.

You'll see many people flailing around making multiple changes at random in the hope that something will work. Don't follow that pattern.

Be methodical. Make single changes and record what you're doing and the outcome. You'll fix the problem much quicker that way.

As a second step, remove -filter:

```
PS C:\> get-wmiobject -class win32_logicaldisk -computername localhost

DeviceID     : A:
DriveType    : 2
ProviderName :
FreeSpace    :
Size         :
VolumeName   :
DeviceID     : C:
DriveType    : 3
ProviderName :
FreeSpace    : 32439992320
Size         : 42842714112
VolumeName   :
DeviceID     : D:
DriveType    : 5
ProviderName :
FreeSpace    :
Size         :
VolumeName   :
```

Wow, that worked! Great. It also contains some interesting information, if you take a moment to look at it. The DriveType property is numeric, but in your original command, the -filter parameter was trying to set DriveType='fixed'—possibly that's the problem. Looking at this output, you can guess that 3 is the numeric type for a fixed disk (it's the numeric type for the C: drive, and we all know that's a fixed disk—see the documentation for the `Win32_LogicalDisk` class on MSDN at http://msdn.microsoft.com/en-us/library/aa394173%28v=vs.85%29.aspx), so try modifying the command:

```
PS C:\> get-wmiobject -class win32_logicaldisk -filter "drivetype='3'"

DeviceID      : C:
DriveType     : 3
ProviderName  :
FreeSpace     : 32439992320
Size          : 42842714112
VolumeName    :
```

Awesome! You've fixed one problem. Let's go back and modify it in the original script, with the following listing showing the revision.

Listing 31.2   Fixing the first problem

```
function Get-DiskInfo {
  [CmdletBinding()]
  param(
    [Parameter(Mandatory=$True,
               ValueFromPipeline=$True,
               ValueFromPipelineByPropertyName=$True)]
    [string[]]$computerName,
    [Parameter(Mandatory=$True)]
    [ValidateRange(10,90)]
    [int]$threshold
  )
  BEGIN {}
  PROCESS {
    foreach ($computer in $computername) {
      $params = @{'computername'=$computer;
                  'filter'="drivetype='3'";          ⟵── Modification
                  'class'='win32_logicaldisk'}
      $disks = Get-WmiObject @params
      foreach ($disk in $disks) {
        $danger = $True
        if ($disk.freespace / $disk.size * 100 -le $threshold) {
          $danger = $False
        }
        $props = @{'ComputerName'=$computer;
                   'Size'=$disk.capacity / 1GB -as [int];
                   'Free' = $disk.freespace / 1GB -as [int];
                   'Danger'=$danger}
        $obj = New-Object -TypeName PSObject -Property $props
        Write-Output $obj
      }
    }
  }
  END {}
}
```

The important thing in listing 31.2 is that you found something that didn't work and that you didn't understand; you didn't just plow ahead and ignore it. You stopped and tried to understand it, and you ended up finding a problem in the script. That's fixed, and so you can move on. You're still on this section:

```
PROCESS {
  foreach ($computer in $computername) {
    $params = @{computername=$computer
               filter="drivetype='3'"
               class='win32_logicaldisk'}
    $disks = Get-WmiObject @params
```

This is just a fragment that won't run on its own because it needs a close to the `foreach` loop. But you can take some of this and run it stand-alone. In the shell, you'll create a variable named `$computer` and then paste in some of the previous code to see if it runs. The result is put into a variable named `$disks`, so you'll check that variable's contents when you're finished to see what it did:

```
PS C:\> $computer = 'localhost'
PS C:\>       $params = @{computername=$computer
>>                  filter="drivetype='3'"
>>                  class='win32_logicaldisk'}
>>       $disks = Get-WmiObject @params
>>

PS C:\> $disks

DeviceID      : C:
DriveType     : 3
ProviderName  :
FreeSpace     : 32439992320
Size          : 42842714112
VolumeName    :
```

Now you know that bit of code works, and you know that it puts something into the `$disks` variable. That's something you should note on your sheet of paper:

$computer = SERVER1
$threshold = 20
$disks = one disk, C:, drivetype=3, size and freespace have values

Now for the next chunk of code:

```
      foreach ($disk in $disks) {
        $danger = $True
        if ($disk.freespace / $disk.capacity * 100 -le $threshold) {
          $danger = $False
        }
```

Here's another `ForEach` loop. Now you know that in your test the `$disks` variable has only one thing in it, so you can just manually assign that to `$disk` and try running this code right in the shell. Even if `$disks` had multiple disks, all you'd need to do would be grab the first one just to run a little test. It looks like this:

```
PS C:\> $disk = $disks[0]
PS C:\> $danger = $True
PS C:\> if ($disk.freespace / $disk.capacity * 100 -le $threshold) {
>>              $danger = $False
>>          }
>>
```

```
Property 'freespace' cannot be found on this object. Make sure that i
t exists.
At line:1 char:19
+         if ($disk. <<<< freespace / $disk.capacity * 100 -le $thres
hold) {
    + CategoryInfo          : InvalidOperation: (.:OperatorToken) []
    , RuntimeException
    + FullyQualifiedErrorId : PropertyNotFoundStrict
```

Whoa, that's not good. The error is saying that there's no `Freespace` property. Okay, send that object to `Get-Member` and see what's happening:

```
PS C:\> $disk | get-member
```

```
Get-Member : No object has been specified to the get-member cmdlet.
At line:1 char:11
+ $disk | gm <<<<
    + CategoryInfo          : CloseError: (:) [Get-Member], InvalidO
    perationException
    + FullyQualifiedErrorId : NoObjectInGetMember,Microsoft.PowerShe
    ll.Commands.GetMemberCommand
```

Looks like your `$disk` variable didn't get populated. Okay, try with the original `$disks` variable; that should contain something:

```
PS C:\> $disks | get-member

   TypeName: System.Management.ManagementObject#root\cimv2\Win32_L...

Name                       MemberType   Definition
----                       ----------   ----------
Chkdsk                     Method       System.Management.Manage...
Reset                      Method       System.Management.Manage...
SetPowerState              Method       System.Management.Manage...
Access                     Property     System.UInt16 Access {ge...
...
```

That worked. So the problem is that because `$disks` contained only one thing, accessing `$disks[0]` probably didn't get any data. So try to create `$disk` again, this time without using the array reference:

```
PS C:\> $disk = $disks
PS C:\> $danger = $True
PS C:\> if ($disk.freespace / $disk.capacity * 100 -le $thresh
old) {
>>              $danger = $False
>>          }
>>
```

```
Property 'capacity' cannot be found on this object. Make sure that it
 exists.
```

```
At line:1 char:37
+         if ($disk.freespace / $disk. <<<< capacity * 100 -le $thres
hold) {
    + CategoryInfo          : InvalidOperation: (.:OperatorToken) []
 , RuntimeException
    + FullyQualifiedErrorId : PropertyNotFoundStrict
```

Well, this is a different problem at least. This time it's telling you there's no `capacity` property. Let's look back to the `Get-Member` output, and it's right. There's no `capacity`. There is, however, `size`. Modify the pasted-in command to try that instead:

```
PS C:\> $danger = $True
PS C:\> if ($disk.freespace / $disk.size * 100 -le $threshold) {
>>          $danger = $False
>>       }
>>
```

```
The variable '$threshold' cannot be retrieved because it has not been
 set.
At line:1 char:62
+         if ($disk.freespace / $disk.size * 100 -le $threshold <<<<
) {
    + CategoryInfo          : InvalidOperation: (threshold:Token) []
 , RuntimeException
    + FullyQualifiedErrorId : VariableIsUndefined
```

Well, you're making progress. This time, the shell says it's upset because `$threshold` doesn't exist. That makes sense because you never created it. You know from your sheet of scratch paper that the variable should contain 20, so set that and try again:

```
PS C:\> $threshold = 20
PS C:\> $danger = $True
PS C:\> if ($disk.freespace / $disk.size * 100 -le $threshold) {
>>          $danger = $False
>>       }
>>

PS C:\> $danger
True
```

Okay, you didn't get any errors this time, and the `$danger` variable contains something. You're not sure it's correct, though, and you know what? This is getting more and more complicated to do by hand. You're trying to keep track of a lot of different values, and you could be introducing errors of your own. So it's time to start using PowerShell to take a load off. First you'll fix the `capacity` thing, so the next listing is your new script.

Listing 31.3   Revising the script to correct another bug

```
function Get-DiskInfo {
  [CmdletBinding()]
  param(
    [Parameter(Mandatory=$True,
             ValueFromPipeline=$True,
             ValueFromPipelineByPropertyName=$True)]
```

```
              [string[]]$computerName,
              [Parameter(Mandatory=$True)]
              [ValidateRange(10,90)]
              [int]$threshold
    )
    BEGIN {}
    PROCESS {
      foreach ($computer in $computername) {
        $params = @{computername=$computer
                    filter="drivetype='3'"
                    class='win32_logicaldisk'}
        $disks = Get-WmiObject @params
        foreach ($disk in $disks) {
          $danger = $True
          if ($disk.freespace / $disk.size * 100 -le $threshold) {        Fixed
            $danger = $False                                               this...
          }
          $props = @{ComputerName=$computer                                ...and
                     Size=$disk.size / 1GB -as [int]                       this
                     Free = $disk.freespace / 1GB -as [int]
                     Danger=$danger}
          $obj = New-Object -TypeName PSObject -Property $props
          Write-Output $obj
        }
      }
    }
    END {}
}
```

31.2 Write-Debug

What you've been doing all along is trying to get inside the script's head, and Power-Shell has some good tools for making that easier, starting with the Write-Debug cmdlet. Because your function uses [CmdletBinding()], the -Debug switch is added automatically, and it controls the Write-Debug output.

> **TIP** It's worth adding [CmdletBinding()] to all your scripts and functions so that you can take advantage of the debug, verbose, and other functionality you gain.

Let's go through the script and add Write-Debug at key points. The cmdlet has two purposes: to output messages and let you know where the script is, and to give you a chance to pause the script, check things out, and resume. You still need to have an expectation of what the script should be doing, because all you're going to be able to do is compare your expectations to reality—and wherever they differ is potentially a bug. The next listing shows where you add Write-Debug.

Listing 31.4 Adding `Write-Debug` statements

```
function Get-DiskInfo {
  [CmdletBinding()]
  param(
```

```
        [Parameter(Mandatory=$True,
                   ValueFromPipeline=$True,
                   ValueFromPipelineByPropertyName=$True)]
        [string[]]$computerName,
        [Parameter(Mandatory=$True)]
        [ValidateRange(10,90)]
        [int]$threshold
    )
    BEGIN {}
    PROCESS {
        Write-Debug "Started PROCESS block"                           ◁──
        foreach ($computer in $computername) {
            Write-Debug "Computer name is $computer"                  ◁──
            $params = @{'computername'=$computer;
                        'filter'="drivetype='3'";                          Added
                        'class'='win32_logicaldisk'}                       Write-
            $disks = Get-WmiObject @params                                 Debug
            Write-Debug "Got the disks"                               ◁──
            foreach ($disk in $disks) {
                Write-Debug "Working on disk $($disk.deviceid)"
                Write-Debug "Size is $($disk.size)"
                Write-Debug "Free space is $($disk.freespace)"
                $danger = $True
                if ($disk.freespace / $disk.size * 100 -le $threshold) {
                    $danger = $False
                }
                Write-Debug "Danger setting is $danger"              ◁──
                $props = @{'ComputerName'=$computer;                       Added
                           'Size'=$disk.size / 1GB -as [int];               Write-
                           'Free' = $disk.freespace / 1GB -as [int];        Debug
                           'Danger'=$danger}
                Write-Debug "Created hash table; will create object next"  ◁──
                $obj = New-Object -TypeName PSObject -Property $props
                Write-Output $obj
            }
        }
    }
    END {}
}
```

Now it's time to run the script:

```
PS C:\> . ./Get-DiskInfo
```

You dot-source the script to load the function:

```
PS C:\> Get-DiskInfo -threshold 20 -computername localhost -debug
DEBUG: Started PROCESS block
Confirm
Continue with this operation?
[Y] Yes  [A] Yes to All  [H] Halt Command  [S] Suspend  [?] Help
(default is "Y"):y
```

This shows you exactly what Write-Debug does: You can see where it's displayed the message, Started PROCESS block, and then paused. You're okay to continue, so you answer "Y" for "Yes" and press Enter, and the script will resume running.

```
DEBUG: Computer name is localhost
Confirm
Continue with this operation?
[Y] Yes  [A] Yes to All  [H] Halt Command  [S] Suspend  [?] Help
(default is "Y"):y
```

Okay, "localhost" is what you expected the computer name to be, so let the script continue:

```
DEBUG: Got the disks
Confirm
Continue with this operation?
[Y] Yes  [A] Yes to All  [H] Halt Command  [S] Suspend  [?] Help
(default is "Y"):s
```

Getting the disk information is a big deal; as you'll recall, you had problems with this earlier when you were testing manually. So enter S to suspend the script. This means the script is still running, but you can get a command-line prompt while still inside the script's scope. The prompt, as you'll see, is slightly different:

```
PS C:\>>> $disks

DeviceID     : C:
DriveType    : 3
ProviderName :
FreeSpace    : 32439992320
Size         : 42842714112
VolumeName   :

PS C:\>>> exit
```

You just displayed the contents of $disks, and they were exactly what you expected. You ran Exit to get out of suspend mode and to let the script continue. Because it had been prompting you whether to proceed, you'll return to that prompt:

```
Confirm
Continue with this operation?
[Y] Yes  [A] Yes to All  [H] Halt Command  [S] Suspend  [?] Help
(default is "Y"):y
```

You answer "Yes" again, and the script proceeds to the next Write-Debug statement:

```
DEBUG: Working on disk C:
Confirm
Continue with this operation?
[Y] Yes  [A] Yes to All  [H] Halt Command  [S] Suspend  [?] Help
(default is "Y"):y
```

After the drive the size is checked:

```
DEBUG: Size is 42842714112
Confirm
Continue with this operation?
[Y] Yes  [A] Yes to All  [H] Halt Command  [S] Suspend  [?] Help
(default is "Y"):y
```

And then the free space:

```
DEBUG: Free space is 32439992320
Confirm
Continue with this operation?
[Y] Yes  [A] Yes to All  [H] Halt Command  [S] Suspend  [?] Help
(default is "Y"):y
```

So you've confirmed the contents of the drive's `Size` and `FreeSpace` properties, which you'd seen earlier anyway when looking at `$disks`. That all looks good—the drive appears to be around 75 percent empty, so it's not in any danger. That should be confirmed by the next debug statement:

```
DEBUG: Danger setting is True
Confirm
Continue with this operation?
[Y] Yes  [A] Yes to All  [H] Halt Command  [S] Suspend  [?] Help
(default is "Y"):s
```

Hold up a minute. Why is the `Danger` setting `True`? That means the `$Danger` variable contains `$True`. You can see in your script where that was set, but you expected that the following math would set it to `$False` because the drive's free space isn't less than the threshold value you specified in `-threshold`. So you're going to suspend the script again and do the math manually:

```
PS C:\>>> $disk.freespace / $disk.size * 100
75.7188077188456
```

Yeah, the drive is about 75 percent free, which is what you expected. So is 75 less than or equal to 20?

```
PS C:\>>> 75 -le 20
False
```

Did you spot the problem? You got the logic backward. You started by assuming that the drive's free space is in danger by setting `$danger` to `$True`. Then, if the drive's free space is less than the threshold value, which in this example isn't the case, you set `$danger` to `$False`. Had to think about that one for a second, but the logic is twisted. So there's no point in continuing. Exit suspend mode:

```
PS C:\>>> exit
Confirm
Continue with this operation?
[Y] Yes  [A] Yes to All  [H] Halt Command  [S] Suspend  [?] Help
(default is "Y"):h
```

And answer `H` to halt the command. This delivers an error message, just letting you know you're the reason things quit running:

```
Write-Debug : Command execution stopped because the user selected the
 Halt option.
At C:\test.ps1:34 char:20
+         Write-Debug <<<< "Danger setting is $danger"
    + CategoryInfo          : OperationStopped: (:) [Write-Debug], P
   arentContainsErrorRecordException
```

```
    + FullyQualifiedErrorId : ActionPreferenceStop,Microsoft.PowerSh
   ell.Commands.WriteDebugCommand
```

Now you need to modify the script, as shown in the following listing.

Listing 31.5 Fixing the logic error

```
function Get-DiskInfo {
  [CmdletBinding()]
  param(
    [Parameter(Mandatory=$True,
               ValueFromPipeline=$True,
               ValueFromPipelineByPropertyName=$True)]
    [string[]]$computerName,
    [Parameter(Mandatory=$True)]
    [ValidateRange(10,90)]
    [int]$threshold
  )
  BEGIN {}
  PROCESS {
    Write-Debug "Started PROCESS block"
    foreach ($computer in $computername) {
      Write-Debug "Computer name is $computer"
      $params = @{computername=$computer
                  filter="drivetype='3'"
                  class='win32_logicaldisk'}
      $disks = Get-WmiObject @params
      Write-Debug "Got the disks"
      foreach ($disk in $disks) {
        Write-Debug "Working on disk $($disk.deviceid)"
        Write-Debug "Size is $($disk.size)"
        Write-Debug "Free space is $($disk.freespace)"
        $danger = $False
        if ($disk.freespace / $disk.size * 100 -le $threshold) {
          $danger = $True
        }
        Write-Debug "Danger setting is $danger"
        $props = @{ComputerName=$computer
                   Size=$disk.size / 1GB -as [int]
                   Free = $disk.freespace / 1GB -as [int]
                   Danger=$danger}
        Write-Debug "Created hashtable; will create object next"
        $obj = New-Object -TypeName PSObject -Property $props
        Write-Output $obj
      }
    }
  }
  END {}
}
```

Used to be
$True

Used to be
$False

You're so confident that this is the right set of changes that you're going to run this again without –Debug and see what happens:

Free	Danger	ComputerName	Size
30	False	localhost	40

Perfect! So you hopefully see the value of `Write-Debug`. With it, you were able to get some visual feedback on the script's execution. You could also suspend and check things out, and eventually you figured out your logic flaw. When you took off the `-Debug` parameter, the script ran normally. You didn't need to pull out all of the `Write-Debug` statements; they're fine staying in there and will be suppressed until you need to debug the script again.

31.3   *Breakpoints*

In a way, what you've done with `Write-Debug` was to manually set a *breakpoint*, a place where your script pauses so that you can take stock and see if everything is running according to expectations. PowerShell v2 introduced another kind of breakpoint, which you can set ahead of time. You can set three kinds of breakpoints:

- A breakpoint that occurs when execution in a script reaches the current line or column. It's similar to using `Write-Debug`, except that you don't have to insert the `Write-Debug` statement into your script.
- A breakpoint that occurs when a specified variable is read, modified, or either. It can be set in the shell globally or can be tied to a specific script filename to just debug that script.
- A breakpoint that occurs when a specified command is run. It can be set in the shell globally or can be tied to a specific script filename to debug just that script.

When any breakpoint occurs, you wind up in the same suspend mode as you saw earlier when you used `Write-Debug`; run `Exit` to let the script resume execution from the breakpoint. In the PowerShell ISE, you can set the line-number style of a breakpoint by going to the line where you want it and pressing F9 (you can also select the Toggle Breakpoint option from the Debug menu). Pressing F9 again on a line where there's a breakpoint set will clear the breakpoint. You can also use a set of cmdlets to manage breakpoints:

- `Set-PSBreakpoint` establishes a new breakpoint; use its parameters to specify the kind of breakpoint, command and variable names, line numbers, and so on.
- `Get-PSBreakpoint` retrieves breakpoints.
- `Remove-PSBreakpoint` removes breakpoints.
- `Enable-PSBreakpoint` and `Disable-PSBreakpoint` work against a breakpoint that you already created; they enable you to turn existing breakpoints on and off temporarily without removing them and having to re-create them.

Here's a quick example of using the breakpoint cmdlets:

```
PS C:\> Set-PSBreakpoint -Line 25 -Script ./get-diskinfo.ps1
   ID Script                Line Command        Variable        Action
   -- ------                ---- -------        --------        ------
    0 get-diskinfo.ps1       25
PS C:\> . .\get-diskinfo.ps1
PS C:\> Get-DiskInfo -computerName localhost -threshold 20
```

```
Entering debug mode. Use h or ? for help.
Hit Line breakpoint on 'C:\scripts\get-diskinfo.ps1:25'
At C:\scripts\get-diskinfo.ps1:25 char:25
+        foreach ($disk in $disks) {
+                        ~~~~~~
PS> $disks
DeviceID     : C:
DriveType    : 3
ProviderName :
FreeSpace    : 165753094144
Size         : 249951154176
VolumeName   :
PS C:\> exit
ComputerName      Danger        Free        Size
------------      ------        ----        ----
localhost         True          154         233
```

You can also set breakpoints in the PowerShell ISE. They work much the same way. In the ISE select the line you want to "break" on and press F9. Or set the breakpoint via the Debug menu by selecting Toggle Breakpoint. You should get something like figure 31.1.

Run your script from within the ISE. If your script contains a single function, as ours does in this example, you won't see anything until you run the command. In the ISE command prompt, run the function and it'll hit the breakpoint, just as it did in the console:

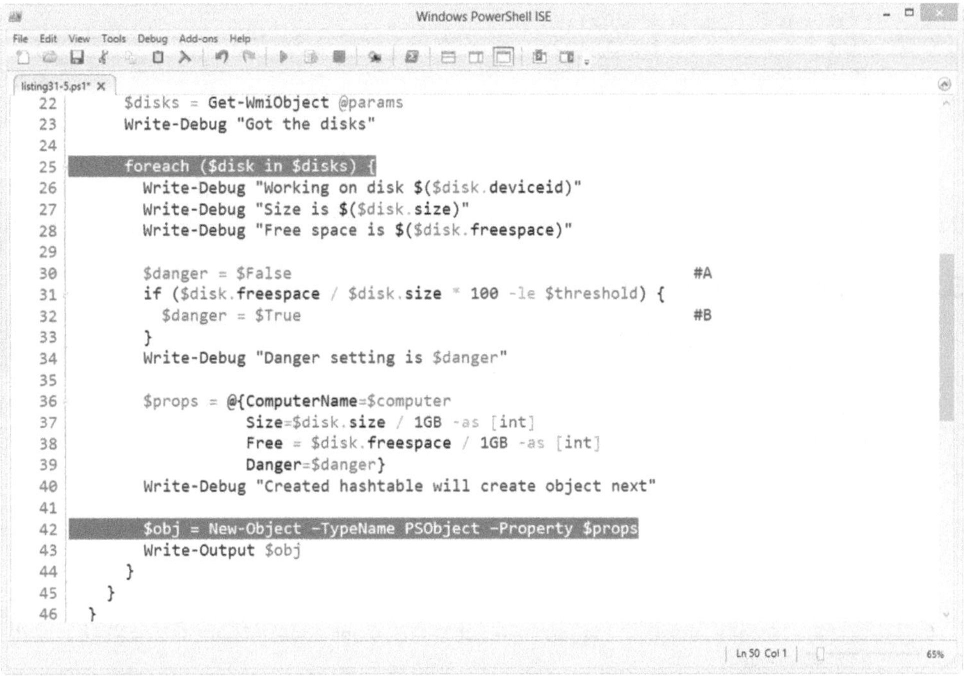

Figure 31.1 ISE breakpoints

```
PS C:\> get-diskinfo -threshold 20 -computerName $env:computername
Hit Line breakpoint on 'C:\Users\...\listing31-5.ps1:25'
[DBG]: PS C:\>>
```

This nested debug prompt has its own set of commands. Type ? at the DBG prompt:

```
[DBG]: PS C:\>> ?

s, stepInto         Single step (step into functions, scripts, etc.)
v, stepOver         Step to next statement (step over functions, scripts,
                    etc.)
o, stepOut          Step out of the current function, script, etc.
c, continue         Continue operation
q, quit             Stop operation and exit the debugger
k, Get-PSCallStack  Display call stack
l, list             List source code for the current script.
                    Use "list" to start from the current line, "list <m>"
                    to start from line <m>, and "list <m> <n>" to list <n>
                    lines starting from line <m>
<enter>             Repeat last command if it was stepInto, stepOver or
                    list
?, h                displays this help message.
```

You can use it much the way you used the prompt in the console. You can look at variables:

```
[DBG]: PS C:\>> $disks

DeviceID     : C:
DriveType    : 3
ProviderName :
FreeSpace    : 165753094144
Size         : 249951154176
VolumeName   :
```

When you're ready to continue, type C. The script will run until it hits another breakpoint or ends. If you wish to end the debug process, type Q at any DBG prompt.

Use the Debug menu to disable breakpoints or remove them altogether. Disabling them saves you from setting them again should the need to debug arise again.

31.4   *Using Set-PSDebug*

Another tool you might want to use is the Set-PSDebug cmdlet. You can use this cmdlet to debug not only scripts but also commands you run directly from the command prompt. The primary way to use it is to turn on tracing by using the –Trace parameter. This parameter accepts three different values:

```
PS C:\> help set-psdebug -parameter Trace

-Trace <Int32>
    Specifies the trace level:
    0 - Turn script tracing off
    1 - Trace script lines as they are executed
    2 - Trace script lines, variable assignments, function calls,
and scripts.
    Required?                  false
    Position?                  named
```

```
      Default value
      Accept pipeline input?       false
      Accept wildcard characters?  False
```

Most of the time, you'll want to use a value of 2:

```
PS C:\> set-psdebug -Trace 2
PS C:\> get-diskinfo -threshold 20 -compu $env:computername

DEBUG:    1+  >>>> get-diskinfo -threshold 20 -compu $env:computername
DEBUG:       ! CALL function '<ScriptBlock>'
DEBUG:   13+    BEGIN  >>>> {}
DEBUG:       ! CALL function 'Get-DiskInfo<Begin>'  (defined in file 'C:\u...
DEBUG:   13+    BEGIN { >>>> }
DEBUG:   14+    PROCESS  >>>> {
DEBUG:       ! CALL function 'Get-DiskInfo<Process>'  (defined in file 'C:...
DEBUG:   15+       >>>> Write-Debug "Started PROCESS block"
DEBUG:   16+     foreach ($computer in  >>>> $computername) {
DEBUG:       ! SET $foreach = 'SERENITY'.
DEBUG:   16+     foreach ( >>>> $computer in $computername) {
DEBUG:       ! SET $foreach = ''.
DEBUG:   46+     >>>> }
DEBUG:   47+    END  >>>> {}
DEBUG:       ! CALL function 'Get-DiskInfo<End>'  (defined in file 'C:\use...
DEBUG:   47+    END { >>>> }
```

The command ran and you can sort of see what it did. What you need to do is also turn on stepping:

```
PS C:\> set-psdebug -step -trace 2
```

Now when you run the command you'll get the same type of interactive debugging we showed you earlier:

```
PS C:\> get-diskinfo -threshold 20 -computer $env:computername
Continue with this operation?
   1+  >>>> get-diskinfo -threshold 20 -computer $env:computername
[Y] Yes  [A] Yes to All  [N] No  [L] No to All  [S] Suspend  [?] Help
(default is "Y"):
DEBUG:    1+  >>>> get-diskinfo -threshold 20 -computer $env:computername
DEBUG:       ! CALL function '<ScriptBlock>'
Continue with this operation?
  13+    BEGIN  >>>> {}
[Y] Yes  [A] Yes to All  [N] No  [L] No to All  [S] Suspend  [?] Help
(default is "Y"):
...
```

When you've finished debugging, you'll need to turn off stepping and tracing:

```
PS C:\> set-psdebug -Off
```

We're not sure the cmdlet adds anything in debugging your scripts than what we've already demonstrated, although there's one other use that might be of value when it comes to writing your scripts. At the beginning of your script, insert this command:

```
set-psdebug -strict
```

This command will force PowerShell to throw an exception if you reference a variable before it has been defined, thus eliminating bugs, often from typos, from the very beginning. But be careful. Set-PSDebug will turn this on for all scopes. In other words, once your script ends, strict mode will still be enabled in your PowerShell session, so this might lead to headaches. The other approach is to use Set-StrictMode –version latest, which works the same as Set-PSDebug –Strict but only for the current scope. Once your script ends, everything goes back to normal.

31.5 *Remote debugging*

So far what we've shown you has been debugging on the local machine. In PowerShell v2 and v3, it wasn't possible to use the PowerShell debugger against remote scripts—that is, you couldn't run the debugger through a PowerShell remoting session. If you needed to debug a script that existed only on the remote machine, you'd have to copy it to your machine or access the remote machine through a Remote Desktop Protocol (RDP) console or similar mechanism.

This changes in PowerShell v4. You can create a remoting session to another machine and debug a script on that machine through the remoting session. You can debug scripts, functions, workflows (we'll cover workflow debugging in the next section), commands, and expressions that are running in the PowerShell v4 console on remote machines.

> **NOTE** Notice the restriction inherent in that last sentence. Debugging remote PowerShell code is a console-only activity. You can't do this through the ISE. The remote computer must be running PowerShell v4.

Debugging, as you've seen, is an interactive activity. You know from chapter 10 that you can use Enter-PSSession to either create a remoting session or use an existing session. You can also use Enter-PSSession to enable you to reconnect to a disconnected session that's running a script on a remote computer. If the script hits a breakpoint, the debugger is started in your session. If the script is paused at a breakpoint, the debugger will be started as you enter the session.

What does this look like in action? To find out, save the contents of listing 31.4 as get-diskinfo.ps1. You can save the code on a remote computer, or if you don't have a remote computer handy, you can simulate this by saving to the local disk. We've saved the code into a folder called TestScripts.

> **NOTE** We chose listing 31.4 deliberately because we know that an error still exists.

Figure 31.2 shows creating the remoting session, changing the working directory, and running the test script.

The first command in figure 31.2 creates the session:

```
Enter-PSSession -ComputerName $env:COMPUTERNAME
```

We change the working folder:

```
cd C:\TestScripts
```

Figure 31.2 Entering a PowerShell remoting session and running the script

We load the function by dot-sourcing it and then we run it:

```
. .\get-diskinfo.ps1
Get-DiskInfo -computerName $env:COMPUTERNAME -threshold 20
```

You can see from the results that free space of 165 GB is being reported on a 232 GB disk. This isn't below the 20 percent threshold, so we need to track the error. You learned in section 31.2 where the errors lie so that you can easily set the appropriate breakpoints. If you were starting the debug process from scratch, you wouldn't have this luxury.

Figure 31.3 shows the breakpoints being added.

You've used `Set-PSBreakpoint` to add breakpoints of the variables `$disk`, `$props`, and `$danger`:

```
Set-PSBreakpoint -Variable disk, props, danger -Script .\get-diskinfo.ps1
```

> **NOTE** When you set breakpoints on variables, use just the variable name, not the $ symbol.

Looking at the code in the script you'd want to see the following:

- The data associated with a disk, including the size and amount of free space
- The variable `$danger` being set to `$True`
- The variable `$danger` being set to `$False` if the criterion on free space is met
- The value of the `$props` variable before the output object is created

```
[RSSURFACEPRO2]: PS C:\TestScripts> Set-PSBreakpoint -Variable disk, props, danger -Script .\get-diskinfo.ps1

ID Script                Line Command        Variable        Action
-- ------                ---- -------        --------        ------
 0 get-diskinfo.ps1                          disk
 1 get-diskinfo.ps1                          props
 2 get-diskinfo.ps1                          danger

[RSSURFACEPRO2]: PS C:\TestScripts>
```

Figure 31.3 Setting breakpoints

You can achieve this by running:

```
Set-PSBreakpoint -Variable disk, props, danger -Script .\get-diskinfo.ps1
```

Now it's time to run the script and step through the debug process. Using the Power-Shell remoting session you created from figures 31.2 and 31.3, start the script as you normally would:

```
[RSSURFACEPRO2]: PS C:\TestScripts> . .\get-diskinfo.ps1
[RSSURFACEPRO2]: PS C:\TestScripts> Get-DiskInfo
➥ -computerName $env:COMPUTERNAME -threshold 20
Entering debug mode. Use h or ? for help.

Hit Variable breakpoint on 'C:\TestScripts\get-diskinfo.ps1:$disk'
➥ (Write access)

At C:\TestScripts\get-diskinfo.ps1:22 char:16
+       foreach ($disk in $disks) {
+                ~
[RSSURFACEPRO2]: [DBG]: PS C:\TestScripts>> $disk

DeviceID      : C:
DriveType     : 3
ProviderName  :
FreeSpace     : 177410433024
Size          : 248951861248
VolumeName    : Windows
```

The script is dot-sourced to load the function, and then the function is called with the local machine name passed to the –computerName parameter and a threshold of 20. The script will run until it hits the first breakpoint; at that point, you see the message Entering debug mode. The information tells you that you've hit a variable breakpoint (shown in bold in the previous code) and indicates the variable that caused the break-point. Notice the prompt change. During normal operations, it includes the computer name, which is standard for remote interactive sessions:

```
[RSSURFACEPRO2]: PS C:\TestScripts>
```

When your session enters debug mode, the prompt changes to this:

```
[RSSURFACEPRO2]: [DBG]: PS C:\TestScripts>>
```

You get a visual indicator that you're in debug mode. You can examine the value of the $disk variable and determine that the data is as expected. Type exit to leave debug mode and move to the next breakpoint:

```
[RSSURFACEPRO2]: [DBG]: PS C:\TestScripts>> exit
Hit Variable breakpoint on 'C:\TestScripts\get-diskinfo.ps1:$danger'
➥ (Write access)

At C:\TestScripts\get-diskinfo.ps1:26 char:9
+         $danger = $True
+          ~
[RSSURFACEPRO2]: [DBG]: PS C:\TestScripts>> $danger
True
[RSSURFACEPRO2]: [DBG]: PS C:\TestScripts>>
```

The second breakpoint is reached and you have the opportunity to examine the $danger variable. As expected, it's set to $True. Type exit to proceed to the next breakpoint:

```
[RSSURFACEPRO2]: [DBG]: PS C:\TestScripts>> exit
Hit Variable breakpoint on 'C:\TestScripts\get-diskinfo.ps1:$props'
➥ (Write access)

At C:\TestScripts\get-diskinfo.ps1:31 char:9
+         $props = @{'ComputerName'=$computer;
+         ~
[RSSURFACEPRO2]: [DBG]: PS C:\TestScripts>> $props

Name                          Value
----                          -----
ComputerName                  RSSURFACEPRO2
Danger                        True
Free                          165
Size                          232

[RSSURFACEPRO2]: [DBG]: PS C:\TestScripts>>
```

This breakpoint is for the $props variable, and you can see that the disk has 165 GB free out of 232 GB. The $danger variable is set to $True but a simple code check shows that it shouldn't be.

As you'll recall, we expected to see four breakpoints. The third should have been when $danger was set to $False. That obviously didn't happen, so you should concentrate on that area, which leads to the discovery of the logic error you saw earlier. Typing exit one last time allows the script to run to completion.

You can remove the breakpoints in bulk like this:

```
Get-PSBreakpoint | Remove-PSBreakpoint
```

You can then exit the remote session or use it for other purposes.

One of the big things in PowerShell v3 was workflows. In that version of PowerShell, you couldn't use the standard debugging cmdlets against workflows. Now you can.

31.6 Debugging workflows

As you learned in chapter 23, PowerShell v4 lets you debug workflows in the console or the ISE. There are some limitations to debugging workflows:

- Although you can *view* workflow variables in the debugger, you can't *set* workflow variables through the debugger.
- Tab completion isn't available in the workflow debugger.
- You can only debug workflows that are running synchronously; you can't debug workflows running as jobs.
- Debugging nested workflows isn't supported.

To illustrate, let's use the simple introductory workflow in listing 23.1. It's repeated here for your convenience:

```
workflow Test-Workflow {
    $a = 1
    $a
    $a++
    $a
    $b = $a + 2
    $b
}
Test-Workflow
```

Save the workflow as testwf.ps1. You can then set a breakpoint:

```
Set-PSBreakpoint -Script .\testwf.ps1 -Line 6
```

This code sets a breakpoint on the line

```
$b = $a + 2
```

Now run the script:

```
PS C:\> .\testwf.ps1
1
2
Entering debug mode. Use h or ? for help.

Hit Line breakpoint on 'C:\TestScripts\testwf.ps1:6'

At C:\TestScripts\testwf.ps1:6 char:10
+       $b = $a + 2
+              ~~~~~~
[WFDBG:localhost]: PS C:\TestScripts>>
```

The first thing to notice is the way the prompt changes to indicate that a workflow ID is being debugged. Once you're in debug mode, you can investigate the value of variables, as you've seen earlier:

```
[WFDBG:localhost]: PS C:\TestScripts>> $a
2
[WFDBG:localhost]: PS C:\TestScripts>> $b
[WFDBG:localhost]: PS C:\TestScripts>>
```

$a has a value of 2, as you'd expect. $b doesn't have a value because entering debug mode through a breakpoint on a line positions you at the start of the line in question that's before that line is executed. You can run that one line of the script by typing s at the prompt:

```
[WFDBG:localhost]: PS C:\TestScripts>> s
At C:\TestScripts\testwf.ps1:7 char:5
+       $b
+        ~~
[WFDBG:localhost]: PS C:\TestScripts>> $b
4
[WFDBG:localhost]: PS C:\TestScripts>>
```

The command s is a shortcut for Step-Into. You've instructed the debugger to execute the next statement and stop. Other commands are available to skip functions, continue to the end of the script, and list the part of the script that's executing. These commands are described in the help file about_debuggers.

In the current example, because the line of code that sets that value has been executed, you can now test the value of $b. You can continue to step through the code or exit debug mode and allow the workflow to complete.

> **NOTE** You can also debug the workflow when it's executing on a remote computer. Set the line breakpoints and then invoke the workflow; you can specify remote computers with the -PSComputername parameter.

Unfortunately, it appears that you can set breakpoints only on line numbers (using Set-PSBreakpoint or the Debug menu in the PowerShell ISE) and not on variables or commands in the workflow.

31.7 *Debugging in third-party editors*

If you're using a third-party scripting editor, you should be able to use the debugging cmdlets and breakpoints we've shown you in this chapter. In fact, most likely the editor will use these tools to provide a debugging feature for their product. Naturally we can't cover how every editor handles debugging, so you'll have to check product documentation.

31.8 *Summary*

Debugging can be tricky, but PowerShell provides straightforward tools that let you quickly compare your expectations to what a script is doing. The tricky part involves coming up with those expectations: If you don't have an idea of what a script should be doing, then debugging it is almost impossible, no matter what tools you have. Finally, if you can prevent bugs from happening in the first place with cmdlets like Set-StrictMode, you'll reduce the amount of time you need to spend debugging. We recommend reading the help file about_Debuggers.

Functions that work like cmdlets

We're not going to introduce any major new concepts or techniques in this chapter. Instead, we'll use this chapter to bring together many of the things that the previous eight or so chapters covered. We'll take a task, write a command to perform that task, and then turn that task into a complete script module, complete with error handling, debugging provisions, a custom default view, a type extension, and lots more. This example is intended to be a soup-to-nuts practical illustration of something you might do on your own.

As we walk you through the various steps, pay close attention to the process we use, as well as the final result of that process. When you're on your own, we're obviously not going to be there with step-by-step instructions. We've tried, in this chapter, to document our way of thinking, and our creation process, so that you can start to adopt them as your own, enabling you to perform this same, build-it-from-scratch process for whatever tasks you need to complete.

We'll present our solution in progressively more complete steps. When we've finished, we'll provide a formal, numbered listing that has the final product. If you're eager to just see the end result, skip ahead to listing 32.1.

Additional steps are required to finalize the module, shown in listings 32.2 to 32.4.

32.1 Defining the task

First, you must define the task. For this example, you'll use a combination of Active Directory and Windows Management Instrumentation (WMI) to write a function that'll accept an organizational unit (OU) name and return all of the nondisabled computers in that OU as well as any child OUs.

> **NOTE** We're assuming that you're using the Microsoft Active Directory cmdlets. If you use the Quest cmdlets, the changes are simple. If you can't use either of these cmdlet sets, it's possible to code this module using Active Directory Service Interfaces (ADSI), but doing so involves more work.

For each computer, you want to display several pieces of information:

- The date the directory object was created
- The date the computer last changed its password
- The computer's operating system, service pack, and version
- The computer's name
- The amount of physical memory installed in the computer
- The number of processors in the computer and the processor architecture (64- or 32-bit)

Most of this information is stored in Active Directory; you'll need to get the memory and processor information by querying the computer from WMI. It's possible, of course, that a computer won't be available for WMI queries when you run your function. If that's the case, you want the function to output the information it has and to leave the memory and processor fields blank.

You want the objects produced by your function to display in a table by default. You'd like that table to list the following, in order:

- Computer name
- Operating system version
- Installed RAM, in gigabytes with up to two decimal places
- Number of processors

The other information won't display by default. You also want these objects to have a `Ping()` method, which will attempt to ping the computer and return either `True` if it can be pinged or `False` if it can't. You want your function to follow all of PowerShell's normal patterns and practices, including displaying help, examples, and so forth.

When you specify the OU that you want the function to query, you want to be able to do so by giving one or more OU names to a parameter or by piping in strings that contain OU names. You expect to provide OU names in a complete distinguished name (DN) format, such as OU=Sales,OU=East,DC=company,DC=com.

32.2   *Building the command*

Let's start by building the command—well, commands, because there will be more than one—that accomplish the task. You'll do so in a script file so that you can easily edit and rerun the commands over and over until you get it right.

> **TIP**   In terms of process, this is an important step: You shouldn't start building the structure of a fancy function, adding error handling and all that other jazz, until you've gotten the basics working properly.

Here's your first attempt:

```
Import-Module ActiveDirectory
$computers = Get-ADComputer -Filter * -SearchBase "dc=company,dc=pri"
$computers
```

Note that you didn't even attempt to add the WMI piece yet. One thing at a time—that's the way to get something done without frustrating yourself. If you approach the problem one step at a time and prove the code works, you limit the troubleshooting and debugging you need to do because any problems will almost always be in the last bit of code you added.

You're storing the retrieved computers in the $computers variable and then simply displaying its contents to check your work. Try running this for yourself, changing the distinguished name of the -SearchBase parameter to match your domain, and you'll notice that your output has a problem:

```
DistinguishedName : CN=WIN-KNBA0R0TM23,OU=Domain
                    Controllers,DC=company,DC=pri
DNSHostName       : WIN-KNBA0R0TM23.company.pri
Enabled           : True
Name              : WIN-KNBA0R0TM23
ObjectClass       : computer
ObjectGUID        : 274d4d87-8b63-4279-8a81-c5dd5963c4a0
SamAccountName    : WIN-KNBA0R0TM23$
SID               : S-1-5-21-29812541-3325070801-1520984716-1000
UserPrincipalName :
```

Doh! You don't have most of the properties you wanted, because you didn't ask the directory service to give them to you. Again, this is why you started small. If you'd simply taken that output and charged ahead with the rest of the script, you'd be spending a good amount of time debugging. As it is, you can immediately check your work, spot your error, and go back and fix it. After a few tries, this is what you come up with:

```
Import-Module ActiveDirectory
$computers = Get-ADComputer -Filter * -SearchBase "dc=company,dc=pri" `
             -Properties Name,OperatingSystem,OperatingSystemVersion,
                    OperatingSystemServicePack,passwordLastSet,
                    whenCreated
```

```
foreach ($computer in $computers) {
  $cs = Get-WmiObject -Class Win32_ComputerSystem `
        -ComputerName $computer.Name
  $properties = @{'ComputerName'=$computer.name
                  'OS'=$computer.OperatingSystem
                  'OSVersion'=$computer.OperatingSystemVersion
                  'SPVersion'=$computer.OperatingSystemServicePack
                  'WhenCreated'=$computer.whenCreated
                  'PasswordLastSet'=$computer.passwordLastSet
                  'Processors'=$cs.NumberOfProcessors
                  'RAM'='{0:N}' -f ($cs.TotalPhysicalMemory / 1GB)
                 }
  $object = New-Object -TypeName PSObject -Property $properties
  Write-Output $object
}
```

You can see that you've added the WMI query in the ForEach loop and that the final object being written to the pipeline has all the information you want:

```
ComputerName     : WIN-KNBA0R0TM23
WhenCreated      : 8/30/2011 1:26:17 PM
RAM              : 1.00
PasswordLastSet  : 10/10/2014 3:37:18 PM
OSVersion        : 6.1 (7601)
OS               : Windows Server 2008 R2 Standard
SPVersion        : Service Pack 1
Processors       : 1
```

(The format of the time and date information is controlled by the settings on our systems, which means that you may see a different format.) At this point, you have your basic functionality working properly. That's the hardest part of a task like this, so you've focused on getting it right, rather than on the structure of a function, or the addition of error handling, or anything else. You'll notice that you've hardcoded the search base, scoping it to the entire domain, and for now you're assuming that every computer will be available for the WMI query.

32.3 *Parameterizing the pipeline*

Our next step will be to find all of the hardcoded information and parameterize it. You've already said that the only input you want to provide is the OU to query, which is the search base, so you'll create a –SearchBase parameter. You'll add the necessary decorators to enable cmdlet-style parameter binding, and you'll make your parameter mandatory. You'll also rig it up to accept pipeline input ByValue so that you can pipe strings into it. We'll highlight the additions and changes in boldface:

```
[CmdletBinding()]
param(
    [Parameter(Mandatory=$true,ValueFromPipeline=$true)]
    [String[]]$searchBase
)
BEGIN {
    Import-Module ActiveDirectory
}
```

```
PROCESS {
    foreach ($ou in $searchBase) {
        $computers = Get-ADComputer -Filter * -SearchBase $ou `
                        -Properties Name,OperatingSystem,
                                    OperatingSystemVersion,
                                    OperatingSystemServicePack,
                                    passwordLastSet,whenCreated
            foreach ($computer in $computers) {
                $cs = Get-WmiObject -Class Win32_ComputerSystem `
                    -ComputerName $computer.name
                $properties = @{'ComputerName'=$computer.name;
                            'OS'=$computer.OperatingSystem;
                            'OSVersion'=$computer.OperatingSystemVersion;
                            'SPVersion'=$computer.OperatingSystemServicePack;
                            'WhenCreated'=$computer.whenCreated;
                            'PasswordLastSet'=$computer.passwordLastSet;
                            'Processors'=$cs.NumberOfProcessors;
                            'RAM'='{0:N}' -f ($cs.TotalPhysicalMemory / 1GB)
                }
                $object = New-Object -TypeName PSObject -Property $properties
                Write-Output $object
            } #end computer foreach
    } #end OU foreach
}
END {}
```

You also adjusted the formatting a bit so that every nested block is properly indented. (We had to reformat slightly just to make everything fit neatly on the page of this book.) But you didn't add any functionality. Let's review what you did:

```
[CmdletBinding()]                              ←——❶ Cmdlet binding
param(
    [Parameter(Mandatory=$true,ValueFromPipeline=$true)]   ❷ Parameter
    [String[]]$searchBase                                     block
)
BEGIN {                                        ←——❸ BEGIN block
    Import-Module ActiveDirectory
}                                              ❹ PROCESS
PROCESS {                                      ←—┘  block       ❺ ForEach
    foreach ($ou in $searchBase) {             ←————              loop
        $computers = Get-ADComputer -Filter * -SearchBase $ou ` ←
                        -Properties Name,OperatingSystem,
                                    OperatingSystemVersion,     ❻ Variable
                                    OperatingSystemServicePack,
                                    passwordLastSet,whenCreated
            foreach ($computer in $computers) {
                $cs = Get-WmiObject -Class Win32_ComputerSystem `
                    -ComputerName $computer.name
                $properties = @{'ComputerName'=$computer.name;
                            'OS'=$computer.OperatingSystem;
                            'OSVersion'=$computer.OperatingSystemVersion;
                            'SPVersion'=$computer.OperatingSystemServicePack;
                            'WhenCreated'=$computer.whenCreated;
                            'PasswordLastSet'=$computer.passwordLastSet;
```

```
                    'Processors'=$cs.NumberOfProcessors;
                    'RAM'='{0:N}' -f ($cs.TotalPhysicalMemory / 1GB)
                }
            $object = New-Object -TypeName PSObject -Property $properties
            Write-Output $object
        } #end computer foreach
    } #end OU foreach
}
END {}
```

7 **END block**

You started the script with the `[CmdletBinding()]` decorator **1**. Doing so allowed you to add information to your parameter. It also supplies access to the common parameters such as -Verbose and -Debug. The parameter itself is declared within a parameter block **2**. You used the `[Parameter()]` decorator (which is legal because you used cmdlet binding) to declare your parameter as mandatory and to indicate that it'll accept input from the pipeline ByValue. The parameter itself is declared as accepting one or more strings, so those strings will be passed along from the pipeline.

Because the ActiveDirectory module needs to be loaded only once, you added a BEGIN block to do that at the start of the execution **3**. The PROCESS block contains the working commands for your script **4**. It'll execute once for every object input from the pipeline.

Because you've set this up to accept one or more search OUs, you need to go through those one at a time, which is what the foreach block does **5**. In it, you'll take one path at a time out of $searchBase and put it in $ou so that you can work with it. You therefore place $ou in the command **6**, instead of your hardcoded search path.

Just for neatness, you included an END block **7**. There's nothing in it, so you could just omit it, but it feels right to add it because you also used BEGIN and PROCESS.

> **TIP** Notice that the closing curly braces for the two foreach loops are labeled with comments. This is a useful technique in long pieces of code so that you're aware of where your loops end. It also helps keep track of the braces because it's easy to leave one out and it can take a while to track down even if you're using the ISE.

It's important to test the script again after making all those changes; a simple typo could mess you up, and it'll be easier to catch it now than later. You'll save the script as Test.ps1 and then test it in four ways:

```
# Make sure you can use a single location with a parameter
./test -searchBase 'dc=company,dc= pri '

# Now multiple values with a parameter
./test -searchBase 'dc=company,dc= pri ','dc=company,dc= pri '

# pipe in one value
'dc=company,dc= pri ' | ./test

# pipe in multiple values
'dc=company,dc= pri ', 'dc=company,dc= pri ' | ./test
```

Notice that you're not trying to be ambitious with your testing. You're still in a test domain (running inside a virtual machine), and it has only one computer in the domain. But the commands work properly: The first and third return one computer, and the second and last return two computers (technically the same one, queried twice).

> **TIP** Put your tests into a script and then you can call a script to test your script! Your tests then become repeatable and are easy to reuse when you change the script. If you want to impress your developer friends, the technique is known as *regression testing*.

If you run this script without supplying the distinguished name of at least one OU, you'll be prompted for values (this is because of the Mandatory=$true statement on the [Parameter()] decorator). The script is set to accept an array, so it'll keep prompting for multiple inputs. Press Enter in the console or click OK at the ISE prompt to tell PowerShell there's no more input.

32.4   *Adding professional features*

Now you can start adding some professionalism to the script. These steps aren't required, but the more you can add to your script, especially so that it acts like a cmdlet, the better your script. You want to make your script as robust as possible as well as easy to troubleshoot or debug.

32.5   *Error handling*

You've said that you want the memory and processor columns to be blank if you can't query a computer via WMI, so let's do that next:

```
[CmdletBinding()]
param(
    [Parameter(Mandatory=$true,ValueFromPipeline=$true)]
    [String[]]$searchBase
)
BEGIN {
    Import-Module ActiveDirectory
}
PROCESS {
    foreach ($ou in $searchBase) {
        $computers = Get-ADComputer -Filter * -SearchBase $ou `
                    -Properties Name,OperatingSystem,
                                OperatingSystemVersion,
                                OperatingSystemServicePack,        ❶ Try block
                                passwordLastSet,whenCreated
        foreach ($computer in $computers) {
            Try {                                                  ❷ Tracking
                $wmi_worked = $true                                  variable
                $cs = Get-WmiObject -Class Win32_ComputerSystem `
                    -ComputerName $computer.name -ErrorAction Stop ❸ Error
            }                                                        action
            Catch {
                $wmi_worked = $false        ❹ Catch
            }                                  block
```

```
            $properties = @{'ComputerName'=$computer.name;
                            'OS'=$computer.OperatingSystem;
                            'OSVersion'=$computer.OperatingSystemVersion;
                            'SPVersion'=$computer.OperatingSystemServicePack;
                            'WhenCreated'=$computer.whenCreated;
                            'PasswordLastSet'=$computer.passwordLastSet
                           }
          if ($wmi_worked) {
            $properties += @{'Processors'=$cs.NumberOfProcessors;
                            'RAM'='{0:N}' -f ($cs.TotalPhysicalMemory / 1GB)
                           }
          } else {
            $properties += @{'Processors'='';
                             'RAM'=''}
          }
            $object = New-Object -TypeName PSObject -Property $properties
            Write-Output $object
          } #end computer foreach
      } #end OU foreach
}
END {}
```

❺ **Error behavior**

Here's what you added:

- You enclosed the WMI query in a `Try` block ❶.
- In the `Try` block, you first set a tracking variable equal to `$True` ❷. You'll use this to keep track of whether the WMI query succeeded.
- You have to tell the `Get-WmiObject` cmdlet to alter its normal error behavior ❸, which is done with the `-ErrorAction` parameter. Setting the parameter to `Stop` will ensure that you get to catch any errors that occur.
- That catching occurs in the `Catch` block ❹, where you're setting your tracking variable to `$False`, indicating that the WMI query failed.
- You also added an `If` construct ❺, which will check the contents of the tracking variable. If it's `$True`, then the WMI query succeeded, and you'll append the WMI information to your hash table. If it's `$False`, then the WMI query failed. You'll still append the two columns to the hash table, but you'll put blank values in them.

Once again, you've made sure to test your script, with both working and nonworking computer names. You added a computer object to the directory and made sure it doesn't exist on the network so that you have a *bad* computer name to query. Here's the test:

```
PS C:\> .\test.ps1 -searchBase "dc=company,dc=pri"
PasswordLastSet : 10/10/2014 3:37:18 PM
WhenCreated     : 8/30/2011 1:26:17 PM
RAM             : 1.00
OSVersion       : 6.1 (7601)
OS              : Windows Server 2008 R2 Standard
Processors      : 1
SPVersion       : Service Pack 1
ComputerName    : WIN-KNBA0R0TM23
PasswordLastSet : 12/1/2011 10:31:46 AM
```

```
WhenCreated       : 12/1/2011 10:31:45 AM
RAM               :
OSVersion         :
OS                :
Processors        :
SPVersion         :
ComputerName      : BAD
```

As you can see, Active Directory returns blank properties for information it doesn't have, such as OSVersion, OS, and SPVersion.

> **NOTE** It's also possible for someone to specify a search base that doesn't exist, which would return an error. You're choosing not to deal with that because the normal PowerShell error message for that situation is pretty descriptive. By not attempting to trap the normal error, you're allowing it to be displayed to the user, who will see it and hopefully know what they've done wrong.

You might also notice at this point that the output from your script doesn't list the properties in the same order in which you defined them. That's okay—PowerShell kind of puts things in whatever order it wants. You can always fix that by piping the output to Select-Object or a Format cmdlet:

```
PS C:\> .\32.ps1 -searchBase "dc=company,dc=pri" |
➥ Format-Table ComputerName,WhenCreated,OSVersion,RAM,Processors,
➥ SPVersion

ComputerName WhenCreated  OSVersion     RAM           Processors SPVersion
------------ -----------  ---------     ---           ---------- ---------
WIN-KNBA0... 8/30/2011... 6.1 (7601)    1.00                   1 Service ...
BAD          12/1/2011...
```

That's the beauty of producing objects as output: You can use all of PowerShell's other capabilities to get the output into whatever form you need it on any given day or for any situation. Alternatively, you can use an ordered hash table for the properties (see chapter 16), which will preserve the order you want.

32.5.1 *Adding verbose and debug output*

While you're at it, you should go ahead and add some verbose and debug output. Right now the script is working fine, but you're not so confident that you think you'll never have to debug it! Adding some debug information right now will save time when the inevitable bugs creep in later. The verbose output will serve to document what the script is doing, as well as provide progress information to someone who's nervous about whether the script is doing anything:

```
[CmdletBinding()]
param(
    [Parameter(Mandatory=$true,ValueFromPipeline=$true)]
    [String[]]$searchBase
)
```

```
BEGIN {
    Write-Verbose "Loading ActiveDirectory module"
    Import-Module ActiveDirectory
}
PROCESS {
    Write-Debug "Starting PROCESS block"
    foreach ($ou in $searchBase) {
        Write-Verbose "Getting computers from $ou"
        $computers = Get-ADComputer -Filter * -SearchBase $ou `
                    -Properties Name,OperatingSystem,
                                OperatingSystemVersion,
                                OperatingSystemServicePack,
                                passwordLastSet,whenCreated
        Write-Verbose "Got $($computers | measure | select -expand count)"
        foreach ($computer in $computers) {
          Try {
            Write-Verbose "WMI query to $computer"
            $wmi_worked = $true
            $cs = Get-WmiObject -Class Win32_ComputerSystem `
                -ComputerName $computer.name -ErrorAction Stop
          } Catch {
            Write-Verbose "WMI query failed"
            $wmi_worked = $false
          }
          Write-Debug "Assembling property hash table"
          $properties = @{'ComputerName'=$computer.name;
                          'OS'=$computer.OperatingSystem;
                          'OSVersion'=$computer.OperatingSystemVersion;
                          'SPVersion'=$computer.OperatingSystemServicePack;
                          'WhenCreated'=$computer.whenCreated;
                          'PasswordLastSet'=$computer.passwordLastSet
                         }
          if ($wmi_worked) {
            $properties += @{'Processors'=$cs.NumberOfProcessors;
                        'RAM'='{0:N}' -f ($cs.TotalPhysicalMemory / 1GB)
                            }
          }
          else {
            $properties += @{'Processors'='';
                            'RAM'=''}
          }
          Write-Debug "Property hash table complete"
          $object = New-Object -TypeName PSObject -Property $properties
          Write-Output $object
        } #end computer foreach
    } # end OU foreach
}
END {}
```

You followed a couple of rules when adding the new output:

- Because you don't have a specific bug you're trying to track down yet, you added `Write-Debug` commands at key points in the script: as the main PROCESS block begins and before and after you create the hash table with your output information. If you need to debug, you expect to have to start with those sections.

- You added `Write-Verbose` calls before any major delays might occur, such as making a WMI query, and before each major section of the script.

Running your script again with the –verbose parameter turns on verbose output. It might surprise you:

```
PS C:\> .\test.ps1 -searchBase "dc=company,dc=pri" -verbose
VERBOSE: Loading ActiveDirectory module
VERBOSE: Importing cmdlet 'Add-ADComputerServiceAccount'.
VERBOSE: Importing cmdlet
'Add-ADDomainControllerPasswordReplicationPolicy'.
...
VERBOSE: Importing cmdlet 'Unlock-ADAccount'.
VERBOSE: Getting computers from dc=company,dc=pri
VERBOSE: Got 2
VERBOSE: WMI query to CN=WIN-KNBA0R0TM23,OU=Domain
Controllers,DC=company,DC=pri

PasswordLastSet : 10/10/2014 3:37:18 PM
WhenCreated     : 8/30/2011 1:26:17 PM
RAM             : 1.00
OSVersion       : 6.1 (7601)
OS              : Windows Server 2008 R2 Standard
Processors      : 1
SPVersion       : Service Pack 1
ComputerName    : WIN-KNBA0R0TM23

VERBOSE: WMI query to CN=BAD,CN=Computers,DC=company,DC=pri
VERBOSE: WMI query failed
PasswordLastSet : 12/1/2011 10:31:46 AM
WhenCreated     : 12/1/2011 10:31:45 AM
RAM             :
OSVersion       :
OS              :
Processors      :
SPVersion       :
ComputerName    : BAD
```

We clipped some of the output in the middle of all that to save space—you can see the "..." we inserted. What happened? Well, when you added the -Verbose switch, it passed that along to the other cmdlets in the script, including `Import-Module ActiveDirectory`. So your verbose output included all the commands that the module was loading. But you can see the output you added yourself! You can tell `Import-Module` to suppress its own verbose output:

```
Import-Module ActiveDirectory -Verbose:$false
```

Test your script again, with verbose output turned on:

```
PS C:\> .\test.ps1 -searchBase "dc=company,dc=pri" -verbose
VERBOSE: Loading ActiveDirectory module
VERBOSE: Getting computers from dc=company,dc=pri
VERBOSE: Got 2
VERBOSE: WMI query to CN=WIN-KNBA0R0TM23,OU=Domain
Controllers,DC=company,DC=pri
PasswordLastSet : 10/10/2014 3:37:18 PM
WhenCreated     : 8/30/2011 1:26:17 PM
```

```
RAM              : 1.00
OSVersion        : 6.1 (7601)
OS               : Windows Server 2008 R2 Standard
Processors       : 1
SPVersion        : Service Pack 1
ComputerName     : WIN-KNBA0R0TM23

VERBOSE: WMI query to CN=BAD,CN=Computers,DC=company,DC=pri
VERBOSE: WMI query failed
PasswordLastSet : 12/1/2011 10:31:46 AM
WhenCreated     : 12/1/2011 10:31:45 AM
RAM              :
OSVersion        :
OS               :
Processors       :
SPVersion        :
ComputerName     : BAD
```

Much better!

32.5.2 Defining a custom object name

You know that you're going to want to create a default view, and a type extension, for your output. To do that, you need to ensure your output object has a unique type name. It takes only one line of code to add it, just after the `New-Object` command and before the `Write-Output` command:

```
$object = New-Object -TypeName PSObject -Property $properties
$object.PSObject.TypeNames.Insert(0,'Company.ComputerInfo')
Write-Output $object
```

Doing this now will set you up for some of your next tasks.

32.6 Making it a function and adding help

You said that you wanted your script to follow PowerShell's best practices and patterns, and displaying help is one of them. Listing 32.1 shows the script again, with the help added.

> **NOTE** Some folks refer to this type of function as a script cmdlet because it looks, feels, and works almost exactly like a real PowerShell cmdlet but was created in a script instead of in Visual Studio.

Listing 32.1 Toolkit.psm1

```
function Get-COComputerInfo {
<#
.SYNOPSIS
Retrieves key computer information from AD and WMI
.DESCRIPTION
Get-COComputerInfo retrieves key computer information from both
Active Directory (AD), and from the computer itself using WMI. In
the case of a computer that is in AD but not available for the WMI
query, certain information in the output may be blank.
```

```
You need to specify a search path, and can specify more than one.
This can be an organizational unit (OU), or an entire domain.
The command will recurse all sub-OUs within whatever path(s) you
specify.
.PARAMETER searchBase
A string, or multiple strings, of locations to start looking for
computer objects in AD. Provide this in DN format, such as:
  'dc=company,dc=com','ou=sales,dc=company,dc=com'
.EXAMPLE
This example searches the Sales OU, and all sub-OUs:
  Get-COComputerInfo -searchBase 'ou=Sales,dc=company,dc=com'
.EXAMPLE
This example reads OU DNs from a text file, and searches them:
  Get-Content paths.txt | Get-COComputerInfo
#>
[CmdletBinding()]
  param(
      [Parameter(Mandatory=$true,ValueFromPipeline=$true)]
      [String[]]$searchBase
  )
  BEGIN {
      Write-Verbose "Loading ActiveDirectory module"
      Import-Module ActiveDirectory -Verbose:$false
  }
  PROCESS {
      Write-Debug "Starting PROCESS block"
      foreach ($ou in $searchBase) {
          Write-Verbose "Getting computers from $ou"
          $computers = Get-ADComputer -Filter * -SearchBase $ou `
                      -Properties Name,OperatingSystem,
                                 OperatingSystemVersion,
                                 OperatingSystemServicePack,
                                 passwordLastSet,whenCreated
          Write-Verbose "Got $($computers | measure | select -expand count)"
          foreach ($computer in $computers) {
            Try {
              Write-Verbose "WMI query to $computer"
              $wmi_worked = $true
              $cs = Get-WmiObject -Class Win32_ComputerSystem `
                    -ComputerName $computer.name -ErrorAction Stop
            } Catch {
              Write-Verbose "WMI query failed"
              $wmi_worked = $false
            }
            Write-Debug "Assembling property hash table"
            $properties = @{'ComputerName'=$computer.name;
                            'OS'=$computer.OperatingSystem;
                            'OSVersion'=$computer.OperatingSystemVersion;
                            'SPVersion'=$computer.OperatingSystemServicePack;
                            'WhenCreated'=$computer.whenCreated;
                            'PasswordLastSet'=$computer.passwordLastSet
                           }
            if ($wmi_worked) {
              $properties += @{'Processors'=$cs.NumberOfProcessors;
                        'RAM'='{0:N}' -f ($cs.TotalPhysicalMemory / 1GB)}
```

```
      } else {
        $properties += @{'Processors'='';
                         'RAM'=''}
      }
      Write-Debug "Property hash table complete"
      $object = New-Object -TypeName PSObject -Property $properties
      $object.PSObject.TypeNames.Insert(0,'Company.ComputerInfo')
      Write-Output $object
    } #end computer foreach
  } #end OU foreach
}
END {}
}
```

You wrapped the contents of the original PowerShell code in a function, named `Get-COComputerInfo`, so that it has a cmdlet-like name, and you added the `CO` prefix to the noun. The pretend organization is just named `company`, so you're prefixing all of its script, cmdlet, and function names with `CO`. Wrapping the script in a function makes it easier to add other functions to the same file, enabling you to build a little library of utilities for yourself.

So that's it. You could now load this script into memory and run `Help Get-COComputerInfo` to display help.

But loading this into memory isn't necessarily easy, because you've encapsulated the code into a function. You can't just run the script and then start using the function. This is probably a good time to make the script into a script module, simply by saving it in a new location and with a new filename. You'll save it in your Documents folder:

```
[My ]Documents\WindowsPowerShell\Modules\Toolkit\Toolkit.psm1
```

> **NOTE** The filename is important for this file. You're naming the module `Toolkit`, and so both the containing folder and the script file have to use that as their filename: Toolkit for the folder and Toolkit.psm1 for the filename. Anything else, and this won't work properly.

Now you can load the script into memory by running `Import-Module Toolkit`, and then either run `Get-COComputerInfo` or run `Help Get-COComputerInfo`. You can remove the module by running `Remove-Module Toolkit`; that'd be necessary if you made any changes to the script and wanted to reload it.

You've also added help capability to the function. You could put the help at the end of the function if you prefer it to be tucked away. See about_Comment_Based_Help for more details.

32.7 *Creating a custom view*

We've already given you a whole chapter (26) on custom views, so please refer back to that for a more detailed breakdown of how to create them. In this chapter, you're just going to create a view to go along with your Toolkit.psm1 script module, specifically to create a default view for your `Company.ComputerInfo` object, which is produced by the `Get-COComputerInfo` function.

Save the view file, shown in the following listing, here:

`[My ]Documents\WindowsPoyourShell\Modules\Toolkit\Toolkit.format.ps1xml`

Listing 32.2   Toolkit.format.ps1xml

```xml
<?xml version="1.0" encoding="utf-8" ?>
<Configuration>
    <ViewDefinitions>
        <View>
            <Name>Company.ComputerInfo</Name>
            <ViewSelectedBy>
                <TypeName>Company.ComputerInfo</TypeName>
            </ViewSelectedBy>
            <TableControl>
                <TableHeaders>
                    <TableColumnHeader>
                        <Label>ComputerName</Label>
                        <Width>14</Width>
                    </TableColumnHeader>
                    <TableColumnHeader>
                        <Label>OSVersion</Label>
                    </TableColumnHeader>
                    <TableColumnHeader>
                        <Label>RAM</Label>
                    </TableColumnHeader>
                    <TableColumnHeader>
                        <Label>Procs</Label>
                    </TableColumnHeader>
                </TableHeaders>
                <TableRowEntries>
                    <TableRowEntry>
                        <TableColumnItems>
                            <TableColumnItem>
                                <PropertyName>ComputerName</PropertyName>
                            </TableColumnItem>
                            <TableColumnItem>
                                <PropertyName>OSVersion</PropertyName>
                            </TableColumnItem>
                            <TableColumnItem>
                                <PropertyName>RAM</PropertyName>
                            </TableColumnItem>
                            <TableColumnItem>
                                <PropertyName>Processors</PropertyName>
                            </TableColumnItem>
                        </TableColumnItems>
                    </TableRowEntry>
                </TableRowEntries>
            </TableControl>
        </View>
    </ViewDefinitions>
</Configuration>
```

You should test this, of course. Load the formatting information into memory and then run your command:

```
PS C:\> Update-FormatData -PrependPath C:\Users\Administrator\Documents\
➥ WindowsPowerShell\Modules\Toolkit\toolkit.format.ps1xml
PS C:\> Get-COComputerInfo -searchBase 'dc=company,dc=pri'

ComputerName    OSVersion         RAM             Procs
------------    ---------         ---             -----
WIN-KNBA0R0...  6.1 (7601)        1.00            1
BAD
```

Looking good! You'll want that formatting information to load automatically, along with the module, but making that happen is the last step you'll take.

32.8   *Creating a type extension*

Reviewing the goals for this script, you also wanted the output objects to have a `Ping()` method that returned `True` or `False`. We covered type extensions in chapter 27, so we'll just jump right in and give you this one (listing 32.3). Save it as

```
[My ]Documents\WindowsPowerShell\Modules\Toolkit\toolkit.ps1xml
```

> **NOTE**   You've used toolkit as the filename for your PSM1 file, this .ps1xml file, and the .format.ps1xml file that you created. You didn't need to be that consistent; PowerShell doesn't care. This file could've been named Fred.ps1xml, and everything would still work the same. But keeping consistent names does make it easier for you to keep track of everything in your head.

Listing 32.3   Toolkit.ps1xml

```xml
<?xml version="1.0" encoding="utf-8" ?>
<Types>
    <Type>
        <Name>Company.ComputerInfo</Name>
        <Members>
            <ScriptMethod>
                <Name>Ping</Name>
                <Script>
                    Test-Connection -computername $this.ComputerName -quiet
                </Script>
            </ScriptMethod>
        </Members>
    </Type>
</Types>
```

You'll load the file in listing 32.3 into memory and then give it a brief test:

```
PS C:\> Update-TypeData -PrependPath C:\Users\Administrator\Documents\
➥ WindowsPowerShell\Modules\Toolkit\toolkit.ps1xml
PS C:\ > Get-COComputerInfo -searchBase 'dc=company,dc=pri' |
➥    foreach-object { $_.ping() }
True
False
```

Okay—not an awesome test, but good enough to prove that your new Ping() method is working correctly. If you want to see the results from multiple computers, you need to be able to link the ping result to the computer name:

```
Get-COComputerInfo -searchBase 'dc=company,dc=pri' |
select ComputerName, @{N="Pingable"; E={$($_.Ping())}}
```

Excellent!

32.9   *Making a module manifest*

Right now, your Toolkit module consists of three parts:

- The script file that contains your function, which is Toolkit.psm1, shown in listing 32.1
- The view file, which is Toolkit.format.ps1xml, shown in listing 32.2
- The type extension, which is Toolkit.ps1xml, shown in listing 32.3

Ideally, you want all three of these files to load and unload as a unit when you run Import-Module or Remove-Module. The way to do that is a module manifest, which you'll call Toolkit.psd1. Now, the filename does matter with this one: Because the module is contained in a folder named toolkit, the manifest filename also has to be toolkit, or PowerShell won't be able to find it.

You'll run the New-ModuleManifest command to create the manifest file. Rather than trying to remember all of its parameters, you'll just let it prompt you for what it wants:

```
PS C:\Users\Administrator\Documents\WindowsPowerShell\Modules\Toolkit> New-
ModuleManifest

cmdlet New-ModuleManifest at command pipeline position 1
Supply values for the following parameters:
Path: toolkit.psd1
NestedModules[0]:
Author: Don, Jeffery, and Richard
CompanyName: PowerShell in Depth
Copyright: Public Domain!
ModuleToProcess: toolkit.psm1
Description: Corporate PowerShell Tools
TypesToProcess[0]: toolkit.ps1xml
TypesToProcess[1]:
FormatsToProcess[0]: toolkit.format.ps1xml
FormatsToProcess[1]:
RequiredAssemblies[0]:
FileList[0]: toolkit.psm1
FileList[1]: toolkit.ps1xml
FileList[2]: toolkit.format.ps1xml
FileList[3]:
PS C:\Users\Administrator\Documents\WindowsPowerShell\Modules\Toolkit>
```

The cmdlet will create the module manifest, included in the next listing so that you can follow along.

Listing 32.4 Toolkit.psd1

```
#
# Module manifest for module 'toolkit'
#
# Generated by: Don, Jeffery, and Richard
#
# Generated on: 12/1/2013
#

@{

# Script module or binary module file associated with this manifest
ModuleToProcess = 'toolkit.psm1'

# Version number of this module.
ModuleVersion = '1.0'
# ID used to uniquely identify this module
GUID = '53901d6b-a07b-4c38-90f3-278737bc910c'
# Author of this module
Author = 'Don, Jeffery, and Richard'
# Company or vendor of this module
CompanyName = 'PowerShell in Depth'

# Copyright statement for this module
Copyright = 'Public Domain!'
# Description of the functionality provided by this module
Description = 'Corporate PowerShell Tools'

# Minimum version of the Windows PowerShell engine required by this module
PowerShellVersion = ''

# Name of the Windows PowerShell host required by this module
PowerShellHostName = ''
# Minimum version of the Windows PowerShell host required by this module
PowerShellHostVersion = ''

# Minimum version of the .NET Framework required by this module
DotNetFrameworkVersion = ''
# Minimum version of the common language runtime (CLR) required by
this module
CLRVersion = ''
# Processor architecture (None, X86, Amd64, IA64) required by this module
ProcessorArchitecture = ''
# Modules that must be imported into the global environment prior to
[CA}importing this module
RequiredModules = @()

# Assemblies that must be loaded prior to importing this module
RequiredAssemblies = @()

# Script files (.ps1) that are run in the caller's environment prior
to importing this module
ScriptsToProcess = @()
# Type files (.ps1xml) to be loaded when importing this module
TypesToProcess = 'toolkit.ps1xml'

# Format files (.ps1xml) to be loaded when importing this module
FormatsToProcess = 'toolkit.format.ps1xml'
```

```
# Modules to import as nested modules of the module specified
in ModuleToProcess
NestedModules = @()
# Functions to export from this module
FunctionsToExport = '*'
# Cmdlets to export from this module
CmdletsToExport = '*'

# Variables to export from this module
VariablesToExport = '*'
# Aliases to export from this module
AliasesToExport = '*'

# List of all modules packaged with this module
ModuleList = @()
# List of all files packaged with this module
FileList = 'toolkit.psm1', 'toolkit.ps1xml', 'toolkit.format.ps1xml'
# Private data to pass to the module specified in ModuleToProcess
PrivateData = ''
}
```

And with that, you've finished. Opening a brand-new shell and running `Import-Module Toolkit` successfully loads your `Get-COComputerInfo` command, its default view, and its type extension (which creates the `Ping()` method on your output objects). Congratulations!

32.10 *Summary*

This chapter has provided a complete, from-scratch look at building a production-quality tool. You added error handling and verbose output, ensured that help was available, and packaged the command as a module that includes a custom default view and a useful type extension. This is what you should aspire to for your PowerShell commands: Make them look, work, and feel just like a native PowerShell command as much as possible. As you've seen, there's a good amount of work involved, but most of it's straightforward. And the payoff is an easier-to-use, more consistent command that works perfectly within the shell.

Tips and tricks for creating reports

This chapter covers

- Working with HTML fragments
- Creating HTML-style reports
- Sending reports by email

There's definitely a trick to creating reports with PowerShell. Remember that PowerShell isn't at its best when it's forced to work with text; objects are where it excels. The more you can build your reports from objects, letting PowerShell take care of turning those into the necessary text, the better off you'll be.

33.1 *What not to do*

Let's start this chapter with an example of what we think is poor report-generating technique. We see code like this more often than we'd like. Most of the time the IT pro doesn't know any better and is perpetuating techniques from other languages such as VBScript. The following listing, which we devoutly hope you'll never run yourself, is a common approach that you'll see less-informed administrators take.

Listing 33.1   A poorly designed inventory report

```
param ($computername)
Write-Host '------- COMPUTER INFORMATION -------'
Write-Host "Computer Name: $computername"
$os = Get-WmiObject -Class Win32_OperatingSystem -ComputerName $computername
Write-Host "   OS Version: $($os.version)"
Write-Host "     OS Build: $($os.buildnumber)"
Write-Host " Service Pack: $($os.servicepackmajorversion)"
$cs = Get-WmiObject -Class Win32_ComputerSystem -ComputerName $computername
Write-Host "          RAM: $($cs.totalphysicalmemory)"
Write-Host " Manufacturer: $($cs.manufacturer)"
Write-Host "        Model: $($cd.model)"
Write-Host "   Processors: $($cs.numberofprocessors)"
$bios = Get-WmiObject -Class Win32_BIOS -ComputerName $computername
Write-Host "BIOS Serial: $($bios.serialnumber)"
Write-Host ''
Write-Host '------- DISK INFORMATION -------'
Get-WmiObject -Class Win32_LogicalDisk -Comp $computername -Filt
'drivetype=3' |
Select-Object @{N='Drive';E={$_.DeviceID}},
              @{N='Size(GB)';E={$_.Size / 1GB -as [int]}},
              @{N='FreeSpace(GB)';E={$_.freespace / 1GB -as [int]}} |
Format-Table -AutoSize
```

The code in listing 33.1 produces a report something like the one shown in figure 33.1.

It does the job, we suppose, but Don has a saying involving angry deities and puppies that he utters whenever he sees a script that outputs pure text like this. First of all, this script can only ever produce output on the screen because it's using `Write-Host`. In most cases, if you find yourself using only `Write-Host`, you're probably doing it

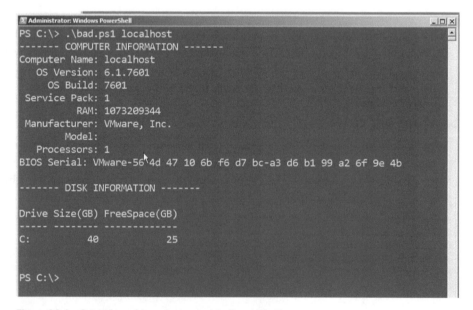

Figure 33.1   A text-based inventory report in PowerShell

wrong. Wouldn't it be nice to have the option of putting this information into a file or creating an HTML page? You could achieve that by just changing all of the `Write-Host` commands to `Write-Output`, but you still wouldn't be doing it the right way.

There are a lot of better ways that you could produce such a report, and that's what this chapter is all about. First, we'd suggest building a function for each block of output that you want to produce and having that function produce a single object that contains all the information you need. The more you can modularize, the more you can reuse those blocks of code. Doing so would make that data available for other purposes, not just for your report. In our example of a poorly written report, the first section, Computer Information, would be implemented by some function you'd write. The Disk Information section is sharing information from only one source, so it's not that bad off, but all of those `Write-Host` commands have to go.

> **Exceptions to every rule**
> There are exceptions to every rule.
>
> One of us (Richard) spends a lot of time having to audit other people's systems. This is done by starting with a standard set of scripts. The scripts are designed to produce output that'll go directly into a Word document to produce the report (either directly written or text files that are copied into the document). In this way, the initial reports can be produced quickly so that the analysis and discussions aren't delayed.
>
> A number of rules are broken in these scripts, including the following:
>
> - Output is a mixture of text and objects.
> - Output is formatted.
>
> This is a deliberate decision because it's known exactly what's wanted out of these scripts and how the report has to look.
>
> So the moral of the story is output objects, but be prepared to step outside of that paradigm when you have an exceptional, and compelling, reason.

In this chapter, we'll focus on a technique that can produce a nicely formatted HTML report, suitable for emailing to a boss or colleague. It's one of our favorite report-production techniques, and it's easily adaptable to a wide variety of situations.

33.2 Working with HTML fragments and files

The trick to our technique lies in the fact that PowerShell's `ConvertTo-HTML` cmdlet can be used in two different ways, which you'll see if you examine its help file. The first way produces a complete HTML page, whereas the second produces an HTML fragment. That fragment is a table with whatever data you've fed the cmdlet. The example produces each section of the report as a fragment and then uses the cmdlet to produce a complete HTML page that contains all of those fragments.

33.2.1 *Getting the information*

You begin by ensuring that you can get whatever data you need formed into an object. You'll need one kind of object for each section of your report, so if you're sticking with Computer Information and Disk Information, that's two objects.

NOTE   For brevity and clarity, we're going to omit error handling and other niceties in this example. You'd add those in a real-world environment.

Get-WmiObject by itself is capable of producing a single object that has all the disk information you want, so you just need to create a function to assemble the computer information, shown in the following listing.

Listing 33.2   Get-CSInfo function

```
function Get-CSInfo {
  param($computername)
  $os = Get-WmiObject -Class Win32_OperatingSystem `
  -ComputerName $computername
  $cs = Get-WmiObject -Class Win32_ComputerSystem `
  -ComputerName $computername
  $bios = Get-WmiObject -Class Win32_BIOS `
  -ComputerName $computername
  #property names with spaces need to be enclosed in quotes
  $props = @{ComputerName=$computername
             'OS Version'=$os.version
             'OS Build'=$os.buildnumber
             'Service Pack'=$os.sevicepackmajorversion
             RAM=$cs.totalphysicalmemory
             Processors=$cs.numberofprocessors
             'BIOS Serial'=$bios.serialnumber}
  $obj = New-Object -TypeName PSObject -Property $props
  Write-Output $obj
}
```

The function uses the Get-WmiObject cmdlet to retrieve information from three different WMI classes on the specified computer. You always want to write objects to the pipeline, so you use New-Object to write a custom object to the pipeline, using a hash table of properties culled from the three WMI classes. Normally we prefer property names to not have any spaces, but because you're going to be using this in a larger reporting context, we're bending the rules a bit.

NOTE   If you already have a function that produces the output you need but the property names aren't formatted in a pretty, report-friendly way, you can always change the property names using Select-Object, as we showed you in chapter 21.

33.2.2 *Producing an HTML fragment*

Now you can use your newly created Get-CSInfo function to create an HTML fragment:

```
$frag1 = Get-CSInfo –computername SERVER2 |
ConvertTo-Html -As LIST -Fragment -PreContent '<h2>Computer Info</h2>' |
Out-String
```

This little trick took us a while to figure out, so it's worth examining:

1 You're saving the final HTML fragment into a variable named $frag1. That'll let you capture the HTML content and later insert it into the final file.

2 You're running Get-CSInfo and giving it the computer name you want to inventory. For right now, you're hardcoding the SERVER2 computer name. You'll change that to a parameter a bit later.

3 You're asking ConvertTo-HTML to display this information in a vertical list rather than in a horizontal table, which is what it'd do by default. The list will mimic the layout from the old, bad-way-of-doing-things report.

4 You're using the –PreContent switch to add a heading to this section of the report. You added the <h2> HTML tags so that the heading will stand out a bit.

5 The whole thing—and this was the tricky part—is piped to Out-String. You see, ConvertTo-HTML puts a bunch of different things into the pipeline. It puts in strings, collections of strings, all kinds of wacky stuff. All of that will cause problems later when you try to assemble the final HTML page, so you're getting Out-String to resolve everything into plain-old strings (but remember it's a string object, *not* a string of text).

You can also go ahead and produce the second fragment. This is a bit easier because you don't need to write your own function first, but the HTML part will look substantially the same. The only real difference is that you're letting your data be assembled into a table rather than as a list:

```
$frag2 = Get-WmiObject -Class Win32_LogicalDisk -Filter 'DriveType=3' `
         -ComputerName SERVER2 |
         Select-Object @{Name='Drive';Expression={$_.DeviceID}},
             @{Name='Size(GB)';Expression={$_.Size / 1GB -as [int]}},
             @{Name='FreeSpace(GB)';Expression={
             $_.freespace / 1GB -as [int]}} |
ConvertTo-Html -Fragment -PreContent '<h2>Disk Info</h2>' | Out-String
```

You now have two HTML fragments, in $frag1 and $frag2, so you're ready to assemble the final page.

33.2.3 *Assembling the final HTML page*

Assembling the final page involves adding your two existing fragments, although you're also going to embed a style sheet. Using Cascading Style Sheet (CSS) language is beyond the scope of this book, but the example in the following listing will give you a basic idea of what it can do. This embedded style sheet lets you control the formatting of the HTML page so that it looks a little nicer. If you'd like a good tutorial and reference to CSS, check out www.w3schools.com/css/.

Listing 33.3 Embedded CSS

```
$head = @'
<style>
```

```
body { background-color:#dddddd;
       font-family:Tahoma;
       font-size:12pt; }
td, th { border:1px solid black;
         border-collapse:collapse; }
th { color:white;
     background-color:black; }
table, tr, td, th { padding: 2px; margin: 0px }
table { margin-left:50px; }
</style>
'@
ConvertTo-HTML -Head $head -PostContent $frag1,$frag2 `
-PreContent "<h1>Hardware Inventory for SERVER2</h1>"
```

You put that style sheet into the variable $head using a here-string to type out the entire CSS syntax you wanted. That gets passed to the -Head parameter and your HTML fragments to the -PostContent parameter. You also add a header for the whole page, where you again hardcode a computer name (SERVER2).

Save the entire script as C:\Good.ps1 and run it like this:

```
./good > Report.htm
```

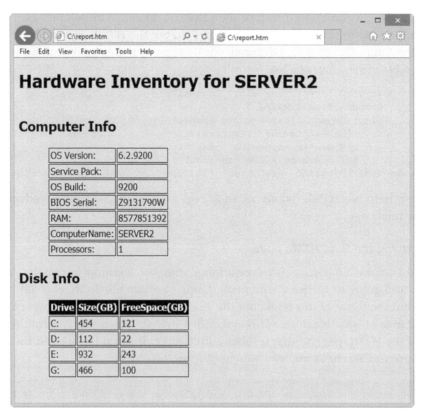

Figure 33.2   An HTML report consisting of multiple HTML fragments

That directs the output HTML to Report.htm, which is incredibly beautiful, as shown in figure 33.2.

Okay, maybe it's no work of art, but it's highly functional and frankly looks better than the on-screen-only report you started with in this chapter. Listing 33.4 shows the completed script, where you're swapping out the hardcoded computer name for a script-wide parameter that defaults to the local host. Notice too that you're including the [CmdletBinding()] declaration at the top of the script, enabling the –verbose parameter. Write-Verbose will document what each step of the script is doing. The next listing is a script you can build on!

Listing 33.4   An HTML inventory report script

```
<#
.DESCRIPTION
Retrieves inventory information and produces HTML
.EXAMPLE
./Good > Report.htm
.PARAMETER
The name of a computer to query. The default is the local computer.
#>
[CmdletBinding()]
param([string]$computername=$env:COMPUTERNAME)
# function to get computer system info
function Get-CSInfo {
  param($computername)
  $os = Get-WmiObject -Class Win32_OperatingSystem `
-ComputerName $computername
  $cs = Get-WmiObject -Class Win32_ComputerSystem -ComputerName $computername
  $bios = Get-WmiObject -Class Win32_BIOS -ComputerName $computername
  $props = @{'ComputerName'=$computername
             'OS Version'=$os.version
             'OS Build'=$os.buildnumber
             'Service Pack'=$os.sevicepackmajorversion
             'RAM'=$cs.totalphysicalmemory
             'Processors'=$cs.numberofprocessors
             'BIOS Serial'=$bios.serialnumber}
  $obj = New-Object -TypeName PSObject -Property $props
  Write-Output $obj
}
Write-Verbose 'Producing computer system info fragment'
$frag1 = Get-CSInfo -computername $computername |
ConvertTo-Html -As LIST -Fragment -PreContent '<h2>Computer Info</h2>' |
Out-String
Write-Verbose 'Producing disk info fragment'
$frag2 = Get-WmiObject -Class Win32_LogicalDisk -Filter 'DriveType=3' `
        -ComputerName $computername |
Select-Object @{Name='Drive';Expression={$_.DeviceID}},
              @{Name='Size(GB)';Expression={$_.Size / 1GB -as [int]}},
        @{Name='FreeSpace(GB)';Expression={$_.freespace / 1GB -as [int]}} |
ConvertTo-Html -Fragment -PreContent '<h2>Disk Info</h2>' |
Out-String
Write-Verbose 'Defining CSS'
```

```
$head = @'
<style>
body { background-color:#dddddd;
       font-family:Tahoma;
       font-size:12pt; }
td, th { border:1px solid black;
         border-collapse:collapse; }
th { color:white;
     background-color:black; }
table, tr, td, th { padding: 2px; margin: 0px }
table { margin-left:50px; }
</style>
'@
Write-Verbose 'Producing final HTML'
Write-Verbose 'Pipe this output to a file to save it'
ConvertTo-HTML -Head $head -PostContent $frag1,$frag2 `
-PreContent "<h1>Hardware Inventory for $ComputerName</h1>"
```

Using the script is simple:

```
PS C:\> $computer = SERVER01
PS C:\> C:\Scripts\good.ps1 -computername $computer |
➥ Out-File "$computer.html"
PS C:\> Invoke-Item "$computer.html"
```

The script runs, produces an output file for future reference, and displays the report. Keep in mind that your work in building the Get-CSInfo function is reusable. Because that function outputs an object, and not just pure text, you can repurpose it in a variety of places where you might need the same information.

To add to this report, you'd just do the following:

1 Write a command or function that generates a single kind of object that contains all the information you need for a new report section.
2 Use that object to produce an HTML fragment, storing it in a variable.
3 Add that new variable to the list of variables in the script's last command, thus adding the new HTML fragment to the final report.
4 Sit back and relax.

Yes, this report is text. Ultimately, every report will be, because text is what we humans read. The point of this one is that everything stays as PowerShell-friendly objects until the last possible instance. You let PowerShell, rather than your own fingers, format everything for you. The working parts of this script, which retrieve the information you need, could easily be copied and pasted and used elsewhere for other purposes (you could even create a module of functions used to retrieve your data that could be used for other purposes). That wasn't as easy to do with our original pure-text report because the working code was so embedded with all that formatted text.

> **NOTE** You can find a free ebook that goes into even greater detail on creating HTML reports at http://powershell.org/wp/ebooks/. Jeff also has a number of examples on his blog here: http://jdhitsolutions.com/blog/?s=html.

33.3 Sending email

What's better than an HTML report? An HTML report that's automatically emailed to whoever needs it!

Fortunately, nothing could be simpler in PowerShell, thanks to its `Send-MailMessage` cmdlet. Just modify the end of your script as follows:

```
Write-Verbose 'Producing final HTML'
Write-Verbose 'Pipe this output to a file to save it'
ConvertTo-HTML -Head $head -PostContent $frag1,$frag2 `
-PreContent "<h1>Hardware Inventory for $ComputerName</h1>" |
Out-File report.htm
Write-Verbose "Sending e-mail"
$params = @{'To'='whomitmayconcern@company.com'
            'From'='admin@company.com'
           'Subject'='That report you wanted'
           'Body'='Please see the attachment.'
           'Attachments'='report.htm'
           'SMTPServer'='mail.company.com'}
Send-MailMessage @params
```

You modify the end of the `ConvertTo-HTML` command to pipe the output to a file. Then you use the `Send-MailMessage` command to send the file as an attachment. If you prefer, you can also send the HTML as the message body itself. You don't need to create the text file but can take the HTML output and use it directly, although you do have to make sure the output is treated as one long string. Here's an alternative example:

```
Write-Verbose 'Producing final HTML'
$body=ConvertTo-HTML -Head $head -PostContent $frag1,$frag2 `
-PreContent "<h1>Hardware Inventory for $ComputerName</h1>" | Out-String
Write-Verbose "Sending e-mail"
$params = @{'To'='whomitmayconcern@company.com'
            'From'='admin@company.com'
           'Subject'='That report you wanted'
           'Body'=$Body
           'BodyAsHTML'=$True
           'SMTPServer'='mail.company.com'}
Send-MailMessage @params
```

Here you build the parameters for `Send-MailMessage` command in a hash table, which is saved into the variable $params. That lets you use the *splat* technique to feed all those parameters to the command at once. There's no difference between what you did and typing the parameters out normally, but the hash table makes the script a bit easier to read.

33.4 Summary

Building reports is a common need for administrators, and PowerShell is well suited to the task. The trick is to produce reports in a way that makes the reports' functional code—the parts that retrieve information and so forth—somewhat distinct from the formatting- and output-creation code. In fact, PowerShell is generally capable of delivering great formatting with little work on your part, as long as you work the way it needs you to.

Part 4

Advanced PowerShell

One of PowerShell's greatest strengths is its ability to connect to other technologies, such as WMI, CIM, COM, .NET, and a host of other acronyms. In part 4, we'll briefly look at each of these and demonstrate how PowerShell can use them. We'll provide one caution: We don't dive as deeply into these as we have the other topics in this book. That's because they *are* external technologies. Although accessed from within PowerShell, they can also be used from a variety of other places, and each could quite easily consume an entire book (and in some cases, others have already written those books—which we'll mention as appropriate within the chapters). Our focus in these chapters will be to look at how PowerShell can use these technologies, give you a starting place for doing so, and then give you direction for further independent exploration.

Having said that, these additional technologies provide a mass of functionality that'll be of great benefit to you in automating tasks in your environment. We encourage you to learn these additional techniques.

Working with the Component Object Model (COM)

This chapter covers

- Discovering what COM is and isn't
- Working with COM objects

Get ready for a blast from the past! Before Microsoft invented the .NET Framework, folks relied on an earlier technology called the Component Object Model (COM). COM is basically a set of rules that enable developers to write software components that can easily interoperate. COM is still in wide use today, although it's considered an older cousin to the .NET Framework. Many technologies you rely on, and use with PowerShell, are still based on COM. Examples include Active Directory Service Interfaces (ADSI) for working with Active Directory, WMI, and the object models that enable you to script against Internet Explorer or the Office products such as Word and Excel. COM is here and unlikely to go away in the foreseeable future. Unlike .NET, whose components can't run without the .NET Framework itself installed, COM doesn't have any specific prerequisites—many pieces of COM software can run on any Windows computer.

Because so much functionality was written in COM, the .NET Framework originally shipped with—and still contains—the ability to load and use those pieces of software that comply with the COM specification. This is done through a .NET

Framework layer called the *interop layer*. PowerShell, through interop, is able to take advantage of many pieces of COM-based software.

34.1 *Introduction to COM objects*

COM software is generally packaged into a dynamic link library (DLL) and is usually written in C++. A given DLL can contain one or more distinct components, usually referred to as *COM objects.* These COM objects are referred to by unique program identifiers (ProgIDs). You don't generally need to know what DLL a COM object lives in or where that DLL is stored. Instead, you ask Windows to load the object by providing Windows with the desired ProgID, like `wscript.shell` or `word.application`. Windows then consults its Registry, which contains cross-references for ProgIDs and their physical DLL locations. Thinking about that process for a moment will tell you an unfortunate fact about COM objects: They have to be explicitly installed and *registered* with Windows so that Windows knows what ProgIDs they use and where the necessary DLL files are kept. This is one of the biggest upsides to COM, because you can look in a single location—the Registry—and see what COM objects are available. It's also one of the biggest downsides, because DLLs must be explicitly registered before being used.

> **NOTE** The process of creating and installing COM DLLs is beyond the scope of this book. Registration is also out-of-bounds for this discussion, although we'll note that many COM-compliant DLLs can be registered by right-clicking them in Windows Explorer and selecting the Register option. You can usually also run the Regsvr32.exe command-line utility, providing it with the complete path and filename of a COM-compliant DLL, to register the COM objects in that DLL.

You can also discover many of the ProgIDs that are available like this:

```
Get-WmiObject -Class Win32_ProgIDSpecification |
sort ProgID | select ProgID, Caption
```

We counted 709 ProgIDs on one of our Windows 8.1 test machines, so expect to spend some time tracking down the exact ProgIDs you'll need.

It isn't enough to know what COM objects are available; you also need to know how to use each one. Many COM-compliant DLLs ship with a *type library*, sometimes stored in a TLB (type library) file, which describes how the COM objects inside that DLL work. Without a type library, you're completely on your own—in fact, for the purposes of this chapter, we're going to assume that any COM object you want to work with comes with a type library. Without one, we'd definitely have to stray far into the realm of C++ development, which is further than we plan, or want, to go with this book.

Ultimately, you're either going to find out about COM object ProgIDs by seeing other people's examples or run across them by using a type library browser. Some commercial script editors—SAPIEN PowerShell Studio is one example—include type library browsers; you can also use your favorite internet search engine to look for "type library browser" or "type library explorer" to find other commercial and free options. These browsers usually display a list of ProgIDs and can be expanded to show the members associated with a ProgID.

> ## What else is out of scope?
>
> There's a lot more that we could cover when it comes to COM, including Distributed COM (DCOM). DCOM, which is needed for WMI calls to remote machines, is the technology that lets you connect to COM objects on remote machines. But we're not going to cover it.
>
> Ultimately, we feel that using COM is something you'll only do when there's not a better, more PowerShell-native option available. In many cases, using COM within PowerShell forces you to adopt a very programmer-like approach, because COM predates PowerShell's pipeline and other command line–oriented approaches. Further, as Microsoft continues to invest in PowerShell, they'll provide all of the functionality you used to get from COM objects as friendlier, better-documented PowerShell commands, providers, and so forth.
>
> COM is, from an administrative viewpoint, extremely incomplete. COM lived at the height of an era where the GUI was king and where automatable components—like COM objects—were very much a second-class effort within Microsoft and other companies. It's rare to find a COM object that can do everything you might need it to do; one of the primary drivers behind PowerShell's existence, in fact, was the scattershot approach known as COM.
>
> Another problem with COM is that .NET's interop layer isn't perfect—and, therefore, PowerShell's ability to use COM objects isn't perfect. Some objects just won't work, forcing you to fall back to an older, COM-based technology like VBScript in order to accomplish your automation goals.
>
> We know a lot of readers may find themselves using a COM object now and again to accomplish some crucial task. That's okay—we know you have to do what you have to do to get the job done. But using COM is stepping firmly outside of PowerShell; you're not using PowerShell at all, except as an access mechanism to the older technology. Because it's outside PowerShell, it's outside what we're going to spend a lot of time on in this book.

There's no global, consolidated list of COM objects—even of the ones made by Microsoft. Most—even Microsoft's—are poorly documented, if they're documented at all. Choosing to use COM is choosing to enter the "here there be dragons" portion of the computing map. You'll often be on your own, at best helped by examples posted by other folks in various online forums and blogs.

Our purpose with this chapter isn't to provide a comprehensive look at everything COM can do. For this chapter, we're assuming you know a few things:

- The ProgID of the COM object you want to use
- The members—that is, the properties and methods—of the COM object that you want to use
- The general functional approach of the COM object you want to use

Our goal with this chapter is to show you how to put that knowledge to use. Because many of the COM-based examples you're likely to find online are based in VBScript, we'll provide some VBScript equivalents to the necessary PowerShell commands, with the hope that our doing so will make those examples easier to translate into PowerShell.

One useful resource for translating VBScript examples into PowerShell is the "The VBScript-to-Windows PowerShell Conversion Guide," which can be found at http://technet.microsoft.com/en-us/library/ee221101.aspx. It does move on a frequent basis so be prepared to search.

> **NOTE** If you're converting WMI-based VBScripts to PowerShell, do not, under any circumstances, follow the methods of displaying the results you'll see in those scripts. Remember that PowerShell emits objects and that the format cmdlets are there to handle your output requirements.

But how do you use COM objects directly in PowerShell?

34.2 *Instantiating COM objects in PowerShell*

Instantiating is the act of loading an object, in this case a COM object, into memory, storing a reference to that object in a variable, and generally preparing to use the COM object.

In VBScript, instantiation is done by using the `CreateObject()` method and the COM object's ProgID:

```
Obj = CreateObject("Wscript.Network")
```

PowerShell's command looks similar:

```
$Obj = New-Object -ComObject "WScript.Network"
```

The `-ComObject` parameter tells PowerShell to fall back to the old COM way of doing things, rather than trying to create an instance of a .NET Framework class. If the `New-Object` command fails, there are several possible reasons to consider:

- The COM object you've selected isn't compatible with PowerShell. There's no real fix for this.

- The ProgID you specified isn't in the Registry, meaning the COM object isn't installed or isn't registered.

- The COM object can't be instantiated in this fashion; it must be created as the result of running some other COM object's methods. You'll need to consult the object's documentation—if you can find it—to learn more.

> **TIP** If you know the ProgID, your best bet if you run into problems is to hop on a search engine and enter that ProgID as a search term. You'll often turn up examples, and possibly even documentation, that way.

Once the object is instantiated and referenced by a variable, you're ready to use it.

34.3 *Accessing and using COM objects' members*

Like the other objects you've used in PowerShell, COM objects have members—primarily properties and methods. Properties may be read-only or may be writable; methods cause the object to execute some task or behavior. One thing you'll see quite commonly when working with COM objects is that properties are in reality other embedded COM objects. At this stage you're digging into the documentation and hoping there are some methods on the object to help you unravel all of this.

Properties are accessed by referring to the object variable and the property name. In VBScript, you'd do this to display the UserName property of the WScript.Network object:

```
objNetwork = CreateObject("WScript.Network")
WScript.Echo objNetwork.UserName
```

Performing the same trick in PowerShell looks almost exactly the same. You use Write-Host to output the property's contents to the screen, because that's what VBScript's WScript.Echo does:

```
$Network = New-Object –Com WScript.Network
Write-Host $Network.UserName
```

> **NOTE** The obj prefix on variable names—such as objNetwork—comes from a coding convention called Hungarian Notation that was popular during VBScript's heyday. Today, most developers prefer not to use those prefixes, although you can obviously do whatever you like. In our PowerShell example, we omitted the obj prefix, but we could've called our variable $objNetwork and the example would've worked the same.

Methods are executed in much the same fashion. For example, WScript.Network has a MapNetworkDrive method that accepts two parameters: the drive letter to use and the Universal Naming Convention (UNC) path to map the drive to. In VBScript, assuming objNetwork already contained the object, you'd do this:

```
objNetwork.MapNetworkDrive("z:\","\\server\share")
```

Once again, PowerShell's syntax looks much the same:

```
$Network.MapNetworkDrive("z:\","\\server\share")
```

There's one important difference between VBScript and PowerShell. With VBScript, you could omit the parentheses from a method that didn't accept any parameters. For example, let's suppose you had an object in the variable objMine, and it had a method named DoSomething, which accepted no input arguments. In VBScript, this would be legal:

```
objMine.DoSomething
```

That's not legal in PowerShell. In PowerShell, you must always provide parentheses immediately after the method name, with no space after the method name, even if the method requires or accepts zero arguments:

```
$mine.DoSomething()
```

That's an important distinction to remember if you're translating VBScript code to PowerShell. One advantage that PowerShell *does* offer, if you have to resort to using COM objects, is that you can interact with them without turning to scripting. Want to know what properties and methods $Network has but your VBScript-foo is a little shaky? Ask PowerShell:

```
PS C:\> $network | Get-Member

    TypeName: System.__ComObject#{24be5a31-edfe-11d2-b933-00104b365c9f}

Name                          MemberType  Definition
----                          ----------  ----------
AddPrinterConnection          Method      void AddPrinterConnection (string...
AddWindowsPrinterConnection   Method      void AddWindowsPrinterConnection ...
EnumNetworkDrives             Method      IWshCollection EnumNetworkDrives ()
EnumPrinterConnections        Method      IWshCollection EnumPrinterConnect...
MapNetworkDrive               Method      void MapNetworkDrive (string, str...
RemoveNetworkDrive            Method      void RemoveNetworkDrive (string, ...
RemovePrinterConnection       Method      void RemovePrinterConnection (str...
SetDefaultPrinter             Method      void SetDefaultPrinter (string)
ComputerName                  Property    string ComputerName () {get}
Organization                  Property    string Organization () {get}
Site                          Property    string Site () {get}
UserDomain                    Property    string UserDomain () {get}
UserName                      Property    string UserName () {get}
UserProfile                   Property    string UserProfile () {get}
```

Unfortunately details may not be as forthcoming as you might wish:

```
PS C:\> $Network.MapNetworkDrive.OverloadDefinitions

void MapNetworkDrive (string, string, Variant, Variant, Variant)
```

If you want to use this method, there are some expected values, but there's no clue as to what they should be. You just have to know or get lucky with an example of someone else's code.

As we've said, we're hoping you only need COM objects to fill a specific need. But don't think they have to exist alone. Once an object exists in PowerShell, you can use it any way you need:

```
PS C:\> $fso=New-Object -Com Scripting.FileSystemObject
PS C:\> $fso.drives | where {$_.drivetype -eq 2} |
>> Select Path,@{Name="SizeGB";Expression={
>> "{0:N2}" -f ($_.TotalSize/1GB)}},
>> @{Name="FreeGB";Expression={ "{0:N2}" -f ($_.FreeSpace/1GB)}},
>> @{Name="UsedGB";Expression={
>> "{0:N2}" -f (($_.TotalSize - $_.FreeSpace)/1GB)}}
>>
```

Path	SizeGB	FreeGB	UsedGB
C:	19.90	4.40	15.50
D:	4.00	2.72	1.28

PowerShell can use the COM object in a pipelined expression just as well as any other type of object.

34.4 *PowerShell and COM examples*

This section won't supply anything like a complete tutorial on using COM objects with PowerShell, but it'll provide a few examples to get you started.

We'll start by looking at the `FileSystem` object. This object was seen a lot in VBScript and still has a few uses. For instance, you can directly see the size of a folder, as the following listing shows.

> **Listing 34.1 Using the `FileSystem` object**

```
$data = @()
$fso = New-Object -ComObject "Scripting.FileSystemObject"
$top = $fso.GetFolder("c:\test")
$data += New-Object PSObject -Property @{
 Path = $top.Path
 Size = $top.Size
}
foreach ($sf in $top.SubFolders) {
 $data += New-Object PSObject -Property @{
  Path = $sf.Path
  Size = $sf.Size
 }
}
$data
```

You instantiate the `FileSystem` object and use the `GetFolder` method on the top-level folder. The `SubFolders` collection is iterated to find the folders and their sizes.

We stated in the introduction that the Microsoft Office products have a COM object model associated with them. The one exception is pre–Office 2013 versions of OneNote, which is XML based. The Office 2013 version of OneNote has a COM-based object model available; see http://msdn.microsoft.com/en-us/library/office/jj680118(v=office.15).aspx for details.

> **NOTE** It's possible to work with the OpenXML format for Word documents, but in many ways this is much harder and has even less documentation and fewer examples. As of this writing, OpenXML isn't fully compatible with Power-Shell v3 or v4, and we don't recommend you use it until this is remedied.

Creating and writing to a Word document can be achieved using the code in listing 34.2.

Listing 34.2   Creating a Word document

```
$word = New-Object -ComObject "Word.application"
$word.visible = $true
$doc = $word.Documents.Add()
$doc.Activate()
$word.Selection.Font.Name = "Cambria"
$word.Selection.Font.Size = "20"
$word.Selection.TypeText("PowerShell")
$word.Selection.TypeParagraph()
$word.Selection.Font.Name = "Calibri"
$word.Selection.Font.Size = "12"
$word.Selection.TypeText("The best scripting language in the world!")
$word.Selection.TypeParagraph()
```

Working with Word in this way quickly gets tedious. You'll most likely want to create functions to handle some of the grunt work. One great use for these techniques is documenting your servers. Use WMI to gather the configuration information and write straight into a Word document. Instant, painless documentation—the admin's dream.

The last example we want to show (listing 34.3) involves Excel.

Listing 34.3   Creating an Excel worksheet

```
$xl = New-Object -comobject "Excel.Application"
$xl.visible = $true
$xlbooks =$xl.workbooks
$wkbk = $xlbooks.Add()
$sheet = $wkbk.WorkSheets.Item(1)
## create headers
$sheet.Cells.Item(1,1).FormulaLocal = "Value"
$sheet.Cells.Item(1,2).FormulaLocal = "Square"
$sheet.Cells.Item(1,3).FormulaLocal = "Cube"
$sheet.Cells.Item(1,4).FormulaLocal = "Delta"
$row = 2
for ($i=1;$i -lt 25; $i++){
$f = $i*$i
    $sheet.Cells.Item($row,1).FormulaLocal = $i
    $sheet.Cells.Item($row,2).FormulaLocal = $f
    $sheet.Cells.Item($row,3).FormulaLocal = $f*$i
    $sheet.Cells.Item($row,4).FormulaR1C1Local = "=RC[-1]-RC[-2]"
$row++
}
```

If you run this, you'll see that it runs painfully slowly. You can watch each entry being made. If you want data in Excel, create a CSV file using Export-CSV and then load the file into Excel.

NOTE If you're looking for more examples of integrating Office applications with PowerShell, visit Jeff's blog and go to http://jdhitsolutions.com/blog/2012/05/san-diego-2012-powershell-deep-dive-slides-and-demos/.

34.5 *Summary*

COM is a technology that you need to be aware of, but it isn't something you'll be using every day unless you're performing a lot of automation based on the Office suite or have a legacy application with a COM interface that you can script. It's a legacy technology that nevertheless will be with us for some time due to the vast number of COM-based applications that have been produced. If you have a .NET-based alternative, we recommend that you use that instead. But in either event, it's all about the objects, and PowerShell makes this a much easier proposition.

Working with
.NET Framework objects

35

One of the most powerful aspects of PowerShell is the fact that it's built on the .NET Framework and that it can access all of the underlying .NET capabilities. The .NET Framework is huge, and it's a good bet that you can find something to do what you need in the event no cmdlet is available for the task at hand.

We have to issue a warning here, though: We're crossing the line. You're no longer using PowerShell as PowerShell; you're diving into the world of .NET programming, and you just happen to be using PowerShell as a way of getting to .NET. You'll need to use programming-style structures, rather than commands. Though this is something PowerShell can do, it isn't something PowerShell necessarily excels at; if you're getting into complex scripts that use .NET heavily, you might have a better experience getting a copy of Visual Studio, which is designed specifically for .NET programming.

> **TIP** PowerShell syntax was created to be deliberately similar to C#. That was done to provide as smooth a transition as possible for the situation

where you need to use a .NET language to get your job done. Having said that, we don't expect many IT pros to progress down that path. It's an option, not a necessity.

We also have to set some scope for this chapter. The Framework is truly massive, and there's no way we can cover all of it. No single book could, let alone a chapter. Our job here is to help you understand some of .NET's terminology, show you how PowerShell accesses .NET, and point you to Microsoft's online documentation for .NET. Beyond that, you're on your own.

35.1 Classes, instances, and members

A *class* is an abstract definition of some functional unit. You've used `Get-Service` for simple examples throughout this book; it produces objects of the type `System.Service-Process.ServiceController`. That's the *type name* of the class. The class is, by and large, just a definition of what such a thing would look like.

An *instance* is some actual, running occurrence of a class. If your machine has 100 services, then it has 100 instances of the `System.ServiceProcess.ServiceController` class. In the case of that particular class, you usually work with the instances that are already running. For other classes, you might first have to create, or *instantiate*, an instance of the class in order to have something to work with. Technically, you have to ask the class to create a new instance of itself, a process called constructing. Classes offer one or more constructors for this purpose, which are essentially a special method that returns a new instance of the class. Some constructors require no extra information in order to get the new instance up and running; other constructors may require additional arguments in order to complete the task.

Part of what the class defines is its *members*. These include its properties, its methods, and the events that it can support. You've seen these before by piping objects to `Get-Member`; now you know why the cmdlet uses the noun "Member".

Typing a class name into your favorite search engine will, often as not, yield Microsoft's documentation for that class. In figure 35.1, we've located the documentation for the `System.ServiceProcess.ServiceController`, which outlines the class's members. You can also see the constructors for the class, which is what you'd call to create a new instance of the class. You can see, for example, that there are three constructors, two of which require additional information in order to execute. The MSDN documentation for .NET shows the latest version by default. You can use the `Other Versions` (immediately below the class name) drop-down to access the documentation for earlier versions of .NET. Appendix C contains information on the .NET version each version of PowerShell expects to work with.

Classes can have two kinds of members. An *instance member* is one that can be accessed only from an instance of the class, and they're the most common types of members. For example, to retrieve the name of a service, you have to have an actual instance of a service to work with. There are also *class members*, also called *static members*, which don't need an instance of the class. For example, .NET's `Math` class offers

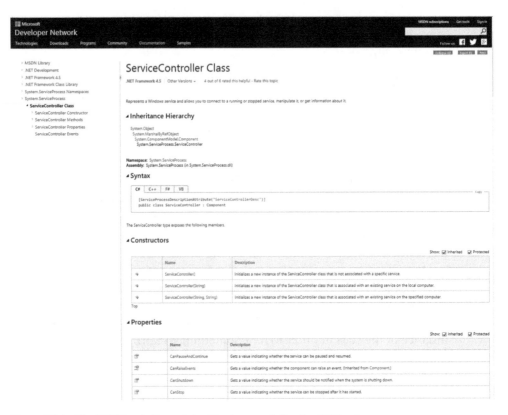

Figure 35.1   The MSDN website contains the documentation for .NET's classes.

static methods for a number of math operations. You don't have to create an instance of the class in order to use them; they're just available to you all the time.

35.2   .NET Framework syntax in PowerShell

PowerShell has specific syntax for working with Framework classes:

- The New-Object cmdlet creates new instances of classes. The -TypeName parameter accepts the type name of the desired class, and -ArgumentList enables you to pass arguments to the class's constructor. Based on the number and data type of the arguments you provide, .NET will automatically select the correct constructor.

NOTE   This "automatic selection" is a standard .NET feature called *overloading*. The arguments accepted by a method, including constructors, collectively form a signature: "This method needs two strings, then a number, then a Boolean value," for example. No constructor can have the same signature as another. Thus, by looking at the values you provide, .NET can figure out which constructor you were trying to run.

- When referring to a class's type name, such as to execute static methods, put the class name in square brackets [].
- Use a period (.) to access the members of a class or instance.
- Follow a class name, in square brackets, with two colons (::) to access static members of the class.

You'll see examples of all of these in the next couple of sections.

35.3 *.NET support in PowerShell*

This heading might seem like an odd one because PowerShell is built from .NET and uses .NET objects (more or less). What this heading means is that a certain amount of the .NET Framework is loaded by default when PowerShell is started. If you need anything else, you must explicitly load it.

If you want to discover the .NET assemblies (often roughly equivalent to namespaces) that are loaded, you can perform this trick:

```
PS C:\> [appdomain]::CurrentDomain.GetAssemblies() | foreach
➥  {$_.Fullname.Split(",")[0]} | Sort

Anonymously Hosted DynamicMethods Assembly
Microsoft.CSharp
Microsoft.Management.Infrastructure
Microsoft.Management.Infrastructure.Native
Microsoft.Management.Infrastructure.UserFilteredExceptionHandling
Microsoft.PowerShell.Cmdletization.GeneratedTypes
Microsoft.PowerShell.Commands.Management
Microsoft.PowerShell.Commands.Utility
Microsoft.PowerShell.ConsoleHost
Microsoft.PowerShell.Security
mscorlib
PSEventHandler
System
System.Configuration
System.Configuration.Install
System.Core
System.Data
System.DirectoryServices
System.Management
System.Management.Automation
System.Numerics
System.Transactions
System.Xml
```

This list is taken from a newly opened PowerShell v4 console on Windows 8.1. Loading other modules will alter the list of loaded assemblies. Other versions of PowerShell on other versions of Windows will give slightly different results.

The `Appdomain` class is a member of the `System` namespace. You should use `[System.AppDomain]` to be 100% correct, but because the `System` namespace is loaded you can omit using `System`. We recommend using the full name, apart from a few well-known classes such as `PSObject` and `Math`. If you're in doubt about whether some part of the .NET Framework is available, you can use this technique to test what's been loaded.

35.4   *Accessing static members*

The -Math class is one you'll commonly see people working with when it comes to static members. Technically, its class name is System.Math, although PowerShell lets you get away with omitting System in class names, because that's one of the default top-level namespaces that PowerShell loads, as you've just seen.

> **NOTE**   A namespace is simply a means of categorizing similar classes. System is one of the top-level categories.

Math doesn't have a constructor, so you're not meant to instantiate it. Instead, you use its many static members, documented at http://msdn.microsoft.com/en-us/library/system.math.aspx. Or you can pipe [math] to Get-Member. When you access a class, you need to put the name inside brackets, so you'd use [Math] rather than Math.

For example, to get the absolute value of a number:

```
PS C:\> [system.math]::Abs(-100)
100
PS C:\> [math]::Abs(-100)
100
```

Here, you're performing the same operation twice, just to demonstrate that both the full class name [System.Math] and the shorter [Math] work identically. As a rule of thumb if the class name starts with System, you can omit it. Abs() is a static method of the [Math] class; methods always include parentheses immediately after the method name. In this case, the method accepts one numeric parameter, which you've given as -100.

> **NOTE**   Get-Member has a number of parameters to help you track down the members you need. -Static will return only static methods The -MemberType property can be used to refine your search.

Math also has some static properties, which are referred to as fields. These contain constant (unchanging) values. For example:

```
PS C:\> [math]::pi
3.14159265358979
```

You can visually differentiate between a method and a property (or field) because methods always have the opening and closing parentheses; properties (and fields) don't.

```
PS C:\> $r=Read-Host "Enter a radius"
Enter a radius: 5
PS C:\> ([math]::Pow($r,2))*[math]::pi
78.5398163397448
```

35.5 Finding the right framework bits

Let's work through an example. Say you'd like to find a way to resolve a hostname into one or more IP addresses by using DNS. This task is certainly possible without resorting to .NET, but it'll make a good exercise for figuring out how to use .NET from within PowerShell.

The toughest aspect of using .NET is finding the part you need, not using it. Fortunately, .NET is well documented, and the internal search engine on http://msdn.microsoft.com and the various public search engines all do a good job. Add "msdn" or ".net" to any search in your favorite search engine to return more Framework-centric results. For example, to find our DNS example, we started with a Bing search for "msdn system.network," guessing that the high-level `System.Network` namespace would be a good starting point (being able to make good guesses definitely shortens the searching process). That search got us the System.Net Namespace page, at http://msdn.microsoft.com/en-us/library/system.net(v=vs.110).aspx, shown in figure 35.2. Note that our guess, `System.Network`, wasn't entirely accurate; the namespace is called `System.Net`. But search engines are often "fuzzy" enough to let a good first guess turn up the right result.

From there, we spotted the `Dns` class, which looked promising.

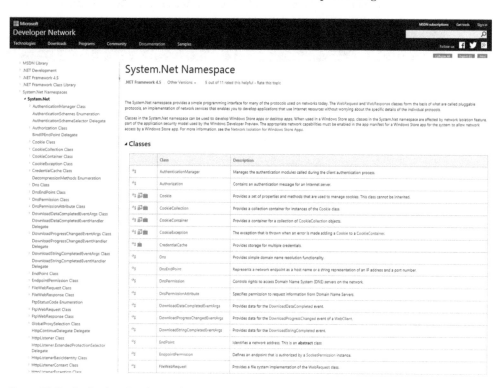

Figure 35.2 Reviewing the classes in the `System.Net` namespace

As you can see if you visit the DNS class' page, at http://msdn.microsoft.com/en-us/library/system.net.dns(v=vs.110).aspx, there's no constructor, meaning we expect all of the members in this class to be static. That's confirmed by the method list, which shows each method with a big red "S" icon, indicating static methods. A bunch of these methods are listed as "Obsolete," which suggests they came from earlier versions of .NET and that we should stay away from them. Fine—that eliminates about half of what's on the page! We eventually found `GetHostAddresses`, which is what we were trying to do. `GetHostByName` was actually our first hit, but it's obsolete, so we kept looking. Clicking on the method name took us to http://msdn.microsoft.com/en-us/library/system.net.dns.gethostaddresses.aspx, shown in figure 35.3.

That took us to the `GetHostAddress` method at http://msdn.microsoft.com/en-us/library/system.net.dns.gethostaddresses(v=vs.110).aspx, as shown in figure 35.4.

Note that the method name is shown as `GetHostAddresses`, not `GetHostAddresses()` with parentheses. Adding the parentheses is something you just have to know to do when you're working from within PowerShell; not every .NET language requires them, but PowerShell does because of its C# background.

This documentation is telling us that the method accepts one argument, a hostname or address, which is a String, and is the hostname or IP address to resolve. It returns an object of `System.Net.IPAddress`. Actually, it says it returns an array of such

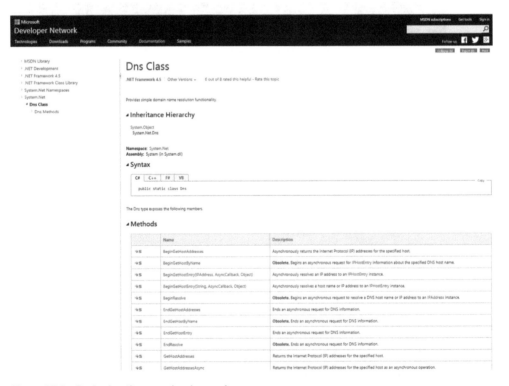

Figure 35.3   Reviewing the `Dns` class's members

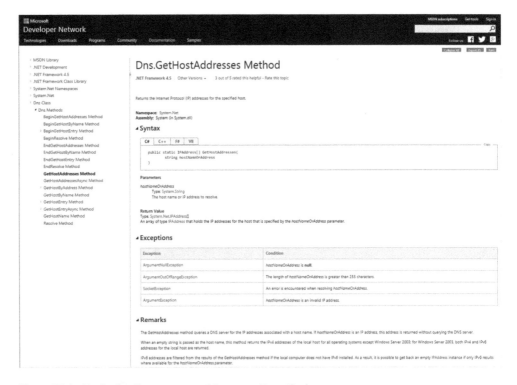

Figure 35.4   Reviewing the `GetHostAddresses()` method

objects, meaning there's the potential for there to be more than one. So before we try this method, we want to see what this `System.Net.IPAddress` looks like. Clicking on that class name under "Return Value" took us to http://msdn.microsoft.com/en-us/library/system.net.ipaddress.aspx, which is shown in figure 35.5.

Constructors are shown here, but we don't need them. We're not going to be creating an instance of this class ourselves; we're going to be getting an instance that was created by our `Dns` method.

The documentation indicates that each `IPAddress` object has an `Address` property but that it's obsolete. Bummer. Scrolling down a bit, we see that there's a `ToString()` instance method, which "Converts an Internet Address to its standard notation." That sounds like what we're after, and the good news is that PowerShell will automatically call `ToString()` when it needs to render a human-readable representation of an object. All objects have a `ToString()` method; you've probably seen them in `Get-Member` output. With all that in mind, let's give this a whirl:

```
PS C:\> [System.Net.Dns]::GetHostAddresses('bing.com')

Address         : 3368374220
AddressFamily   : InterNetwork
ScopeId         :
IsIPv6Multicast : False
```

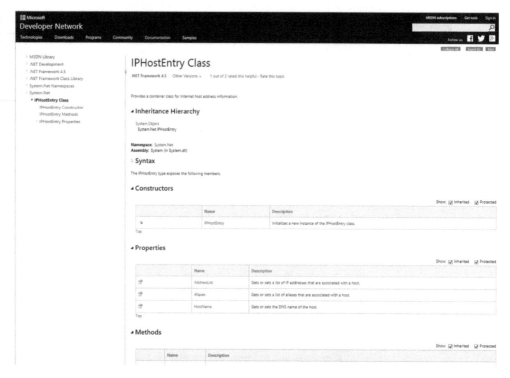

Figure 35.5   Reviewing the `System.Net.IPAddress` class documentation

```
IsIPv6LinkLocal    : False
IsIPv6SiteLocal    : False
IsIPv6Teredo       : False
IsIPv4MappedToIPv6 : False
IPAddressToString  : 204.79.197.200
```

Cool. That `IPAddressToString` is even better—it's exactly what we wanted. But it's not listed in the MSDN web page—where did it come from? A quick pipe to `Get-Member` reveals the truth:

```
PS C:\> [System.Net.Dns]::GetHostAddresses('bing.com') | get-member

   TypeName: System.Net.IPAddress

Name               MemberType   Definition
----               ----------   ----------
Equals             Method       bool Equals(System.Object comparand)
GetAddressBytes    Method       byte[] GetAddressBytes()
GetHashCode        Method       int GetHashCode()
GetType            Method       type GetType()
MapToIPv4          Method       ipaddress MapToIPv4()
MapToIPv6          Method       ipaddress MapToIPv6()
ToString           Method       string ToString()
Address            Property     long Address {get;set;}
AddressFamily      Property     System.Net.Sockets.AddressFamily Addr...
IsIPv4MappedToIPv6 Property     bool IsIPv4MappedToIPv6 {get;}
```

```
IsIPv6LinkLocal     Property     bool IsIPv6LinkLocal {get;}
IsIPv6Multicast     Property     bool IsIPv6Multicast {get;}
IsIPv6SiteLocal     Property     bool IsIPv6SiteLocal {get;}
IsIPv6Teredo        Property     bool IsIPv6Teredo {get;}
ScopeId             Property     long ScopeId {get;set;}
IPAddressToString   ScriptProperty System.Object IPAddressToString {get=...
```

Ah, it's a `ScriptProperty`. That's something added by PowerShell. So the clever Power-Shell team, or someone at Microsoft, suspected we might be using this class method and added a handy conversion that gets us the IP address in a string format. So we can just select it to get the address:

```
PS C:\> [System.Net.Dns]::GetHostAddresses('bing.com') | Select -Property
➥    IPAddressToString

IPAddressToString
-----------------
204.79.197.200
```

Or, if we just want the string all by itself:

```
PS C:\> [System.Net.Dns]::GetHostAddresses('bing.com') | Select
➥   -ExpandProperty IPAddressToString
204.79.197.200
```

> **DNSClient module**
>
> We used the `[System.Net]` class for demonstration purposes only. There's a DNSClient module you can use to do things like resolving hostnames. As a rule, you should always look for a cmdlet before turning to a .NET class.
>
> ```
> PS C:\> Resolve-DnsName -Name bing.com | Format-List
>
> Name       : bing.com
> Type       : A
> TTL        : 82
> DataLength : 4
> Section    : Answer
> IPAddress  : 204.79.197.200
> ```
>
> The DNSClient module is available in PowerShell v3 and v4 but only on Windows 8/Windows Server 2012 and Windows 8.1/Windows Server 2012 R2, respectively. It's a CDXML-based module (see chapter 39) that relies on WMI classes that aren't available on legacy versions of Windows.
>
> Using .NET as we've shown here is your get-out-of-jail card when working on older versions of Windows.

35.6 Creating and working with instances

That's a great static method example—but what about classes that require you to create an instance? We struggled a bit to find something that wasn't covered by a Power-Shell command, and in the end we decided to show you how to access the properties

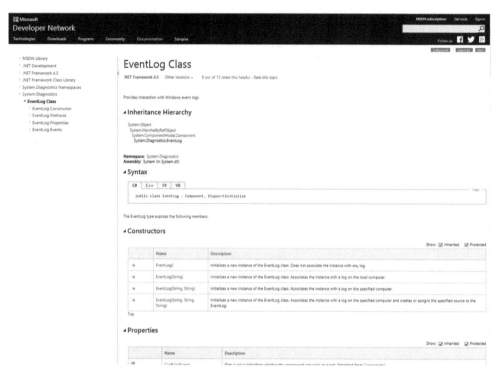

Figure 35.6   Reviewing the `EventLog` class documentation

of a Windows event log. Yes, you can do this with cmdlets already, but it's still a good example of the process you'd use for other .NET stuff. And, because all Windows computers have event logs, anyone can test this out and get used to it.

We needed to start by finding the necessary class. A Bing search for ".NET event log" turned up hits for the `EventLog` class; switching the search to ".NET eventlog class" got us to http://msdn.microsoft.com/en-us/library/system.diagnostics.eventlog.aspx, which is shown in figure 35.6.

Looking at the constructors, we see that the second one accepts a string, which is the name of an event log on the computer. The third constructor does the same thing while also accepting a remote computer name, which is useful to know about—we'll file that away for later. We can also see that the complete type name for the class is `System.Diagnostics.EventLog`. So here goes:

```
PS C:\> $log = New-Object -TypeName System.Diagnostics.EventLog
➥    -ArgumentList 'Security'
PS C:\> $log

  Max(K) Retain OverflowAction          Entries Log
  ------ ------ --------------          ------- ---
  20,480      0 OverwriteAsNeeded         7,448 Security
```

Cool. So our `$log` variable now contains a reference to the Security log. It's common to store object instances in a variable, as we've done, so that you can easily refer to the instance later. The MSDN web page shows several properties, a few of which were output by default when we displayed $log. There are also methods, including the Clear() method:

```
PS C:\> $log.clear()
```

No errors usually means it works—and hope we meant to do that! Note that methods have no -confirm or -whatIf parameter, as a cmdlet would, so you'd better be careful with what you try.

.NET limitations

If you've ever wondered why there isn't a PowerShell cmdlet to back up an event log before clearing it, the answer is that the underlying .NET class doesn't supply a method to perform backups.

```
PS C:\> Get-EventLog -List | gm

    TypeName: System.Diagnostics.EventLog
```

This result indicates that the PowerShell event log cmdlets use the same .NET class we've shown you here, which if you check the documentation doesn't have a backup method.

If you want to back up an event log, you need to use WMI.

We've often heard comments like "PowerShell should be able to do X and it can't." It's usually not a PowerShell limitation but a limitation of the underlying .NET class—and that's something much harder to get changed.

Honestly, that's about it. There's no specific need to "release" the $log variable, although we can certainly do so if we're done with it:

```
PS C:\> del variable:log
```

or use Remove-Variable, which does the same thing:

```
PS C:\> remove-variable log
```

Deleting it from the VARIABLE: drive releases its resources and will free up some memory (although not necessarily right away; .NET itself will take care of the memory management when it feels the need and has a spare moment, in a process called garbage collection).

35.7 *Summary*

Working with the .NET Framework from within PowerShell is easy—once you know what part of .NET you want and how to use it. As with everything else in PowerShell, knowing how to do what you want is the tough challenge; getting PowerShell to do it is a bit easier. But just because you can doesn't always mean you should. Wherever possible, look for cmdlets that you can work with and use the "raw" .NET Framework to fill in the gaps.

Remember in chapter 21 we showed you how to create your own .NET class for the objects that you need to output from your scripts. That chapter would be worth rereading in the light of what you've learned here. We also recommend chapter 19 of *PowerShell Deep Dives* (Manning, 2013) if you want to learn more about using .NET code with PowerShell.

We'd love to direct you to a book that's just about .NET, but there aren't any. Most will include .NET in the context of a language, like C# or Visual Basic. If you decide to pick one up, go with C#, as its syntax is closest to PowerShell, but understand that you won't be able to run code examples from the book as is. Microsoft's own MDSN Library (start in http://msdn.microsoft.com/en-us/library/190bkk9s.aspx) might be the best starting point to help you become more familiar with what .NET has to offer.

Accessing databases

This chapter covers

- Using the .NET Framework to connect to a database
- Querying databases with PowerShell
- Adding, deleting, and modifying databases with PowerShell
- Running stored procedures with PowerShell

It's not uncommon to need to access something that's in some kind of a database, so that's what we'll show you in this chapter. Now, as with many other chapters, we need to set some boundaries for what we're going to cover (and not cover). This chapter won't teach you the SQL query language, nor will it teach you how to create, maintain, or manage a database. This chapter is about using PowerShell to access the data that's in a database and nothing more. We also assume you already have the necessary database drivers installed on your computer and that you can physically connect to whatever database you need. You don't need any particular commands or extensions—you don't have to install SQL Server's PowerShell stuff, for example—but if you're accessing a database such as Oracle or MySQL, you'll need the appropriate drivers installed for .NET. Having said that, if you can get your hands on the SQL server tools it'll make your life much easier when accessing SQL Server databases.

Something else to keep in mind is that there are no native database access commands in PowerShell. Instead, we'll be using the underlying .NET Framework classes, which means the information in this chapter will look a lot like .NET Framework programming. Right now, PowerShell has no help for that.

36.1   *Native SQL vs. OLEDB*

The first thing you'll need to decide is what kind of database you'll be connecting to. At this point, the decision comes down to two simple choices: Microsoft SQL Server and everything else. The .NET Framework has specific code built into it for accessing SQL Server (called SQL Server Native Client); everything else gets access through Object Linking & Embedding Database (OLEDB), and you'll have to have the appropriate .NET Framework–compatible OLEDB drivers installed.

For most of this chapter, we're going to focus on Microsoft SQL Server. That means you'll see .NET class names like `System.Data.SqlClient.SqlConnection`; if you wanted to change any of those examples to OLEDB, simply change `SqlClient` to `OleDb` and change `Sql` to `OleDb`. In other words, if you wanted to work with an Oracle database, instead of using the `System.Data.SqlClient.SqlConnection` class in your PowerShell expressions, you'd use `System.Data.OleDb.OleDbConnection`. It's that easy!

36.2   *Connecting to data sources*

Your first step will be to connect to a database. To do this, you need to know four things:

- The server name where the database lives (and it might be something like "localhost" if it's on the same machine). In the case of SQL Server, which can run multiple named copies of itself on a computer, you may also need to know the instance name you want to connect to. For example, SQL Server Express installs, by default, to a named instance called SQLEXPRESS, meaning the total server name might look something like SERVER\SQLEXPRESS. You can see the instance names by running `Get-Service` in PowerShell and looking for SQL Server services; there will be one service per instance, and the service name will be something like "SQLSERVER$SQLEXPRESS" with a dollar sign between the service name and the instance name. You just need the instance name—in this case, SQLEXPRESS.
- The name of the database you want to connect to.
- Whether or not you're using Windows integrated security (an option SQL Server provides) or standard security (which could be SQL Server or almost anything else).
- If you're using standard security, then you'll also need a username and password.

If you don't know all this information, you'll need to speak with whoever "owns" the database, or database server, to get it.

Once you have that information, you'll use it to build a *connection string*. That's a set of instructions that tells .NET what kind of database you're using and passes along the information. We never remember the syntax for these things—we always look them up at http://ConnectionStrings.com.

> **TIP** You will find many variations on a theme when looking at code for connecting to databases. We use the approach presented here because it works for us. If you prefer a slightly different way of coding, please feel free to use it. The basic ideas are the same however you end up cutting the code.

Once you have the correct connection string, you'll fill in the information and create a `Connection` object. Set its `ConnectionString` property to your connection string, and you're ready to go. For example, a SQL Server (2008 and later) connection, using standard security, might look like this:

```
PS C:\> $connection = New-Object
    -TypeName System.SqlClient.SqlConnection
    -Property @{'ConnectionString'='Data Source=myServerAddress;
     InitialCatalog=myDataBase;
     User Id=myUsername;Password=myPassword;'}
```

And a connection that uses Windows integrated security might look like this:

```
PS C:\> $connection = New-Object
    -TypeName System.Data.SqlClient.SqlConnection
    -Property @{'ConnectionString'=' Data Source=myServerAddress;
    InitialCatalog=myDataBase;
    Integrated Security=SSPI;'}
```

Both of these create the `Connection` object, assign its connection string, and put the resulting object into the `$connection` variable. From there, you just need to open the connection to start using it:

```
PS C:\> $connection.Open()
```

At some point, make sure you close it, too—otherwise you'll use all the connections and whoever runs the database will likely get extremely upset with you:

```
PS C:\> $connection.Close()
```

A single connection can only be held open for a single operation. That is, if you're using a connection to read data out of the database, you can't use that same connection to send changes back to the database. So it's not uncommon to have two connections open: one for reading and another for writing. Just be sure you put each into its own variable, and make sure you close them both when you've finished!

> **TIP** We add the `Close()` command to our scripts as soon as we open the database so that we don't forget it!

36.3   *Querying data*

To read data from the database, you send a SQL language query to the database and then read through whatever comes back. SQL is largely the same across different database platforms, but not entirely. Though there are standards for the language, different vendors implement different levels of the standard, leaving a bit of inconsistency between database products. If you're not familiar with the language, www.w3schools.com/SQl/default.asp is a good place to start. It does a fine job of pointing out the minor—but obviously important—differences between various platforms and covers the syntax quite well, with lots of great examples.

There are two broad techniques for reading data with .NET. The first involves something called a `DataReader` object, whereas the second involves something called a `DataAdapter`. We're going to show you both of them, but we tend to prefer the `DataAdapter` approach, so we'll start there.

Either way, we suggest getting your SQL language query into a variable. Keep in mind that PowerShell lets you do some fancy variable-replacement tricks when you use double quotes. That's convenient, because SQL delimits strings in single quotes, so you can build queries like this:

```
PS C:\> $query = "SELECT computername,version
    FROM inventory
    WHERE version = $version
    AND manufacturer = '$mfg'"
```

This gets you a completed query in the `$query` variable. The capitalization of `SELECT`, `FROM`, and `WHERE` isn't strictly necessary, but it does make the query easy to read. Notice that the values within `$version` and `$mfg`, which you've presumably populated elsewhere, are inserted into this query. You need to be careful that `$version` and `$mfg` don't contain any single quotation marks, or it'll mess up the final query syntax.

> **WARNING** Dynamically building a query by inserting variables' contents into the query can be dangerous. If you're populating those variables from user-provided input, you're leaving yourself open to a kind of attack called SQL injection, in which a malicious user deliberately corrupts a query in order to delete data, queries data they shouldn't, and more. We're assuming you're the only one populating your query's contents, and so you can make sure you're not doing anything stupid. But if you plan to accept input from outside, untrusted sources, just be aware of the danger.

With your query in a variable, you're ready to begin.

36.3.1   *Databases with DataAdapters*

`DataAdapters` are neat because they basically turn the data into a set of objects, not unlike importing a CSV file into PowerShell. We think that makes the resulting data a lot easier to work with. Here's how you create one with your query (assuming your opened connection object is in the variable `$connection` and your query is in `$query`):

```
$command = $connection.CreateCommand()
$command.CommandText = $query
$adapter = New-Object System.Data.SqlClient.SqlDataAdapter $command
$dataset = New-Object System.Data.DataSet
$adapter.Fill($dataset)
$table = $dataset.Tables[0]
Write-Output $table
```

That code will output one object for each row of data your query returned, and each column you queried will become a property of those objects. You could use a ForEach construct (or the ForEach-Object cmdlet) to enumerate those rows and do something with each one in turn. We'll get into a more complete example toward the end of this chapter, when we provide you with some wrapper functions to make Data-Adapters even easier to work with.

36.3.2 *Databases with DataReaders*

DataReaders are a slightly more procedural way of getting to data. You'll start with the same connection (in $connection for this example) and SQL query (in $query). Again, make sure the connection is opened first:

```
$command = New-Object System.Data.SqlClient.SqlCommand
$command.Connection = $connection
$command.CommandText = $query
$reader = $command.ExecuteReader()
while ($reader.Read()) {
  $reader.GetValue(0)
}
$reader.Close()
```

The $reader.GetValue(0) is reading the data from a column, in this case the first column you queried. In our example, that would be the computerName column of the table, because that's the first column listed in the query string. You'd change the 0 to 1 to read the second column, and so forth. The $reader.Read() method will move you to the next row and return $True if there's another row waiting after that. So, in your While loop, you're basically reading through all available rows. The important thing to remember with a DataReader is that it's a one-way street—you can't go backward.

36.4 *Adding, changing, and deleting data*

Changes to databases are made with INSERT, UPDATE, and DELETE queries. Again, our goal isn't to teach you that query syntax—you need to either know it already or learn it on your own. Our goal is to show you how to use these queries with PowerShell. There's one simple technique we'll show you. Again, assuming you have a connection object in $connection and your query in $query, you'd do this:

```
$command = $connection.CreateCommand()
$command.CommandText = $query
$command.ExecuteNonQuery()
```

And that's it.

36.5   *Calling stored procedures*

Many databases include *stored procedures*, which are bits of code, usually written in SQL, that run on the database server itself. These are often an effective way to accomplish tasks, because the procedure can bundle up all the necessary business logic needed. You can kind of think of a procedure as a sort of server-side SQL command: You need to know the command name and its parameters, and then you can run it. Sadly, there's no built-in help, so you'll have to know what you're doing up front to make use of them. Procedures are also a safer way to execute code that contains user-provided input, because they're less susceptible to SQL injection attacks.

Let's assume you have a stored procedure (or *stored proc*, as database folks like to call them) named DoSomething that you want to run. It has a single input argument, which expects a computer name. Assuming you have an open connection in $connection, here's how you'd execute the procedure:

```
$command = $connection.CreateCommand()
$command.commandText = 'DoSomething'
$param = New-Object System.Data.SqlClient.SqlParameter '@computer',
    'localhost'
$command.Parameters.Add($param)
$command.ExecuteNonreader()
```

You've used ExecuteNonReader() assuming that the procedure does something but doesn't return any rows of data. Plenty of procedures do return data, though—so to capture that output you'd do something like this instead:

```
$command = $connection.CreateCommand()
$command.commandText = 'DoSomething'
$param = New-Object System.Data.SqlClient.SqlParameter '@computer',
    'localhost'
$command.Parameters.Add($param)
$adapter = New-Object System.Data.SqlClient.SqlDataAdapter
$adapter.SelectCommand = $command
$dataset = New-Object System.Data.DataSet
$adapter.Fill($dataset)
$table = $dataset.Tables[0]
```

This syntax isn't all that different from what we showed you earlier; there's just a bit extra involved to add the parameter to the procedure before running it to get the results.

36.6   *A module to make it easier*

Dealing with the database code can be ugly sometimes, and so to make things easier we proudly present the DataAccess module! Just save the following listing in your user PowerShell modules folder in a folder called DataAccess. You should end up with a path like \Users\<*username*>\Documents\WindowsPowerShell\Modules\DataAccess\ DataAccess.psm1.

Listing 36.1   DataAccess.psm1

```
function Get-DatabaseData {
 [CmdletBinding()]
 param (
  [string]$connectionString,
  [string]$query,
  [switch]$isSQLServer
 )
 if ($isSQLServer) {
  Write-Verbose 'in SQL Server mode'
  $connection = New-Object -TypeName System.Data.SqlClient.SqlConnection
} else {
  Write-Verbose 'in OleDB mode'
  $connection = New-Object -TypeName System.Data.OleDb.OleDbConnection
 }
 $connection.ConnectionString = $connectionString
 $command = $connection.CreateCommand()
 $command.CommandText = $query
 if ($isSQLServer) {
  $adapter = New-Object System.Data.SqlClient.SqlDataAdapter $command
 } else {
  $adapter = New-Object System.Data.OleDb.OleDbDataAdapter $command
 }
 $dataset = New-Object -TypeName System.Data.DataSet
 $adapter.Fill($dataset)
 $dataset.Tables[0]
}
function Invoke-DatabaseQuery {
 [CmdletBinding()]
 param (
  [string]$connectionString,
  [string]$query,
  [switch]$isSQLServer
 )
 if ($isSQLServer) {
  Write-Verbose 'in SQL Server mode'
  $connection = New-Object -TypeName System.Data.SqlClient.SqlConnection
 } else {
  Write-Verbose 'in OleDB mode'
  $connection = New-Object System.Data.OleDb.OleDbConnection
 }
 $connection.ConnectionString = $connectionString
 $command = $connection.CreateCommand()
 $command.CommandText = $query
 $connection.Open()
 $command.ExecuteNonQuery()
 $connection.close()
}
```

Whenever you need to use these commands, just run `Import-Module DataAccess` to load them into the shell. They're designed to work with either SQL Server or OLEDB connection strings; you'll pass in the connection string that you want to use.

For example, suppose you have a SQL Server Express instance running on the local computer. Because you're an admin, you can rely on Windows authentication to get you into it. In the database, you have a table named Computers. That table has several columns: Computer (which you expect to contain computer names), as well as OSVersion, BIOSSerial, OSArchitecture, and ProcArchitecture. Here's how you might use the DataAccess module to query all of the computer names:

```
Import-Module DataAccess
Get-DatabaseData -verbose –connectionString `
'Server=localhost\SQLEXPRESS;Database=Inventory;Trusted_Connection=True;' `
-isSQLServer -query "SELECT * FROM Computers"
```

> **WARNING** The connection strings were kind of long, so to make all of this fit in the book we had to use PowerShell's escape character. Make sure you type that "backtick" correctly and that it's immediately followed by a carriage return—no tabs or spaces after it, please!

Here's how you'd insert a new computer into the table:

```
Invoke-DatabaseQuery -verbose –connectionString `
'Server=localhost\SQLEXPRESS;Database=Inventory;Trusted_Connection=True;' `
-isSQLServer -query "INSERT INTO Computers (computer) VALUES('win7')"
```

And finally, re-query the computers to see that your addition is in there:

```
Get-DatabaseData -verbose –connectionString `
'Server=localhost\SQLEXPRESS;Database=Inventory;Trusted_Connection=True;' `
-isSQLServer -query "SELECT * FROM Computers"
```

So you basically have two functions, `Get-DatabaseData` and `Invoke-DatabaseQuery`. The first is for reading data with a SELECT query (or to execute a stored procedure that returns data), and the second is for running INSERT, UPDATE, and DELETE queries (or a stored procedure that doesn't return data). Each has a `-connectionString` parameter and a `-query` parameter, and each has a `-isSQLServer` switch that you use when the connection string points to a SQL Server machine. Omit `-isSQLServer` if you're providing an OLEDB connection string.

36.7 *Summary*

We've given you a concise introduction to using databases. Our expectation is that you're a general-purpose administrator and that databases aren't your first love—and they might even just be a necessary evil! Hopefully, the DataAccess module we've given you will make it even easier to incorporate databases into your scripts.

Oh, and before we forget—don't forget to check that you've closed all the database connections you opened.

Proxy functions

This chapter covers
- Understanding proxy functions
- Creating proxy functions
- Adding and removing parameters

Proxy functions are a neat—if little-used—aspect of PowerShell. A proxy is someone with the authority to act as you. A proxy function lets you replace a PowerShell command or function with a custom version while leveraging the internal functionality of the original. They've also been called "wrapper functions," which is a good description, because they "wrap around" existing commands to provide a sort of custom interface to them.

37.1 The purpose of proxy functions

Proxy functions are often used as a way of restricting or enhancing a PowerShell command. For example, you might take away parameters from a command so that potentially dangerous functionality is disabled. Or you might add parameters to a command, enhancing its functionality.

PowerShell's implicit remoting capability, which we discussed in chapter 10, uses proxy functions. When you import commands from a remote computer, you're creating local proxy functions. They're very sparse functions: They contain enough functionality to take whatever parameters you type, pass them to the remote machine, and execute the command there. But they make it look like the commands are available locally on your computer.

37.2 *How proxy functions work*

Proxy functions take advantage of PowerShell's command-name conflict-resolution system. When you load multiple commands having the same name, PowerShell defaults to running the one most recently loaded or defined. So if you create a function named `Get-Content`, it'll "override" the original `Get-Content` for the current PowerShell session. That lets you add or remove parameters and enhance the command's functionality. Also at play is the fact that when you run a command, PowerShell first matches against aliases, then against functions, then against cmdlets—so a function will always "override" a cmdlet.

There are a few caveats here. In a normal shell, you can't stop someone from unloading or otherwise removing your proxy function, which then gives them access to the original command. You also can't stop someone from explicitly accessing the original command using fully qualified command names, such as `ActiveDirectory\Get-ADUser`. So from this perspective, proxy functions aren't a security mechanism—they're a convenience feature.

There's also a caveat related to the help system. When it finds two commands with the same name, such as a proxy function and the original underlying cmdlet, it'll list them both when asked for help on either. So proxy functions can make it a bit trickier to get to the help for the original command.

It might seem, with these caveats, that proxy functions aren't helpful, but they're useful when combined with custom PowerShell Remoting endpoints. As we described in chapter 10, a custom endpoint—or custom configuration, to use PowerShell's technical term—can be restricted. You can set it up so that only your proxy functions can run, thus restricting access to the original, underlying cmdlet and providing a much better security mechanism. In fact, it's when combined with those custom endpoints that proxy functions start to become intriguing.

37.3 *Creating a basic proxy function*

To demonstrate, you'll be extending the `ConvertTo-HTML` cmdlet via a proxy function. Now, you're not going to name your proxy function `ConvertTo-HTML`; instead, you'll create a proxy function named `Export-HTML`. Your goal is to both convert the data and write it out to a file, instead of having to pipe the HTML to `Out-File` on your own. So your proxy function will pick up a new parameter, `-FilePath`, that accepts the name of an output file. Because you're not overriding its name, the original cmdlet will remain available for someone who needs it in its original form.

Start by creating the shell for the proxy function:

```
PS C:\> $metadata = New-Object System.Management.Automation.CommandMetaData
➥   (Get-Command ConvertTo-HTML)
```

The metadata you're creating looks like this:

```
Name                     : ConvertTo-Html
CommandType              :
                           Microsoft.PowerShell.Commands.ConvertToHtmlCommand
DefaultParameterSetName  : Page
SupportsShouldProcess    : False
SupportsPaging           : False
PositionalBinding        : True
SupportsTransactions     : False
HelpUri                  : http://go.microsoft.com/fwlink/?LinkID=113290
RemotingCapability       : None
ConfirmImpact            : Medium
Parameters               : {[InputObject,
                           System.Management.Automation.ParameterMetadata],
                           [Property,
                           System.Management.Automation.ParameterMetadata],
                           [Body,
                           System.Management.Automation.ParameterMetadata],
                           [Head,
                           System.Management.Automation.ParameterMetadata]
                           ...}
```

The `Parameters` section stores the parameter definitions—for instance:

```
PS C:\>  $metadata.Parameters["InputObject"]

Name            : InputObject
ParameterType   : System.Management.Automation.PSObject
ParameterSets   : {[__AllParameterSets,
                  System.Management.Automation.ParameterSetMetadata]}
IsDynamic       : False
Aliases         : {}
Attributes      : {__AllParameterSets}
SwitchParameter : False
```

Once you've generated the metadata, it's time to create the proxy function:

```
PS C:\> [System.Management.Automation.ProxyCommand]::Create($metadata) |
➥ Out-File Export-HTML.ps1
```

As you'll see, this is digging pretty deeply into PowerShell's internals. The result of these two commands is a file, Export-HTML.ps1, which contains your proxy function's starting point, as shown in listing 37.1. Compare the metadata for the parameters to what's written out to your proxy function.

Listing 37.1 A new proxy function's starting point

```
[CmdletBinding(DefaultParameterSetName='Page',
             HelpUri='http://go.microsoft.com/fwlink/?LinkID=113290',
             RemotingCapability='None')]
param(
    [Parameter(ValueFromPipeline=$true)]
    [psobject]
    ${InputObject},
    [Parameter(Position=0)]
```

```
        [System.Object[]]
        ${Property},
        [Parameter(ParameterSetName='Page', Position=3)]
        [string[]]
        ${Body},
        [Parameter(ParameterSetName='Page', Position=1)]
        [string[]]
        ${Head},
        [Parameter(ParameterSetName='Page', Position=2)]
        [ValidateNotNullOrEmpty()]
        [string]
        ${Title},
        [ValidateNotNullOrEmpty()]
        [ValidateSet('Table','List')]
        [string]
        ${As},
        [Parameter(ParameterSetName='Page')]
        [Alias('cu','uri')]
        [ValidateNotNullOrEmpty()]
        [System.Uri]
        ${CssUri},
        [Parameter(ParameterSetName='Fragment')]
        [ValidateNotNullOrEmpty()]
        [switch]
        ${Fragment},
        [ValidateNotNullOrEmpty()]
        [string[]]
        ${PostContent},
        [ValidateNotNullOrEmpty()]
        [string[]]
        ${PreContent})
begin
{
    try {
        $outBuffer = $null
        if ($PSBoundParameters.TryGetValue('OutBuffer', [ref]$outBuffer))
        {
            $PSBoundParameters['OutBuffer'] = 1
        }
        $wrappedCmd =
➡  $ExecutionContext.InvokeCommand.GetCommand('ConvertTo-Html',
➡  [System.Management.Automation.CommandTypes]::Cmdlet)
        $scriptCmd = {& $wrappedCmd @PSBoundParameters }
        $steppablePipeline =
➡  $scriptCmd.GetSteppablePipeline($myInvocation.CommandOrigin)
        $steppablePipeline.Begin($PSCmdlet)
    } catch {
        throw
    }
}
process
{
    try {
        $steppablePipeline.Process($_)
    } catch {
```

```
            throw
        }
    }
}
end
{
    try {
        $steppablePipeline.End()
    } catch {
        throw
    }
}
<#
.ForwardHelpTargetName ConvertTo-Html
.ForwardHelpCategory Cmdlet
#>
```

There's some cool stuff here. There are three script blocks named BEGIN, PROCESS, and END—just like the advanced functions we showed you in earlier chapters (24 and 32). Those manage the execution of the original, underlying cmdlet. There's also, at the end, some comment-based help that forwards to the original cmdlet's help. This is technically an advanced script, because it isn't contained within a function; scripts are a bit easier to test, so we'll leave it that way for now.

37.4 Adding a parameter

Start by adding the definition for a mandatory -FilePath parameter to the top of the parameter block (shown in bold in the following code):

```
param(
    [Parameter(Mandatory=$true)]
    [string]
    $FilePath,
    [Parameter(ValueFromPipeline=$true)]
    [psobject]
    ${InputObject},
    [Parameter(Position=0)]
    [System.Object[]]
    ${Property},
    [Parameter(ParameterSetName='Page', Position=3)]
    [string[]]
    ${Body},
    [Parameter(ParameterSetName='Page', Position=1)]
    [string[]]
    ${Head},
    [Parameter(ParameterSetName='Page', Position=2)]
    [ValidateNotNullOrEmpty()]
    [string]
    ${Title},
    [ValidateNotNullOrEmpty()]
    [ValidateSet('Table','List')]
    [string]
    ${As},
    [Parameter(ParameterSetName='Page')]
    [Alias('cu','uri')]
```

```
[ValidateNotNullOrEmpty()]
[System.Uri]
${CssUri},
[Parameter(ParameterSetName='Fragment')]
[ValidateNotNullOrEmpty()]
[switch]
${Fragment},
[ValidateNotNullOrEmpty()]
[string[]]
${PostContent},
[ValidateNotNullOrEmpty()]
[string[]]
${PreContent})
```

You now have a few things that you need to code:

- You need to strip off your -FilePath parameter before the underlying cmdlet is run, because it won't understand that parameter and will throw an error. This happens in the BEGIN block.
- You need to call the underlying cmdlet and pipe its output to Out-File.

Within the proxy function, you have access to a variable called $wrappedCmd, which is the original cmdlet. That variable is set up for you by the generated proxy function code. You also have access to a hash table called $PSBoundParameters, which contains all the parameters that your proxy function was run with. You'll use those two variables to do your magic; the entire script appears in the following listing.

Listing 37.2   Export-HTML.ps1

```
[CmdletBinding(DefaultParameterSetName='Page',
               HelpUri='http://go.microsoft.com/fwlink/?LinkID=113290',
               RemotingCapability='None')]
param(
    [Parameter(Mandatory=$true)]
    [string]
    $FilePath,                                          ◁──┐ Added new
    [Parameter(ValueFromPipeline=$true)]                   │ parameter
    [psobject]
    ${InputObject},
    [Parameter(Position=0)]
    [System.Object[]]
    ${Property},
    [Parameter(ParameterSetName='Page', Position=3)]
    [string[]]
    ${Body},
    [Parameter(ParameterSetName='Page', Position=1)]
    [string[]]
    ${Head},
    [Parameter(ParameterSetName='Page', Position=2)]
    [ValidateNotNullOrEmpty()]
    [string]
    ${Title},
    [ValidateNotNullOrEmpty()]
    [ValidateSet('Table','List')]
```

```
        [string]
        ${As},
        [Parameter(ParameterSetName='Page')]
        [Alias('cu','uri')]
        [ValidateNotNullOrEmpty()]
        [System.Uri]
        ${CssUri},
        [Parameter(ParameterSetName='Fragment')]
        [ValidateNotNullOrEmpty()]
        [switch]
        ${Fragment},
        [ValidateNotNullOrEmpty()]
        [string[]]
        ${PostContent},
        [ValidateNotNullOrEmpty()]
        [string[]]
        ${PreContent})
begin
{
    try {
        $outBuffer = $null
        if ($PSBoundParameters.TryGetValue('OutBuffer', [ref]$outBuffer))
        {
            $PSBoundParameters['OutBuffer'] = 1
        }
        $wrappedCmd =
        $ExecutionContext.InvokeCommand.GetCommand('ConvertTo-Html',
        [System.Management.Automation.CommandTypes]::Cmdlet)
        $PSBoundParameters.Remove('FilePath') | Out-Null
        $scriptCmd = {& $wrappedCmd @PSBoundParameters |
          Out-File -FilePath $FilePath }
# $scriptCmd = {& $wrappedCmd @PSBoundParameters }
        $steppablePipeline =
        $scriptCmd.GetSteppablePipeline($myInvocation.CommandOrigin)
        $steppablePipeline.Begin($PSCmdlet)
    } catch {
        throw
    }
}
process
{
    try {
        $steppablePipeline.Process($_)
    } catch {
        throw
    }
}
end
{
    try {
        $steppablePipeline.End()
    } catch {
        throw
    }
}
```

Added this code

Commented out

```
<#
.ForwardHelpTargetName ConvertTo-Html
.ForwardHelpCategory Cmdlet
#>
```

In listing 37.2 you added only two lines and commented out one line. You used the splatting technique to pass all your parameters, except -FilePath, to the underlying cmdlet. Now you can test it:

```
PS C:\> get-process | .\Export-HTML.ps1 -filepath procs.html
```

It works perfectly, creating an HTML file with the designated filename.

37.5   *Removing a parameter*

Suppose, for some internal political reasons in your company, you don't want anyone setting the -Title parameter of the output HTML. Instead, you always want the HTML page title to be "Generated by PowerShell." Simple enough. Start by removing the -Title parameter from the parameter declaration block in your script. Then, programmatically add the parameter when your function is run, passing a hardcoded value. The next listing shows the new version.

Listing 37.3   Export-HTML.ps1, version 2

```
[CmdletBinding(DefaultParameterSetName='Page',
               HelpUri='http://go.microsoft.com/fwlink/?LinkID=113290',
               RemotingCapability='None')]
param(
    [Parameter(Mandatory=$true)]
    [string]
    $FilePath,
    [Parameter(ValueFromPipeline=$true)]
    [psobject]
    ${InputObject},
    [Parameter(Position=0)]
    [System.Object[]]
    ${Property},                                                  Changed
    [Parameter(ParameterSetName='Page', Position=2)]              this
    [string[]]
    ${Body},
    [Parameter(ParameterSetName='Page', Position=1)]
    [string[]]
    ${Head},
    #[Parameter(ParameterSetName='Page', Position=2)]
    #[ValidateNotNullOrEmpty()]                                   Commented
    #[string]                                                     this out
    #${Title},
    [ValidateNotNullOrEmpty()]
    [ValidateSet('Table','List')]
    [string]
    ${As},
    [Parameter(ParameterSetName='Page')]
    [Alias('cu','uri')]
```

```
        [ValidateNotNullOrEmpty()]
        [System.Uri]
        ${CssUri},
        [Parameter(ParameterSetName='Fragment')]
        [ValidateNotNullOrEmpty()]
        [switch]
        ${Fragment},
        [ValidateNotNullOrEmpty()]
        [string[]]
        ${PostContent},
        [ValidateNotNullOrEmpty()]
        [string[]]
        ${PreContent})
begin
{
    try {
        $outBuffer = $null
        if ($PSBoundParameters.TryGetValue('OutBuffer', [ref]$outBuffer))
        {
            $PSBoundParameters['OutBuffer'] = 1
        }
        $wrappedCmd =
        $ExecutionContext.InvokeCommand.GetCommand('ConvertTo-Html',
        [System.Management.Automation.CommandTypes]::Cmdlet)
            # we added this
            $PSBoundParameters.Remove('FilePath') | Out-Null
            $PSBoundParameters.Add('Title','Generated by PowerShell')
            $scriptCmd = {& $wrappedCmd @PSBoundParameters |
            Out-File -FilePath $FilePath }
            # end of what we added
            # we commented out the next line
            # $scriptCmd = {& $wrappedCmd @PSBoundParameters }
            $steppablePipeline =
        $scriptCmd.GetSteppablePipeline($myInvocation.CommandOrigin)
            $steppablePipeline.Begin($PSCmdlet)
    } catch {
        throw
    }
}
process
{
    try {
        $steppablePipeline.Process($_)
    } catch {
        throw
    }
}
end
{
    try {
        $steppablePipeline.End()
    } catch {
        throw
    }
}
```

Added this

```
<#
.ForwardHelpTargetName ConvertTo-Html
.ForwardHelpCategory Cmdlet
#>
```

Notice that you left the parameter in and just commented it out. That way, if you ever change your mind about something so goofy, it's easy to put back in. Also notice that you needed to change the position of the -Body parameter from 3 to 2. -Title used to be in 2, and you can't have a position 3 without a 2, so -Body had to be moved up.

37.6   *Turning it into a function*

From a practical perspective, you probably should turn this script into a function so that it can be put into a module and loaded on demand. That's easy: You just need to add the function keyword, the function's name, and the opening and closing curly brackets:

```
Function Export-HTML {
...
}
```

The following listing shows the final result, which you should save as a script module named ExtraTools.

Listing 37.4   ExtraTools.psm1

```
function Export-HTML {
[CmdletBinding(DefaultParameterSetName='Page',
              HelpUri='http://go.microsoft.com/fwlink/?LinkID=113290',
              RemotingCapability='None')]
param(
    [Parameter(Mandatory=$true)]
    [string]
    $FilePath,
    [Parameter(ValueFromPipeline=$true)]
    [psobject]
    ${InputObject},
    [Parameter(Position=0)]
    [System.Object[]]
    ${Property},
    [Parameter(ParameterSetName='Page', Position=3)]
    [string[]]
    ${Body},
    [Parameter(ParameterSetName='Page', Position=1)]
    [string[]]
    ${Head},
    #[Parameter(ParameterSetName='Page', Position=2)]
    #[ValidateNotNullOrEmpty()]
    #[string]
    #${Title},
    [ValidateNotNullOrEmpty()]
    [ValidateSet('Table','List')]
    [string]
    ${As},
    [Parameter(ParameterSetName='Page')]
```

```
    [Alias('cu','uri')]
    [ValidateNotNullOrEmpty()]
    [System.Uri]
    ${CssUri},
    [Parameter(ParameterSetName='Fragment')]
    [ValidateNotNullOrEmpty()]
    [switch]
    ${Fragment},
    [ValidateNotNullOrEmpty()]
    [string[]]
    ${PostContent},
    [ValidateNotNullOrEmpty()]
    [string[]]
    ${PreContent})
begin
{
    try {
        $outBuffer = $null
        if ($PSBoundParameters.TryGetValue('OutBuffer', [ref]$outBuffer))
        {
            $PSBoundParameters['OutBuffer'] = 1
        }
        $wrappedCmd =
➥   $ExecutionContext.InvokeCommand.GetCommand('ConvertTo-Html',
➥   [System.Management.Automation.CommandTypes]::Cmdlet)
        # we added this
        $PSBoundParameters.Remove('FilePath') | Out-Null
        $PSBoundParameters.Add('Title','Generated by PowerShell')
        $scriptCmd = {& $wrappedCmd @PSBoundParameters |
        Out-File -FilePath $FilePath }
        # end of what we added
        # we commented out the next line
        # $scriptCmd = {& $wrappedCmd @PSBoundParameters }
        $steppablePipeline =
➥   $scriptCmd.GetSteppablePipeline($myInvocation.CommandOrigin)
        $steppablePipeline.Begin($PSCmdlet)
    } catch {
        throw
    }
}
process
{
    try {
        $steppablePipeline.Process($_)
    } catch {
        throw
    }
}
end
{
    try {
        $steppablePipeline.End()
    } catch {
        throw
    }
```

```
}
<#
.ForwardHelpTargetName ConvertTo-Html
.ForwardHelpCategory Cmdlet
#>
}
```

Once the module in listing 37.4 is imported into your PowerShell session, you have access to the function. Tab completion works as well. If you try to tab-complete `-Title`, it won't work because it has been removed. But tab completion for `-FilePath` will work.

There's one final item we want to bring to your attention and that's help. If you ask for help on `Export-HTML`, you'll get complete help for `ConvertTo-HTML`. This is because help requests are forwarded:

```
<#
.ForwardHelpTargetName ConvertTo-Html
.ForwardHelpCategory Cmdlet
#>
```

The net result is that you won't see the new `-FilePath` parameter and `-Title` will still be visible, although unusable, which might cause some confusion. You can delete these lines and the help URI in the `cmdletbinding` block:

```
[CmdletBinding(DefaultParameterSetName='Page',
            HelpUri='http://go.microsoft.com/fwlink/?LinkID=113290',
            RemotingCapability='None')]
```

Now you can create and insert comment-based help directly in the function, perhaps copying and pasting help information from `ConvertTo-HTML`. See chapter 29 for more information on writing help for your PowerShell scripts and functions.

37.7 *Summary*

This chapter demonstrated a useful way to employ proxy functions: to add functionality to a cmdlet without removing access to the original cmdlet. You could've simply added a `-FilePath` parameter to `ConvertTo-HTML` (this example was inspired by fellow PowerShell MVP Shay Levy, who took that approach for his own example at http://blogs.technet.com/b/heyscriptingguy/archive/2011/03/01/proxy-functions-spice-up-your-powershell-core-cmdlets.aspx). But doing so would've been inconsistent with the ConvertTo verb in PowerShell; by creating a new function with the proper Export verb, you maintained consistency within the shell and gained a useful command that Microsoft should have written for you. But now you don't need to wait for them to do so!

Shay and another PowerShell MVP, Kirk Munro, have created a set of PowerShell extensions that make working with proxy functions much easier. If this is an area you want to explore, then download PowerShell Proxy Extensions from http://pspx.codeplex.com/.

Building a GUI

Although PowerShell is obviously all about the command line, there may well be times when you want to create a script that displays a graphical user interface (GUI), perhaps for less technically proficient colleagues or end users. Fortunately, PowerShell is built atop the .NET Framework, which offers not one but two ways of displaying a GUI.

As with some of the other chapters in the latter part of this book, we need to set some expectations. Creating and programming a GUI is pure .NET Framework programming, plain and simple. Entire, massive books exist on the topic, so there's no way we can cover all that material in this chapter. Instead, we'll show you how PowerShell connects to these technologies and uses them. If you'd like to explore further, we recommend that you pick up a dedicated book on the topic. One thing we're going to make sure we cover, though, is some tips for translating the C#-based examples you'll run into elsewhere (including in Microsoft's documentation) into PowerShell's scripting language. That way, as you start to explore beyond the simple examples here, you'll be ready to leverage the enormous set of examples that other folks have already written.

For Windows Forms programming, which is what we'll cover first, we recommend *Programming Microsoft Windows Forms* by Charles Petzold (Microsoft Press, 2005). It's an older book, but still very accurate. Another title is *Windows Forms in Action, Second Edition* by Erik Brown (Manning, 2006). For Windows Presentation Foundation, the topic of this chapter's second half, consider *WPF in Action with Visual Studio 2008* by Arlen Feldman and Maxx Daymon (Manning, 2008).

As those book titles imply, PowerShell has two means of raising a GUI: Windows Forms, which is the original GUI technology built into .NET, and Windows Presentation Foundation (WPF), which is a newer technology introduced in .NET Framework 3.5. WPF is more modern, more modular, and somewhat more complex; Windows Forms (or WinForms) is a bit more classic, a bit simpler to use, and still very much in use by all kinds of developers. We'll start with it.

38.1   *WinForms via PowerShell Studio*

In WinForms, you create your GUI programmatically—that is, you create instances of objects like buttons, windows, check boxes, and so forth and set their properties to position them on the screen. This gets tedious, especially in PowerShell where you spend a lot of trial-and-error time tweaking positions and so on. To make the process easier, we tend to use PowerShell Studio (formerly known as PrimalForms) from SAPIEN Technologies (http://primaltools.com). This is a commercial product, meaning you have to pay for it, although you might still be able to find the free Community Edition on the SAPIEN site. The free edition provides a lot of functionality but obviously not all the bells and whistles of the commercial product. If you need to develop graphical PowerShell scripts, this tool is well worth your investment.

We'll focus on the basics and create a simple GUI tool. You can do a lot more with PowerShell Studio (and WinForms), and the product's documentation provides a good starting point. You'll also find the company's blog to be an excellent source of examples (http://www.sapien.com/blog/) for PrimalForms, aka PowerShell Studio, including complex tasks like building data grids and other GUI elements.

> **NOTE**   PowerShell Studio projects can become terrifically complex, including multiple windows and lots of GUI elements. We'll keep it simple, just to illustrate the basics and cover some of what you can do. Otherwise, this chapter could easily become its own book!

By the way, it's completely possible to create an entire WinForms-based script without a tool like PowerShell Studio. PowerShell Studio just makes it a million times easier. But, toward the end of our upcoming example, we'll show you what the final code looks like and walk you through some key pieces of it. That'll get you started on hand-coding a GUI, if you'd prefer to take that time-consuming, laborious, and highly manual approach. Which we obviously wouldn't do ourselves!

WARNING   Like many third-party tools, PowerShell Studio does quite a bit when it installs. One of the things it sets up is a set of Windows Firewall exceptions. Just make sure you review what it's done after it installs, and be sure you're comfortable with those changes. Obviously, you can disable or remove anything you don't like, but you may impact certain product features. We don't work for SAPIEN, but we do find their support team to be responsive, so if you run into trouble with the application, start at http://support.sapien.com for help.

38.1.1   Creating the GUI

Your first step, after installing the product, will be to start a new project and create a GUI. You do need to plan ahead a bit. What will your final script do? What information will you need to collect, and how will you display it? You might even sit down with a pencil and paper and sketch out your GUI in advance so that you can work more efficiently once you begin in earnest. When you're ready, start by creating a new Form Project, as shown in figure 38.1. We're using a beta version of PowerShell Studio 2014, so your results might vary.

TIP   We strongly recommend you have a PowerShell script or function that already works from the command console. You'll find it much easier to build a GUI that incorporates your code than trying to create the graphical elements and your code at the same time. You'll also end up with two versions of the same tool, one for console use and one graphical, which is exactly the PowerShell model.

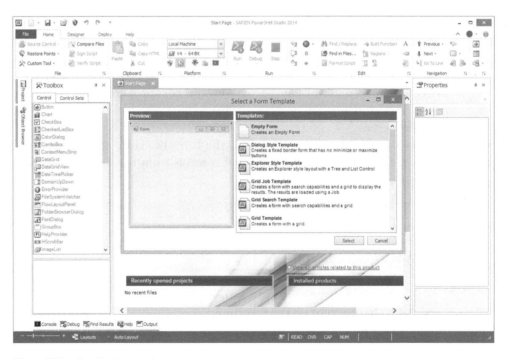

Figure 38.1   Creating a new form

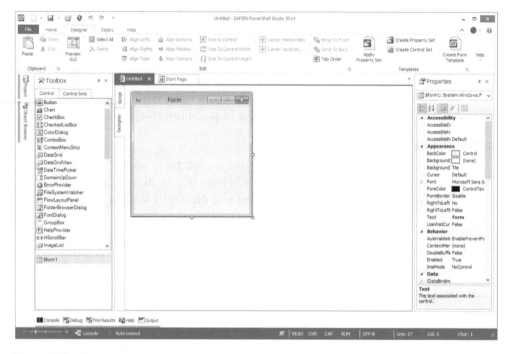

Figure 38.2 An empty form

PowerShell Studio offers a number of form templates. We started with a totally blank slate, as shown in figure 38.2.

Use the right-hand Properties Explorer to set properties of the form itself. For this example, set ControlBox to False, FormBorderStyle to FixedDialog, and Start Position to CenterScreen, and type `QueryEvents` for the Text property. Also pin open the Toolbox on the left-hand side, as shown in figure 38.3. Use the Toolbox to configure element properties.

Now you'll add several controls to the form to create the display shown in figure 38.4. Drag and drop the individual controls from the Toolbox to the form. For this example:

- Add a Label, and set the following:
  - TextAlign to MiddleRight
  - Text to `Log to Display`
- Add a Combo Box, and set the following:
  - Name to `comboEventLogList`
  - DropDownStyle to DropDownList
- Add a button, and set the following:
  - Text to `Display` (which causes PowerShell Studio to set Name to button-Display automatically)

- Add a second button, and set the following:
  - Text to `Close` (which causes PowerShell Studio to set Name to buttonClose automatically)
- Resize the form by dragging its edges. Then, set the following in the Form properties under Misc:
  - AcceptButton to buttonDisplay (which will activate buttonDisplay if the user presses Enter)
  - CancelButton to buttonClose (which will activate buttonClose if the user presses Esc)

The GUI after the completion of these steps is shown in figure 38.4.

The Name properties are crucial. Any control that a user might interact with needs a meaningful name. PowerShell Studio will create variables that make each control easier to reference; the variable names come from the control's Name property. So your buttonDisplay button will be referenced via a `$buttonDisplay` variable. If you don't set the name, you get meaningless variable names like `$combobox1`, which are a lot harder to work with when you get into the code.

38.1.2 Adding the code

After you've finished drawing the GUI, you can start adding code and PowerShell commands to make it function. The first thing you'll do is right-click the form and select

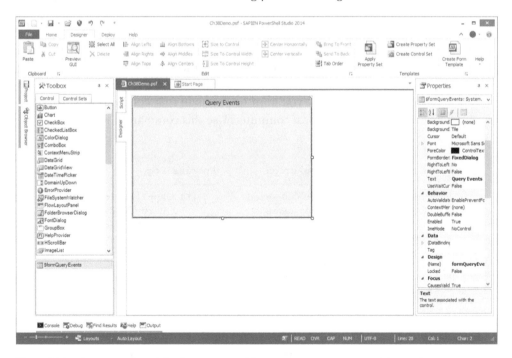

Figure 38.3 Set properties of the form to control its appearance, startup position, and so on.

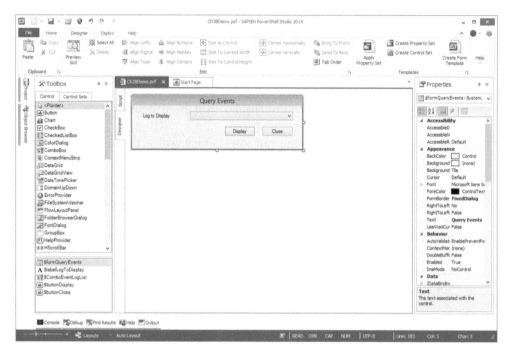

Figure 38.4   Getting the rest of the GUI in place. You can rearrange and resize until you're happy with the results.

Edit Default Event to open a code editor with the form's Load event. Here you'll add the commands that you want to run when the form loads (see figure 38.5); that's when you start the GUI application.

When this form loads, you want to populate that combo box with whatever event logs are present on the local computer. Use this command to do so:

```
PS C:\> Get-EventLog -List

  Max(K) Retain OverflowAction          Entries Log
  ------ ------ --------------          ------- ---
  20,480      0 OverwriteAsNeeded         9,817 Application
  20,480      0 OverwriteAsNeeded             0 HardwareEvents
     512      7 OverwriteOlder                0 Internet Explorer
  20,480      0 OverwriteAsNeeded             0 Key Management Service
     128      0 OverwriteAsNeeded           175 OAlerts
  20,480      0 OverwriteAsNeeded        31,223 Security
  20,480      0 OverwriteAsNeeded         4,979 System
  15,360      0 OverwriteAsNeeded        17,668 Windows PowerShell
```

So it's the Log property that you want added to the list. You need to figure out how to do that, so in your favorite search engine enter msdn winforms combobox (MSDN gets you to Microsoft's site, WinForms narrows you down to a particular technology, and ComboBox is the name of the control you're trying to manipulate). The result

Figure 38.5   You can unpin the side panels to give yourself more room for code.

is http://msdn.microsoft.com/en-us/library/system.windows.forms.combobox.aspx, shown in figure 38.6. Looking at the list of methods, you don't see anything that looks like "add an item to the list." Back in the Properties list, you do see Items, which "Gets an object representing the collection of items contained in this ComboBox."

Clicking the Items property takes you to http://msdn.microsoft.com/en-us/library/ system.windows.forms.combobox.items.aspx, which lists a handy C# code example for adding items to the box:

```
private void addButton_Click(object sender, System.EventArgs e) {
    comboBox1.Items.Add(textBox1.Text);
}
```

This looks like an example of how to have an item added when a button is clicked. The single line of code within that function is the only part you care about. It looks like you refer to the combo box (which in your PowerShell project will be $combo-EventLogList, because that's the name you gave it). You refer to its Items property, execute the Add() method, and pass in the text you want to add.

When you read down in the PowerShell code a bit, you realize that PowerShell Studio has created a Load-ComboBox function for you. Wow. Reading the comment-based help, it looks like all you need to do is provide a –ComboBox parameter and a list of items to add. PowerShell Studio has a built-in place to add code like this to initialize controls when the form is loaded.

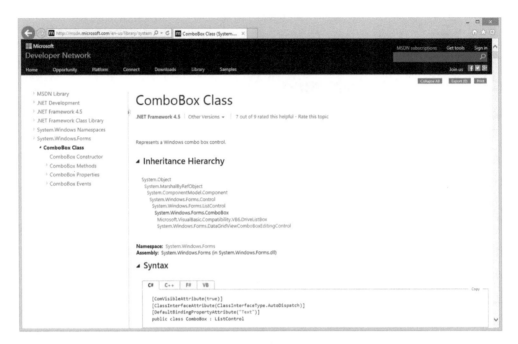

Figure 38.6   Figuring out how to use a ComboBox in WinForms

```
$formQueryEvents_Load={
    #TODO: Initialize Form Controls here
    Load-ComboBox -ComboBox $comboEventLogList -Items (
    Get-EventLog -list | Select-Object -expandProperty Log
      )
}
```

Figure 38.7 shows your code.

All you have to do now is test what you have so far by clicking Run Project in the Ribbon. As you can see in figure 38.8, your list populated correctly.

Now you need to do something with whatever log the person selects. That'll happen when they click the Display button you created. So, stop the script (there's a button in the Ribbon for this action) or click the Close button because you've already told the form that's the default Cancel button. Then go back to the Designer tab to display your form. Right-click the Display button and choose Edit Default Event. Or because this is a simple form, you can scroll down in the Script pane until you find the `$buttonDisplay_Click` script block.

You'll need to access whatever item has been selected in the combo box. In the MDSN documentation, you'll find a `SelectedItem` property that'll contain whatever item is currently selected, so you'll use that:

```
$buttonDisplay_Click={
    Get-EventLog -LogName ($comboEventLogList.SelectedItem) |
    Out-GridView
}
```

```
      12   └ }
      13
      14
      15 ⊟ function OnApplicationExit {
      16       #Note: This function is not called in Projects
      17       #Note: This function runs after the form is closed
      18       #TODO: Add custom code to clean up and unload modules when the application exits
      19
      20       $script:ExitCode = 0 #Set the exit code for the Packager
      21   └ }
      22
      23 ⊟ $formQueryEvents_Load={
      24       #TODO: Initialize Form Controls here
      25       Load-ComboBox -ComboBox $comboEventLogList -Items (
      26       Get-EventLog -list | Select-Object -expandProperty Log
      27       )
      28
      29   └ }
      30     |
      31
      32 ⊟ #region Control Helper Functions
      33   function Load-ComboBox
      34 ⊟ {
      35 ⊟ <#
      36       .SYNOPSIS
      37           This functions helps you load items into a ComboBox.
      38
      39       .DESCRIPTION
      40           Use this function to dynamically load items into the ComboBox control.
      41
      42       PARAMETER   ComboRox
```

Figure 38.7   **Adding code that'll run when the form loads**

Notice that you're piping the result to Out-GridView. Doing so gives you an easy way of displaying the results, but it does require that the Windows PowerShell ISE be installed on the system. For this example, we'll assume you've already done that, so

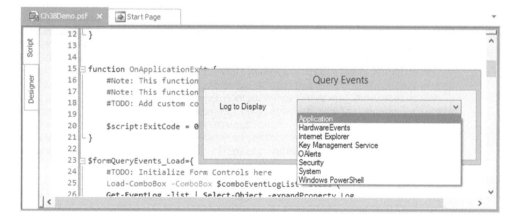

Figure 38.8   **Testing the project as you complete each step is a good way to avoid complex bugs.**

you're good to go. In this particular scenario, you probably don't need to define it, but your last step might be to make the Close button do something:

```
$buttonClose_Click={
    $MainForm.Close()
}
```

With that, you've made the entire thing work.

NOTE PowerShell Studio provides the ability to run scripts in both 32-bit and 64-bit shells. You have to be careful to select the right one, especially if your script will use extensions that are available in only one architecture. A drop-down box in the Ribbon lets you select one or the other each time you run.

38.1.3 *Using the script*

Obviously, you don't want your users to have to install PowerShell Studio just to run your script, so you'll need to export your project. Your two main choices are to create a stand-alone script or to create a packaged executable. Either route still requires PowerShell to be installed on users' machines in order to run; this isn't compilation à la Visual Studio. Use the Deploy tab in the Ribbon. The following listing shows the complete, deployed script from our example.

Listing 38.1 Our example project code

```
#-------------------------------------------------------------------------
# Source File Information (DO NOT MODIFY)
# Source ID: 97f0343b-2da0-4a16-9bc1-c88987f99cc0
# Source File: C:\Users\Jeff\Dropbox\PowerShell In Depth 2nd\Chapter
# 38\Ch38Demo.psf
#-------------------------------------------------------------------------
#region File Recovery Data (DO NOT MODIFY)
<#RecoveryData:
WhAAAB+LCAAAAAAABADNmFtv2jAUx98n7TtYeUaQCylUgkgQijSNbllh3d4qJzmhXp0Y2U7b7
NPPudC1pCwJKmhCQtic4/+5/HwiGF2Dzx6ApzMsMVIfBGHxWDM15+MHhEZfOVmTGNM5ofAFR+C
4d9ZwBhHrbkQ461W+Lpy8X+BLJNMNjLVlKiRE3R8kDtij6M4Zj4r3Dnrrqw66KWPod/Xs1UFuQ
mXCYRxDIjmmHXSVeJT4nyFdsXuIx95ggG3fPjPOrT7ow3MNxSqUsRaq8741KrWLB4il0JB/R2j
AlYfmslhyRkWRpQr5irMNcJmWrhPfh42cJlKyeGujrK4hBOXvQ2nm5QYzIjYUpxrqbU/rbY/bc
7yL1Rm04fEuZQLaHE6JSndJfoPm9I1hBxm6Ve9UFGTKnjRnjqmAWo+sW1PGA+BLmVKlNSdPEMw
pmxd65yxojk7Dar1WkrM5RUTRJKsbq5yUuo+B4hrfVfwJDUnV0P75PL90n7BcFCJ8DbbHfXyxd
apHvaiz0fH/RUt+1Gvlqbo2TUIJayqmrNZKU7VbcF8XDTCMo0OsvUGPkXfX0TawKcgeWB3kFnl
+I1GY+9THIDiuJF1jkXTUL4LuCEiwTRHfor9e5dRxjVnxZM3bkyvYOM/JeV5bJ2UFdMcHsBKGe
sxaTEb09I8mHa87EwgNcf9+50C3OabOxOoNWYuizymRv3RQcuF81gXbL0gQraETS1n7DEuHzDb
ZXZQg+JnyWApSby+iLFHIdhf9r20Gn1TPT/7jWmtJNyYWNPuK2SNVshWrduzsMAe0KODQDMVVZ
IVO2jqvBwfqh9NLnbRj4pu434Yut56hDSZasUIUSEhyVDzoDK3CSVrVYJLEgQUFhBW4XrV/teL
iRAQqV6B2NqWO6lT9v4Sx3gNkWK3O0kki/KK/2XAaMqAZXihNbTPcGCd9cGyR71npV3lSPiMU+
K9A2n/UCnyO4XGu9+fesXsZ9tphDh+VLP0EC3dCu1wEBpGYOvYwvVaPyN6mpwIVxeE8XQJ/IH4
cFDLWmfnMg4nSa/MSg0JldoRcnteFlNl1Hv5X4LzBxptjfRaEAAA
#>
#endregion
#=========================================================================
# Code Generated By: SAPIEN Technologies, Inc., PowerShell Studio 2014
# v4.1.36
```

```
# Generated On: 2/17/2014 4:57 PM
# Generated By: Jeff Hicks
#=======================================================================
#-----------------------------------------------
#region Application Functions
#-----------------------------------------------

function OnApplicationLoad {
    #Note: This function is not called in Projects
    #Note: This function runs before the form is created
    #Note: To get the script directory in the Packager use:
    Split-Path $hostinvocation.MyCommand.path
    #Note: To get the console output in the Packager
    (Windows Mode) use: $ConsoleOutput
    (Type: System.Collections.ArrayList)
    #Important: Form controls cannot be accessed in this function
    #TODO: Add modules and custom code to validate the application load

    return $true #return true for success or false for failure
}

function OnApplicationExit {
    #Note: This function is not called in Projects
    #Note: This function runs after the form is closed
    #TODO: Add custom code to clean up and unload
    modules when the application exits

    $script:ExitCode = 0 #Set the exit code for the Packager
}

#endregion Application Functions

#-----------------------------------------------
# Generated Form Function
#-----------------------------------------------
function Call-Ch38Demo_psf {

    #-----------------------------------------------
    #region Import the Assemblies
    #-----------------------------------------------
    [void][reflection.assembly]::Load('mscorlib,
➡      Version=4.0.0.0, Culture=neutral,
➡      PublicKeyToken=b77a5c561934e089')
    [void][reflection.assembly]::Load('System,
➡      Version=2.0.0.0, Culture=neutral,
➡      PublicKeyToken=b77a5c561934e089')
    [void][reflection.assembly]::
➡      Load('System.Windows.Forms, Version=2.0.0.0,
➡      Culture=neutral, PublicKeyToken=b77a5c561934e089')
    [void][reflection.assembly]::Load('System.Data,
➡      Version=2.0.0.0, Culture=neutral,
➡      PublicKeyToken=b77a5c561934e089')
    [void][reflection.assembly]::Load('System.Drawing,
➡      Version=2.0.0.0, Culture=neutral,
➡      PublicKeyToken=b03f5f7f11d50a3a')
    [void][reflection.assembly]::Load('System.Xml,
➡      Version=2.0.0.0, Culture=neutral,
```

```
➥    PublicKeyToken=b77a5c561934e089')
[void] [reflection.assembly]::
➥    Load('System.DirectoryServices, Version=2.0.0.0,
➥    Culture=neutral, PublicKeyToken=b03f5f7f11d50a3a')
[void] [reflection.assembly]::Load('System.Core,
➥    Version=3.5.0.0, Culture=neutral,
➥    PublicKeyToken=b77a5c561934e089')
[void] [reflection.assembly]::
➥    Load('System.ServiceProcess, Version=2.0.0.0,
➥    Culture=neutral, PublicKeyToken=b03f5f7f11d50a3a')
#endregion Import Assemblies

#-----------------------------------------------
#region Generated Form Objects
#-----------------------------------------------
[System.Windows.Forms.Application]::EnableVisualStyles()
$formQueryEvents = New-Object 'System.Windows.Forms.Form'
$buttonClose = New-Object 'System.Windows.Forms.Button'
$buttonDisplay = New-Object 'System.Windows.Forms.Button'
$ComboEventLogList = New-Object 'System.Windows.Forms.ComboBox'
$labelLogToDisplay = New-Object 'System.Windows.Forms.Label'
$InitialFormWindowState = New-Object
'System.Windows.Forms.FormWindowState'
#endregion Generated Form Objects

#-----------------------------------------------
# User Generated Script
#-----------------------------------------------

$formQueryEvents_Load={
    #TODO: Initialize Form Controls here
    Load-ComboBox -ComboBox $comboEventLogList -Items (
    Get-EventLog -list | Select-Object -expandProperty Log
    )
}

#region Control Helper Functions
function Load-ComboBox
{
<#
    .SYNOPSIS
        This functions helps you load items into a ComboBox.

    .DESCRIPTION
        Use this function to dynamically load
        items into the ComboBox control.

    .PARAMETER  ComboBox
        The ComboBox control you want to add items to.

    .PARAMETER  Items
        The object or objects you wish to load
        into the ComboBox's Items collection.

    .PARAMETER  DisplayMember
        Indicates the property to display for the
        items in this control.
```

```
    .PARAMETER  Append
        Adds the item(s) to the ComboBox without
        clearing the Items collection.

    .EXAMPLE
        Load-ComboBox $combobox1 "Red", "White", "Blue"

    .EXAMPLE
        Load-ComboBox $combobox1 "Red" -Append
        Load-ComboBox $combobox1 "White" -Append
        Load-ComboBox $combobox1 "Blue" -Append

    .EXAMPLE
        Load-ComboBox $combobox1 (Get-Process) "ProcessName"
#>
    Param (
        [ValidateNotNull()]
        [Parameter(Mandatory=$true)]
        [System.Windows.Forms.ComboBox]$ComboBox,
        [ValidateNotNull()]
        [Parameter(Mandatory=$true)]
        $Items,
        [Parameter(Mandatory=$false)]
        [string]$DisplayMember,
        [switch]$Append
    )

    if(-not $Append)
    {
        $ComboBox.Items.Clear()
    }

    if($Items -is [Object[]])
    {
        $ComboBox.Items.AddRange($Items)
    }
    elseif ($Items -is [Array])
    {
        $ComboBox.BeginUpdate()
        foreach($obj in $Items)
        {
            $ComboBox.Items.Add($obj)
        }
        $ComboBox.EndUpdate()
    }
    else
    {
        $ComboBox.Items.Add($Items)
    }

    $ComboBox.DisplayMember = $DisplayMember
}
#endregion

$buttonDisplay_Click={
    #TODO: Place custom script here
        Get-EventLog -LogName ($comboEventLogList.SelectedItem) |
    Out-GridView
```

```
    }

    # --End User Generated Script--
    #-----------------------------------------------
    #region Generated Events
    #-----------------------------------------------

    $Form_StateCorrection_Load=
    {
        #Correct the initial state of the form to
            prevent the .Net maximized form issue
        $formQueryEvents.WindowState = $InitialFormWindowState
    }

    $Form_Cleanup_FormClosed=
    {
        #Remove all event handlers from the controls
        try
        {
            $buttonDisplay.remove_Click($buttonDisplay_Click)
            $formQueryEvents.remove_Load($formQueryEvents_Load)
            $formQueryEvents.remove_Load($Form_StateCorrection_Load)
            $formQueryEvents.remove_FormClosed($Form_Cleanup_FormClosed)
        }
        catch [Exception]
        { }
    }
    #endregion Generated Events

    #-----------------------------------------------
    #region Generated Form Code
    #-----------------------------------------------
    $formQueryEvents.SuspendLayout()
    #
    # formQueryEvents
    #
    $formQueryEvents.Controls.Add($buttonClose)
    $formQueryEvents.Controls.Add($buttonDisplay)
    $formQueryEvents.Controls.Add($ComboEventLogList)
    $formQueryEvents.Controls.Add($labelLogToDisplay)
    $formQueryEvents.AcceptButton = $buttonDisplay
    $formQueryEvents.CancelButton = $buttonClose
    $formQueryEvents.ClientSize = '418, 103'
    $formQueryEvents.ControlBox = $False
    $formQueryEvents.FormBorderStyle = 'FixedDialog'
    $formQueryEvents.Name = "formQueryEvents"
    $formQueryEvents.StartPosition = 'CenterScreen'
    $formQueryEvents.Text = "Query Events"
    $formQueryEvents.add_Load($formQueryEvents_Load)
    #
    # buttonClose
    #
    $buttonClose.DialogResult = 'Cancel'
    $buttonClose.Location = '321, 50'
    $buttonClose.Name = "buttonClose"
    $buttonClose.Size = '75, 23'
```

```
    $buttonClose.TabIndex = 3
    $buttonClose.Text = "Close"
    $buttonClose.UseVisualStyleBackColor = $True
    #
    # buttonDisplay
    #
    $buttonDisplay.DialogResult = 'Cancel'
    $buttonDisplay.Location = '228, 50'
    $buttonDisplay.Name = "buttonDisplay"
    $buttonDisplay.Size = '75, 23'
    $buttonDisplay.TabIndex = 2
    $buttonDisplay.Text = "Display"
    $buttonDisplay.UseVisualStyleBackColor = $True
    $buttonDisplay.add_Click($buttonDisplay_Click)
    #
    # ComboEventLogList
    #
    $ComboEventLogList.DropDownStyle = 'DropDownList'
    $ComboEventLogList.FormattingEnabled = $True
    $ComboEventLogList.Location = '142, 14'
    $ComboEventLogList.Name = "ComboEventLogList"
    $ComboEventLogList.Size = '254, 21'
    $ComboEventLogList.TabIndex = 1
    #
    # labelLogToDisplay
    #
    $labelLogToDisplay.Location = '22, 13'
    $labelLogToDisplay.Name = "labelLogToDisplay"
    $labelLogToDisplay.Size = '100, 23'
    $labelLogToDisplay.TabIndex = 0
    $labelLogToDisplay.Text = "Log to Display"
    $labelLogToDisplay.TextAlign = 'MiddleLeft'
    $formQueryEvents.ResumeLayout($false)
    #endregion Generated Form Code

    #---------------------------------------------

    #Save the initial state of the form
    $InitialFormWindowState = $formQueryEvents.WindowState
    #Init the OnLoad event to correct the initial state of the form
    $formQueryEvents.add_Load($Form_StateCorrection_Load)
    #Clean up the control events
    $formQueryEvents.add_FormClosed($Form_Cleanup_FormClosed)
    #Show the Form
    return $formQueryEvents.ShowDialog()

} #End Function

#Call OnApplicationLoad to initialize
if((OnApplicationLoad) -eq $true)
{

    Call-Ch38Demo_psf | Out-Null        ◁─┐ Form created
    #Perform cleanup                       │ here
    OnApplicationExit
}
```

You can see what a massive amount of code PowerShell Studio has created. In particular, notice the area of code where the GUI is programmatically created. Without a tool like PowerShell Studio, this is what you're left to create by hand—no thank you!

> **NOTE**   Your own project scripts will look a lot different. PowerShell Studio adds "control helper functions," like the `LoadComboBox` function we used, based on the controls you add to your form. Add different controls and you'll pick up different helper functions, so it's worth browsing the code listing in PowerShell Studio to see what it's added. We'll include our PowerShell Studio source file as part of the chapter downloads if you want to load it up and try it out yourself.

At this point, all you need to do is distribute the PS1 file and it can be executed like any other PowerShell script.

38.2   *Windows Presentation Foundation (WPF) and ShowUI*

WPF is the other, newer means of producing a GUI in .NET. We're not aware of a tool exactly like PowerShell Studio for WPF, but you may not feel you need one. You see, WPF doesn't create the GUI programmatically like WinForms does. Instead, the GUI definition is contained in an XML file (technically, the specific XML format is called XAML, for Extensible Application Markup Language). You can get any of the free "Express" editions of Visual Studio and use their built-in WPF forms-building tool, which looks a lot like PowerShell Studio, to produce the XAML file. Then, you just tell PowerShell (well, you tell .NET) to load the XAML and do something with it.

The next listing shows an example of what we're talking about.

Listing 38.2   Sample XAML

```
<?xml version="1.0" encoding="utf-16"?>
<Window
xmlns="http://schemas.microsoft.com/winfx/2006/xaml/presentation"
xmlns:x="http://schemas.microsoft.com/winfx/2006/xaml"
Title="Newest 100" Height= "200" Width="400"
>
<Canvas Width="300" Height="100"
 xmlns:sma="clr-namespace:System.Management.Automation;assembly=
System.Management.Automation"
 >
  <Canvas.Resources>
  </Canvas.Resources>
  <Label Canvas.Left="45" Canvas.Top="10">
    <Label.Resources>
    </Label.Resources>log to display</Label>
  <ComboBox IsEditable="False" Text="Application"
Name="comboBoxLogName" Canvas.Left="130" Canvas.Top="10">
    <ComboBox.Resources>
    </ComboBox.Resources>
  </ComboBox>
  <Button IsDefault="True" Canvas.Left="50" Canvas.Top="50"
```

```
Name="Display" ToolTip="Show last 100 entries">
    <Button.Resources>
    </Button.Resources>Display</Button>
  <Button Canvas.Left="175" Canvas.Top="50" Name="Close"
ToolTip="Quit">
    <Button.Resources>
    </Button.Resources>Close</Button>
</Canvas>
</Window>
```

Creating the XML in listing 38.2 isn't easy for most IT pros. And to run it takes even more work, as shown in the following listing.

Listing 38.3   Running sample WPF

```
Add-Type -AssemblyName PresentationFramework                    ⟵  Load required
                                                                   .NET assembly

[xml]$xaml = Get-Content -Path c:\scripts\sample-wpf.xml        ⟵  Create XML
                                                                   document

$reader = New-Object system.xml.xmlnodereader $xaml            ⟵  Create XML
                                                                   reader object

$form = [windows.markup.xamlreader]::Load($reader)       ⟵  Create form


                                                               ⟵  Add click events
                                                                   to buttons
$btnDisplay = $form.findname("Display")
$btnDisplay.Add_Click({ Get-Eventlog -LogName $($combo.Text) -Newest 100 |
Out-GridView -Title "Recent Entries"})

$btnClose = $form.FindName("Close")
$btnClose.Add_Click( {$form.close()})

$combo = $form.FindName("comboBoxLogName")
get-eventlog -List | foreach {                                     Populate
 $combo.items.Add($_.logDisplayname) | Out-Null              ⟵    combo box
}

#select the first item
$combo.SelectedIndex=0
                                                               Display
$form.showDialog() | Out-Null                            ⟵    form
```

But you don't have to mess with XAML if you don't want to—and frankly we don't. An easier way to integrate WPF into PowerShell is the free ShowUI module, available at http://showui.codeplex.com/. This module contains a bunch of commands like `New-Label` and `New-ComboBox` that let you run PowerShell-like commands to output WPF GUIs.

The website for the project has some quick examples, so we'll let you go straight there to get them. They'll be more up-to-date than anything we could put into this book. But, for the sake of comparison, we put together a ShowUI version of the WinForms script in the next listing.

Listing 38.4   A ShowUI script

```
<#
 This must be run in the ISE or in a PowerShell console session started
 with -STA
#>

Import-Module ShowUI

New-Canvas -ControlName "Newest 100" -Height 100 -Width 300 -children {
 New-Label -content "log to display" -left 45 -top 10
 New-ComboBox -IsEditable:$false -SelectedIndex 0
➥   -Top 10 -left 130 -Name comboBoxLogName
➥   -ItemsSource @(Get-eventlog -list |
Select -ExpandProperty Log)
 New-Button "Display" -isDefault -Top 50 -left 50  -On_Click {
     Get-Eventlog -logname $($comboBoxLogName.SelectedItem)
➥     -Newest 100 |
     Out-GridView -Title "Newest 100"
   }
 New-Button "Close" -Top 50 -left 175 -On_Click { Close-Control}
 } -Show
```

There's still quite a bit of trial and error to position all the elements, but when you run the script in listing 38.4 you get a form like figure 38.9. This is the same thing you'd have seen if you'd run the "native" WPF sample in listing 38.3.

If you want to use WPF, we think a tool like ShowUI is essential, but expect to invest some time in figuring out how to use it.

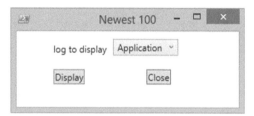

Figure 38.9   A ShowUI form

38.3   *WinForms vs. WPF*

One advantage of WPF is that it's a bit more self-contained and modular than Win-Forms, and using XAML lets you separate your GUI (which is defined in the XML) from the code and commands that make the GUI functional. But as a PowerShell admin, you just might not care—that kind of "separation of layers" is something developers love to go on about, but for simple admin utilities it's kind of a pointless argument. But keep in mind that in the latest version of Windows Server, you can't rely on a GUI being present at all. And, when the operating system's Minimal Server GUI mode is enabled, only WPF is supported—not WinForms. So if you need to make a GUI that must run *on* a server, WPF might be a better selection. That said, you shouldn't be writing GUIs to run on servers. Write the GUI to run on your client and send commands to the server via Remoting. That's Microsoft's model going forward, and you should adopt it, too.

Apart from those considerations, from the perspective of an admin, there aren't going to be a lot of differences between WinForms and WPF. With a great WinForms tool like PowerShell Studio, you might feel that WinForms is the way to go—and we'd have trouble arguing you out of it. Don't get us wrong: Some of our fellow MVPs and PowerShell enthusiasts will argue for *hours* about WinForms versus WPF, each raising perfectly valid arguments. But those respected colleagues are developers, and about 5 minutes into the argument we're usually at the bar ordering a refill or three while they go on and on about stuff we can barely comprehend. Ask us which to choose, and the answer is, "Whichever gets the job done faster, and another glass of wine, please."

The one advantage we'll admit to regarding WPF is that, because it's newer, it gets more attention. That means there are a ton of third-party add-in controls—graphs, charts, slick-looking buttons, you name it—that you could use. But again, from an admin perspective, you're unlikely to be using those things. If you're sticking purely with the basic controls—text boxes, labels, check boxes, buttons, lists, and the like—either WinForms or WPF will get the job done.

38.4　*Ideas for leveraging a GUI tool*

One of the main reasons we see administrators creating GUI tools is to give end users, or less-privileged technicians, the ability to perform some task that they wouldn't ordinarily have permission to perform. This is where the packaging capabilities of a product like PowerShell Studio can come in handy: You can have the package run under previously specified credentials, and users can perform only what the GUI enables them to do.

PowerShell's remoting capabilities (which we discussed in chapter 10) raise other, interesting possibilities. For example, consider this approach:

1 On a server, set up a custom remoting endpoint. Limit the commands available within the endpoint to just those commands needed to complete some specific task.

2 Configure the endpoint to use Run As credentials (you do this by using `Register-PSSessionConfiguration` or `Set-PSSessionConfiguration`). Also configure the security descriptor on the endpoint to allow the necessary users to connect.

3 You probably don't want to teach your users how to manually enter a remoting session and run commands, but your GUI can do that. Run the GUI on users' computers, and have the GUI establish a remoting connection to your custom endpoint.

4 Your GUI can then send commands to the custom endpoint for execution. They'll run under the endpoint's Run As credentials, meaning you can run commands that a user couldn't normally run. Because the endpoint is restricted to a limited set of commands, it doesn't matter if some clever user bypasses your GUI and connects to the endpoint manually; they'll still only have the capabilities that the GUI ordinarily surfaces.

We think there are a lot of clever possibilities here, and you're going to see Microsoft and other software vendors taking advantage of this approach. Why not use it yourself?

38.5   *Summary*

In this chapter, we've presented you with an overview of two means of creating a GUI from a PowerShell script. Although we realize there's a huge amount of additional exploration and explanation you might be hungry for, we feel that you should first choose one of these two methods, WinForms or WPF, to focus on. Then, set yourself up with some good training or books on that specific method. Given what we've shown you about connecting those technologies to PowerShell, you should be ready to start expanding your skills and capabilities and creating ever-more-complex GUIs.

WMI and CIM

This chapter covers

- Introducing WMI
- Understanding the WMI and CIM cmdlets
- Working with CIM sessions and CDXML

Including a chapter on Windows Management Instrumentation (WMI) and the Common Information Model (CIM) in an advanced PowerShell book may seem to be an odd move, but in reality PowerShell and WMI are closely linked—we've written much on using WMI with PowerShell, two powerful technologies that combine to give a huge amount of functionality. PowerShell makes this combination even more powerful because 60% of the new PowerShell cmdlets delivered in the Windows 8/Windows Server 2012 family of products are produced from WMI classes as "cmdlets over objects," which we'll cover near the end of the chapter.

The chapter starts with an overview of WMI and explains the relationship between WMI and CIM. PowerShell cmdlets have been available to work with WMI since PowerShell v1. We provide an overview of those cmdlets that focuses on the issues and intricacies of using them rather than detailed explanations.

The bulk of this chapter is taken up with a detailed examination of the Power-Shell CIM cmdlets, which were introduced with PowerShell v3. These are analogous to the WMI cmdlets but extend the range of functionality. Closely related to the CIM cmdlets are CIM sessions, which are similar to the PowerShell Remoting session and provide an easy way to remove the dependence on the Distributed Component Object Model (DCOM) for accessing WMI on remote systems.

PowerShell v3 introduced technology to wrap WMI classes in XML. You save the file with a .cdxml extension and you can use it as a PowerShell module. This technology provides huge gains in terms of ease of use. As we stated earlier, much of the new PowerShell functionality introduced in Windows Server 2012 is delivered through using these "cmdlets over objects." As we mentioned, the chapter closes by examining how this technology can be accessed. We offer an example to help the explanation.

Before we get to the new stuff, let's spend a little time recapping the fundamentals by considering just exactly what WMI is.

39.1   *What is WMI?*

Before we discuss using WMI with PowerShell, we must define WMI. And where does CIM come into the picture?

WMI is Microsoft's implementation of the Common Information Model (CIM), which is an industry standard produced by the Distributed Management Task Force (DMTF). According to www.dmtf.org/standards/cim, "CIM provides a common definition of management information for systems, networks, applications and services, and *allows for vendor extensions*" (our emphasis). WMI was introduced back in the days of Windows NT 4. WMI is what allows you to manage Windows-based systems.

If you try this code:

```
PS C:\> Get-WmiObject -List *OperatingSystem | select Name
```

you'll see the following returned:

```
Name
----
CIM_OperatingSystem
Win32_OperatingSystem
Win32_SystemOperatingSystem
```

Ignore the last entry—it's a WMI link class between the operating system and the computer system. The important classes are CIM_OperatingSystem and Win32_Operating-System. The first is the base class that represents an operating system as defined by the DMTF, and the second is Microsoft's implementation of that class in WMI.

If you try this:

```
PS C:\> Compare-Object -ReferenceObject (Get-WmiObject CIM_OperatingSystem)
     -DifferenceObject (Get-WmiObject Win32_OperatingSystem)
```

you'll discover that there's no apparent difference between the classes. If you dig a little further:

```
PS C:\> Get-WmiObject CIM_OperatingSystem | get-member |
     Select TypeName -unique
```

```
TypeName
--------
System.Management.ManagementObject#root\cimv2\Win32_OperatingSystem

PS C:\> Get-WmiObject win32_Operatingsystem | get-member |
➥ Select TypeName -unique

TypeName
--------
System.Management.ManagementObject#root\cimv2\Win32_OperatingSystem
```

you'll find that the WMI and CIM classes are effectively identical. Why have both? The answer is so that the CIM information can be accessed from non-Windows implementations of CIM.

Starting with PowerShell v3, Microsoft began moving back toward the DTMF standards and introducing a new API for accessing WMI—which is why there are WMI cmdlets and CIM cmdlets. We'd expect any future development to be concentrated on the CIM cmdlets rather than the WMI cmdlets. Because the WMIcmdlets have been around the longest, we'll start with a quick look at how to use them.

39.2 *WMI cmdlets*

Now that you know what WMI is, let's look at how you can use PowerShell to work with WMI. The WMI cmdlets in PowerShell v3 and v4 are identical to those in PowerShell v2, so this discussion applies to all versions. We'll concentrate on some areas that might cause you problems rather than provide a full detailed description.

The most important point to know is that working with WMI in Windows is COM-based. This means that to access remote machines you need the DCOM service running on the remote system and you need to configure any firewalls to allow DCOM, WMI, and Remote Management access. You can accomplish this by using Group Policy, the GUI, `netsh`, or the PowerShell cmdlets in the NetSecurity module if you're using Windows 8/Windows Server 2012 or later.

Once that's complete, you can use WMI with PowerShell. The WMI cmdlets are as follows:

```
PS C:\> Get-Command *WMI* -CommandType cmdlet | select Name

Name
----
Get-WmiObject
Invoke-WmiMethod
Register-WmiEvent
Remove-WmiObject
Set-WmiInstance
```

Four of them work directly with WMI objects, whereas the fifth (`Register-WmiEvent`) works with events. The cmdlets all have a `-ComputerName` parameter so they can work with remote machines (remember that's via DCOM). Let's see some examples of these cmdlets in action.

39.2.1 *Get-WmiObject*

Get-WmiObjectdoes exactly what it says: it gets WMI objects. This is probably the WMI cmdlet you'll use the most (it was the only WMI cmdlet in PowerShell v1 and the only way to interact with remote systems in PowerShell v1). You've seen examples of it at work throughout the book, so we'll just provide a quick recap:

```
PS C:\> Get-WmiObject -Class Win32_ComputerSystem

Domain              : WORKGROUP
Manufacturer        : Microsoft Corporation
Model               : Surface Pro 2
Name                : RSSURFACEPRO2
PrimaryOwnerName    : Richard
TotalPhysicalMemory : 8506142720
```

You could also write a query as you might have done in VBScript:

```
PS C:\> Get-WmiObject -Query "SELECT * FROM Win32_ComputerSystem"
```

The query is written in WMI Query Language (WQL), which is a subset of SQL. A detailed description of WQL is available at http://msdn.microsoft.com/en-us/library/windows/desktop/aa394552(v=vs.85).aspx. You may see comments regarding speed differences depending on whether you use a query. In reality, our tests show little difference between the two approaches, though using the query involves more typing. But where you can see performance gains is with filtering.

For example, if you use WMI to look at logical disks:

```
PS C:\> Get-WmiObject -Class Win32_LogicalDisk
```

you'll get data returned for your hard drives as well as CD/DVD drives. The way to differentiate between the two types of disk is to use the value of the DriveType property. A value of 3 indicates a hard disk and 5 indicates it's a CD/DVD.

> **NOTE** Many WMI properties are numeric values that need to be interpreted. The WMI documentation on MSDN—we recommend starting at http://msdn.microsoft.com/en-us/library/aa394572(v=vs.85).aspx—is the best source for this information.

You can restrict or filter the results in a number of ways. The most obvious to PowerShell novices would be to use Where-Object:

```
PS C:\> Get-WmiObject -Class Win32_LogicalDisk | where DriveType -eq 3

DeviceID     : C:
DriveType    : 3
ProviderName :
FreeSpace    : 181799030784
Size         : 248951861248
VolumeName   : Windows
```

We actively discourage this approach because it means retrieving all the data and then performing the filter action. This isn't too bad on the local machine, but it's a bad idea when pulling data back from multiple machines across the network. The better approach is to let Get-WMIObject do the filtering for you on the remote machine. Luckily, WQL can help. You might use a query:

```
PS C:\> Get-WmiObject -Query "SELECT * FROM Win32_LogicalDisk WHERE
⇒  DriveType = 3"
```

If you're using a string value in your filter, then put the value in single quotes:

```
PS C:\> Get-WmiObject -Query
⇒   "SELECT * FROM Win32_LogicalDisk WHERE DeviceId = 'C:'"
```

This approach works and is perfectly acceptable, but our preferred technique will save you some typing:

```
PS C:\> Get-WmiObject -Class Win32_LogicalDisk -Filter "DriveType = 3"
```

The -Filter parameter takes the WHERE clause from the WQL query (everything after the WHERE keyword) and delivers the same results. When you apply filtering, either with a query or the parameter, it's done on the source machine. So if you query a remote machine for processes that meet some criteria, the processing happens remotely, not on your machine, which makes PowerShell much more efficient. One thing to be careful of when using filters is that the operators are the legacy operators, not the new PowerShell operators.

Get-WmiObject also has an interesting set of parameters, as you'll discover when you read the help file. A few of them leap out and require a bit of explanation or commentary, as shown in table 39.1.

Table 39.1 Important Get-WmiObject **parameter descriptions**

Parameter	Comments
ComputerName	Enables access to WMI classes on remote machines. Uses DCOM as connectivity protocol. DCOM must be running on remote machine and firewalls must be configured to allow DCOM transactions.
AsJob	The WMI processing runs as a job. The *-Job cmdlets have to be used to access the data.
ThrottleLimit	Use with the AsJob parameter to control the number of simultaneous actions.
EnableAllPrivileges	Ensures that all of your user privileges are enabled. Use this parameter in addition to running PowerShell with elevated privileges.
Amended	Enables access to some extra information such as a class description that's normally too expensive to retrieve.
Authentication	This is the DCOM authentication level. Use a value of 6 (packet privacy) when accessing remotely through providers such as IIS or Clustering that require it. Not required for accessing data on a local machine.

Table 39.1 Important `Get-WmiObject` parameter descriptions *(continued)*

Parameter	Comments
DirectRead	Indicates whether direct access to the WMI provider is requested for the specified class without any regard to its base class or to its derived classes; restricts output to just the class asked for. Very rarely used; usually doesn't make any difference.
Impersonation	Default value is `impersonate`, which allows objects to use the credentials of the caller. Nothing more is usually required.

For most of your WMI work, you probably won't need to use most of the parameters in table 39.1 and can instead stick with their defaults.

As you can see, retrieving WMI objects is straightforward. But sometimes you may need to remove WMI objects once you've found them.

39.2.2   *Remove-WmiObject*

The `Remove-WmiObject` cmdlet has to be used with care. If you remove the WMI object for a critical service, your system will become unstable and probably crash. This cmdlet can be used like this:

```
PS C:\> $p = Get-WmiObject -Class Win32_Process -Filter "Name='calc.exe'"
PS C:\> Remove-WmiObject -InputObject $p
```

Or you could take this approach:

```
PS C:\> Get-WmiObject -Class Win32_Process -Filter "Name='calc.exe'" |
    Remove-WmiObject
```

Both techniques work. We recommend the second approach for two reasons. First, you can use the `Get-WmiObject` call to double-check that you're deleting the correct object and save yourself from those embarrassing "oops" moments. Second, it's a bit less typing, which will increase your productivity over the long run.

> **NOTE** In the previous examples, terminating the calc.exe process would also remove the WMI object. From our experience, you shouldn't need to remove WMI objects directly from the CIM repository that often. `Remove-WmiObject` should be for those special cases. The cmdlet also supports `-WhatIf` and `-Confirm`.

Occasionally you may need to modify a WMI object rather than deleting it.

39.2.3   *Set-WmiInstance*

`Set-WmiInstance` is used to modify one or more properties on a WMI object. As an example, let's look at changing the label on a disk volume. Say your test system doesn't have a label for its C: drive.

```
PS C:\> Get-WmiObject -Class Win32_Volume -Filter "Name = 'C:\\'" |
    Format-table Name, Label -autosize
```

```
Name Label
---- -----
C:\
```

The use of \\ always catches people new to PowerShell and WMI. It's required because WMI uses \ as an escape character and needs the second \ to escape it so that it's used as a literal character. Performing the change is simply a matter of piping the Win32_Volume object into Set-WmiInstance:

```
PS C:\> Get-WmiObject -Class Win32_Volume -Filter "Name = 'C:\\'" |
➥   Set-WmiInstance -Arguments @{Label="WmiTest"}
```

> **NOTE** You'll need to run PowerShell with elevated privileges to make this change. And yes, for a local system you could've used the Label command.

You can rerun the test to observe the change:

```
PS C:\> Get-WmiObject -Class Win32_Volume -Filter "Name = 'C:\\'" |
➥   Format-table Name, Label -autosize

Name Label
---- -----
C:\  WmiTest
```

You'll find that many, if not most, of the properties on WMI classes are read-only (check the class documentation on MSDN if in doubt), so don't expect to spend a lot of time modifying property values. You can't change the size of the disk this way!

> **TIP** Piping the results of a WMI query into Get-Member will show that many properties are labeled get and set, which you may take to mean they can be overwritten. Don't believe it; check the documentation.

Many WMI classes provide methods for performing administrative tasks. A number of PowerShell cmdlets, like Stop-Computer, are based on these methods. If you can find a cmdlet that accomplishes what you need, use it. Otherwise, you need to turn your attention elsewhere.

39.2.4 *Invoke-WmiMethod*

In PowerShell v1 you only had the Get-WmiObject cmdlet. This meant that if you wanted to utilize a WMI method, you had to create a variable for the object and then call the method:

```
PS C:\> $proc = Get-WmiObject -Class Win32_Process -Filter
➥   "Name='calc.exe'"
PS C:\> $proc.Terminate()

__GENUS          : 2
__CLASS          : __PARAMETERS
__SUPERCLASS     :
__DYNASTY        : __PARAMETERS
__RELPATH        :
__PROPERTY_COUNT : 1
```

```
__DERIVATION     : {}
__SERVER         :
__NAMESPACE      :
__PATH           :
ReturnValue      : 0
PSComputerName   :
```

NOTE When you're working with WMI methods, a return code of 0 indicates success. Any other result indicates that the method call has failed.

This approach still works even in PowerShell v4, but you have a better way of doing things:

```
PS C:\> proc = Get-WmiObject -Class Win32_Process -Filter
➥  "Name='calc.exe'"
PS C:\> Invoke-WmiMethod -InputObject $proc -Name Terminate
```

An even better way is to pipe the results of your search into `Invoke-WmiMethod`:

```
PS C:\> Get-WmiObject -Class Win32_Process -Filter "Name='calc.exe'" |
➥  Invoke-WmiMethod -Name Terminate
```

You can also work with methods that take parameters:

```
PS C:\> Invoke-WmiMethod -Class Win32_Process -Name Create `
-ArgumentList 'calc.exe', 'c:\scripts'
```

The method arguments are provided as an array to the cmdlet. There's an issue regarding the use of arguments with `Invoke-WmiMethod` that comes up quite regularly. As an example, consider formatting a disk:

```
PS C:\> $vol = Get-WmiObject -Class Win32_Volume -Filter "DriveLetter='H:'"
PS C:\> $vol.Format("FAT", $true, 4096, "", $false)
```

The arguments correspond to the filesystem to use, whether to perform a quick format, the cluster size to use, the volume label, and whether compression is enabled. The logical assumption would be that you could change the code to this:

```
PS C:\> Get-WmiObject -Class Win32_Volume -Filter "DriveLetter='H:'" |
➥  Invoke-WmiMethod -Name Format -ArgumentList "FAT", $true, 4096, "",
➥  $false
```

Unfortunately it doesn't work and you get the following error message:

```
Invoke-WmiMethod : Input string was not in a correct format.
```

If you modify the order of the arguments, it'll work:

```
PS C:\> Get-WmiObject -Class Win32_Volume -Filter "DriveLetter='H:'" |
➥  Invoke-WmiMethod -Name Format -ArgumentList 4096, $false, "FAT", "",
➥  $true
```

The differences between the documented order of arguments and the order expected by `Invoke-WmiMethod` are illustrated in table 39.2.

Table 39.2 Order of arguments as documented and as expected by `Invoke-WmiMethod`

Using method as documentation	Using `Invoke-WmiMethod`
FileSystem	ClusterSize
QuickFormat	EnableCompression
ClusterSize	FileSystem
Label	Label
EnableCompression	QuickFormat

The argument list as documented can be derived using this:

```
(Get-WmiObject -Class Win32_Volume -Filter "DriveLetter='H:'").Format
```

This code will show the order required by `Invoke-WmiMethod`:

```
([wmiclass]"Win32_Volume").GetMethodParameters('Format')
```

The [wmiclass] type accelerator instructs PowerShell to treat "Win32_Volume" as a WMI class object. The object has a method called `GetMethodParameters` that we're invoking to get the parameters for the `Format` method.

The easy way to remember parameter order is that method parameters for `Invoke-WmiMethod` are in alphabetical order. Don't ask us why; we suspect it's a .NET thing.

> **NOTE** The new `Get-CimClass` cmdlet also gives the correct order for `Invoke-WmiMethod`. Use `(Get-CimClass-ClassNameWin32_Volume).CimClass-Methods['Format'].Parameters`. We recommend using `Invoke-CimMethod` in Power-Shell v3 and v4 because the argument names and values are required, which removes issues regarding their order.

Another issue arises when you're dealing with arguments that take arrays of values. This works:

```
PS C:\> $nic = Get-WmiObject -Class Win32_NetworkAdapterConfiguration
➥   -Filter "Index=7"
PS C:\> $nic.SetDNSServerSearchOrder("10.10.54.201")
```

Using `Invoke-WmiMethod` failed. After discussions with fellow PowerShell MVP Bartek Bielawski and a bit more digging, we found that for multiple DNS servers this would work:

```
PS C:\> $dnsserver = "10.10.54.201", "10.10.54.98"
PS C:\> Get-WmiObject -Class Win32_NetworkAdapterConfiguration -Filter
➥   "Index=7" | Invoke-WmiMethod -Name SetDNSServerSearchOrder
➥   -ArgumentList (,$dnsserver)
```

It's necessary to create an array as the input argument (,$variable)—it's a unary array, that is, a one-element array. If you want to use just a single DNS server, then you need to use the unary array trick twice: once when you create the variable and again when you use Invoke-WmiMethod. Messy, but it works:

```
PS C:\> $dnsserver = (,"10.10.54.201")
PS C:\> Get-WmiObject -Class Win32_NetworkAdapterConfiguration -Filter
➥ "Index=7" | Invoke-WmiMethod -Name SetDNSServerSearchOrder
➥ -ArgumentList (, $dnsserver)
```

To jump ahead slightly (we'll cover the CIM cmdlets in greater detail later in the chapter), if you want to use the CIM cmdlets, it's easy if you have multiple DNS servers:

```
PS C:\> $dnsserver = "10.10.54.201", "10.10.54.98"
PS C:\> Get-CimInstance -ClassName Win32_NetworkAdapterConfiguration
➥ -Filter "Index=7" | Invoke-CimMethod -MethodName
➥ SetDNSServerSearchOrder -Arguments @{DNSServerSearchOrder =
➥ $dnsserver}
```

If you just have a single one, you need to create a unary array on the Arguments parameter:

```
PS C:\> $dnsserver = "10.10.54.201"
PS C:\> Get-CimInstance -ClassName Win32_NetworkAdapterConfiguratio
➥ -Filter "Index=7" | Invoke-CimMethod -MethodName
➥ SetDNSServerSearchOrder -Arguments @{DNSServerSearchOrder =
➥ (,$dnsserver)}
```

This isn't satisfactory because you have to adopt different techniques depending on the number of DNS servers you need to put into the property. This is *not* a PowerShell issue; it's a WMI issue because the IP address that you saw last time also takes an array and it was happy with a single value. Hopefully, this isn't something that will come up too often, but be aware of these options when working with WMI methods.

> **TIP** We recommend using the networking cmdlets in Windows 8 and later to modify the DNS server search order.

Last but not least in our consideration of the WMI cmdlets is how you work with events.

39.2.5 *Register-WmiEvent*

WMI has a rich, event-driven environment that you can access through the PowerShell eventing engine. Using Get-WmiObject-List*Event* will generate a long list of classes, most of which are related to events. Three classes of note are as follows:

- __InstanceCreationEvent
- __InstanceModificationEvent
- __InstanceDeletionEvent

Using these classes involves creating a WQL query and registering the event:

```
PS C:\> $q = "SELECT * FROM __InstanceModificationEvent WHERE
➥ TargetInstance ISA 'Win32_LocalTime'"
PS C:\> Register-WmiEvent -Query $q
```

The results are obtained using the PowerShell event cmdlets:

```
PS C:\> Get-Event | select TimeGenerated
TimeGenerated
-------------
05/02/2014 15:52:18
05/02/2014 15:52:19
05/02/2014 15:52:20
05/02/2014 15:52:21
05/02/2014 15:52:22
05/02/2014 15:52:23
05/02/2014 15:52:24
05/02/2014 15:52:25
05/02/2014 15:52:26
05/02/2014 15:52:27
05/02/2014 15:52:28
```

A new event is generated every second as the system time changes. The results are from a machine configured for UK date format. As always, you should remove registrations and events when you've finished processing:

```
PS C:\> Unregister-Event *
PS C:\> Get-Event | Remove-Event
```

The WMI cmdlets provide a huge amount of functionality. They were joined in Power-Shell v3 by the CIM cmdlets, which provide alternative routes to that same functionality but also expand what you can achieve in PowerShell when you're working with WMI.

> **NOTE** PowerShell includes several WMI type accelerators such as [wmi] and [wmisearcher]. These are intended to provide shortcuts to WMI objects—in other words, to save some typing. The type accelerators assume you have solid WMI knowledge and thus are a bit more complicated to use. We typically don't use them because Get-WmiObject is so easy to use and flexible. Frankly, we're not sure they offer a lot of value, which is why we aren't covering them in this chapter. There's not much more we could add than what's already documented in About_WMI_cmdlets.

39.3 *CIM cmdlets*

As we stated in the introduction, WMI is the Microsoft implementation of CIM. In the PowerShell v3 wave of products (including Windows 8 and Windows Server 2012), a new API was introduced for accessing CIM (WMI). This API replaces the COM-based API that we grew to know and love in PowerShell v1 and v2.

> **NOTE** In the rest of this chapter, we'll use WMI and CIM interchangeably unless we're discussing the new API or cmdlets. They're the same thing.

The new API generated the need for a new set of cmdlets. As you've seen, the WMI cmdlets of PowerShell v2 are still available and, more important, still as valid.

TIP If you have a lot of scripts using the WMI cmdlets, don't rush to modify them to use the CIM cmdlets. They'll still work in PowerShell v3 and v4. Consider modifying them when you have to make major changes.

The CIM cmdlets mirror the WMI cmdlets, as you can see in table 39.3. One important point to note is that the CIM cmdlets can be used to work with legacy existing WMI classes and the new classes Microsoft introduced with Windows 8/Server 2012 and later. The WMI cmdlets will work with the new classes, but they aren't as flexible when working with remote machines.

Table 39.3 Comparing WMI and CIM cmdlets

WMI cmdlet	CIM cmdlet
	Get-CimClass
	New-CimInstance
Get-WmiObject	Get-CimInstance
	Get-CimAssociatedInstance
Set-WmiInstance	Set-CimInstance
Invoke-WmiMethod	Invoke-CimMethod
Remove-WmiObject	Remove-CimInstance
Register-WmiEvent	Register-CimIndicationEvent

The use of `Get-`, `Set-`, and `Remove-CimInstance` is directly comparable to the corresponding WMI cmdlets. `Get-CimAssociatedInstance` is a new and improved way to work with WMI class associations. There's an invoke cmdlet for CIM methods that's similar to `Invoke-WmiMethod`. You can also work with CIM events through `Register-CimIndicationEvent`.

A couple of cmdlets don't have corresponding WMI equivalents. `Get-CimClass` is a discovery tool that opens the CIM classes in a way that's much easier to use. `New-CimInstance` can be used to create new instances of CIM classes but only under certain circumstances. In most cases you're better served by using the class's `Create` method via `Invoke-CimMethod`. We won't say anything else about `New-CimInstance`.

The other big difference is the way that the CIM cmdlets access remote systems. You'll recall the WMI cmdlets use DCOM for remote connectivity. When you use the CIM cmdlets, the default method of connecting to remote machines is Web Services-Management (WSMAN). This is exactly the same protocol that PowerShell Remoting uses. You need to have the remoting service (WinRM) running and configured on the remote machine. You don't have to enable the full remoting capability (by running `Enable-PSRemoting`), but remember it's enabled by default on the latest versions of Windows servers.

NOTE You can use the WSMAN cmdlets to retrieve WMI data from remote machines. The syntax of these cmdlets is difficult, and we recommend using them only as a last resort. If you want to learn more about the WSMAN cmdlets, check out chapter 17 of *PowerShell and WMI* (Manning, 2012). The CIM cmdlets combine the firewall-friendly nature of the WSMAN cmdlets with the syntax simplicity of the WMI cmdlets. Best of both worlds.

The CIM cmdlets don't use PowerShell Remoting but they can use CIM sessions, which are analogous to remote PowerShell sessions (which we describe in the next section). You can still use DCOM in a CIM session, but it's a fallback for accessing legacy systems that don't have PowerShell v3 or v4 installed. The remote connectivity options are listed in table 39.4.

Table 39.4 Connectivity options when using CIM cmdlets

Scenario	Protocol
Local machine—`computername` parameter not used	DCOM
Local machine—`computername` parameter used	WSMAN
Remote machine—`computername` parameter used	WSMAN
Remote machine—CIM session with default options	WSMAN
Remote machine—CIM session with DCOM protocol specified	DCOM

One big difference is the type of objects returned by the two groups of cmdlets. Try running this code:

```
PS C:\> Get-WmiObject -Class Win32_ComputerSystem | Get-Member

TypeName: System.Management.ManagementObject#root\cimv2\
➥   Win32_ComputerSystem

Name                      MemberType      Definition
----                      ----------      ----------
PSComputerName            AliasProperty   PSComputerName = __SERVER
JoinDomainOrWorkgroup     Method          System.Management…
Rename                    Method          System.Management…
SetPowerState             Method          System.Management…
UnjoinDomainOrWorkgroup   Method          System.Management…
AdminPasswordStatus       Property        uint16 AdminPasswordStatus
AutomaticManagedPagefile  Property        boolAutomaticManagedPagefile
…
```

Now compare those results to this:

```
PS C:\> Get-CimInstance -ClassName Win32_ComputerSystem | Get-Member

TypeName: Microsoft.Management.Infrastructure.CimInstance#
➥   root/cimv2/Win32_ComputerSystem

Name      MemberType   Definition
----      ----------   ----------
Clone     Method       System.ObjectICloneable.Clone()
```

```
Dispose                        Method      void Dispose()
Equals                         Method      boolEquals(System.Objectobj)
GetCimSessionComputerName      Method      string GetCimSessionComputerName()
GetCimSessionInstanceId        Method      guidGetCimSessionInstanceId()
GetHashCode                    Method      intGetHashCode()
GetObjectData                  Method      void GetObjectData...
GetType                        Method      type GetType()
ToString                       Method      string ToString()
AdminPasswordStatus            Property    uint16 AdminPasswordStatus {get;}
AutomaticManagedPagefile       Property    boolAutomaticManagedPagefile
AutomaticResetBootOption       Property    boolAutomaticResetBootOption
...
```

The first point to note is that the object type changes. Get-WmiObject returns a System
.Management.ManagementObject type object, but the object returned from Get-
CimInstance is from the Microsoft.Management.Infrastructure.CimInstance class.
This is part of the new API for working with CIM we mentioned earlier.

The other big difference is that the WMI cmdlet returns a set of methods that are
part of the WMI class:

- JoinDomainOrWorkgroup
- Rename
- SetPowerState
- UnjoinDomainOrWorkgroup

A variable can be created to reference the object and the methods called on that
object, such as:

```
PS C:\> $comp = Get-WmiObject -Class Win32_ComputerSystem
PS C:\> $comp.Rename("Newname", "password", "username")
```

This approach will *not* work with the CIM cmdlets because the objects that are
returned are inert; they don't give access to the WMI class methods. If you need to use
the methods, you have to use Invoke-CimMethod as described later in the chapter.

An apparent, but important, difference is that the WMI cmdlets use -Class but the
CIM cmdlets use -ClassName. However, the CIM cmdlets will accept -Class as an
abbreviated parameter name so this shouldn't be too difficult to use.

The only way to learn about the CIM cmdlets is to use them, so let's start by looking
at how you discover information on the CIM classes.

39.3.1 Get-CimClass

This cmdlet alone makes the move to the CIM API worthwhile. It opens up WMI classes
to discovery in a simple way. Here's the default information returned by the cmdlet:

```
PS C:\> Get-CimClass -Class Win32_ComputerSystem

NameSpace: ROOT/cimv2

CimClassName                 CimClassMethods         CimClassProperties
------------                 ---------------         ------------------

Win32_ComputerSystem         {SetPowerState, R...    {Caption,Description...}
```

You can dig into the detailed information:

```
PS C:\> $class = Get-CimClass -Class Win32_ComputerSystem
PS C:\> $class.CimClassMethods

Name                     ReturnType Parameters         Qualifiers
----                     ---------- ----------         ----------
SetPowerState            UInt32 {PowerState...    {}
Rename                   UInt32 {Name...          {Implemented, ValueMap}
JoinDomainOrWorkgroup    UInt32 {AccountOU...     {Implemented, ValueMap}
UnjoinDomainOrWorkgroup  UInt32 {FUnjoinOptions...{Implemented, ValueMap}
PS C:\> $class.CimClassProperties

Name              : Caption
Value             :
CimType           : String
Flags             : Property, ReadOnly, NullValue
Qualifiers        : {MaxLen, read}
ReferenceClassName :
...
```

Probably the most useful part is when you drill down into the methods and get to understand the parameters:

```
PS C:\> $class.CimClassMethods["Rename"].Parameters

Name                     CimType Qualifiers
----                     ------- ----------
Name                     String {ID, In}
Password                 String {ID, In}
UserName                 String {ID, In}
```

You get the parameter name and, more important, the type of data the method expects for that parameter. This information can be difficult to obtain using the WMI cmdlets, and most people resort to the documentation.

If you need them, you can access the system properties for the class by using `$class.CimSystemProperties`.

Unfortunately, there's one gap in the information provided by `Get-CimClass`: You can't get to the amended properties. Some properties are buried deep in the WMI database and involve relatively expensive processing to reach. The most common reason for accessing these properties is to read the class description. With the WMI cmdlets, you'd do this:

```
PS C:\> (Get-WmiObject -List Win32_ComputerSystem -Amended).Qualifiers |
➥   where Name -eq "Description" | select -ExpandProperty Value

The Win32_ComputerSystem class represents a computer system operating
in a Win32 environment.
```

There's no equivalent mechanism using the CIM cmdlets to retrieve this information.

Now that you've seen how to discover information about the CIM classes, how do you retrieve information about the instances of those classes?

39.3.2 *Get-CimInstance*

If we'd asked you to tell us how to access a WMI class in PowerShell v2, you'd have told us to use Get-WmiObject. Table 39.3 shows that the equivalent CIM cmdlet is Get-CIMInstance, which is used exactly as you'd expect:

```
PS C:\> Get-CimInstance -ClassName Win32_ComputerSystem

Name             PrimaryOwnerName  Domain     TotalPhysicalMemory  Model
----             ----------------  ------     -------------------  -----
RSSURFACEPRO2 Richard              WORKGROUP 8506142720            Surface Pro 2
```

The Manufacturer property has been removed to fit the page size. One thing to be aware of is that the default formatting has changed for many standard classes. The information is still there; it's just formatted slightly differently.

The techniques you used with Get-WmiObject still work. You can use the -Filter parameter:

```
PS C:\> Get-CimInstance -ClassName Win32_Process -Filter "Name =
➥ 'powershell.exe'"

ProcessId Name          HandleCount  WorkingSetSize  VirtualSize
--------- ----          -----------  --------------  -----------
4060      powershell.exe  700        124346368       310177792
```

Alternatively, you can use a query:

```
PS C:\> Get-CimInstance -Query "SELECT * FROM Win32_Process WHERE Name =
➥ 'powershell.exe'"

ProcessId Name          HandleCount  WorkingSetSize  VirtualSize
--------- ----          -----------  --------------  -----------
4060      powershell.exe  732        124186624       310177792
```

If you want to access a machine by name, local or remote:

```
PS C:\> Get-CimInstance -Query "SELECT * FROM Win32_Process WHERE Name =
➥ 'powershell.exe'" -ComputerName RSLAPTOP01

ProcessId Name          HandleCount  PSComputerName
--------- ----          -----------  --------------
4060      powershell.exe  802        RSLAPTOP01
```

WorkingSetSize and VirtualSize properties were removed from the display for the sake of brevity.

You can even use -ResourceURI in a manner similar to the WSMAN cmdlets if you wish. We don't recommend that approach; the syntax is more convoluted.

One great thing about the CIM cmdlets is that the data can be refreshed. Follow through this example on your machine to see what we mean. First, create an object representing the PowerShell process running on your machine. You can then display KernelModeTime, which is a measure of the time that the CPU spends on PowerShell:

```
PS C:\> $p = Get-CimInstance -ClassName Win32_Process -Filter "Name =
➥ 'powershell.exe'"
PS C:\> $p | format-table Name, KernelModeTime -AutoSize
```

```
Name             KernelModeTime
----             --------------
powershell.exe        31356201
```

If you pipe that object through `Get-CimInstance`, the values are refreshed:

```
PS C:\> $p | Get-CimInstance |
➥ format-table Name, KernelModeTime -AutoSize

Name             KernelModeTime
----             --------------
powershell.exe        31824204
```

Note that the original object, $p, remains the same; it's just the data you're displaying that gets refreshed. There's no comparable way of doing this with the WMI cmdlets.

WMI classes may be associated with other classes. A typical example is the association between the `Win32_NetworkAdapter` and the `Win32_Network-Adapter-Configuration` classes. The first holds hardware information on your network card, and the second holds the TCP/IP configuration data. You'll often need to retrieve information on the configuration based on the adapter. For example, you can find the wireless adapter using the WMI cmdlets:

```
PS C:\> $nic = Get-WmiObject -ClassName Win32_NetworkAdapter -Filter
➥    "NetEnabled = $true AND NetConnectionID LIKE '%Wireless%'"
```

Now you need to find its TCP/IP address, which is stored on the `Win32_Network-AdapterConfiguration` class:

```
PS C:\> Get-WmiObject -Query "ASSOCIATORS OF
➥    {Win32_NetworkAdapter.DeviceID=$($nic.DeviceID)}
➥    WHERE ResultClass = Win32_NetworkAdapterConfiguration
"
DHCPEnabled       : True
IPAddress         : {192.168.1.2, fe80::6d95:b824:6a72:a0a9}
DefaultIPGateway  : {192.168.1.1}
DNSDomain         : tiscali.co.uk
ServiceName       : athr
Description       : Atheros AR5007 802.11b/g WiFi Adapter
Index             : 11
```

You can do the same thing with the CIM cmdlets but in a slightly different way:

```
PS C:\> $nic = Get-CimInstance -ClassName Win32_NetworkAdapter
➥    -Filter "NetEnabled = $true AND NetConnectionID LIKE '%Wireless%'"
PS C:\> Get-CimAssociatedInstance -CimInstance $nic -ResultClassName
➥    Win32_NetworkAdapterConfiguration | select IPAddress

IPAddress
---------
{192.168.1.2, fe80::6d95:b824:6a72:a0a9}
```

Using the CIM cmdlets is cleaner and simpler. Anything that removes the need to remember the query syntax for WMI associations has to be a bonus.

Sometimes you find CIM instances on your systems that you don't want or no longer need. You can use the CIM cmdlets to remove those instances.

39.3.3 *Remove-CimInstance*

Every system you touch has a number of processes running that consume resources. Sometimes other admins may leave processes running that they shouldn't have—we know you wouldn't do that. There are a couple of ways to remove those processes.

The simplest method of using `Remove-CimInstance`, and the one we recommend, is to use `Get-CimInstance` first and pipe the results into `Remove-CimInstance`:

```
PS C:\> Get-CimInstance -ClassName Win32_Process -Filter "Name =
➥    'calc.exe'" | Remove-CimInstance
```

This approach has the advantage of allowing you to correctly identify the instance you want to remove before performing the deletion. The alternative approach is to perform a query and remove the results:

```
PS C:\> Remove-CimInstance -Query "SELECT * FROM Win32_Process WHERE Name =
➥    'calc.exe'"
```

If you look at the help for `Remove-Ciminstance`, you'll see that a `-WhatIf` parameter is available:

```
PS C:\> Remove-CimInstance -Query "SELECT * FROM Win32_Process WHERE Name =
➥    'calc.exe'"  -WhatIf

What if: Performing operation "Remove-CimInstance" on Target
 "Win32_Process: calc.exe (Handle = "3600")".
```

This parameter depends on the underlying functionality within the WMI provider. If the provider supports `-WhatIf`, then the parameter works properly. In the case of the provider not supporting `-WhatIf`, either you'll get an error or the parameter is ignored and the cmdlet does its job. We haven't seen any documentation describing which providers support `-WhatIf` and which don't, so your mileage may vary.

Sometimes you don't want to remove a CIM instance; you just want to modify it.

39.3.4 *Set-CimInstance*

Modifying the value of a CIM instance isn't a task that comes up every day, but you need to be able to do it when required. There's a cmdlet for this called `Set-CimInstance`. A simple example is to look at the label on the disk volume holding the C: drive:

```
PS C:\> Get-CimInstance -ClassName Win32_Volume -Filter "Name = 'C:\\'" |
Format-table Name, Label -autosize

Name Label
---- -----
C:\
```

As with the WMI version of this example from earlier in the chapter, the \ needs to be escaped. Changing the label is just a matter of piping the results into `Set-CimInstance`:

```
PS C:\> Get-CimInstance -ClassName Win32_Volume -Filter "Name = 'C:\\'" |
➥    Set-CimInstance -Property @{Label="CimTest"}
```

The result can be tested:

```
PS C:\> Get-CimInstance -ClassName Win32_Volume -Filter "Name = 'C:\\'" |
➥   Format-table Name, Label -autosize

Name Label
---- -----
C:\  CimTest
```

A more common scenario is working with the methods on the WMI classes to perform changes. Whereas you used Invoke-WMIMethod earlier in the chapter, the corresponding CIM cmdlet is Invoke-CimMethod.

39.3.5 *Invoke-CimMethod*

CIM provides a huge repository of information that you can tap into to discover what's happening on your systems. It also provides the opportunity to manage those systems through the methods on the CIM classes. You saw earlier that there are a few issues with using Invoke-WmiMethod. Those issues don't exist when you use Invoke-CimMethod.

As we explained, you can use Get-CimClass to discover the parameter information you need about a method. Let's create a process:

```
PS C:\> $class = Get-CimClass -ClassName Win32_Process
PS C:\> $class.CimClassMethods["Create"].Parameters

Name                          CimType  Qualifiers
----                          -------  ----------
CommandLine                   String   {ID, In, MappingStrings}
CurrentDirectory              String   {ID, In, MappingStrings}
ProcessStartupInformation     Instance {EmbeddedInstance, ID, In,...
ProcessId                     UInt32   {ID, MappingStrings, Out}
```

You need to provide a command-line command to start the process and a directory. The parameters are supplied as a hash table using the parameter name you've discovered and the value. The hash table can be built separately or as part of the cmdlet call; we prefer to do it separately because it makes the code more readable. You can then invoke the method as shown here:

```
PS C:\> $params = @{CommandLine = "calc.exe"; CurrentDirectory =
➥   "c:\scripts"}
PS C:\> Invoke-CimMethod -ClassName Win32_Process -MethodName Create
➥   -Arguments $params

   ProcessId    ReturnValue  PSComputerName
   ---------    -----------  --------------
        2040              0
```

As with calling any WMI method, a return code of 0 means success. Anything else is a failure. Some methods, such as the Terminate method of Win32_Process, don't have any arguments. In these cases, you have a couple of options. Option one is to get the instance and pipe it into Invoke-CimMethod:

```
PS C:\> Get-CimInstance -Class Win32_Process -Filter "Name = 'calc.exe'" |
➥   Invoke-CimMethod -MethodName terminate
```

Alternatively, you can create a variable for the instance and use that instance as follows:

```
PS C:\> $inst = Get-CimInstance -Class Win32_Process -Filter "Name =
➥ 'calc.exe'"
PS C:\> Invoke-CimMethod -InputObject $inst -MethodName Terminate
```

39.3.6 *Register-CimIndicationEvent*

Windows is an event-driven operating system. PowerShell provides a good way of working with the event engine. WMI provides events. You can put all of that together to work with WMI events. If you've worked with WMI events using `Register-WmiEvent` you'll notice a few differences. A number of CIM classes deal with events in general:

```
PS C:\> Get-CimClassCIM_Inst* | Select -expand CimClassname
CIM_InstIndication
CIM_InstCreation
CIM_InstModification
CIM_InstDeletion
CIM_InstalledSoftwareElement
CIM_InstalledOS
```

You may also find classes that deal with explicit events, such as `Win32_VolumeChange-Event`, `Win32_ComputerShutdownEvent`, or `RegistryKeyChangeEvent`. The first thing you should do when working with events is register the event you need:

```
PS C:\> $q = "SELECT * FROM CIM_InstModification WHERE TargetInstance ISA
➥ 'Win32_LocalTime'"
PS C:\> Register-CimIndicationEvent -Query $q
```

In this case you'll get an event every second as the system time changes. You can see the results by using PowerShell's `Get-Event` cmdlet:

```
PS C:\> Get-Event | select TimeGenerated
```

When you've finished with the event, you should unregister it and tidy up by clearing out the event queue:

```
PS C:\> Unregister-Event *
PS C:\> Get-Event | Remove-Event
```

The CIM cmdlets provide an alternative and, in many cases, a better way of working with WMI. We've mentioned several times that the CIM cmdlets can use the Power-Shell remoting protocols to access remote systems. It's time we had a look at how that works.

39.4 *CIM sessions*

As shown in table 39.4, the CIM cmdlets use WSMAN to access remote systems by default, either through the –ComputerName parameter or by using a CIMsession using the –CimSession parameter. These options are exactly analogous to PowerShell Remoting. Use the –ComputerName parameter when you want to access the remote machine only once, and use a CIMsession when you want to perform a number of actions on the remote system.

Connecting to a remote machine using the -ComputerName parameter is exactly the same as for any other cmdlet with this capability:

```
PS C:\> Get-CimInstance -ClassName Win32_OperatingSystem -ComputerName
➥  webr201 | Select PSComputerName, LastBootUpTime
```

A CimSession is created and used like this:

```
PS C:\> $sw = New-CimSession -ComputerName webr201
PS C:\> Get-CimInstance -ClassName Win32_OperatingSystem -CimSession $sw |
➥   Select PSComputerName,LastBootUpTime
```

This creates a CimSession using WSMAN. How can you tell?

```
PS C:\> $sw
Id           : 1
Name         : CimSession1
InstanceId   : 2e1cf2b0-96e5-4fdd-90e9-f18948846500
ComputerName : webr201
Protocol     : WSMAN
```

Look at the session information and it'll tell you the protocol. This is great, but you can only use WSMAN with a CimSession against PowerShell v3 or v4. Look at the WSMAN information for the webr201 system used in the earlier example:

```
PS C:\> Test-WSMan -ComputerName webr201

wsmid            : http://schemas.dmtf.org/wbem/wsman/identity/1/
                   wsmanidentity.xsd
ProtocolVersion : http://schemas.dmtf.org/wbem/wsman/1/wsman.xsd
ProductVendor   : Microsoft Corporation
ProductVersion  : OS: 0.0.0 SP: 0.0 Stack: 3.0
```

This is version 3 of WSMAN that's installed with PowerShell v3 and v4. Look at a system running PowerShell v2:

```
PS C:\> Test-WSMan -ComputerName server02

wsmid            : http://schemas.dmtf.org/wbem/wsman/identity/1/
                   wsmanidentity.xsd
ProtocolVersion : http://schemas.dmtf.org/wbem/wsman/1/wsman.xsd
ProductVendor   : Microsoft Corporation
ProductVersion  : OS: 0.0.0 SP: 0.0 Stack: 2.0
```

If you try to use a CIM session over WSMAN to a system running WSMAN version 2.0, *it will fail.* What's the answer? Drop back to DCOM:

```
PS C:\> $o = New-CimSessionOption -Protocol DCOM
PS C:\> $sd = New-CimSession -ComputerName server02 -SessionOption $o
PS C:\> Get-CimInstance -ClassName Win32_OperatingSystem -CimSession $sd |
➥   Select PSComputerName,LastBootUpTime
```

The only difference is that a session option to use the DCOM protocol has been used. If you create a session using the DCOM protocol, you automatically get packet privacy enabled. This provides remote access to WMI providers such as IIS or clustering that demand the packet privacy level of encryption.

NOTE If you use a WSMAN-based CIM session, you don't need to worry about packet privacy; you aren't using DCOM, so it's not an issue.

Other `CIMSession` options include `UICulture`, skipping of certificate checks, password authentication mechanisms, proxy types, and WMI impersonation (or packet privacy–level encryption), although you should be able to use most default settings. The complete help file for this cmdlet is a recommended read, and there's no reason for us to rehash it here.

One of the good things about CIM sessions is that they can be combined. You can achieve this by explicitly specifying the sessions you want to use:

```
PS C:\> Get-CimInstance -ClassName Win32_OperatingSystem -CimSession $sw,
➥ $sd | Select PSComputerName, LastBootUpTime
```

The end result is getting `Win32_OperatingSystem` information from multiple CIM sessions. Alternatively, this can be done implicitly by piping all of the available CIM sessions to `Get-CimInstance`:

```
PS C:\> Get-CimSession | Get-CimInstance -ClassName Win32_OperatingSystem |
➥   Select PSComputerName,LastBootUpTime
```

Our favorite thing regarding CIM sessions is that if you use WSMAN (which was revised for PowerShell v3; PowerShell v4 uses the same versions of WSMAN) the session can survive a reboot of the remote machine, as illustrated in figure 39.1.

You're given a warning that you have up to four minutes to reconnect after you attempt to reconnect to the remote machine. If you're restarting a system that runs Microsoft Exchange or another application that takes a long time to restart, your session may time out. In that case you'll need to re-create it.

The CIM cmdlets and CIM sessions come as "out-of-the-box" technology. Microsoft's long-term strategy is to use CIM in place of the WMI technologies you're familiar with. So we encourage you to take the time to begin learning and using these new cmdlets.

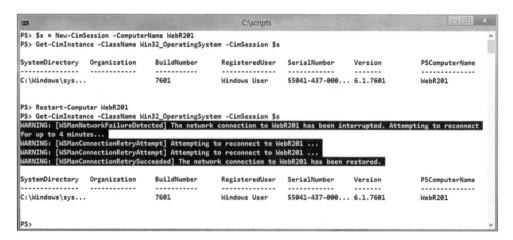

Figure 39.1 Reconnecting a WSMAN-based CIM session

One last piece of CIM-related functionality that we want to cover enables you to create your own cmdlets from CIM classes.

39.5 *"Cmdlets over objects"*

This topic may be stretching the envelope a bit for a lot of IT pros, but it's a powerful way to deliver easy-to-use CIM-based functionality. It's also critical to understand because 60% of the PowerShell functionality in both Windows Server 2012 and Windows Server 2012 R2 is delivered using this technique. The basis of the technique is that you take a CIM class, wrap some XML around the properties and methods, save it as a CDXML file, and publish it as a PowerShell module.

That's right; we did say XML. An example is shown in listing 39.1, which takes the `Win32_LogicalDisk` class and creates two cmdlets for your module. The first cmdlet enables you to filter by disk type, using words instead of the integer codes WMI expects, and the second invokes the `Chkdsk` method.

Listing 39.1   Cmdlet over object code

```
<?xml version="1.0" encoding="utf-8"?>
<PowerShellMetadataxmlns="http://schemas.microsoft.com/cmdlets-over-
    objects/2009/11">
<Class ClassName="root\cimv2/Win32_LogicalDisk">          ❶ Header, class
<Version>1.0</Version>                                         definition
<DefaultNoun>LogicalDisk</DefaultNoun>
<InstanceCmdlets>
<GetCmdletParametersDefaultCmdletParameterSet="ByName">
<QueryableProperties>
<Property PropertyName="Name">                           ❷ Filter by
<Type PSType = "System.String"/>                             name
<RegularQuery>
<CmdletParameterMetadataPSName="Name"
    ValueFromPipelineByPropertyName="true" CmdletParameterSets="ByName" />
</RegularQuery>
</Property>
<Property PropertyName="DriveType">                      ❸ Filter by
<Type PSType = "DJRPID.Disk.DriveType"/>                     drive type
<RegularQuery>
<CmdletParameterMetadataPSName="DriveType"
    CmdletParameterSets="ByType" />
</RegularQuery>
</Property>
<Property PropertyName="FreeSpace">                      ❹ Filter by
<Type PSType="System.UInt64" />                              free space
<MaxValueQuery>
<CmdletParameterMetadataPSName="MaxFreeSize"
    CmdletParameterSets="BySize" />
</MaxValueQuery>
<MinValueQuery>
<CmdletParameterMetadataPSName="MinFreeSize"
    CmdletParameterSets="BySize" />
</MinValueQuery>
</Property>
```

```
</QueryableProperties>
</GetCmdletParameters>
<Cmdlet>
<CmdletMetadata Verb="Invoke" Noun="LogicalDiskChkdsk"
    ConfirmImpact="Medium"/>
<Method MethodName="Chkdsk">                                    Chkdsk method
<ReturnValue>                                                   definition
<Type PSType="System.UInt32"/>
<CmdletOutputMetadata>
</CmdletOutputMetadata>
</ReturnValue>
<Parameters>                                                    Method
<Parameter ParameterName="FixErrors">                          parameters
<Type PSType="Boolean" />
<CmdletParameterMetadataPSName="FixErrors" />
</Parameter>
<Parameter ParameterName="ForceDismount">
<Type PSType="Boolean" />
<CmdletParameterMetadataPSName="ForceDismount" />
</Parameter>
<Parameter ParameterName="OkToRunAtBootUp">
<Type PSType="Boolean" />
<CmdletParameterMetadataPSName="OkToRunAtBootUp" />
</Parameter>
<Parameter ParameterName="RecoverBadSectors">
<Type PSType="Boolean" />
<CmdletParameterMetadataPSName="RecoverBadSectors" />
</Parameter>
<Parameter ParameterName="SkipFolderCycle">
<Type PSType="Boolean" />
<CmdletParameterMetadataPSName="SkipFolderCycle" />
</Parameter>
<Parameter ParameterName="VigorousIndexCheck">
<Type PSType="Boolean" />
<CmdletParameterMetadataPSName="VigorousIndexCheck" />
</Parameter>
</Parameters>
</Method>
<GetCmdletParametersDefaultCmdletParameterSet="ByName">
<QueryableProperties>
<Property PropertyName="Name">
<Type PSType = "System.String"/>
<RegularQuery>
<CmdletParameterMetadataPSName="Name"
    ValueFromPipelineByPropertyName="true" CmdletParameterSets="ByName" />
</RegularQuery>
</Property>
</QueryableProperties>
</GetCmdletParameters>
</Cmdlet>
</InstanceCmdlets>
</Class>                                                        Enumeration
<Enums>                                                         definition
<EnumEnumName="DJRPID.Disk.DriveType" UnderlyingType="System.UInt32">
<Value Name="RemovableDisk" Value="2" />
```

```
<Value Name="HardDisk" Value="3" />
<Value Name="NetworkDrive" Value="4" />
<Value Name="CD" Value="5" />
<Value Name="RAMDisk" Value="6" />
</Enum>
</Enums>
</PowerShellMetadata>
```

This listing should be saved with a CDXML extension. The filename will eventually be used as the module name, so plan accordingly. If you want PowerShell to be able to easily find it, then create an appropriately named subfolder in your module path. We'll show you how to import this later.

For now let's look at this file, which appears a lot more complicated than it actually is. The listing starts with some header lines ❶. Here you provide the CIM class you'll be using—in this case, Win32_LogicalDisk. The namespace is expected as part of the class information. The version can be provided by any scheme you use in your organization. The last part of this area supplies the default noun. This is what will be used by the Get cmdlet you'll create. Our recommendation is to relate the noun to the class. Use the full class name or the part after the Win32_. We've used LogicalDisk, which is descriptive, informative, and singular.

The next sections of the list provide the search properties used with your new Get-LogicalDisk cmdlet. For example, if you just use the cmdlet name, all logical disks are returned:

```
PS C:\> Get-LogicalDisk | format-table DeviceId, DriveType, Size, FreeSpace
➡   -autosize

DeviceId DriveType       Size      FreeSpace
-------- ---------       ----      ---------
C:              3 249951154176 163819159552
E:              5
F:              5
```

Your cmdlet has three defined search properties. The first uses the name ❷ of the logical disk—that is, the drive letter:

```
PS C:\> Get-LogicalDisk -Name c: | format-table DeviceId, DriveType, Size,
➡   FreeSpace -autosize

DeviceId DriveType       Size      FreeSpace
-------- ---------       ----      ---------
C:              3 249951154176 163819200512
```

The second parameter allows you to search by disk type ❸. You can do so using the WMI integer code:

```
PS C:\> Get-LogicalDisk -DriveType 3 | Format-table DeviceId, DriveType,
➡   Size, FreeSpace -autosize

DeviceId DriveType       Size      FreeSpace
-------- ---------       ----      ---------
C:              3 249951154176 163819659264
```

Better still, you can use a descriptive term to indicate the type of disk you require:

```
PS C:\> Get-LogicalDisk -DriveTypeHardDisk | format-table DeviceId,
    DriveType, Size, FreeSpace -autosize

DeviceId DriveType          Size      FreeSpace
-------- ---------          ----      ---------
C:               3 249951154176 163819659264
```

The translation between the numerical value and the descriptive term is managed by the DJRPID.Disk.DriveType enumeration, which is provided at the end of the list ❼ in the enums section.

Searching on the amount of free space available on the disk is managed slightly differently ❹. Two parameters are supplied: one for a search based on the maximum amount of free space available and the other on the minimum amount of free space required. Their use needs a little bit of thinking about:

```
PS C:\> Get-LogicalDisk -MinFreeSize 150GB | format-table DeviceId,
    DriveType, Size, FreeSpace -autosize

DeviceId DriveType          Size      FreeSpace
-------- ---------          ----      ---------
C:               3 249951154176 163817295872
PS C:\> Get-LogicalDisk -MinFreeSize 200GB | format-table DeviceId,
    DriveType, Size, FreeSpace -autosize
```

A disk has to have at least the requested amount of free space available for it to be returned when the –MinFreeSpace parameter is used. The opposite is true when using the –MaxFreeSpace parameter:

```
PS C:\> Get-LogicalDisk -MaxFreeSize 150GB | format-table DeviceId,
    DriveType, Size, FreeSpace -autosize
PS C:\> Get-LogicalDisk -MaxFreeSize 200GB | format-table DeviceId,
    DriveType, Size, FreeSpace -autosize

DeviceId DriveType          Size      FreeSpace
-------- ---------          ----      ---------
C:               3 249951154176 163817295872
```

The disk has to have less than the value supplied to the –MaxFreeSpace parameter for it to be returned.

Each method on the CIM class can be used to create another cmdlet ❺. A name can be supplied for the noun that'll be applied to the cmdlet. It doesn't have to match the method name, but we recommend incorporating the method name as done in this example. The parameters of the Chkdsk method can be found using Get-CimClass:

```
PS C:\> (Get-CimClass -ClassName
    Win32_LogicalDisk).CimClassMethods["ChkDsk"].Parameters

Name                                            CimType Qualifiers
----                                            ------- ----------
FixErrors                                       Boolean {ID, in}
ForceDismount                                   Boolean {ID, in}
OkToRunAtBootUp                                 Boolean {ID, in}
```

```
RecoverBadSectors                                          Boolean {ID, in}
SkipFolderCycle                                            Boolean {ID, in}
VigorousIndexCheck                                         Boolean {ID, in}
```

The parameters are coded individually ❻ with the cmdlet name for the parameter, the data type, and the parameter name as defined in the class supplied.

To use the CDXML file, import it as a module as you would any other PowerShell module. The same module rules apply. To make it easier, save the file as Logicaldisk.cdxml in a folder called LogicalDisk under your Modules folder:

```
PS C:\> Import-Module Logicaldisk
PS C:\> get-command -Module Logicaldisk

CommandType     Name                                   ModuleName
-----------     ----                                   ----------
Function        Get-LogicalDiskLogicaldisk
Function        Invoke-LogicalDiskChkdskLogicaldisk
```

Or you can specify the full path of the file:

```
PS C:\> import-module c:\devwork\logicaldisk.cdxml
```

Using CDXML should be regarded as an advanced technique, and we recognize that not everyone will want to code XML in this manner. You can find more CDXML examples in chapters 18 and 19 of *PowerShell and WMI* or on Richard's blog at http:// richardspowershellblog.wordpress.com/. Finally, a PowerShell community project is in the process of starting to provide a number of modules for the common legacy WMI classes, so don't feel you need to reinvent the wheel.

39.6   *Summary*

Knowing how to use WMI and CIM with PowerShell is a critical skill for IT pros. Most management tasks you'll need to undertake will use WMI and CIM. Using the WMI cmdlets will continue to work for all versions of PowerShell. So if you have WMI-based management scripts in place, don't feel you need to rewrite them. Because Microsoft's long-term strategy for remote management centers around CIM, it's to your benefit to begin using these cmdlets now. You can use CIM with systems running PowerShell v2— just remember that you'll need to use DCOM for your CIMSessions to these machines.

Working with the web

This chapter covers

- Getting data from a website
- Working with JSON
- Working with REST services

Web protocols have given us incredible access to data. Whether you're consuming an XML feed from an internal web service, scraping HTML pages from the public internet, or interacting with REST services on a partner extranet, web technologies help make it happen. PowerShell is well connected to these technologies, too, meaning you can use it as a tool for automating those interactions.

> **NOTE** This chapter in particular focuses on Windows PowerShell v3 and v4. Much of what we're discussing can be performed in older versions, but the shell itself lacks the commands. Instead, you end up working with the raw .NET Framework to accomplish these tasks. Cmdlets are always easier than raw .NET code.

At first glance this may seem to be a developer-oriented topic, but the administration tools of many software products within our environments are increasingly exposed as web services. As an administrator, you need to know how to access those services. First, though, how do you access a simple website?

40.1   Getting data from the web

PowerShell's Invoke-WebRequest command is designed to send an HTTP request to a web server and to download the results. For example, if you run Invoke-WebRequest -Uri http://manning.com, you'll get back a result object. That object includes a number of useful properties:

- StatusCode contains 200 if the request completed normally; other HTTP error numbers like 404 (not found) are possible. You'll find a list of possible status codes along with their descriptions and meanings here: www.w3.org/Protocols/rfc2616/rfc2616-sec10.html. Individual web servers won't necessarily implement all status codes or instance those implemented by Internet Information Services (IIS), as explained at http://support.microsoft.com/kb/943891.

- StatusDescription contains OK if the request is successful. StatusDescription is tightly coupled with StatusCode and is explained in the URL given in the StatusCode item.

- Content contains the actual content of the response, which in this case would be the HTML for the web page. PowerShell doesn't *render* the web page because it isn't a browser, but it does give you access to the raw HTML. The default display will show you only the beginning of the HTML; to see the whole page's worth, use Invoke-WebRequest -Uri http://manning.com | select -ExpandProperty Content.

- RawContent includes not only the HTML but also the raw HTTP response headers. Those headers can include information on the web server, cookies, cache information, and more.

- Forms is a collection of objects that contain the HTML for any input forms defined in the document. Similarly, Images contains the HTML for any images on the page, InputFields contains input fields, Links contain HTML hyperlinks, and so on.

- Headers provides a collection of HTTP response headers. These are parsed from the RawContent property, and they're easier to work with because they're all nicely broken out into a collection.

- ParsedHTML is a reference to a Component Object Model (COM) object that provides access to the Document Object Model (DOM) of the page. We'll work with this property a bit later in this chapter.

Keep in mind that the command's job is to send a request to a URL and then save whatever comes back. What you do with those results depends on your goals, and how you work with the results depends on what the web server sent you. We'll explore those topics later in this chapter.

> **NOTE** PowerShell uses the term *Uniform Resource Identifier* (URI) in most of its web-friendly cmdlets. We tend to use the term *Uniform Resource Locator* (URL) in this book. A URL is one kind of URI: in addition to idenifying a resource,

the URL tells the computer how to get to that resource, often by providing a protocol handler like http://. We won't be working with any examples that use URIs other than URLs.

40.2 *Using web sessions*

The back-and-forth between web servers and browsers (or PowerShell) isn't technically a conversation, although we often refer to it that way. In a conversation, someone says something to you, and you reply. They remember your reply (unless maybe you're at a really wild party), and craft their next response based on that reply.

When a browser (or PowerShell) sends a request to a web server, though, the web server has no idea who it's talking to—even if it just sent that same web browser a response a few seconds ago. Every request-response exchange starts from scratch, with no context as to what has happened in the past. Imagine the difficulty this presents: You send your username and password to a website in order to log in and the website sends you a "logged in" web page. You then send a request to access, say, your account details, and the web server says, "Wait, who are you again?"

Cookies help solve that problem. A *cookie* is a small piece of information, such as a unique identifier, sent by the web server to you. You're supposed to send it back to the web server with each subsequent request, helping the server remember who you are and what you were both talking about. Cookies help create a conversational thread, or context, that lets you work with a web server. Together with some other pieces of information, cookies form a *web session*. If you need to automate some back-and-forth with a web server by using PowerShell, you'll need to manage web sessions.

To help demonstrate this, we've set up a page at http://powershell.org/cookietest .php. This page attempts to send two cookies to you and also displays any cookies you sent it. Try this:

```
PS C:\> Invoke-WebRequest -Uri http://powershell.org/cookietest.php |
➥ Select -expandproperty content

<h1>Enter Details</h1>
<form name="testform" action="cookietest.php" method="post">
      <input type="text" name="field1">
      <input type="text" name="field2">
</form>
```

The test page has a form named testform, which contains two input fields, named field1 and field2, which is what you see as returned content. Eventually, you should see cookie information. Our goal will be to capture the web session so that subsequent attempts will show that we correctly re-sent the cookies back to the server. To simulate the process of logging into a web page, we're pretending that the input fields in the form are for username and password.

We start by retrieving the page and capturing the response to a variable. That'll make it easier to work with:

```
$response = Invoke-WebRequest -Uri http://powershell.org/cookietest.php
➥ -SessionVariable session
```

Our variable response contains data like this:

```
StatusCode        : 200
StatusDescription : OK
Content           : <h1>Enter Details</h1>
                    <form name="testform" action="cookietest.php"
                        method="post">
                        <input type="text" name="field1">
                        <input type="text" name="field2">
                    </form>
RawContent        : HTTP/1.1 200 OK
                    Transfer-Encoding: chunked
                    Connection: keep-alive
                    Content-Type: text/html; charset=UTF-8
                    Date: Sat, 14 Dec 2013 09:48:38 GMT
                    Set-Cookie: __cfduid=ddb23833cf32b002cb11ba618b3283304...
Forms             : {testform}
Headers           : {[Transfer-Encoding, chunked], [Connection,
                        keep-alive], [Content-Type, text/html;
                        charset=UTF-8],
                    [Date, Sat, 14 Dec 2013 09:48:38 GMT]...}
Images            : {}
InputFields       : {@{innerHTML=; innerText=;
                    outerHTML=<INPUT name=field1>; outerText=;
                    tagName=INPUT; name=field1},
                    @{innerHTML=; innerText=;
                    outerHTML=<INPUT name=field2>;
                    outerText=; tagName=INPUT;
                    name=field2}}
Links             : {}
ParsedHtml        : mshtml.HTMLDocumentClass
RawContentLength  : 165
```

Next we want to get the forms so that we can log in. For now, we're pretending that we don't care about whatever cookies were sent. We know in our human brains that this is our first visit to the website. You'll notice, however, that we did capture the web session in $session. There's no typo there: When you provide a variable name to -Session-Variable, it only wants the variable name, which doesn't include a dollar sign. The contents of the $session variable are as follows:

```
PS C:\> $session

Headers              : {}
Cookies              : System.Net.CookieContainer
UseDefaultCredentials : False
Credentials          :
Certificates         :
UserAgent            : Mozilla/5.0 (Windows NT; Windows NT 6.3; en-GB)
                       WindowsPowerShell/4.0
Proxy                :
MaximumRedirection   : -1
```

So, to get that form:

```
$form = $response.forms[0]
```

we did need to analyze the web page ahead of time to determine that the first form (index 0) is the one we want. (You can view the available forms using `$response.Forms`.) Now that we have that form, we can fill in the fields:

```
$form.fields['field1'] = 'myname'
$form.Fields['field2'] = 'mypassword'
```

We can now send the form back to the server:

```
$r = Invoke-WebRequest -Uri http://powershell.org/cookietest.php
    -WebSession $session -Method POST -Body $form.fields
```

A lot went on there.

> **NOTE**   We used the –WebSession parameter with our session variable, including the $ prefix. –Sessionvariable is used for the first request with just the variable name (no $). Subsequent sessions use –WebSession with the variable including $.

We sent our web session object back, and we needed to specify the POST method as opposed to the default GET. A GET request is a simple URL, perhaps with parameters embedded in that URL (such as http://mysite.com/page.aspx?this=that&these=those). A POST request, on the other hand, can contain an entire body of information, which in this case is the filled-in form fields.

HTTP verbs

A number of standard HTTP verbs (also known as method definitions) are defined here: www.w3.org/Protocols/rfc2616/rfc2616-sec9.html. The common verbs you'll meet are as follows:

- GET—Used for reading information
- POST—Used for creating information
- PUT—Used for changing information
- DELETE—Used for removing information

Other verbs you may come across include:

- OPTIONS—Gets information on communication options
- HEAD—Same as GET but contains no message body in the response
- TRACE—Invokes a remote, application-layer loopback of the request
- CONNECT—Reserved for use with a proxy

When you're using PowerShell, the HTTP verbs can be used in a case-insensitive manner —that is, *GET* and `get` will both work. Other clients may not be so generous, so we recommend that you capitalize the verb.

Let's run the following to see what we got back:

```
$r.Content
```

In our run-through, here's what we got:

```
You sent cookie 'test1' containing 'value1' <br>
You sent cookie 'test2' containing 'value2' <br>
You sent cookie '__cfduid' containing
➥ 'd43e5b7c0e2de81022570ddeb3f54ff8a1386698974876' <br>
You sent field 'field1' containing 'myname' <br>
You sent field 'field2' containing 'mypassword' <br>
<h1>Enter Details</h1>
<form name="testform" action="cookietest.php" method="post">
    <input type="text" name="field1">
    <input type="text" name="field2">
</form>
```

Great! Our cookies made it to the server, and so did our form fields. Now we can keep passing those cookies back with each request. Keep in mind that the server might well send new cookies or change the ones it sent us; we'd need to use -WebSession to capture the new web session with each request, while at the same time sending the last session we got:

```
$r2 = Invoke-WebRequest -Uri http://powershell.org/cookietest.php
➥ -WebSession $session -Method Post -Body $form.fields
```

That way, $session is being continually updated with whatever the server sent back.

40.3   *Working with web responses*

So you've sent a request, and you've gotten a response, and you want to work with the content. What do you do? Well, that depends on what the content is. If it's XML, you can just cast it as XML:

```
[xml]$xml_response = $response.content
```

and then work with the XML as normal XML data (see chapter 14 for details). But sometimes, you might be "scraping" a web page and need to work with the raw HTML; other times, you might be getting a JavaScript Object Notation (JSON) result that you'll need to work with.

40.3.1   *Working with HTML documents*

There are two ways to work with HTML. Some web pages are in XHTML, which is an XML-friendly version of HTML. Those pages can be cast as XML and you can treat them as normal XML documents. Other HTML pages might not be explicitly XML-friendly, but you can try casting them as XML anyway. If it works, manipulating XML is the easiest way to go. If it doesn't work, you'll just get an error.

Your last choice—when the HTML page can't be cast as XML—is to work with the web page's DOM. Unfortunately, this requires that you have Internet Explorer (IE) installed locally, which might be a problem on a server (especially a Server Core server). IE provides the COM code that works with the DOM, but if you have IE, the DOM can be an interesting and straightforward way to manipulate a web page.

NOTE   This isn't a book on HTML DOM, which is a massive topic all by itself. Suffice it to say that the DOM takes a structured document and creates a hierarchical object model out of it, which you can manipulate programmatically. You'll find Microsoft's HTML DOM reference at http://msdn.microsoft.com/en-us/library/windows/apps/br212882.aspx. We're going to focus on a simple example that shows how PowerShell can access the DOM, but then you're on your own.

Let's take our cookietest.php page as an example. It contains a heading that's styled with the HTML <H1> tag. How can we extract its contents so that we can display the actual heading text?

First, get the page and its DOM object:

```
PS C:\> $page = Invoke-WebRequest -Uri http://powershell.org/cookietest.php
PS C:\> $dom = $page.ParsedHtml
PS C:\> $dom.getElementsByTagName('H1') | Select -Expand innerText
```

This code selects the <H1> tag (it'd select them all, if there were more than one) and expands its innerText property, which contains the text within the tag. Of course, given that this is PowerShell, there's always more than one way to solve a problem: We could've found that heading text by using a regular expression with the page content:

```
$page.Content -match "<H1>(?<heading>.*)?</H1>"
$matches['heading']
```

The point is that HTML is just text. You can work with it via regular expressions, treat it as XML, or treat it like an HTML DOM. But PowerShell isn't a browser—it's not going to run embedded JavaScript, display graphics, or anything else.

40.3.2   *Working with JSON data*

When PowerShell needs to save a static representation of an object in a textual format, it uses XML. Actually, the underlying .NET Framework does so, in a process called *serialization*. For example, when PowerShell Remoting sends result objects across the network, those are serialized into XML, because XML is easy to transmit across a network—it's just text! Turning the XML back into a programmatic object is called *deserialization*.

JavaScript, the language of web browsers and client-side web programming, doesn't use XML as much. Instead, it serializes to something called JSON. Here's a snippet of JSON, created by piping a Windows service (the BITS service) to ConvertTo-JSON:

```
PS C:\> Get-Service -Name bits | ConvertTo-Json
{
    "CanPauseAndContinue":  false,
    "CanShutdown":  false,
    "CanStop":  false,
    "DisplayName":  "Background Intelligent Transfer Service",
    "DependentServices":  [

                        ],
    "MachineName":  ".",
    "ServiceName":  "bits",
```

There's a lot more data, including the required and dependent services. JSON isn't as verbose as XML, but you still get a lot of text. You'd use JSON if you needed to send something to a web server that was expecting JSON, or if you wanted to consume an object that a web server sent to you in JSON format. JSON would be the content of your web response, so you'd use `Invoke-WebRequest` to send the request and get the response, and then run the content of the response through `ConvertFrom-Json`. The result would be an object you could manipulate in PowerShell.

Jeff's blog has a function that returns JSON, so we can use that to play with. We'll start by asking his server for the data we want:

```
$json = Invoke-WebRequest -DisableKeepAlive -UseBasicParsing
➥ -Uri http://jdhitsolutions.com/blog/?json=get_tag_index
```

This code is supposed to return a list of tags from his blog, including their names, internal ID numbers, the number of posts using each tag, and so on. We've told PowerShell to not try and parse the resulting HTML (-UseBasicParsing) because the result isn't HTML—it's JSON. `$json` now contains a web response; let's convert the JSON content to PowerShell objects:

```
$tags = $json.content | ConvertFrom-Json | select -ExpandProperty tags
```

That gives us a bunch of tag objects. Looking in `$tags`, we'll find objects like the following:

```
id           : 443
slug         : sid
title        : SID
description  :
post_count   : 1

id           : 338
slug         : smbit
title        : smbit
description  :
post_count   : 2

id           : 432
slug         : snapshot
title        : snapshot
description  :
post_count   : 1
```

You could then do whatever you wanted with the objects:

```
PS C:\> $tags | sort post_count -Descending | select -First 5 |
➥ Format-Table -AutoSize

id slug       title       description post_count
-- ----       -----       ----------- ----------
 4 powershell PowerShell              380
 8 scripting  Scripting               181
19 wmi        WMI                      63
32 functions  functions                62
10 books      Books                    43
```

Not surprisingly, Jeff writes a lot about PowerShell. This was just meant to be a quick example; remember, JSON is just a data format and not a service discovery mechanism. In other words, there's no way to tell whether a website accepts or produces JSON, or even what that JSON means, except for trial and error or previous knowledge of the website.

As a further example, the feature on Jeff's blog that provides JSON can return data based on a search result, but you have to know in advance how to construct the URI. In this example, we'll get some recent blog posts on PowerShell:

```
$uri="http://jdhitsolutions.com/blog/?json=get_search_results&search=
➥ powershell"
```

Using `Invoke-WebRequest` we'll retrieve HTML content:

```
$results = Invoke-WebRequest -Uri $uri -DisableKeepAlive
```

As before, the results are converted from JSON:

```
$converted = $results.Content | ConvertFrom-Json
```

If we pipe `$converted` to `Get-Member`, we can discover what type of object we have to work with:

```
   TypeName: System.Management.Automation.PSCustomObject

Name          MemberType   Definition
----          ----------   ----------
Equals        Method       bool Equals(System.Object obj)
GetHashCode   Method       int GetHashCode()
GetType       Method       type GetType()
ToString      Method       string ToString()
count         NoteProperty System.Int32 count=5
count_total   NoteProperty System.Int32 count_total=486
pages         NoteProperty System.Int32 pages=98
posts         NoteProperty System.Object[] posts=System.Object[]
status        NoteProperty System.String status=ok
```

The `posts` property, which we've boldfaced, appears to be a collection of posts. What does this object look like?

```
PS C:\> $converted.posts | Get-Member

   TypeName: System.Management.Automation.PSCustomObject

Name          MemberType   Definition
----          ----------   ----------
Equals        Method       bool Equals(System.Object obj)
GetHashCode   Method       int GetHashCode()
GetType       Method       type GetType()
ToString      Method       string ToString()
attachments   NoteProperty System.Object[] attachments=System.Object[]
author        NoteProperty System.Management.Automation.PSCustomObject
                           author=@{id=1; slug=administrator; name=Jeffery Hicks;...
```

```
categories      NoteProperty System.Object[] categories=System.Object[]
comments        NoteProperty System.Object[] comments=System.Object[]
comment_count   NoteProperty System.Int32 comment_count=4
comment_status  NoteProperty System.String comment_status=open
content         NoteProperty System.String content=<!—
                google_ad_section_start -->The other day Distinguished
                Engineer and ...
custom_fields   NoteProperty System.Management.Automation.PSCustomObject
                custom_fields=@{tt_auto_tweet=System.Object[]; tt_auto...
date            NoteProperty System.String date=2013-12-09 11:59:15
excerpt         NoteProperty System.String excerpt=<!—
                google_ad_section_start -->The other day Distinguished
                Engineer and ...
id              NoteProperty System.Int32 id=3573
modified        NoteProperty System.String modified=2013-12-09 11:59:15
slug            NoteProperty System.String slug=updated-console-graphing-in-
                powershell
status          NoteProperty System.String status=publish
tags            NoteProperty System.Object[] tags=System.Object[]
title           NoteProperty System.String title=Updated Console Graphing in
                PowerShell
title_plain     NoteProperty System.String title_plain=Updated Console
                Graphing in PowerShell
type            NoteProperty System.String type=post
url             NoteProperty System.String
                url=http://jdhitsolutions.com/blog/2013/12/updated-console-
                graphing-in-powershell/
```

As you're developing scripts or tools that rely on the cmdlets we're covering in this chapter, you'll need to spend some time exploring results with Get-Member.

Now that we have the data, we can use it like we would any other object from PowerShell.

```
#a regex to strip out html tags
[regex]$rx="<(.|\n)+?>"

$converted.posts | Select Title,
@{Name="Excerpt";Expression={$rx.Replace($_.excerpt,"")}},Url,
@{Name="Date";Expression={[datetime]$_.Date}} | Format-List
```

You can see the result in figure 40.1.

Most of the time, though, you probably won't need to use the JSON cmdlets much. Let's look at another web cmdlet, Invoke-RestMethod, that attempts to do much of the heavy lifting for you.

40.4   Using REST services

Invoke-RestMethod is designed to interact with Representational State Transfer (REST) websites. For IT pros, all you need to know is that this cmdlet will return rich and often hierarchical content from a website.

> **NOTE**   REST is an architecture, not a technology, so expect a lot of variation in the way URIs are constructed between different REST web services.

Figure 40.1   Converted JSON data

The cmdlets will attempt to "decode" the content and give you an appropriate
PowerShell object. If you use the cmdlets to get an RSS feed, you might get XML. If
you query a site using JSON, the cmdlets will attempt to convert it from JSON for
you. You shouldn't need to use `ConvertFrom-Json`. As a last resort, the cmdlet
should give you the same type of content you'd get with `Invoke-WebRequest`. Let's
look at a few examples.

First, let's get the feed from PowerShell.org:

```
$feed = Invoke-RestMethod -Method GET -Uri http://powershell.org/wp/feed/
```

You don't have to use the –`Method` parameter because it defaults to GET, but if you
develop the habit of using it you won't forget when you need to use another HTTP
verb, such as POST, with a REST web service.

If you pipe `$feed` to `Get-Member`, you'll discover it's an XML object. Here's a sample:

```
PS C:\> $feed[0]

title       : Episode 250 - PowerScripting Podcast - Julian Dunn from Ch...
link        : http://powershell.org/wp/2013/12/11/episode-250-powerscrip...
comments    : {http://powershell.org/wp/2013/12/11/episode-250-powerscri...
pubDate     : Thu, 12 Dec 2013 02:16:51 +0000
creator     : creator
category    : {category, category, category, category}
guid        : guid
description : description
encoded     : encoded
commentRss  : http://powershell.org/wp/2013/12/11/episode-250-powerscrip...
enclosure   : enclosure
```

Figure 40.2 An RSS feed from `Invoke-RestMethod`

Because this is XML, we have a hierarchical object:

```
PS C:\> $feed[0].description

#cdata-section
--------------
A Podcast about Windows PowerShell. Listen: In This Episode Tonight on the
PowerScripting Podcast, we talk to Julian Dunn abou...
```

So with a little work, we can transform `$feed` into something useful:

```
$feed | Select Title,
@{Name="Description";Expression={($rx.Replace($_.Description.InnerText,""))
➥ .Trim()}},
@{Name="Published";Expression={$_.PubDate -as [datetime]}},
Link,
@{Name="Category";Expression={$_.Category.innertext -join ","}}
```

We're using the same regex pattern from earlier (see figure 40.2) to strip out any HTML tags in the description.

We could've achieved a similar result with `Invoke-WebRequest`, but we would've either had to parse the DOM data or taken additional steps to turn the results into XML. `Invoke-RestMethod` did all of the hard work for us. The following listing puts all of this together into a function called `Get-RSS`.

Listing 40.1 The `Get-RSS` function

```
Function Get-RSS {
[cmdletbinding()]
Param (
[Parameter(Position=0,ValueFromPipeline=$True,
```

```
    ValueFromPipelineByPropertyName=$True)]
    [ValidateNotNullOrEmpty()]
    [ValidatePattern("^http")]
    [Alias('url')]
    [string[]]$Path="http://powershell.org/wp/feed/"
    )

Begin {
    Write-Verbose -Message "Starting $($MyInvocation.Mycommand)"

    [regex]$rx="<(.|\n)+?>"                              ◁─┐  Strip out
} #begin                                                    HTML tags

Process {
    foreach ($item in $path) {
        $data = Invoke-RestMethod -Method GET -Uri $item
        foreach ($entry in $data) {
            #link tag might vary
            if ( $entry.origLink) {
                $link = $entry.origLink
            }
            elseif ($entry.Link) {
                $link = $entry.link
            }
            else {
                $link = "undetermined"
            }
                                                         ◁─┐  Determine
            if ($entry.description -is [string]) {          description type
                $description =
➥ $rx.Replace($entry.Description.Trim(),"").Trim()
            }
            elseif ($entry.description -is [System.Xml.XmlElement]) {
                $description =
➥ $rx.Replace($entry.Description.innerText,"").Trim()
            }
            else {
                                                         ◁─┐  Use description
                $description = $entry.description
            }

            [pscustomobject][ordered]@{                  ◁─┐  Use customobject
                Title = $entry.title
                Published = $entry.pubDate -as [datetime]
                Description = $description
                Link = $Link
            } #hash
        } #foreach entry
    } #foreach item

} #process

End {
    Write-Verbose -Message "Ending $($MyInvocation.Mycommand)"
} #end

} #end Get-RSS
```

RSS feeds can vary, and we've tried to accommodate as much as possible, but there's no guarantee the function will work perfectly. In those cases, you'll need to examine the results from `Invoke-RestMethod` to discover the correct property names and types. In the meantime, you can try it out with these commands:

```
Get-RSS -Path http://powershell.org/wp/feed/
Get-RSS -Path http://mcpmag.com/rss-feeds/prof-powershell.aspx
Get-RSS -Path http://windowsitpro.com/rss.xml
Get-RSS -Path "http://richardspowershellblog.wordpress.com/feed/"
```

Finally, we'll take the JSON queries we discussed earlier but modify them to use `Invoke-RestMethod`:

```
PS C:\> (Invoke-RestMethod
➥ "http://jdhitsolutions.com/blog/?json=get_tag_index").tags |
➥ sort Post_count -desc | select -First 5 |
➥ Format-Table ID,Title,Post_Count

id title        post_count
-- -----        ----------
 4 PowerShell        380
 8 Scripting         181
19 WMI                63
32 functions          62
10 Books              43

PS C:\> [regex]$rx="<(.|\n)+?>"
PS C:\> (Invoke-RestMethod
➥ "http://jdhitsolutions.com/blog/?json=get_search_results&search=
➥ powershell").posts | Select Title,
➥ @{Name="Excerpt";Expression={$rx.Replace($_.excerpt,"")}},Url,
➥ @{Name="Date";Expression={[datetime]$_.Date}} | Format-List

title   : Updated Console Graphing in PowerShell
Excerpt : The other day Distinguished Engineer and PowerShell Godfather
          Jeffrey Snover posted a blog article about the evils of
          Write-Host. His take, which many agree with, is that Write-Host
          is a special case cmdlet. In his article he mentions
          console graphing as an example. I wrote such a script earlier
          this year. Mr. Snover&#8217;s post drove [&hellip;]
          Share this:EmailPrintPinterest
url     : http://jdhitsolutions.com/blog/2013/12/updated-console-graphing-
          in-powershell/
Date    : 12/9/2013 11:59:15 AM
...
```

We get the same results as before, but without having to deal with converting JSON data.

By now you're probably wondering when you should use `Invoke-WebRequest` and when you should use `Invoke-RestMethod`. The answer: It depends. If you definitely know you're dealing with a RESTful website, then `Invoke-RestMethod` is the way to go. If you're pulling information from an RSS feed, use `Invoke-RestMethod` first. Otherwise, you'll need to spend some time testing both cmdlets and deciding how to best parse or use the results. But there's one more type of web resource you might want to take advantage of in PowerShell: SOAP.

40.5   *Using SOAP web services*

The Simple Object Access Protocol (SOAP) puts a wrapper around the whole serialization and deserialization thing. Essentially, SOAP allows PowerShell to "see" a web service as if it was a locally installed piece of software. You get an instance of the object—much like running `Get-Service` to get instances of service objects—and then you can play with the properties and methods of that object. Under the hood, it's all XML and HTTP, but that's all handled for you.

Let's experiment with the IP-to-location web service, located at www.webservicex .net/geoipservice.asmx, which is referred to as the *endpoint* for the service. We have to start by creating a local web service proxy, which will serve as the translator between us and the web service. Doing so is easy:

```
$px = New-WebServiceProxy "http://www.webservicex.net/geoipservice.asmx?WSDL"
```

This code asks the service for its Web Services Description Language (WSDL), which describes how the service wants to be used. PowerShell constructs a local proxy, which we've saved in $px. We can easily see what the service is capable of now by simply piping $px to `Get-Member`:

```
$px | Get-Member -MemberType Method
```

We're only interested in the methods, but you could run this yourself and see what else is available. We got back a list with several methods, including `GetGeoIP()` among others (the list is a bit long; run the commands yourself to see the full output). We also see that `GetGeoIP()` accepts a string. Let's try it, using the IP address of Google's public DNS server, 8.8.8.8:

```
$IPAddress="8.8.8.8"
$px.GetGeoIP($IPAddress)
```

We get this result:

```
ReturnCode        : 1
IP                : 8.8.8.8
ReturnCodeDetails : Success
CountryName       : United States
CountryCode       : USA
```

Neat! So basically, $px—our local web service proxy—is acting like a piece of locally installed software. In reality, it's doing all the under-the-hood magic needed to query information from the web server. It gives us an object that works like any other PowerShell object. We can, for example, select properties:

```
$px.GetGeoIP($IPAddress) | Select IP,Country*
```

Unfortunately, there's no central directory of every SOAP-enabled web service out there. The WebServiceX.net website publishes a lot of public web services, and they maintain a list of them all. You can also use search engines to find them, and you may have use for SOAP when working with internal web services inside your organization.

40.6 *Just in case*

We referred to a cookietest.php page several times in this chapter; in the event it becomes unavailable online, the following listing contains the PHP source code for it.

Listing 40.2   CookieTest.php

```php
<?php
setcookie('test1','value1');
setcookie('test2','value2');
foreach ($_COOKIE as $key=>$value) {
    echo "You sent cookie '$key' containing '$value' <br>\n";
}
foreach ($_POST as $key=>$value) {
    echo "You sent field '$key' containing '$value' <br>\n";
}
?>
<h1>Enter Details</h1>
<form name="testform" action="cookietest.php" method="post">
<input type="text" name="field1">
<input type="text" name="field2">
</form>
```

You can drop the code on any web server that supports PHP (including Windows' own IIS) and it should work with the examples in this chapter.

40.7 *Summary*

Using the web cmdlets opens up many possibilities for IT pros. You'll have to set aside some time to figure out the correct approach given the web resource, data, and what you intend to do with it. Despite the concept of web standards, we've seen enough variation in web content that it's hard to come up with a one-size-fits-all script or function to consume web resources.

We didn't cover every single parameter or feature of these cmdlets because some of them are for special-use cases. But we wanted to give you enough of a taste to whet your appetite. As with everything in this book, be sure to read the full cmdlet help and examples.

Desired State Configuration

Desired State Configuration (DSC) was introduced in Windows PowerShell v4 as part of the Windows Management Framework 4.0. That means it's available on Windows Server 2008 R2 and later, although as you'll learn in this chapter its usefulness is determined by the compatible resources available on a given computer. DSC is heavily tilted toward server management rather than client management, but as you'll see, it has applications for clients as well.

41.1 What is DSC?

DSC is an attempt by Microsoft to provide *declarative configuration management* in a standards-based fashion. There's an important distinction here: with *declarative* configuration, you give a computer a description of what you want that computer to look like. You don't worry about how it gets that way—you just tell it what you want. That's different from the more familiar *imperative* configuration, where you write a script that makes whatever changes necessary to make a computer look the way you want.

Here's a noncomputer example: with imperative management, you might tell your teenaged son to go outside, get in the car, start the car, drive out of the driveway, turn left at the stop light, park at the convenience store, go inside, get a container of milk, and return to the house. You have to detail each step, and your ability to do so depends on your son knowing how to follow each step. For example, if he isn't sure about what type of milk to buy, then you'll have to dig even deeper and lay out the exact steps needed to do so. Imperative management makes it easy to get buried in implementation details. When the underlying technology changes—say, you buy a new car that has a pushbutton start—you have to rewrite the directions.

With declarative management, you'd simply tell your son, "Make sure there's always at least a quarter-full container of milk in the fridge." Your son's underlying intelligence (hah) would kick in and make sure that was true, including running out to the store when necessary to replenish the milk. Bet you're wishing your son had declarative management now, right?

Traditionally, Windows administrators have written scripts in the imperative mode, meaning each script had to be finely crafted and tuned, and often changed when versions of Windows changed, to perform each task. It was time-consuming as heck. With DSC, we're shifting over to declarative management, meaning we write "scripts" that tell the computer what to be, and the computer takes care of it. And they're not "scripts" in the traditional sense, because they contain little programming. They use a specialized set of instructions that both you and the computer can understand.

41.2 DSC architecture

DSC consists of two main layers. The *configuration script* is the declarative statement of what you want the computer to look like. "I want you to be a web server, I want you to have *this* set of files, and I want your firewall to have *these* ports open." DSC compiles that script into a Managed Object Format (MOF) file. A MOF file is a text-based file that represents information in the Common Information Model (CIM), an open standard managed by the Distributed Management Task Force (DMTF). The DMTF is an industry working group, meaning we're working in the world of open standards that can, potentially, work across platforms.

The MOF file is then deployed to the computers that you want it to apply to. We'll cover how that happens later in this chapter, but the short story is that either a computer can *pull* the MOF file from a URL, or you can *push* the MOF file to the computer in a one-time operation.

> **NOTE** It is also possible to pull the MOF file from an SMB share but most people we've talked to use a URL.

Once the computer has the MOF file, DSC evaluates it on a schedule. If you pushed the file, that's every 15 minutes by default; if you have the computer pulling the file, it'll check every 30 minutes. That runs as a Windows Scheduled Task.

When the computer evaluates the MOF file, the second main layer of DSC comes into play: *DSC resources*. Each resource is, essentially, a PowerShell module that implements three specific functions. So, if the configuration MOF says, "You should be a web server," then a DSC resource capable of installing roles and features will load up, determine whether the computer meets that criteria, and install the IIS role if needed. A DSC resource has the ability to test a configuration element as well as remediate it, or set it to a specific state (such as installed or not installed).

These resources are where the magic happens—they're the imperative part of the equation that implements the declarative configuration that you provide. Microsoft and third-party vendors can provide these resources, so you don't have to worry about how to implement specific configurations—you just have to tell DSC what you want done. You can also author your own DSC resources as PowerShell script modules if you like; we'll cover that later.

NOTE The usefulness of DSC depends on the availability of resources that can configure whatever it is you need. For example, DSC can't do anything with Microsoft Exchange Server unless you have an Exchange-related set of resources. So DSC will get more useful over time, as more resources are developed and released.

Windows Management Framework 4.0 shipped with a number of basic DSC resources:

- *Archive*—Uncompresses zip files.
- *Environment*—Manages environment variables.
- *File*—Manages files and folders.
- *Group*—Manages local groups.
- *Log*—Writes to the Microsoft-Windows-Desired State Configuration/Analytic log but only when you are using push mode. In pull mode, an event appears in the log to state that the resource is writing to the log but the message doesn't get written.
- *Package*—Installs and manages Windows Installer and Setup.exe packages.
- *Process*—Configures Windows processes.
- *Registry*—Manages Registry keys and values.
- *Role*—Adds and removes Windows roles and features.
- *Script*—Runs a PowerShell script.
- *Service*—Manages Windows services.
- *User*—Manages local user accounts.

Microsoft is releasing additional DSC resources "out-of-band," meaning they'll be released for download rather than made part of a future OS release. You can find the out-of-band resources on TechNet: http://gallery.technet.microsoft.com/site/search?query=dsc%20resource%20kit&f%5B0%5D.Value=dsc%20resource%20kit&f%5B0%5D.Type=SearchText&ac=2. The resources are released in waves; the appearance of a new wave is announced on the PowerShell team blog (http://blogs.msdn.com/b/powershell/). Look for posts about the DSC Resource Kit.

NOTE The resources in the DSC Resource Kit are supplied as is with no warranty and the caveat that support for the Resource Kit may be withdrawn in future versions of Windows if these resources become part of the Windows Server install.

The DSC resources in the resource kit all have an "x" (for experimental) as a prefix to indicate that they are part of the Resource Kit. Another source of DSC resources, in some cases modified versions of those in the Resource Kit, can be found at https://github.com/PowerShellOrg/DSC. The resources here are all prefixed with a "c" (for community).

NOTE If you're using the experimental, or community, resources, remember that they're supplied as is and it's your responsibility to test them thoroughly in your environment.

Future versions of Windows and other Microsoft products may also include resources, and third-party software vendors can include or provide resources. Note that a resource may have a dependency on a specific product version. For example, if Exchange Server 2016 (assuming there is such a product) ships with a bunch of DSC resources, those might be compatible only with that version of Exchange. It'll all depend on the product.

So how do you deploy resources once you get them? You don't! Just as a computer can pull its MOF from a URL, DSC knows how to check a URL for resources that it's missing. It can download them—as zip files, which it knows how to uncompress—and install them locally when it needs them. That means you get the desired MOF (or MOFs) to your computers, and they'll take care of the rest, including grabbing any DSC resources referenced by those MOFs.

NOTE You can find the official documentation for resources here: http://technet.microsoft.com/en-us/library/dn282125.aspx. The site includes a list of built-in resources as well as information on developing custom resources.

41.3 Writing the configuration script

So it all begins—assuming you have the resources you need—with a configuration script. Remember, you're using PowerShell syntax, but the result will be translated into a MOF file, because that's what DSC uses under the hood.

Why MOF?

This is probably a good time to explore why Microsoft decided to do the PowerShell-to-MOF conversion, rather than simply letting DSC use a PowerShell "script" directly. Why the middleman format?

Mainly because, believe it or not, Microsoft is trying hard to play better with others in the datacenter. The protocol used by PowerShell Remoting, WS-Management, is an open standard, and in theory you could use Remoting to send commands to a Linux

(continued)

box or an IBM AS/400, assuming someone had implemented the protocol on those operating systems. And someone could do that, if they wanted, without violating any Microsoft patents or other intellectual property—that's what "open standard" means.

So it is with MOF. You can write a configuration script in PowerShell, turn it into a MOF, and send it to a Linux machine, provided you're using DSC through WMF 5.0 and have loaded the appropriate packages on your Linux machine. Once WMF 5.0 is complete, you can do cross-platform managing right from PowerShell. Similarly, DSC can consume a MOF generated by something other than PowerShell, too, which means you could potentially use non-Microsoft, cross-platform software to generate MOFs and send them to a Windows computer, and DSC could follow the instructions in that MOF to configure the computer.

The investment in MOF is, therefore, all about enabling better cross-platform management of heterogeneous datacenters. That might seem totally un-Microsoft-like, but these days it's where the company is headed.

The following listing shows a sample configuration "script."

Listing 41.1   Sample DSC Configuration

```
Configuration IISWebsite
{
    Node @("Server1","Server2")
    {
        WindowsFeature IIS
        {
            Ensure    = "Present"
            Name      = "Web-Server"
        }

        WindowsFeature ASP
        {
            Ensure    = "Present"
            Name      = "Web-Asp-Net45"
        }
    }
}
```

This example is straight from the PowerShell team's blog (http://blogs.msdn.com/b/ powershell/archive/2013/11/01/configuration-in-a-devops-world-windows-powershell-desired-state-configuration.aspx), and it's a great introduction to writing these scripts.

It starts with the `Configuration` keyword. Everything related to this configuration will be contained within the `Configuration` construct. Within the construct, you can define one or more `Node` sections, and each node defines the computers that it'll apply to. In this case, there's one node, and it applies to two computers: Server1 and

Server2. If you specify more than one computer for the node, you need to use an explicit array as you did in listing 41.1.

What's neat is that you can also provide a script block instead of a static list of computer names. Even better, you can parameterize the node name. Here's an example:

```
Configuration IISWebsite
{
        Param($NodeList)

        Node $NodeList
        {
```

In this snippet, you've replaced the static array of computer names with a parameter, and you've defined that parameter in a `Param()` block. When you run this configuration to translate it to MOF, you can provide a list of computer names, perhaps queried from Active Directory or a database of some kind.

Within the `Node` block, you can have one or more configuration items. Each starts with a keyword that maps to a DSC resource—in the example, `WindowsFeature`. This example uses the arbitrary names `IIS` and `ASP`—DSC doesn't care what you name the sections. Inside, each one provides the name of a role and specifies that each of them is to be present on the computer. Exactly what you put into these configuration items will vary a bit, because different resources may require different pieces of information. The practical upshot of this entire example is that the ASP.NET 4.5 and IIS roles will be installed on the server, if they aren't already. If someone later removes one of the roles, DSC will reinstall them in its next scheduled evaluation of the MOF, if you've configured DSC to do so.

DSC behavior

You can configure DSC to behave in one of three ways:

- `ApplyOnly`—You apply the configuration to the node once and DSC has no further interest in the machine unless you create a new configuration for that machine.
- `ApplyAndMonitor`—You apply the configuration to the node once and DSC will monitor any changes to that configuration but won't do anything about them.
- `ApplyAndAutoCorrect`—The configuration is applied to the node and DSC will periodically test the configuration (the default is 15 minutes). If it finds that the configuration has changed, it will reapply the DSC configuration to correct any changes.

These behaviors apply to both push and pull modes.

Next, you have to compile the script—technically, it's translating, not "compiling" in the software development sense—into a MOF. To do so, you just run the configuration like you'd run a function. Assuming you're in the PowerShell ISE, run the PowerShell configuration script, or dot-source it. Like workflows, configurations are a new command type:

```
PS C:\> Get-Command -CommandType Configuration

CommandType     Name                                      ModuleName
-----------     ----                                      ----------
Configuration   IISWebsite
```

The command even has help (see figure 41.1)!

Now you can run it like any other command. Assuming you left the `NodeList` parameter in the example, you might run this:

```
IISWebsite –NodeList (Get-ADComputer –filter *
➡   -SearchBase "ou=WebServers,dc=domain,dc=pri" |
➡   Select-Object -ExpandProperty Name)
```

That code would compile the MOF and target every computer in the WebServers organizational unit (OU) of the domain.pri Active Directory domain. This example assumes that your computer has the Microsoft ActiveDirectory module installed, which can be found in the Remote Server Administration Tools (RSAT).

By default PowerShell will create a subdirectory named after the configuration and store the new MOF files there. The directory is created at your current location. If you'd run the previous example in the root of C:\, you'd have seen a folder called IISWebSite and MOF for every computer from your Active Directory query. You can specify a different path using the `OutPath` parameter, which you can see from the help screen. The bottom line is pay attention to where you're executing the configuration.

There's a bit more you can put into the configuration if you like. For example, if you intend for DSC to periodically review and reapply your configuration, you can

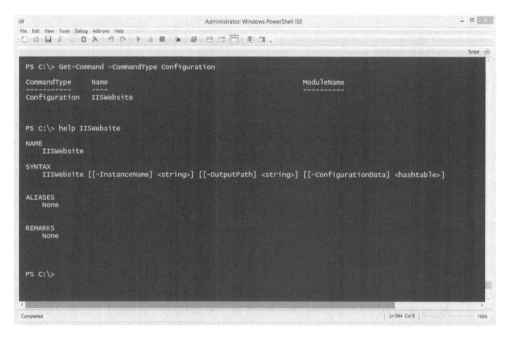

Figure 41.1   DSC Configuration Help

control some of its behavior for doing so. Within a `Node` construct, add a section of instructions to the Local Configuration Manager (or LCM, the piece of DSC that does all the actual work):

```
Node $NodeList
{
    LocalConfigurationManager
    {
        RebootNodeIfNeeded = $True
        ConfigurationMode = "ApplyAndAutoCorrect"
        ConfigurationModeFrequencyMins = 15
    }
}
```

Here, you've said that you want the final MOF applied, and then reapplied every 15 minutes. You want the target computer rebooted automatically, if that's required to complete the configuration. This Local Configuration Manager section applies to the *entire node*, and it's not unusual to place this in a `Node` construct of its own. You can't have a different setting for some configuration items; whatever you set the LCM to do will be in effect for *all* DSC configurations targeted at that computer. If you have the LCM set to use a pull server and then manually push a configuration to that server, the node's behavior will switch accordingly.

> **NOTE** There's a more substantial configuration example at http://blogs .technet.com/b/keithmayer/archive/2013/11/06/why-r2-automated-server-self-provisioning-and-remediation-with-desired-state-configuration-dsc-in-powershell-4-0.aspx#.UpzV66UbM_4, if you're interested in seeing something that installs roles, manages services, and even runs a custom script.

41.4 Getting the configuration to the computer

You have two ways of getting the MOF files to their intended computers: push or pull. Push is the easiest to explain, so we'll start with it.

Assuming that you've enabled PowerShell Remoting between the computers on your network, and assuming you have permission to remote into the targeted computers, you can deploy the MOFs as follows:

```
Start-DSSCConfiguration -Path .\IISWebsite -Wait -Verbose -Force
```

This will look in the IISWebsite subfolder of the current folder for MOF files, read them to figure out who they're supposed to go to, and then transfer them to those computers. (If you've specified a different output path, change the command accordingly.) The targeted computers' LCM will then process the MOF files and start configuring the computer to look the way the MOF file demands.

> **NOTE** The IISWebsite folder name came from the name of our original `Configuration` element. In it, a MOF file will exist for each computer targeted. So, following our example, that would be each computer in the Web-Servers OU.

If you're deploying an LCM configuration, you'll deploy that part somewhat differently:

```
Set-DscLocalConfigurationManager –Path .\IISWebsite –Verbose
```

This code reads the MOF that you created on your computer, contacts the target computers, and updates their LCM configuration. Because this is a separate step, you'll often build this into a completely independent `Configuration` element so that you can apply it to an independent block of servers.

The push model has some downsides and general considerations:

- Each configuration generates one MOF file per targeted computer, so you can wind up with a load of MOF files floating around. It's perfectly fine to send multiple MOFs to a single target—they'll all apply.
- The dependency on WS-Management for communications can be problematic, especially across domain boundaries where the protocol requires a lot of extra setup (like SSL certificates).
- If you want to change a configuration, you have to go through this whole process: update your script, compile the MOFs, and redeploy the MOFs. That can be a pain in the neck if you're doing it a lot.

In most environments you'll probably want to investigate the pull model.

> **NOTE**   Microsoft made some last-minute changes to DSC between the initial release of Windows Server 2012 R2 and the general availability release. If you try pushing a configuration to a server that's running a pre-General Availability (GA) version of Windows Server 2012 R2, you may get errors about missing DSC resources. If so, you'll need to download and install the patch for KB2883200. See http://support.microsoft.com/kb/2883200 for more details.

41.4.1   Pull model

With the pull model, you get several advantages over the push model, and there's only a small amount of additional setup:

- Communications happen over HTTP(S), because the pull server is just a web server.
- It's easier for managed nodes to find and download DSC resources, because they can be hosted on the same web server.
- Multiple computers can pull from a single MOF file, making file management easier.
- Computers can periodically check their MOF files for changes, making it easier to reconfigure a bunch of computers at once.
- Computers become responsible for getting their MOFs, rather than you being responsible for making sure the push operation completed successfully.

In the pull model, you still run your configuration to produce a MOF file. That MOF simply needs to live on a web server. One difference in the configuration file—the only difference—is that you provide a globally unique identifier (GUID) instead of node names. That's because a MOF intended for the pull model doesn't target specific computers; it just sits on the web server waiting to be pulled. You then tell your computers which MOFs to grab, and the way you do that is by matching up the GUIDs. "Hey, servers 1 through 52, you go get configuration 1C707B86-EF8E-4C29-B7C1-34DA2190AE24, okay?" That means your node names, inside the configuration script, tend to be static:

```
Configuration SimpleConfigurationForPullSample
{
    Node 1C707B86-EF8E-4C29-B7C1-34DA2190AE24
    {
```

NOTE If you want to create a GUID, you can use the Guidgen.exe tool. Search the internet for it (it's free) if it isn't already on your computer. If you know a bit about programming, you can also use the `NewGuid()` method of the .NET Framework `Guid` class.

That gets you your MOF files, suitable for pulling. How do you tell computers to pull them? Follow these steps:

1 Run your configuration, which will produce a folder that has your configuration name as the folder name, and a file that also has the GUID as the filename and that has a .MOF filename extension.

2 You need to generate a checksum for the MOF file, which will allow remote computers' LCM to verify the integrity of the file. To do so, in PowerShell run the following command (note that `MyExampleConfiguration` should be replaced with your configuration folder name):

```
New-DSCCheckSum -Configuration .\MyExampleConfiguration
➥ -Outpath .\MyExampleConfiguration
```

3 Configure each computer to pull the MOF (and its checksum) from the pull server. To do so, you have to push a MOF to the target, and that MOF has to configure the LCM. We call this the *meta-configuration MOF*. The following listing shows an example a meta-configuration MOF (we'll cover these options in a bit).

Listing 41.2 A meta-configuration MOF

```
instance of MSFT_KeyValuePair as $keyvaluepair1
{
    key = "ServerUrl";
        value = "http://pullserver:8080/PSDSCPullServer/PSDSCPullServer.svc";
};

instance of MSFT_KeyValuePair as $keyvaluepair2
{
    key = "AllowUnsecureConnection";
    value = "true";
};
```

```
instance of MSFT_DSCMetaConfiguration
{
   ConfigurationID = "1C707B86-EF8E-4C29-B7C1-34DA2190AE24";
   RefreshMode="PULL";
   DownloadManagerName="WebDownloadManager";
   RebootNodeIfNeeded=True;
   RefreshFrequencyMins = 15;
   ConfigurationModeFrequencyMins = 30;
   ConfigurationMode = "ApplyAndAutoCorrect";
   DownloadManagerCustomData = {$keyvaluepair1,$keyvaluepair2};
};

instance of OMI_ConfigurationDocument
{
   Version="1.0.0";
   Author="DonJ";
};
```

4 Now you need to set up a pull server. That's a normal server that has the DSC
   Pull Service installed (run `Add-WindowsFeature Dsc-Service` to install it; it'll
   install IIS automatically if needed). The example we're using uses port 8080 (so
   it won't conflict with a web server that might be installed on that computer) and
   doesn't require SSL. The server also needs an IIS endpoint for the DSC Pull Service (this is all handled by IIS at the end of the day).

5 Put the MOF and checksum files onto the pull server. That's usually in
   C:\Program Files\WindowsPowerShell\DscService\Configuration. Both the MOF
   and the checksum need to have the same base filename (e.g., My.MOF and
   My.MOF.checksum).

6 With your LCM meta-configuration MOF in hand (from step 3), run the following to push the LCM configuration to the targeted computers. Notice in this
   example that we've manually copied the MOF file to the computer, and we're
   running this locally, so we just use localhost for the computer name and assume
   that the MOF file is in the current folder and named localhost.meta.mof:

```
Set-DscLocalConfigurationManager -ComputerName localhost
➥   -Path . -Verbose
```

NOTE   There's nothing stopping you from copying a meta-configuration MOF
via WS-Management, but if that's not enabled, then this one-time process is
required to get pull working. If you come up with a standard MOF, you could
even include that in your master image for new virtual machine deployments,
making it easy to script this step.

Okay, let's dive into that meta-configuration MOF for a bit. Here's the first section:

```
instance of MSFT_KeyValuePair as $keyvaluepair1
{
     key = "ServerUrl";
     value =
➥ "http://pullserver:8080/PSDSCPullServer/PSDSCPullServer.svc";
};
```

This code is pretty boilerplate, with the exception of `pullserver:8080`. That obviously needs to be the URL (and, if it isn't port 80, the port number) of your pull server. This assumes the IIS endpoint was named `PSDSCPullServer`. On to the next section:

```
instance of MSFT_KeyValuePair as $keyvaluepair2
{
        key = "AllowUnsecureConnection";
        value = "true";
};
```

This code permits non-SSL connections. Next is the good stuff:

```
instance of MSFT_DSCMetaConfiguration
{
        ConfigurationID = "1C707B86-EF8E-4C29-B7C1-34DA2190AE24";
        RefreshMode="PULL";
        DownloadManagerName="WebDownloadManager";
        RebootNodeIfNeeded=True;
        RefreshFrequencyMins = 15;
        ConfigurationModeFrequencyMins = 30;
        ConfigurationMode = "ApplyAndAutoCorrect";
        DownloadManagerCustomData = {$keyvaluepair1,$keyvaluepair2};
};
```

That `ConfigurationID` is the GUID you made up when you created your configuration in the first place—this is how you tell the computer which configuration to grab. You'll leave most of this section alone otherwise, although you can obviously adjust the refresh intervals if you like.

The creation of this meta-configuration MOF and the need to manually deploy it is the weak link in DSC right now. For new servers, it's not that significant. For existing servers, it's no big deal if WS-Management is working between them all. In an environment without WS-Management (e.g., PowerShell Remoting) set up, pushing this MOF to all your servers can be a bit of a hassle.

> **NOTE** You'll find another excellent walkthrough of setting up a pull server here: http://powershell.org/wp/2013/10/03/building-a-desired-state-configuration-pull-server/. That example uses different values for things like the configuration folder, so you can see how to change those things if you like. And over at http://blogs.msdn.com/b/powershell/archive/2013/11/21/powershell-dsc-resource-for-configuring-pull-server-environment.aspx, you'll find a DSC configuration script (and MOF) that completely handles setting up a pull server.

If you set up a DSC pull server, you'll notice that the default folder C:\Program Files\ WindowsPowerShell\DSCService has a subfolder for modules. That's where you put your DSC resources so that pull clients can find any resources they're missing.

41.5 Creating and testing a DSC pull server

As we explained in the previous section, you can create a server from which other machines can *pull* their configuration. The pull server can be used to provide the configuration information to initially configure your server and, if that's the way you want to operate your environment, enforce that configuration. But how do you set up a pull server?

You have three choices for creating a DSC pull server:

- Perform all the steps manually, using web-based documentation and blog posts to give you guidance.
- Run the scripts and follow the instructions in this section.
- Use the DSC Resource Kit download from http://gallery.technet.microsoft.com/ xPSDesiredStateConfiguratio-417dc71d to use DSC to configure the pull server.

We recommend that you create at least one DSC pull server in a lab environment before you turn to the DSC Resource Kit. This approach will give you a full understanding of the steps being performed and aid in any troubleshooting you may need to perform.

Listing 41.3 shows the control script for creating the DSC pull server and installing the Windows Backup feature on a server to test that everything is working correctly. You could install part of RSAT if you want to use something less intrusive for your test. The script in listing 41.3 calls a number of other scripts. We'll describe this main script first so that you have an overview of the process and then provide code and descriptions of the other scripts.

Listing 41.3   SetupDSC.ps1, the control script for creating a DSC pull server

```
Function New-Hash {                                             Create
    param($algorithm,$path)                                  ❶ new hash
    $fileStream = [IO.File]::OpenRead((Resolve-Path $path))
    $hasher = [Security.Cryptography.HashAlgorithm]::Create($algorithm)
    $hash = $hasher.ComputeHash($filestream)
    $filestream.close()
    $filestream.dispose()
    return $hash
}                                                              Create new
Function New-ChecksumFile {                                  ❷ checksum
    param($path)
    $hash = New-Hash -algorithm sha256 -path $path
    $hashStr = [system.bitconverter]::tostring($hash).replace('-','')
    [IO.File]::WriteAllText("$($Path).checksum",$hashStr)     Install DSC
}                                                            ❸ service

.\InstallPullServerConfig -DSCServiceSetup                    Generate
                                                           ❹ MOF file
.\SampleConfig.ps1

Copy-Item -Path .\Dsc\PullDemo\MEMBER2.mof `                  Copy
  -Destination c:\ProgramData\PSDSCPullServer\Configuration\ ❺ MOF file
  ➥ e528dee8-6f0b-4885-98a1-1ee4d8e86d82.mof

Get-ChildItem -Path C:\ProgramData\PSDSCPullServer\Configuration ` Create
-Filter *.mof |                                            ❻ checksum
ForEach-Object { New-ChecksumFile -path $_.FullName }
```

```
.\SampleSetPullMode.ps1

Invoke-CimMethod -ComputerName MEMBER2 `
  -Namespace root/microsoft/windows/desiredstateconfiguration `
  -Class MSFT_DscLocalConfigurationManager `
  -MethodName PerformRequiredConfigurationChecks `
  -Arguments @{Flags = [uint32]1} -Verbose
```

Configure client machine ⑦

Force client configuration ⑧

The script starts by defining two functions. If you plan on making heavy use of DSC, you should think about making these functions always available in your PowerShell sessions. The first function creates a hash of a file ❶ by creating a value that represents the file. If the file is changed, the hash of the changed file won't match the original and DSC will reject the file.

The function accesses .NET classes to compute the hash value. An alternative is to use the Get-FileHash cmdlet:

```
PS C:\> Get-FileHash -Path logv0.6.txt | fl *

Algorithm : SHA256
Hash      :
➥ A486B8873D1000541D95756F78D7256FF6971A714C58DFE3B959A6278D9A95DC
Path      : C:\MyData\SkyDrive\Data\scripts\logv0.6.txt
```

By default, Get-FileHash uses the SHA256 algorithm as used in the script. If you just want the hash value, use the following:

```
PS C:\> (Get-FileHash -Path logv0.6.txt).Hash
A486B8873D1000541D95756F78D7256FF6971A714C58DFE3B959A6278D9A95DC
```

The second function ❷ creates a checksum file that contains the hash value you calculated in the New-Hash function. System.IO.File is used rather than the PowerShell cmdlets to ensure there isn't any whitespace in the file that would stop it from being effective.

The main part of the script does five things through scripts that it calls:

1 Configures the DSC pull server (listing 41.4) ❸
2 Generates a MOF file for installing Windows Backup (listing 41.5) ❹
3 Copies the MOF file to the configuration folder ❺
4 Creates a checksum file for the MOF file ❻
5 Pushes the MOF file to the server ❼

A final step ❽ is to use WMI to force the configuration on to the remote server. The WMI namespace is new for DSC. You can see the other methods on the class by using Get-CimClass:

```
Get-CimClass `
-Namespace  root/microsoft/windows/desiredstateconfiguration `
-ClassName MSFT_DscLocalConfigurationManager |
select -ExpandProperty CimClassMethods
```

You can test whether the remote server has pulled, and applied, the configuration:

```
Get-WindowsFeature -Name Windows-Server-Backup -Computer MEMBER2
```

Now that you have an overview of the process, let's look at the details, starting with configuring the pull server (including the initial installation of the DSC service).

41.5.1   *Configuring a DSC pull server*

You can configure a DSC pull server by using the InstallPullServerConfig.ps1 script in listing 41.4.

> **NOTE** The script in listing 41.4 uses the PSWSIISEndpoint.psm1 module. We'll discuss the appropriate functions from that module, but we won't cover everything in the module. The module will be available in the download for the book, as will the scripts in this chapter.

Listing 41.4   InstallPullServerConfig.ps1, a script for creating a DSC pull server

```
[CmdletBinding()]
Param(                                                         ←┐  Define
        [Int]$Port = 8080,                                    ① parameters
        [switch]$DSCServiceSetup,
        [String]$iisroot = "$env:HOMEDRIVE\inetpub\wwwroot",
        [String]$rootdatapath = "$env:PROGRAMDATA"
 )

                                                               ←┐  Set
$pathPullServer     =                                         ② variables
    "$pshome\modules\PSDesiredStateConfiguration\PullServer"

$scriptDir          = Split-Path $MyInvocation.MyCommand.Path
Import-Module $scriptDir\PSWSIISEndpoint.psm1 -force

$siteName           = "PSDSCPullServer"
$iisPullServer      = Join-Path $iisroot $siteName
$psdscserverpath    = Join-Path $rootdatapath $siteName

$configurationpath  = Join-Path $psdscserverpath "Configuration"
$modulepath         = Join-Path $psdscserverpath "Modules"

$jet4provider       = "System.Data.OleDb"
$jet4database       = "Provider=Microsoft.Jet.OLEDB.4.0;
     ⇒                  Data Source=
     ⇒                  $env:PROGRAMDATA\PSDSCPullServer\Devices.mdb;"

if($DSCServiceSetup)                                          ③ Install DSC
{                                                             ←┐  service
    Add-WindowsFeature Dsc-Service
}
                                                             ④ Create
Create-PSWSEndpoint        -site $siteName `                 ←┐  website
                           -path $iisPullServer `
                           -cfgfile "$pathPullServer\PSDSCPullServer.config" `
                           -port $Port `
                           -applicationPoolIdentityType LocalSystem `
                           -app $siteName `
                           -svc "$pathPullServer\PSDSCPullServer.svc" `
                           -mof "$pathPullServer\PSDSCPullServer.mof" `
                           -dispatch "$pathPullServer\PSDSCPullServer.xml" `
                           -asax "$pathPullServer\Global.asax" `
```

```
                                    -dependentBinaries  "$pathPullServer\
  ➥                                 Microsoft.Powershell.DesiredStateConfiguration.
  ➥                                 Service.dll"
New-Item -path $rootdatapath -itemType "directory" -Force
```

```
Set-Webconfig-AppSettings `
                          -path $iisPullServer `
                          -key "dbprovider" `
                          -value $jet4provider
```
❺ Set web config—
database

```
Set-Webconfig-AppSettings `
                          -path $iisPullServer `
                          -key "dbconnectionstr" `
                          -value $jet4database
```

```
$repository = Join-Path $rootdatapath "Devices.mdb"
Copy-Item "$pathPullServer\Devices.mdb" $repository -Force
```
❻ Copy
database

```
New-Item -path "$configurationpath" -itemType "directory" -Force
```

```
Set-Webconfig-AppSettings `
                          -path $iisPullServer `
                          -key "ConfigurationPath" `
                          -value $configurationpath
```
Set web
config—
application
❼ configuration

```
New-Item -path "$modulepath" -itemType "directory" -Force
```

```
Set-Webconfig-AppSettings `
                          -path $iisPullServer `
                          -key "ModulePath" `
                          -value $modulepath
```

```
Set-Webconfig-AppSettings `
                          -path $iisPullServer `
                          -key "ApplicationBase" `
                          -value $iispullserver
```

```
Set-Webconfig-AppSettings `
                          -path $iisPullServer `
                          -key "TestConfigPath" `
                          -value $iispullserver
```

The script starts with a set of parameters ❶. The parameters have defaults; a switch parameter always defaults to $false. The other parameters define the port for the website and the paths for the website virtual directory and DSC data folder.

A set of variables is defined ❷. The variables specify:

- The path to source files
- Commands that perform the DSC installation
- Website and data folder configuration

Install the DSC service if required ❸, and then create the website ❹. Create-PSWSEndpoint is in the PSWSIISEndpoint.psm1 module (see listing 41.5). With the site created, it's time to configure the application directory and define the DSC configuration repository ❺. The configuration database ❻ is copied into the configuration folder.

A final set of modifications to the web config file ❼ can be made when testing. `Set-Webconfig-Appsettings` is also available in the PSWSIISEndpoint.psm1 module (see listing 41.6)

We mentioned the `Create-PSWSEndpoint` function earlier. This has been extracted from the PSWSIISEndpoint.psm1 module, as you can see in listing 41.5.

Listing 41.5   Function that creates a website

```
function Create-PSWSEndpoint
{
    param (

        # Unique Name of the IIS Site
        [parameter(mandatory = $true)]
        [ValidateNotNullOrEmpty()]
        [String] $site,

        # Physical path for the IIS Endpoint on the machine
        (under inetpub/wwwroot)
        [parameter(mandatory = $true)]
        [ValidateNotNullOrEmpty()]
        [String] $path,

        # Web.config file
        [parameter(mandatory = $true)]
        [ValidateNotNullOrEmpty()]
        [String] $cfgfile,

        # Port # for the IIS Endpoint
        [parameter(mandatory = $true)]
        [ValidateNotNullOrEmpty()]
        [Int] $port,

        # IIS Application Name for the Site
        [parameter(mandatory = $true)]
        [ValidateNotNullOrEmpty()]
        [String] $app,

        # IIS App Pool Identity Type - must be one of LocalService,
        LocalSystem, NetworkService, ApplicationPoolIdentity

        [ValidateSet('LocalService', 'LocalSystem', 'NetworkService',
        'ApplicationPoolIdentity')]
        [String] $applicationPoolIdentityType,

        # WCF Service SVC file
        [parameter(mandatory = $true)]
        [ValidateNotNullOrEmpty()]
        [String] $svc,

        # PSWS Specific MOF Schema File
        [parameter(mandatory = $true)]
        [ValidateNotNullOrEmpty()]
        [String] $mof,

        # Global.asax file [Optional]
        [ValidateNotNullOrEmpty()]
        [String] $asax,
```

```
        # PSWS Specific Dispatch Mapping File [Optional]
        [ValidateNotNullOrEmpty()]
        [String] $dispatch,

        # PSWS Test Specific RBAC Config File [Optional when using
         the Pass-Through Plugin]
        [ValidateNotNullOrEmpty()]
        [String] $rbac,

        # Any dependent binaries that need to be deployed to the
         IIS endpoint, in the bin folder
        [ValidateNotNullOrEmpty()]
        [String[]] $dependentBinaries,

        # Any dependent PowerShell Scipts/Modules that need to
         be deployed to the IIS endpoint application root
        [ValidateNotNullOrEmpty()]
        [String[]] $psFiles,

        # True to remove all files for the site at first, false otherwise
        [Boolean]$removeSiteFiles = $false)

    $script:wshShell = New-Object -ComObject wscript.shell
    $script:appCmd = "$env:windir\system32\inetsrv\appcmd.exe"
    $script:SrvMgr = $null
    $script:netsh = "$env:windir\system32\netsh.exe"

    Log ("Setting up test site at
    http://$env:COMPUTERNAME.$env:USERDNSDOMAIN:$port")

    ParseCommandLineAndSetupResouce -site $site -path $path
    -cfgfile $cfgfile -port $port -app $app
    -applicationPoolIdentityType $applicationPoolIdentityType
    -svc $svc -mof $mof -asax $asax -dispatch $dispatch
    -rbac $rbac -dependentBinaries $dependentBinaries
    -psFiles $psFiles -removeSiteFiles $removeSiteFiles

    CreateFirewallRule $port

    PerformActionOnAllSites start
}
```

The function uses appcmd.exe to perform the configuration. You could also use the IIS cmdlets. If you don't know your way round the IIS cmdlets, we recommend Jason Helmick's *Learn Windows IIS in a Month of Lunches* (Manning, 2014).

The other function from the PSWSIISEndpoint.psm1 module you need to see is Set-Webconfig-Appsettings (listing 41.6).

Listing 41.6 Function that configures the website

```
function Set-Webconfig-AppSettings
{
    param (
        # Physical path for the IIS Endpoint on the machine
         (possibly under inetpub/wwwroot)
        [parameter(mandatory = $true)]
        [ValidateNotNullOrEmpty()]
        [String] $path,
```

```
        # Key to add/update
        [parameter(mandatory = $true)]
        [ValidateNotNullOrEmpty()]
        [String] $key,

        # Value
        [parameter(mandatory = $true)]
        [ValidateNotNullOrEmpty()]
        [String] $value

        )

    Log ("Setting options at $path")

    $webconfig = Join-Path $path "web.config"
    [bool] $Found = $false

    if (Test-Path $webconfig)
    {
        $xml = [xml](get-content $webconfig);
        $root = $xml.get_DocumentElement();

        foreach( $item in $root.appSettings.add)
        {
            if( $item.key -eq $key )
            {
                $item.value = $value;
                $Found = $true;
            }
        }

        if( -not $Found)
        {
            $newElement = $xml.CreateElement("add");
            $nameAtt1 = $xml.CreateAttribute("key")
            $nameAtt1.psbase.value = $key;
            $newElement.SetAttributeNode($nameAtt1);

            $nameAtt2 = $xml.CreateAttribute("value");
            $nameAtt2.psbase.value = $value;
            $newElement.SetAttributeNode($nameAtt2);

            $xml.configuration["appSettings"].AppendChild($newElement);
        }
    }

    $xml.Save($webconfig)
}
```

The function reads the web configuration file as an XML document and then performs the required modifications before writing the new file.

Once you have your DSC pull server configured, you need to create your DSC configuration files.

41.5.2   *Sample configuration*

The configuration file in listing 41.7 installs the Windows Backup feature on to a server called MEMBER2.

Listing 41.7 DSC config file that installs Windows Backup

```
Configuration PullDemo
{
  Node MEMBER2
  {
    WindowsFeature Backup
    {
      Ensure = 'Present'
      Name   = 'Windows-Server-Backup'
    }
  }
}
PullDemo
```

The final piece in the DSC configuration puzzle is to ensure your client machines use the pull server.

41.5.3 Configuring a machine to use the pull server

Listing 41.8 shows how to configure a machine to use the pull server.

Listing 41.8 Configuring your DSC client to use the pull server

```
configuration  SetPullMode
{
  Node MEMBER2
  {
    LocalConfigurationManager
    {
      ConfigurationMode = 'ApplyOnly'
      ConfigurationID = 'e528dee8-6f0b-4885-98a1-1ee4d8e86d82'
      RefreshMode = 'Pull'
      DownloadManagerName = 'WebDownloadManager'
      DownloadManagerCustomData = @{
      ServerUrl = 'http://pull1.lab.pri:8080/PSDSCPullServer.svc';
      AllowUnsecureConnection = 'true' }
      RefreshFrequencyMins = 15
    }
  }
}

SetPullMode
Set-DSCLocalConfigurationManager -Computer MEMBER2 -Path ./SetPullMode -Verbose
```

The important parts of the configuration are the URL of the server and `ConfigurationID`, which has to be a GUID. If you're creating new machines, you could create a new GUID using the following:

```
PS C:\> [Guid]::NewGuid()

Guid
----
5ef37a69-35ab-4331-ab28-6ee9f5ee8146
```

Alternatively, for an existing machine that's already in Active Directory, you could use the `ObjectGUID` property from the computer object. You need to use `Set-DSCLocalConfigurationManager` to configure the machine. WMF 4 must be installed on a machine that runs Windows Server 2012 or Windows Server 2008 R2.

DSC has some resources available when you install. Others are available through the Resource Kit. You'll end up writing your own if what you need isn't available.

41.6   *Writing DSC resources*

So let's say you need to configure a server and you don't have a DSC resource that can do it. Maybe you want to use DSC to manage some internal line-of-business application, for example. Microsoft won't provide a resource for that, of course, but you can author your own.

> **NOTE**   We'll provide a high-level walkthrough of DSC resource authoring. Most of the complexity of authoring comes from whatever it is you're trying to configure; we'll focus only on the resource structure. We'll take the bare-bones approach to authoring; you can also check out http://blogs.msdn.com/ b/powershell/archive/2013/11/19/resource-designer-tool-a-walkthrough-writing-a-dsc-resource.aspx for an overview of the DSC Resource Designer Tool, which can take care of some of the nitty-gritty for you.

DSC resources are merely PowerShell script modules, which we've covered elsewhere in this book. What makes them different is that they have to follow a specific internal pattern, providing specific, predefined functions that DSC knows to execute. Within those functions, you do whatever is necessary to implement whatever it is you're configuring.

> **NOTE**   If you're using the documentation at http://technet.microsoft.com/ en-us/library/dn249927.aspx, you'll see the word *provider* a lot. Before releasing PowerShell v4 and DSC, Microsoft referred to DSC resources as providers. The term changed by the time it was released, but the docs haven't been updated as of this writing.

41.6.1   *Create the MOF Schema*

You'll need to start with a MOF schema, which defines the properties of the resource. When you use your resource in a configuration script, you assign values to these properties. In the examples in this chapter, for example, we had properties like:

```
WindowsFeature IIS
{
    Ensure = "Present"
    Name = "Web-Server"
}
```

Ensure and Name are both properties that are defined in the MOF schema. So your MOF might look something like this (pulled from the official documentation):

```
[ClassVersion("1.0.0"), FriendlyName("Website")]
class Demo_IISWebsite : OMI_BaseResource
```

```
{
  [Key] string Name;
  [write] string PhysicalPath;
  [write,ValueMap{"Present", "Absent"},Values{"Present", "Absent"}] string
➥ Ensure;
  [write,ValueMap{"Started","Stopped"},Values{"Started", "Stopped"}] string
➥ State;
  [write,ValueMap{"http", "https"},Values{"http", "https"}] string
➥ Protocol[];
  [write] string BindingInfo[];
  [write] string ApplicationPool;
  [read] string ID;
};
```

Each line in that construct—let's call it Schema.mof—is essentially a property, or a piece of information that your resource needs to operate. `Name` is a string, and it's the *key*, meaning whatever values go into `Name` will uniquely identify something. For example, in our previous example, `Web-Server` was a value provided to a `Name` property, because it uniquely identified the role to install.

Everything else gets tagged as readable or writable, and you'll typically see mostly writable properties. Those are ones that can accept values from your configuration scripts. Many will be simple strings; others, as in this example, are *value maps*. Notice this one:

```
[write,ValueMap{"Present", "Absent"},Values{"Present", "Absent"}] string
➥ Ensure;
```

This value map offers two options, `Present` and `Absent`, which map to the internal values `Present` and `Absent`. In this case, the options and their underlying values are the same; sometimes it might map options like `Started` and `Stopped` to internal values like `0` and `1`. It all depends how you're using the data. In that example, if someone used your resource in a configuration and passed `Stopped`, your code would see `1`.

The `FriendlyName` property at the top of the MOF defines the name that a configuration script would use to call on this resource. In our previous configuration script examples, you saw `WindowsFeature`, which is a friendly name defined by the Role resource. So, to use this "Website" resource in a configuration script, you might see:

```
Configuration My-Config {
  Node WWW1 {
    Website {
      Name = 'www'
      PhysicalPath = 'c:\inetpub\www3\'
      Ensure = 'Present'
      State = 'Started'
      Protocol = 'http'
    }
  }
}
```

There's the `Website` friendly name, and within its construct are the properties defined in the schema (well, most of them), along with values for each.

NOTE   Microsoft-authored resources use an Ensure property, which usually accepts the values Present and Absent, as a way of indicating whether the configuration should be installed. You don't have to follow that pattern, but doing so will make your resources more consistent.

41.6.2   *Create the script module*

Your schema MOF defines your resource's friendly name and the properties it accepts from a configuration script. You also need a script module, which takes those property values and implements the configuration. Resource script modules must implement three functions:

- Test-TargetResource—This function does the same thing as Get-Target-Resource, but returns $True or $False, depending on whether the configuration item is configured as specified in the parameters.
- Set-TargetResource—This function does whatever is necessary to put the configuration item in whatever state is specified by the parameter values. For example, if a website doesn't exist, it would be created. If it exists, it would be updated to reflect the passed-in configuration.
- Get-TargetResource—This function tests the current state of the configuration item. If the item exists, the returned object must have all the properties defined in the schema MOF, with values filled in for the existing configuration item. Most of these properties are empty if the configuration doesn't exist.

Each of those functions must have a parameter set that matches the properties defined in your schema MOF—that is, if you were using the website example schema MOF, your three functions would each need a parameter set like this:

```
param
(
    [ValidateSet("Present", "Absent")]
    [string]$Ensure = "Present",

    [Parameter(Mandatory)]
    [ValidateNotNullOrEmpty()]
    [string]$Name,

    [Parameter(Mandatory)]
    [ValidateNotNullOrEmpty()]
    [string]$PhysicalPath,

    [ValidateSet("Started", "Stopped")]
    [string]$State = "Started",

    [string]$ApplicationPool,

    [string[]]$BindingInfo,

    [string[]]$Protocol
)
```

This parameter set matches the properties in the schema MOF. When DSC runs the function, it'll take the values assigned to the properties (in the configuration script) and match them up to these parameters. In this way, the functions get the data they need to implement the configuration.

Save the module file as `ResourceName.psm1`, replacing `ResourceName` with the name of your resource.

41.6.3 Create the module manifest

You use PowerShell's `New-ModuleManifest` command to create a new manifest. Name it the same as the script module, only with a .psd1 filename extension—Website.psd1 to go with Website.psm1, for example. When creating the manifest:

- You can use the `-RequiredModules` parameter to specify the names of any PowerShell modules that must be loaded in order for your module to work properly.
- Use `-NestedModules` to specify the name of your script module—Website.psm1, for example.
- It's okay for your module to include functions beyond the three required ones, and that's a good way to modularize any functionality you need the module to perform. If you do this, use the `-FunctionsToExport` parameter to export `Get-TargetResource`, `Set-TargetResource`, and `Test-TargetResource`.

41.6.4 Putting it all together

Keep in mind that *you'll never run this module* except to test it! These functions are all called by DSC. Here's how it works: Suppose you create a resource using the schema MOF we outlined earlier. You complemented it with a script module and manifest, implementing the three required functions and the necessary parameter sets. Assume the MOF looked like listing 41.9.

Listing 41.9   Demo_IISWebsite.schema.mof

```
[ClassVersion("1.0.0"), FriendlyName("Website")]
class Demo_IISWebsite : OMI_BaseResource
{
  [Key] string Name;
  [write] string PhysicalPath;
  [write,ValueMap{"Present", "Absent"},Values{"Present", "Absent"}] string
⇨ Ensure;
  [write,ValueMap{"Started","Stopped"},Values{"Started", "Stopped"}] string
⇨ State;
  [write,ValueMap{"http", "https"},Values{"http", "https"}] string
⇨ Protocol[];
  [write] string BindingInfo[];
  [write] string ApplicationPool;
  [read] string ID;
};
```

NOTE   For consistency, we're using the same example as in the documentation at http://technet.microsoft.com/en-us/library/dn249927.aspx. Notice that the schema MOF filename is in a particular format: *resourcename*.schema.mof. The class name in the MOF uses the same resource name.

You could then back that up with a script module, as shown in listing 41.10.

Listing 41.10   Demo_IISWebsite.psm1

```
function Get-TargetResource
{
    param
    (
        [ValidateSet("Present", "Absent")]
        [string]$Ensure = "Present",

        [Parameter(Mandatory)]
        [ValidateNotNullOrEmpty()]
        [string]$Name,

        [Parameter(Mandatory)]
        [ValidateNotNullOrEmpty()]
        [string]$PhysicalPath,

        [ValidateSet("Started", "Stopped")]
        [string]$State = "Started",

        [string]$ApplicationPool,

        [string[]]$BindingInfo,

        [string[]]$Protocol
    )

        $getTargetResourceResult = $null;

        <# YOUR CODE HERE - assume $Website is a valid object #>
        $getTargetResourceResult = @{
                Name = $Website.Name;
                Ensure = $ensureResult;
                PhysicalPath = $Website.physicalPath;
                State = $Website.state;
                ID = $Website.id;
                ApplicationPool = $Website.applicationPool;
                Protocol = $Website.bindings.Collection.protocol;
                Binding = $Website.bindings.Collection.bindingInformation
        }

        $getTargetResourceResult;
}

function Set-TargetResource
{
    [CmdletBinding(SupportsShouldProcess=$true)]
    param
    (
        [ValidateSet("Present", "Absent")]
        [string]$Ensure = "Present",

        [Parameter(Mandatory)]
        [ValidateNotNullOrEmpty()]
        [string]$Name,
```

```
        [Parameter(Mandatory)]
        [ValidateNotNullOrEmpty()]
        [string]$PhysicalPath,

        [ValidateSet("Started", "Stopped")]
        [string]$State = "Started",

        [string]$ApplicationPool,

        [string[]]$BindingInfo,

        [string[]]$Protocol
    )
    <# Your code here #>
}
function Test-TargetResource
{
    [CmdletBinding(SupportsShouldProcess=$true)]
    param
    (
        [ValidateSet("Present", "Absent")]
        [string]$Ensure = "Present",

        [Parameter(Mandatory)]
        [ValidateNotNullOrEmpty()]
        [string]$Name,

        [Parameter(Mandatory)]
        [ValidateNotNullOrEmpty()]
        [string]$PhysicalPath,

        [ValidateSet("Started", "Stopped")]
        [string]$State = "Started",

        [string]$ApplicationPool,

        [string[]]$BindingInfo,

        [string[]]$Protocol
    )
    <# Your code here #>
}
```

NOTE These three functions aren't complete—remember, we're just trying to show you the structure of a resource. In reality, Microsoft already gives you a resource that handles websites.

You could then create a manifest like the one shown in listing 41.11.

Listing 41.11   Demo_IISWebsite.psd1

```
@{

# Script module or binary module file associated with this manifest.
# RootModule = ''

# Version number of this module.
ModuleVersion = '1.0'
```

```
# ID used to uniquely identify this module
GUID = '6AB5ED33-E923-41d8-A3A4-5ADDA2B301DE'

# Author of this module
Author = 'Contoso'

# Company or vendor of this module
CompanyName = 'Contoso'

# Copyright statement for this module
Copyright = 'Contoso. All rights reserved.'

# Description of the functionality provided by this module
Description = 'This Module is used to support the creation and
➥    configuration of IIS Websites through Get, Set and Test API
➥    on the DSC managed nodes.'

# Minimum version of the Windows PowerShell engine required by this module
PowerShellVersion = '4.0'

# Minimum version of the common language runtime (CLR) required by this module
CLRVersion = '4.0'

# Modules that must be imported into the global environment prior to
# importing this module
RequiredModules = @("WebAdministration")

# Modules to import as nested modules of the module specified in RootModule/
    ModuleToProcess
NestedModules = @("Demo_IISWebsite.psm1")

# Functions to export from this module
FunctionsToExport = @("Get-TargetResource", "Set-TargetResource",
"Test-TargetResource")

# Cmdlets to export from this module
#CmdletsToExport = '*'

# HelpInfo URI of this module
# HelpInfoURI = ''
```

With all of that in place, you could then write a configuration script that uses this resource, as shown in listing 41.12.

Listing 41.12   MyConfig.ps1

```
Configuration MyConfig {
  Node WWW1 {
    Website {
      Name = 'Sample Website'
      PhysicalPath = 'C:\Webfiles\Sample'
      Ensure = 'Present'
      State = 'Started'
      Protocol = 'http'
      ApplicationPool = 'MyAppPool'
    }
  }
}
```

Let's say you then ran the configuration to create MyConfig\WWW1.MOF, and you pushed that MOF file to the computer WWW1. For the sake of argument, let's also assume that you'd already deployed Demo_IISWebsite.psm1, Demo_IISWebsite.schema.mof, and Demo_IISWebsite.psd1 to the computer WWW1, putting them in the correct paths. That computer's LCM would read the MOF, see that the Website resource was needed, and go find your Demo_IISWebsite.psm1 module.

The LCM would pull the values from the WWW1.MOF—the site name, physical path, state, protocol, and all that. It'd then run `Test-TargetResource`, passing along those values to the parameters of `Test-TargetResource`. If `Test-TargetResource` returned `$True`, the LCM would stop, because nothing else would need to be done. If it returned `$False`, the LCM would call `Set-TargetResource`, again passing in the MOF property values to the function's parameters. `Set-TargetResource` would then need to do whatever was necessary to get things configured as specified.

41.7 DSC vs. Group Policy

We're often asked about the relationship between DSC and Group Policy, and it's an easy answer: there isn't one.

Group Policy is still the winner for client configuration. Clients typically belong to a domain, and Group Policy depends on the domain to target computers and apply policy. Client computers move around a lot: they're laptops, they get reassigned, their users relocate, and so on. Group Policy is built to understand that, and it has flexible options for applying policy to various computers based on detailed criteria. The PowerShell product team hasn't—so far—spent much time making DSC better than Group Policy when it comes to client management. Group Policy *is* declarative, after all, so it already meets a similar need.

But servers are a little different. Servers are static—they don't move around much, and we don't reassign them much. Servers tend to live in one place, and we know about every single one of them. Servers are less likely to belong to a domain than a client machine, because there are numerous scenarios—think public web servers—where belonging to a domain is impractical. DSC has no dependency on a domain: as long as you can communicate between computers, it'll work, and those communications can be configured to work across domain and workgroup boundaries.

This is why, at present, most of the focus on DSC is for servers, especially servers in mass-scale environments like cloud hosting providers. That isn't to say DSC can't replace Group Policy, but right now Group Policy definitely has some capabilities that are difficult to re-create in DSC. Eventually, we can foresee DSC picking up some of Group Policy's richer targeting and application capabilities and eventually supplanting Group Policy, but that might be a little ways off. DSC does have a few things going for it that Group Policy doesn't: First, DSC resources are easy to create and deploy, whereas extending Group Policy is extremely complex. Second, DSC's ability to operate without domain dependencies can be beneficial. Third, a DSC script is more human-readable than a raw Group Policy file, making it easy to version-control configurations, test them offline, and so on.

41.8   *Summary*

This chapter was written for the first release of DSC, which was in the Windows Management Framework 4. We already know that the PowerShell product team is actively working on the next version of DSC, so stay tuned for more. There's also an active community building around DSC—you'll find some at PowerShell.org, and there's a DSC-related coding project happening on PowerShell.org's GitHub repository at https://github.com/PowerShellOrg/DSC. DSC is bound to be a big part of your future, so make sure you're connecting and keeping up!

appendix A
Best practices

This chapter covers

- General best practices
- Scripting best practices
- PowerShell in the enterprise best practices

Throughout this book, we've noted—and sometimes hinted at—practices you can follow to make your PowerShell efforts, especially scripts, more maintainable, better performing, and more flexible than you ever thought possible. In this appendix, we'll reiterate and organize those suggestions for easier reference. The number one recommendation is to use PowerShell every day. The following recommendations aren't in any particular order of importance.

PowerShell general best practices

These recommendations are designed for you to get the best out of PowerShell:

- Read the help files—there's a mass of good information, especially in the examples.
- In PowerShell v3 and later, set up a schedule to update help on a regular basis. Just remember that if you're saving help in a mixed-version environment you must keep saved help in separate locations. Monitor the PowerShell help versions RSS feed at http://sxp.microsoft.com/feeds/msdntn/PowerShellHelpVersions for news of revised help files being available.

- Set your script execution policy to RemoteSigned (at the least).
- Use the pipeline—PowerShell is designed for pipeline usage. If you apply coding styles from older scripting languages, you'll lose a lot of functionality and create work for yourself. That said, don't feel you have to do everything in one-line commands. Sometimes it's helpful to break long commands into several steps, each still using the pipeline.
- Give variables meaningful names, such as `$computer` rather than `$c`.
- Avoid variables with spaces or special symbols in their names, such as `${my odd variable}`.
- Never set `$ErrorActionPreference` (or `$VerbosePreference` or any other "preference" variable) globally in the shell or in a script or function. Instead, use parameters, such as a cmdlet's `-ErrorAction` parameter or a function's `-Verbose` parameter, to set the preference on an as-needed basis.
- Avoid enumerating collections—using `ForEach-Object` or the `ForEach` scripting construct—unless there's no other way to accomplish your task.
- Use single quotes unless you explicitly need the variable-replacement and expression-evaluation capabilities of double quotes. If you're working with SQL Server databases, remember that they use single quotes for strings.
- String substitution (or multiplication) is much easier than string concatenation.
- Use the built-in numeric constants—PowerShell understands KB, MB, GB, TB, and PB.
- Avoid using native .NET classes and methods unless there's no cmdlet alternative. The exception is for large-scale enterprise scripting where you might see some performance gains using native .NET classes. You have to be willing to trade simplicity for performance.
- Be careful with code downloads from the internet and always double-check what the code is doing—your environment may be different enough from the author's that you'll encounter problems. When pasting downloaded or copied code from a web page, watch out for curly single and double quotes. Change them to single quotes.
- Filter early and format late. Restrict the data set as soon as possible, but don't format the data until you're just about to display your data.

PowerShell scripting best practices

These recommendations are designed for you to get the best out of PowerShell scripts:

- Give variables a type, such as `[string] $logfile`, especially if they're parameters.
- Avoid using variables that haven't first been given a value within the current scope.
- Give functions and workflows cmdlet-style, verb-noun names such as `Get-DiskInfo`.
- When a script performs a given task, rather than having it just acting as a container for several functions, give the script a cmdlet-style, verb-noun name such as Set-UserAttribute.ps1.

- When naming functions and scripts with a verb-noun style name, apply a two- or three-character prefix to the noun. This will generally be a prefix that relates to your company. For example, a company named Great Things, Inc. might name a function `Get-GTUserInfo` or might name a script Set-GTUserInfo.ps1. Alternatively, apply a prefix when loading the module.

- If you create private (that is, nonexported) variables in a script module, give those variables distinct names. Many developers will use an underscore for this distinction, such as `$_private` or `$_counter`.

- When defining script or function parameters, use parameter names that correspond to native cmdlet parameters that have a similar purpose. For example, a parameter intended to collect computer names would be `-Computername` rather than `-host` or `-machine`, because native PowerShell cmdlets use `-Computername`. You can always define a parameter alias for alternate or shorter parameter names such as `-host`.

- Avoid using `Write-Host` unless your sole purpose is to produce output that will only ever need to be seen onscreen. If you use `Write-Host`, use a foreground or background color so your messages can be distinguished from your output.

- Use `[CmdletBinding]` in your scripts and functions to give easy access to verbose messages, debugging, and other advanced functionality.

- If your script or function will change the system, add support for `-Whatif` and `-Confirm`.

- Use `Write-Verbose` to produce "progress information," such as messages that tell you what a script or function is about to attempt.

- Use `Write-Debug` to produce messages intended to assist with the debugging process, keeping in mind that `Write-Debug` will pause the script and offer an opportunity to suspend it.

- Remember that `Write-Warning` exists for those times when you need to output informational messages to screen.

- Scripts and functions should produce one, and only one, kind of output. That output should usually be an object and may be a custom object that combines information from multiple sources.

- Always define help for scripts and functions, even if it's just comment-based help. XML-based help files are often only needed when you need to provide help messages in multiple languages.

- Avoid changing aliases, variables, and other scoped elements of a scope other than the current one.

- Break tasks into distinct, small units of functionality and implement each as a function. For example, a script that performs 10 different things should be broken up into 10 functions, with a script that calls those functions in the proper sequence.

- Sign code examples that you plan to share with the public. Yes, it'll require a code-signing certificate and we're not kidding ourselves about the likelihood of people following this advice. But it's a good way to help the public confirm that your code hasn't been tampered with by someone else.

- Avoid using Hungarian notation for variable names; conventions like `$strName` and `$intCounter` are outdated and unnecessary.
- Indent the contents of a script block, such as the `{contents}` of an `If` construct, loop, or other scripting construct.
- Consider using `Write-Verbose`, `Write-Debug`, and so forth to provide inline documentation for scripts and functions, rather than using inline comments for that purpose.
- In a script, function, or workflow, avoid aliases (except for widely understood ones like `Dir`) and truncated parameter names. Spell out full cmdlet and parameter names for better readability and maintainability.
- Avoid using the backtick (`` ` ``) character at the end of a line so that you can continue the command on the next physical line. Instead, break lines at "natural" PowerShell points. Hitting Enter after any of these characters will allow the line to be continued on the next (`{` , `;` `|`.
- If you use proxy functions, make sure you publish them with your module.
- Remember `Test-Path` and use it to test for file or folder existence or any provider path.
- `Try...Catch...Finally` should be used anywhere that exceptions could cause problems in your processing.
- Don't use `Trap`—`Try...Catch` is easier and better.
- Keep your logic simple—for example, avoid double negatives in `If` statements.
- Don't use Notepad as a script editor, except for the most minimal of scripts. At the very least use the Windows PowerShell ISE. Notepad is good for quickly viewing code because PowerShell files open in Notepad by default.
- Avoid using the `Return` keyword. Instead, think about writing objects to the pipeline.

PowerShell in the enterprise best practices

These recommendations are designed for you to make the best use of PowerShell in the enterprise:

- Use Group Policy to configure and enforce PowerShell Remoting and script execution.
- Use a Remoting or CIM session if you're accessing a remote machine more than once.
- Use PowerShell jobs for long-running tasks.
- Use PowerShell workflows where you need the ability to interrupt or restart scripts or use parallel execution.
- Store scripts in a source control solution so that you have both a backup and a way to roll back to a previous version if you mess something up.

- Restrict access to your production scripts to just those who need it.
- Use `Test-Connection` to test the availability of a remote machine before attempting a lot of processing.
- Make sure PowerShell Remoting is enabled on your servers.
- Credentials should be created before being used—don't create them in your command, especially if you need them more than once.
- Use WSMAN rather than DCOM for CIM sessions if at all possible.
- Develop a standardized script template and style, especially when a team of administrators will be developing PowerShell scripts.
- Consider an enterprise execution policy of AllSigned, and use a code-signing certificate from your Active Directory PKI.
- Create shared scripts that define common functions, aliases, and variables you might need for your team. Store these scripts centrally, such as on a UNC, and then dot-source them in your profile script.
- Use PowerShell Web Access to provide additional remote access, and administration, capabilities.
- Use PowerShell Web Access and restricted endpoints to delegate permission to junior admins where appropriate.
- Use Desired State Configuration to create, and maintain, you server configurations. Use a Pull server to minimize manual intervention.
- We hope this goes without saying, but test *everything* in a nonproduction environment. With the widespread adoption of virtualization, there's no reason you can't. You don't need a Hyper-V farm and a 10 TB SAN; you can get started with the open source VirtualBox and trial versions from Microsoft.

appendix B
PowerShell Web Access

PowerShell Web Access (PWA) was introduced as part of Windows Server 2012 and enhanced in Windows Server 2012 R2. Strictly speaking, it isn't part of PowerShell but is a feature of Windows Server that enables you to connect to a PowerShell Remoting endpoint from a web browser. That web browser can be on a Windows device, a non-Windows tablet, on even a smart phone if your eyesight is good enough to deal with the tiny screen. PWA brings mobile remoting to administrators using PowerShell. In this appendix, we'll give you an overview of setting up PWA and then conclude by working through a script that will set up PWA on a remote machine.

The first thing you need to do is install PWA. The PWA server would normally sit in your organization's DMZ. Connectivity is supplied to the corporate LAN so that you can create remote connections from the PWA server to machines in your domain. In this first example, we assume that the machine is in the domain.

PWA is a Windows feature and isn't installed by default. You also need to ensure that IIS, .NET 4.5, and PowerShell 3.0 (Windows Server 2012), 4.0 (Windows Server 2012 R2), or 5.0 (the next version of Windows Server) are installed.

You can use Server Manager to perform the install or better still use PowerShell:

```
Install-WindowsFeature -Name WindowsPowerShellWebAccess `
-IncludeAllSubFeature -IncludeManagementTools -Restart
```

This code will install PWA and the required subfeatures, and then force the machine to restart. The supporting roles and features should be installed for you. If you want to ensure you have full control over the install process, you can specifically state what you want installed:

```
Install-WindowsFeature -Name Web-WebServer, Web-Mgmt-Console,
NET-Framework-45-ASPNET, Web-Net-Ext45, Web-ISAPI-Ext,
Web-ISAPI-Filter, Web-Default-Doc, Web-Http-Errors,
Web-Http-Redirect, Web-Static-Content,
Web-Filtering, WindowsPowerShellWebAccess -Confirm:$false
```

The installation routine adds a PowerShell module for managing PWA:

```
PS C:\> Get-Command -Module PowerShellWebAccess

CommandType     Name
-----------     ----
Function        Install-PswaWebApplication
Function        Uninstall-PswaWebApplication
Cmdlet          Add-PswaAuthorizationRule
Cmdlet          Get-PswaAuthorizationRule
Cmdlet          Remove-PswaAuthorizationRule
Cmdlet          Test-PswaAuthorizationRule
```

These cmdlets exist to test and administer the PWA service. You still need to have the correct modules, or scripts, installed on the machines you're going to manage via PWA.

Your next step is to create the PWA web application:

```
Install-PswaWebApplication -WebApplicationName PSG `
  -UseTestCertificate
```

Give the application a name and in this case use a self-generated test certificate.

> **WARNING** Do not use this technique in a production environment; use a proper SSL certificate.

You now need to add a rule to enable a user or group to access a server:

```
Add-PswaAuthorizationRule -RuleName "RS Server 02 Full" `
-ComputerName server02.manticore.org        `
-UserName manticore\richard `
-ConfigurationName microsoft.powershell
```

This command has created a rule that allows a user called Richard to access the default remoting endpoint on an individual server—in this case, server02. No other users can access that endpoint and server pairing through PWA until they are *explicitly* granted the rights to do so. To minimize administration, use groups rather than individuals.

This is an important point and needs to be repeated. Users (or groups of users) are explicitly granted access through PWA to specific remoting endpoints on specific servers. If you aren't part of a PWA authorization rule, either individually or through a group, you don't get access. If you attempt to access a server through PWA where a rule doesn't exist to give you access, your connection attempt will be refused by the system. If you look at the syntax of Add-PswaAuthorizationRule, you'll see that you can use groups of computers as well as groups of users:

```
PS C:\> Get-Command Add-PswaAuthorizationRule -Syntax

Add-PswaAuthorizationRule -ComputerGroupName <string>
-ConfigurationName <string> -UserGroupName <string[]>
[-Credential <pscredential>] [-RuleName <string>]
[-Force] [<CommonParameters>]
```

```
Add-PswaAuthorizationRule [-UserName] <string[]>
-ComputerGroupName <string> -ConfigurationName <string>
[-Credential<pscredential>] [-RuleName <string>]
[-Force] [<CommonParameters>]

Add-PswaAuthorizationRule -ComputerName <string>
-ConfigurationName <string> -UserGroupName <string[]>
[-Credential<pscredential>] [-RuleName <string>]
[-Force] [<CommonParameters>]

Add-PswaAuthorizationRule [-UserName] <string[]>
[-ComputerName] <string> [-ConfigurationName] <string>
[-Credential<pscredential>] [-RuleName <string>]
[-Force] [<CommonParameters>]
```

Consult the cmdlet documentation (remember to use `Update-Help`) for full details.

You can examine the rules enabled on a PWA box:

```
PS C:> Get-PswaAuthorizationRule | Format-List *

Id                  : 0
RuleName            : RS Server 02 Full
User                : manticore\richard
UserType            : User
Destination         : manticore\server02
DestinationType     : Computer
ConfigurationName   : microsoft.powershell
```

And you can test those rules:

```
Test-PswaAuthorizationRule -ComputerName server02 `
-UserName manticore\richard
```

This command tests whether a particular user can access a particular computer through PWA. If the answer is yes, you see the rule information; otherwise, no data is returned.

If you install PWA on a computer called Win12R2, you can access it like this:

```
https://win12r2/PSG
```

where `PSG` is the name of the web application that we created earlier. When accessing PWA, you'll have to log in with your credentials and give the name of the server to which you'll connect. PWA connections are made to a single server at a time. You can't get access to multiple servers because you're connecting to specific remoting endpoints on specific servers. Figure B.1 shows the PWA logon screen.

In figure B.1 one set of credentials is supplied. These are domain credentials that allow access to all computers in the domain. If you're accessing non-domain-joined computers, or you're using local accounts for any reason, you'll need to supply appropriate credentials for the server to which you're connecting.

Your browser will display a PowerShell console with an area at the bottom to type your commands and a results pane above it, as shown in figure B.2.

NOTE Tab completion doesn't fully work in the PWA console. It works for cmdlet names but not other items, such as environment variables or cmdlet parameters.

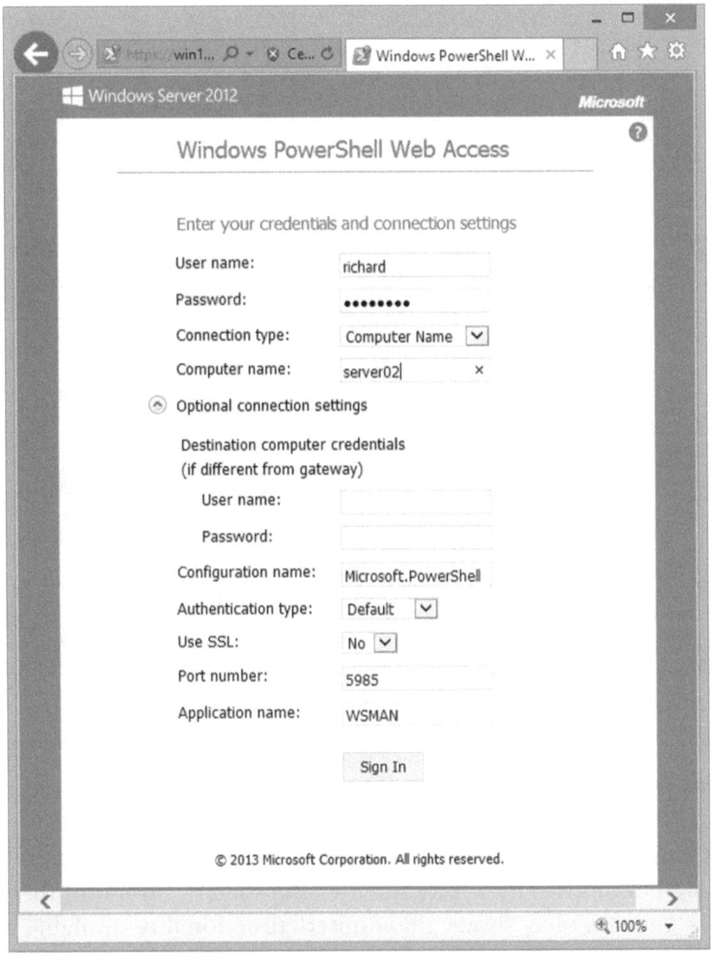

Figure B.1 Logging into PowerShell Web Access

The PWA console has an Exit button in the bottom-right corner that you click to close the connection (see figure B.2). You'll be returned to the logon screen (figure B.1). You can then close the browser or connect to another machine.

So far you've exposed the whole of the functionality available through PowerShell to the user via PWA. You may want to limit the activities the user can perform, in which case you need to create a constrained endpoint as you saw in chapter 10. As an example, assume you have a constrained endpoint that provides access only to the Active Directory cmdlets. To make this available through PWA, you need to create a rule:

```
Add-PswaAuthorizationRule -RuleName "server02 AD admin only" `
-ComputerName server02.manticore.org `
-UserName manticore\methul -ConfigurationName ADPS
```

If you test the rule:

```
Test-PswaAuthorizationRule  -UserName manticore\methul `
 -ConfigurationName * -ComputerName server02
```

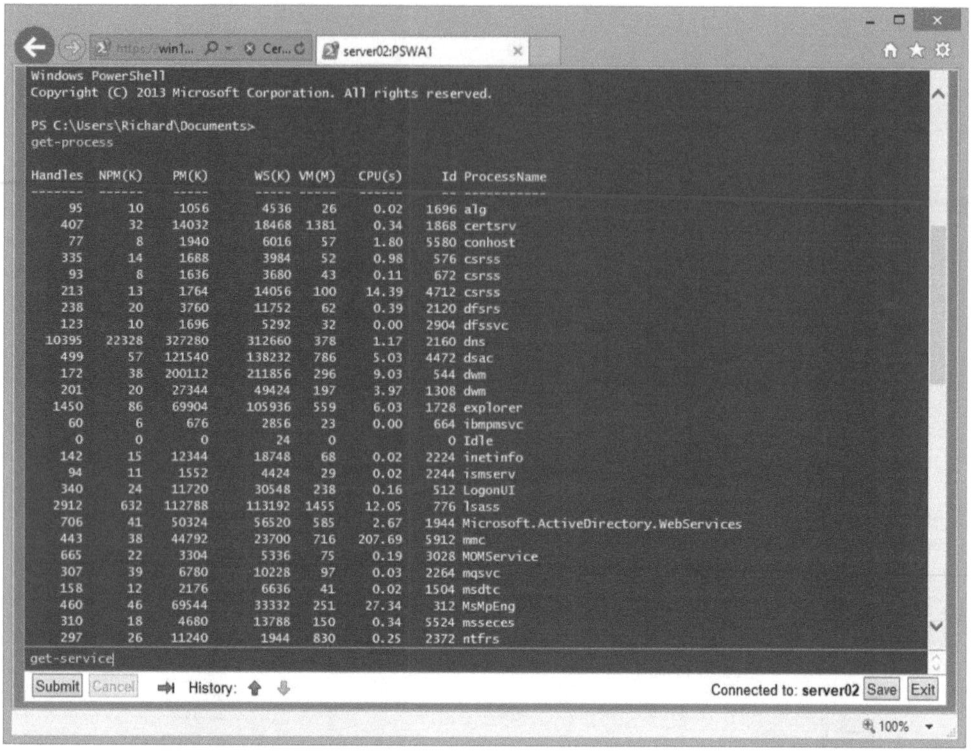

Figure B.2   Using PowerShell Web Access

you'll see that the user is granted access to only the ADPS configuration on server02.

When users sign in to PWA, they have to enter the specific endpoint they want to access. Running `Get-Command` shows the limited functionality available through the endpoint.

PWA has a lot more options that you can discover in the documentation at http:// technet.microsoft.com/en-us/library/hh831611.aspx. We strongly recommend reading this documentation before implementing PWA.

appendix C
PowerShell versions

There have been four versions of PowerShell since the original release in November 2006 that was announced at TechEd Europe in Barcelona. You're likely to meet, at least, versions 2 through 4 in your work. In this appendix, we'll provide information on the various PowerShell versions so that you are aware of the capabilities of each. You can use this information to determine how you'll administer your environment and possibly modify your approach to manage the differences between versions.

The four PowerShell releases are outlined in table C.1. The table includes release date, required .NET version, and where you can find the download, as of this writing.

Table C.1   The four PowerShell releases

Version	Release date	.NET version	Download
PowerShell v1	October 2006	,NET 2.0	Windows Vista http://support.microsoft.com/kb/928439 Windows Server 2003 and XP http://support.microsoft.com/kb/926139
PowerShell v2	October 2009	.NET 2.0 ISE needs .NET 3.5	http://support.microsoft.com/kb/968929
PowerShell v3	September 2012	.NET 4.0	www.microsoft.com/en-us/download/details.aspx?id=34595
PowerShell v4	October 2013	.NET 4.5	www.microsoft.com/en-us/download/details.aspx?id=40855

Starting with Windows Server 2008, PowerShell became part of the operating system. The details of which versions of Windows support which versions of PowerShell are supplied later in this appendix.

PowerShell, as we've pointed out numerous times, is based on the .NET Framework. The version of .NET required by PowerShell changes as you progress through the versions. Notice that PowerShell v2 requires .NET 2.0 only if you're using the console. You'll need .NET 3.5 if you intend to use ISE or the Out-GridView cmdlet.

The PowerShell download for Windows Vista wasn't released until January 2007, so you may see references in the literature to PowerShell being released in 2007.

There was a significant change in terminology between PowerShell versions 1 and 2. Starting with v2, PowerShell became part of the Windows Management Framework (WMF). This meant that you got PowerShell and a set of supporting, or parallel, technologies that you need to manage your Windows environment. Table C.2 outlines the major components in each release.

Table C.2   Download contents

Version	Download contents
PowerShell v1	PowerShell 1.0
PowerShell v2	Windows Management Framework 2.0 PowerShell 2.0 　　WinRM 2.0 BITS 4.0 (Not on Windows Server 2003 or XP)
PowerShell v3	Windows Management Framework 3.0 　　PowerShell 3.0 　　WinRM 3.0 　　CIM (WMI) 　　Management Odata IIS Extension 　　Server Manager CIM Provider
PowerShell v4	Windows Management Framework 4.0 　　PowerShell 4.0 　　WinRM 3.0 　　Windows PowerShell Web Services (Odata) 　　Desired State Configuration

PowerShell v2 introduced remote administration over the WinRM service. This service had a version change in version 3. Note that PowerShell v4 is still using WinRM 3.0. You can successfully perform PowerShell remoting between WinRM 2.0 and 3.0, meaning that any combination of PowerShell v2, v3, or v4 can be used as the local and remote machines.

The same can't be said of the CIM cmdlets introduced in PowerShell v3. They default to WSMAN (WinRM) for making remote connections and are version-specific in expecting WinRM 3.0. You can't upgrade WinRM independent of PowerShell, so if you need to use the CIM cmdlets against a system running PowerShell v2, you must revert to using DCOM for remote connectivity by creating a `CIMSessionOption`. Of course, you can simplify your PowerShell experience by making sure all your systems are running at least PowerShell v3.

PowerShell is part of the Windows operating system now, and each new version of Windows is accompanied by a new version of PowerShell. We often see questions in the forums about using PowerShell's feature "X" on a particular version of Windows. Very often that feature can't be used because you can't install the particular version of PowerShell you need on the version of Windows you are dealing with. Table C.3 shows which versions of Windows can support a particular version of PowerShell.

Table C.3   PowerShell and operating system support matrix

Operating System	PowerShell v1	PowerShell v2	PowerShell v3	PowerShell v4
Windows Server 2012 R2	Not installable	Not installable	Not installable	Installed (not on server core)
Windows 8.1	Not installable	Not installable	Not installable	Installed
Windows Server 2012	Not installable	Not installable	Installed (not on server core)	Download
Windows 8	Not installable	Not installable	Installed	Not installable (upgrade to Windows 8.1)
Windows Server 2008 R2	Not installable	Installed (ISE optional but not on server core)	Download Need SP1	Download
Windows 7	Not installable	Installed	Download Need SP1	Download
Windows Server 2008 (Not Server Core)	Installed as optional feature	Download Need SP1 or SP2	Download Need SP2	Not installable
Windows Vista	Download	Download Need SP1 or SP2	Not installable	Not installable
Windows Server 2003 R2	Download	Download Need SP2	Not installable	Not installable
Windows Server 2003	Download Need SP2	Download Need SP2	Not installable	Not installable
Windows XP	Download Need SP3	Download Need SP3	Not installable	Not installable

Keep these points in mind:

- PowerShell v4 can't be installed on Itanium (IA64) versions of Windows Server 2012 or Windows Server 2008 R2.

- PowerShell can't be installed on Windows Server 2008 Server Core. A number of people published hacks showing how it could be achieved. Running Power-Shell on Windows Server 2008 Server Core isn't supported by Microsoft and isn't a recommended practice.
- The support plan roughly follows the pattern that the latest version of Power-Shell is installed as part of the latest versions on Windows and downloads are provided for the previous two releases of Windows. There are exceptions—for example, you can't install PowerShell v4 on Windows 8.

IT pros usually want the latest and greatest set of features—which means upgrading the instance of PowerShell on your older versions of Windows subject to availability, as shown in table C.3.

There's a problem. Some other applications are tied to particular versions of .NET, and if you try to upgrade PowerShell on a system with these applications installed, you'll cause problems and may need to completely rebuild your system. The known incompatibilities are listed in table C.4.

Table C.4   Known incompatibilities

Application	PowerShell v1	PowerShell v2	PowerShell v3	PowerShell v4
System Center 2012 Config-uration Manager	N/A	N/A	Incompatible	Incompatible
System Center Virtual Machine Manager	N/A	N/A	Incompatible	N/A
System Center Virtual Machine Manager 2008 R2	N/A	N/A	Incompatible	Incompatible
Exchange Server 2013	N/A	N/A		Incompatible
Exchange Server 2010	N/A	N/A	Incompatible	Incompatible
Exchange Server 2007	N/A	N/A	Incompatible	Incompatible
SharePoint 2013	N/A	N/A	N/A	Incompatible
SharePoint 2010	N/A	N/A	Incompatible	Incompatible

In some cases, a service pack for the application will allow the application to be installed on a system with a previously incompatible version of PowerShell. Exchange 2013 SP1, for instance, enables the application to be installed on Windows Server 2012 R2, which means that it can co-exist with PowerShell v4.

> **TIP**   The bottom line here is to not perform a PowerShell upgrade but upgrade the whole system so that you don't break your application. In many cases, upgrading may not be possible, so you'll need to work around missing functionality.

Table C.5 shows how the main functionality groups map to the sequence of Power-Shell releases.

Table C.5   PowerShell functionality matrix

Functionality	PowerShell v1	PowerShell v2	PowerShell v3	PowerShell v4
Core PowerShell engine	Yes	Yes	Yes	Yes
WMI cmdlets	Get-WmiObject Only	Yes	Yes	Yes
PowerShell Remoting	N/A	Yes	Yes	Yes
WSMAN 2.0	N/A	Yes	Yes	Yes
PowerShell Jobs	N/A	Yes	Yes	Yes
BITS cmdlets	N/A	Yes	Yes	Yes
Advanced functions	N/A	Yes	Yes	Yes
Modules	N/A	Yes	Yes	Yes
Eventing engine	N/A	Yes	Yes	Yes
ISE	N/A	Yes	Yes	Yes
CIM API	N/A	N/A	Yes	Yes
CIM cmdlets	N/A	N/A	Yes	Yes
CDXML	N/A	N/A	Yes	Yes
PowerShell workflow	N/A	N/A	Yes	Yes
PowerShell scheduled jobs	N/A	N/A	Yes	Yes
PowerShell Web Access	N/A	N/A	Yes	Yes
Module Auto-loading	N/A	N/A	Yes	Yes
Updatable Help	N/A	N/A	Yes	Yes
Desired State Configuration	N/A	N/A	N/A	Yes

You can get a full list of the new features, bug fixes, and enhancements in PowerShell v3 and v4 from http://technet.microsoft.com/en-us/library/hh857339.aspx. Also check out this help file: about_Windows_PowerShell_4.0.

One thing that seems to be causing a lot of confusion is the number of modules, and corresponding functionality, installed with PowerShell v3 and v4. What you get depends on the operating system version you're using.

If you run this:

```
Get-Module -ListAvailable
```

on a Windows 8.1 system (PowerShell v4), you'll find a total of 58 modules installed in $pshome\modules—that is, C:\windows\system32\WindowsPowerShell\v1.0\Modules.

NOTE   This result is assuming a new, clean install. If you've installed any features such as Hyper-V, you may have more.

These are the modules installed as part of PowerShell. Right?

Compare this with a Windows 7 machine that's been upgraded to PowerShell v4. Repeating the exercise, you'll find a grand total of 15 modules. So where has the other 75 percent of your functionality gone?

This is the breakdown of the modules installed on the Windows 7 machine. The terminology is ours (feel free to disagree with the groupings):

Core PowerShell:

- Microsoft.PowerShell.Diagnostic
- Microsoft.PowerShell.Host
- Microsoft.PowerShell.Management
- Microsoft.PowerShell.Security
- Microsoft.PowerShell.Utility
- CimCmdlets
- ISE
- Microsoft.WSMan.Management

File Transfer module

- BitsTransfer

Troubleshooting:

- PSDiagnostics
- TroubleshootingPack

Other related engines:

- PSDesiredStateConfiguration
- PSScheduledJob
- PSWorkflow
- PSWorkflowUtility

And that's it. Everything else as far as we can determine is CDXML-based and therefore can't be made available on legacy systems. The modules in table C.6 are included in that category.

Table C.6   CDXML modules in PowerShell v3 and v4

AppBackgroundTask	AppLocker	Appx
AssignedAccess	BitLocker	BranchCache
Defender	DirectAccessClientComponents	Dism
DnsClient	International	iSCSI
Kds	MMAgent	MsDtc
NetAdapter	NetConnection	NetEventPacketCapture
NetLbfo	NetNat	NetQos

Table C.6 CDXML modules in PowerShell v3 and v4 (continued)

NetSecurity	NetSwitchTeam	NetTCPIP
NetWNV	NetworkConnectivityStatus	NetworkTransition
PcsvDevice	PKI	PrintManagement
ScheduledTasks	SecureBoot	SmbShare
SmbWitness	StartScreen	Storage
TLS	TrustedPlatformModule	VpnClient
Wdac	WindowsDeveloperLicense	WindowsErrorReporting
WindowsSearch		

As you saw in chapter 39, a CDXML-based module is produced by taking a CIM (WMI) class and wrapping it in some simple XML and saving it as a CDXML file. This file can then be published as a PowerShell module. The CIM classes won't be made available on down-level systems, so you won't find this functionality on anything earlier than Windows 8 or Windows Server 2012.

If you need the functionality supplied by these modules, you'll have to use either the old command-line tools or a WMI class. Much of the functionality of the Net-Adapter and NETCPIP modules, for instance, can be duplicated using Win32_Network-Adapter and Win32_NetworkAdapterConfiguration.

So where does this leave you? We'd like to say upgrade everything to the latest available operating system so that you can get the latest version of PowerShell, but that's an unrealistic expectation. If at all possible, install PowerShell v3 on all of your servers with Remoting enabled so that you can manage them from your desktop. On your desktop, at a minimum we think you need PowerShell v3, although v4 with RSAT installed would be even better. If you are stuck with legacy systems, try to get at least v2 installed so that you can perform some basic remote management and use WMI. And if you're stuck with systems that are PowerShell v1, well, you have our sympathy and you'll have to accept the fact that your management options will be extremely limited.

With that, we'll say good luck!

index

MANNING

The Manning Early Access Program

Don't wait to start learning! In MEAP, the Manning Early Access Program, you can read books as they're being created and long before they're available in stores.

Here's how MEAP works.

- **Start now.** Buy a MEAP and you'll get all available chapters in PDF, ePub, Kindle, and liveBook formats.

- **Regular updates.** New chapters are released as soon as they're written. We'll let you know when fresh content is available.

- **Finish faster.** MEAP customers are the first to get final versions of all books! Pre-order the print book, and it'll ship as soon as it's off the press.

- **Contribute to the process.** The feedback you share with authors makes the end product better.

- **No risk.** You get a full refund or exchange if we ever have to cancel a MEAP.

Explore dozens of titles in MEAP at www.manning.com.

Hands-on projects for learning your way

liveProjects are an exciting way to develop your skills that's just like learning on-the-job.

In a Manning liveProject you tackle a real-world IT challenge and work out your own solutions. To make sure you succeed, you'll get 90 days full and unlimited access to a hand-picked list of Manning book and video resources.

Here's how liveProject works:

- **Achievable milestones.** Each project is broken down into steps and sections so you can keep track of your progress.

- **Collaboration and advice.** Work with other liveProject participants through chat, working groups, and peer project reviews.

- **Compare your results.** See how your work shapes up against an expert implementation by the liveProject's creator.

- **Everything you need to succeed.** Datasets and carefully selected learning resources come bundled with every liveProject.

- **Build your portfolio.** All liveProjects teach skills that are in-demand from industry. When you're finished, you'll have the satisfaction that comes with success and a real project to add to your portfolio.

Explore dozens of data, development, and cloud engineering liveProjects at www.manning.com!